business ethics

MANAGING CORPORATE CITIZENSHIP AND SUSTAINABILITY IN THE AGE OF GLOBALIZATION

business ethics

Managing Corporate Citizenship and Sustainability in the Age of Globalization

third edition

ANDREW CRANE
DIRK MATTEN

OXFORD
UNIVERSITY PRESS

OXFORD
UNIVERSITY PRESS

Great Clarendon Street, Oxford, OX2 6DP,
United Kingdom

Oxford University Press is a department of the University of Oxford.
It furthers the University's objective of excellence in research, scholarship, and education by publishing worldwide. Oxford is a registered trade mark of Oxford University Press in the UK and in certain other countries

First Published 2004
Second Edition 2007
Third Edition 2010

British Library Cataloguing in Publication Data
Data available

Library of Congress Cataloguing in Publication Data
Data available

Special Student Editon

Exclusive Distributed Title

St Martin's Books (a division of A. M. Inc.)

CONTENTS

DETAILED CONTENTS

9 Suppliers, Competitors, and Business Ethics 389

10 Civil Society and Business Ethics 439

LIST OF FIGURES

LIST OF BOXES

Ethics in Action

Ethical Dilemma

Ethics on Screen

Ethics Online

GUIDE TO THE BOOK

Each chapter includes the following pedagogical features:

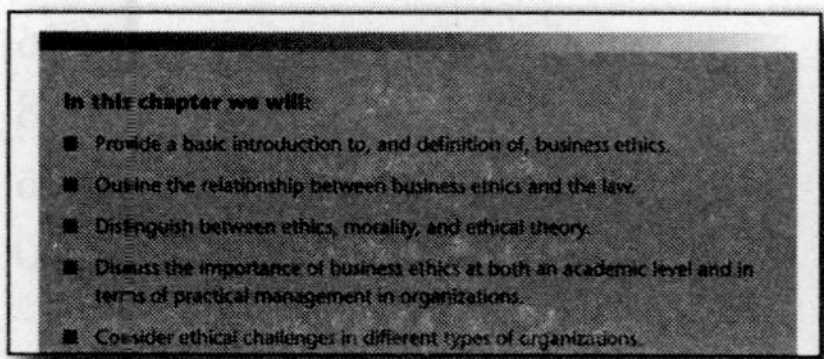
In this chapter we will:

- Provide a basic introduction to, and definition of, business ethics.
- Outline the relationship between business ethics and the law.
- Distinguish between ethics, morality, and ethical theory.
- Discuss the importance of business ethics at both an academic level and in terms of practical management in organizations.
- Consider ethical challenges in different types of organizations.

Learning Objectives

Each chapter starts with a set of bulleted learning outcomes, which indicate what you can expect to learn from the chapter

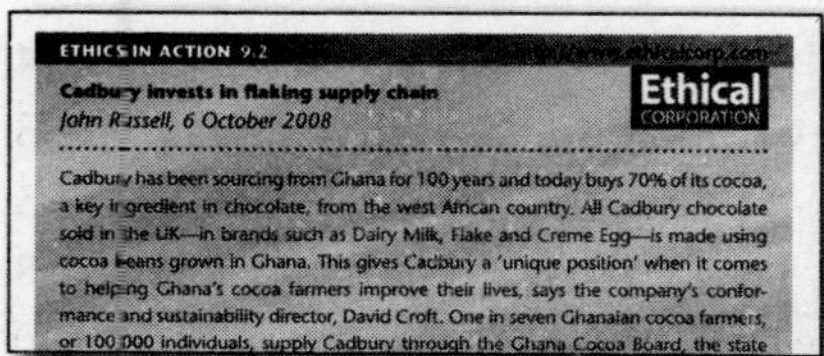
ETHICS IN ACTION 9.2

Cadbury invests in flaking supply chain

John Russell, 6 October 2008

Cadbury has been sourcing from Ghana for 100 years and today buys 70% of its cocoa, a key ingredient in chocolate, from the west African country. All Cadbury chocolate sold in the UK—in brands such as Dairy Milk, Flake and Creme Egg—is made using cocoa beans grown in Ghana. This gives Cadbury a 'unique position' when it comes to helping Ghana's cocoa farmers improve their lives, says the company's conformance and sustainability director, David Croft. One in seven Ghanaian cocoa farmers, or 100 000 individuals, supply Cadbury through the Ghana Cocoa Board, the state

Ethics in Action

These are short articles, primarily drawn from Ethical Corporation magazine, which showcase current ethical problems faced by business, leading edge initiatives, or high profile scandals that have hit the headlines.

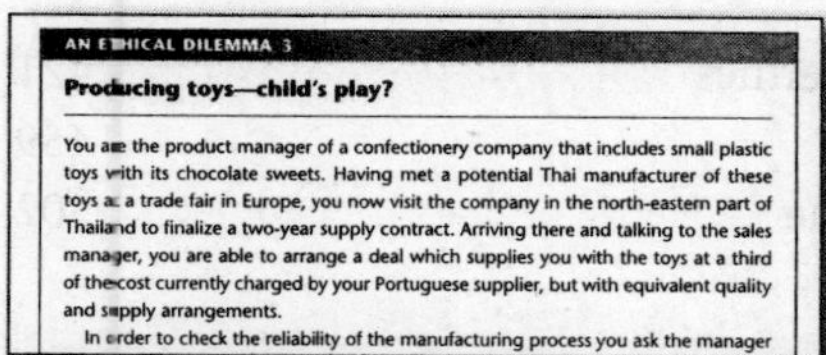
AN ETHICAL DILEMMA 3

Producing toys—child's play?

You are the product manager of a confectionery company that includes small plastic toys with its chocolate sweets. Having met a potential Thai manufacturer of these toys at a trade fair in Europe, you now visit the company in the north-eastern part of Thailand to finalize a two-year supply contract. Arriving there and talking to the sales manager, you are able to arrange a deal which supplies you with the toys at a third of the cost currently charged by your Portuguese supplier, but with equivalent quality and supply arrangements.

In order to check the reliability of the manufacturing process you ask the manager

An Ethical Dilemma

These describe a hypothetical ethical scenario, typically derived from real life incidents, and provide you with the opportunity to think about what you would do in a typical business ethics situation in a structured way.

CLICK HERE for links to useful sources of further information

ETHICS ON SCREEN 5

Wal-Mart: The High Cost of Low Price

An engrossing, muckraking documentary about the retail giant that's been calle[d the] world's largest, richest and probably meanest corporation.'

Kenneth Turan, *Los A*

Named after its founder Sam Walton (but trading under the Asda brand name in the UK), the US-based Wal-Mart is the world's largest retailer, and America's biggest employer. But along with commercial success, inevitably

Ethics on Screen

These provide reviews of a topical film selected because it helps to bring to life some of the key issues discussed in the respective chapter.

ETHICS ONLINE 1

Ethical fashion for ethics girls

Want to buy a new pair of skinny jeans but also care about how much the workers were paid to make them? Think there may be space in your life for a solar-powered MP4 player? Well, being ethical doesn't have to mean being unfashionable any more, at least not according to the Ethics Girls, a UK-based organization launched online in 2007. The Ethics Girls website seeks, as they put it, to

Unlike some ethical shopping sites, such as the Ethical Consumer organization's online buyers' guides (which provide detailed scorecards for a wide range of products in numerous categories), Ethics Girls do not claim to have a particularly robust research methodology. Their approach is style-led rather than research-led, with an emphasis on lifestyle journalism and the promotion of positive

Ethics Online

This is a new feature in the 3rd edition. These provide explanations of how business ethics issues discussed in the chapter have been dealt with on the web and through social media.

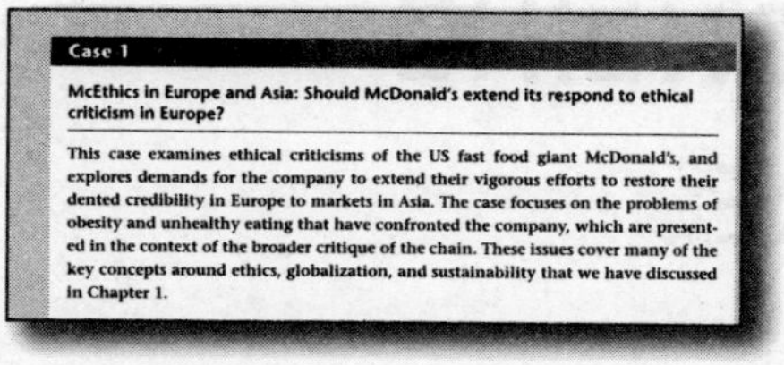
Case 1

McEthics in Europe and Asia: Should McDonald's extend its respond to ethical criticism in Europe?

This case examines ethical criticisms of the US fast food giant McDonald's, and explores demands for the company to extend their vigorous efforts to restore their dented credibility in Europe to markets in Asia. The case focuses on the problems of obesity and unhealthy eating that have confronted the company, which are presented in the context of the broader critique of the chain. These issues cover many of the key concepts around ethics, globalization, and sustainability that we have discussed in Chapter 1.

Case Studies

At the end of each chapter is an extended case study that describes in detail the ethical issues faced by well-known companies. They provide an excellent opportunity to use the material covered in the chapter to conduct a critical analysis of a real-life situation.

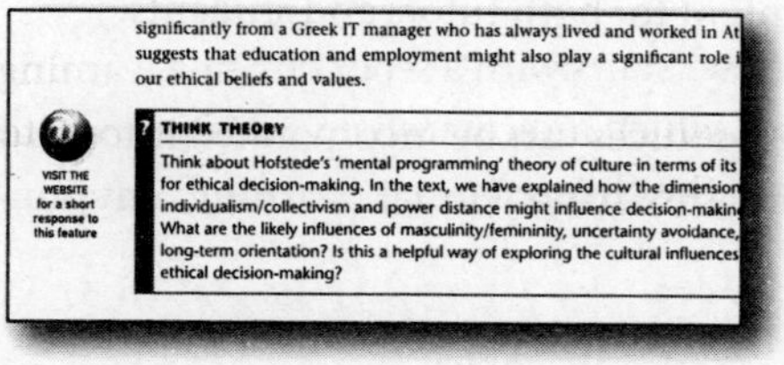
significantly from a Greek IT manager who has always lived and worked in At
suggests that education and employment might also play a significant role i
our ethical beliefs and values.

THINK THEORY

Think about Hofstede's 'mental programming' theory of culture in terms of its for ethical decision-making. In the text, we have explained how the dimension individualism/collectivism and power distance might influence decision-makin What are the likely influences of masculinity/femininity, uncertainty avoidance, long-term orientation? Is this a helpful way of exploring the cultural influences ethical decision-making?

Think Theory

Throughout the text are call-out boxes that encourage you to stop and think about how the theories discussed in the book apply to real world examples.

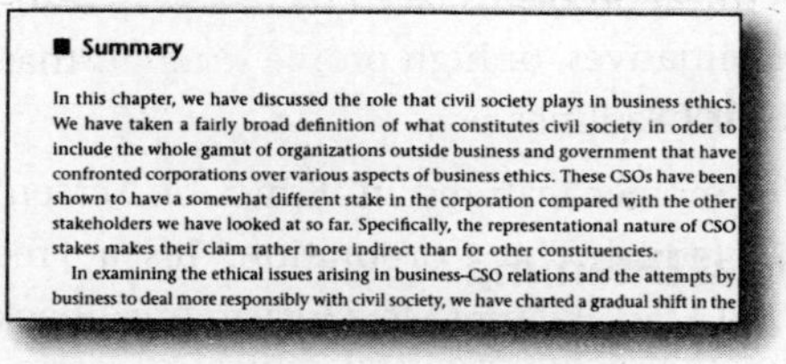
■ Summary

In this chapter, we have discussed the role that civil society plays in business ethics. We have taken a fairly broad definition of what constitutes civil society in order to include the whole gamut of organizations outside business and government that have confronted corporations over various aspects of business ethics. These CSOs have been shown to have a somewhat different stake in the corporation compared with the other stakeholders we have looked at so far. Specifically, the representational nature of CSO stakes makes their claim rather more indirect than for other constituencies.

In examining the ethical issues arising in business-CSO relations and the attempts by business to deal more responsibly with civil society, we have charted a gradual shift in the

Chapter Summary

The chapter summary provides a brief overview of the issues covered in a particular chapter, helping you to review what you have learned.

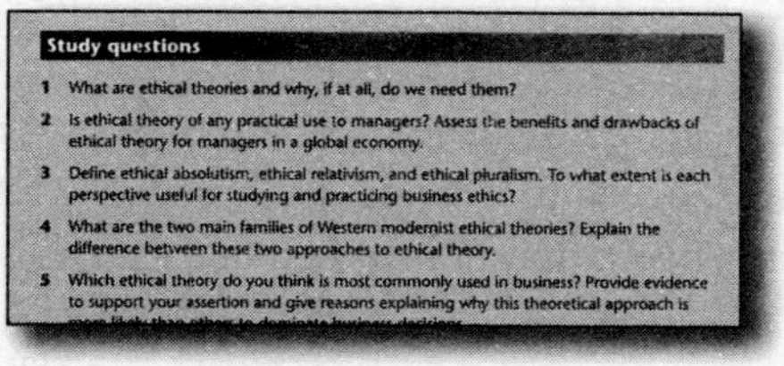
Study questions

1 What are ethical theories and why, if at all, do we need them?
2 Is ethical theory of any practical use to managers? Assess the benefits and drawbacks of ethical theory for managers in a global economy.
3 Define ethical absolutism, ethical relativism, and ethical pluralism. To what extent is each perspective useful for studying and practicing business ethics?
4 What are the two main families of Western modernist ethical theories? Explain the difference between these two approaches to ethical theory.
5 Which ethical theory do you think is most commonly used in business? Provide evidence to support your assertion and give reasons explaining why this theoretical approach is

Study Questions and Research Exercise

At the end of each chapter we provide readers with the opportunity to test their knowledge and understanding of the material covered so far in a format commonly used in course assignments and exams.

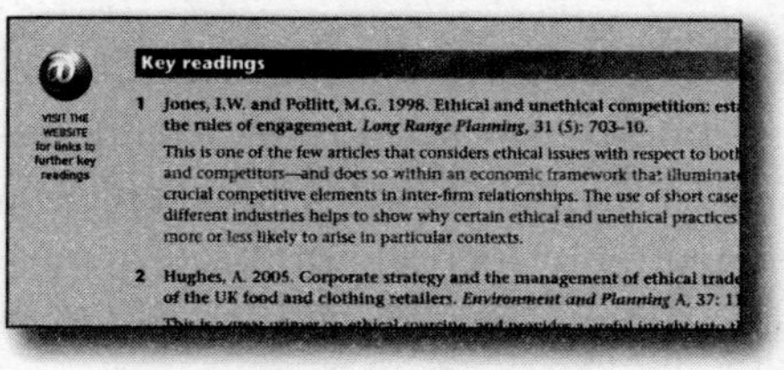

Key readings

1 Jones, I.W. and Pollitt, M.G. 1998. Ethical and unethical competition: est the rules of engagement. *Long Range Planning*, 31 (5): 703–10.

This is one of the few articles that considers ethical issues with respect to both and competitors—and does so within an economic framework that illuminat crucial competitive elements in inter-firm relationships. The use of short case different industries helps to show why certain ethical and unethical practices more or less likely to arise in particular contexts.

2 Hughes, A. 2005. Corporate strategy and the management of ethical trad of the UK food and clothing retailers. *Environment and Planning* A, 37: 1

Key Readings

At the end of each chapter, we select two articles that we believe provide the best insight into some of the issues we have discussed. Annotated with helpful comments about their content, these will help prioritize additional reading and research.

HOW TO USE THE ONLINE RESOURCE CENTRE

http://www.oxfordtextbooks.co.uk/orc/cranebe3e/

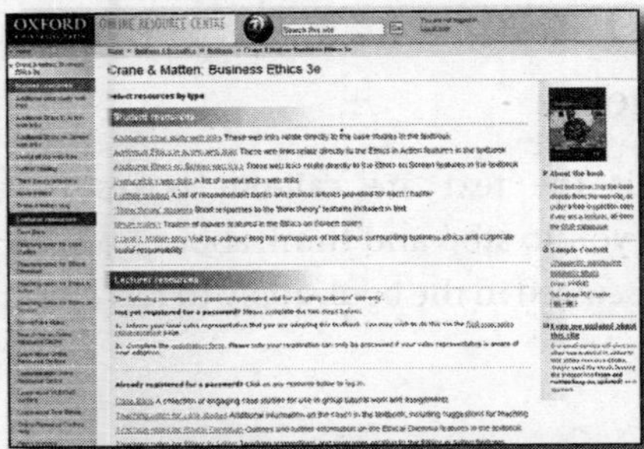

To support this text, there is a wide range of web-based content for both tutors and students.

All these resources can be incorporated into your institution's existing virtual learning environment.

■ For students

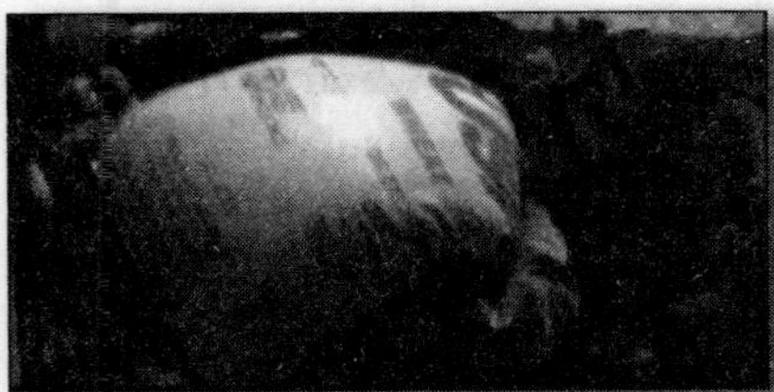

Film trailers

Trailers of movies featured in 'Ethics on Screen' boxes, including The Corporation, It's a Free World, Wal-Mart, Picture Me, Orgasm Inc., Black Gold and Battle in Seattle.

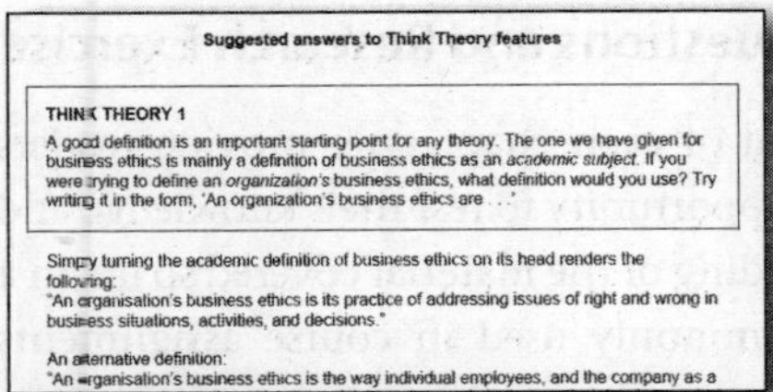

Suggested answers to Think Theory features

THINK THEORY 1

A good definition is an important starting point for any theory. The one we have given for business ethics is mainly a definition of business ethics as an *academic subject*. If you were trying to define an *organization's* business ethics, what definition would you use? Try writing it in the form, 'An organization's business ethics are . . .'

Simply turning the academic definition of business ethics on its head renders the following:
"An organisation's business ethics is its practice of addressing issues of right and wrong in business situations, activities, and decisions."

An alternative definition:
"An organisation's business ethics is the way individual employees, and the company as a

Think Theory solutions

Attempt to answer them yourself and then check your knowledge with suggested solutions for all the Think Theory questions posed in each chapter.

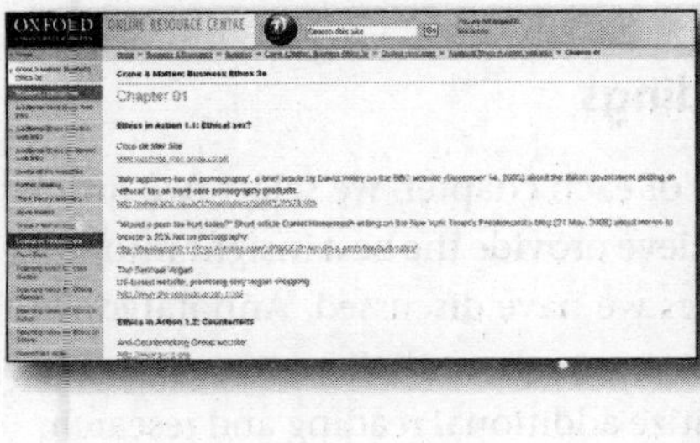

Annotated web links

Links to websites relevant to all the cases, Ethics in Action, Ethics on Screen, and ethics online features included in the chapters, providing you with the opportunity for exploring issues in more depth and getting updates of latest developments.

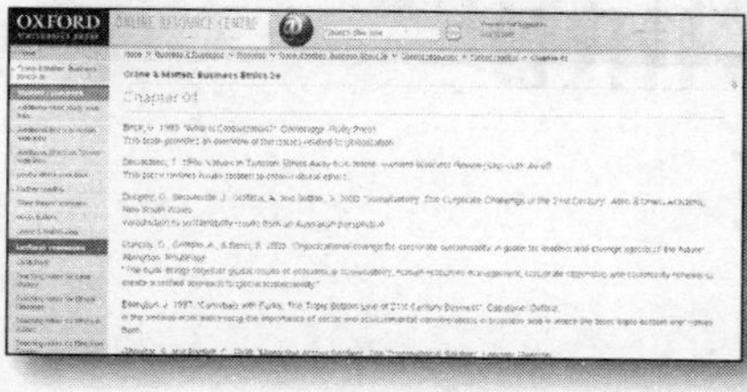

Recommended reading

Annotated links for additional readings providing you with orientation through the literature in order to enhance your understanding of key conceptual issues and selected applications.

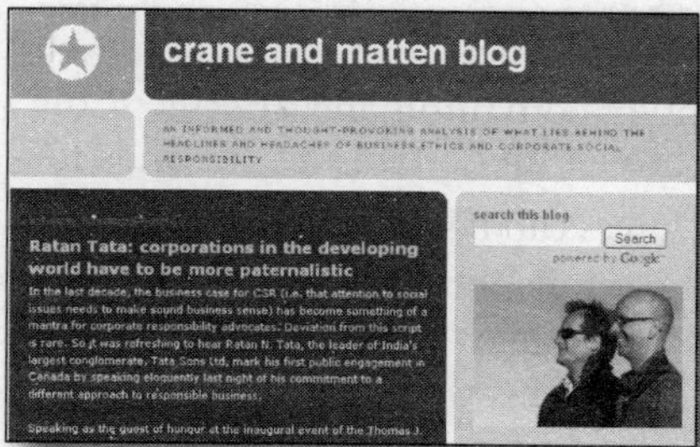

Crane and Matten blog

Follow the authors' commentary on all the latest business ethics issues and trends, and take the opportunity to contribute your own perspective though online comments.

■ For registered adopters

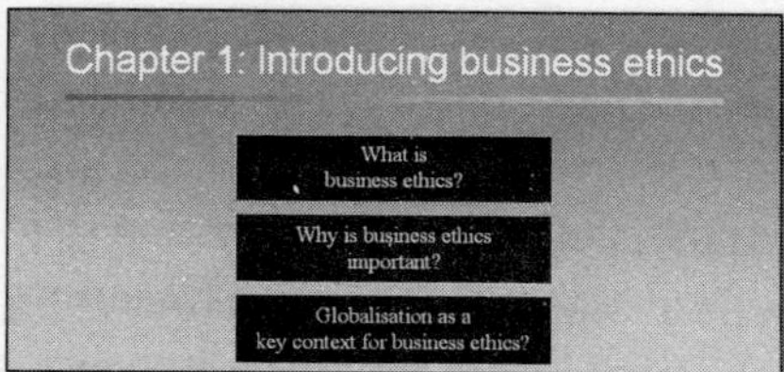

Powerpoint® slides

A full set of chapter-by-chapter lecture slides including all the main points and figures in the text, fully customizable to suit your own presentation style.

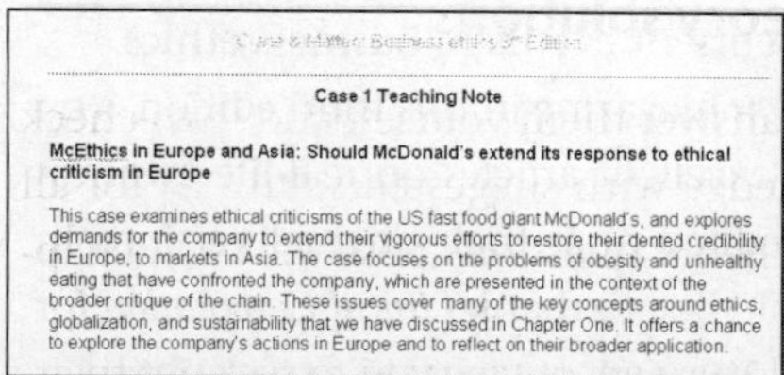

Teaching notes

Suggested answers, teaching suggestions, and further resources for all Ethics in Action features, Ethical Dilemmas, Ethics on Screen, and end-of-chapter cases.

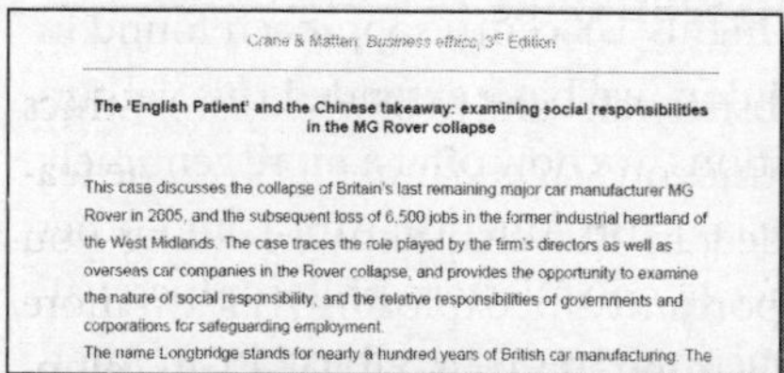

Case bank

Repository of all the cases (with teaching notes) from the previous editions of Crane and Matten, so that you can still get access to all the tried and tested cases you've used in the past.

PREFACE TO THE THIRD EDITION

This third edition of *Business Ethics* is published at the close of the first decade of the millennium. It seems that there could hardly have been a time when the demands for a renewed focus on business ethics—and even for a new contract between business and society—have been more visible. With the financial crisis of the late 2000s, widespread scandals around executive pay and corporate irresponsibility, and growing concerns about climate change, food security, and global health, the whole issue of business ethics has become a matter of widespread debate and consideration across the globe. Such events have also brought home just how inescapable the global context of business ethics has become, and how critical it is to integrate questions of business ethics with broader concerns around corporate citizenship and sustainability.

In this third edition, we continue to bring these diverse perspectives together in order to offer a comprehensive and holistic account of contemporary business ethics. We have also thoroughly revised the text to ensure that it remains the freshest, most engaging, and illuminating book for students of business ethics on the market. New subjects covered in this edition include the ethics of private equity, social enterprise, the business of water, and the impact of global religions. We include new cases and examples throughout and have introduced a new pedagogical feature 'Ethics Online' that discusses the increasing prominence of ethics issues on the web. You will also notice that we have revamped and expanded the online resource centre, and now complement the textbook with an ongoing Crane and Matten blog, where we provide our personal take on current events in business ethics.

We are very pleased to partner with *Ethical Corporation* magazine in this third edition. You will find that we have reproduced a number of their excellent articles on real-life business ethics cases. In some cases, these have been slightly edited from their original versions in the interests of length and temporal accuracy. We would like to thank *Ethical Corporation* for their permission to use and edit this material, and would also encourage you to seek out their magazine and website to explore all the latest developments in the world of business ethics.

The success of the earlier editions of the text confirmed for us the demand for a fresh perspective on business ethics that avoided the usual highly US-centric approach found in most other business ethics textbooks. In this third edition, we have extended this yet further. In place of the European focus of the first two editions, we now offer a more genuinely global perspective. We have even more content on Asia, Latin America, Africa, and other regions; we provide greater emphasis on the importance of non-Western philosophies, values, and religions on business ethics; and we couch our analysis of the subject in an international comparative framework that enables students from one culture to see how and why accounts may differ in other regions and contexts. Nonetheless, the book does still retain a distinct European flavour, not least because this is where the text has its origins.

ACKNOWLEDGEMENTS

First off, we would like to thank all of our readers, students, and fellow-instructors who over the years have provided such great feedback in developing the successive editions of *Business Ethics*. Without all your enthusiasm and encouragement, the book would never have taken off in the way that it has. We are also grateful to the legions of anonymous OUP reviewers who have taken the time to provide detailed comments and suggestions on the book throughout its three editions. We'd also like to thank Aliyah Ahmed and Salman Sabri who helped with some of the new research and updating.

Our sincere thanks go to the Schulich School of Business for providing us with the time, resources, and support without which the book would not have been possible. We would also like to thank Stephanos Anastiadis for all his hard work in updating the Online Resource Centre materials, and Mary Rizzo for assisting with permissions and other administrative details. Others who have provided help are acknowledged at the relevant places in the book. Finally, we would like to thank the team at OUP, especially our dedicated editor Fran Griffin, who succeeded so ably where Nicki Sneath left off, as well as Jo Hardern and Katy Duff who were responsible for production and marketing respectively. We are always surprised by how much work each new edition entails for us as authors, but our team at OUP always provides wonderful support and service along the way.

Andrew Crane & Dirk Matten

January 2010

Front cover: A woman sells fruit from the roadside, a small business that was made possible by microfinance business schemes in Luanda, Angola. For more on microfinance, see case 8 (383–387), *Targeting the poor with microfinance: hype or hope for poverty reduction?*

Credit: Thomas Havisham/Panos

Paper: This book is printed on paper which has been accredited by the Forest Stewardship Council. FSC members comprise a diverse group of representatives from environmental and social groups, the timber trade, paper industry, forestry profession, indigenous people's organisations, community forestry groups and forest product certification organisations from around the world. It is their job to ensure that the forests are managed to protect wildlife habitat and respect the rights of local communities.

All products carrying the FSC Logo have been independently certified as coming from forests that meet the internationally recognized FSC Principles and Criteria of Forest Stewardship. Certification involves inspection and auditing of the land from which the timber and pulpwood originate and tracking it through all the steps of the production process until it reaches the end user. The Forest Stewardship Council (FSC) is an international non-profit organisation founded in 1993 to support the world's forests.

The FSC is an example of a business-CSO collaboration, as discussed in chapter 10. See pages 470–4 for more information.

PART A

Understanding Business Ethics

1

Introducing Business Ethics

In this chapter we will:

- Provide a basic introduction to, and definition of, business ethics.
- Outline the relationship between business ethics and the law.
- Distinguish between ethics, morality, and ethical theory.
- Discuss the importance of business ethics at both an academic level and in terms of practical management in organizations.
- Consider ethical challenges in different types of organizations.
- Present globalization as an important, yet contested, concept that represents a critical context for business ethics.
- Discuss different international perspectives on business ethics, including European, Asian, and North American perspectives.
- Present the 'triple bottom line' of sustainability as a key goal for business ethics.

What is business ethics?

'A book on business ethics? Well that won't take long to read!'

'You're taking a course on business ethics? So what do you do in the afternoon?'

'Business ethics? I didn't think there were any!'

These are not very good jokes. Still, that does not seem to have stopped a lot of people from responding with such comments (and others like them) whenever students of business ethics start talking about what they are doing. And even if these are not particularly funny things to say, nor even very original, they do immediately raise an important problem with the subject of business ethics: some people cannot even believe that it exists!

Business ethics, it has been claimed, is an oxymoron (Collins 1994). By an oxymoron, we mean the bringing together of two apparently contradictory concepts, such as in 'a cheerful pessimist' or 'a deafening silence'. To say that business ethics is an oxymoron suggests that there are not, or cannot be, ethics in business: that business is in some way unethical (i.e. that business is inherently bad), or that it is, at best, amoral (i.e. outside of our normal moral considerations). For example, in the latter case, Albert Carr (1968) notoriously argued in his article 'Is Business Bluffing Ethical' that the 'game' of business was not subject to the same moral standards as the rest of society, but should be regarded as analogous to a game of poker, where deception and lying were perfectly permissible.

To some extent, it is not surprising that some people think this way. Various scandals concerning undesirable business activities, such as the polluting of rivers with industrial chemicals, the exploitation of sweatshop workers, the payment of bribes to government officials, and the deception of unwary consumers, have highlighted the unethical way in which some firms have gone about their business. However, just because such malpractices take place does not mean that there are not some kinds of values or principles driving such decisions. After all, even what we might think of as 'bad' ethics are still ethics of a sort. And clearly it makes sense to try and understand why those decisions get made in the first place, and indeed to try and discover whether more acceptable business decisions and approaches can be developed.

Revelations of corporate malpractice should not therefore be interpreted to mean that thinking about ethics in business situations is entirely redundant. After all, as various writers have shown, many everyday business activities require the maintenance of basic ethical standards, such as honesty, trustworthiness, and co-operation (Collins 1994; Watson 1994). Business activity would be impossible if corporate directors always lied; if buyers and sellers never trusted each other; or if employees refused to ever help each other.

Similarly, it would be wrong to infer that scandals involving corporate wrongdoing mean that the *subject* of business ethics was in some way naïve or idealistic. Indeed, on the contrary, it can be argued that the subject of business ethics primarily exists in order to provide us with some answers as to *why* certain decisions should be evaluated as ethical or unethical, or right or wrong. Without systematic study, how are we able to offer anything more than vague opinions or hunches about whether particular business activities are acceptable?

Whichever way one looks at it then, there appears to be good reason to suggest that business ethics as a phenomenon, and as a subject, is not an oxymoron. Whilst there will inevitably be disagreements about what exactly constitutes 'ethical' business activity, it is possible at least to offer a fairly uncontroversial definition of the subject itself. So, in a nutshell, here is what we regard the subject of business ethics as:

> **Business ethics is the study of business situations, activities, and decisions where issues of right and wrong are addressed.**

It is worth stressing that by 'right' and 'wrong' we mean morally right and wrong, as opposed to, for example, commercially, strategically, or financially right or wrong. Moreover, by 'business' ethics, we do not mean only commercial businesses, but also government organizations, pressure groups, not-for-profit businesses, charities, and other organizations. For example, questions of how to manage employees fairly, or what constitutes deception in advertising, are equally as important for organizations such as Greenpeace, the University of Stockholm, or the German Christian Democrat Party as they are for Shell, Volvo, or Deutsche Bank (see pp. 15–17 for detailed discussion of ethics in different types of organizations).

? THINK THEORY

A good definition is an important starting point for any theory. The one we have given for business ethics is mainly a definition of business ethics as an *academic subject*. If you were trying to define an *organization's* business ethics, what definition would you use? Try writing it in the form, 'An organization's business ethics are . . .'

VISIT THE WEBSITE for a short response to this feature

Business ethics and the law

Having defined business ethics in terms of issues of right and wrong, one might quite naturally question whether this is in any way distinct from the law. Surely the law is also about issues of right and wrong. This is true, and there is indeed considerable overlap between ethics and the law. In fact, the law is essentially an institutionalization or codification of ethics into specific social rules, regulations, and proscriptions. Nevertheless, the two are not equivalent. Perhaps the best way of thinking about ethics and the law is in terms of two intersecting domains (see **Figure 1.1**). The law might be said to be a definition of the minimum acceptable standards of behaviour. However, many morally contestable issues, whether in business or elsewhere, are not explicitly covered by the law. For example, just as there is no law preventing you from being unfaithful to your girlfriend or boyfriend (although this is perceived by many to be unethical), so there is no law in many countries preventing businesses from testing their products on animals, selling landmines to oppressive regimes, or preventing their employees from joining a union—again, issues which many feel very strongly about. Similarly, it is possible to think of issues that are covered by the law, but which are not really about ethics.

AN ETHICAL DILEMMA 1

No such thing as a free drink?

A good friend of yours, who studies at the same university, has been complaining for some time to you that he never has any money. He decides that he needs to go out and find a job, and after searching for a while is offered a job as a bartender in the student bar at your university. He gladly accepts and begins working three nights a week. You too are pleased, not only because it means that your friend will have more money, but also because the fact is that you often go to the student bar already and so will continue to see him quite frequently despite him having the new job.

The extra money is indeed much welcomed by your friend (especially as he has less time to spend it now too), and initially he seems to enjoy the work. You are also rather pleased with developments since you notice that whenever you go up to the bar, your friend always serves you first regardless of how many people are waiting.

After a time though, it becomes apparent that your friend is enjoying the job rather less. Whenever you see him, he always seems to have a new story of mistreatment at the hands of the bar manager, such as getting the worst shifts, being repeatedly chosen to do the least popular jobs, and being reprimanded for minor blunders that go uncensored for the rest of the staff.

This goes on for a short while and then one day, when you are in the bar having a drink with some of your other friends, your friend the bartender does something that you are not quite sure how to react to. When you go up to pay for a round of four beers for you and your other friends, he discretely only charges you for one. Whilst you are slightly uncomfortable with this, you certainly don't want to get your friend into any kind of trouble by mentioning it. And when you tell your friends about it, they of course think it is very funny and congratulate you for the cheap round of drinks! In fact, when the next one of your friends goes up to pay for some drinks, he turns around and asks you to take his money, so that you can do the same trick for him. Although you tell him to get his own drinks, your friend the bartender continues to undercharge you whenever it is your turn to go to the bar. In fact this goes on for a number of visits, until you resolve to at least say something to him when no one else behind the bar is listening. However, when you do end up raising the subject he just laughs it off and says, 'Yeah, it's great isn't it? They'll never notice and you get a cheap night out. Besides, it's only what this place deserves after the way I've been treated.'

Questions

1 Who is wrong in this situation—your friend for undercharging you, you for accepting it, both of you, or neither of you?

2 Confronted by this situation, how would you handle it? Do nothing or ask your friend to stop undercharging you? If you take the latter option, what would you do if he refused?

3 To what extent do you think that being deliberately undercharged is different from other forms of preferential treatment, such as serving you in front of other waiting customers?

4 Does the fact that your friend feels aggrieved at the treatment he receives from his boss condone his behaviour at all? Does it help to explain either his or your actions?

For example, the law prescribes whether we should drive on the right or the left side of the road. Although this prevents chaos on the roads, the decision about which side we should drive on is not an ethical decision as such.

In one sense then, business ethics can be said to begin where the law ends. Business ethics is primarily concerned with those issues not covered by the law, or where there is no definite consensus on whether something is right or wrong. Discussion about the ethics of particular business practices may eventually *lead* to legislation once some kind of consensus is reached, but for most of the issues of interest to business ethics, the law typically does not currently provide us with guidance. For this reason, it is often said that business ethics is about the 'grey areas' of business, or where, as Treviño and Nelson (2007: 3) put it, 'values are in conflict'. **Ethical Dilemma** 1 presents one such situation that you might face where values are in conflict. Read through this and have a go at answering the questions at the end.

As we shall see many times over in this book, the problem of trying to make decisions in the grey areas of business ethics, or where values may be in conflict, means that many of the questions posed are *equivocal*. What this suggests is that there simply may not be a definitive 'right' answer to many business ethics problems. And as is the case with issues such as the testing of products on animals, executive compensation packages,

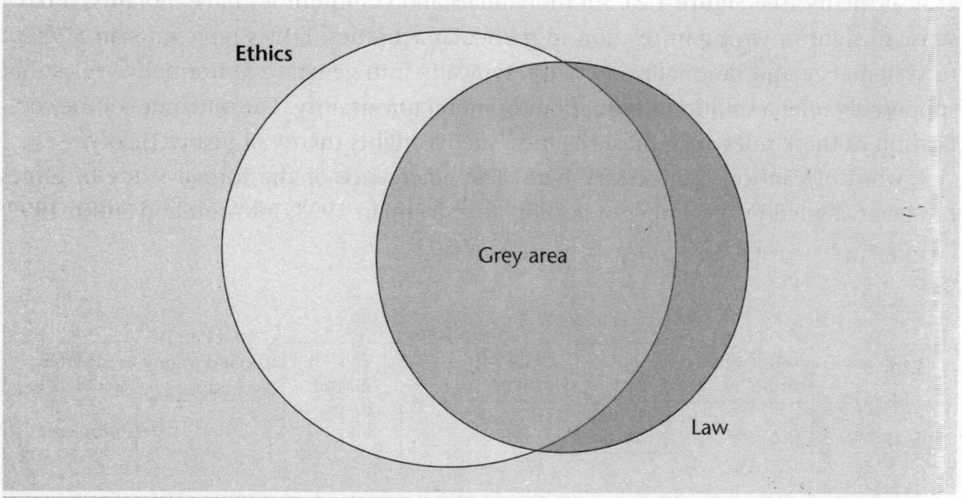

Figure 1.1. The relationship between ethics and the law

persuasive sales techniques, or child labour, business ethics problems also tend to be very controversial and open to widely different points of view. In this sense, business ethics is not like subjects such as accounting, finance, engineering, or business law where you are supposed to learn specific procedures and facts in order to make objectively correct decisions. Studying business ethics should help you to make *better* decisions, but this is not the same as making unequivocally *right* decisions.

Defining morality, ethics, and ethical theory

Some of the controversy regarding business ethics is no doubt due to different understandings of what constitutes morality or ethics in the first place. Before we continue then, it is important for us to sort out some of the terminology we are using.

In common usage, the terms 'ethics' and 'morality' are often used interchangeably. This probably does not pose many real problems for most of us in terms of communicating and understanding things about business ethics. However, in order to clarify certain arguments, many academic writers have proposed clear differences between the two terms (e.g. Crane 2000; Parker 1998b). Unfortunately, though, different writers have sometimes offered somewhat different distinctions, thereby serving more to confuse us than clarify our understanding.[1] Nonetheless, we do agree that there are certain advantages in making a distinction between 'ethics' and 'morality', and following the most common way of distinguishing them, we offer the following definitions:

Morality is concerned with the norms, values, and beliefs embedded in social processes which define right and wrong for an individual or a community.

Ethics is concerned with the study of morality and the application of reason to elucidate specific rules and principles that determine right and wrong for a given situation. These rules and principles are called ethical theories.

According to this way of thinking, morality precedes ethics, which in turn precedes ethical theory (see **Figure 1.2**). All individuals and communities have morality, a basic sense of right or wrong in relation to particular activities. Ethics represents an attempt to systematize and rationalize morality, typically into generalized normative rules that supposedly offer a solution to situations of moral uncertainty. The outcomes of the codification of these rules are ethical theories, such as rights theory or justice theory.

A word of caution is necessary here. The emergence of the formal study of ethics has been aligned by a number of authors (e.g. Bauman 1993; Johnson and Smith 1999;

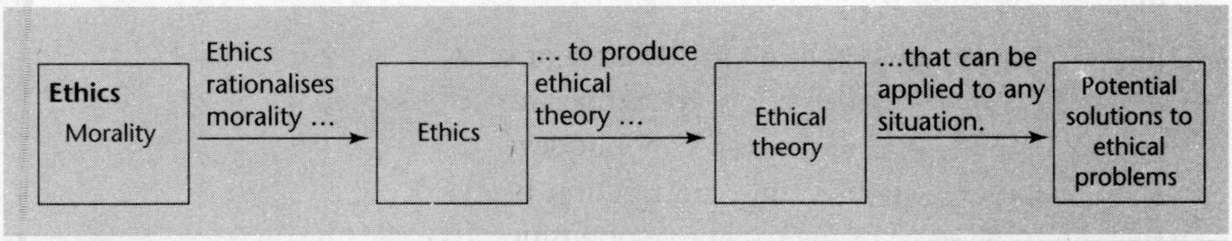

Figure 1.2. The relationship between morality, ethics, and ethical theory

Parker 1998b) with the modernist Enlightenment project, and the idea that moral uncertainty can be 'solved' with recourse to human rationality and abstract reasoning. As we shall show in Chapters 3 and 4, this has come under increasing attack from a number of quarters, including feminists and postmodernists. However, it is important at this stage to recognize that *ethics* is about some form of rationalization of *morality*. The importance of this distinction will hopefully therefore become clearer, and will certainly become more pertinent, as we start to examine these and other theories (in Chapter 3), as well as assessing how they feed into ethical decision-making in business (in Chapter 4). Indeed, contributing to the enhancement of ethical decision-making is one of the primary aims of this book, and of the subject of business ethics more generally. In the next section, we shall briefly review this and some of the other reasons why studying business ethics is becoming increasingly important today across the globe.

■ Why is business ethics important?

Business ethics is currently a very prominent business topic, and debates and dilemmas surrounding business ethics have attracted a lot of attention from various quarters. For a start, consumers and pressure groups have increasingly demanded that firms seek out more ethical and ecologically sounder ways of doing business. The media has also kept a constant spotlight on corporate abuses and malpractices. And even firms themselves appear to be increasingly recognizing that being ethical (or at the very least, being seen to be ethical) may actually be good for business. Ethical issues confront organizations whatever line of business they might be in. **Ethics in Action 1.1**, for example, provides an illustration of how Sam Roddick has taken the unusual step of opening an ethical 'erotic boutique' aimed at the luxury end of the sex toys and erotic lingerie market.

There are therefore many reasons why business ethics might be regarded as an increasingly important area of study, whether as students interested in evaluating business activities or as managers seeking to improve their decision-making skills. In summary, we can suggest the following reasons why a good understanding of business ethics is important:

1 The power and influence of business in society is greater than ever before. Evidence suggests that many members of the public are uneasy with such developments (Bernstein 2000). For instance, one recent poll of more than 20 leading economic nations revealed that almost 75% of residents believed large companies had too much influence on the decisions of their government (Cywinski 2008). Business ethics helps us to understand why this is happening, what its implications might be, and how we might address this situation.

2 Business has the potential to provide a major contribution to our societies, in terms of producing the products and services that we want, providing employment, paying taxes, and acting as an engine for economic development, to name just a few examples. How, or indeed whether, this contribution is made raises significant ethical issues that go to the heart of the social role of business in contemporary society. As a 2008 global survey conducted by McKinsey shows, about 50% of business executives think that corporations make a mostly or somewhat positive contribution to society, whilst

VISIT THE WEBSITE for links to useful sources of further information

ETHICS IN ACTION 1.1

Ethical sex?

Most people will have heard of Anita Roddick, the charismatic founder of the Body Shop chain of shops, and one of the best-known advocates of ethical business. Although Anita died unexpectedly in 2008, her daughter Sam Roddick looks set to carry her mother's torch and challenge ideas of ethical business all over again. For Sam is the founder of Coco de Mer, a self-proclaimed 'erotic boutique' with branches in London and Los Angeles that has taken a novel approach to the usually seedy sex industry by loudly broadcasting its firm ethical stance along with its X-rated products.

The shop sells a variety of sexually oriented material, from lingerie to bondage gear, designer sex toys, erotic literature, 'erotic jewel tools', and salons that provide 'lessons in the art of loving'. It aims very much at the top end of a lucrative market, with a hand-crafted silver leather dog mask setting you back some US$450 and a JimmyJane-designed gold vibrator with diamonds costing an eyebrow-raising US$2,750! However, Roddick has identified a clear market niche by targeting the kind of people that would not be seen dead in a back-street sex shop, but will happily sign up for one of the shop's courses on 'tricks to please a man' or a 'spanking skills salon' at its fashionable Covent Garden or Melrose Avenue stores. Not only this, but Roddick has recognized that many people are uncomfortable with the whiff of exploitation that taints the traditional sex industry, and so has set about developing an 'ethical' approach to the business that offers a clear alternative to most of the rest of the market.

'We have very strong and clear ethics at Coco de Mer,' the firm's website boasts, 'All our products are made with the consideration of environmental and human rights. We invest in the talents of local artisans. When we seek a skill abroad, we work with small Fair Trade projects or cottage industries.' Not only this, but along with an educational approach to sex among its customers, Coco de Mer also operates an 'activist arm' called Bondage for Freedom, which provides a free creative service for organizations fighting for human or environmental rights.

For some commentators, the whole idea of trying to marry business ethics with the business of sex is too much of a contradiction in terms to make any real sense. With its 'tasteful' erotica featuring topless models and full frontal nudity, and a product range that celebrates the full range of (legal) sexual activity in explicit detail, there is a significant portion of society that would simply brand the whole endeavour as objectionable and obscene, especially within the usually prudish British and American cultures. And in much the same way that the anti-smoking lobby will not countenance the possibility of there being an ethical cigarette firm, so too there are problems in establishing a credible ethical sex shop.

Perhaps unsurprisingly then, Roddick's Coco de Mer shop appears to be something of a pioneer within the sex industry—just as much as her mother was in the fledgling 'green' toiletries industry of the 1970s and 1980s. Maybe the ethical approach to sex will also catch on like the Body Shop approach did—but until it does, it seems like you'd have a hard job finding anywhere else that sold dildos with conflict-free diamonds, sustainable wood spanking paddles, or fairly traded condoms that protect the livelihoods of rubber plantation workers.

Sources

Macalister, T. 2005. Ethical erotica. *Guardian*, Saturday 15 January. http://www.guardian.co.uk; http://www.coco-de-mer.com.

? THINK THEORY

If, as we have argued, business ethics is not an oxymoron, then is it necessarily true of *any* business, regardless on the industry it is in? Think about the reasons for and against regarding Coco de Mer as an ethical organization. Would the same arguments hold for an 'ethical' land mine manufacturer, or an 'ethical' animal testing laboratory?

VISIT THE WEBSITE for a short response to this feature

some 25% believe that their contribution is mostly or somewhat negative (*McKinsey Quarterly* 2008).

3 Business malpractices have the potential to inflict enormous harm on individuals, on communities and on the environment. Through helping us to understand more about the causes and consequences of these malpractices, business ethics seeks, as the founding editor of the *Journal of Business Ethics* has suggested (Michalos 1988), 'to improve the human condition'.

4 The demands being placed on business to be ethical by its various stakeholders are constantly becoming more complex and more challenging. Business ethics provides the means to appreciate and understand these challenges more clearly, in order that firms can meet these ethical expectations more effectively.

5 Few businesspeople have received formal business ethics education or training. Business ethics can help to improve ethical decision-making by providing managers with the appropriate knowledge and tools to allow them to correctly identify, diagnose, analyse, and provide solutions to the ethical problems and dilemmas they are confronted with.

6 Ethical violations continue to occur in business, across countries and across sectors. For example, a recent survey of over 1,000 UK employees working in public and private sectors found that one in three workers did not consider their employers to be fair.[2] Another survey of nearly 2,000 Hong Kong executives revealed that more than 40% of those with operations in China had encountered fraud.[3] Business ethics provides us with a way of looking at the reasons behind such infractions, and the ways in which such problems might be dealt with by managers, regulators, and others interested in improving business ethics.

7 Business ethics can provide us with the ability to assess the benefits and problems associated with different ways of managing ethics in organizations.

VISIT THE WEBSITE for links to useful sources of further information

ETHICS ON SCREEN 1

Blood Diamond

Blood Diamond means well, but it also means box-office business.

Manohla Dargis, *New York Times*

Blood Diamond, a thriller set against the backdrop of the civil war in Sierra Leone in the 1990s, provides a fast-paced, action-filled Hollywood-style perspective on the issues surrounding 'conflict diamonds'. Defined by the United Nations as '... diamonds that originate from areas controlled by forces or factions opposed to legitimate and internationally recognized governments', conflict diamonds are essentially those mined and traded by rebel military forces in order to fund conflict in war-torn areas, particularly in central and western Africa. The proceeds from the sale of conflict diamonds go towards purchasing arms and other illegal activities that sustain rebel militia units. Brutal conflicts in Angola and Sierra Leone brought conflict diamonds to the United Nations' attention and subsequently led to targeted UN sanctions prohibiting the importing of diamonds originating from rebel sources.

It is in this context that the events in the movie *Blood Diamond* are situated. The narrative centres around the discovery of a huge pink diamond by a Sierra Leonean fisherman, Solomon Vandy (played by Djimon Hounsou), who has been taken from his family and forced to work in the diamond fields. Following an attack by government troops on the rebel mining camp, Vandy is forced to hide the diamond in the jungle before being captured and thrown into jail. It is here that he meets Danny Archer (Leonardo DiCaprio), a cynical Zimbabwean diamond smuggler, linked through a South African mercenary to a Western diamond company. Archer and Vandy agree an uneasy alliance to retrieve the diamond, and set off on a perilous journey back into the conflict zone.

Blood Diamond does not go into detail on the issues surrounding conflict diamonds, but uses the issue as a springboard for developing an exotic action adventure with plenty of thrills and spills and even a slice of romance in the form of a beautiful American journalist, played by Jennifer Connelly, who Archer meets along the way. In so doing, it clearly brings a relatively obscure business ethics issues to a wide mainstream cinema audience in a way that a book, a news segment, or factual documentary never could. In watching the film, the terrible consequences of civil war, and the role of the diamond trade in fuelling such conflict, simply cannot be ignored. Critics, however, have also criticized the film for its rather crude politics and easy moralizing, its simplistic portrayal of the complex issues involved, and its readiness to reduce African problems to Hollywood-style solutions.

Warner Bros./The Kobal Collection

The release of the film also met some controversy within the global diamond industry. With its Christmas theatrical release in the US coinciding with the main diamond-buying season in the world's largest diamond jewellery market, the diamond industry launched an estimated $15m public-relations and education campaign to combat the movie's negative images of the industry. The World Diamond Council (WDC) created a website, DiamondFacts.org, to communicate to the public about reforms in the 2000s that led to a substantial decline in the global trade in conflict diamonds. As a result of a UN-backed initiative called the Kimberley Process that was launched in 2003, the share of conflict diamonds in the global industry is estimated to have fallen to less than 1% of total trade from a high of around 4% at the end of the 1990s when *Blood Diamond* is set.

The WDC also distributed information packs for retailers and customers and hired a crisis-management firm to direct its educational efforts, including full-page ads in US newspapers such as the *Los Angeles Times*, *The New York Times*, and *USA Today*. In a particularly successful PR coup, the industry enlisted Nelson Mandela to talk about the economic benefits of diamond mining for the African population. For their part, the studio behind the film's release maintained that it was a fictionalized account set at a particular time in history, whilst the director, Edward Zwick, was widely reported to have refused to add a disclaimer requested by the WDC to inform audiences that voluntary reforms had since stamped out most conflict diamonds.

Blood Diamond went on to box office success and even garnered Oscar nominations for the two male leads. Perhaps most importantly, it also brought some critical ethical issues into the mainstream. Whilst the movie itself employs little subtlety in highlighting the problems of conflict diamonds, it shows that business ethics can even prove to be a hit at the multiplex—providing you are prepared to disguise it as an action adventure and lace it with a typical Hollywood ending.

Sources

Dargis, M. 2006. Diamonds and the devil, amid the anguish of Africa. *New York Times*, 6 December.
Stanley, T.L. 2006. Gem sellers launch blitz against 'Blood Diamond'. *Advertising Age*, 11 December: p. 12.
http://www.diamondfacts.org.
http://www.un.org/peace/africa/Diamond.html.

8 Finally, business ethics is also extremely interesting in that it provides us with knowledge that transcends the traditional framework of business studies and confronts us with some of the most important questions faced by society. The subject can therefore be richly rewarding to study because it provides us with knowledge and skills that are not simply helpful for doing business, but rather, by helping us to understand modern societies in a more systematic way, can advance our ability to address life situations far beyond the classroom or the office desk.

Having identified some of the reasons why business ethics is important, we should also make it clear that this does not necessarily mean that there are not also a number of problems with the subject of business ethics. Indeed, these have prompted writers such as Andrew Stark (1994) to pose the question 'what's the matter with business ethics?' and Tom Sorrell (1998) to pronounce on the 'strange state of business ethics'. After all, despite many years of business ethics being researched and taught in colleges and universities, ethics problems persist and the public remains sceptical of the ethics of business. However, in the main, these concerns are directed at how theories of business ethics have been developed and applied, rather than questioning the importance of business ethics as a subject per se.

Indeed, there does seem to be a growing consensus regarding the importance of addressing questions of business ethics, whether on the part of students, academics, governments, consumers, or, of course, businesses. There are now modules in business ethics being run in universities across Europe, the US, and much of the rest of the world.

VISIT THE WEBSITE for links to useful sources of further information

ETHICS ONLINE 1

Ethical fashion for ethics girls

Want to buy a new pair of skinny jeans, but also care about how much the workers were paid to make them? Think there may be space in your life for a solar-powered MP4 player? Well, being ethical doesn't have to mean being unfashionable any more, at least not according to the Ethics Girls, a UK-based organization launched online in 2007. The Ethics Girls website seeks, as they put it, to 'set the example' in 'ethical fashion, shopping and ideas'. Featuring a shop, magazine, product reviews, and an easy-to-read jargon buster, the site promises to 'take the guilt out of ethical consumption, to make life and our choices simpler'.

Unlike some ethical shopping sites, such as the Ethical Consumer organization's online buyers' guides (which provide detailed scorecards for a wide range of products in numerous categories), Ethics Girls do not claim to have a particularly robust research methodology. Their approach is style-led rather than research-led, with an emphasis on lifestyle journalism and the promotion of positive choices among young women. And perhaps more than anything, it shows the continuing transformation and maturation of the internet as a place for ethical shoppers of all kinds—and not just diehard activists—to go for advice, information, and inspiration.

Sources

Ethics Girls website: http://www.ethicsgirls.co.uk.
Ethical Consumer website: http://www.ethicalconsumer.org.

As *The Times* newspaper put it, 'business schools are talking up their ethics courses in the wake of recent corporate scandals' (Dearlove 2006). There has also been an outpouring of books, magazine, journal, and newspaper articles on the subject, as well as web pages, blogs, and other electronic publications—amazon.com currently lists more than 14,000 books related to business ethics, whilst a Google search on 'business ethics' returns more than 4 million hits at the time of writing. Even through television and cinema, business ethics issues are reaching a wide audience. Movies such as the Hollywood feature, *Blood Diamond,* the subject of **Ethics on Screen 1**, raise a number of critical business ethics issues and have played them out to millions of viewers across the globe.

Similarly, the last few years have witnessed significant growth in what might be regarded as the business ethics 'industry', i.e. corporate ethics officers, ethics consultants, ethical investment trusts, ethical products and services, and activities associated with ethics auditing, monitoring, and reporting. One annual UK survey, for instance, estimates the country's 'ethical market' (i.e. consumer spending on ethical products and services) to be worth something like £35bn annually (The Co-operative Bank 2008). The ethical market ranges from organic and fair trade foods to responsible holidays, energy efficient products, ethical banking, and ethical clothes. As **Ethics Online 1** shows, organizations such as Ethics Girls have sprung up to help consumers navigate these new market niches—and to promote the idea that ethics is also for those who 'love to shop'!

What is clear then is that business ethics has not only been recognized as increasingly important, but has also undergone rapid changes and developments during the past decade or so. This has been the case not only in large corporations, but also in small- and medium-sized enterprises (SMEs), and in public and non-profit organizations too. Let's now take a closer look at how business ethics issues might be manifested in these rather different organizational contexts.

■ Business ethics in different organizational contexts

It should be clear by now that whatever else we may think it of it, business ethics clearly matters. But it matters not just for huge multinational corporations like McDonald's, Nestlé, Shell or HSBC, but also for a range of other types of organizations. Some of the issues will inevitably be rather similar across organizational types. **Figures 1.3 and 1.4**, for example, show that employees from business, government, and civil society organizations (by this we mean non-profit, charity, or non-governmental organizations) observe similar types of ethical misconduct in the workplace—and at similar intensities. Indeed, despite some historical differences, the level of ethical violations observed by employees in different sectors appears to be converging. Nonetheless, there are also a number of critical differences, which are worth elaborating on a little further (and which are summarized in **Figure 1.5**).

Business ethics in large versus small companies

Small businesses (often referred to as SMEs or small and medium-sized enterprises) typically differ in their attention and approach to business ethics. As Laura Spence (1999) suggests, these differences include the lack of time and resources small business managers have

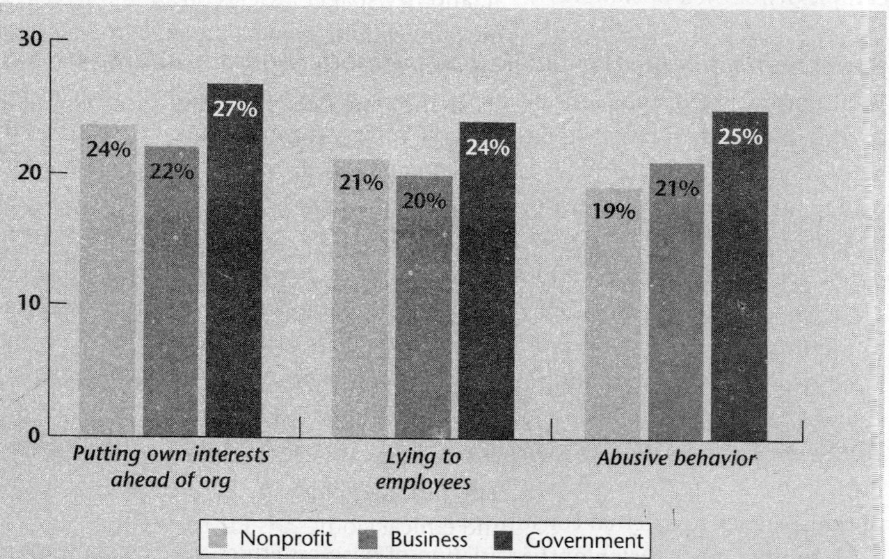

Figure 1.3. Types of misconduct across sectors

Source: Ethics Resource Center (2008), 2007 *National Nonprofit Ethics Survey: An Inside View of Nonprofit Sector Ethics*, Arlington, VA: Ethics Resource Center: p.16. Reprinted with permission.

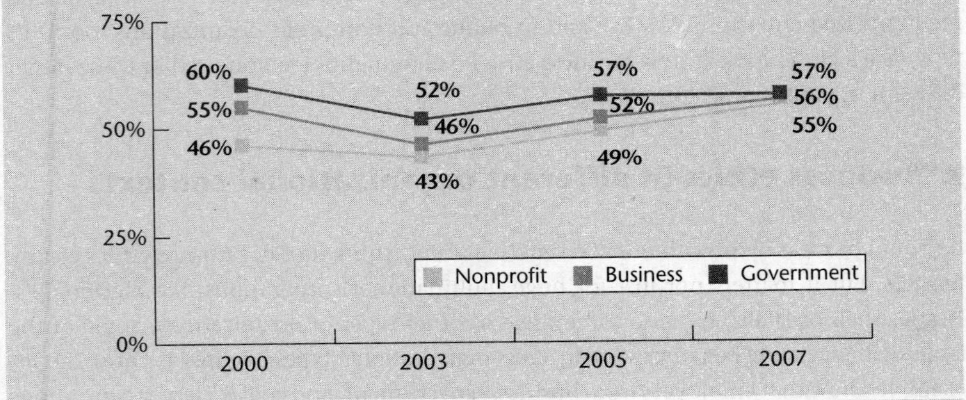

Figure 1.4. Observed ethical misconduct across sectors

Source: Ethics Resource Center (2008), 2007 *National Nonprofit Ethics Survey: An Inside View of Nonprofit Sector Ethics*, Arlington, VA: Ethics Resource Center: p.3. Reprinted with permission.

available to focus on ethics, their autonomy and independence with respect to responsibilities to other stakeholders, and their informal trust-based approach to managing ethics. They have also been found to assess their employees as their single most important stakeholder (Spence and Lozano 2000). Large corporations, on the other hand, tend to have much more formalized approaches with considerably more resources available to develop sophisticated ethics management programmes. That said, they are constrained by the need to focus on profitability and shareholder value, as well as the very size and complexity of their operations.

Business ethics in private, public, and civil society organizations

Whilst private sector companies will tend to be responsible primarily to their shareholders or owners, the main responsibilities of civil society organizations (CSOs) are to the constituencies they serve (and also to their donors). In the public sector, more attention is paid to higher level government and the general public. Typical ethical issues prioritized by government agencies will be those of rule of law, corruption, conflicts of interest, public accountability, and various procedural issues involved in ensuring that resources are deployed fairly and impartially (Moilanen and Salminen 2007). This is usually reflected in a formalized and bureaucratic approach to ethics management. CSOs, on the other hand, will often be more informal in their approach, emphasizing their mission and values. CSOs may be limited in terms of the resources and training they may typically be able to deploy in relation to managing ethics, whereas, on the other hand, government organizations are often restricted by a heavy bureaucracy that breeds inertia and a lack of transparency to external constituencies.

This rather quick sketch of the variation of business ethics across organizational contexts should give you some of the flavour of the challenges that managers may face in each type of organization. In this book, we will generally focus more on large corporations than the other types—principally because most of our readers will probably end

	Large corporations	Small businesses	Civil society organizations	Public sector organizations
Main priorities in addressing ethical issues	Financial integrity, employee/ customer issues	Employee issues	Delivery of mission to clients; integrity of tactics; legitimacy and accountability	Rule of law, corruption, conflicts of interest; procedural issues, accountability
Approach to managing ethics	Formal, public relations and/or systems-based	Informal, trust-based	Informal, values-based	Formal, bureaucratic
Responsible and/or accountable to	Shareholders and other stakeholders	Owners	Donors and clients	General public, higher level government organizations
Main constraints	Shareholder orientation; size and complexity	Lack of resources and attention	Lack of resources and formal training	Inertia, lack of transparency

Figure 1.5. Differences in business ethics across organizational types

up working in such an organization. However, as we go through, we will also highlight issues pertinent to small firms, and in the latter part of the book in particular, we will discuss in much fuller detail business ethics and CSOs (Chapter 10) and government (Chapter 11). Before we move on though, we need to consider another important context—namely the global nature of business ethics today.

■ Globalization: a key context for business ethics?

Globalization has become one of the most prominent buzzwords of recent times. Whether in newspaper articles, politicians' speeches, or business leaders' press conferences, the 'G-word' is frequently identified as one of the most important issues in contemporary society. In the business community, in particular, there has been considerable enthusiasm about globalization. For instance, as chairman of Goldman Sachs in 2001, Hank Paulson talked of 'the gospel of globalization' in praising the increasingly interconnected world economy and its benefits for economic growth, global welfare, democracy, and world peace (Paulson 2001). However, Paulson also had the pleasure of witnessing the more ambiguous 'blessings' of globalization in his role as US Treasury Secretary in 2008, when he was in charge of taming the disastrous effects of the global financial crisis on the US economy. It is hardly surprising then to learn that business leaders have also started to recognize the increased risks that globalization can bring to their operations. As William Parrett, the Chief Executive Officer at Deloitte Touche Tohmatsu (one of the 'Big Four' accounting firms), commented at the 2006 World Economic Forum (WEF) in

Davos: 'One effect of globalization has been that risk of all kinds—not just fiscal, but also physical—have increased for businesses, no matter where they operate. Information travels far and fast, confidentiality is difficult to maintain, markets are interdependent and events in far-flung places can have immense impact virtually anywhere in the world.'

So, globalization clearly has some downsides, even for the business community. But beyond this, it is significant that we have witnessed the rise of a new worldwide culture of 'anti-globalization' campaigners and critics. Various meetings of the World Economic Forum, the WTO, the IMF, and the World Bank, as well as the summits of G8 or EU leaders, have been accompanied by criticism and occasionally even violent protest against the 'global world order', 'global capitalism', the 'dictate of the multinationals', and so on. Riots in Seattle, Davos, Prague, and Genoa in the late 1990s and early 2000s made the public aware that globalization was a hotly contested topic on the public agenda, and successive battles over fair trade, poverty, food prices, water access, and financial stability have kept the ethical spotlight on the process of globalization.

In the context of business ethics, this controversy over globalization plays a crucial role. After all, corporations—most notably multinational corporations (MNCs)—are at the centre of the public's criticism on globalization. They are accused of exploiting workers in developing countries, destroying the environment, and, by abusing their economic power, engaging developing countries in a so-called 'race to the bottom'. This term describes a process whereby MNCs pitch developing countries against each other by allocating foreign direct investment to those countries that can offer them the most favourable conditions in terms of low tax rates, low levels of environmental regulation, and restricted workers' rights. However true these accusations are in practice, there is no doubt that globalization is the most current and demanding arena in which corporations have to define and legitimate the 'rights and wrongs' of their behaviour.

What is globalization?

Globalization is not only a very controversial topic in the public debate; it is also a very contested term in academic discourse.[4] Apart from the fact that—mirroring the public debate—the camps seem to be divided into supporters and critics, there is some doubt about whether globalization is really even happening at all. So, for example, some argue that there is nothing like a 'global' economy, because roughly 90% of world trade only takes place either within or between the three economic blocs of the EU, North America, and Asia, leaving out most other major parts of the globe (World Trade Organization 2008). Obviously, we have to examine the 'globalization' buzzword more carefully, and to develop a more precise definition if we want to understand its character and its implications for business ethics.

Globalization as a new phenomenon has often been mixed up or confounded with a host of other related phenomena (Scholte 2005). One aspect is *'internationalization'*, which is a part of globalization, but not a new process as such: at the end of the nineteenth century, the percentage of cross-border transactions worldwide was not considerably lower than at the end of the twentieth century (Moore and Lewis 1999). Others see globalization essentially as some form of '*Westernization*', since it seemingly results in the export of Western culture to other, culturally different, world regions. Again, this is not a new phenomenon at all: the era of colonization in the nineteenth century resulted in the export of various facets of Western culture to the colonized countries, evidenced for example by the British legacy in countries such as India, the Spanish legacy in South America, and the French legacy in Africa.

All of these views of globalization describe some of the more visible features of globalization. They are certainly important issues, but as Jan Aart Scholte (2005) shows, they do not characterize the significantly *new* aspects of globalization. If we want to get a grip on the decisive features of globalization, he suggests we can start by looking at the way social connections have traditionally taken place. These connections, be they personal relations with family members or friends, or economic relations such as shopping or working, previously took place within a certain territory. People had their family and friends in a certain village; they had their work and business relations within a certain town or even country. Social interaction traditionally needed a certain geographical space to take place. However, this link between social connections and a specific territory has been continuously weakened, with two main developments in the last few decades being particularly important.

The first development is *technological* in nature. Modern communications technology, from the telephone, to radio and television, and now the internet, open up the possibility of connecting and interacting with people despite the fact that there are large geographical distances between them. Furthermore, the rapid development of global transportation technologies allows people to easily connect with other people all over the globe. While Marco Polo had to travel for many months before he finally arrived in China, people today can step on a plane and, after a passable meal and a short sleep, arrive some time later on the other side of the globe. Territorial distances play a less and less important role today. The people we do business with, or that we make friends with, no longer necessarily have to be in the same place as we are.

The second development is *political* in nature. Territorial borders have been the main obstacles to worldwide connections between people. Only 20 years ago, it was still largely impossible to enter the countries in the Eastern bloc without lengthy visa procedures, and even then, interactions between people from the two sides were very limited. With the fall of the iron curtain, and substantial liberalization efforts elsewhere (for instance within the EU), national borders have been eroded and, in many cases, have even been abolished. In Europe, you can drive from Lapland to Sicily without stopping at a single national border.

These two developments mainly account for the massive proliferation and spread in supra-territorial connections. These connections may not always necessarily have a global spread in the literal sense of worldwide coverage. The new thing though about these connections is that they no longer need a geographical territory to take place and they are not restricted by territorial distances and borders any more. Scholte (2005) thus characterizes globalization as '*deterritorialization*', suggesting that we can define globalization as follows:

Globalization is a process which diminishes the necessity of a common and shared territorial basis for social, economic, and political activities, processes, and relations.

Let us have a look at some examples of globalization according to this definition:

- Due to the modern communication infrastructure, many of us can closely follow the 2010 FIFA World Cup in South Africa live on TV—regardless of where we are located at the time that it takes place. Such events are global not in the sense that they actually happen all over the world, but in the sense that billions of people follow them, and to some extent take part in them, regardless of the fact that they are standing in Milan, Manchester, or Manila.

- We can potentially drink the same Heineken beer, drive the same model of Toyota car, or buy the same expensive Rolex watch almost wherever we are in the world—we do not have to be in Amsterdam, Tokyo, or Geneva. Certain global products are available all over the world and going for a 'Chinese', 'Mexican', or 'French' meal indicates certain tastes and styles, rather than a trip to a certain geographical territory.

- Our banks no longer store or provide access to our money in a single, geographic location. We can quite easily have a credit card that allows us to withdraw money all over the world, we can pay our bills at home in Europe, via internet banking while sitting in an internet café in India, or even order our Swiss private banking broker to buy an option on halved pigs at the Chicago exchange without even moving our feet from the sofa. On the downside, as we saw in the late 2000s, a country's economic security is linked as much to global financial interactions as it is to national laws and policies.

Global communications, global products, and global financial systems and capital markets are only the most striking examples of deterritorialization in the world economy. There are many other areas where globalization in this sense is a significant social, economic, and political process. As we shall now see, globalization also has significant implications for business ethics.

Globalization and business ethics: a new global space to manage

Globalization as defined in terms of the deterritorialization of economic activities is particularly relevant for business ethics, and this is evident in three main areas—culture, law, and accountability.

Cultural issues

As business becomes less fixed territorially, so corporations increasingly engage in overseas markets, suddenly finding themselves confronted with new and diverse, sometimes even contradictory ethical demands. Moral values that were taken for granted in the home market may get questioned as soon as corporations enter foreign markets (Donaldson 1996). For example, attitudes to racial and gender diversity in Europe may differ significantly to those in Middle Eastern countries. Similarly, Chinese people might regard it as more unethical to sack employees in times of economic downturns than would be typical in Europe. Again, whilst Europeans tend to regard child labour as strictly unethical, some Asian countries might have a more moderate approach (for further examples, see

Kline 2005). Consider the case of *Playboy*, the US adult magazine, which had to suspend its Indonesian edition and vacate the company premises in 2006 in the wake of violent protests by Islamic demonstrators—even though the Indonesian edition was a toned-down version that did not show nudity.[5]

The reason why there is a potential for such problems is that whilst globalization results in the deterritorialization of some processes and activities, in many cases there is still a close connection between the local culture, including moral values, and a certain geographical region. For example, Europeans largely disapprove of capital punishment, whilst many Americans appear to regard it as morally acceptable. Women can freely sunbathe topless on most European beaches, yet in some states of America they can be fined for doing so—and in Pakistan would be expected to cover up much more. This is one of the contradictions of globalization: on the one hand, globalization makes regional difference less important since it brings regions together and encourages a more uniform 'global culture'. On the other hand, in eroding the divisions of geographical distances, globalization reveals economic, political, and cultural differences and confronts people with them. This dialectical effect has been a growing subject for research over the past decade (see, for instance, Boli and Lechner 2000).

> **? THINK THEORY**
>
> Capital punishment and topless sunbathing are interesting issues to think about globalization theory and cultural dimensions of ethics, but have little to do with business responsibility as such. Can you think of some similar examples that a business might have to deal with?

VISIT THE WEBSITE for a short response to this feature

Legal issues

A second aspect is closely linked to what we said previously about the relationship between ethics and law. The more economic transactions lose their connection to a certain regional territory, the more they escape the control of the respective national governments. The power of a government has traditionally been confined to a certain territory; for example, French laws are only binding on French territory, UK laws on UK territory, and so on. As soon as a company leaves its home territory and moves part of its production chain to, for example, a third world country, the legal framework becomes very different. Consequently, managers can no longer simply rely on the legal framework when deciding on the right or wrong of certain business practices. If, as we said earlier (pp. 5–8), business ethics largely begins where the law ends, then deterritorialization increases the demand for business ethics because deterritorialized economic activities are beyond the control of national (territorial) governments. For example, global financial markets are largely beyond the control of any national government, and the constant struggle of governments against issues such as child pornography on the internet shows the enormous difficulties in enforcing national laws in deterritorialized spaces. **Ethics in Action 1.2** provides a popular example of the ethical issue of counterfeiting, which has become a major business problem for many big brands in the West.

VISIT THE WEBSITE for links to useful sources of further information

ETHICS IN ACTION 1.2 http://www.ethicalcorp.com

Counterfeits—knock-offs no bargain

Stephen Gardner, 6 March 2008

Ethical CORPORATION

In more innocent times, counterfeiting and intellectual property theft were the preserve of hawkers of dodgy copies of dubious videos and bootleg concert recordings at car boot sales. But what was once a cottage industry has become a multi-tentacled international operation.

There has been an explosion in both the range and quantity of counterfeit goods. British authorities in 2006 and 2007 seized counterfeit designer sportswear, mineral water, cigarettes, razorblades, blood pressure tablets, skin-lightening creams, motorbikes, crane parts and a Dalek. Almost everything is being faked.

The fake trade rides on the back of globalisation. But while world trade has expanded by about 500 per cent in the past two decades, the International AntiCounterfeiting Coalition says that counterfeiting has shot up by as much as 10,000 per cent.

For business this is clearly bad news. Figures cited by the UK government's Intellectual Property Office in its 2007 report show that counterfeit toys in Spain reduced the sales of Spanish toymakers by 11 per cent. British American Tobacco chairman Jan du Plessis, speaking in April 2007, called counterfeiters 'one of our biggest global competitors'.

But a deeper understanding of the issues around counterfeiting is emerging, which connects the fight against fake goods to corporate responsibility agendas. Among business, governments and law enforcement agencies there is 'pretty major acceptance that we've got a big problem', says Ruth Orchard of the Anti-Counterfeiting Group, which has a 200-strong membership, illustrating how much is at stake. It includes big sports names such as Adidas, Nike and Manchester United, pharmaceutical firms such as GlaxoSmithKline and Proctor & Gamble, and luxury brands such as Breitling, Cartier and Louis Vuitton.

Tackling counterfeiting means addressing both supply and demand. On the demand side, consumers have an ambiguous relationship with counterfeiters, often knowingly breaking the law to get what is seen as a bargain. But as counterfeiting expands there is a growing awareness of the drawbacks. Fake razorblades break; fake soap contains mercury; fake cigarette lighters explode; fake car brake pads turn out to be made from compressed sawdust.

On the supply side, counterfeiting can be an industry of misery. John Trew, senior adviser on child labour for humanitarian organisation Care, says he sees 'linkages' between people smuggling, child labour and counterfeiting. In south-east Asia especially, 'trafficking brokers' promise villagers better lives for their children, but those children end up as part of a 'very organised underground sector' producing fake goods. It is an issue that 'affects the poor disproportionately', says Trew, citing Cambodia, China and Laos as countries where there is a particular problem.

The cost of fakes

For business therefore, campaigning against counterfeiting is both a way to protect brands and to promote responsibility. Action has so far concentrated on the demand side. The Anti-Counterfeiting Group's Ruth Orchard, says tackling demand for fakes is 'much more effective'. She adds: 'We can keep chopping hydra heads off but [the counterfeiters] keep growing another one.' Awareness-raising plans being mooted include a marketing campaign aimed at universities, anti-counterfeiting blogs, and creative competitions targeting art school students. Ebay is one corporation that has expressed interest.

Broadly, Orchard says, the phenomenon of counterfeiting is the developing world supplying what the developed world wants. Much counterfeiting activity can be traced to China. A European Commission survey of customs seizures in 2006 found that 79 per cent of counterfeits came from China. There is a 'different attitude' in China where the lines between real and fake are blurred, says Orchard.

But work to tackle the supply side should not be neglected, says John Trew of Care. The first concern, he says, should be to quantify the problem and establish the links between counterfeiting and child labour. 'Our main goal is to focus on gaining credible data that validates the business point of view' on the supply-side damage done by counterfeiting. 'The private sector needs to be proactive in its response,' Trew adds.

Sources

Ethical Corporation, Stephen Gardner, 6 March 2009, http://www.ethicalcorp.com.

? THINK THEORY

Explain the link between in rise of globalization and the surge in counterfeit products. From a cultural and legal perspective, how would you evaluate counterfeiting as an ethical issue for businesses (a) in the West and (b) in the developing world? What potential solutions could we think of to address counterfeiting?

VISIT THE WEBSITE for a short response to this feature

Accountability issues

Taking a closer look at global activities, one can easily identify corporations as the dominant actors on the global stage: MNCs own the mass media that influence much of the information and entertainment we are exposed to, they supply global products, they pay our salaries, and they pay (directly or indirectly) much of the taxes that keep governments running. Furthermore, one could argue that MNCs are economically as powerful as many governments. For example in 2008, the gross domestic product (GDP) of Greece was about the same as the revenue of Wal-Mart (both around US$400bn). However, whereas the Greek government has to be accountable to the Greek people and must face elections on a regular basis, the managers of Wal-Mart are formally accountable only to the relatively small group of people who own shares in the company. The communities in the US, China, or the UK that depend directly on Wal-Mart's investment decisions, however, have next to no influence on the company and, unlike a regional or national government, Wal-Mart is, at least in principle, not legally accountable to these constituencies.

What this means is that the more economic activities get deterritorialized, the less governments can control them, and the less they are open to democratic control by the affected people. Consequently, the call for direct (democratic) accountability of MNCs has become louder in recent years, evidenced, for example, by the anti-globalization protests that we mentioned before. Put simply, globalization leads to a growing demand for *corporate accountability*. We shall examine this argument fully in the next chapter, but clearly, it is exactly here where business ethics is increasingly in demand since it offers the potential for corporations to examine and respond to the claims made on them by various stakeholders. Indeed, globalization can be seen to affect *all* stakeholders of the corporation, as we shall discuss in Part II of the book. Some examples of these impacts are presented in **Figure 1.6**.

Globalization and business ethics: new local challenges to address

So far in this section we have accentuated the homogenizing effects of globalization: it creates a new deterritorialized space where business faces similar ethical questions worldwide. Paradoxically though, globalization also has an opposite effect on business: the more business becomes global, the more it gets exposed to regions and countries where ethical values and practices are still vastly different. From this perspective it is important to note that the formal academic subject of business ethics is largely a North American invention and has most of its roots and a large part of its traditions in the US. The reception of business ethics in other parts of the world is, however, fairly young; for instance in Europe it only became visible from the beginning of the 1980s (van Luijk 2001). In presenting a text from an international perspective, we believe that although many of the original ideas in business ethics have been, and still are, very useful in, say, the African, Latin American, or Asian context, there are definite limits to the transfer of North American approaches into a context often denoted as 'ROW' (i.e. 'rest of the world'). For instance, the European context poses some distinctly different questions, which are not necessarily on the agenda from an American perspective (Spence 2002). Likewise, Asia has quite a distinct historical, philosophical, and religious legacy, giving rise to a different approach to the study, as well as the practice, of business ethics in Asia (Elankumaran, Seal, and Hashmi 2005; Ip 2009; Romar 2004). At another level, it is also critical to think beyond developed countries in shaping our knowledge and understanding of business ethics. After all, it is in emerging economies and the developing world where many ethical issues in business are most pressing (Visser 2008), and insights from

Stakeholders	Ethical impacts of globalization
Shareholders	Globalization provides potential for greater profitability, but also greater risks. Lack of regulation of global financial markets, leading to additional financial risks and instability
Employees	Corporations outsource production to developing countries in order to reduce costs in global marketplace—this provides jobs, but also raises the potential for exploitation of employees through poor working conditions
Consumers	Global products provide social benefits to consumers across the globe, but may also meet protests about cultural imperialism and westernization. Globalization can bring cheaper prices to customers, but vulnerable consumers in developing countries may also face the possibility of exploitation by MNCs.
Suppliers and competitors	Suppliers in developing countries face regulation from MNCs through supply chain management. Small scale indigenous competitors are exposed to powerful global players
Civil society (pressure groups, NGOs, local communities)	Global business activity brings the company in direct interaction with local communities thereby raising the possibility for erosion of traditional community life. Globally active pressure groups emerge with aim to 'police' the corporation in countries where governments are weak and corrupt
Government and regulation	Globalization weakens governments and increases the corporate responsibility for jobs, welfare, maintenance of ethical standards, etc. Globalization also confronts governments with corporations from regions with different cultural expectations about issues such as bribery, corruption, taxation, and philanthropy.

Figure 1.6. Examples of the ethical impacts of globalization on different stakeholder groups

Asian, African, and Latin American ethical perspectives are therefore essential for situating business ethics in a truly global context.

International variety in approaches to business ethics

Various authors have claimed that there are certain fundamental differences in the way in which business ethics is practised and studied in different parts of the world. Much of this work initially focused on *Europe* (e.g. Koehn 1999; van Luijk 1990; Vogel 1992, 1998), but in the last few years, there has been a flurry of studies emerging from *Africa* (Rossouw 2005; Visser et al. 2006), *Australasia* (Kimber and Lipton 2005; Moon 1995), *Latin America* (Haslam 2007; Puppim de Oliveira and Vargas 2006), and *South, East and South-East Asia* (Donleavy et al. 2008; Ip 2009; Kimber and Lipton 2005). In this section, we shall look at these differences in relation to six key questions and discuss some of the specifics of business ethics in various regions or countries globally. An example of this discussion with regard to three key regions can is summarized in **Figure 1.7**. In so doing, we recognize that, given their cultural and geographical breadth, some regions such as Africa or Asia are perhaps harder to generalize about than Europe or North America. However, the point is not to make an absolutely definitive statement about business ethics in different regions of the world, but to show that any approach to business ethics is likely to be driven by the cultural and historical context of the region or country.

Who is responsible for ethical conduct in business?

The US is typically said to exhibit a strong culture of individualism, suggesting that individuals are responsible for their own success. Hence, if there are demands for solving ethical questions, it would be the individual who is usually expected to be responsible for making the right choices. There is an impressive literature dealing with individual ethical decision-making emanating from the US (as we shall discuss in Chapter 4), and many US textbooks focus on decision-making at this level (Ferrell et al. 2008; Treviño and Nelson 2007). In Asia, however, hierarchy is much more important, and so top management is typically seen as responsible for ethical conduct. Similar perspectives can be found in Africa or India, where long-standing tribal and close-knit family-based communities tend to embed the individual in a broader social context in which responsibility for decisions is more a collective than an individual matter. Somewhat similar, in Europe it has traditionally been thought that it is not the individual businessperson, nor even the single company, that is primarily expected to be responsible for solving ethical dilemmas in business. Rather, it is a collective and overarching institution, usually the state. European business ethics has therefore tended to focus more on the choice *of* constraints compared with the US approach of focusing on choice *within* constraints

	Europe	North America	Asia
Who is responsible for ethical conduct in business?	Social control by the collective	The individual	Top management
Who is the key actor in business ethics?	Government, trade unions, corporate associations	The corporation	Government, corporations
What are the key guidelines for ethical behaviour?	Negotiated legal framework of business	Corporate codes of ethics	Managerial discretion
What are the key issues in business ethics?	Social issues in organizing the framework of business	Misconduct and immorality in single decisions situations	Corporate governance and accountability
What is the dominant stakeholder management approach?	Formalized multiple stakeholder approach	Focus on shareholder value	Implicit multiple stakeholder approach, benign managerialism

Figure 1.7. Regional differences from a business ethics perspective: the example of Europe, North America, and Asia

(Enderle 1996). A specific flavour of this approach can then be found in Eastern Europe and other post-communist countries where individuals tend to assign responsibility for ethical behaviour primarily to the larger collective or bureaucratic entities that govern economic or social life (Lewicka-Strzalecka 2006).

Who is the key actor in business ethics?

In the US, in most (but not all) areas, the institutional framework of business ethics has traditionally been fairly loose so that the key actor has tended to be the corporation. This, at least partly, explains a the rather practical approach to business ethics evident in the US approach (Enderle 1996). Similarly, given that business ethics is particularly important when the law has not yet codified the 'right' or 'wrong' of a certain action, this would also seem to partially explain the longer legacy of business ethics as an academic subject in the US. However, the identification of the corporation as the key actor in the US also means that corporate misconduct tends to face greater enforcement and harsher penalties (Vogel 1992).

Conversely, in most European countries there is quite a dense network of regulation on most of the ethically important issues for business. Workers' rights, social and medical care, and environmental issues are only a few examples where European companies could be said to have traditionally not had to consider so very much the moral values that should guide their decisions. These questions have, at least in principle, been tackled by the government in setting up a tight institutional framework for businesses. Examples range from the Scandinavian welfare state, to the German cohabitation system, and the strong position of trade unions and workers' rights in France (Matten and Moon 2008).

In Europe, governments, trade unions, and corporate associations have therefore been key actors in business ethics. A similar focus on government tends to be evident in the Asian perspective, although it is corporations, rather than trade unions that have typically been involved with governments in this activity. For example, in Japan, firms are interconnected with one another and with the government through *keiretsu* arrangements, whilst South Korea exhibits a similar *chaebol* structure. In China, many large corporations are still state-owned. Hence, engagements with business ethics in Asia often look to both governments and corporations as key actors.

Moving to developing countries in Africa or Latin America, however, the so-called third sector, i.e. non-governmental organizations (NGOs), is often a key player within the arena of business ethics. One of the reasons for this lies in the fact that governments in these countries often are underfunded or even corrupt, and therefore provide limited guidance or legal frameworks for ethical decision-making. In Latin America, for instance, NGOs are the key players in organizing, incentivizing, or coordinating ethical initiatives by business (Haslam 2007). NGOs also partner with business (and governments) in public-private partnerships to address urgent ethical issues, such as poverty, disease, or lack of education—as we will discuss in more detail in Chapter 10.

What are the key ethical guidelines for ethical behaviour?

The differing character and extent of the legal frameworks globally to some degree necessitates different approaches to business ethics. Similarly, it also suggests that whereas the key practical guidelines for ethical behaviour in some countries, such as in Europe, tend to be codified in the negotiated legal framework of business, in Asia, there is greater managerial discretion, giving rise to a more organic and flexible approach to ethical decision-making that places considerable emphasis on personal virtues and collective responsibility and relationships (Koehn 1999). Notably, personal and professional life are not seen to be distinct, as is typically the case in the US and Europe (Parker 1998a: 128). Indeed, in the US, there is a strong reliance on rules and guidelines for business conduct, but rather than coming from government (as in Europe), these tend to come from businesses themselves, in the form of corporate codes of ethics and internal compliance programmes (Enderle 1996). Nonetheless, these are often put in place to avoid the potentially hefty fines that accompany breaches of the US federal sentencing guidelines (Vogel 1992). As the Asian context suggests, these differences become even more pronounced once we leave the context of Western and industrialized countries. Deon Rossouw (2005: 98), for instance, argues that business ethics in the African context is predicated on the philosophy of *Ubuntu*, a value system in which the 'commitment to co-existence, consensus, and consultation' is prized as the highest value in human interaction. While Rossouw infers that Ubuntu explains the absence of shareholder supremacy in African corporate governance, the somewhat similar Chinese notion of *Guanxi* exposes a general tension with these traditional values: they sometimes fly in the face of certain fundamental Western ethical beliefs. The Guanxi idea puts close, reciprocal, trusting interpersonal ties at the core of human interaction, which has led some commentators to question whether in Chinese business relations, the Guanxi-informed practice of gift-giving in fact amounts to little less than an indifference to bribery (Chenting 2003).

What are the key issues in business ethics?

This contrast is often manifested in the types of issues deemed important within business ethics in different contexts. This becomes evident when looking at contemporary US business ethics textbooks, since they tend to accord a considerable amount of space to issues such as privacy, workers' rights, salary issues, and whistleblowing, to name just a few. These are deemed to be the responsibility of the individual company, since the state, in principle, does not take full responsibility for regulating these issues. The European approach, in contrast, has tended to focus more on social issues in organizing the framework of business. Hence, European business ethics textbooks have tended to include greater consideration of subjects such as the ethics of capitalism and economic rationality (Enderle 1996). In Asia, concerns about the responsible organization of business have given rise to a focus on ethical issues in relation to corporate governance and the accountability of management for practices such as mismanagement and corruption. Specifically in China, the latter issue is high on the agenda of the government, exemplified by the fact that some of the most recent business ethics scandals to hit the country around food and drug safety have led to recalls, arrests, and even executions of corrupt officials (Ip 2009). In the developing world in general, there seems to be a predominant focus on the ethical obligations of business to provide jobs that pay a living wage, and to provide fairly priced goods and services (Visser 2008). Next to these basic economic functions of business, ethical considerations in the developing world place a particular expectation on multinationals—particularly foreign ones—to contribute to local development, healthcare, and education.

What is the most dominant stakeholder management approach?

Another important aspect that follows from the above is the different character of European and other corporations (Whitley 1992). European corporations in general are smaller than their US counterparts, and may be more likely to see multiple stakeholders (as opposed to simply shareholders) as the focus of corporate activity. European, African, and Asian models of capitalism are not so dominated by the drive for shareholder value maximization compared with American companies. European companies are often managed by large executive and supervisory boards, with a considerable amount of interlocking ownership structures between companies and close bank relations (van Luijk 1990). Asian companies also feature a great deal of structural integration, but the interests of employees and other stakeholders are often promoted through cultural norms of trust and implicit duties, rather than formal governance mechanisms (Johnson and Scholes 2002: 199). This sort of arrangement might be thought of as a form of 'benign managerialism' (Parkinson 2003: 493), an approach that has a long-standing tradition in countries such as India, where companies like Tata have attempted to honour ethical obligations to multiple stakeholders for decades (Elankumaran et al. 2005). This approach is also visible in Latin America, where much of the economy is dominated by smaller, often family-owned firms and where the key stakeholder from a business ethics perspective is the employee (Vives 2007).

Sources of difference between different regions globally

From where have such differences emerged? Comparing the US and Europe—two otherwise very similar contexts seen from a global perspective—can serve as an instructive backdrop in answering this question. Many of these differences in business ethics are rooted in the differing cultural, economic, and religious histories of the Europe and the US (Palazzo 2002). One argument here is that the influence of the Catholic and Lutheran Protestant religions in Europe led to a collective approach to organizing economic life, whereas the individual focus of the Calvinist-Protestant religion in the US led to the rise of a distinctly different capitalist (in the original sense) economic system (Weber 1905). Even though today we tend to talk about much of Europe and the US as secularized countries, there are significant differences in the religious legacies of the two regions—which in turn have a significant impact on the different approaches to business ethics in different regions.

This becomes even more pronounced in other parts of the world where the active practice of religion is sometimes still more embedded than in the West. In Asia, the influence of Hinduism, Buddhism, and Confucianism, for example, could be said to have led to a more pragmatic, relational, and flexible approach to ethical decision-making (Koehn 1999). The Muslim world, although diverse in its spread over three continents, is characterized by a number of ethical principles, of which justice/fairness, trusteeship and integrity ('unity') can be considered core (Rice 1999). Such religiously informed ethical values sometimes can have far-reaching implications for business, as the example of Islamic financial systems shows (Nomani 2008).

Next to religious influence, differences in business ethics can also have other historic roots. Georges Enderle (1996) suggests that the interest in broader macro issues of business ethics in Europe can also be partly traced to the need to rebuild institutions after the Second World War and in the aftermath of economic and political restructuring in Eastern Europe. Moreover, Vogel (1992) argues further that the focus on individual action and codes of conduct in the US has been substantially driven by the impact of widely publicized corporate scandals that have focused attention on the need to avoid ethical violation at the firm level (see also Verstegen Ryan 2005). In a similar vein, many of the specific challenges for business ethics in the developing world, be it poor governance, extreme poverty, or violence, can be understood as a heritage from colonial times (Banerjee 2009), as is particularly visible in countries such as South Africa, Brazil, or Myanmar (Burma). In some countries such as Canada or Australia, it is mining companies—rather than just governments—that are exposed to ethical claims, based, for instance, on past and current discrimination against indigenous groups (Lertzman and Vredenburg 2005).

Globalization and the assimilation of different global regions

As we can see then, there are a number of reasons that can be advanced to explain differences in business ethics across countries and regions of the globe. But does this mean the differences are likely to be sustained, given the ongoing processes of globalization? Certainly, globalization has quite significantly reduced and mitigated some of the peculiarities of business systems globally. This is maybe nowhere more visible than in Europe (Whittington and Mayer 2002). Therefore, however important it is to see the differences between the US and other regions, there is a clear tendency of assimilation in the different business systems. In Europe, this has been manifested in a decrease in the importance of (especially national) governmental regulation for business. Globalization has resulted in a rapid and comprehensive move towards deregulation of business activities, which increasingly puts businesses in contexts similar to the American version of capitalism (Matten and Moon 2008). This is even more the case if we focus on Eastern Europe and former communist countries: economies in transition are typically characterized by a weak state, and a deficit in law enforcement, which together leave a growing number of ethical issues to be tackled by businesses (Lang 2001). This trend towards a greater convergence of business systems and firm characteristics is visible in most parts of the world (Whitley 1999); however, we also see that certain fundamental characteristics and differences remain and will continue to have relevance (Sorge 2005).

In this book, we therefore shall provide the following balance between the different positions on the main differences in business ethics evident in different parts of the globe:

- Rather than selecting either one or the other, we will consider both the individual decision-maker and the corporation itself as responsible for ethical conduct—and consider both top managers, as well as rank-and-file organization members. Although it is clearly individuals in organizations who ultimately make business ethics decisions, many non-US perspectives suggest that we also have to look at the context that shapes those decisions. Moreover, most of us quite naturally regard corporations as significant actors in business ethics. If there is an incident of industrial pollution or it is revealed that children are being used in an overseas factory, it is usually the company as a whole that we criticize, rather than any specific manager(s).
- We will focus on the corporation in its relations with other key actors such as government, NGOs, and trade unions.
- We will provide a critical perspective on both managerial discretion and ethical guidelines (such as codes of conduct), and broader forces shaping ethical decision-making, such as product and financial markets, supply chains, civil society, and systems of governance.
- The morality of single business situations will be considered in the context of corporate governance and the broader organizing framework of business.
- A multiple stakeholder approach that includes shareholders as a particularly important constituency will be taken. As we will outline in Chapter 2, this assumes some intrinsic rights for stakeholders, rather than focusing only on their role in affecting shareholder value.

Sustainability: a key goal for business ethics?

At the same time that these new challenges of globalization have emerged, considerable interest has also been directed towards the development of new ways of addressing the diverse impacts of business in society. Many of these impacts are far-reaching and profound. To mention just a few, one only needs to think of impacts such as:

- The environmental pollution, in particular the effects on climate change, caused by the production, transportation, and use of products such as cars, refrigerators, or newspapers.
- The ever increasing problems of waste disposal and management as a result of excessive product packaging and the dominance of the 'throwaway culture'.
- The devastating consequences for individuals and communities as a result of plant closures and 'downsizing' as experienced throughout Europe, from South Wales in the UK all the way to the accession countries of Central and Eastern Europe.
- The erosion of local cultures and environments due to the influx of mass tourism in places as diverse as Thai fishing villages, Swiss alpine communities, or ancient Roman monuments.

Company	Sustainability statement	Source
BP	'At BP we define sustainability as the capacity to endure as a group: by renewing assets; creating and delivering better products and services that meet the evolving needs of society; attracting successive generations of employees; contributing to a sustainable environment; and retaining the trust and support of our customers, shareholders and the communities in which we operate.'	Sustainability Report, 2007
DeBeers	'Addressing sustainability issues means enhancing our relationship with host and partner governments, building consumer confidence in diamonds, and ensuring our activities contribute positively to the livelihoods of both present and future generations.'	www.debeersgroup.com 2009
Nokia	'Corporate responsibility (CR) at Nokia is a collective effort. We believe that management of CR issues is most effective when sustainability policies and programs are embedded in every aspect of our operations.'	Nokia CSR Report 2007
Toyota	'Since its foundation, Toyota has conducted business with 'contributing to the development of a prosperous society through the manufacture of automobiles' as a guiding principle. 'Contributing to the development of a prosperous society' means 'contributing to the sustainable development of the earth.'	Sustainability Report 2008
Volkswagen	'Values, social responsibility and active sustainability are integral characteristics of our company culture. We are future-oriented in our approach to important issues such as climate change. We operate a broad range of research and development activities and provide trend-setting approaches to the mobility of tomorrow.'	www.volkswagenag.com, 2009

Figure 1.8. Corporate commitments to sustainability

Faced with such problems (and many more besides), it has been widely suggested that the goals and consequences of business require radical re-thinking. Following the Rio Earth Summit of 1992, one concept in particular appears to have been widely promoted (though not unilaterally accepted) as the essential new conceptual frame for assessing not only business activities specifically, but industrial and social development more generally. That concept is *sustainability*.

Sustainability has become an increasingly common term in the rhetoric surrounding business ethics, and has been widely used by corporations, governments, consultants, pressure groups, and academics alike. **Figure 1.8** provides some examples of sustainability being used in the corporate reports and other business communications of some major multinational firms.

Despite this widespread use, sustainability is a term that has been utilized and interpreted in substantially different ways (Dobson 1996). Probably the most common usage of sustainability, however, is in relation to *sustainable development*, which is typically defined as 'development that meets the needs of the present without compromising the ability of future generations to meet their own needs' (World Commission on Environment and Development 1987). This, however, is only the core idea of an elusive and widely contested concept—and one which has also been subject to a vast array of different conceptualizations and definitions (Gladwin, Kennelly, and Krause 1995). So whilst we would caution against any unreserved acceptance of any particular interpretation, at a very basic level, sustainability appears to be primarily about system maintenance, as in ensuring that our actions do not impact upon the system—for example, the Earth or the biosphere—in such a way that its long-term viability is threatened. By focusing sustainable development on the potential for future generations to satisfy their needs, sustainability also raises considerations of *intergenerational equity*, i.e. equality between one generation and another.

With its roots in environmental management and analysis, for a long time sustainability as a concept was largely synonymous with environmental sustainability. More recently, though, the concept of sustainability has been broadened to include not only environmental considerations, but also economic and social considerations (Elkington 1998). This is shown in **Figure 1.9**.

This extension of the sustainability concept arose primarily because it is not only impractical, but even sometimes impossible, to address the sustainability of the natural environment without also considering the social and economic aspects of relevant communities and their activities. For example, whilst environmentalists have opposed road-building programmes on account of the detrimental impact of such schemes on the environment, others have pointed to the benefits for local communities of lower congestion in their towns and extra jobs for their citizens. Another argument for this extension is the consideration that if equity is to be extended to future generations, then logically it should also be extended to all those in the current generation. Hence, one of the World Commission on Environment and Development's primary espoused aims was the eradication of world poverty and inequity.

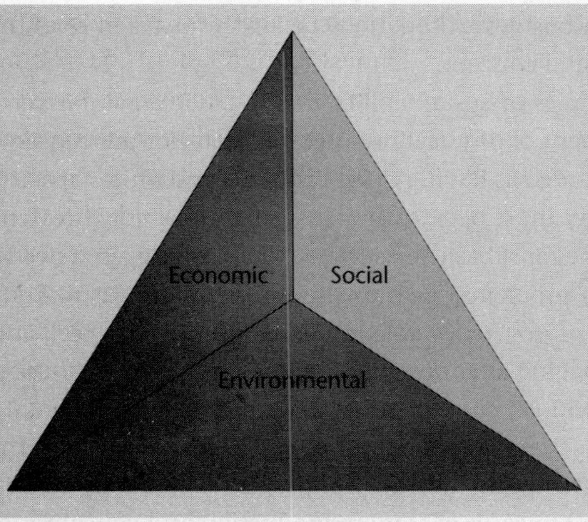

Figure 1.9. The three components of sustainability

As we see it then, sustainability can be regarded as comprising three components—environmental, economic, and social. This suggests the following definition:

Sustainability refers to the long-term maintenance of systems according to environmental, economic and social considerations.

Whilst we regard this definition as sufficient for determining the essential content of the sustainability concept, it is evident that sustainability as a phenomenon also represents a specific goal to be achieved. The framing of sustainability as a goal for business is encapsulated most completely in the notion of a 'triple bottom line'.

The triple bottom line

The triple bottom line (TBL) is a term coined by, and vigorously advocated by, John Elkington, the Director of the SustainAbility strategy consultancy and author of a number of influential books on corporate environmentalism. His view of the TBL is that it represents the idea that business does not have just one single goal—namely adding economic value—but that it has an extended goal set which necessitates adding environmental and social value too (Elkington 1998). From this perspective, it should be clear why we have highlighted sustainability as a potentially important new goal for business ethics. However, in order to develop a clearer picture of just what the three components of sustainability actually represent in terms of a goal for business ethics, we shall have to examine each of them in turn.

Environmental perspectives

As we mentioned briefly above, the concept of sustainability is generally regarded as having emerged from the environmental perspective, most notably in forestry management and then later in other areas of resource management (Hediger 1999). Indeed, it would probably be true to say that, at the present moment, there is still a fairly widespread conception within business (though we believe a mistaken one) that sustainability is a purely environmental concept.

The basic principles of sustainability in the environmental perspective concern the effective management of physical resources so that they are conserved for the future. All biosystems are regarded as having finite resources and finite capacity, and hence sustainable human activity must operate at a level that does not threaten the health of those systems. Even at the most basic level, these concerns suggest a need to address a number of critical business problems, such as the impacts of industrialization on biodiversity, the continued use of non-renewable resources, such as oil, steel, and coal, as well as the production of damaging environmental pollutants like greenhouse gases and CFCs from industrial plants and consumer products. At a more fundamental level though, these concerns also raise the problem of economic growth itself, and the vexed question of whether future generations can really enjoy the same living standards as us without a reversal of the trend towards ever more production and consumption.

Economic perspectives

The economic perspective on sustainability initially emerged from economic growth models that assessed the limits imposed by the carrying capacity of the earth.[6] The recognition that continued growth in population, industrial activity, resource use, and pollution could mean that standards of living would eventually decline led to the emergence of sustainability as a way of thinking about ensuring that future generations would not be adversely disadvantaged by the activities and choices of the present generation. Economists such as Kenneth Arrow (Arrow and Hurwicz 1977), Herman Daly (Daly 1991; Daly and Cobb 1989), and David Pearce (1999) have since been highly influential in advancing the agenda for a macroeconomic understanding of sustainability.

The implications for business ethics of such thinking occur on different levels. A narrow concept of economic sustainability focuses on the economic performance of the corporation itself: the responsibility of management is to develop, produce, and market those products that secure the long-term economic performance of the corporation. This includes a focus on those strategies which, for example, lead to a long-term rise in share price, revenues, and market share rather than short-term 'explosions' of profits at the expense of long-term viability of success. An example of an unsustainable approach in this perspective would be the 'dot.com bubble' at the beginning of this century.

A broader concept of economic sustainability would include the company's attitude towards and impacts upon the economic framework in which it is embedded. Paying bribes or building cartels, for instance, could be regarded as economically unsustainable because these activities undermine the long-term functioning of markets. Corporations that attempt to avoid paying corporate taxes through subtle accounting tricks might be said to behave in an unsustainable way: if they are not willing to fund the political institutional environment (such as schools, hospitals, the police, and the justice system), they erode one of the key institutional bases of their corporate success. The international pressure group, the Tax Justice Network,[7] has therefore formed a coalition of researchers and activists with a shared concern about such issues to raise awareness and stimulate action against the harmful impacts of tax avoidance, tax competition, and tax havens.

Social perspectives

The development of the social perspective on sustainability has tended to trail behind that of the environmental and economic perspectives (Scott, Park, and Cocklin 2000) and remains a relatively new development. The explicit integration of social concerns into the business discourse around sustainability can be seen to have emerged during the 1990s, primarily, it would seem, in response to concerns regarding the impacts of business activities on indigenous communities in less developed countries and regions. It would be wrong to assume though that this means that, until this time, local community claims on business (and other social issues) went entirely unheard by business, or unexamined by business ethics scholars. Indeed, in Chapter 2 we shall be tracing the rather impressive literature dealing with such issues. However, the inclusion of social considerations such as these within the specific domain of sustainability marked a significant shift in the way that notions of sustainability were conceptualized.

The key issue in the social perspective on sustainability is that of *social justice*. Despite the impressive advances in standards of living that many of us have enjoyed, a recent UN Report on the World Social Situation identified persistent and deepening inequality across the globe. With 80% of the world's gross domestic product belonging to the 1 billion people living in the developed world and the remaining 20% shared by the 5 billion people living in developing countries, the report suggested that 'failure to address this inequality predicament will ensure that social justice and better living conditions for all people remain elusive, and that communities, countries, and regions remain vulnerable to social, political and economic upheaval' (UN 2005: 12). In particular, the report highlighted 'the widening gap between skilled and unskilled workers, the chasm between the formal and informal economies, and the growing disparities in health, education and opportunities for social and political participation' (p. 3). As one of the main engines of economic development, business is increasingly bound up in such debates. Therefore, a more just and equitable world, whether between rich consumers in the West and poor workers in developing countries, between the urban rich and the rural poor, or between men and women, remains the central concern in the social perspective on sustainability.

How exactly business should respond to such a challenge remains open to question, but the goals at least have received some clarification in recent years with the publishing of the UN's Millennium Development Goals. These set out the main social and developmental challenges facing the world at the present time, and articulate specific targets and indicators to be achieved by 2015. The eight Millennium Development Goals are to:

- Eradicate extreme poverty and hunger.
- Achieve universal primary education.
- Promote gender equality and empower women.
- Reduce child mortality.
- Improve maternal health.
- Combat HIV/AIDS, malaria, and other diseases.
- Ensure environmental sustainability.
- Develop a global partnership for development.

Although the goals and targets identified by the UN are essentially the responsibility of *governments* to achieve, some of them have very direct implications for business, whilst others relate more broadly to the broader environment in which companies have to operate (Newell and Frynas 2007). Ultimately, as Nelson and Prescott (2003) argue, 'all of them are relevant for the private sector in today's interdependent global economy'—a point borne out by the attempt by some companies, such as Nestlé, to issue reports on their contribution to the Millennium Development Goals.

> **? THINK THEORY**
>
> Consider each of the Millennium Development Goals and set out how business could reasonably contribute to progress towards them.

VISIT THE WEBSITE for a short response to this feature

Implications of sustainability for business ethics

Given this extended set of expectations placed on business according to the triple bottom line of sustainability, there are clearly significant implications for how we should look at business ethics. Issues of an ethical nature, be they plant closures, product accessibility issues, or industrial pollution, demand that we consider a diverse and complex range of considerations and concerns. However, to achieve genuine sustainability in any of the three areas, let alone in *all* of them, is perhaps expecting too much. After all, there are few, if any, products, businesses, or industries that can confidently claim to be sustainable in the full sense of the word. However, with the notion of sustainability widely promoted by governments, businesses, NGOs, and academia, it is clearly vital that we understand its full implications and evaluate business ethics practices according to their performance along, and trade-offs between, the different dimensions of sustainability. As Elkington (1998) suggests, the TBL is less about establishing accounting techniques and performance metrics for achievements in the three dimensions (which we shall look at in Chapter 5), and more about revolutionizing the way that companies think about and act in their business. It is these challenges, as they are framed according to each of the corporation's stakeholders, that we shall be examining in the second part of the book.

■ Summary

In this chapter, we have defined business ethics, and set it within a number of significant currents of thinking. First, we have shown the importance of business ethics to current business theory and practice, suggesting that knowledge of business ethics is vital in the contemporary business environment. Secondly, we have argued that business ethics has been fundamentally recontextualized by the forces of globalization, necessitating a distinctly global view of ethical problems and practices in business. Finally, we have identified sustainability as a crucial concept that helps to determine and frame the goals of business activities from an ethical perspective. In the rest of the book, we shall revisit these themes of globalization, international diversity, and sustainability many more times in order to expand, refine, and contextualize the initial arguments put forward here. In the next chapter though, we shall move on to consider specifically the social role and responsibilities of the corporation, and examine the emerging concept of corporate citizenship.

Study questions

1 Critically evaluate the proposition that business ethics is an oxymoron.

2 'Business ethics is of no practical importance to managers. Debates about right and wrong should be left in the classroom.' Critically evaluate this statement using examples where appropriate.

3 What is the relationship between business ethics and the law?

4 'Business ethics do not really matter to small firm owners. They will get away with whatever they can in order to succeed.' Critically examine why such a view of small firms might be pervasive and whether it is likely to be accurate.

5 What is globalization and why is it important for understanding business ethics? Select one multinational corporation based in your home country and set out the different ways in which globalization might have implications for business ethics in that corporation.

6 What is sustainability? To what extent do you think it is possible for corporations in the following industries to be sustainable? Explain your answers.

(a) Tobacco industry.

(b) Oil industry.

(c) Car industry.

Research exercise

Business ethics issues are reported on regularly in the media. Conduct a thorough investigation of all the incidents that have been reported on the web during the past two weeks.

1 List the incidents that you have unearthed, and identify the main issues and criticisms in each case.

2 To what extent is it possible to classify these as ethical as opposed to legal violations?

3 Which companies have been implicated in each case? Are these large or small companies, local or international in scope? Explain your findings.

4 In which country has each incident taken place? Can you identify any national or regional influences on the types of cases that have come to light?

Key readings

VISIT THE WEBSITE for links to further key readings

1 **Collins, J.W. 1994. Is business ethics an oxymoron? *Business Ho izons*, September–October: 1–8.**

This paper is very readable and provides a good overview of the challenge facing business ethics. It goes on to identify a route forward that emphasizes the importance of managers in building trust and creating value.

2 **Cullum, L., Darbyshire, C.C., Delgado, R., and Vey, P.C. 2005. Executives behaving badly. *Ha a Business Re iew*, September: 106–7.**

Humour is a great way to start thinking about business ethics. This article presents cartoons focusing on the theme of executives behaving badly in the work environment, and provides a good platform for thinking about why the idea that business ethics is an oxymoron is so embedded in organizational life. Read the cartoons, have a laugh, and then consider what needs to change in organizations in order to get people to take ethics more seriously.

Case 1

McEthics in Europe and Asia: should McDonald's extend its response to ethical criticism in Europe?

VISIT THE WEBSITE for links to useful sources of further information

This case examines ethical criticisms of the US fast food giant McDonald's, and explores demands for the company to extend their vigorous efforts to restore their dented credibility in Europe to markets in Asia. The case focuses on the problems of obesity and unhealthy eating that have confronted the company, which are presented in the context of the broader critique of the chain. These issues cover many of the key concepts around ethics, globalization, and sustainability that we have discussed in Chapter 1.

McDonald's is truly a multinational corporation. By 2009, the firm was operating some 31,000 restaurants in 118 countries, serving almost 60 million customers a day. The market leader in its industry, and one of the most vigorous exponents of a global business approach, McDonald's has pioneered an innovative business model that has since been widely imitated in the fast food industry and beyond.

However, there are many who are not so positive about the corporation's approach and criticisms of McDonald's have been a common feature of the past three decades. Nowhere has this been more evident than in Europe, where McDonald's became the bête noir of environmentalists and social justice campaigners in the 1980s and 1990s. Not only did the company gain the distinction of being the subject of England's longest ever trial—the by now legendary McLibel case—but anti-globalization campaigners in France and elsewhere famously targeted the company with store occupations and assaults. More recently, nutritionists and healthy eating campaigners roundly criticized the company for its standard fare of high calorie burgers and fries that many saw as a major cause of spiralling obesity rates, especially among young people. With a loss of market share to apparently healthier offerings, and governments pushing for increasing regulation of fast food advertising to children, McDonald's reached a crisis that saw it attempt an ethical makeover in the mid-2000s. In came healthy options, such as fresh salads and fruit, as well as sports campaigns for young people, and enhanced nutritional labelling. Meanwhile, with increasing affluence in Asia leading to a wave of diet-related problems similar to those in Europe—such as escalating rates of obesity and diabetes in children and young adults—some started to question whether the new directions McDonald's was starting to take in Europe shouldn't be replicated in India, China, and other developing countries.

Big Mac under attack

When the epic McLibel trial came to an end in 1997, after more than three years of hearings, court proceedings, and deliberation, the McDonald's corporation must have thought that things couldn't have got any worse. Although the company was partly vindicated by the judge's verdict concerning the veracity of some of the claims made by an obscure London activist group in the late 1980s, the two unemployed campaigners that the huge company had spent millions of dollars taking to court were ruled to have proven several of their claims. These included accusations that the company 'exploits children' with its advertising; was 'culpably responsible' for cruelty to animals; 'strongly antipathetic' to unions; paid its workers low wages; falsely advertised its food as nutritious; and risked the health of its most regular, long-term customers—hardly a positive message to be sending to its millions of customers and critics across the world. The trial attracted massive international publicity, and even sparked the publication of an acclaimed book, a TV programme, a documentary film, and most damaging of all, the McSpotlight website, which immediately made a wealth of information critical of McDonald's, much of it used in the trial, freely available to an international audience.

More trouble was soon to come for the company from across the channel, when Jose Bové and his radical farmers' union, the Confederation Paysanne, made international headlines for his campaign to defend small, local producers and resist the march of the American multinational in France. McDonald's continued to meet resistance within France and other parts of the world throughout the 2000s, due to an upsurge in anti-American feeling following the invasion and occupation of Iraq. However, probably the biggest ethical challenge faced by McDonald's in Europe and other developed countries concerned issues of health and nutrition. With critics claiming that a diet of fast food had been a major contributor to escalating rates of obesity, McDonald's, as the world's leading fast food company, inevitably found itself first in the firing line. Among the arguments made by its critics were that the company had failed to provide a balanced menu, that it provided insufficient nutritional information and guidance, and that it actively encouraged consumers (especially children) to make unhealthy choices, for example by promoting 'supersize' portions.

The hauling over the coals of the company's nutritional record continued with the box office success of the film *Supersize Me* across much of Europe and the US in the mid-2000s. In the movie, the filmmaker Morgan Spurlock experiments with eating nothing but McDonald's for a month and records the subsequent effects on his health. Whilst the company was aggressive in its response to the film in the US, its European response was considerably more accommodating, suggesting on a website specifically launched to provide 'a balanced debate' on the nutrition issues raised by Spurlock that 'What may surprise you is how much of the film we agree with'.

Meanwhile, European governments also started to tackle the fast food industry in efforts to address health and nutrition issues. The UK government, for example, initiated a Commons Health Committee inquiry into obesity that saw executives from McDonald's and other food companies giving evidence. In France, meanwhile, the government introduced a tax on all food and drink advertising not bearing a health message.

Big Mac fights back

In the face of such sustained criticism, McDonald's did not stand idly by, especially once profits looked to be at risk. The chain launched a substantial turnaround strategy in 2003 where, to many people's surprise, the firm dropped its supersizing options, and put a range of new healthy options on the menu, including salads and grilled chicken flatbreads, porridge for breakfast, and even the opportunity for concerned parents to replace fries with carrot sticks and fruit in the ubiquitous children's 'happy meals'. A huge advertising campaign emphasizing the firm's fresh and healthy new approach accompanied the menu changes, with the slogan 'McDonald's. But not as you know it' splashed across close-up pictures of fruit and salad. The campaign was also backed by booklets detailing the new menus and healthy options for children, which were sent to 17m households across the UK and elsewhere. Extended in-store nutritional labelling also followed—a move once vigorously resisted by the company.

Beyond its own stores, McDonald's also launched exercise and sports initiatives especially targeted at young people. Promoted under the theme of 'balanced lifestyles', the company sought to show young people the two sides to a healthy lifestyle—a balanced diet and exercise. Country websites in Europe began including sports sections in addition to the usual information about stores and menus, and have now become a standard feature on national websites. For instance, in France in 2009 the company was promoting its 'McDo Sports Tour', which enables children to try out Olympic sports for free across the country, as well as the 'McDo Kids Iron Tour', a series of triathlons for the under twelves. And not to miss out on Europe's passion for its favourite sport, the firm also sponsored the UEFA EURO 2008 Football Championship and introduced partnerships with football associations in the UK to train community football coaches and make coaching more widely accessible to young people.

Initially, such developments were viewed with considerable scepticism, especially when it was revealed that one of the new salads, the Chicken Caesar salad, had more fat and calories than the much maligned hamburger. However, to this and many other criticisms the company was quick to respond (in the case of the Chicken Caesar salad by introducing a lower-fat dressing). Over time it has become clear that the shifts under way at McDonald's are part of a long-term strategic realignment towards changing societal values and expectations. This was further emphasized by 2007 commitments to only serve 100% Rainforest Alliance-certified sustainably grown coffee in its UK restaurants, as well as switching its delivery trucks to biodiesel made from its own reprocessed used cooking oil.

In most respects, McDonald's strategy appears to have been a success. Even though evidence suggests that the vast majority of McDonald's customers still order a burger, fries, and cola, it clearly feels more acceptable to eat at McDonald's again in Europe because the menu is healthier, and families especially have greater opportunity now to provide their children with a more balanced meal under the golden arches. Even the firm's fiercest critics seemed to have lost their momentum, with the anti-McDonald's site McSpotlight apparently abandoned in 2005. Notably, the strategy seems to have contributed to a turnaround in the firm's faltering prospects. From a slump in the early to mid-2000s, sales rebounded following the menu relaunch—and even in the downturn of the late 2000s, the company was able to maintain steady growth in profits. Although its ethical commitments had led to some cost increases and a diversion from its standardized model, the firm's commitment to good value continued to attract price-conscious consumers. Remarkably, by 2009 Europe was the firm's highest growth region, driven in part by considerable popularity in food-loving France, where according to *The Times*, the chain had become the country's 'worst-kept dirty secret'.

Big Mac goes East

However, despite the apparent success of the McDonald's turnaround in Europe, many of the same threats to its reputation have returned to haunt the company in Asia. With increasing prosperity in emerging economies such as India and China, the demand for eating out and for a whole range of convenience foods has expanded substantially in recent years. In both India and China, the market for eating out now exceeds $120bn a year, much of it in fast-food restaurants, with further growth widely predicted across Asia. Capitalizing on this trend, McDonald's announced in 2009 plans to open a further 500 restaurants in China over the next three years, including more drive-in formats and 24-hour delivery. But as eating habits are changing, so too are health problems. Rates of obesity in China have doubled in the last ten years, and even though only a few decades ago famine was a more common threat, the country is said now to be facing an oncoming obesity epidemic. Other diet and exercise-related problems such as diabetes and heart disease are also on the rise.

To date, activists and regulators have not challenged fast food companies such as McDonald's to the same extent that they were attacked in Europe, but growing pressure is clearly evident. A 2008 report by the group Consumers International claimed that global brands take advantage of lax laws in Asian countries to promote calorie-dense and nutrition-poor foods to children. A follow-up by *Ethical Corporation* magazine revealed that, although widespread in Europe, nutritional information was absent on McDonald's websites for the Philippines, Hong Kong, and China. Moreover, practices now halted in Europe appeared to be much in use in Asia—such as dedicated online kids' zones where the company has been accused of targeting young children with unhealthy food.

The company this time has been less slow to respond to its critics—a healthy option corn soup has emerged on the menu in China, a vegetarian burger features in India, and the games, competitions, and special offers featured on the company's Asian kids' zones have largely been scaled back. But the overall emphasis on healthy eating, exercise, and a balanced lifestyle has yet to be actively promoted to anything like the same extent as in Europe. Whether this means that the company is planning a different strategy in Asia or is simply rolling out a global ethical response over time, remains to be seen.

Questions

1 Set out the main criticisms that have been levelled at McDonald's in Europe. To what extent are these criticisms likely to be replicated in Asia? What differences can be predicted?

2 Describe and evaluate the tactics used by McDonald's in responding to their critics in Europe? Will these work to the same degree in Asia?

3 Should McDonald's offer healthy alternatives to the same extent in all the countries in which it operates, or just those where it has been criticized in the past, or is it expecting further regulation? What if customers overseas do not want healthy options?

4 How could McDonald's seek to avoid further criticism in the future? Can the company realistically present itself as an ethical corporation?

5 How sustainable is the fast food industry from the point of view of the triple bottom line?

Sources

Chhabara, R. 2008. Brand marketing—catering for local tastes. *Ethical Corporation*, 13 November: http://www.ethicalcorp.com/content.asp?ContentID=6200.

Choueka, E. 2005. Big Mac fights back. *BBC News*, 8 July: http://www.bbc.co.uk/news.

Frean, A. 2009. McDonald's sales driven by French hunger. *The Times,* 10 August: http://www.timesonline.com.

Schiller, B. 2006. Consumer health: food fears. *Ethical Corporation,* 19 June: http://www.ethicalcorp.com.

The Economist. 2004. Big Mac's makeover—McDonald's turned around. *The Economist,* 16 October.

Yan, F. and Li, H. 2009. McDonald's eye 500 stores in China in 3 years: exec. *Reuters,* 18 February: http://www.reuters.com.

Notes

1 For example, Kelemen and Peltonen (2001) analyse the different usage of the concepts of 'ethics' and 'morality' in the writings of Michel Foucault and Zygmunt Bauman, two leading authors in the area of postmodern business ethics. They reveal strikingly different distinctions that in fact virtually provide a direct contradiction to one another.

2 GoodCorporation/GfK Fairness Index Survey: http://www.goodcorporation.com.

3 KPMG, Fraud and misconduct in Hong Kong: 2006 findings, http://www.kpmg.com.cn.

4 There is a wide range of literature addressing globalization and its meaning. A good introduction is provided by Scherer and Palazzo (2008a).

5 See Anon. 2006. *Playboy* halts operations in Indonesia after protests. *Hindustan Times*, 21 April: 15.

6 For an early articulation of this relationship, see Meadows et al. (1974). Whilst many of their initial predictions of growth limits proved to be overly pessimistic, the basic principle of carrying capacity has become largely accepted.

7 See http:// www.taxjustice.net.

2

Framing Business Ethics

CORPORATE RESPONSIBILITY, STAKEHOLDERS, AND CITIZENSHIP

In this chapter we will:

- Analyse the notion of responsibility as it applies to corporations.
- Distinguish the various concepts of corporate social responsibility.
- Present the stakeholder theory of the firm as key concept in business-society relations.
- Outline the concept of corporate accountability, and establish its importance in understanding the political role of the firm in society.
- Critically examine the notion of corporate citizenship and assess its contribution to the framing of business ethics.
- Discuss throughout the chapter the implication of these—mostly US-born—concepts for different parts of the global economy.

■ Towards a framework for business ethics

In Chapter 1, we defined the subject of business ethics as 'the study of business situations, activities, and decisions where issues of right and wrong are addressed'. In order to address issues of right and wrong, the crucial starting point for businesses is the question of whether companies are actors that have to make decisions beyond simply producing goods and services on a profitable basis. After all, if companies provide us with great products that we want to buy, employ workers to produce them, and pay taxes to government, aren't they already providing a sufficient contribution to society? It is the definition and justification of these potentially wider responsibilities that is the subject of this chapter. We begin by addressing the fundamental nature of the modern corporation in order to answer the question of whether corporations can have a moral responsibility in the same way as individual people do. We then proceed to discuss key themes in the literature on the social role of business, namely corporate social responsibility, stakeholder theory, and corporate accountability. We finish the chapter by exploring the notion of corporate citizenship. We argue that although this is a new concept to have emerged from the literature, and it can be interpreted in a number of different ways, in its fullest sense it can be extremely useful for framing some of the problems of business ethics in the global economy raised in Chapter 1.

■ What is a corporation?

It may seem like an obvious question, but the practical and legal identification of the corporation within any given society has significant implications for how, and indeed whether, certain types of responsibility can be assigned to such an entity. Corporations are clearly not the same as individual people, and before we can decide what responsibilities they might have, we need to define exactly what they are, and why they exist in the first place.

The corporation is by far the dominant form of business entity in the modern global economy. Although not all businesses (such as sole traders) are corporations, and many corporations (such as charities and universities) are not-for-profit businesses, we shall be primarily concentrating on business in the corporate form.

Key features of a corporation

So what is it then that defines a corporation? A corporation is essentially defined in terms of legal status and the ownership of assets. Legally, corporations are typically regarded as independent from those who work in them, manage them, invest in them, or receive products or services from them. Corporations are separate entities in their own right. For this reason, corporations are regarded as having *perpetual succession*, i.e. as an entity, they can survive the death of any individual investors, employees, or customers—they simply need to find new ones.

This legal status leads on to the second key defining feature of corporations. Rather than shareholders or managers owning the assets associated with a corporation, *the corporation itself* usually owns those assets. The factories, offices, computers, machines, and other assets operated by, say, the Anglo-Dutch consumer products giant, Unilever, are the property of Unilever, not of its shareholders. Shareholders simply own a share in the company that entitles them to a dividend and some say in certain decisions affecting the company. They could not, for instance, arrive at Unilever's HQ and try to remove a computer or a desk and take it home, because it is Unilever that owns that computer or desk, not the shareholder. Similarly, employees, customers, suppliers, etc., deal with, and agree contracts with, the corporation, not with shareholders.

The implications of this situation are extremely significant for our understanding of the responsibilities of corporations:

- **Corporations are typically regarded as 'artificial persons' in the eyes of the law.** That is, they have certain rights and responsibilities in society, just as an individual citizen might.
- **Corporations are notionally 'owned' by shareholders, but exist independently of them.** The corporation holds its own assets and shareholders are not responsible for the debts or damages caused by the corporation (they have limited liability).
- **Managers and directors have a 'fiduciary' responsibility to protect the investment of shareholders.** This means that senior management is expected to hold shareholders' investment in trust and to act in their best interests. As we shall see in Chapter 6, the exact nature of the duty this imposes on managers and how it is legally structured actually varies across different parts of the world.

This establishes a legal framework for corporations to be opened up to questions of responsibility in that a company is legally responsible for its actions in the eyes of the law. However, this is not quite the same as assigning a *moral* responsibility to corporations. After all, it is one thing to say that a person feels a sense of moral responsibility for their actions, and can feel pride or shame in doing the right or wrong thing, but clearly, we cannot claim the same for inanimate entities such as corporations. Hence, we need to look a little more closely at the specific nature and responsibilities of corporations.

Can a corporation have social responsibilities?

In 1970, just after the first major wave of the business ethics movement in the US, the Nobel-Prize-winning economist Milton Friedman published an article that has since become a classic text, questioning the alleged social role of corporations. Under the provocative title 'The social responsibility of business is to increase its profits', he vigorously protested against the notion of social responsibilities for corporations. He based his argument on three main premises:

- **Only human beings have a moral responsibility for their actions.** His first substantial point was that corporations are not human beings and therefore cannot assume true moral responsibility for their actions. Since corporations are set up by individual human beings, it is those human beings who are then individually responsible for the actions of the corporation.
- **It is managers' responsibility to act solely in the interests of shareholders.** His second point was that as long as a corporation abides by the legal framework society has set up for business, the only responsibility of the managers of the corporation is to make profit, because it is for this task that the firm has been set up and the managers have been employed. Acting for any other purpose constitutes a betrayal of their special responsibility to shareholders and thus essentially represents a 'theft' from shareholders' pockets.
- **Social issues and problems are the proper province of the state rather than corporate managers.** Friedman's third main point was that managers should not, and cannot, decide what is in society's best interests. This is the job of government. Corporate managers are neither trained to set and achieve social goals, nor (unlike politicians) are they democratically elected to do so.

We will deal with the second and third points shortly. First, however, we will examine the proposition that a company cannot be morally responsible for what it does, since its decisions are essentially those of individual people.

Can a corporation be morally responsible for its actions?

Is a corporation just a collection of individuals who work together under the same roof, or is the corporation not only a *legal* entity in its own right, but also a *moral* one? Can a corporation actually assume moral responsibility for the rights and wrongs of its actions? The debate regarding the assignation of moral responsibilities to corporations is a long and complex one,[1] and has received renewed attention in recent years following the publication of Joel Bakan's (2004) controversial book, *The Corporation*, which went on to form the basis of a hard-hitting documentary released in 2004 (see **Ethics on Screen 2**). Bakan's basic premise is that the legal designation of the corporation makes it unable to act except in thoroughly self-interested ways—that, in effect, the corporation is an unfeeling psychopath, which is 'by any reasonable measure hopelessly and unavoidably demented'.

Whilst Bakan's conclusion regarding the inability of corporations to act upon moral reasons to refrain from harming others is a powerful one, there is general support from the business ethics literature for some degree of responsibility to be accredited to corporations. Nevertheless, this is not the same, and almost certainly weaker, than the moral responsibility of individuals.

These arguments are primarily based on the idea that in order to assign responsibility to corporations, it is necessary to show that in addition to legal independence from their members (as discussed above), they also have *agency* independent of their members (Moore 1999a). There are two main arguments in support of this point. The first argument looks at the fact that apart from individuals taking decisions within companies, every organization has a *corporate internal decision structure* that directs corporate decisions in line with pre-determined goals (French 1979). Such an internal decision structure is manifested in various elements which, acting together, result in a situation whereby the majority of corporate actions cannot be assigned to any individual's decisions—and therefore responsibility—alone. The corporate internal decision structure is evident in the organization chart, as well as in the established corporate policies that determine the company's actions far beyond any individual's contribution. This view does not exclude the fact that individuals still act independently within the corporation and that there are still quite a number of decisions that can be directly traced back to individual actors. The crucial point is that corporations normally have an organized framework of decision-making that, by establishing an explicit or implicit *purpose* for decisions, clearly transcends the individual's framework of responsibility.

A second argument supporting the moral dimension of corporate responsibility is the fact that all companies not only have an organized corporate internal decision structure, but furthermore manifest a set of beliefs and values that set out what is generally regarded as right or wrong in the corporation—namely, the *organizational culture* (G. Moore 1999). As we shall see in Chapter 4, these values and beliefs are widely believed to be a strong influence on the individual's ethical decision-making and behaviour. Hence, many of the issues discussed in this book for which corporations receive either praise or blame can be traced back to the company's culture. For example, many commentators attributed Levi Strauss & Co.'s progressive response to child labour and other human rights problems in developing countries to the firm's ethical beliefs and espoused core values (see, e.g. Donaldson 1996: 54).

We can therefore conclude that corporations do indeed have some level of moral responsibility that is more than the responsibility of the individuals constituting the corporation. Not only does the legal framework of most developed countries treat the corporation as a 'legal' or 'artificial' person that has a legal responsibility for its actions, but the corporation also appears to have moral agency of sorts that shapes the decisions made by those in the corporation.

In the following sections, we will take a closer look at the second argument brought forward by Friedman (and many of his followers). This questions any social responsibilities a corporate manager might have beyond those which are based on the duty to produce profits for shareholders. In order to do so, we shall primarily discuss probably the two most influential concepts to have arisen from the business ethics literature to date: corporate social responsibility and stakeholder theory.

VISIT THE WEBSITE for links to useful sources of further information

VISIT THE WEBSITE to see a trailer for 'the corporation'

ETHICS ON SCREEN 2

The Corporation

A surprisingly rational and coherent attack on capitalism's most important institution.

The Economist

The Corporation is a multi-award winning documentary based on the book of the same name written by Law professor Joel Bakan. Made by Bakan in collaboration with fellow Canadians Mark Achbar and Jennifer Abbott, the film was released in 2004 to critical and commercial success on both sides of the Atlantic.

The film presents a thoroughly researched, and thought-provoking analysis of the nature of the corporation, and the implications this might have for corporate responsibility. Taking its lead from the scandals that rocked corporate America in the early 2000s, and which continued to be played out in the courts for some years after, it asks us to consider if unethical practices are simply the fault of a few rogue individuals or whether there is a problem at the heart of the corporate form.

The film details the emergence and history of the legal status of the corporation in America and notes the key nineteenth-century legal innovation that led to the idea that, in the eyes of the law, companies could be regarded as artificial persons. However, the main message of the film is that, by their very nature, corporations are unable to act in any other way than to selfishly pursue their own self-interests. Using psychological profiling based on case studies of corporate misbehaviour, the filmmakers argue that if corporations are to be regarded as people, then the only recognizable model that they follow is that of the psychopath! The problem with corporations, they contend, is that they are legally instituted to act as 'externalising machines' that inevitably disregard their social impacts on society.

The film is particularly powerful in that it presents its case through interviews with a wide range of business executives and well-known experts, including such influential figures as Milton Friedman, Noam Chomsky, Michael Moore, Robert Monks, the former boss of Shell, Sir Mark Moody-Stuart, and the pioneering CEO of Interface Carpets, Ray Anderson. These are supported by a cast of typically unseen figures operating in the worlds of undercover marketing, advertising to children, competitive intelligence gathering, and commodity broking. The picture that emerges is not that the people inside companies are evil, but that the corporate form itself is so anti-social that it dehumanizes those that work in them in its relentless pursuit of profit and power.

Courtesy Mark Achbar, Big Picture Media Corporation, www.TheCorporation.com

Ultimately then, the film portrays a pretty bleak picture of the corporation, but not one that is completely irredeemable. In the final part of the film, something of a manifesto for action is presented that offers some food for thought on how we might proceed out of our current predicament. Perhaps what is most striking about the film though is how much it focuses on the specifically Anglo-American form of the joint-stock corporation, which differs from the continental European or East Asian models in a number of important ways. Similarly, it takes little account of privately held firms, which are very common in other parts of the world, most notably Asia, nor of co-operatives which are particularly prominent in Italy for example. Taking these alternative models into account, we might arguably find a corporation that is rather less conspicuously psychotic.

Sources

Bakan, J. 2004. *The corporation: the pathological pursuit of profit and power*. London: Constable and Robinson.

The Economist. 2004. The lunatic you work for. *The Economist*, 6 May: http://www.theeconomist.com

http://www.thecorporation.com (where you can watch the film online for free).

■ Corporate social responsibility

The systematic reasoning about a conceptual framework for corporate social responsibility (CSR) started in the US half a century ago (Carroll 2008). During this time many different concepts and principles have been aired and debated in relation to CSR. Such debates have focused on two key questions:

1 Why might it be argued that corporations have social as well as financial responsibilities?

2 What is the nature of these social responsibilities?

Let us look at each of these two questions in turn.

Why do corporations have social responsibilities?

This first question has raised enormous amounts of controversy in the past, but it is by now fairly widely accepted that businesses do indeed have responsibilities beyond simply making a profit. This is based on a number of distinct, but related, arguments,[2] many of which tend to be couched in terms of *enlightened self-interest*, i.e. the corporation takes on social responsibilities insofar as doing so promotes its own self-interest. For example:

- Corporations perceived as being socially responsible might be rewarded with extra and/or more satisfied customers, whilst perceived irresponsibility may result in boycotts or other undesirable consumer actions. In a 2008 survey, *The Economist* (2008a: 13) found that for more than 50% of global business leaders the prime reason to engage in CSR is 'having a better brand reputation'. For companies with a strong global brand, consumer pressure can be the key driver towards more responsible practices, as the example of Nike has probably most vividly demonstrated (Zadek 2004).
- Similarly, employees might be attracted to work for, and even be more committed to, corporations perceived as being socially responsible (Greening and Turban 2000). In a 2008 survey in 18 countries worldwide, the top reason for people to perceive a company as socially responsible has been 'fair employee treatment'.[3]
- Voluntarily committing to social actions and programmes may forestall legislation and ensure greater corporate independence from government (Moon and Vogel 2008).
- Making a positive contribution to society might be regarded as a long-term investment in a safer, better-educated and more equitable community, which subsequently benefits the corporation by creating an improved and stable competitive context in which to do business (Porter and Kramer 2006).

These are primarily good *business* reasons why it might be advantageous for the corporation to act in a socially responsible manner. In arguing against CSR, Friedman (1970) in fact does not dispute the validity of such actions, but rather says that when they are carried out for reasons of self-interest, they are not CSR at all, but merely profit-maximization 'under the cloak of social responsibility'. This may well be true, and to a large extent depends on the *primary motivations* of the decision-maker (Bowie 1991). It is not so much a matter of whether profit subsequently arises from social actions, but whether profit or altruism was the main reason for the action in the first place. However, corporate motives are difficult, sometimes impossible, to determine. Moreover, despite numerous academic studies, a direct relationship between social responsibility and profitability has been almost impossible to unambiguously 'prove'.[4] Even though the overall weight of evidence seems to suggest some kind of positive relationship, there is still the issue of causality (Orlitzky 2008). When successful companies are seen to be operating CSR programmes, it is just as reasonable to suggest that CSR does not contribute to the success, but rather the financial success frees the company to indulge in the 'luxury' of CSR.

Hence, in addition to these business arguments for CSR, it is also important to consider further *moral* arguments for CSR:

- Corporations cause social problems (such as pollution), and hence have a responsibility to solve those they have caused and to prevent further social problems arising.
- As powerful social actors, with recourse to substantial resources, corporations should use their power and resources responsibly in society.
- All corporate activities have social impacts of one sort or another, whether through the provision of products and services, the employment of workers, or some other corporate activity. Hence, corporations cannot escape responsibility for those impacts, whether they are positive, negative, or neutral.
- Corporations rely on the contribution of a much wider set of constituencies, or stakeholders in society (such as consumers, suppliers, local communities), rather than just shareholders, and hence have a duty to take into account the interests and goals of these stakeholders as well as those of shareholders.

Given this range of moral and business arguments for CSR, the case for CSR is on a reasonably secure footing, although as we shall discuss later in the chapter, there are also problems with this, particularly in terms of the accountability of corporations (pp. 67–73). Our next question though is: if corporations have some type of social responsibility, what form does that responsibility take?

VISIT THE WEBSITE for a short response to this feature

? THINK THEORY

Theories of CSR suggest there are both business and moral reasons for engaging in social initiatives. Go to the website of one or two companies of your choice and find the section dealing with social issues (the page may be headed CSR or sustainability, or perhaps corporate citizenship) and see what kinds of reasons the corporations give for their involvement in CSR. Is there a balance of business and moral reasons, or does one type of reason predominate? How do you explain this?

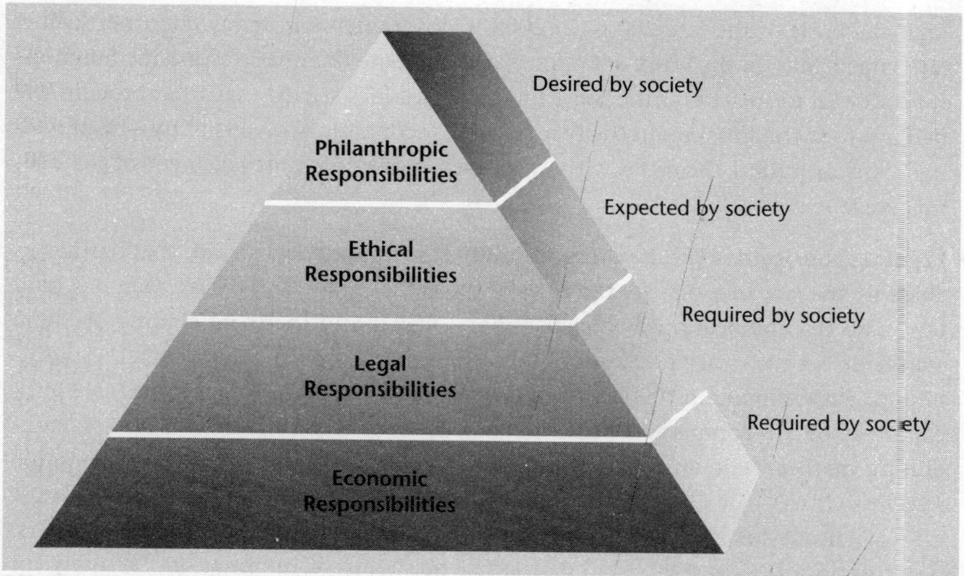

Figure 2.1. Carroll's four-part model of corporate social responsibility
Source: Adapted from Carroll, A. B. 1991. The pyramid of corporate social responsibility: towards the moral management of organizational stakeholders. *Business Horizons* (Jul–Aug): 42, Fig. 3.

What is the nature of corporate social responsibilities?

Probably the most established and accepted model of CSR that addresses our second question is the 'Four-part model of corporate social responsibility', as initially proposed by Archie Carroll (1979), and subsequently refined in later publications (e.g. Carroll 1991; Carroll and Buchholtz 2009). This model is depicted in **Figure 2.1.**

Carroll regards CSR as a multi-layered concept, which can be differentiated into four interrelated aspects—economic, legal, ethical, and philanthropic responsibilities. He presents these different responsibilities as consecutive layers within a pyramid, such that 'true' social responsibility requires the meeting of all four levels consecutively. Hence, Carroll and Buchholtz (2009: 44) offer the following definition:

> **Corporate social responsibility includes the economic, legal, ethical, and philanthropic expectations placed on organizations by society at a given point in time.**

- **Economic responsibility.** Companies have shareholders who demand a reasonable return on their investments, they have employees who want safe and fairly paid jobs, they have customers who demand good quality products at a fair price, etc. This is, by definition, the reason why businesses are set up in society and so the first responsibility of business is to be a properly functioning economic unit and to stay in business. This first layer of CSR is the basis for all the subsequent responsibilities, which rest on this (ideally) solid basis. According to Carroll (1991), the satisfaction of economic responsibilities is thus *required* of all corporations. This became especially evident during the financial crisis of the late 2000s. In 2008/9, governments in many countries 'bailed out' large banks on the brink of failure exactly because their basic economic functions were so vital to society. At the same time, many critics argued that what brought the banks into such diffuclties in the first place was economic irresponsibility—by providing loans or trading securities without proper, professional management of the risks involved.

- **Legal responsibility**. The legal responsibility of corporations demands that businesses abide by the law and 'play by the rules of the game'. Laws, as we have seen in Chapter 1, are the codification of society's moral views, and therefore abiding by these standards is a necessary prerequisite for any further reasoning about social responsibilities. For example, in the last few years a number of high profile firms have been convicted of anti-competitive behaviour as a result of illegal strategies aimed at maintaining market share and profitability (i.e. focusing excessively on their economic responsibilities). The US software giant Microsoft has faced a long-running anti-trust case in Europe for abusing its monopolistic position to disadvantage competitors, resulting in a fine of €280.5m for insufficient supply of information. Similarly, in 2007 the EC Directorate General for Competition targeted cartel activity, issuing fines of more than €3.3bn. These decisions involved 41 companies in industries ranging from German escalator manufacturing, to Dutch beer, and bitumen production in Spain.[5] As with economic responsibilities, then, Carroll (1991) suggests that the satisfaction of legal responsibilities is *required* of all corporations seeking to be socially responsible.

- **Ethical responsibility**. These responsibilities oblige corporations to do what is right, just, and fair even when they are not compelled to do so by the legal framework. A good example of ethical responsibilities is the issue of climate change for companies in North America, where unlike in Europe, a consistent regulatory framework has yet to be developed. Nevertheless, companies feel the mounting pressure from consumers, the general public, and employees to reduce greenhouse gas emissions, leading to a number of voluntary initiatives in Canada and the US (Eberlein and Matten 2009). Carroll (1991) argues that ethical responsibilities therefore consist of what is generally *expected* by society over and above economic and legal expectations.

- **Philanthropic responsibility**. Lastly, at the tip of the pyramid, the fourth level of CSR looks at the philanthropic responsibilities of corporations. The Greek word 'philanthropy' means literally 'the love of the fellow human'. By using this idea in a business context, the model incorporates activities that are within the corporation's discretion to improve the quality of life of employees, local communities, and ultimately society in general. This aspect of CSR addresses a great variety of issues, including things such as charitable donations, the building of recreation facilities for employees and their families, support for local schools, or sponsoring of art and sports events. According to Carroll (1991: 42), philanthropic responsibilities are therefore merely *desired* of corporations without being expected or required, making them 'less important than the other three categories'.

The benefit of the four-part model of CSR is that it structures the various social responsibilities into different dimensions, yet does not seek to explain social responsibility without acknowledging the very real demands placed on the firm to be profitable and legal. In this sense, it is fairly pragmatic.

However, its main limitation is that it does not adequately address the problem of what should happen when two or more responsibilities are in conflict. For example, the threat of plant closures and/or job losses often raises the problem of balancing economic responsibilities (of remaining efficient and profitable) with ethical responsibilities to provide secure jobs to employees. So for instance in the economic downturn of 2008, many car manufacturers, such as General Motors, Daimler, and Ford, made thousands of workers in their Canadian plants redundant. What trade unions condemned as blatant greed for profit was defended by the companies as an indispensable measure for economic survival.[6]

A second problem with the model, and indeed with much of the CSR literature, is that it is strongly biased towards the US context, as we shall now discuss.

CSR in an international context

CSR as a view of business responsibility in society has been particularly strong as a concept in the US, from where much of the literature, authors, and conceptualizations have emerged. In Europe and other areas of the globe, however, the concept of CSR has only more recently become so influential. The main reason for this is that the US (and other countries) tend to leave more discretion over their social responsibilities. This has led to a model of *explicit* CSR, which means CSR as an explicit activity of private companies. Other countries have operated more of an *implicit* CSR model that sees social responsibilities of business tightly embedded in the legal and institutional framework of society (Matten and Moon 2008). In Europe this has been achieved mainly through regulation, whereas in countries in Africa or Asia other, softer institutions such as religious, customary, or tribal traditions have shaped expectations on business. Generally, then, whilst one could argue that all levels of CSR play a role outside the US, they clearly have different significance and, furthermore, are interlinked in a somewhat different manner.

- The aspect of *economic* responsibility in the US is strongly focused on the profitability of companies and thus chiefly looks at the responsibility to shareholders. As we shall explain in more detail in Chapter 6, the dominant model of capitalism in much of Europe and Asia has traditionally been somewhat different. This model tends to define economic responsibility far more broadly and focuses, at least to the same extent (if not more), on the economic responsibility of corporations to employees and local communities as well. Examples include the fairly extensive healthcare and other social provisions by German or French companies, encompassing a very elaborate system of mandatory workers' rights and collective bargaining. In a similar vein, the Indian multinational Tata has a more than 100-year-old tradition of giving back to the community by investing in a range of educational and social projects wherever the company operates. As Wayne Visser (2005) argues with regard to the African context, these philanthropic responsibilities in fact are nearly as important as the economic level of the Carroll pyramid.

- The element of *legal* responsibility is often regarded as the basis of every other social responsibility in Europe, particularly given the prominent role of the state in regulating corporate practice. Continental European thinking tends to see the state in the role of enforcing the accepted rules of the game, whereas in the Anglo-American worldview, governmental rules are more likely to be regarded as an interference with private liberty. In many developing countries with weak or corrupt governments, compliance at the legal level is often not a very reliable standard of responsible behaviour.
- As we discussed in Chapter 1, different regions of the world differ significantly as to local ethical values and preferences. For instance, it has been found that Europeans tend to exhibit far greater mistrust in modern corporations than North Americans (Wootliff and Deri 2001). Hence, a general disquiet about corporations, even if they are running properly in economic terms and comply with the law, suggests the need for constant reaffirmation of their social legitimacy. Thus, nuclear power, genetic engineering, and animal testing have always been issues far higher up the public agenda in Europe than in other parts of the world (Dawson 2005). Similar differences apply to the developing world. For African companies, ethical expectations focus on good governance and avoiding corrupt practices. In the developing world in general, as Visser (2008) has argued, ethical expectations are less prevalent compared to the expectation that corporations assume their economic and philanthropic responsibilities.
- With regard to *philanthropic* responsibility, the US has a long-standing tradition of successful companies or rich capitalists such as Bill Gates donating large sums to the funding of art, higher education, or local community services—just to name a few examples (Brammer and Pavelin 2005). In Europe, by contrast, income and corporate taxes are generally higher than in the US and funding of the cited activities is more an expectation directed towards governments. In countries such as India or China, we see that against the backdrop of widespread poverty, companies are increasingly expected to 'share' their wealth with local communities. A landmark event here was the 2008 earthquake in Western China which saw an unprecedented outpouring of philanthropic donation by Chinese companies and entrepreneurs (French 2008). **Ethics in Action 2.1**, however, points to the limits of an approach to CSR that focuses exclusively on philanthropy in the Indian context.

As we can see then, whilst the four levels of responsibility are still largely valid in most international contexts, they take on different nuances, and may be accorded different significance. For example, Isabelle Maignan (2001) found that while US consumers stress the economic responsibilities of companies, their French and German counterparts tend to be far more concerned about companies complying with social norms and laws relating to social performance. These types of differences are yet more evident if we take the concept of CSR even further afield. For example, Visser (2006) has shown that in Africa, 'economic responsibilities still get the most emphasis. However, philanthropy is given second highest priority, followed by legal and then ethical responsibilities.' Moreover, as Visser shows, the various responsibilities may take on different orientations in such contexts. Noting that the economic contribution of companies in Africa is 'highly prized', he contends that the economic contribution of multinationals such as Anglo American (the UK-based mining company) in Africa exceeds the GDP of many individual African countries.

Thus, CSR, even if neatly defined along the lines of Carroll's model, still remains a relatively vague and in many respects arbitrary construct. This has led to the demand to reframe CSR as a more strategic concept of *corporate social responsiveness*, or as one CSR advocate puts it, not so much a question of whether to do CSR, but of how to do it (N.C. Smith 2003).

? THINK THEORY

Think about the theory of CSR in the context of a multinational. To what extent can a multinational corporation operate a global CSR programme, or is it necessary for such companies to operate on a more national or regional basis?

VISIT THE WEBSITE for a short response to this feature

CSR and strategy—corporate social responsiveness

The idea of corporate social responsiveness conceptualizes the more strategic and processual aspects of CSR, as in how corporations actively respond to social concerns and expectations. It has often been presented as the action phase of CSR (Carroll 1979; Wood 1991). Frederick (1994) thus defines corporate social responsiveness in the following way:

> **Corporate social responsiveness refers to the capacity of a corporation to respond to social pressures.**

Again, Archie Carroll has been very influential in setting out modes of social responsiveness and his delineation of four 'philosophies' or strategies of social responsiveness (Carroll 1979) have been widely cited.[7] These are:

- **Reaction**—the corporation denies any responsibility for social issues, for example, by claiming that they are the responsibility of government, or by arguing that the corporation is not to blame.
- **Defence**—the corporation admits responsibility, but fights it, doing the very least that seems to be required. Hence, the corporation may adopt an approach based mainly on superficial public relations rather than positive action.
- **Accommodation**—the corporation accepts responsibility and does what is demanded of it by relevant groups.
- **Pro-action**—the corporation seeks to go beyond industry norms and anticipates future expectations by doing more than is expected.

VISIT THE WEBSITE for links to useful sources of further information

ETHICS IN ACTION 2.1 http://www.ethicalcorp.com

Satyam fraud—responsibility issues in India

Rajesh Chhabara, 9 March 2008

Ethical CORPORATION

The billion-dollar fraud at Satyam should sound a warning bell for Indian companies to reassess their approach to corporate responsibility. It has raised serious questions about how Indian companies define and practise corporate responsibility. In January 2009, Satyam Computer Services, India's fourth largest information technology outsourcing company, revealed that it had lied about nearly £1bn of non-existent cash on its books.

Until 2009, Satyam had enjoyed a reputation as a leader in corporate responsibility among Indian companies. Its now disgraced chairman and founder, B. Ramalinga Raju, used to head the corporate responsibility committee of the Confederation of Indian Industries, India's business lobby group. The committee mainly encouraged members to pursue community development programmes. Raju also established the Satyam Foundation, which the company describes as its 'corporate social responsibility arm'. Its philanthropy helped Satyam win several domestic corporate responsibility awards.

Such a narrow definition of corporate responsibility as charity is common among Indian companies. When talking about responsible business, most exclude key issues such as transparency, ethics, governance, anti-corruption and accountability to stakeholders. Most list only charity projects as their corporate responsibility programmes. But the moral outrage that greeted Satyam's revelations has been so strong that it could force Indian companies to re-evaluate their position. Now they will have to focus on corporate governance and transparency if they are to convince the public of their ethical credentials.

Increased scrutiny

India's massive IT outsourcing industry, which handles sensitive information and data for mostly multinational clients, is particularly under pressure after the Satyam scandal and a disclosure in January 2009 by Wipro, the country's third largest technology firm, that the World Bank banned it last year for four years for providing improper benefits to bank staff. Incidentally, Satyam was blacklisted for eight years by the World Bank in December 2008 for similar charges. Alerted by the scandals, multinational clients have subsequently introduced greater scrutiny of Indian IT vendors' governance practices. A senior manager at Wipro, who requested anonymity, says several of the company's clients—many on the Fortune 500 list of the world's biggest corporations—have asked recently for detailed information about its corporate governance arrangements since the Satyam scandal broke.

India's top property companies, including DLF and Unitech, are also feeling the heat. A report by investment bank Credit Suisse in early 2009 highlights an unusual proportion of 'related party' transactions. These are transactions with other firms directly or indirectly owned by management personnel, and so are potential grounds for conflicts of interest. The report says that following the Satyam incident, it is clear that investors should focus on corporate governance issues.

While Indian regulators have pledged to introduce tougher governance rules to prevent a repeat of the Satyam experience, much responsibility lies with Indian companies to raise standards of corporate responsibility. But already several business leaders and associations have called the Satyam fraud a one-off incident, which should not prompt wholesale change. Some outsiders feel that the reputation of Indian business, and India's ability to attract foreign investment, hang in the balance in the aftermath of the scandals. Mary Longhurst, managing director of UK-based public relations firm Epoch Strategic Communications, who works in India, warns: 'If Indian companies develop a reputation for not taking corporate responsibility seriously, the Indian corporate brand image will be damaged'.

Sources

Ethical Corporation, Rajesh Chhabara, 9 March 2009, http://www.ethicalcorp.com.

? THINK THEORY

What levels of CSR are mentioned in this example from India? What could be reasons for the alleged imbalanced approach of Indian companies towards CSR?

VISIT THE WEBSITE for a short response to this feature

Many corporations appear to have a shifting strategy of social responsiveness. For example, in the past, tobacco companies have outright denied a link between smoking and health problems such as lung cancer (reaction). Once the health link had been publicly accepted, however, tobacco firms still fought anti-tobacco campaigners by allegedly denying knowledge of the addictive properties of nicotine, lobbying against further government regulation, and delaying litigation cases (defence). More recently, the weight of evidence against the industry has arguably led to a more accommodative stance, with firms such as BAT now admitting they are in a 'controversial' industry marketing 'risky' products, and Phillip Morris rolling out a youth smoking-prevention programme. Some suggestion of a more pro-active strategy might even be said to be emerging. BAT, for example, claim that they are changing some of the ways they address issues of concern by introducing 'stakeholder dialogue', whereby stakeholders have allegedly helped shape BAT's business principles. Additionally, they have produced an annual social report that follows the AA1000 assurance standard for accountability, and the Global Reporting Initiative guidelines for sustainability reporting (see Chapter 5: p. 217 for more detail on these standards). However, given the tobacco industry's strategies of responsiveness in the past, it is perhaps not surprising that such moves are still often interpreted as defensive tactics by their critics.[8]

Such difficulties in identifying clear-cut strategies of social responsiveness have led to the development of ways of conceptualizing observable outcomes of business commitment to CSR, namely *corporate social performance*.

Outcomes of CSR: corporate social performance

If we are able to measure, rate, and classify companies on their economic performance, why should it not be possible to do the same with its 'societal' performances as well? The answer to this question has been given by the idea of *corporate social performance* (CSP) and again, the debate about adequate constructs has been long and varied in output. Donna Wood (1991) has presented a model which by many is regarded as the state-of-the-art concept and has been extensively cited in the CSR literature. Following her model, corporate social performance can be observed as the *principles* of CSR, the *processes* of social responsiveness, and the outcomes of corporate behaviour. These outcomes are delineated in three concrete areas:

- **Social policies**—explicit and pronounced corporate social policies stating the company's values, beliefs, and goals with regard to its social environment. For example, most major firms now explicitly include social objectives in their mission statements and other corporate policies. Some corporations also have more explicit goals and targets in relation to social issues, such as BP's company-wide emissions targets. Back in 1997, it sought to achieve a 10% reduction in its 1990 levels of greenhouse gas emissions, which it achieved in 2001, nine years ahead of schedule. Now the company has invested nearly £300m in a programme to continue improving energy efficiency and reduce emissions by a further four million tonnes before 2010.[9]

- **Social programmes**—specific social programmes of activities, measures, and instruments implemented to achieve social policies. For example, many firms have implemented programmes to manage their environmental impacts, based around environmental management systems such as ISO 14000 and EMAS (Environmental Management and Auditing Scheme) that include measures and instruments that facilitate the auditing of environmental performance.
- **Social impacts**—social impacts can be traced by looking at concrete changes the corporation has achieved through the programmes implemented in any period. Obviously this is frequently the most difficult to achieve, since much data on social impacts is 'soft' (i.e. difficult to collect and quantify objectively), and the specific impact of the corporation cannot be easily isolated from other factors. Nevertheless, some impacts can be reasonably well estimated. For example: policies aimed at benefiting local schools can examine literacy rates and exam grades; environmental policies can be evaluated with pollution data; employee welfare policies can be assessed with employee satisfaction questionnaires; and equal opportunity programmes can be evaluated by monitoring the composition of the workforce and benchmarking against comparable organizations.

Clearly then, whilst the outcomes of CSR in the form of CSP is an important consideration, the actual measurement of social performance remains a complex task. We shall be discussing some of the potential tools and techniques for achieving this in more detail in Chapter 5. A more immediate problem, however, is to define not only what the corporation is responsible for, but who it is responsible to. This is the task of stakeholder theory.

■ Stakeholder theory of the firm

The stakeholder theory of the firm is probably the most popular and influential theory to emerge from business ethics (Stark 1994). Whilst the use of term 'stakeholder' in business was first noted in the 1960s, the theoretical approach was in the main developed and brought forward by Edward Freeman (1984) in the 1980s. Unlike the CSR approach, which strongly focuses on the corporation and its responsibilities, the stakeholder approach starts by looking at various groups to which the corporation has a responsibility. The main starting point is the claim that corporations are not simply managed in the interests of their shareholders alone, but that there is a whole range of groups, or stakeholders, that have a legitimate interest in the corporation as well.

Although its basic premise is simple and readily understood, there are numerous different definitions as to who or what constitutes a stakeholder, some of which are shown in **Figure 2.2**. This range of definitions makes it difficult to get a generally agreed upon idea of what a stakeholder actually is. However, Freeman's (1984: 46) original idea of a stakeholder focused on any group or individual who can affect, or is affected by, the achievement of the organization's objectives. To actually determine who in a specific situation can be considered as a stakeholder, Evan and Freeman (1993) suggest we can

Author	Definition
Stanford memo 1963 (cited in Freeman 1984).	'those groups without whose support the organization would cease to exist.'
Freeman 1984.	'can affect or is affected by the achievement of the organization's objectives.'
Evan and Freeman 1993.	'benefit from or are harmed by, and whose rights are violated or respected by, corporate actions.'
Hill and Jones 1992.	'constituents who have a legitimate claim on the firm . . . established through the existence of an exchange relationship' who supply 'the firm with critical resources (contributions) and in exchange each expects its interests to be satisfied.'
Clarkson 1995.	'have, or claim, ownership, rights, or interests in a corporation and its activities.'

Figure 2.2. Some early definitions of stakeholders

apply two simple principles. The first is the *principle of corporate rights*, which demands that the corporation has the obligation not to violate the rights of others. The second, the *principle of corporate effect*, says that companies are responsible for the effects of their actions on others. In the light of these two basic principles, we can define a stakeholder in this slightly more precise way:

> **A stakeholder of a corporation is an individual or a group which either: is harmed by, or benefits from, the corporation; *or* whose rights can be violated, or have to be respected, by the corporation.**

This definition makes clear that the range of stakeholders differs from company to company, and even for the same company in different situations, tasks, or projects. Using this definition, then, it is not possible to identify a definitive group of relevant stakeholders for any given corporation in any given situation. However, a typical representation is given in **Figure 2.3**.

Figure 2.3(a) shows the traditional model of managerial capitalism, where the company is seen as only related to four groups. Suppliers, employees, and shareholders provide the basic resources for the corporation that then uses these to provide products for consumers. The shareholders are the 'owners' of the firm and they consequently are the dominant group, on behalf of whose interests the firm should be run.

In **Figure 2.3(b)**, we find the stakeholder view of the firm, where the shareholders are one group among several others. The company has obligations not only to one group, but also to a whole variety of other constituencies that are affected by its activities. The corporation is thus situated at the centre of a series of interdependent two-way relationships.

It is important to remember though that stakeholder groups also might have duties and obligations to their *own* set of stakeholders, and to the other stakeholders of the corporation. This gives rise to a *network model* of stakeholder theory (Rowley 1997), which is shown in **Figure 2.3(c)**.

VISIT THE WEBSITE for a short response to this feature

? THINK THEORY

The network model of stakeholder theory suggests that firms have indirect relationships with a whole range of constituencies via their immediate stakeholders. To what extent should corporations also have to respect the rights of these indirect stakeholders? Think, for example, about the case of a company's supply chain and all the different tiers of supplier stakeholders that are involved. Does a company have responsibilities to suppliers at all tiers?

Why stakeholders matter

If we go back to our discussion earlier in the chapter regarding Milton Friedman's arguments against social responsibility, his second main objection was that businesses should only be run in the interests of their owners. This correlates with the traditional stockholder model of the corporation, where managers' only obligation is to shareholders. Indeed, in legal terms, we have already seen that in most developed nations, managers

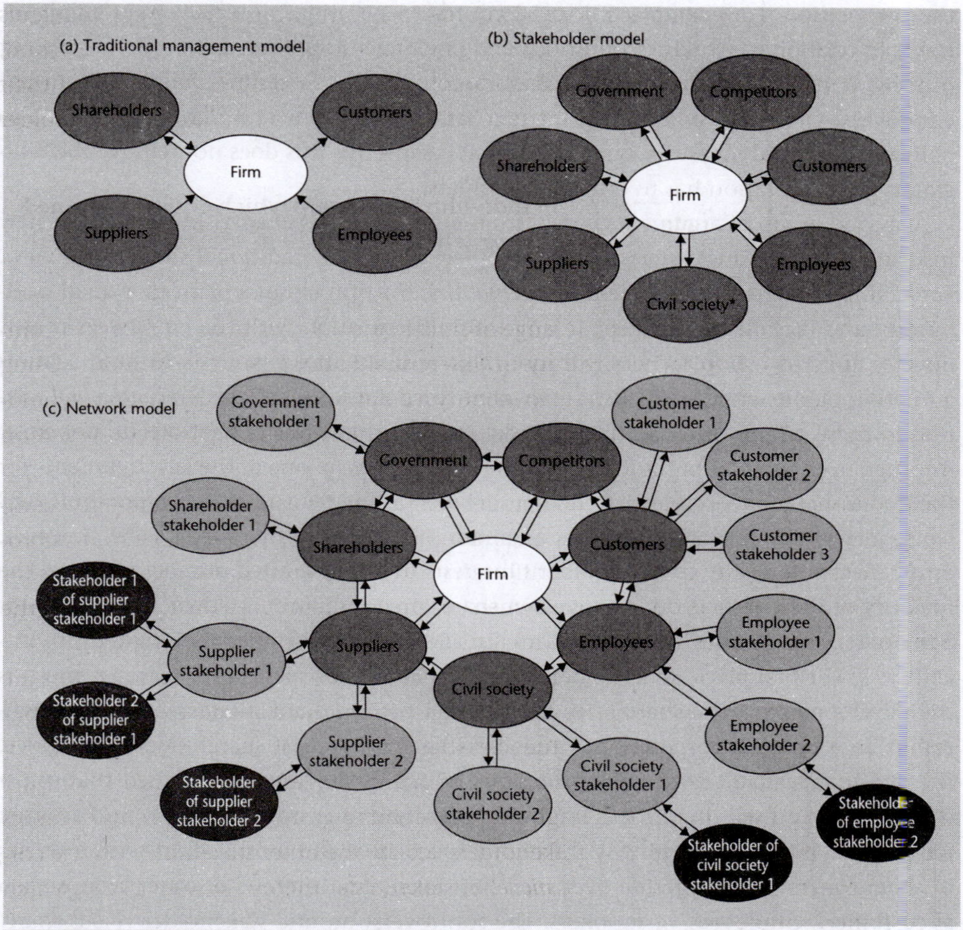

Figure 2.3. Stakeholder theory of the firm

have a special *fiduciary relationship* with shareholders to act in their interests. Stakeholder theory therefore has to provide a compelling reason why other groups also have a legitimate claim on the corporation.

Freeman (1984) himself gives two main arguments. First, on a merely descriptive level, if one examines the relationship between the firm and the various groups to which it is related by all sorts of contracts, it is simply not true to say that the only group with a legitimate interest in the corporation are shareholders. From a *legal perspective*, there are far more groups apart from shareholders that appear to hold a legitimate 'stake' in the corporation since their interests are already protected in some way. There are not only legally binding contracts to suppliers, employees, or customers, but also an increasingly dense network of laws and regulations enforced by society, which make it simply a matter of fact that a large spectrum of different stakeholders have certain rights and claims on the corporation. For example, EU social contract legislation protects certain employee rights in relation to working conditions and pay, suggesting that, from an ethical point of view, it has already been agreed that corporations have certain obligations toward employees. Of course, among this broader set of obligations and rights, there are also obligations toward investors, but from a legal perspective this does not remove the obligation the corporation has to other stakeholders.

A second group of arguments comes from an *economic perspective*. In the light of new institutional economics, there are further objections to the traditional stockholder view. For example, there is the problem of *externalities*: if a firm closes a plant in a small community and lays off the workers, it is not only the relation with the employees that is directly affected—shop owners will lose their business, tax payments to fund schools and other public services will also suffer—but since the company has no *contractual* relation to these groups, the traditional model suggests that these obligations do not exist. Another, even more important aspect is the *agency problem*: one of the key arguments for the traditional model is that shareholders are seen as the owners of the corporation, and consequently the corporation has its dominant obligation to them. This view, however, only reflects the reality of shareholder's interests in a very limited number of cases. The majority of shareholders do not invest in shares predominantly to 'own' a company (or parts of it), nor do they necessarily seek for the firm to maximize its long-term profitability. In the first place, shareholders often buy shares for speculative reasons, and it is the development of the share price that is their predominant interest—and not 'ownership' in a physical corporation. In his trenchant critique of shareholder dominance, the late management guru Sumantra Ghoshal (2005: 80) therefore argued that 'most shareholders can sell their stocks far more easily than most employees can find another job'. Hence, it is not evident why the highly speculative and mostly short-term interests of shareowners should preside over the often long-term interests of other groups such as customers, employees, or suppliers. The controversy around stakeholder versus shareholder dominance is ongoing and has flared up publicly again in the financial crisis of the late 2000s. Among the most noted voices was the one of former General Electric CEO Jack Welch—a long-standing poster boy of the shareholder value advocates—telling the *Financial Times* that shareholder value as a strategy 'is a dumb idea' and that 'your main constituencies are your employees, your customers and your products' (Guerrera 2009).

A new role for management

According to Freeman, this broader view of responsibility towards multiple stakeholders assigns a new role to management. Rather than being simply agents of shareholders, management has to take into account the rights and interests of all legitimate stakeholders. Whilst they still have a fiduciary responsibility to look after shareholders' interests, managers must balance this with the competing interests of other stakeholders for the long-term survival of the corporation, rather than maximizing the interest for just one group at a time. We shall look at some of the ways in which managers can achieve this in Chapter 5, but clearly, the task of balancing different stakeholder expectations is a major challenge.

Furthermore, since the company is obliged to respect the rights of all stakeholders, this could suggest a further obligation to allow stakeholders to take part in managerial decisions that substantially affect their welfare and their rights. In this sense, there is a case for suggesting some model of *stakeholder democracy* that gives stakeholders an opportunity to influence and control corporate decisions—although, as we shall see later in the book, different stakeholders will have different expectations in this respect and different forms of participation in the corporate decisions will be possible (see Matten and Crane 2005b). This also includes the idea of a model or a legally binding code of *corporate governance*, which codifies and regulates the various rights of the stakeholder groups. This, as we shall now see, appears to be more developed in other parts of the world than it is in the US, where stakeholder theory originated.

Stakeholder thinking in an international context

Stakeholder theory is a very simple, straightforward approach to the modern corporation. Therefore, in the second part of the book we will have a detailed look at major stakeholders of the company and provide an in-depth analysis of the company's obligations and managerial approaches towards these different stakeholders. Nevertheless, it is important to frame stakeholder thinking from an international perspective. As we indicated above, the shareholder domination of the model of managerial capitalism has never been as strongly developed in continental Europe, Korea, or Japan as it has in the Anglo-American tradition. Therefore, a general 'shift' towards other stakeholders has not been seen as so much of a necessity in those other parts of the world. Furthermore, with state influence on corporations—or even direct ownership—still playing a considerable role in countries such as France, Germany, or China—one of the major 'shareholders', government, automatically represents a large variety of 'stakeholders'—at least in principle. The result of this is that the rights of social groups other than the direct contractual partners of the firm have traditionally been fairly well respected anyway in these countries. This typically applies to European countries such as France and Germany, but also to many Asian economies, in particular Japan. It applies as well to many economies in transition from communism, where the large state-owned industrial entities always had a strong commitment to all sorts of groups other than their owners—a pattern that still survives to some extent despite the recent phase of privatization (Edwards and Lawrence 2000).

In a certain sense then, one could argue that although the *terminology* of stakeholder theory is relatively new outside the US, the general principles have actually been *practised* in many countries for some time. Let's just consider two examples:

- The vision of stakeholder democracy reads as something of a blueprint for the German model of industrial relations: on the supervisory board of large public shareholder-owned corporations, at least one-third of the board members have to be representatives of the employees—and in some industries they even have up to 50% of the votes. Furthermore, there is a very dense 'corporate law' of governance that codifies far-reaching rights of co-determination within the company. Although one might argue that this is only focusing on just one stakeholder group, namely employees, this example is representative of a generally broader orientation of corporations towards stakeholders in many European countries.

- Most explicitly in Japan, but to a lesser degree in China, India, Korea, or Taiwan, we see a specific form of business organization in large conglomerates (Carney 2008). These networks of banks, manufacturing companies, suppliers, and service providers (e.g. *keiretsu* in Japan, *chaebol* in Korea) reflect a view of the firm where suppliers, creditors, and customers represent the most important stakeholders. In particular in Japan and Korea, this wider focus on who could be important stakeholders has also included the employee, where traditionally companies offered lifetime employment so that 'salary men' worked for just one company throughout their entire life.

Although some of these entrenched patterns of stakeholder orientation have waned in the process of globalization, this absence of shareholder dominance is still strongly influencing approaches to corporate governance in these parts of the world. We will look at further aspects of stakeholder management, inclusion, and participation in the second part of the book, when we move on to focusing on each stakeholder group individually. However, at this stage, it is important to recognize that there are not only different ways in which a stakeholder approach can be implemented, but there are actually quite different *forms* of the theory itself.

Different forms of stakeholder theory

The popularity of stakeholder theory in the business ethics literature has meant that quite different forms of the theory have emerged, and it is important to be able to distinguish between them.[10] Thomas Donaldson and Lee Preston (1995) provide a convincing argument that there are in fact three forms of stakeholder theory:

- **Normative stakeholder theory**—this is theory that attempts to provide a reason why corporations *should* take into account stakeholder interests.
- **Descriptive stakeholder theory**—this is theory that attempts to ascertain whether (and how) corporations *actually do* take into account stakeholder interests.
- **Instrumental stakeholder theory**—this is theory that attempts to answer the question of whether it is *beneficial for the corporation* to take into account stakeholder interests.

In the preceding discussion, we have mainly used the first two types of argument to present the case for a stakeholder approach—that managers should and indeed do (at least to some extent) take into consideration interests beyond narrow shareholder concerns. However, we will develop a deeper normative basis for our arguments regarding specific stakeholder groups in Part II of the book. The instrumental argument—that considering the interests of stakeholders is in the best interests of the corporation—is largely akin to the argument for enlightened self-interest that we presented earlier in this chapter on p. 51.

By now, it should be fairly evident that Friedman's (1970) first and second arguments against the social role and responsibilities of the corporation face considerable dissent from those advocating a CSR and/or stakeholder position. However, there is still one final aspect of his argument that we have not yet addressed. This is the issue of corporate accountability.

■ Corporate accountability—the firm as a political actor

In Friedman's view, corporations should not undertake social policies and programmes because this is the task of government; and since corporate managers are acting on behalf of shareholders, rather than being elected by the general public, their accountability is primarily to shareholders not to the public. It is important that we make it clear what we mean by accountability in this context. Hence, for our purposes:

> **Corporate accountability refers to whether a corporation is answerable in some way for the consequences of its actions.**

In arguing against the inclusion of a social role in corporate activity, Friedman was therefore suggesting that corporations should only be involved in commercial activities and hence should, and indeed could, only be answerable to their shareholders. Although it could potentially be argued that Friedman's argument was defensible when his article was published, more recently the question of corporate accountability has become far more vexed. This is because it has been increasingly recognized that despite this apparent lack of accountability with respect to their social consequences, corporations have begun to be involved in numerous social activities and have actually taken up many of the functions previously undertaken by governments. Firms have thus begun to take on the role of political actors.

Since the late 1980s, we have witnessed a growing tendency toward the 'privatization' of many political functions and processes formerly assigned to governments. There have been two major reasons for this development:

- Governmental failure.
- Increasing power and influence of corporations.

Both developments assign to business a considerably widened array of political responsibilities, which in turn result in a growing demand for corporate accountability with regard to the use of this power. Whilst we shall refrain from an extended discussion of the specific relations between business and government at this stage (this is the subject of Chapter 11), it is important to briefly set out these two underlying processes that are driving demands for greater corporate accountability.

Governmental failure: 'risk society' and the institutional failure of politics

In 1986, the German sociologist Ulrich Beck published a book under the title of *Risk Society*[11] that, in close dialogue with British authors such as Anthony Giddens, has laid the basis for a new view on industrial societies in the late twentieth and early twenty-first centuries. Beck starts by describing the way various threats to the survival of mankind and its natural environment are becoming increasingly dominant on the public agenda. Examples are the risks of nuclear power, the risks of global warming, the risks of industrial agriculture, and the risks inherent in new technologies such as genetic engineering, just to name a few. In Europe, such risks certainly came dramatically to the attention of the general public with the landmark experience of the nuclear accident in Chernobyl in 1986, followed by the BSE crisis, the international SARS outbreak of 2003, and the 'bird flu' scare of 2006, not to mention the increasing concerns around climate change risk that came to prominence in the late 2000s.

Normally, these problems are the classic tasks for governments and politicians to deal with, causing them to issue laws that regulate these phenomena and protect citizens. However, the crucial point in these cases is that governments have been largely unable to protect their citizens; on the contrary, most of these risks and catastrophes happened with the government either being equally affected or, as the BSE case shows, being one of the main actors responsible for the problem. Beck and Giddens in their theory then conclude that this leads us to a general problem of modern societies: as well as providing their citizens with an abundance of goods and services, modern industrial societies also confront their citizens with severe risks to their health, their environment, even to the survival of mankind as such on the planet. At the same time, we see that the political institutions of modern societies are not able to protect their citizens from these self-imposed consequences of industrialization.

Why do governments fail?

There are numerous reasons why governments are not able to do their job here. Sometimes, as already indicated, they are too much part of the problem to be able to be part of the solution. More often, tackling these issues would result in severe changes in the lifestyle of modern society and in a decrease of public welfare—something politicians are quite reluctant to impose on their electorate. Sometimes these risks are even beyond the control of a single government, as the example of Chernobyl or the risk of global warming shows. Beck talks of an 'organized irresponsibility' in this context and analyses some other ways of coping with these hazards that have started to emerge as a consequence.

In particular, Beck suggests that in many important areas, political action is obviously no longer a task carried out exclusively by politicians. In the case of numerous social and environmental issues, non-governmental organizations (NGOs) such as Greenpeace or Friends of the Earth, or else protest groups and campaigners such as anti-road protestors, have also been important political actors (see Chapter 10 for more discussion of the role of such groups). Beck speaks of a new political arena, which he calls 'subpolitics', meaning political action that is taken by actors, as it were, 'below' the level of traditional governmental politics. **Case 2** describes the area of global conservation and management of water resources, where companies attempt to address this issue together with NGOs. We could find numerous other examples (e.g. **Cases 3, 5, 9, 10** in this book) that would show us that governments in many respects have lost some of their traditional capability to solve major issues in modern industrial societies. Crucially though, at the same time as we have witnessed a *weakened state*, we have also witnessed a parallel development, which has seen a massive *rise in corporate power and influence*.

Corporate power on the rise

The rise in corporate power and influence over the past 20 years or so has been receiving growing attention from academics and the general public alike. We have seen various street demonstrations against growing corporate power (see **Ethics on Screen 10**), as well as targeted attacks on specific corporations such as McDonald's (see **Case 1**) and Nestlé (Case 2). Moreover a number of influential books such as Joel Bakan's (2004) *The Corporation*, Naomi Klein's (2007) *The Shock Doctrine*, and Robert Reich's (2007) *Supercapitalism* have argued that the big corporations have gained ever more influence in society and in particular in politics. There is, however, considerable controversy in the literature about this thesis: whilst a growing body of work sees a problem in the extended power residing in the corporate sector, some mainstream business writers still contend that even large MNCs are relatively weak and politically dependent on national governments (e.g. Rugman 2000).

The crucial point in the critical view is the argument that across the globe, people's lives are increasingly controlled and shaped no longer only by governments but also by corporations. Let us have a look at some examples:

- The liberalization and deregulation of markets and industries during the rule of centre-right governments in many countries since the 1980s has given more influence, liberty, and choice to private actors. The more strongly the market dominates economic life, the weaker governmental intervention and influence is. The struggle of many governments to address the financial crisis in the late 2000s and regain control of financial markets is just the latest illustration of this point.
- The same period resulted in a huge privatization of major public services and formerly public-owned companies. Major industries such as media, telecommunications, transport, and utilities are now dominated by private actors.
- Most industrialized countries are to varying degrees struggling with unemployment. Although governments are made responsible for this, they cannot directly control employment levels because decisions over employment, relocation, or lay-offs are taken by corporations.
- Globalization facilitates relocation and potentially makes companies able to engage governments in a 'race to the bottom', i.e. it has been argued that corporations have continually relocated to 'low-cost' regions where they are faced with lower levels of regulation (or at least enforcement) of pay and working conditions, environmental protection, and corporate taxation (Scherer and Smid 2000).
- Since many of the new risks emergent in industrial society (as discussed above) are complex and far-reaching (often beyond the scope of individual countries), they would require very intricate laws, which in turn would be very difficult to implement

and monitor. Hence, corporations have increasingly been set the task of regulating themselves, rather than facing direct government regulation (see Chapter 11 for a more detailed discussion). For example, in various legislative projects, the European Union has set incentives for companies or industry to come up with self-regulation and self-commitments, rather than imposing a law upon them from above. Consequently, companies—or bodies of organized corporate interests—are increasingly assuming the role of political actors in the sphere of social and environmental issues.

We could easily add to this list and will come back to these issues throughout the book. **Ethical Dilemma 2**, for example, describes another situation where business might be involved in taking over previously governmental functions, namely the funding of universities.

The central problem behind these trends, however, is clearly visible: the idea of democracy is to give people control over the basic conditions of their lives and the possibility to choose the policies that they regard as desirable. However, since many such decisions are no longer taken by governments (and hence, indirectly by individual citizens) but by corporations (who are not subject to democratic election), the problem of democratic accountability becomes crucial.

VISIT THE WEBSITE for a short response to this feature

? THINK THEORY

Think about the concept of globalization that was discussed in Chapter 1, and our characterization of globalization as *deterritorialization*, namely 'the progressive eroding of the relevance of territorial bases for social, economic and political activities, processes and relations'. How might this influence the failing of government and increasing power of corporations?

The problem of democratic accountability

The central points here are the questions of *who controls corporations and to whom are corporations accountable*. There are those like Friedman, as discussed above, who see it as a given that corporations are only accountable to their shareholders, and furthermore, are accountable to obey and comply with the laws of the countries in which they do business. However, there are also good arguments for the view that since corporations now shape and influence so much of public and private life in modern societies, in effect they are already *de facto* political actors, so they have to become more accountable to society.

One argument, offered by Hertz (2001a) and others, is that given the power of large corporations, there is more democratic power in an individual's choice as a consumer (for or against certain products) than in their choice at the ballot box. As Craig Smith (1990) contends, consumption choices are to some extent 'purchase votes' in the social control of corporations. However, as we shall discuss in more detail in Chapter 8 when we cover business relations with consumers, one should also recognize the limitations of the individual's power to affect corporate policy through purchase choices. There is little guarantee that consumers' social choices will be reflected in their consumer choices, nor that such social choices will be even recognized, never mind acted on, by corporations. After all, not only do corporations benefit from a massive power imbalance compared with individual consumers, but consumers are also constrained in executing their voting rights by the choices offered by the market. Perhaps most importantly, consumers are just one of the multiple stakeholders that corporations might be expected to be accountable to.

This has led to further questions regarding how corporations can be made more accountable to the broad range of relevant stakeholders for their actions. One important stream of literature has examined the possibility for corporations to audit and report on their social, ethical, and environmental performance through new accounting procedures, such as environmental accounting and social reporting (Owen and O'Dwyer 2008). Another important stream of literature has looked at broader issues of communication with stakeholders, and development of stakeholder dialogue and stakeholder partnerships (e.g. Bendell 2000b; Crane and Livesey 2003). We shall look at these developments, which have been largely pioneered by European academics, institutions, and corporations, in more detail later in the book, most notably in Chapters 5 and 10. However, the key issue here is that in order to enhance corporate accountability, corporate social activity, and performance should be made more visible to those with a stake in the corporation. The term usually applied to this is **transparency**.

Although transparency can relate to any aspect of the corporation, demands for transparency usually relate primarily to social as opposed to commercial concerns, since traditionally corporations have claimed that much of their data are commercially confidential. However, it is evident that many social issues cannot be easily separated from commercial decisions. For example, Nike long claimed that the identity and location of their suppliers could not be revealed because it was commercially sensitive information that their competitors could exploit. However, concerns over working conditions in these factories led to demands for Nike to make the information public, which in 2005 they eventually agreed to do. Similarly, manufacturers and retailers of cars, CDs, and other consumer products have traditionally kept a close guard on information relating to costs. However, in the face of accusations regarding consumer exploitation as a result of collusion amongst competitors to produce artificially inflated prices, pressure has been put on firms in these industries to make their cost structures more transparent.

Clearly then, we need to take a fairly broad view of transparency in this regard, giving rise to the following definition:

Transparency is the degree to which corporate decisions, policies, activities, and impacts are acknowledged and made visible to relevant stakeholders.

Whilst increased transparency is certainly no panacea for restoring public trust (see, for example, O'Neill 2002), the tenor of current demands for greater corporate accountability and transparency, particularly as exemplified by the protest movement against global capitalism, MNCs, and global background institutions such as the IMF or the World Bank, suggests that increased attention to issues of transparency might no longer be just an option for many corporations. Increasingly, corporate accountability and transparency

AN ETHICAL DILEMMA 2

When good results are bad results?

Professor Ballistico is scratching his head. Looking at the results of last month's series of experiments makes him feel a bit uneasy. He has been sitting in his office for hours now trying to analyse the spreadsheets from every possible angle—but without success. He even had an argument with his research assistant, accusing her of having prepared the results incorrectly—but she had been right all along.

Not that Ballistico is particularly unhappy about his project. It is actually quite a successful piece of research looking at the various side effects of food additives in frozen food. The two-year project has already produced some very good publications; he has even been invited several times to give interviews on the television and in the press about the results. However, this time round he has a strange feeling. The thing that is making him feel uneasy is that according to the results of the latest tests, two substances involved in the study, called 'Longlife' and 'Rotnever', appear to quite significantly increase the risk of human allergies for long-time consumers of the additives. And however he turns and interprets the results, his assistant really seems to have delivered solid work on the data analysis.

Normally such surprising results would be good news. Solid results of this kind would make for sensational presentations at the next conference of the World Food Scientist Federation. On top of that, 'Longlife' and 'Rotnever' are very common additives in the products of the large food multinational Foodcorp, which is the market leader in frozen food in his country. His results could really make big headlines.

There is one little problem though: Professor Ballistico is director of the Foodcorp Centre for Food Science at BigCity University. Three years ago, the food company donated €2.3m to BigCity University in order to set up the research centre and to fund its activities. The company felt that as 'a good corporate citizen we should give something back to society by funding academic research for the benefit of future generations'. They also had signalled that they saw this as a continuous engagement over time . . . and Ballistico is only too aware that the decision about the next €2m funding will be imminent three months from now.

Professor Ballistico has a major dilemma: if he publishes his results, Foodcorp might get into serious trouble. He also knows that this will be quite embarrassing at the next meeting with his sponsor, and it will most certainly influence the company's decision to further fund the centre. And he hardly dares to think of his next meeting with the president of the university, who is always so proud of BigCity having such excellent ties to companies and scoring highest in the country in terms of its ability to secure external funding. Should he therefore just tell Foodcorp privately about his results so that they can take appropriate action to deal with Rotnever and Longlife?

Questions

1 What are the main ethical issues for Professor Ballistico here?

2 What options are open to him? How would you assess these options?

3 How should Ballistico proceed, and what can he realistically do to prevent similar problems arising in the future?

4 What are the wider ethical concerns regarding corporate involvement in funding universities and other public institutions?

5 In the light of this case, give a critical assessment of the potential as well as the limits of corporations stepping into roles often played by governments, such as the funding of higher education.

are being presented as necessities, not only from a normative point of view, but also with regard to the practical aspects of effectively doing business and maintaining public legitimacy. In the face of such developments, we have witnessed increasing emphasis being placed on the notion of *corporate citizenship*—a relatively new, but potentially important addition to the lexicon of business ethics. In the last main section of the chapter then, we shall examine this new term and assess its significance for the conceptualization of the social role of the corporation.

■ Corporate citizenship

Towards the middle of the 1990s, the term 'corporate citizenship' (CC) emerged as a new way of addressing the social role of the corporation. Initially favoured primarily by practitioners (Altman and Vidaver-Cohen 2000), corporate citizenship has also increasingly been introduced into the academic literature. Although again, the shift in terminology largely started in the US, numerous companies in Europe, Asia, and elsewhere have since committed themselves to CC (see **Figure 2.4**), and various consultancies and research centres based around the concept of CC have been founded across the globe.

A major landmark in this process was the joint statement on 'Global Corporate Citizenship—The Leadership Challenge for CEOs and Boards' that was signed by CEOs from around 40 of the world's largest MNCs at the annual World Economic Forum, among them major European companies such as ABB, Deutsche Bank, Diageo, Phillips, Renault, and UBS (World Economic Forum 2002). Given such emphasis being placed on CC, we need to be clear about what exactly it means. This task, however, is complicated by the different meanings implied by those employing the term, as we shall now see.

Defining corporate citizenship: three perspectives

As we have already seen, CC is currently a prominent term in key debates about business ethics globally. Therefore, much of the discussion in this book is framed around the concept of CC. However, as the literature on CC is relatively new, and a widely accepted definition of CC has yet to be established, we first of all need to develop a working definition of the term that can be used in the subsequent chapters of the book. In order

Company	Industry and country of origin	Corporate citizenship (emphasis added)	Source
BHP Billion	Mining, Australia	When operating effectively, the Company's community investment programmes should create sustainable, long-term value for our host communities and demonstrate the Company's *citizenship*. The critical question in regard to our success is whether we have managed to leave a lasting positive legacy in the communities where we operate.	Sustainability Report 2008
Citibank	Banking and Financial Services, USA	We define *citizenship* as the positive impact that Citi has on society and the environment through its core business activities, philanthropy, diversity efforts, volunteerism, and public policy engagement, as well as the philanthropic initiatives undertaken by the Citi Foundation.	2007 Citizenship report
Microsoft	Software, USA	Microsoft's endorsement of the UN Global Compact signifies that we are committed to aligning our business operations and strategies with 10 established principles [...] Principles—which correspond with Microsoft's *global corporate citizenship* values—help guide our efforts to achieve greater accountability and drive continuous improvement of our business practices.	Citizenship Report 2009
Total	Oil and Gas, France	Total is committed to contributing to the sustainable development of host communities around the world. In addition to being a normal part of **good corporate citizenship**, this policy fosters good relationships with neighbours and greater acceptance of our operations.	Corporate Social Responsibility Report 2007
Toyota	Automobiles, Japan	The **Corporate Citizenship Division** was organized in January 2006 as a specialized division to reinforce corporate social contribution activities and integrate corporate social contribution functions that had been performed by multiple divisions.	Sustainability Report 2008

Figure 2.4. Commitments to corporate citizenship

	Limited view	Equivalent view	Extended view
Focus.	Philanthropy, focused on projects, limited scope.	All areas of CSR.	Citizenship: social, political, and civil rights.
Main stakeholder group.	Local communities, employees.	Broad range of stakeholders.	Broad range of citizens; society in general.
Motivation.	Primarily philanthropic; also economic where citizenship is 'strategic'.	Mixed—economic, legal, ethical, philanthropic.	Political.
Moral grounding.	Reciprocity, i.e. 'putting something back'.	Duty to be responsible and avoid harms to society.	Grounding is not moral, but comes from changes in the political arena.

Figure 2.5. Three views of corporate citizenship

to do so, we will first have to delineate our definition of CC within other definitions typically employed either explicitly or implicitly elsewhere. Currently, the literature on CC reveals three different perspectives (Crane, Matten, and Moon 2008):

- **A limited view of CC**—this equates CC with corporate philanthropy.
- **An equivalent view of CC**—this equates CC with CSR.
- **An extended view of CC**—this acknowledges the extended political role of the corporation in society.

We shall briefly discuss each of these three perspectives—**Figure 2.5** provides an overview. However, it is important to realize that in many respects, the language of CC is simply a new terminology for existing ideas. As will become evident, although the first two views are by far the most common in popular usage, only the extended view of CC actually offers anything genuinely new to the terms and concepts already discussed in this chapter. The extended view is also, we suggest, probably the most significant and appropriate way of employing CC from a *descriptive perspective* to frame the debate about corporate accountability.

Limited view of CC

Initially, CC was, and in many instances still is, used to identify the philanthropic role and responsibilities the firm voluntarily undertakes in the local community, such as charitable donations. The limited view of CC tends to focus nearly completely on the direct physical environment of the company, resulting in a strong focus on local communities as the main stakeholder of the firm. Carroll (1991), for example, identifies 'being a good corporate citizen' with his fourth level of CSR, namely philanthropic responsibilities. Accordingly, Carroll (1991) places CC at the top level of his CSR pyramid, suggesting that it is a discretionary activity beyond that which is expected of business.

Citizenship in this respect is essentially about putting something back into the community, and is based on the corporation receiving from society with the one hand and giving to society with the other. For example, the UK organization Business in the Community is one of the world's largest national networks of companies aiming to make a positive impact on society in this way. The organization was set up in 1982 against a backdrop of enormously high levels of unemployment and urban rioting in the UK. Advocating the idea that 'healthy high streets rely on healthy back streets', companies were enlisted to join the network and make more positive impacts on their communities because in the long run this would be better for business.

Although academics and managers discussing corporate citizenship often imply this philanthropic meaning, we might question whether the limited view of CC really justifies the invention and usage of a new terminology. There is little that is genuinely new here and only very limited reference to the usage of the term 'citizenship'.

Equivalent view of CC

The second common understanding of CC consists in a somewhat updated label for CSR (or sometimes stakeholder management), without attempting to define any new role or responsibilities for the corporation. The most striking example for this use of CC is probably Carroll himself who, in a paper entitled 'The four faces of corporate citizenship' (Carroll 1998), defines CC exactly the same way as he initially defined CSR two decades ago! Similarly, Isabelle Maignan and her colleagues (e.g. Maignan and Ferrell 2000, 2001; Maignan, Ferrell, and Hult 1999) have defined CC as 'the extent to which businesses meet the economic, legal, ethical and discretionary responsibilities imposed on them by their stakeholders'—essentially a repackaging of Carroll's (1991) definition of CSR.

Clearly, this is a very common way of employing the terminology of CC, but given that it creates quite a bit of conceptual confusion, is not particularly helpful from an academic point of view. However, it is perhaps understandable given that CC is a concept that is mainly used and understood by practitioners, and hence academics, consultants, and others seeking to influence corporations might expect their ideas to be better understood and received in the corporate world by framing them in recognized practitioner terminology. Nonetheless, a significantly new conception of the social role and responsibilities of corporations can be discerned within the emerging debate on corporate citizenship, and it is to this that we shall now turn.

An extended view of CC

Whilst there has been only fairly limited discussion of an extended view of CC, it has recently received some more attention (Scherer and Palazzo 2008b), and has been more fully set out in Matten and Crane (2005a) and Crane et al. (2008).

The extended view takes as its starting point the notion of 'citizenship'. The current understanding of citizenship that is dominant in most industrialized societies is based on the liberal tradition, where citizenship is defined as a set of individual rights (Faulks 2000: 55–82). Following the still widely accepted categorization by T.H. Marshall (1965), liberal citizenship comprises three different aspects of entitlements:

- **Social rights**—these provide the individual with the *freedom to* participate in society, such as the right to education, healthcare, or various aspects of welfare. These are sometimes called 'positive' rights since they are entitlements towards third parties.
- **Civil rights**—these provide *freedom from* abuses and interference by third parties (most notably the government); among the most important are the rights to own property, to engage in 'free' markets, or exercise freedom of speech. These are sometimes called 'negative' rights since they protect the individual against the interference of stronger powers.
- **Political rights**—these include the right to vote or the right to hold office and, generally speaking, enable the individual to participate in the process of governance beyond the sphere of his or her own privacy.

The key actor for governing these rights for citizens is the government. Thus, at first glance, it is somewhat hard to make any sense of something like 'corporate citizenship' since citizenship is about relations between individuals and governments. Although, as we saw earlier, corporations are regarded as 'artificial persons' and so do enjoy some of the rights and obligations of other citizens (rights to own property, for example), it is hard to imagine corporations claiming most of the social and political rights that individual citizens enjoy. We would argue though that corporations enter the picture not because they have an entitlement to certain rights as a 'real' citizen would, but as powerful public actors that—for better or for worse—can have a significant impact on those 'real' citizen's rights. Similarly, as we have discussed above in relation to corporate accountability, the failure of governments to fulfil some of their traditional functions, coupled with the rise in corporate power, has meant that corporations have increasingly taken on a role in society which is similar to that of traditional political actors. Hence, corporations enter the arena of citizenship at the point where traditional governmental actors start to fail to be the only 'counterpart' of citizenship. Quite simply, they can be said to partly take over those functions with regard to the protection, facilitation, and enabling of citizen's rights—formerly an expectation placed solely on the government. Let us consider some examples:

- **Social rights.** Many companies have pursued initiatives formerly within the province of the welfare state: feeding homeless people, helping headteachers in managing school budgets, enhancing the employability of the unemployed, or improving deprived neighbourhoods. For example, the British retailer Marks and Spencer runs its 'Marks and Start' programme to help unemployed and homeless people gain work experience and skills that improve their employment prospects.[12] Similarly, in developing countries where governments simply cannot (or do not want to) afford a welfare state, the task of improving working conditions in sweatshops, ensuring employees a living wage, providing schools, medical centres, and roads, or even providing financial support for the schooling of child labourers are all activities in which corporations such as Shell, Nike, Levi Strauss, and others have engaged under the label of CC.

- **Civil rights.** Governmental failure again becomes particularly visible in developing or transforming countries in the arena of civil rights. Drastic examples, such as the role of Shell in Nigeria and its apparent role in the restriction of civil rights of the Ogoni people (see Boele et al. 2000), show that corporations might play a crucial role in either discouraging (as with Shell) or encouraging governments to live up to their responsibility in this arena of citizenship. A positive example for the latter might be General Motors and other corporations in South Africa during the apartheid period, which after being pressurized by their own stakeholders, eventually exerted some pressure of their own on the South African government to desist from violating the civil rights of black South Africans.
- **Political rights.** Voter apathy in national elections has been widely identified in many industrialized countries, yet there appears to be a growing willingness on the part of individuals to participate in political action *aimed at corporations rather than at governments* (Hertz 2001a). Whether through single-issue campaigns, anti-corporate protests, consumer boycotts, or other forms of sub-political action, individual citizens have increasingly sought to effect political change by leveraging the power, and to some extent vulnerability, of corporations. Returning to the McEurope case in Chapter 1, when anti-obesity campaigners sought to draw attention to the social problems of poor health and nutrition among young people, they achieved international coverage for their efforts not by tackling the American or the UK governments, but by attacking the McDonald's corporation.

Hence, given this emerging role for corporations in the administration of civil, social, and political rights, the extended view of CC suggests the following definition:

> **Corporate citizenship describes the corporate function for governing citizenship rights for individuals.**

These rights are governed by the corporation in different ways. With regard to social rights, the corporation basically either supplies or does not supply individuals with social services and hence largely takes on either a *providing* or an *ignoring role*. In the case of civil rights, corporations either capacitate or constrain citizens' civil rights, and thus can be viewed as assuming more of an *enabling* or a *disabling role*. Finally, in the realm of political rights, the corporation is essentially an additional conduit for the exercise of individuals' political rights—hence, the corporation primarily assumes a *channelling* or a *blocking role*. This extended conceptualization of corporate citizenship is shown in **Figure 2.6**.

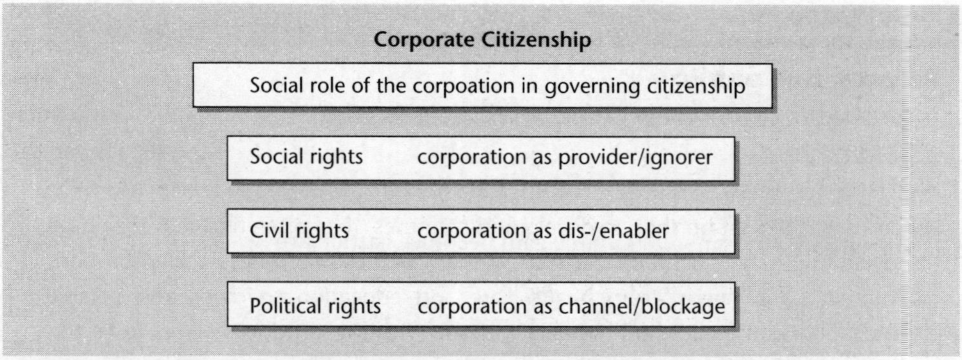

Figure 2.6. An extended view of corporate citizenship

It is evident that corporate citizenship may be the result either of a voluntary self-interest-driven corporate initiative, or of a compulsory, public pressure-driven corporate reaction—either way it places corporations squarely in a political role rather than just an economic one. Most firms actually claim to not want to take on such a political role in society, yet it seems that increasingly they do, either because of pressure from activists, or sometimes simply out of necessity. If an apparel company needs to make sure the children of its staff working in a poor African community get an education, they may need to build their own schools centre because the local authorities may simply just not have the resources to do so. The point is that we do not need to know the motivation to label something an act of 'extended' CC. This is because this view of CC is essentially a *descriptive* conceptualization of what does happen, rather than a *normative* conceptualization of what should happen. **Ethics in Action 2.2** provides the opportunity to examine this perspective in the context of corporate initiatives in developing countries.

Assessing corporate citizenship as a framework for business ethics

Having set out these three views of CC, we need to consider whether the concept of corporate citizenship really represents a useful new way of framing business ethics—or at least whether it offers us anything different or better compared with CSR, stakeholder theory, and the other concepts we have discussed in this chapter.

Our view is that CC as it is *typically* used by academics and managers—which is either in the 'limited' or the 'equivalent' sense—doesn't really add anything to our understanding of business ethics. Essentially, it is just a new buzzword to describe existing ideas about business-society relations.

However, in the 'extended' view that we have described here, CC does seem to add something significant that helps us frame business ethics in new ways. There are a number of respects in which it does this:

VISIT THE WEBSITE for links to useful sources of further information

ETHICS IN ACTION 2.2 http://www.wsj.com

Private, but public

Mike Valente and Andrew Crane, Wall Street Journal, 23 March 2009

When companies set up shop in developing countries, they often find that they have to do a lot more than just run a business. In many of these countries, local institutions can't meet basic needs, from health care and education to roads and reliable electricity. But companies can't operate without a healthy, productive work force and solid infrastructure—so, more and more of them are taking matters into their own hands. Companies are laying down roads and water pipes, setting up schools and hospitals and bankrolling a range of social programs. In other words, increasingly companies are taking on functions typically handled by the public sector.

This new role, however, isn't easy. Companies are struggling to figure out how to help locals without making them too dependent, while finding ways to placate shareholders back home who may not see the value of all these pricey investments.

Into the Breach

In many cases, companies directly take on public-service roles, even when these have little relationship to their core business. For instance, a mining company might build schools, health-care facilities or general infrastructure—things that have nothing to do with the job of mining but are essential to creating an environment for doing business.

Consider Magadi Soda Co. When the mining company—a part of India's TATA Chemicals Ltd.—set up operations in Kenya, it discovered that almost all government-funded public programs in the region were centered on the city of Nairobi. But the company was outside city limits—and lacked the infrastructure it needed for its operations. So, Magadi Soda started building. It extended the 75-mile (120-kilometer) road from the southern edges of Nairobi to the company's facilities in Lake Magadi, and built and operated an extension of the Kenyan railway line to transport soda ash to the port of Mombasa. It also introduced a passenger coach to offer transport services to the public along the route. The road and railway are now used by Kenyans with little relationship to the company, and the company helps the community maintain rural access roads.

Meanwhile, Magadi Soda bolstered its work force by ensuring the health and safety of local residents. The company constructed water-treatment plants and extended water distribution to surrounding communities. It also built up local housing, health care and education facilities, as well as supporting other local schools and providing scholarships for students.

But taking on a big public role carries risks. For one thing, activists may derail well-meaning programs by questioning why companies are acting like governments—with few, if any, measures in place to ensure accountability. Then there's the question of creating dependency among local communities. Once made, public commitments may escalate and be difficult to reverse. Companies can face a backlash if they retrench investments because of difficult financial times, or pressure from shareholders or a parent firm.

One way to avoid these concerns is to take on a sweeping role only when the lack of public services represents an immediate threat to the surrounding community or the company, such as a famine or drought. In fact, that's the strategy some big companies favor in developing countries. Still, even if companies aren't planning long-term social efforts, just emergency relief, they should keep community concerns in mind and involve locals in decision making as early as possible.

Working Through Others

Another solution to the problems encountered above is to rely on other organizations to provide necessary services. With this approach, companies help establish local groups, or bolster existing ones, that make decisions about public welfare and implement social programs. These groups take on the responsibility and accountability for providing necessities, leaving the company in a purely support role, such as providing funds. This might not be an answer to immediate problems—such as helping a community deal with drought—but it can build up long-term capabilities, so communities can eventually handle crises themselves.

That's what Magadi Soda ended up doing. The company eventually became uncomfortable with the government-like role it was playing. So, senior executives helped set up a county council and brought the local community on board to prioritize the company's public programs. This reduced the company's costs and minimized its obligation to operate activities in which it had little expertise.

Or consider a Russian aluminum producer that found itself facing a host of problems in the communities where it operated. Pressure was on to hire and source supplies locally. But public health and education were deteriorating—hurting the potential work force—and there were few small businesses to draw on. The company decided to help the communities help themselves. It organized nongovernmental organizations, or NGOs, and community foundations in and around the regions it operated, and then provided funding for critical programs. The result? The groups partnered with local communities to launch educational and health-care facilities, and nurture small businesses that ended up in the company's supply chain.

Again, though, companies that adopt this approach face a number of challenges. Unlike the strategy Magadi Soda used at first, which brings immediate results, this approach requires a longer-term investment of resources. And that can lead to grumbling from shareholders back home or local communities in need. What's more, companies must be careful to build good relationships in the community. If they don't take the time to learn local concerns, they may end up fostering groups and programs that don't really address what communities need, potentially leading to friction. In our research in Africa, for instance, CEOs commented on the importance of regularly visiting communities and senior chiefs to gain sensitivity to their ways of life.

Sources

Ethical Corporation, Mike Valente and Andrew Crane, *Wall Street Journal*, 23 March 2009, http://www.wsj.com.

VISIT THE WEBSITE for a short response to this feature

> **? THINK THEORY**
>
> In which way are the companies in Kenya and Russia mentioned in this case implementing the 'extended view of corporate citizenship'? What are the new responsibilities arising from this role and what are the limits of this approach?

- The extended view of CC helps us to see better the *political role* of the corporation and clarifies the demand for *corporate accountability* that is such a prominent feature of contemporary business ethics thinking.
- By providing us with a way of understanding business in relation to common rights of citizenship across cultures, CC in this sense also helps us to better understand some of the challenges presented by the new context of *globalization*.
- These rights of citizenship, which include rights to equality, participation, and a safe and clean environment, also have strong links to the new goal for business ethics of *sustainability*.
- Finally, although the notion of CSR has been widely adopted all over the world, the extended view of CC provides us with a more critical perspective on the social role of business that is more in keeping with non-US ways of thinking about business ethics.

Of course, the downside to the extended view of CC is that it is both new and not yet widely accepted within the mainstream discourse of business ethics. As **Ethics Online 2** highlights, many of these issues are not even too well represented in the mainstream media—with the result that many of the problematic implications of the shift towards more corporate political influence are hotly debated and showcased on various platforms on the internet. Hence, in the remainder of the book, although we shall mainly refer to CC in this extended sense, we shall also where relevant refer to the other meanings that we have outlined here.

■ Summary

In this chapter, we discussed business ethics in relation to the social role of the corporation. We outlined the nature of corporations and argued that confining corporations to their initial purpose of producing goods and services in a way that yields a maximal profit for the shareholders of the corporation is too limited. We subsequently analysed different perspectives on CSR, stakeholder theory, and corporate accountability, and assessed their relevance in an international context. This was complemented with insights into recent changes in the political framework of many societies and how globalization results in assigning a political role to corporations. Finally, we highlighted the current debate in business ethics and discussed corporate citizenship as the latest concept in the field.

ETHICS ONLINE 2

The conspicuous rise of the political side of the corporation

The government-like role of the modern corporation, as well as issues of social responsibility, transparency, and corporate accountability that we discussed in this chapter, are hotly debated on the web. Many of the new trends which find attention in print or other media were first featured online. And indeed the richness of resources here is quite impressive.

A good example is the 2005 PBS film *Private Warriors* as part of the *Frontline* documentary series in the US, which investigated the extent of privatization of the war in Iraq. The documentary, which is now to be found streamed online on the PBS website, was among the first to highlight the significant problems of this shift in the Pentagon strategy since the Bush administration took over. Here the web is particularly apt to serve as a channel since its content cannot easily be controlled and suppressed by companies who own the mainstream private media—or otherwise influence media content through their advertising money.

This is yet more evident when taking the more critical scene of corporate activists and critics into account. One of the most prominent members of this movement, the Canadian journalist Naomi Klein, has her own website to pass on the message. Moreover, when her 2007 book, *The Shock Doctrine*, was published, she streamed a seven-minute short film based on the book (directed by Alfonso Cuarón), which has since been viewed hundreds of thousands of times on Youtube. But this applies not only to activists. Organizations such as the UN increasingly use the internet as a platform to further its goals for the role of business. An example is the United Nations Development Program (UNDP) initiative 'Growing Inclusive Markets', which aims to change corporate behaviour towards a more equitable capitalism. 'We believe that in the race to achieve the Millennium Development Goals (MDGs) by 2015, the greatest untapped resource is the private sector', the website says. It offers all sorts of information, tools, advice, and research for business to do exactly what governments fail to deliver in many places: microcredit in Guatemala, water access in Haiti, or access to telecommunication in South Africa. In a world where media space and time is increasingly controlled by private corporations and their short-term interests, it is all too often the internet that not only provides the platform to highlight some of the problematic sides of the rise in corporate power but at the same time provides a platform for attempting to develop positive solutions.

Sources

Growing Inclusive Markets website: http://www.growinginclusivemarkets.org.
Klein, N. (2007). *The shock doctrine: the rise of disaster capitalism.* Toronto: Alfred A. Knopf Canada.
PBS website: http://www.pbs.org/wgbh/pages/frontline/shows/warriors/view/.
The Shock Doctrine Clip: http://www.naomiklein.org (or search on http://www.youtube.com)

VISIT THE WEBSITE for links to useful sources of further information

Our argument is that the shifts and changes in the global economy in recent years have brought to the surface the necessity for a new framing of business ethics. However, CC as used by practitioners and academics alike is presently still a rather messy concept. Our extended perspective on CC—which ultimately sees the corporation as a political actor governing the citizenship of individual stakeholders—helps to bring some much needed definitional clarity to the CC debate. Perhaps more importantly though, it helps us to conceptualize the emerging role of corporations in the global economy, as well as to clarify the ethical expectations increasingly placed upon them.

Study questions

1 What are the main implications of the *legal status* of corporations for notions of corporate social responsibility?

2 'Only human beings have a moral responsibility for their actions.' Critically assess this proposition in the context of attempts to ascribe a moral responsibility to corporations.

3 What is enlightened self-interest? Compare and evaluate arguments for corporate social responsibility based on enlightened self-interest with more explicitly moral arguments.

4 According to Archie Carroll, what are the four levels of corporate social responsibility? How relevant is this model in a European, Asian, or an African context?

5 Explain the difference between normative, descriptive, and instrumental versions of stakeholder theory. To what extent do stakeholders have intrinsic moral rights in relation to the management of the corporation?

6 Define the extended view of corporate citizenship. Give examples to illustrate the concept.

Research exercise

Select one of the following companies:

(a) Microsoft (www.microsoft.com).

(b) Toyota (www.toyota.com).

(c) L'Oréal (www.loreal.com).

Investigate the company's website and set out the main aspects of their corporate responsibility, sustainability, or corporate citizenship programmes. Which aspects of their programmes might be said to be formerly governmental responsibilities? What are the benefits and drawbacks of the corporation taking over these responsibilities?

Key readings

VISIT THE WEBSITE for links to further key readings

1 **Carroll, A.B. 2008. A history of corporate social responsibility: concepts and practices. In A. Crane, A. McWilliams, D. Matten, J. Moon, and D. Siegel (eds.), *The Oxford handbook of corporate social responsibility*: 19–46. Oxford: Oxford University Press.**

This provides a broad overview of the development of CSR theory and practice (albeit from a predominantly US perspective) from one of the field's most well-known scholars.

2 **Matten, D. and Crane, A. 2005. Corporate citizenship: towards an extended theoretical conceptualization. *Academy of Management Review*, 30 (1): 166–79.**

This article sets out the main arguments presented in the last part of this chapter in more detail and is useful if you want to follow up the citizenship perspective more fully.

Case 2

The business of water

VISIT THE WEBSITE for links to useful sources of further information

This case explores some of the more recent developments in the world on corporate social responsibility and business ethics. Water as an increasingly scarce and contested resource has become an issue where businesses find themselves more and more confronted by new expectations and demands from society. Whether on the supply side, as providers of drinking water and sanitation or whether on the demand side, as users or marketers of water, private corporations have become key players in addressing needs that sometimes extend substantially beyond their initial economic interests.

Water has increasingly become a contentious political issue—and a hot issue for business ethics. Water is considered a basic human need, and so access to clean water is typically considered to be a fundamental human right. However, although it appears to be abundant, humans can actually only use 1% of global water resources for drinking. While most developed countries have decent access, 18% of the world's population have no access to basic safe drinking water and 40% have no access to basic sanitation. A person living in sub-Saharan Africa has to get by with between 10–20 litres of water per day—by comparison, the average Canadian uses more than 300 litres of water a day. To meet the UN Millennium Development Goals, which aim to achieve access to safe water for all by 2015, we would need to create access to safe water for 300,000 new people every day.

With an issue this contentious, it is no surprise that water has also increasingly become an ethical issue for business. Business is deeply involved in the world of water, either on the supply side as a provider of safe drinking water and sanitation, or on the demand side as a major user of water as a raw material, or as a product to sell.

Privatizing water utilities

On the supply side, we have seen a marked increase in privatization of water utilities over the last 30 years. The global market here is dominated by two French MNCs, Suez and Vivendi, and a handful of other players who have become increasingly involved in the water business in developing countries. The privatization of water supply, however, has become an ever more heated issue. There are, of course, often good grounds for privatization: municipal water companies have often proved to be inefficient and overly bureaucratic, if not outright corrupt and even failing, as has sometimes been the case in developing countries. Bringing in the private sector, so the argument goes, can increase efficiency, improve service levels, and even help to address poor access to water in the developing world.

The reality, however, yields a rather mixed picture. While proponents such as Globalisation Institute fellow, Misha Balen, argue that the majority of privatizations have actually improved water provision, a number of high profile, and rather spectacular, failures have made activists and politicians more and more opposed to the idea.

According to the critics, at the heart of the problem with privatized water supply is the fact that private companies entering the market for water only do so in the long run if they apply what is called in the industry 'full cost recovery'. One case that hit the headlines in the early 2000s is that of the South African township Ngwelezane in the state of Kwazulu Natal. When the government started to charge full cost recovery for water (allegedly to prepare the water supply system for sale to a private company), the mostly poor and disease-stricken inhabitants of the township could not afford their water anymore. As a result, they resorted to a nearby lake, which led to a cholera epidemic that killed 300 people.

Even more famous are the two so-called 'Water Wars' in Bolivia in 2000 and 2005. The World Bank had given the country a loan for improving the water system and as in most contracts, the Bank demanded privatization of the system (in 2002, more than four-fifths of World Bank contracts required privatization). The system in Bolivia's capital La Paz was ultimately taken over by a subsidiary of the US multinational Bechtel, which found it hard in the beginning to recoup their investments because the system they inherited was in such a dismal state. Since the World Bank contract ruled out government subsidies, the only way to 'full cost recovery' were some changes in the pricing and in the law. Finally, not without some lobbying, Law 2029 was passed, which granted private water companies monopoly rights in the ridings they operated in. This implied that people were no longer allowed to use water for free out of their wells or even to collect rainwater. Law 2029 led to long and violent riots in La Paz and gave rise to a political movement on the left, which culminated in the overthrow of the government in 2006. The privatization of the water system was terminated and reversed in that same year.

But problems with privatized supply are not exclusive to the developing world. In 2006, Thames Water, the private company that serves London and the South East of England, was fined for the second time for missing the government target for cutting down leakages in its drinking-water supply network—still a whopping 894m litres a day at the time. This did not, however, prevent the company from declaring a 31% rise in pre-tax profits of £347m, while customers saw prices rising by 20% from 2005 to 2009. In France, large water companies have, over the last few years, faced multiple allegations and even some convictions for bribery of municipal governmental officials, and similar cases of corruption are reported from other European countries. In the US, the city of Atlanta stands as a salutary example of some of the limitations of water privatization. Here, privatization in 1999 (to the French company Suez) led to low service levels, exclusion of poor consumers, and higher prices so that the system was ultimately put back into public management in 2003.

Serving an insatiable thirst

A slightly different set of issues enters the corporate agenda on the demand side of the story. As with privatization, these issues are particularly acute in the developing world, where Western MNCs can be seen as competing with local business and the indigenous population for the use of often scarce water resources. The issue is particularly salient for industries with high usage of water, such as mining and of course, the drinks industry.

Perhaps the most well-known and best-reported incident concerned Coca-Cola's bottling plant in Kerala in Southern India. As one of the company's more recent expansions, Coca-Cola is estimated to have invested over $1bn in its Indian business between 1993 and 2004, thus contributing roughly a fifth of the entire foreign direct investment to the country. Against this backdrop, it came as quite a surprise to the company when in 2004 a High Court in the southern province of Kerala ordered the closure of a Coca-Cola bottling plant in the village of Palchimada. The ruling followed three years of campaigning by local villagers, national NGOs, and research institutes, displaying a truly multifaceted arsenal of campaign tactics, reaching from local demonstrations, sit-ins at the plant gate, and human chains, to ten-day marches between various Coke plants, nationwide 'Quit India' campaigns, and political lobbying (the Indian parliament subsequently banned the company's products from its cafeteria).

The central issue of the campaign, at least initially, was the fact that since the Kerala plant opened in 2000, groundwater levels had fallen by 25–40 feet, resulting in severe water shortages for rural neighbours of the plant. Harvests allegedly fell by 80–90% and the remaining water became undrinkable in a region where most people are extremely poor and dependent on small-scale local agriculture.

Coca-Cola, who extracted about 510,000 litres of water per day from the groundwater around the plant, initially blamed the decline in water on poor rainfalls in the region during the preceding years, and dismissed the protest as 'anti-capitalist'. Still though, the company set up a tanker service providing people around the plant with a daily supply of water. The court, however, ruled that groundwater is a public good and Coca-Cola, in the aftermath of the ruling, had to reorganize its water supply from other parts of India into the plant. As of 2006, Coca-Cola has reduced its water use by 24% and installed rainwater-harvesting systems in 26 of their plants.

Ultimately, Coca-Cola became something of a leader in water management practices, including the introduction of a far-reaching Global Water Stewardship Initiative. In India, this entailed, amongst other things, a commitment to replace all groundwater used in its beverages and their production by 2009. Globally, the firm struck a water conservation partnership with the World Wide Fund for Nature (WWF), which in 2007 led to the firm's CEO announcing an ambitious goal to return to communities and to nature an amount of water equivalent to what they used in all of their beverages and their production. As the firm says, 'this means reducing the amount of water used to produce our beverages, recycling water used for manufacturing processes so it can be returned safely to the environment, and replenishing water in communities and nature through locally relevant projects'. The latter included a $30m 'Replenish Africa Initiative' that aims at providing drinking water to the towns and villages where the company has bottling plants.

Usually, Coca-Cola works in these projects in partnership with local and international NGOs, community groups, and international aid agencies. Since 1997, the company has successfully engaged in a number of projects in countries such as Angola, Ethiopia, Mozambique, Nigeria, and Rwanda, and effectively brought water supply to many places where governments hitherto had failed to deliver. Similar projects have been started by Nestlé, the beer conglomerate SABMiller, and a number of mining companies.

The increasing involvement of business in the management of global water resources has led the UN Global Compact (see **Ethics in Action 11.2**) to set up a special forum called 'The CEO Water Mandate'. Here, CEOs of many major companies, including those mentioned in this case, have committed themselves to implement sustainable water management practices in their operations.

The world of water though remains an ambiguous terrain for companies. While implementing fairly wide-ranging measures around the conservation and accessibility of water, even the best-managed companies continue to demand ever more water as their markets grow. Moreover, beverage companies have raised further criticism for their heavy investment in another increasingly contentious business, bottled water. For Nestlé, for example, its main beverage business is in bottled water, and the firm markets more than 70 brands globally, including the iconic Perrier and Vittel brands. The main ethical concerns faced by companies such as Nestlé in the marketing of bottled water centre around issues of wastefulness (it currently takes approximately three litres of water to produce one litre of bottled water), packaging, transport costs, the exploitation of non-renewable aquifers (such as the water from the Fiji Islands), and, more generally, the fact that in most developed countries where bottled water is sold, tap water is a perfectly healthy and adequate alternative.

Activists have long campaigned against the growth of the bottled water business, and some governments have begun to act. For instance in Canada, 12 municipalities, including the City of Toronto, had initiated bans on bottled water on municipal premises by 2009. Nestlé, which has instituted a range of water conservation initiatives across its global businesses, nonetheless reacted rather aggressively to the new hard-line direction of regulators. Not only did they hire lobbyists to manipulate the municipal bans, but the firm also placed contentious advertisements in the Canadian press which raised widespread allegations of greenwash. Perhaps this was not so surprising given that among the claims panned by the critics was Nestlé's contention that 'bottled water is the most environmentally responsible consumer product in the world'! Further embarrassments ensued for the company in 2008 when a Swiss television station revealed that Nestlé had hired a security firm to spy on the NGO ATTAC, with a particular focus on a Brazilian activist who had targeted the company's bottled water operations in Brazil.

Questions

1 Who are the main stakeholders of beverage companies such as Coca-Cola and Nestlé in this case? How would you prioritize their stakes and how legitimate are the different stakes?

2 Think of the role of Nestlé in this case in terms of Carroll's pyramid of CSR. Which responsibilities does it live up to and where would you see space for improvement?

3 Think of the privatized water companies in this case in terms of the 'extended view of corporate citizenship' as discussed in this chapter. What are the specific governmental roles they have taken on? Evaluate their performance from this perspective.

4 How do you evaluate the growing expectations and the changing role of companies in the arena of water management? What are the consequences for accountability, transparency, and participation of stakeholders? Discuss the potential and the limits of what corporations can ultimately achieve in the business of water.

Sources

Anon. 2006. Thames Water misses leak target. *BBC News*, 22 June: http://www.bbc.co.uk.

Balen, M. 2006. Debate: water and the private sector: the case for privatization. *Ethical Corporation*, 25 May.

Chenoweth, J. and Bird, J. (eds.). 2005. *The business of water and sustainable development*. Sheffield: Greenleaf.

Carty, B. 2003. The water barons: a look at the world's top water companies. *CBC Radio Canada*: http://www.cbc.ca/news/features/water/business.html.

Christian Aid. 2004. *Behind the mask: the real face of corporate social responsiblity*. London: Christian Aid.

Girard, R. 2009. Nestlé's sinking division. *Polaris Institute*: http://www.polarisinstitute.org.

Reichardt, M. 2009. Water in Africa—business turns on the tap. *Ethical Corporation*, 12 June.
Rose, J. 2004a. Cola companies in more strife in India. *Ethical Corporation*, 10 November.
—— 2004b. Further protests against Coca-Cola in India. *Ethical Corporation*, 18 November.
—— 2004c. Indian campaign to kick cola out. *Ethical Corporation*, 23 September.
The Center for Public Integrity. 2003. *The water barons*. Washington: The Center for Public Integrity.
http://thewaterproject.org.
http://www.nestle-waters.com.
http://www.thecoca-colacompany.com.
http://www.unglobalcompact.org.

Notes

1 There are numerous authors who have argued for and against the assignation of moral responsibility to corporations—see Moore (1999) for a review.
2 These arguments have been widely presented in the CSR literature, but are largely derived from the work of Davis (1973) and Mintzberg (1983). See also Kurucz et al. (2008) for an overview.
3 Globescan CSR Monitor 2008, http://www.globescan.com.
4 This relationship has been examined at least since the early 1970s, with interest apparently unabated despite (or perhaps because) of the somewhat equivocal findings so far. Good overviews of this literature are provided in the articles by Griffin and Mahon (1997), McWilliams and Siegel (2000), and Waddock and Graves (1997), with a meta-analysis of previous studies provided by Orlitzky et al. (2003).
5 European Commission. 2007. Report on Competition Policy 2007. Brussels: European Commission.
6 Bronski, C. 2008. Layoffs and plant closures ravage Canada's auto industry. *World Socialist Web Site*, 8 November: http://www.wsws.org.
7 Carroll's (1979) four modes of social responsiveness were, in fact, derived from the work of Ian Wilson. They have subsequently been applied by Wartick and Cochran (1985), and Clarkson (1995) among others. Wood (1991), in contrast, provides a critique of this typology, and develops a different categorization based on specific processes, namely, environmental assessment, stakeholder management, and issues management.
8 For more argument from both sides on these issues, you may want to visit the websites of ASH, the anti-smoking lobby group (http://www.ash.org.uk) and BAT, the UK-based tobacco giant (http:// www.bat.com).
9 *The Telegraph*. 2005. BP tackles climate change threat with £200m boost for energy efficiency, 25 October: http://www.telegraph.co.uk/money.
10 There are a number of excellent papers which offer reviews of stakeholder theory, in particular Donaldson and Preston (1995) and Stoney and Winstanley (2001).
11 Published 1992 in English translation—see Beck (1992).
12 For more information, see http://www.marksandspencer.com.

3

Evaluating Business Ethics

NORMATIVE ETHICAL THEORIES

In this chapter we will:

- Locate the role of normative ethical theory for ethical decision-making in business.
- Highlight the international differences in perspectives on normative ethical theory.
- Provide a critical overview of Western modernist ethical theories, such as utilitarianism, ethics of duty, and rights and justice.
- Explore the potential of contemporary views on ethical theories for business, such as virtue ethics, feminist ethics, discourse ethics, and postmodernism.
- Suggest that the most appropriate usage of normative ethical theory is in a pragmatic and pluralistic fashion that contributes to, rather than dictates, ethical decision-making.

■ Introduction

In our everyday lives, we constantly come up against situations where values are in conflict and where we have to make a choice about what is right or wrong. Whether it is a question of whether to lie about something in order to protect a friend's feelings, driving over the speed limit when rushing to avoid being late for a date, or thinking about whether to report a classmate you have seen cheating on their assignment, we all have some prior knowledge of what is right or wrong that helps us to decide what to do. Most of the situations like this that we are faced with in our personal lives are pretty much within the scope of what a typical person would be able to decide. In a business context, however, situations might become considerably more complex.

We could think for example of the situation of a multinational company intending to establish a subsidiary in a developing country: not only do we have to cope with a number of ethical problems at the same time—maybe paying bribes for planning permission, deciding on the wage level for the workers, or establishing a minimum age for workers, etc.—but we also face the problem that a variety of people will be involved, all of whom might have different views and attitudes towards these moral issues. Consequently, coming to an ethical conclusion in business situations is far more complex than in most of the situations where we as private individuals have to make ethical decisions.

Perhaps more importantly, in a business context, there is often a need for these decisions to be based on a systematic, rational, and widely understandable argument so that they can be adequately defended, justified, and explained to relevant stakeholders. Similarly, if we believe that what an organization has done is wrong, we need some concrete basis from which to argue our case. After all, at what point can we say that a particular behaviour is more than just *different* from what we would have done, but in some way actually *wrong*? This is the point where normative ethical theories come into play. By normative, we mean ethical theories that propose to prescribe the morally correct way of acting. Such ethical theories, as we set out in Chapter 1, can be defined as follows:

Ethical theories are the rules and principles that determine right and wrong for a given situation.

In this chapter, we will take a look at the major ethical theories and analyse their value and potential for business ethics. To begin with, though, we first need to be clear about how exactly we shall be using ethical theory in the context of this chapter, and in the rest of the book that follows.

■ The role of ethical theory

In locating a place for ethical theory, Richard De George (1999) suggests that two extreme positions can be imagined:

- **Ethical absolutism.** On the one side of the spectrum would be a position of ethical absolutism, which claims that there are eternal, universally applicable moral principles. According to this view, right and wrong are *objective* qualities that can be rationally determined.

- **Ethical relativism.** The other extreme would be a position of relativism, which claims that morality is context-dependent and *subjective*. Relativists tend to believe that there are no universal right and wrongs that can be rationally determined—it simply depends on the person making the decision and the culture in which they are located. In its most well-known form, the notion of relativism occurs in international business issues, where it is argued that a moral judgement about behaviour in another culture cannot be made from outside because morality is culturally determined. Ethical relativism is different from *descriptive relativism*: whilst the latter merely suggests that different cultures *have* different ethics, the former proposes that both sets of beliefs can be equally *right*. Ethical relativism then is still a normative theory (De George 1999).

? THINK THEORY

Think about the concepts of absolutism and relativism in the context of bribery. How would each theory conceptualize the problem of bribery and what course of action might they suggest for someone faced with a corrupt official?

VISIT THE WEBSITE for a short response to this feature

Most traditional *Western modernist* ethical theories tend to be absolutist in nature. They seek to set out universal rules or principles that can be applied to any situation to provide the answer as to what is right or wrong. Contemporary ethical theories provide us with some *alternative perspectives* on ethical theory. They often tend towards a more relativistic position. However, in the course of this chapter, we want to show that for the practical purposes of making effective decisions in business, both of these positions are not particularly useful.

Our position therefore is one of **pluralism**. This occupies something of a middle ground between absolutism and relativism. Pluralism accepts different moral convictions and backgrounds, while at the same time suggesting that a consensus on basic principles and rules in a certain social context can, and should, be reached. Ethical theories, as we shall show, can help to clarify different moral presuppositions of the various parties involved in a decision—as one person may tend to think in terms of one theory, whilst another might think in terms of a different theory. In making good business decisions, we need to understand this range of perspectives in order to establish a consensus on the solution to ethical problems (Kaler 1999). Rather than establishing a single universal theory, in this chapter we will present the different theoretical frameworks as complementary resources or conceptual tools that help us make a practical, structured, and systematic assessment of the right and wrong in particular business decisions. Theory can help to clarify these situations and each theory highlights different aspects that need to be considered.

This view rests on two basic things that John Kaler (1999) suggests we already know about morality before we even try to introduce ethical theory into it. First, morality is foremost a *social phenomenon*. We apply morality because we constantly have to establish the rules and arrangements of our living together as social beings. It seems reasonable to accept the argument of *descriptive relativism*—that there is a diversity of moral convictions, be they religiously, philosophically, or otherwise ideologically grounded, is a given. Hence, even if there were one and only one 'objectively' right moral conviction, it is simply a matter of fact that this is not widely agreed upon. It only takes a quick visit to the pub or café to listen in to the conversations around us to discover that people from the same street or place of work differ considerably in their moral views and convictions. From a business angle, this gets even more important due to globalization, since this multiplies the relevant 'supply' of moralities by the sheer number of different cultural contexts playing a role in business decisions. As morality seeks to solve questions of right and wrong in organizing social life, we cannot realistically rely on an absolutist position, since empirically we see a variety of moral convictions. If we are to make good decisions that are acceptable to others, we obviously need to develop some knowledge of the different moralities that we are likely to be faced with.

The second of Kaler's (1999) assumptions is that morality is primarily about *harm and benefit*. Right and wrong are largely about avoiding harm and providing benefits. After all, if we didn't dislike harm or value benefits, there would simply be no need for morality. As we will see further on, 'benefit' and 'harm' are matters that are conceptualized differently by various ethical theories. Nevertheless, we argue that there is a certain consensus about the fact that morality should ultimately help a society to avoid harm and provide benefits for its members. Given this focus, it is possible to partly refute the position of the relativists and claim that morality is more than a subjective feeling or opinion since it is about actual harms and benefits that we need to address. Ultimately, the logic of relativism is that everything is just different and nothing is wrong (Donaldson 1996). This 'anything goes' approach to morality is not very helpful when we see genuine harm being inflicted on people.

However, as the relativists suggest, this second assumption also necessarily places ethical theories in a pragmatic context: even the most subtle theory is used by individuals in a concrete business situation where most people have a basic 'gut' feeling about the right and wrong of the situation based on the perceived harms and benefits (Treviño and Nelson 2007). Therefore, narrowly and rigidly applying one theory and treating the theory as the only authority in questions of right and wrong would give ethical theory a status that it will never actually have in practical business decisions. The immense value though of ethical theories lies in the fact that they help to rationalize—and by this understand—this gut feeling. Furthermore, they make it possible to engage in a rational discourse between individuals whose moral values are different from each other. **Ethics Online 3** provides an overview of numerous blogs on business ethics where one can see how some of the principles outlined in this chapter are applied to real-life events in the business ethics world.

■ Normative ethical theories: North-American and European origins and differences

In Chapter 1 under the section on globalization and business ethics (pp. 17–31), we argued that business ethics thinking varies from region to region globally. This is particularly the case in the use of ethical theories. It is, however, probably fair to say that the academic debate on business ethics has so far been largely dominated by thinking originating in Europe and North America. In fact, more narrowly, most of the literature available in English is more or less dominated by an Anglo-American view, whereas many of the continental European or Asian approaches are less widely received since

ETHICS ONLINE 3

The world of business ethics blogs

The growth of the blogosphere has not gone unnoticed by the business ethics community. There are now a considerable number of blogs concerned with applying ethical theories and principles to the latest business issues and scandals, both in English as well as increasingly in other languages too, such as French, German, Spanish, or Portuguese.

The value of following these blogs for business ethics students is manifold. Many business ethics blogs comment on current events using the types of theories and concepts discussed in this chapter. They also feature interesting links, provide opinion, and offer food for thought—all of which helps to highlight the exciting contemporary relevance of the topic. Blogs can be very helpful for applying what you read in your business ethics textbook, or what you learn in your ethics class, to what is happening right now in the business world.

Not all business ethics blogs showcase the theoretical thinking discussed in this chapter, but those written by academics tend to offer the most thorough ethical analysis—and are often the most relevant for applying the lessons learnt in the classroom. So, for instance, Chris MacDonald's Business Ethics Blog, which claims to be the longest-running such blog, has included a range of ethical analyses. In one week in May 2009, this included the ethics of executive compensation, anti-union activities at Starbucks, and the rights and wrongs of restaurants serving *foie gras*. Meanwhile, the same week, the Professional Ethics Network blog, based in Leeds University in the UK, dissected the ethics of politicians' expenses accounts and the dumping of toxic waste in Cote d'Ivoire. You will also find many more examples of business ethics theories applied to contemporary events in our own blog.

Most bloggers, however, are not academics—and yet in their assessment of business ethics issues, many of the ideas discussed in the classroom tend to get aired. Popular bloggers include professional commentators or journalists (e.g. Mallen Baker or Toby Webb), NGO activists (e.g. Wayne Visser), and consultants and practitioners (e.g. Lauren Bloom). Such blogs may be light on ethical theory, but they are high on practical insight and advice, and help to give a more rounded picture of the business ethics issues currently hitting the headlines.

Featured blogs

http://craneandmatten.blogspot.com (Andrew Crane and Dirk Matten)
http://csrinternational.blogspot.com/ (Wayne Visser)
http://ethicalcorp.blogspot.com/ (Toby Webb)
http://www.businessethics.ca/blog/ (Chris MacDonald)
http://www.idea.leeds.ac.uk/penblog/ (Professional Ethics Network)
http://www.mallenbaker.net/csr/blog.php (Mallen Baker)
http://www.thebusinessethicsblog.com/ (Lauren Bloom)

VISIT THE WEBSTE for links to useful sources of further information

most of the literature is published in languages other than English. And although we find several continental European approaches also in American and British textbooks, the general use and the necessity for theory in business ethics is fairly different on both sides of the Atlantic. Though our core focus in this chapter is on European and North American approaches, we acknowledge that there is a growing debate and literature on African, Asian, and Latin-American perspectives on business ethics.

We believe it is helpful, then, to highlight some relevant differences in the mainstream debate in Europe and North America as they most commonly appear in the published literature (see Palazzo 2002)—albeit with a note of caution about the dangers of generalizing such a rich and diverse body of work.

- **Individual versus institutional morality.** As we saw in Chapter 1, some approaches to studying business ethics tend to have a more individualistic perspective on morality (e.g. the US), whilst others (such as in Europe) tend to focus more on the economic system and the wider governing institutions. Therefore, normative ethical theories in the US tend to be more applicable to *individual behaviour*, whereas in Europe the *design of institutions* in the economic system seems to be the main influence in developing and applying theory.

- **Questioning versus accepting capitalism.** Most of the mainstream business ethics literature in the US does not particularly question the existing framework of management, but rather sees ethical problems occurring *within the capitalist system*, which it treats as a given. In Europe, relevant parts of business ethics focus on *questioning the ethical justification of capitalism*. Hence, considerable effort in business ethics theory has been dedicated to defending or refining the ethical legitimacy of capitalist economic thought. Although one has to say that not all of this work has been immediately helpful in solving day-to-day issues in business life, it nevertheless helps to develop a more critical and distanced approach to the institutions that govern and determine business decisions, and by this to provide substantial help in understanding and theorizing a number of ethical dilemmas in business life, including corporate governance, employee rights, and stakeholder involvement.

- **Justifying versus applying moral norms.** Although some of the religious roots in both continents are still remarkably influential on the institutional fabric of economic life, substantial processes of secularization—i.e. movement towards a *non-religious* form of organizing—have taken place. In Europe, most notably in the northern parts, this secularization process has opened the door to a variety of other ideological and philosophical approaches. In general, Sweden, Germany, and the Netherlands, for example, are characterized by a strong pluralism of moral convictions and values. Therefore, the challenge for business ethics on the theoretical level consists to a strong degree in the *justification and ethical legitimation of norms* for addressing ethical dilemmas in business situations. In the US, however, judging by most American business ethics textbooks, these issues do not seem to take such a dominant position: apart from a section on normative theories in business, most textbooks seem to treat the question of moral values as a given and focus chiefly on the *application of morality* to business situations. American society—at least as far as the dominant white majority is concerned—seems to rest on a quite rigid set of mostly Christian-based values, which are accepted as a given code of moral values and are therefore not put under further scrutiny. This seems to have been further reinforced by the recent rise of the evangelical far right and neoconservative movements.

Notwithstanding these differences, it is important to recognize that no single normative theory can be 'claimed' or attributed to any individual country or region. As we shall now see, most of the traditional theories routinely embraced by American authors are in fact European in origin. And, as indicated in Chapter 1, there is of course a wealth of ethical thinking in business beyond the North American and European context. However, in terms of theoretical approaches to the field, the debate beyond this context is rather limited, albeit with some important additions to the debate concerned with Asian and other approaches to business ethics. A key difference to the approaches discussed later in this chapter is that much of the thinking in Asian business ethics, for example, is either informed by religion, such as Islam (Wienen 1999) or Buddhism (Gould 1995), or traditional community values, such as the Chinese *Guanxi* approach (Chenting 2003). European and North American approaches, in contrast, are mainly based on philosophical arguments, as we will discover in the following sections.

■ Western modernist ethical theories

In Western societies, the ethical theories traditionally regarded as appropriate for application to business contexts are based on philosophical thinking generated in Europe and North America beginning with the enlightenment in the eighteenth century. This age is often referred to also as 'modernity' as it modernized a lot of traditional thinking dominated by religious approaches throughout the Middle Ages. We refer to these theories therefore as 'Western modernist'. They generally offer a certain rule or principle that one can apply to any given situation—hence, they are *absolutist* in intention. These theories are normative because they start with an assumption about the nature of the world, and more specific assumptions about the nature of human beings. Consequently, the degree to which we can accept the theory and the outcome of its application to particular business situations depends chiefly on the degree to which we share their underlying assumptions. As they have a rather well-defined rule of decision, the main advantage of these theories is the fact that they normally provide us with a fairly *unequivocal solution* to ethical problems.

These theories generally can be differentiated into two groups (see **Figure 3.1**). On the right-hand side of Figure 3.1 we have theories that base moral judgement on the outcomes of a certain action. If these outcomes are desirable, then the action in question is morally right; if the outcomes of the action are not desirable, the action is morally wrong. The moral judgement in these *consequentialist theories* is thus based on the intended

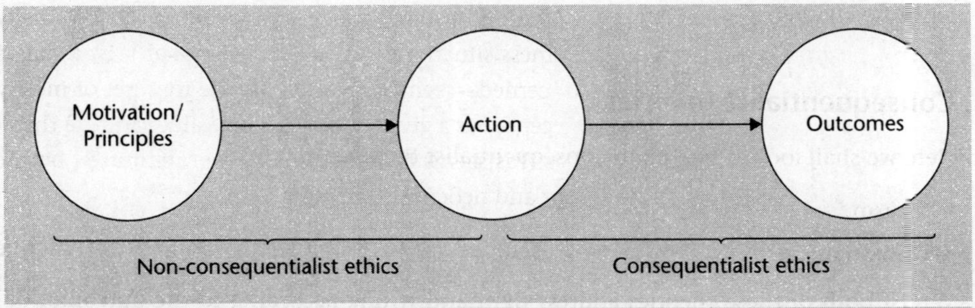

Figure 3.1. Consequentialist and non-consequentialist theories in business ethics

	Egoism	Utilitarianism	Ethics of duties	Rights and justice
Contributors	Adam Smith.	Jeremy Bentham, John Stuart Mill.	Immanuel Kant.	John Locke, John Rawls.
Focus	Individual desires or interests.	Collective welfare.	Duties.	Rights.
Rules	Maximization of desires/ self-interest.	Act/rule utilitarianism.	Categorical imperative.	Respect for human beings.
Concept of human beings	Man as an actor with limited knowledge and objectives.	Man is controlled by avoidance of pain and gain of pleasure ('hedonist').	Man is a rational moral actor.	Man is a being that is distinguished by dignity.
Type	Consequentialist.	Consequentialist.	Non-consequentialist.	Non-consequentialist.

Figure 3.2. Major normative theories in business ethics

outcomes, the aims, or the goals of a certain action. Therefore, consequentialist ethics is often also referred to by the term *teleological*, based on the Greek word for 'goal'.

On the other hand, we have those theories that base the moral judgement on the underlying principles of the decision-maker's motivation. An action is right or wrong, these theories suggest, not because we like the consequences they produce, but because the underlying principles are morally right. These *non-consequentialist* approaches are quite closely linked to Judeo-Christian thinking and start from reasoning about the individual's rights and duties. These philosophic theories, also called *deontological* (based on the Greek word for 'duty'), look at the desirability of principles, and based on these principles, deduce a 'duty' to act accordingly in a given situation, regardless of the desirability of the consequences.

In the following, we will have a closer look at both families of philosophic theories and analyse their potential for solving various business decisions. **Figure 3.2** gives a short overview of the relevant philosophical schools and the basic elements of their thinking. In explaining these theories, we shall use them to reflect on a particular business problem, as presented in **Ethical Dilemma 3**. We suggest you read this before continuing with the chapter.

Consequentialist theories

Here we shall look at two main consequentialist theories:

- Egoism.
- Utilitarianism.

Whilst both of these theories address right and wrong according to the outcomes of a decision, we shall see that they address those outcomes in different ways—egoism by

AN ETHICAL DILEMMA 3

Producing toys—child's play?

You are the product manager of a confectionery company that includes small plastic toys with its chocolate sweets. Having met a potential Thai manufacturer of these toys at a trade fair in Europe, you now visit the company in the north-eastern part of Thailand to finalize a two-year supply contract. Arriving there and talking to the sales manager, you are able to arrange a deal that supplies you with the toys at a third of the cost currently charged by your Portuguese supplier, but with equivalent quality and supply arrangements.

In order to check the reliability of the manufacturing process you ask the manager to show you around the place. You are surprised to find out that there is no real workshop on the premises. Rather, the production process is organized such that at 6am, about 30 men line up at the company's gate, load large boxes with toy components on their little carts or motor-scooters and take the material to their homes.

Your prospective supplier then takes you to one of these places where you see a large family, sitting in a garage-like barn assembling the toys. Not only are the mother and father doing the job, but also the couple's six children, aged 5 to 14, who are working busily—and from what you see, very cheerfully—together with the parents, while the grandmother is looking after the food in an adjacent room. In the evening, at around 8pm, the day's work is done, the assembled toys are stored back in the boxes and taken to the workshop of the company, where the men receive their payment for the finished goods. At the end of the week, the toys are shipped to the customers in Europe.

As you have never come across such a pattern of manufacturing, your Thai partner explains to you that this is a very common and well-established practice in this part of the country, and one which guarantees a good level of quality. Satisfied, you tell the Thai manager that you will conclude the paperwork once you get back home, and you leave the company offices happy in the knowledge of the cost savings you're going to make, and quietly confident that it will result in a healthy bonus for you at the end of the year.

On your way back, while buying some souvenirs for your 5- and 7-year-old nieces at the airport, you suddenly start wondering if you would like to see them growing up the same way as the child workers that you have just employed to make your company's toys.

Questions

1 Reading the case and putting yourself in the role of the product manager, what would your immediate gut reaction be?

2 Based on your spontaneous immediate decision, can you set out the reasons for your choice? Also, can you relate those reasons back to some underlying values or principles that are obviously important to you?

focusing on the outcomes for the *decision-maker*, utilitarianism by focusing on the wider *social outcomes within a community*.

Egoism

Egoism is one of the oldest philosophical ideas, and it was already well known and discussed by ancient Greek philosophers such as Plato. In the last three centuries, it has been quite influential in modern economics, particularly in relation to Adam Smith's (1723–90) ideas about the design of liberalist economics. Egoism can be defined as follows:

> **Following the theory of egoism, an action is morally right if the decision-maker freely decides in order to pursue either their (short-term) desires or their (long-term) interests.**

The justification for egoism lies in the underlying concept of man: as man has only limited insight into the consequences of his actions, the only suitable strategy to achieve a good life is to pursue his own desires or interests. Adam Smith (1793) argued that in the economic system, this pursuit of individual self-interest was acceptable because it produced a morally desirable outcome for society through the 'invisible hand' of the marketplace. Smith's argument may thus be summarized as saying that one is likely to find a moral outcome as the end-product of a system based on free competition and good information. For example, if a producer makes and sells shoddy or faulty products, then consumers may suffer in the short term as a result of the lack of fitness of the products that they have bought. However, in the longer run, providing consumers know about alternative choices, the producer's trade will suffer as consumers turn to other producers. Hence, the producer will avoid producing shoddy goods for their own self-interest, thus producing a situation that is beneficial to all. Because of his aim to produce wider social benefits, some have likened Smith's theory to 'egoist practices for utilitarian results' (Beauchamp and Bowie 1997: 18).

It is important to distinguish egoism based on desire from *selfishness*. Whereas the egoist can be moved by pity for others in seeking to remove his own distress caused by their plight, the selfish person is insensitive to the other. So, for example, a good deal of what we discussed as voluntary elements in the concept of corporate social responsibility or corporate citizenship in Chapter 2 can be perfectly in line with an egoistic philosophy as long as the company, or the rich philanthropist, chooses to donate to a worthy cause (because it makes them feel better or because it is for the ultimate benefit of the company), rather than voting themselves a pay rise.

Within moral philosophy, an important criticism of egoism *based on desire* is that it renders patently different approaches to life as being equivalent; thus in this view, the life of the student who just gets drunk every night in the bar is as admirable as the student who works hard for a first class degree, if both followed their desire. Therefore, within this school of philosophy, an egoism *based on the pursuit of interests* is the ultimate rendering of this concept (Graham 1990). The idea of interests based on the pursuit of one's long-term well-being enables one to distinguish between the life of the hard-drinking student and that of the hard-working student. In this formulation, a gap opens up between desire (or longing) and what is in one's ultimate interests, such that one can say that it is not in the interest of the drinking student to give in to immediate desires. An egoism based on interests therefore approaches the idea of objective value—as in, that one way of acting is objectively better or 'more ethical' than another.

This leads to the notion of '*enlightened egoism*', which is quite often discussed in the context of business ethics. We have come across it already in Chapter 2 when discussing 'enlightened self-interest'. For example, corporations might invest in the social environment, for instance by supporting schools or sponsoring a new ambulance for the local health service, because an improved level of social services is in the interest of workforce retention and satisfaction.

If we apply this theory to the case in Ethical Dilemma 3, we would have to look at the actors involved and analyse if they freely pursue their own desires or interests in engaging in the deal. This certainly applies to the manager and his Thai partner, and by the looks of the case, it could also apply to the parents of the family business. As for the children, it could be that they are quite happy to help the parents and just take it for granted that things work like this in their world. From this perspective, an egoistic look at the situation might consider the deal as morally right. One might, however, wonder if it is in the children's long-term interest to engage in this type of work: although one could argue that it prevents them from being forced into far less desirable forms of work, moral concerns arise when considering that this type of work prevents them from going to school, exposes them to fairly hard working hours, all of which casts some doubt on whether they really are able to freely pursue their own interests. The latter considerations then would tend to suggest that from an egoistic point of view this action might be immoral.

It doesn't take much thought to discover certain weaknesses in egoist ethics. To begin with, this theory works fine if there is a mechanism in society that makes sure that no individual egoist pursues his or her own interests at other egoists' expense. In Adam Smith's thinking, this mechanism would be the market. Although in a great number of cases we can see that the market works perfectly well, there are numerous situations where this does not seem to be the case, and where the egoism of single actors leads to unfavourable results. The current anti-globalization movement is largely fuelled by the fact that on a global level markets are not functioning perfectly and we thus witness a blatantly unequal distribution of wealth across the globe. Another example would be the sustainability debate: the victims of today's resource depletion or global climate change are future generations, which are not yet present to take part in any kind of market. This clearly shows some initial limitations of egoist theory.

Utilitarianism

The philosophy of utilitarianism has been one of the most commonly accepted ethical theories in the Anglo-Saxon world. It is linked to the names of the British philosophers and economists Jeremy Bentham (1748–1832) and John Stuart Mill (1806–1873) and has been influential in modern economics in general. The basic principle of utilitarianism could be defined as follows:

According to utilitarianism, an action is morally right if it results in the greatest amount of good for the greatest amount of people affected by the action.

This principle, also called the '*greatest happiness principle*' is the ultimate consequentialist principle as it focuses solely on the consequences of an action, weighs the good results against the bad results, and finally encourages the action that results in the greatest amount of good for all people involved. Unlike egoism, it does not only look at each individual involved, and ask whether their individual desires and interests are met, but it focuses on the collective welfare that is produced by a certain decision.

The underlying idea is the notion of utility, which Bentham sees as the ultimate goal in life. Man is seen as a hedonist, whose purpose in life is to maximize pleasure and minimize pain. In this hedonistic rendition of utilitarianism, utility is measured in terms of *pleasure and pain* (the 'hedonistic' view). Other interpretations of utility look at *happiness and unhappiness* (the 'eudemonistic' view), while others take a strongly extended view that includes in the equation not only pleasure or happiness, but ultimately all *intrinsically valuable human goods* (the 'ideal' view). These goods then would typically include aspects such as friendship, love, trust, etc. The latter view in particular makes utilitarianism open to a great number of practical decision situations and prevents it from being rather narrowly focused on pleasure and pain only.

Utilitarianism has been very powerful since it puts at the centre of the moral decision a variable that is very commonly used in economics as a parameter, which measures the (economic) value of actions: 'utility'. Regardless of whether one accepts that utility really is quantifiable, it comes as no surprise to find that utilitarian analysis is highly compatible with the quantitative, mathematical methodology of economics. So, in analysing two possible actions in a single business decision, we can assign a certain utility to each consequence and each person involved, and the action with the highest aggregate utility can be determined to be morally correct. Ultimately utilitarianism then comes close to what we know as *cost-benefit analysis*.

Typical situations where utilitarian analysis can be very helpful are situations such as animal testing for medical research: although this inflicts considerable pain on animals, utilitarianists argue that it is still morally right as the pain of these animals has to be weighed against the fact that it prevents far greater pain on behalf of all those humans that profit from the tested drugs. Ultimately, utilitarian thinking has been used in very extreme situations: so, for example, the group of German generals and intellectuals who conspired to assassinate Hitler in 1944 justified their attempt on utilitarian grounds as the murder (pain) of one person opened the way to reducing the pain of millions of other people.

If we apply this theory to the situation described in Ethical Dilemma 3, we first of all have a look at all the actors involved and analyse their potential utility in terms of the pleasure and pain involved in different courses of action, say either going ahead with the deal (action one) or not doing the deal (action two). We could set up a simple balance sheet, such as that depicted in **Figure 3.3.**

After analysing all the good and bad effects for the persons involved, we can now add up 'pleasure' and 'pain' for action 1, and the result will be the *utility* of this action. After having done the same for action 2, the moral decision is relatively easy to identify: the greatest utility of the respective actions is the morally right one. In our hypothetical case, the decision would probably go in favour of action 1 (doing the deal) as it involves the most pleasure for all parties involved, whereas in action 2 (not doing the deal), the pain seems to dominate the analysis.

	Action 1: doing the deal		Action 2: not doing the deal	
	Pleasure	**Pain**	**Pleasure**	**Pain**
Product manager	Good deal for the business; potential for personal bonus.	Bad conscience; possible risk for company reputation.	Good conscience; less risk.	Loss of a good deal.
Thai dealer	Good deal.			Loss of a good deal; search for a new customer in Europe.
Parents	Secure the family's income.	Limited prospects for children.		Search for other sources of income.
Children	Feeling of being needed, being 'grown up'; approval of the parents.	Hard work; no chance of school education.	No hard work; time to play and go to school.	Potentially forced to do other, more painful work.
Grandmother	Family is able to support her.			Loss of economic support.

Figure 3.3. Example of a utilitarian analysis

This example shows already some of the more complicated issues with utilitarian philosophy. The main *problems with utilitarianism* are:

- **Subjectivity.** Clearly when using this theory you have to think rather creatively, and assessing such consequences as pleasure or pain might depend heavily on the subjective perspective of the person who carries out the analysis.
- **Problems of quantification.** Similarly, it is quite difficult to assign costs and benefits to every situation. In the example, this might be quite easy for the persons directly involved with the transaction, but it is certainly difficult to do so for the children involved, since their pleasure and pain is not quantifiable. Especially in these cases, it might be quite difficult to weigh pleasure against pain: is losing a good contract really comparable to forcing children into labour? Similarly, under utilitarianism, health and safety issues in the firm require 'values' of life and death to be quantified and calculated, without the possibility of acknowledging that they might have an intrinsic worth beyond calculation.
- **Distribution of utility.** Finally, it would appear that by assessing the greatest good for the greatest number, the interests of minorities are overlooked. In our example, a minority of children might suffer so that the majority might benefit from greater utility.

Of course, utilitarians were always aware of the limits of their theory. The problem of subjectivity, for example, led to a refinement of the theory, differentiating between what has been defined as 'act utilitarianism' versus 'rule utilitarianism':

Act utilitarianism looks to single actions and bases the moral judgement on the amount of pleasure and the amount of pain this single action causes.

Rule utilitarianism looks at classes of action and asks whether the underlying principles of an action produce more pleasure than pain for society in the long run.

Our utilitarian analysis of Ethical Dilemma 3 used the principle of act utilitarianism by asking whether just in that *single situation* the collective pleasure exceeded the pain inflicted. Given the specific circumstances of the case, this might result in the conclusion that it is morally right, because the children's pain is considerably small, given the fact, for instance, that they might have to work anyway or that school education might not be available to them. From the perspective of **rule utilitarianism**, however, one would have to ask whether child labour *in principle* produces more pleasure than pain. Here, the judgement might look considerably different, since it is not difficult to argue that the pains of child labour easily outweigh the (mainly) economic benefits of it. Rule utilitarianism then relieves us from examining right or wrong in every single situation, and offers the possibility of establishing certain principles that we then can apply to all such situations.

Non-consequentialist theories

Here we shall look at the two main types of non-consequentialist ethical theories that have been traditionally applied to business ethics:

- Ethics of duties.
- Ethics of rights and justice.

These two approaches are very similar, stemming from assumptions about basic universal principles of right and wrong. However, whilst rights-based theories tend to start by assigning a right to one party and then advocating a corresponding duty on another party to protect that right, ethics of duties *begin* with assigning of the duty to act in a certain way.

Rights and duty have also been central to many religious perspectives on business ethics, and remain important influences on business decision-makers worldwide, especially in regions with high rates of religious adherence, such as Latin America, the US, the Middle East, and Africa. Such approaches start from the basis of divine revelation, as found, for instance, in the religious tracts of the three monotheistic religions of Judaism, Christianity, and Islam, which ascribe enduring duties to God, or conversely, 'God-given rights'. In such a revelation of what is right or wrong human behaviour has its divine, eternal validity—regardless of whether the outcomes in given situation are in anybody's self-interest (egoism) or result in more pleasure or pain (utilitarianism), as consequentialist approaches would suggest. This said, we do not imply that religion is entirely oblivious of outcomes—but as we shall specifically see in the context of Kant's ethics of duties—many religions ground ethical behaviour in some eternally valid principles, which are derived from a duty to others, or to a specific deity.

Ethics of duties

In business ethics, the most influential theory to come from the perspective of ethics of duty derives from the work of the German philosopher Immanuel Kant (1724–1804). Kant argued that morality and decisions about right and wrong were not dependent on a particular situation, let alone on the consequences of one's action. For Kant, morality was a question of certain eternal, abstract, and unchangeable principles—a set of a priori moral laws—that humans should apply to all ethical problems. As a key Enlightenment thinker, Kant was convinced that human beings do not need God, the church, or some other superior authority to identify these principles for ethical behaviour. He saw humans as *rational* actors who could decide these principles for themselves. Hence, humans could therefore also be regarded as independent *moral actors* who made their own rational decisions regarding right and wrong.

Kant subsequently developed a theoretical framework through which these principles could be derived, called the '*categorical imperative*'. By this he meant that this theoretical framework should be applied to every moral issue regardless of who is involved, who profits, and who is harmed by the principles once they have been applied in specific situations.

The categorical imperative consists of three parts, which Kant puts forward as follows (see De George 1999):

Maxim 1: Act only according to that maxim by which you can at the same time will that it should become a universal law.

Maxim 2: Act so that you treat humanity, whether in your own person or in that of another, always as an end and never as a means only.

Maxim 3: Act only so that the will through its maxims could regard itself at the same time as universally lawgiving.

According to Kant, these three maxims can be used as tests for every possible action, and an action is to be regarded as morally right if it 'survives' all three tests. This suggests that morality is characterized by three important elements, each of which is tested by one of these maxims.

Maxim 1 checks if the action could be performed by everyone and reflects the aspect of consistency, as in an action can only be right if everyone could follow the same underlying principle. So, for example, murder is an immoral action because if we allowed everybody to murder there would be no possibility of human life on earth; lying is immoral, because if everybody were allowed to lie, the entire notion of 'truth' would be impossible, and an organized and stable human civilization would not be imaginable.

Maxim 2 focuses on Kant's view that humans deserve respect as autonomous, rational actors, and that this *human dignity* should never be ignored. We all use people as means, as soon as we employ them or pay them to provide us with goods or services. However, this does not mean we should *only* treat them as means to achieve what we want and just forget about their own needs and goals in life, and their expectations to make their own choices.

The third maxim scrutinizes the element of *universality*. I might come to the conclusion that a certain principle could be followed consistently by every human being; I could also come to the conclusion that in following that principle, I respect human dignity and do not just 'use' people as a means only. But then Kant wants us to check if the principles of our actions would be acceptable for every human being. This test therefore tries to overcome specifically the risk of *subjectivity* inherent in the utilitarian analysis, since it asks us to check if other rational actors would endorse our judgement of a certain situation. In other contexts, this point has been referred to as the 'New York Times test' (Treviño and Nelson 2004: 99)—namely, if you would be uncomfortable if your actions were reported in the press, you can be fairly sure that they are of doubtful moral status.

As some have argued, Kant's categorical imperative, in particular maxim 1, comes closest to a core tenet of many religions, otherwise also referred to as the '*golden rule*': 'Treat others as you wanted to be treated yourself' (Brammer et al. 2007: 231). This core principle is more or less explicitly embedded not just in the three monotheistic religions, but also in Buddhism, Hinduism, and Confucianism amongst others (Romar 2004). **Figure 3.4** in fact shows that the golden rule is a common feature of various belief systems across the world.

Figure 3.4. The Golden Rule in different belief systems

Source: Reproduced with permission from Scarboro Missions.

The core difference between a religious and a Kantian approach to the golden rule is that while religion 'recognizes God as the ultimate source of value' (Pava 1998: 504), Kant's approach reflects a different assumption: if God is the creator of rational human beings, then these human beings should also be able to rationally understand and decide whatever is the morally right or wrong thing to do in a given situation—rather than just being told what to do by a divine authority.

If we apply Kant's moral 'test' to Ethical Dilemma 3, we get the following insights:

- According to *maxim 1*, the first question would be to ask if we would want everybody to act according to the principles of our action. Obviously, as the product manager you are already uncomfortable about applying the principle of exploiting child labour from a third world context to your own family back home in Europe. You probably would not like this to become a universal law, which would then suggest that this activity could be deemed immoral on the basis of inconsistency.
- Regarding *maxim 2*, it is questionable whether the children have freely and autonomously decided to work. By making use of their labour, you could be said to be largely treating them as cheap labour for your own ends, rather than as 'ends in themselves', suggesting that their basic human dignity was not being fully recognized and respected.
- Looking at *maxim 3*, there is also the question of whether you would like your friends and family to know about your decision. In other words, it would seem rather doubtful that every rational human being would universally come to the same conclusion that child labour is a principle that should be followed on a general basis.

Kant's theory is quite extensive, and for the purpose of this book, we do not want to dig any deeper into it beyond these three basic principles. But already these can be quite helpful in practical situations and have had a considerable influence on business ethics thinking. For example, in Chapter 2 we discussed the *stakeholder concept* of the firm. Evan and Freeman (1993) argue that the ethical basis of this concept has been substantially derived from Kantian thinking. Hence, in order to treat employees, local communities, or suppliers not only as means, but also as constituencies with goals and priorities of their own, Evan and Freeman suggest that firms have a fundamental *duty* to allow these stakeholders some degree of influence on the corporation. By this they would be enabled to act as free and autonomous human beings, rather than being merely factors of production (employees), or sources of income (consumers), etc.

? THINK THEORY

Stakeholder theory has also been considered from other theoretical perspectives. How would you apply utilitarianism for instance to the concept of stakeholder theory? Do you think that the two different perspectives would suggest different obligations towards stakeholders?

VISIT THE WEBSITE for a short response to this feature

There are, however, also *problems with ethics of duty*.

- **Undervaluing outcomes.** Obviously one of these problems is that there is rather too little consideration of the outcomes of one's actions in ethics of duty. Although Kant would argue that you can consider consequences providing you would agree that everyone should do so when faced with similar situations, it gives you no real way of assessing these outcomes, and they do not form a fundamental part of the theory itself. They *may* be incorporated, but then again, they may not.

- **Complexity.** Secondly, whilst the basic idea of ethics of duty is quite simple—basically, is this action right, and is it my duty to do it—specific formulations such as Kant's categorical imperative can be quite complicated to apply. His principles-based way of evaluating a decision requires a certain amount of abstraction and it is this level of intellectual scrutiny that one cannot take for granted in each and every case.
- **Optimism.** Furthermore, Kant's theory is quite optimistic: his view of man as a rational actor who acts consequently according to self-imposed duties seems more of an ideal than a reality with regard to business actors. In contrast, the strength of egoism is that it is a concept of humans that is generally quite well confirmed by the conventional pattern of business behaviour.

Ethics of rights and justice

In Chapter 2, we briefly discussed the notion of citizenship as defined in terms of a set of individual rights. Actually, this notion of rights goes back to an entire philosophical school initially linked to another modernist thinker, the British philosopher John Locke (1632–1714). He conceptualized the notion of 'natural rights', or moral claims, that humans were entitled to, and which should be respected and protected (at that time, primarily by the state). Among the most important rights conceived by Locke and subsequent rights theorists were *rights to life, freedom, and property*. These have since been extended to include rights to freedom of speech, conscience, consent, privacy, and the entitlement to a fair legal process among others.

In terms of an ethical theory, we could define rights along the following lines:

Natural rights are certain basic, important, unalienable entitlements that should be respected and protected in every single action.

The general significance of the notion of rights in terms of an ethical theory lies in the fact that these rights typically result in the duty of other actors to respect them. In this respect, rights are sometimes seen as related to duties, since the rights of one person can result in a corresponding duty on other persons to respect, protect, or facilitate these rights. My right to property imposes a duty on others not to interfere with my property or take it away. My right to privacy imposes a duty on others to refrain from gathering personal information about my private life without my consent. Rights and duties are therefore frequently seen as two sides of the same coin.

This link to corresponding duties makes the theory of rights similar to Kant's approach. The main difference is that it does not rely on a rather complex process of determining the duties by applying the categorical imperative. Rather, the notion of rights is based on a certain axiomatic claim about human nature that rests mostly on various philosophical approaches of the Enlightenment, often backed up by certain religious views, such as the approach of Catholic social thought. Natural rights, or human rights, as they are referred to mostly today, are based on a certain consensus of all human beings about the nature of *human dignity*.

Despite its lack of a complicated theoretical deduction—or maybe even just because of its rather simple and plausible viewpoint—the rights approach has been very powerful throughout history and has substantially shaped the constitutions of many modern states. This includes the Declaration of the Rights of Man that was influential during the period of the French Revolution (1789), and the American Constitution, which is largely based on notions of rights. These ideas have also led to the United Nations Declaration of Human Rights, issued in 1948, which has been a powerful standard of worldwide enforcement of various rights. Another source of deducting human rights, of course, can also be found in religion. So, for instance, the Interfaith Centre for Corporate Responsibility (ICCR), a pan-religious American lobby group for CSR, makes its case for human rights on the basis that man is created in the image of God and therefore has some fundamental dignity, which is the basis for assigning and protecting some basic human rights for individuals.[1] Another, more secular manifestation of rights thinking is the Charter of Fundamental Human Rights for the European Union agreed as part of the Nice Treaty in 2000. Based on the original idea of 'natural rights', these entitlements have been applied to many different areas of social, political, and economic life, leading to various civil, social, and political rights, which ultimately define the notion of modern (liberal) citizenship.

Today, basic human rights would include a right to life, liberty, justice, education, fair trial, freedom of belief, association, and expression, to name just a few. It is this background that makes the entire notion of human rights one of the most common and important theoretical approaches to business ethics on a practical level. Corporations, especially multinationals, are increasingly judged with regard to their attitude to human rights and how far they respect and protect them. The Business and Human Rights Resource Centre, for example, established that nearly 250 companies had published policies on human rights by 2009[2]—some examples of which are given in **Figure 3.5**.

The perspective of human rights certainly provides the most straightforward answer to Ethical Dilemma 3. In using child labour, the product manager could be said to violate the rights of the children to education, and arguably to infringe the right to freedom of consent. Furthermore, a human rights perspective would cast doubt on the issue of an individual's right to a living wage, as it would appear that poor wages could have necessitated the engagement of the entire family in employment over long hours of work rather than paying one parent a suitable wage to provide for his or her family.

Ethical theories based on rights are very powerful because of their widely acknowledged basis in fundamental human entitlements. However, the theoretical basis is one of plausibility rather than a deep theoretical methodology. Moreover, perhaps the most substantial limitation of this approach is that notions of rights are quite strongly located in a Western view of morality. A considerable amount of friction might occur if these ideas were to be directly transferred, if not imposed, on communities with a different cultural and religious legacy.

Company	Human rights statement	Source
Body Shop.	We aim to ensure that human and civil rights, as set out in the Universal Declaration of Human Rights, are respected throughout our business activities. We will establish a framework based on this declaration to include criteria for workers' rights embracing a safe, healthy working environment, fair wages, no discrimination on the basis of race, creed, gender or sexual orientation, or physical coercion of any kind.	'Trading charter': www.thebodyshopinternational.com
Novartis.	We seek to promote and protect the rights defined in the Universal Declaration of Human Rights of the United Nations within our sphere of influence. We do not tolerate human rights abuses within our own business operations.	'Policy on Corporate Citizenship 2003': www.novartis.com
Philips.	Philips supports and respects human rights and strives to ensure that its activities do not make it an accessory to infringements of human rights.	'General business principles': www.philips.com
Skanska.	We respect the United Nations Universal Declaration of Human Rights and recognize our responsibility to observe those rights that apply to our performance toward our employees and the communities we work and live in.	'Skanska Code of Conduct: www.skanska.com
Toshiba.	Toshiba Group Companies shall accept the different values of individuals and respect differences in character and personality based on a fundamental respect for human rights.	'Toshiba Group Standards of Conduct': www.toshiba.com

Figure 3.5. Human rights statements by multinationals

The problem of justice

The approach of human rights to ethics has a particular relation to economic and business decisions. Whenever two parties enter an economic transaction there has to be agreement on a fair distribution of costs and benefits between the parties. This is what contracts are for, or most commonly, this is achieved by means of the market. Problems of distribution, however, do not only occur in transactions, but on a wider scale as well:

- How should a company pay its shareholders, executives, office workers, and manual staff so that everybody gets a fair compensation for their input into the corporation?
- How should a company take into account the demands of local communities, employees, and shareholders when planning an investment with major impacts on the environment?
- How should a government allocate money for education so that every section of society gets a fair chance of a good education?

We could easily multiply these examples, but what becomes clear is that individual rights have to be realized in a certain social context in such a way that they are addressed and respected equally and fairly. This is where the issue of justice arises.

Justice can be defined as the simultaneously fair treatment of individuals in a given situation with the result that everybody gets what they deserve.

The crucial moral issue here however is the question of what exactly 'fairness' means in a given situation and by which standards we can decide what a person might reasonably deserve. According to Beauchamp and Bowie (1997), theories of justice typically see fairness in two main ways:

- **Fair procedures.** Fairness is determined according to whether everyone has been free to acquire rewards for his or her efforts. This is commonly referred to as *procedural justice.*
- **Fair outcomes.** Fairness is determined according to whether the consequences (positive and negative) are distributed in a just manner, according to some underlying principle such as need or merit. This is commonly referred to as distributive justice.

Most views of justice would ideally seek to achieve both types of fairness, but this is not always possible. Consider the case of access to higher education. Say it was discovered that certain ethnic groups were under-represented in your university's degree programmes. Given that ethnicity is not correlated with innate intelligence, we might seek to solve this problem by reserving a certain number of places for under-represented groups to make sure that educational rewards were *distributed* fairly amongst these different sections of society. However, this would impose a potentially unfair *procedure* on the university's admissions, since 'over-represented' groups would be excluded from applying for the reserved places. This debate was ignited recently in India in the face of plans to extend the country's quota system reserving places for lower caste Hindus in government-funded academic institutions. The announcement of the plans led to massive street demonstrations by angry students at some of the country's most élite institutions, and even doctors at major hospitals went on strike to show solidarity (Majumder 2006). Generally, one can argue that justice and fairness in business transactions have also been at the core of the debate on religious foundations of business ethics. As Beekun and Badawi (2005) have argued, justice and fairness in fact are amongst the core tenets of any economic activity in Islam. A similar focus is also present in other religions, such as Buddhism, Christianity, and Judaism (Gould 1995; Pava 1998).

Notions of justice have been widely applied in business ethics problems, notably in relation to employment practices and the question of discrimination. Justice has also been a key feature of debates about globalization and sustainability. Here, the main concern is about issues of social and economic justice—themes that have long pervaded reasoning about the ethics of economic systems.

This problem of a just distribution of wealth in and between societies has been addressed in numerous ways, although historically answers have tended to fall somewhere between two extreme positions: *egalitarianism and non-egalitarianism.*

The *egalitarian* approach claims that justice is the same as equality—burdens and rewards should be distributed equally and deviations from equality are unjust (Beauchamp and Bowie 1997). Revelations that the poorest 40% of the world's population accounts for just 5% of global income, whilst the richest 20% accounts for three-quarters of world income would therefore clearly be seen as unjust by an egalitarian.[3] The most common example of an egalitarian position in designing a just economic system may be seen in the work of Karl Marx (see Wray-Bliss and Parker 1998). Living during the industrial revolution in nineteenth-century Britain and Germany, Marx identified the exploitation of the 'working class' in a labour process that provided excess wealth to the owners of the means of productions ('the capitalists'). As an ultimate solution to this problem, Marxist thinking suggests that a just society would be one where the working classes would collectively own the means of production themselves and thus would be the immediate beneficiaries of the economic outcomes of their work in the production process.

With the collapse of the Eastern bloc and China's opening up to market reforms at the end of the twentieth century, Marxist thinking, at least in its real-world manifestations, has somewhat lost momentum. Recently though, Marx's ideas have been reinvigorated in the context of globalization, where the relations between, for instance, consumers and workers in the global South and large Western MNCs mirror fairly closely his initial analysis of the oppression of the working classes by capitalism (Jones et al. 2005: 96–111).

However, egalitarian approaches have problems with the fact that there are differences between people. For instance, should someone who works hard earn the same as a lazy person? Are all skills really worth the same? Egalitarian approaches also tend to be inefficient, since there are no incentives for innovation and greater efficiency because everyone is rewarded equally anyway. Furthermore, they can lead to restrictions in individual freedom, since freedom to engage in economic transactions, for instance, could again lead to inequality among the actors involved, as the free market system clearly demonstrates.

The *non-egalitarian* approach, at the other end of the spectrum, would claim that justice in economic systems is ultimately a product of the fair process of free markets. Actors with certain needs would meet actors who can answer their needs, and if they agree on a transaction, justice is determined by the market forces of supply and demand. One of the more influential thinkers in business ethics along these lines is Robert Nozick (1974). He argues that a distribution of wealth in society is just as long as it has been brought about by just transfers and just original acquisition. For example, Bill Gates' personal wealth as the richest individual on the planet would be perfectly justifiable if the way he had set up Microsoft initially was without fraud or coercion and all other subsequent business transactions had been compliant with the same standards. Nozick's theory is often dubbed 'entitlement theory', as he considers wealth distribution as morally acceptable as long as 'everyone is entitled to the holdings they possess' (Nozick, cited in Boatright 2009: 75). Strong resonance of non-egalitarian thinking, finally, can be found in some religious systems, most notably the Calvinist protestant tradition. Based on a particular focus on the individual's responsibility to a personal god, Calvinism has laid the ground for what many now see as America's 'secular religion' of modern capitalism (Palazzo, 2002).

As discussed in Chapter 2, this free market approach has been popular over the last couple of decades. However, some have also argued that it has led to considerable inequality. This has been particularly visible in the so-called 'economies in transition' in the former Communist bloc or countries such as India, which traditionally had a rather strong socialist (i.e. egalitarian) approach to economics and business. **Ethics in Action 3.1** illustrates fairly commonplace contentions and dilemmas for governments and business in shifting the economy towards more competitiveness, while at the same time living up to the challenges of protecting the basic rights of individuals and notions of justice and fairness within society.

The notion of the market presupposes equal participants in the market in order to produce a just system. But insofar as people differ in income, ability, health, social and economic status, etc., markets can lead to results that some people would no longer regard as fair. On a global level, this has become visible when poor, underdeveloped countries have tried to compete with highly industrialized countries: it is as if in Formula One we allowed a bicycle to start next to a Ferrari: even with the fairest rules, the driver on the bicycle would be doomed to lose.

Obviously, the two extreme answers to the question of what exactly justice means in an economic context are unsatisfactory. The answer might well lie in between the two. A very popular approach to this problem has been proposed by the American John Rawls (1971). In his '*theory of justice*' he suggests two criteria—two 'tests' as it were—to decide whether an action could be called just. According to Rawls, justice is achieved when:

1 Each person is to have an equal right to the most extensive total system of basic liberties compatible with a similar system of liberty for all.

2 Social and economic inequalities are to be arranged so that they are both:

   (a) to the greatest benefit of the least advantaged; and

   (b) attached to offices and positions open to all under conditions of fair equality of opportunity.

The first principle is the most important one: before allowing for any inequalities, we should ensure that the basic freedoms are realized to the same degree for everyone affected by the decision. The first condition thus looks to general human rights and requires their fulfilment before we can proceed to the next step.

The second test is based on the assumption that inequalities are unavoidable in a free and competitive society. However, two conditions should be met. First, an arrangement is just when even the one who profits least from it is still better off than they would be without it. This, for example, would suggest that high salaries for corporate leaders might be acceptable providing that employees at the bottom of the corporate hierarchy were also better off as a result—say, because the high salary for the leader led to better corporate performance, which in turn could be translated into higher wages for the least paid. The second condition, again following this example, would be met if not only a privileged few could ascend the corporate ladder, but everyone had a fair chance of doing so, regardless of gender, race, appearance, etc.

VISIT THE WEBSITE for links to useful sources of further information

ETHICS IN ACTION 3.1 http://www.ethicalcorp.com

Ethical CORPORATION

India's special economic zones—an ethics black hole

Rajesh Chhabara, 5 June 2007

India's government, facing imminent election defeat in several important states and violent protests against forced acquisition of farmland, announced in February 2007 that states could no longer acquire land. Instead, new regulations will allow developers to buy land directly from farmers for special economic zones (SEZs)—regions with liberal economic laws designed to encourage investment, especially by foreign companies. State governments had previously bought land under the Land Acquisition Act of 1894—dating from the colonial era. The law gave governments absolute authority to unilaterally target, price, and acquire any agricultural land for industrial projects. Following China's example, India plans to create more than 500 SEZs across the country. Commerce minister Kamal Nath has championed SEZs as 'engines of growth' which will help boost exports, spur inward foreign investment, and create thousands of jobs. Not everyone agrees. Human rights groups are outraged by the large-scale displacements and loss of livelihood that the SEZs will cause. They also criticize the government for giving generous fiscal incentives to industry, while cutting subsidies on food. Human rights activist Medha Patkar says: 'The government is distributing land to private companies, which is against the farmers and workers of the country.' Himanshu Thakkar, the founder of South Asia Network on Dams, River and People, says: 'The conversion of land to SEZ would mean destruction of groundwater recharge systems, contamination by release of industrial effluent and crisis of water for the neighboring communities'. More than 86,000 hectares of land will be required for the 237 SEZs approved so far. Most of this will have to be bought from farmers, displacing an estimated 1 million people. Hungry for investment and export markets, the government is tempting companies with controversial non-fiscal concessions. Freedom of association and collective bargaining rules, as well as the Environment Protection Act, will not apply to SEZs. Companies will be able to hire and fire as they wish. Neither will they be required to obtain environmental clearance for their projects.

Economic free-for-all

Companies including Salem, Reliance, Tata, Arcelor Mittal, and Posco are already under fire after state governments forcibly tried to acquire land for their projects. At least 21 protestors have died in resulting clashes with police. In general, companies have relied on the police to help them take possession of the allotted land rather than trying to engage the affected communities to address their concerns. Now India's government has cleverly eased itself out of the controversy by amending the law. This will introduce layers of middlemen into the land acquisition process and could send land prices rocketing. While companies may end up paying more for the land, farmers will not necessarily receive a higher price. The property business in India is notorious for its nexus between developers and politicians, police, bureaucrats, and local goons—popularly termed as 'land mafia'. Critics say SEZ policy allows developers to possess large chunks of land at throw-away prices. They claim extensive tax breaks are fuelling speculative investment, causing fears of a real estate bubble. Developers can use up to 50% of land for non-industrial purposes, which may include building residential complexes, malls, hotels, recreation clubs, and so on.

Responsibility opportunity

The question is whether companies will act responsibly while buying the land directly from farmers. Will they succeed where the government has failed? The biggest challenge before the companies is to create a climate of trust and to engage with a range of stakeholders. It will not be easy given the extensive resentment and bitterness among farmers and NGO scepticism of the SEZ model of development. An accurate understanding of deep-rooted cultural aspects of land ownership in India will be a key advantage for any company wanting effective engagement with farmers. Farmers will expect what they regard as fair compensation and rehabilitation benefits. Companies willing to offer training and employment opportunities to displaced families will score an advantage. Companies will also need to address NGO concerns about mass displacement and lack of rehabilitation measures, fair treatment of workers and environmental impacts of SEZs. Smart companies can use the amended land rules to strengthen their position in the Indian market by constructively engaging in the real issues and finding innovative solutions. Shareholders, as well as stakeholders, will be watching closely.

Sources

Ethical Corporation, Rajesh Chhabara, 5 June 2007, http://www.ethicalcorp.com.

? THINK THEORY

Think about the situation of rural landowners/farmers in contemporary India. What in your view would be a just and fair approach to implement the SEZ concept of the Indian government? Would your judgement change if you applied consequentialist theories of business ethics?

VISIT THE WEBSITE for a short response to this feature

There are, of course a couple of more considerations, conditions, and elements to Rawls' theory that we will not go into here. Even in this simplified form, though, we can usefully apply some of its basic findings to various business situations in order to determine 'just' treatment of stakeholders.

If we look to our example in Ethical Dilemma 3, the first test would be to ask if all people involved (including the product manager) were in possession of the same basic liberty. Apart from the cultural differences between Europe and Thailand, this is certainly not the case for the children, since they are obviously not allowed to have even a basic education. The second principle could conceivably allow for a more tolerant approach to child labour: the first criterion for inequality would be to ask if the children are worse or better off with the arrangement. One might reasonably argue here that children are often forced into worse things in developing countries than assembling plastic toys. Prostitution, begging, and theft might be other alternatives, suggesting that the children would be better off if you concluded the deal. However, if concluding your deal meant that the children would miss schooling that they otherwise would have had, the arrangement is definitely not benefiting the least well off. The second criterion, though, poses even more of a problem, since without access to education the children do not have a realistic chance of achieving the position that the better-off parties such as yourself have. Hence, they are definitely not 'under conditions of fair equality of opportunity'.

If we extend our view slightly more broadly, Rawls' view of justice can actually be used to justify multinationals' exploitation of low wages and poor conditions in less developed countries—at least under certain conditions. For example, some MNCs have taken it upon themselves to cater for school education or basic healthcare in less developed manufacturing locations. By this, MNCs still take advantage of lower wages in these countries, but by providing a 'system of basic liberties compatible with a similar system of liberty for all' and creating 'conditions of fair equality of opportunity' (at least on a local level), one might argue that the resulting inequalities are still 'to the greatest benefit of the least advantaged'. After all, without the manufacturing plant, local people would probably face greater poverty and less opportunity for development than they would with it.

VISIT THE WEBSITE for a short response to this feature

? THINK THEORY

In Chapter 2, in the context of the extended conceptualization of corporate citizenship, we have discussed the role of companies in the provision of basic entitlements such as water, security, and health. From the perspective of John Rawls' theory of justice, could you imagine a situation in which the involvement of private corporations in the provision of public services (such as the provision of water) could be considered as morally just?

Limits of Western modernist theories

If we look back to these major Western modernist ethical theories, we could argue that they present a quite comprehensive view of humans and society, and based on various assumptions, they come up with actionable principles to answer ethical questions. In presenting such a closed 'model' of the world, these theories have the substantial advantage that they can come up with a solution to every possible situation. They have, however, the big disadvantage that their view of the world only presents one aspect of human life, while reality normally tends to be more complex than the simplified view of these ethical theories.

In the previous discussions, we have outlined some of the main benefits and drawbacks of each of these main ethical theories. However, the very approach of *all* Western modernist theories is open to criticism. As largely absolutist theories based on objective reason, a number of drawbacks for approaching business ethics problems through theory of this sort can be identified.

The main criticisms of Western modernist ethical theories are:

- **Too abstract.** Stark (1994) suggests that traditional ethical theories are too theoretical and impractical for the pragmatic day-to-day concerns of managers. In real life, managers are unlikely to apply abstract principles derived from long-dead philosophers when dealing with the concrete problems of business. The business context has its own values, structures, and practices that need to be taken into account (Furman 1990).

- **Too reductionist.** Kaler (1999) argues that each theory tends to focus on one aspect of morality at the cost of all the rest of morality. Why choose consequences, duties, *or* rights when *all* are important?

- **Too objective and élitist.** Parker (1998) suggests that ethical theories attempt to occupy a rarefied high ground, such that those specialist ethicists and philosophers who know and understand the theories can pronounce on the right and wrong of other people without any subjective experience of the situation they are faced with. Just because Crane and Matten know the difference between utilitarianism and justice, why should that mean that we can decide for you whether a product manager in Thailand is doing the right thing?

- **Too impersonal.** By focusing on abstract principles, traditional ethical theories do not take account of the personal bonds and relationships that shape our thoughts and feelings about right and wrong (Gilligan 1982).

- **Too rational and codified.** Ethical theories try and distil right and wrong down to codified rational rules of behaviour. Bauman (1993) contends that this suppresses our moral autonomy and denigrates the importance of our moral feelings and emotions, all of which he claims are crucial for acting morally towards others.

- **Too imperialist.** Why assume that ethical theories from the West are suitable for business people everywhere else in the world? What about the ethical teachings of classical Asian or traditional African philosophy, for instance—do these not also have something useful to say about modern-day business ethics?

Clearly, then, there are certain problems associated with these Western modernist theories (see also Jones et al. 2005). Many of these stem from their emphasis on the more absolutist approach to ethical theory. As a result, there have been a number of more recent attempts to develop or resurrect alternative ethical theories that emphasize greater flexibility, as well as including consideration of decision-makers, their context, and their relations with others, as opposed to just abstract universal principles. Although these are also open to criticism, they help to enrich the choice of perspectives we could take on ethical issues in business.

■ Alternative perspectives on ethical theory

Alternative, more contemporary perspectives on ethical theories are those that have either been developed or brought to prominence in the business ethics field over the past two decades or so. As such, they much less commonly appear in business ethics texts, yet we would suggest that they offer an important alternative perspective that should not be ignored, and which, we would suspect, may become increasingly more influential in the business ethics literature. We shall be looking at four main contemporary ethical theories:

- Ethical approaches based on character and integrity.
- Ethical approaches based on relationships and responsibility.
- Ethical approaches based on procedures of norm generation.
- Ethical approaches based on empathy and moral impulse.

Ethical approaches based on character and integrity

Up to now, we have chiefly looked at right and wrong according to the ethics of particular *actions*. However, much attention in recent years has focused on approaches that start from a different perspective: rather than checking every single action according to its outcomes, or its underlying principles, these approaches look to the character or integrity of the *decision-maker* (Nielsen 2006). Focusing on the integrity of individuals clearly has a strong resonance in a business context, especially when considering the ethics of professionals such as doctors, lawyers, and accountants who rely on their moral probity for maintaining legitimacy and gaining clients. Attention to character as a foundation for business ethics has also arisen in non-Western contexts, such as Africa, where it has been argued that its humanistic approach is more easily acceptable in African culture than rules-based approaches (Gichure 2006).

Character and integrity-based approaches to business ethics have mainly drawn on one of the earliest ethical theories, that of **virtue ethics**. In virtue ethics, the main message is that 'good actions come from good persons'. We could therefore define virtue ethics along the following lines:

> **Virtue ethics contends that morally correct actions are those undertaken by actors with virtuous characters. Therefore, the formation of a virtuous character is the first step towards morally correct behaviour.**

Virtues are a set of acquired traits of character that enable a person to lead a good life. Virtues can be differentiated into *intellectual virtues*—'wisdom' being the most prominent one—and *moral virtues*, which comprise a long list of possible characteristics such as honesty, courage, friendship, mercy, loyalty, modesty, patience, etc. All these virtues are manifested in actions that are a habitual pattern of behaviour of the virtuous person, rather than just occurring once or in one-off decisions. As these traits are not ours by birth, we acquire them by learning, and most notably in business, by being in relationships with others in a community of practice (MacIntyre 1984).

Central to the ethics of virtue is the notion of a 'good life'. For Aristotle, one of the original proponents of virtue ethics, this consists of happiness—not in a limited hedonistic, pleasure-oriented sense, but in a broader sense. This most notably includes virtuous behaviour as an integral part of the good life: a happy businessperson would not only be one who finally makes the most money, but one who does so whilst at the same time savouring the pleasures of a virtuous manner of achieving their success. In a business context, the 'good life' means far more than being a profitable company. Virtue ethics takes a much more holistic view by also looking at the way this profit is achieved, and most notably, by claiming that economic success is just one part of the good business life—with satisfaction of employees, good relations among all members of the company, and harmonious relations with all stakeholders being equally important (J. Collier 1995).

From this point of view, the virtuous product manager in Ethical Dilemma 3 could take in different perspectives, depending on the community from which the notion of a virtuous manager was derived. On the one hand, you could be compassionate and considerate with the situation of the suppliers. Taking into account their need for work and money, as well as the children's need for education, you perhaps would try to do business with them while, at the same time, assuming responsibility for the children's education. For instance, you could support a local school, or pay sufficiently high wages to allow the family to send their children to school, rather than making use of them as cheap labour. On the other hand, you might also think that the 'good life' in rural Thailand might in fact consist of an entire family working happily together and that Western concepts of education, professionalization, and efficiency are a different concept of a 'good life' that might not be appropriate to the Thai approach to life. Typically, though, virtue ethics in a business context such as this would suggest that the solution to many of the problems faced by managers are located in the culture and tradition of the relevant community of practice. The product manager should determine what a 'virtuous' product manager would do from his or her professional code of conduct, from virtuous role models, or from professional training.

It doesn't take long to see what the main drawback of virtue ethics is (see also Jones et al. 2005: 56–68): how do we determine which community ideal of good practice to consult? And, in the absence of a clear code of conduct from our relevant communities, how do we translate ideas of virtuous traits into ethical action? Still, the relevance of virtue ethics for business ethics is that it reminds us that right and wrong cannot simply be resolved by applying a specific rule or principle, but that we need to cultivate our knowledge and judgement on ethical matters over time through experience and participation (Nielsen 2006).

Ethical approaches based on relationships and responsibility

This eschewal of a principle-based approach to ethical problems has also been taken up by other alternative frameworks, which focus not on character, but on relationships. One notable example of this approach is *feminist ethics*, which starts from the assumption that men and women have fairly different attitudes towards organizing social life, with significant impact on the way ethical conflicts are handled (Gilligan 1982).

In addressing ethical problems, traditional ethical theory has looked for rules and principles to be applied in a fair, objective, and consistent way. This approach has been almost exclusively established and promulgated by male philosophers and thinkers such as Kant, Locke, Bentham, Smith, and Mill. The 'ethics of rights', as this view sometimes is called (Maier 1997), tries to establish legitimate grounds for claims and interests of individuals in situations of social conflicts.

Feminist ethics, on the other hand, has a different approach that sees the individual deeply embedded in a network of interpersonal relations. Consequently, responsibility for the members of this network and maintenance of connectedness, rather than allegiance to abstract moral principles, is the predominant concern of feminist ethics. This approach, often therefore called an *ethics of care*, consequently results in significant differences in the view of ethical issues (Maier 1997; Rabouin 1997). Moral problems are conflicts of responsibilities in relationships rather than conflicts of rights between individuals and therefore can only be solved by personal, subjective assessment that particularly stresses the importance of emotion, intuition, and feeling. Whilst traditional approaches would focus on 'fair' results, feminist perspectives stress social processes and particularly aim at the achievement of harmony, empathy, and integration with regard to ethical issues. The main goal is to avoid harm and maintain healthy relationships. Following this description, we might suggest the following definition:

> **Feminist ethics is an approach that prioritizes empathy, harmonious and healthy social relationships, care for one another, and avoidance of harm above abstract principles.**

While some of the literature on feminist perspectives of business ethics—as outlined above—focuses on gender differences and embeds the ethical approach in a gender-specific context (e.g. Maier 1997), the more recent debate has moved beyond those simple ways of essentializing a 'female' approach to ethics. Rather, as Janet Borgerson (2007) has argued, feminist perspectives on business ethics highlight some general principles, which are relevant beyond a narrow concern with 'gender', 'care', or other simple reductions of a feminist perspective. Key elements of a feminist approach then would include the following (Borgerson, 2007):

- **Relationships.** While many of the Western modernist theories focus on the individual person trying to enact ethical behaviour, feminist perspectives put an emphasis on the fact that ethical decisions are taken in a specific context of personal human interrelations. Such a perspective then would emphasize the impact of ethical decision-making on the web of interpersonal relations of the decision-maker.

- **Responsibility.** Rather than just 'having' responsibility in a given context, feminist perspectives would suggest that ethical decision-making asks for an active 'taking' of responsibility. Thus, in a given situation, rather than defensively acting to live up to external demands or pressures, feminist perspectives suggest an *active* involvement in and assumption of responsibilities for the ethical implications of business activities.

- **Experience.** Feminist perspectives highlight the fact that in decision-making, including ethical decisions, human beings are intricately determined by past experiences. So rather than applying 'principles' or 'rules' in an abstract way, this approach would encourage one to learn and develop from experiences in the past.

> **? THINK THEORY**
>
> Think about the ethical arguments used by family members, friends, or colleagues. Can you see any differences between the arguments used by men and women? What does this say about the potential contribution of feminist ethics?

VISIT THE WEBSITE for a short response to this feature

This focus on relationships and responsibilities is also evident in some non-Western ethical frameworks. For example, in *Buddhist approaches to business ethics*, as Gould (1995) points out, there is an emphasis on considering 'everyone as our father, mother, brother or sister', blaming yourself rather than others, and focusing on personal growth and fulfilment as basic tenets of ethical decision-making. Ultimately, the Buddhist perspective highlights the interconnectedness and web of relationships in which ethical decision-making takes place. Similarly, there is a focus on relationships as the basis for ethical conduct in *Confucian approaches to business ethics* (Romar 2004).

Applying a relationships approach to the case in Ethical Dilemma 3 would in a certain sense require far more knowledge about the case than we can acquire from just reading about it. A relationships-oriented perspective would cause the product manager to try to get a closer view of the family involved and see if the children are really happy in this situation. It would also involve a better understanding of the social and economic constraints that cause the family to embark on this particular production pattern. Ironically, a feminist perspective would not necessarily argue categorically against any involvement of children in the process, as long as the inter-familiar relationships are functioning well, and the children are not forced, exploited, or compelled to work beyond their physical capacities. As the latter conditions probably might not be fulfilled, relational approaches would probably tend to object to child labour as well—however, not so very much because it violates certain (Western) principles, but because of the likely distress and suffering of the children. Furthermore, feminist theories would also look at the situation of the other actors involved and scrutinize, for example, the question of whether the money earned by the assembling of toys is spent and how the income in the family is distributed, etc.

Ethical approaches based on procedures of norm generation

All the theoretical approaches we have discussed so far start from a certain perspective on humans, on the values or goals governing their decisions, and a few other assumptions that in essence are all normative in nature. By normative, remember that we mean prescriptions of right and wrong action. Having said 'normative', however, we might step back for a minute and ask if this starting point is, in fact, a very useful way to solve ethical conflicts in business. After all, we cannot take it for granted in a given situation that everybody shares, for instance, the notion of humans being hedonistic, or of rights or feminist values being the most appropriate ones to address ethical problems in business. This is already problematic in a group of relatively homogeneous people; say the marketing department of a Swedish car company. But it gets even more complicated if there is a meeting of all marketing directors of the company worldwide, since this could conceivably include participants as diverse as evangelical fundamentalists from the US, atheists from Russia, Muslims from Egypt and Buddhists from Japan. In these situations, the most significant problems arise from the diverging normative perspectives that the different people might bring to the table.

It is at this point that theoretical approaches based on norm generation might come into the picture. These approaches seek ethical behaviour not in applying ethical principles, but in generating norms that are appropriate and acceptable to those who need to resolve a particular problem. There are various forms such practices could take, including for instance the traditional African institution of the palaver, where the relevant parties would be brought together under a 'palaver tree' and be allowed to speak freely in order to generate appropriate principles for decision-making (Gichure 2006). However, probably the best-known approach to norm generation in business ethics is that of *discourse ethics*.

The philosophical underpinning of discourse ethics is the argument that norms ultimately cannot be justified by rational arguments, but that they have to be generated and applied to solve ethical conflicts on a day-to-day basis (Preuss 1999). Horst Steinmann and Albert Löhr (1994), who are among the main proponents of a discourse approach to business ethics, argue that ethical reflection has to start from real-life experiences (rather than belief systems, which could be too diverse). They contend that the ultimate goal of ethical issues in business should be the *peaceful settlement of conflicts*.

With this goal in mind, different parties in a conflict should sit together and engage in a discourse about the settlement of the conflict, and ultimately provide a solution that is acceptable to all. This 'ideal discourse', as it is usually called, is more than an occasional chat or business meeting; it particularly has to answer certain philosophical criteria, such as impartiality, non-persuasiveness, non-coercion, and expertise of the participants (Habermas 1983). This would particularly include the injunction that those who are more powerful in a certain situation refrain from imposing their values on others, and using their power to solve the ethical conflict according to their own belief systems. Such a discourse then would lead to norms for a specific situation that are an expression of the rational consensus of all affected persons or represented parties. In establishing a rational 'ideal discourse' about specific problems, this approach is thus supposed to be *norm generating*.

Given this brief outline, we might usefully posit the following basic definition:

> **Discourse ethics aims to solve ethical conflicts by providing a process of norm generation through rational reflection on the real life experience of all relevant participants.**

Discourse ethics, then, is more a recipe for practical conflict solution than an ethical theory comparable to those discussed above. In simple terms, the only condition for it to work is the assumption that all rational human beings share the experience, and that the norm of peaceful resolution of conflict is the best way to organize social interaction. It is based on rationality and requires a dialogue in which people are able and willing to exchange arguments and follow the 'non-coercive coercion of the best argumentation' (Habermas 1983). There are understandably certain practical limits to this approach, especially the considerable amount of time it involves, and the fairly optimistic assumptions about rational human behaviour in discourses. Nevertheless, discourse ethics has been the underlying concept for the settlement of numerous disputes about environmental impacts of corporate decisions, in which various stakeholders with completely divergent value systems had to come to a common decision on certain controversial projects (Renn et al. 1995). See **Ethics in Action 3.2** for an illustration of where an approach akin to discourse ethics has been applied in the generation of a global standard on CSR.

If we apply a norm-generating approach such as discourse ethics to Ethical Dilemma 3, it lies in the nature of the concept that we are not able to say if this would influence in any way the resulting decision of the parties involved. It would, however, suggest that all parties involved, starting with the Thai trading company, the confectionery manufacturer, the parents, the children, but potentially also the consumers in Europe, should meet together to enter a 'norm-generating' discourse on the topic. Apart from the fact that this shows some of the practical difficulties of the concept, the idea does open the way to a solution that could be closest to the interests of all parties involved.

Ethical approaches based on empathy and moral impulse

Finally, there is a school of thought in business ethics that takes up a point that we have already touched upon when discussing discourse ethics in the previous section. Often referred to as *'postmodern business ethics'*, this school of thought fundamentally questions the link between rationality and morality that is inherent in all the Western modernist ethical theories discussed earlier in this chapter. These traditional theories have their origins in modernism, which emerged roughly during the eighteenth-century Enlightenment era. 'Modern' thinkers strove for a rational, scientific explanation of the world and aimed at comprehensive, inclusive, theoretically coherent theories to explain nature, man, and society. In the area of the social sciences, one of the results of this was the development of various theories, commonly in the form of certain '–isms', such as liberalism, communism, socialism, rationalism, capitalism, etc. Postmodern thinkers contend that these comprehensive theories, these 'grand narratives' of society (Lyotard 1984), are too ambitious, optimistic, and reductionist, ultimately failing to explain the complex reality of human existence.

While postmodernism tends to embrace a whole range of theoretical propositions and arguments, postmodern thinkers have been particularly influential in ethics, since they identify the specific danger of rational approaches to morality. Zygmunt Bauman (1993), one of the best-known proponents of postmodern ethics, argues that by codifying morality within specific rules and codes of behaviour (as, for example, exemplified in bureaucratic organizations), rational approaches deny the real source of morality, which is rooted in a 'moral impulse' towards others. This is a subjective, emotional conviction that humans have about right and wrong, based on their experiences, sentiments, and instincts. Moral judgement, then, is a gut feeling more than anything else, but this is inevitably nullified

VISIT THE WEBSITE for links to useful sources of further information

ETHICS IN ACTION 3.2 http://www.ethicalcorp.com

Standards: ISO steps towards social responsibility

Ethical CORPORATION

Paul Hohnen, 22 September 2008

The ISO Social Responsibility Working Group took a small—but potentially historic—step forward at its meeting in Santiago de Chile on 1–5 September 2008. Nearly 400 experts and observers from around the world agreed that sufficient progress had been made in developing the draft international standard on social responsibility (ISO 26000) for the 'working draft' to be taken to 'committee draft' level. In the process of ISO standards' development, this takes the draft standard one stage closer to the wider consultation and voting phases that could see it available for public use globally in 2010. For readers unfamiliar with these negotiations, a short history of a long story is in order.

Long road

Best known for its widely used technical and management standards, ISO embarked in 2005 on its first 'soft' standard—on social responsibility. As a new and controversial subject area for ISO, the mandate given to the working group was to develop a standard by late 2008 that would provide voluntary guidance to all organizations, public and private. While there were proponents (especially from developing countries) who wanted a standard that could be used for certification purposes—to demonstrate their world class performance to increasingly picky northern consumers and investors—others argued that ethical issues were too soft and culture-defined for certification. As a result, it was agreed that the standard would not be a management system standard (like the popular ISO 14001 standard), and could not be used for certification. Since March 2005, there have been six negotiating sessions of the Working Group on Social Responsibility. Experts and observers from six groups—government, industry, labour, consumer organizations, NGOs, and a group of academic, consultant, standards, and other bodies—have been working intensively on reaching consensus on what 'social responsibility' means, and what should go in the world's first standard on the subject. Arriving in Santiago, it was not clear to many negotiators whether their Carmenera was half empty or half full. To many, the working draft before them was over due, over long, and over done.

Kitchen sink

Difficulties in getting agreement on scope and content issues had already meant that the original 2008 deadline would not be met. Coming in at over 80 pages, excluding annexes, there was also hand-wringing about whether all but the largest organizations would be inclined to read the standard. Moreover, there was a sense that apart from not mentioning the kitchen sink, the draft seemed dauntingly comprehensive. On the other hand, there was a sense that important and hard-won consensus had been achieved on a number of fronts. For all its length, the draft contained valuable and well-written guidance on core social responsibility subjects. These included organizational governance, human rights, labour practices, the environment, fair operating practices, consumer issues, and community involvement. Moreover, it was common ground that the definition of social responsibility—embracing such notions as the importance of sustainable development, stakeholder expectations, compliance with national and international law, and the need for organization-wide integration—provided a much needed level of clarity. While everyone could point to weaknesses in the text, there was a general sense that real progress had been made, and that it was time to take the draft to a wider audience. By agreeing to move the draft to 'committee draft' status, following further amendments recommended at the Santiago meeting, the draft standard will now be opened to comments from ISO's 84 participating (and thus voting) national standards bodies for comment. How quickly ISO can complete this process remains to be seen.

Sources

Ethical Corporation, Paul Hohnen, 22 September 2008, http://www.ethicalcorp.com.

? THINK THEORY

How far can we interpret the process of developing the new ISO 26000 standard as an application of discourse ethics? What are the advantages of this approach and what could be seen as drawbacks and risks?

VISIT THE WEBSITE for a short response to this feature

when people enter organizations and become distanced from the people who are actually going to experience the consequences of their decisions, such as consumers, investors, suppliers, and others. These ideas lead us to the following definition:

> **Postmodern ethics is an approach that locates morality beyond the sphere of rationality in an emotional 'moral impulse' towards others. It encourages individual actors to question everyday practices and rules, and to listen to and follow their emotions, inner convictions, and 'gut feelings' about what they think is right and wrong in a particular situation.**

Ultimately, postmodernists are rather sceptical about the entire venture of business ethics (ten Bos and Willmott 2001), since ethical theories aim to find 'rules and principles that determine right or wrong' (our definition in Chapter 1). Postmodernists tend to suggest otherwise, such that 'the foolproof—universal and unshakably founded—ethical code will never be found' (Bauman 1993). A postmodern perspective on business ethics does not then provide us with any rule or principle, not even a 'recipe' for ethical decision-making, such as discourse ethics. However, postmodern ethics have quite significant implications for ethical decisions in business.[4] Gustafson (2000: 21), for example, suggests that postmodern business ethics emphasizes the following:

- **Holistic approach.** As morality is an inner conviction of individual actors, there is no separation between the private and professional realm. Postmodernists argue that modernist theories of ethical behaviour lead to an abstract and distant view of ethical issues that ultimately causes actors to follow different standards in their professional and private lives. For business organizations, such a view of ethical decision-making could unleash a quite subversive potential to business ethics, as it might question the beliefs and practices held by the organization (Bauman 1993).
- **Examples rather than principles.** As morality is not based on rational theories, ethical reasoning is not embodied in principles and rules. Rather, it is based on narratives of experience, relies on metaphors to explain inner convictions, and suggests persons and role models of certain virtues that the individual could point to as an embodiment of his/her 'moral instinct'. Of all the theories discussed so far, virtue ethics therefore has the strongest affiliation to postmodern ethics (Shaw 1995).
- **'Think local, act local'.** Modernist theories and '–isms' are aimed at general principles that are applicable to each and every situation. Postmodernists think that ethical reasoning has to be far more modest: it would be realistic to expect ethics to come up with local rules applicable to single issues and situations. Rather than finding one principle for multiple situations, business ethics focuses on deciding one issue after another. This does not mean that postmodernists do not take their decisions seriously and could decide on an issue in one way today and in another way tomorrow. It rather highlights the fact that no one situation is the same, and that different actors, power relations, cultural antecedents, and emotional contexts might lead to different judgements in situations that could, in the abstract, be regarded as being in the same 'class' and subject to the same 'principles'.
- **Preliminary character.** Postmodern ethicists are often seen as more pessimistic than their modern counterparts. They know that ethical decisions are subject to non-rational processes, and thus less controllable and predictable. Ethical reasoning therefore is a constant learning process, an ongoing struggle for the solutions that have a better fit, or for reasoning that just makes more sense and works better than the approaches tried out so far.

From the nature of a postmodern view on business ethics, it might already be clear that the notion of discussing the abstract case of Ethical Dilemma 3 is a nearly impossible venture. Indeed, postmodernist thinkers are sceptical of the vignette or hypothetical case method of learning about business ethics, preferring instead to engender moral commitment to others through real-life encounters (McPhail 2001). We would at best only be able to come up with some form of judgement if we travelled to Thailand, visited the site, talked to the people, and emphatically immersed ourselves in the real-life situation. We would then have a 'moral impulse' about what to feel about the situation and could come up with what we would regard as the moral way to decide in this situation.

However, the example does gives us a few indications, and as good postmodernists, we would be well aware of the limitations of our present view on the issue and would try to suggest a preliminary view of what we would do in the situation of the product manager. We might, for example, at least suggest that we as the product manager have made the right first move in actually going to the site of production and facing those who will be affected by our decisions rather than staying at home and simply dismissing them as faceless 'suppliers'. We might also point to our attempt to make our own autonomous decision based on the situation faced in the specific culture of Thailand, rather than relying on a corporate code of ethics, particularly one which is intended to have universal application. However, postmodernists would also question the extent to which you as the product manager are so steeped in a corporate mentality that you immediately think in terms of costs and bonuses, rather than people and their lives.

Ultimately, it is of the nature of postmodernism that we are not able to finally decide on the situation for the manager, since we lack the contextual nuances of the situation and we are not aware of the extent to which a genuine 'moral impulse' is possible in this context.

Summary: towards a pragmatic use of ethical theory

The array of ethical theories discussed in this chapter provides us with a rich source of assistance in making morally informed decisions. However, the discussion of our case, Ethical Dilemma 3, has brought to the surface quite a variety of different views and normative implications depending on the theoretical approach that has been chosen. Sometimes these views provide quite widely contradictory results.

As we have already indicated earlier in this chapter, we will not suggest one theory or one approach as the best or true view of a moral dilemma. **Figure 3.6** shows this

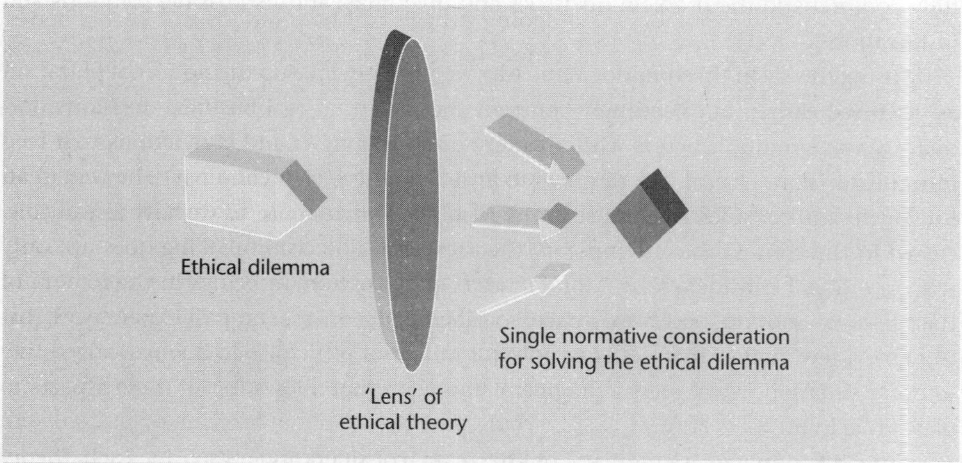

Figure 3.6. A typical perspective on the value of ethical theory for solving ethical dilemmas in business

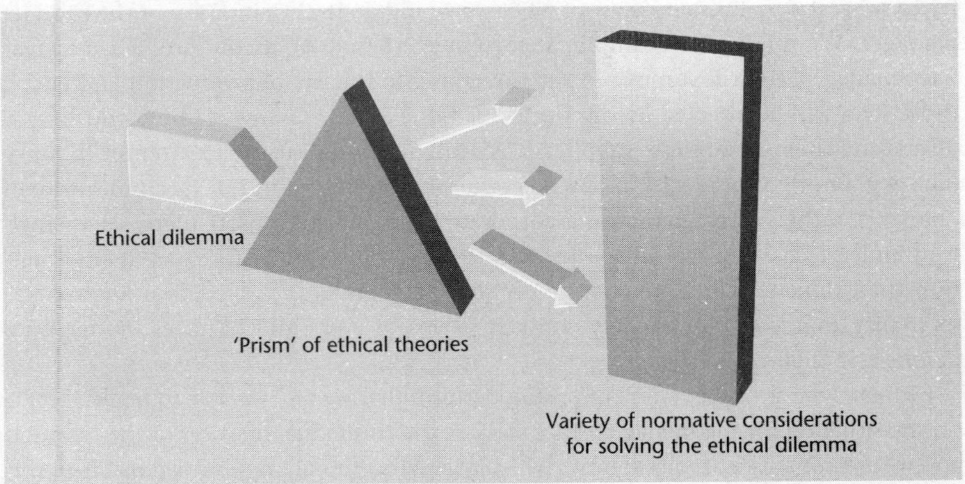

Figure 3.7. A pluralistic perspective on the value of ethical theories for solving ethical dilemmas in business

approach, where ethical theory is seen as a kind of 'lens' through which to focus ethical decision-making on a specific consideration, such as rights, duties, discourse, or whatever.

We would rather suggest that all of the theoretical approaches we have discussed throw light from different angles on one and the same problem and thus work in a complementary rather than a mutually excluding fashion. **Figure 3.7** elucidates this role of ethical theories: by viewing an ethical problem through the 'prism' of ethical theories, we are provided with a variety of considerations pertinent to the moral assessment of the matter at hand. Based on this 'spectrum' of views, the business actor then is able to fully comprehend the problem, its issues and dilemmas, and its possible solutions and justifications.

By using theory in this non-dogmatic way we not only take up the notion of pluralism as discussed earlier, but genuinely confront the issue that real business decisions normally involve multiple actors with a variety of ethical views and convictions that feed into the decision. Ethical theories help to articulate these views and pave the way to an intelligent and considered response to the problem. Furthermore, as we have already discussed in the context of contemporary theories, ethical decision-making does not only rely on rational considerations. Moral matters embrace human beings in the totality of their reason, emotion, bodily existence, social embeddedness, and past experiences, just to name a few. Rather than looking only for universal principles to dogmatically apply to every situation, we suggest a pragmatic approach that allows for all these aspects to play a role in business ethics.

Figure 3.8 provides a summary of the main consideration raised by each theory discussed in this chapter. Although we would draw back from advocating something akin to a 'ten-point plan' for ethical decision-making, you might want to use this figure

Consideration	Typical question you might ask yourself	Theory
One's own interests.	Is this really in my, or my organization's, best long-term interests? Would it be acceptable and expected for me to think only of the consequences to myself in this situation?	Egoism.
Social consequences.	If I consider all of the possible consequences of my actions, for everyone who is affected, will we be better or worse off overall? How likely are these consequences and how significant are they?	Utilitarianism.
Duties to others.	Who do I have obligations to in this situation? What would happen if everybody acted in the same way as me? Am I treating people only to get what I want for myself (or my organization) or am I thinking also of what they might want too?	Ethics of duty.
Entitlements of others.	Whose rights do I need to consider here? Am I respecting fundamental human rights and people's need for dignity?	Ethics of rights.
Fairness.	Am I treating everyone fairly here? Have processes been set up to allow everyone an equal chance? Are there major disparities between the 'winners' and 'losers' that could be avoided?	Theories of justice.
Moral character.	Am I acting with integrity here? What would a decent, honest person do in the same situation?	Virtue ethics
Care for others and relationships.	How do (or would) the other affected parties feel in this situation? Can I avoid doing harm to others? Which solution is most likely to preserve healthy and harmonious relationships among those involved?	Feminist ethics.
Process of resolving conflicts.	What norms can we work out together to provide a mutually acceptable solution to this problem? How can we achieve a peaceful settlement of this conflict that avoids 'railroading' by the most powerful player?	Discourse ethics.
Moral impulse and emotions.	Am I just simply going along with the usual practice here, or slavishly following the organization's code, without questioning whether it really feels right to me? How can I get closer to those likely to be affected by my decision? What do my emotions or gut feelings tell me once I'm out of the office?	Postmodern ethics.

Figure 3.8. Considerations in making ethical decisions: summary of key insights from ethical theories

as a checklist of potential ways of addressing business ethics problems and dilemmas. The movie *It's a Free World*, reviewed in **Ethics on Screen 3**, provides a good example of how ethical decision-making in complex situations and webs of relationships can benefit from multiple perspectives.

In fact, there is actually a school of *ethical pragmatism* that is becoming more and more influential in business ethics thinking, and there is an ongoing debate in the literature

VISIT THE WEBSITE for links to useful sources of further information

VISIT THE WEBSITE to see a trailer for 'It's a Free World . . .'

ETHICS ON SCREEN 3

It's a Free World...

Loach again gives us much to think about.

Nick Clarke, *Socialist Review*

It's a Free World... is another one of British veteran director Ken Loach's typical films focusing on the life and struggles of ordinary workers in today's global economy. The film starts and ends in Eastern Europe and follows (mostly illegal) immigrants to London where they find work in clothing factories and on construction sites. The central character of the film is Angie, a cocky and entrepreneurial single mother, who runs her own recruitment agency from the backroom of a pub. The film, awarded Best Screenplay at the 2007 Venice film festival, is fast paced and quite gripping to watch, not at least due to Kierston Wareing's stunning debut performance as Angie's character.

In her early thirties, the rather likeable and attractive Angie faces the typical pressures of a working-class single mother. However, after being sexually harassed by her former boss, she sets up her own business with her friend Rosie: there is a huge demand for cheap labour from Eastern Europe and she sees a lucrative business opportunity in providing firms with suitable immigrant workers. Alas, there are a few corners to be cut. Many of the workers she uses are in the UK illegally and this makes them exploitable in various ways. Angie works with all sorts of seedy characters at construction sites, including a guy who can get forged passports for her workers.

The film follows Angie down the slippery slope of the illegal work and immigration business and while she is aware of what she is doing, she also rationalizes her business: 'We're giving people a chance'! The grey zone is further extended when Angie and Rosie start having sex with some of those workers who completely depend on them. This said though, the film carefully avoids black and white stereotyping: it also follows Angie's struggle to be a responsible and caring mother to her son. After all, the viewer learns that she is as much a victim of the circumstances as she is responsible for the plight of her workers. One day she gives a lift home to one of her Iranian workers and after seeing the dismal conditions in which he lives with his family, she invites them home for a meal and finds them a better place to stay. The film culminates when one of Angie's clients suddenly disappears without paying her the wages for the workers. While Angie tries to get away with not paying her recruitees, the angry workers follow her home and threaten her and her son's life.

Courtesy Sixteen Films

The film is a nice backdrop for understanding the value of having multiple ethical lenses on an issue. While utilitarian perspectives would probably render Angie's business as an operation that makes everyone involved better off, non-consequential perspectives would help us identify doubts about the correctness of her actions. Trafficking workers, housing them like animals, cheating on their pay, or forging documents are all activities which violate human dignity and human rights. To understand Angie, contemporary perspectives on ethics prove equally helpful. She in fact thinks carefully about her relationships (most notably with her son and her friend Rosie), but she also actively assumes responsibility for the plight of some of her workers.

Ultimately, the film talks directly to the 'moral impulse' of the viewer: exploitation of desperate workers from poor countries is an intricate element of the global economy and many goods and services we enjoy are only possible with the active 'use' of these workers. The film, however, lifts the veil of long supply chains and anonymous market transactions by exposing the real lives of these people—without whom, for instance, the construction industry in most Western countries would be unthinkable today.

Sources

Clarke, N. 2007. It's a free world... *Socialist Review*, September.

Mangan, L. 2007. Last night's TV: It's a free world. *Guardian*, 25 September.

Simon, A. 2007. It's a free world... *Variety*, 1 September, http://www.variety.com.

Solomon, J. 2007. Loach film stirs new controversy. *Guardian*, 2 September, http://www.sixteenfilms.co.uk.

about the necessity for opening up ethical decision-making to embrace not only rational theoretical reasoning, but a variety of individual and situational aspects of human existence (Rosenthal and Buchholz 2000). Without going to the postmodern extreme of denying the relevance of rationality for moral reasoning and locating these decisions mostly in the emotional sphere, there is a growing insight into the necessity of, for instance, combining reason and emotion in business ethics (ten Bos and Willmott 2001). The pragmatic approach we would like to advocate welcomes theoretical approaches in normative business ethics in their variety, while at the same time accepting that they play a role alongside personal, cultural, psychological, cognitive, and context-related factors, all of which ultimately feed into a moral decision in business. Therefore, in the next chapter, we will focus more on these factors that shape how we *actually* make ethical decisions in organizations.

Study questions

1. What are ethical theories and why, if at all, do we need them?
2. Is ethical theory of any practical use to managers? Assess the benefits and drawbacks of ethical theory for managers in a global economy.
3. Define ethical absolutism, ethical relativism, and ethical pluralism. To what extent is each perspective useful for studying and practicing business ethics?
4. What are the two main families of Western modernist ethical theories? Explain the difference between these two approaches to ethical theory.
5. Which ethical theory do you think is most commonly used in business? Provide evidence to support your assertion and give reasons explaining why this theoretical approach is more likely than others to dominate business decisions.

6 Read the following case:

You are the manager of FoodFile, a busy city-centre restaurant catering mainly to local office workers at lunchtimes and an eclectic, fashionable crowd of professionals in the evenings. You are proud of your renowned food and excellent service. Most of your staff have been with you since you opened three years ago—unusual in an industry characterized by casual labour and high turnover. You consider this to be one of the key factors in your consistency and success. Now, your head chef has come to you and told you, in confidence, that she is HIV positive. She is very distressed and you want to reassure her. However, you are troubled about her continuing to work in the kitchens and are concerned about the effect this news could have on the other staff, or even on your customers should they find out about her situation.

(a) Set out the main ethical considerations that are suggested by each of the theories covered in this chapter.

(b) Which theories are most persuasive in dealing with this dilemma?

(c) What would you do in this situation and why?

Research exercise

Select a business ethics problem or dilemma that you have faced or which has arisen in an organization of which you have been part, either as an employee, a student, or a manager.

1 Briefly describe the basic details of the case, and identify and discuss the main business ethics issues involved.
2 Set out the main responses, solutions, or courses of action that *could* have been considered in relation to this problem.
3 Evaluate these options using theory discussed in this chapter.
4 What decision was finally made? To what extent do you believe that this was the best option, and why?

Key readings

VISIT THE WEBSITE for links to further key readings

1 Kaler, J. 1999. What's the good of ethical theory? *Business hics: A u opean Re iew*, 8 (4): 206–13.

This paper questions the value and the function of ethical theories and in so doing is very readable and thought provoking. In combination with a reply by Tom Sorrell in a later issue of the same journal, this debate helps you to understand the potential and the limits of the theories discussed in this chapter (see Sorrell, T. 2000. The good of theory: a reply to Kaler. *Business Ethics: A European Review*, 9 (1), 51–7).

2 Parker, M. 1998. Business ethics and social theory: postmodernizing the ethical. *B i ish Jou nal of Manage en* , 9 (special issue): 27–36.

This article provides you a deeper background for most of the more contemporary theories in business ethics. It is not the easiest read but elucidates some of the more general points we have made in the second half of the chapter.

Case 3

British petroleum and the BTC pipeline: Turkish delight or Russian roulette?

VISIT THE WEBSITE for links to useful sources of further information

This case analyses BP's social responsibility initiatives in the context of one of the largest construction projects in recent history, the Baku-Tblisi-Ceyhan pipeline. It exposes the ethical problems and dilemmas faced by a large Western multinational operating in a host country environment characterized by corruption, poor governance, and potential human rights abuses. It allows us to examine the ethical basis of claims for corporate responsibility and highlights questions regarding the boundaries of responsibility for corporations.

It is not often that a large industrial project features centre stage in a blockbuster movie. But this was exactly what happened to the Baku-Tbilisi-Ceyhan (BTC) pipeline project when the 1999 instalment of James Bond, *The World Is Not Enough*, with Pierce Brosnan and Sophie Marceau, was plotted around a terrorist coup on the massive oil pipeline project in the Caucasus that has strategic importance to the West (and therefore, of course, to the British secret service MI6!).

On its completion in 2006, the €2.61bn BTC pipeline, linking the world's third largest oil reserves in the Caspian Sea near Baku in Azerbaijan to the Turkish port of Ceyhan on the Mediterranean cost, was considered the world's largest private construction project, designed to transport 1m barrels a day over a distance of some 1,100 miles. The strategic importance of the project lies in reducing Western dependency on Middle Eastern oil, while at the same time providing safe access to energy through NATO member Turkey and NATO candidate Georgia, while avoiding exposure to the political instability of post-Soviet Russia. Ultimately, the pipeline is designed also to provide access to oil reserves in Kazakhstan and other central Asian countries.

The BTC project is privately operated by a consortium of 11 large oil MNCs from countries including the US, Japan, France, Norway, and Italy, with British Petroleum (BP) as the leading partner, owning 30.1%. BP is a major player in the Azeri oil fields and sees this area as one of its major strategic business units. The project is also a crucial source of revenue—estimates talk of $150bn over the next 20 years—for the Azerbaijan, Georgian, and Turkish governments through whose territories the pipeline runs. Given the expected economic knock-on effects, the project was dubbed the 'silk road of the 21st century' by the Turkish government.

Pipeline problems

It is perhaps no surprise that a project of such magnitude has raised all sorts of concerns on the part of campaigners and civil society groups. First, such a project has significant environmental impacts through the disruption caused during the building phase. There were concerns about the coating of the pipeline and the risks of leakages, in particular in Georgia, where oil spills might significantly impact the country's strategic water resources in the Bojorni National Park. Concerns were also raised over the fact that the pipeline runs through earthquake zones, with campaigners claiming that this would make leakages nearly inevitable. Secondly, throughout the project, campaigners have highlighted the prospect of up to 30,000 civilians along the pipeline being (at least temporarily) relocated. Furthermore, the high ranking in the Transparency International Corruption Perception

Index (for details, see Chapter 11) of Azerbaijan (ranked 158 in 2008) or Turkey (58 in 2008) gave little hope for a spread of the wealth in a way that would benefit a largely poor rural population. Finally, on the political level, with civil unrest and wars in the region—the pipeline passes within only a few miles of the war-torn area of Nagorno-Karabakh—the project had always been accompanied by considerable fears of terrorist attacks.

BP's introduces its CSR programme

Whilst it clearly has its detractors, BP was considered at the time of the pipeline's construction to be one of the leading companies in embracing sustainability and corporate social responsibility (CSR), certainly in comparison to its oil industry rivals. In had been one of the more prominent corporations involved in initiatives around renewable energy, climate change, human rights, and corruption prevention, among others. In line with these policies, but also in response to the expectation of the investors in the project (such as the European Bank for Reconstruction and Development), BP set up a Regional Sustainability Development Program (RSDP) from the early stages of the project in order to proactively address critical social, ethical, and environmental issues.

The RSDP consists of three parts. The first is an Environmental Investment Program aimed at dealing with ecological issues. The second is a Community Investment Program (CIP), which with a budget of about $20m, mostly addressed social issues during the construction phase. And the third is the more long-term Regional Development Initiative (RDI), which has a similar budget of about $25m, and is designed to accompany the project over a ten-year life span after its opening. Interestingly, only two other companies out of the 11 running the project joined BP in these efforts.

The CIP has been set up in such a way that the delivery of the project is carried out in partnership with NGOs and other organizations, such as universities and private consulting firms in the respective countries. In Azerbaijan and Georgia, this included only international groups, such as the International Rescue Committee (IRC), Save the Children, and Care International, while in Turkey, the CIP was mainly implemented with local Turkish organizations. BP also set up a group of local co-ordinators in the towns and villages affected by the pipeline, and in consultation with local community representatives, implemented a whole range of projects. Most of these focused on improvement of the local infrastructure in building and repairing roads, schools, utilities, and even graveyards, while other projects aimed at local economic development, focusing on agriculture and skill development. In Turkey, for instance, the programme resulted in the first commercial strawberry farm for export. In an attempt to secure transparency and accountability, BP also set up a monitoring and complaints procedure, run by the American billionaire George Soros' Open Society Institution, in co-operation with more than 30 local NGOs.

While many of these projects and initiatives led to fairly immediate impacts, the CIP was also hampered by a number of issues. Collaboration between all these different actors proved difficult, with many local actors competing against each other and communication with local, often illiterate, landowners on the issue of compensation proved difficult. In relying on local actors in the delivery of the CIP, BP was also exposed to an environment threatened by corruption, which in turn led to complaints from locals, in particular in Azerbaijan and Georgia. In Turkey, where the national oil company ran the scheme, miscommunication between the contractors and the local authorities led to complaints about the approach from the donors in implementing the projects. In many communities, the efforts were also hampered by local political divisions and in one case, even a blood feud between the dominant families.

For campaigners such as Friends of the Earth, Amnesty International, and Bankwatch, the BTC project is to some extent evidence that much of BP's talk about CSR and sustainability is little more than 'greenwash'. They, for instance, blamed the company for signing a Host Country Agreement (HGA) with Turkey which 'blatantly disregards the European Convention on Human Rights', as Professor Sheldon Leader, the legal advisor to Amnesty International, put it. They also criticized the company for the alleged torture of human rights activists and critics of the BTC project by local police in Turkey. They also reported cases where landowners had been apparently threatened into accepting inappropriately low compensation settlements.

Many of the issues were made public in the 2006 documentary film *Zdroj (Source)* by Czech filmmakers Martin Mareček and Martin Skalský. The film documents not only the devastating social and environmental consequences of Caspian oil production (where BP is a major player), but also serious human rights abuses through the BTC project. The film features a great number of local residents who claim never to have been compensated for their land, let alone to have been asked for permission to use their property. It also alleges corruption among the Azerbaijan governing elite, which in turn impedes a broader spread of the wealth generated by the oil, and suppresses opposition by civil society groups.

Operations commence, yet ethical challenges persist

Despite these problems, the pipeline went into operation in 2006 and BP has been in charge of running the Azeri and Georgian parts of the pipeline, while the Turkish section is run by the state oil company Botas. However, the external Caspian Development Advisory Panel (CDAP), appointed in 2003 by then CEO of BP, Lord Browne to ensure that BP lived up to its aspirations for the BTC project, warned in its March 2007 report that BP needed to recognize that it faced ongoing challenges in the operations phase. These included such diverse challenges as government and state oil company misuse of revenues accruing directly and indirectly from the pipeline, growing community resentment of a pipeline that passes underfoot, but provides no discernible local benefits, and alleged human rights abuses by the state security organizations charged with pipeline security.

The CDAP recommended a number of specific actions, including:

- Continuing the RDI.
- A centralized coordinating structure for the RDI, which is now organized as a set of different country-based initiatives, and the adoption of sustainable development as a cross-cutting theme for the RDI as a whole (access to energy, enterprise development, and effective governance).
- Appointment by BTC of independent ombudsmen in Azerbaijan and Georgia to hear complaints from individuals who believe their human rights have been abused by state security personnel protecting the pipeline, and engagement of the Turkish authorities to encourage the creation of a comparable institutional vehicle in Turkey.

- The appointment of an independent external body to conduct periodic reviews of BP's performance on the ground in the Caspian region.

BP's response to these recommendations was largely positive, and the company subsequently committed $41m to the RDI for the three years 2006–8 and gained an additional $70m from other sources. BP itself committed an additional $7m for regional projects, and maintained networks of Community Liaison Officers in Azerbaijan and Georgia to engage in capacity-building with local organizations, and to provide direct communications between BTC and the communities through which the pipeline passes.

Efforts to integrate the RDI in all three countries were mostly hampered by the governments of the three countries who preferred to not give up control of these issues to a third party on a transnational level. Despite this, BP engaged in a number of agricultural projects in Turkey, even though they were not running this part of the pipeline. However, with the 2007 resignation of Lord Browne, a noted supporter of CSR and sustainability, doubts were raised about the ongoing momentum behind BP's social initiatives in support of the BTC pipeline. Indeed, since this time, prominent NGOs such as The Corner House in the UK have continued to highlight a number of human rights and environmental concerns during the operation phase of the BTC project.

Beyond these problems in enacting its social responsibility initiatives, ongoing political tensions in the region have also continued to bedevil the BTC project. In August 2008, the pipeline again made headlines when an explosion, allegedly set up by the Kurdistan Workers Party (PKK), ruptured the pipeline, leading to a six-day fire and the spillage of 12,000 barrels of oil. While the route of the pipeline makes a considerable detour around the Kurdish territory, the risk of sabotage through the PKK remains. And then, only two days after this fire, the pipeline again drew attention when Russian planes dropped bombs dangerously close to its route in the South Ossetia conflict between Russia and Georgia. It appeared that despite the efforts of BP to address the social, ethical, and environmental issues around the pipeline, it would continue to be a project as much suited to James Bond as to a CSR manager.

Questions

1 What are the main ethical issues and dilemmas BP faces in this case?

2 How would you evaluate BP's approach to the social, environmental, and economic impacts of the project for local communities? Assess the approach from the perspective of utilitarianism and deontology (ethics of duties) first. Will the assessment differ from a rights- and justice-based perspective?

3 This case raises questions about the scope of responsibility for a Western MNC operating in environments with corruption and poor governance. What is your opinion on how far a company such as BP should go in this case? Can they really be made responsible for the actions of local officials and governments? Try to base your answer on arguments derived from one or more ethical theories.

4 What is the appropriate way for BP to respond to its ongoing criticism? Base your answer on the contemporary ethical theories, in particular virtue ethics, discourse ethics, and postmodern ethics.

Sources

Hildyard, N., Yildiz, K., Paluello, M.M., Kochladze, M., and Rau, N. 2008. Open letter to ECGD: BTC pipeline: resurgence of regional conflicts—concerns over ECGD due diligence and implications for human rights of affected communities. *The Corner House*, 28 August: http://www.thecornerhouse.org.uk.

International Finance Corporation. 2006. The Baku-Tblisi-Ceyhan pipeline project. *Lessons of Experience*, September 2006 (2).

Macalister, T. 2003. Amnesty calls for action on Caspian. *Guardian*, 20 May.

Tran, M. 2005a. Caspian oil pipeline opens. *Guardian*, 25 May.

—— 2005b. Q&A: The Baku-Tbilisi-Ceyhan pipeline. *Guardian*, 26 May.

http://www.automatfilm.cz.

http://www.bp.com.

http://www.bankwatch.org.

http://www.caspsea.com.

We also acknowledge the support provided by Ms Deniz Tura through her MBA Dissertation at Royal Holloway, University of London (based on field research in Azerbaijan and Turkey in Summer 2005 including 65 interviews with project managers of the RSDI and locally based NGO activists) as well as insights from our colleague Eleanor Westney during numerous opportunities to jointly teach this case at the Schulich School of Business.

Notes

1 See http://www.iccr.org.

2 See http://www.business-humanrights.org.

3 Data from the Human Development Report (HDR) (2007), United Nations Development Program, 27 November, p. 25.

4 In some ways, then, postmodern approaches to ethics resonate quite substantially with some Asian ethical frameworks, particularly those such as Buddhism or Taoism. Rather that the monotheistic 'book religions', which in different degrees have entire dogmas of right and wrong built around them, these Eastern philosophies seek to go beyond rationality and instead emphasize qualities such as compassion or spontaneity.

4

Making Decisions in Business Ethics

DESCRIPTIVE ETHICAL THEORIES

In this chapter we will:

- Examine the question of why ethical and unethical decisions get made in the workplace.
- Determine what an ethical decision is.
- Review prominent ethical decision-making models and delineate key elements in terms of individual and situational influences on ethical decision-making.
- Discuss the importance of differences between individuals in shaping ethical decision-making, comparing demographic, cultural, experiential, cognitive, and imaginative aspects.
- Critically evaluate the importance of situational influences on ethical decision-making, delineating between issue-based and context-based factors.
- Identify points of leverage for managing and improving ethical decision-making in business, and posit the concept of ethical culture as a prominent focus for such discussions.

Introduction

When BP, one of the world's largest corporations, announced in 2008 that it had sacked nearly 1,500 people during the previous year for 'non-compliance or unethical behaviour'—a more than 500% increase in four years—the company made it clear that driving out corruption across its global businesses was no easy matter. As Lord Browne, the former chief executive, had said a few years earlier when the number of dismissals was but 250 a year, 'human ingenuity will always find something to get up to. It is our job to track it down'.[1]

But is unethical behaviour simply a matter of individual human ingenuity to do wrong, or can we also put such problems down to other factors? Perhaps corruption is as much due to the culture of certain countries as it is to personal characteristics. And the escalating incidence of ethical misconduct uncovered by BP could be more attributable to institutionalized norms of behaviour in the company than any individual wrongdoing.

This chapter looks at the issue of ethical decision-making in organizations to begin to answer some of these questions about the causes of misbehaviour. In so doing, we will seek to provide the tools to explain why some businesspeople make what appear to be the right ethical choices, whilst others do things that are unscrupulous or even illegal. We will also address the question of whether people who make these unethical decisions are inherently bad, or whether there are other reasons that can explain the incidence of ethics problems in business. The chapter provides a way of addressing these questions by examining what are called *descriptive* ethical theories.

Descriptive business ethics theories seek to describe how ethical decisions are actually made in business, and what influences the process and outcomes of those decisions.

Descriptive ethical theories provide an important addition to the *normative* theories covered in the previous chapter: rather than telling us what businesspeople *should* do (which is the intention of normative theory), descriptive theories seek to tell us what business people *actually* do—and more importantly, they will help to explain *why* they do it.

Understanding the reasons why people make certain decisions is clearly important from a business ethics perspective, not least because it helps us to comprehend the factors that lead to ethical and unethical decisions. From a practical point of view, though, this is also useful for attempts to manage and improve business ethics. Obviously, we first need to know what shapes ethical decision-making before we can try and influence it. Therefore, descriptive theories can be said to provide a practical understanding of how the ethical theories covered in the previous chapter can be applied, as well as assisting in identifying points of leverage for managing business ethics, as will be discussed in the next chapter.

We begin by looking at what exactly an ethical decision is and then go on to examine the various models that have been put forward to explain the process of ethical decision-making in the workplace. This shows us that although ethical decision-making is very complex, extensive research over the years from psychologists, sociologists, management scholars, and others has provided us with a relatively clear picture of the important stages and influences that are central to understanding the ethical decision-making process. We proceed to summarize and evaluate current knowledge about these stages and influences, covering issues of the cognitive and emotional processes individuals go through in making ethical evaluations, as well as the situational influences that shape the decisions and actions they actually come to make.

■ What is an ethical decision?

On the face of it, this is a very simple question. After all, we have already said in Chapter 1 that ethical decisions are concerned with a judgement about right and wrong. But as Morris (2004) suggests, by using the language of right and wrong, we have already identified that a situation is moral in nature. So, there is an important process of identification that goes *before* this, whereby we examine situations and determine whether they are characterized by such considerations in the first place. Imagine, for example, a situation where you are downloading a copy of Kanye West's latest album from your friend. Are you faced with a moral dilemma? Is this an ethical decision? Perhaps, for you, this is simply a normal practice that has no apparent moral dimensions. But Mercury Records, West's label, may take a very different perspective. They may argue that there is a very important moral dimension to this decision, since you are not only breaking the law, but are 'stealing' intellectual copyright for free and depriving the company and the artist of their rightful return on their investment. So how do we objectively decide whether a situation should be assigned moral status in the first place?

There are a number of factors we might identify here, the most important of which are these:

- **The decision is likely to have significant effects on others.** As we saw in the last chapter, two of the most critical aspects of morality are that it is concerned with harms and benefits, and that it is about considerations of social good, i.e. considerations of others beyond the self. Even egoism is concerned with others in that one is expected to act in one's own self-interest because that is for the *good of society*. Copying an album does have material affects on others, namely the record label, the musicians, and other organizations that have contributed their time and effort to its production.
- **The decision is likely to be characterized by choice, in that alternative courses of action are open.** A moral decision requires that we have a choice. For argument's sake, if you accidently copied the Kanye West album without realizing it, then you could not be said to have had much of a choice in the matter. In the normal course of affairs, however, you have the option to copy it or not copy it. When decision-makers actually recognize that they have ethical choices, then they face an *ethical dilemma*.

- **The decision is perceived as ethically relevant by one or more parties.** Regardless of whether the decision-maker sees a decision as having ethical content, if others do, then the decision immediately incurs some degree of ethicality. When a bank provides a loan for a new dam project, this might seem like an ethically neutral act, but campaigners against the dam who are concerned about its impacts on local people and the environment might regard it as highly ethically significant. Similarly, just because someone copies albums all the time without ever considering it to be an ethical decision, this does not mean that they are engaging in an ethically neutral act.

Now that we have identified the basic characteristics of an ethical decision, let us look at how we can model the decision process that we go through in responding to the decision.

■ Models of ethical decision-making

If we think about times when we have been confronted with an ethical dilemma, we might well now be able to recognize what kind of normative principles we were employing—perhaps we were mainly concerned with possible consequences, or maybe we were thinking mainly about rights or relationships. However, we are probably less likely to know why we in fact thought about it in this way, or why we even saw it as an ethical issue in the first place. This, however, is the purpose of descriptive models of ethical decision-making. Various such models have been presented in the literature, and by far the most widely cited ones have been derived from the work of psychologists.

Many of the models most influential in business ethics have appeared in the mainstream management literature, and include those by Linda Treviño (1986) and Thomas Jones (1991). Important contributions have also been made in the marketing literature (which in itself is strongly influenced by psychology), such as the models by Hunt and Vitell (1986) and by O.C. Ferrell and colleagues (Ferrell and Gresham 1985; Ferrell, Gresham, and Fraedrich 1989). These models are not necessarily competing models, since they draw extensively upon one another and are often presented as 'extensions' to, or a 'synthesis' of, earlier models.

In general, all of these models primarily seek to represent two things:

- The different stages in decision-making people go through in responding to an ethics problem in a business context;
- The different influences on that process.

We shall briefly look at each of these two aspects in turn and link them together to form a framework for understanding ethical decision-making in business.

Stages in ethical decision-making

In a review of research on ethical decision-making in business, Loe, Ferrell, and Mansfield (2000: 186) suggest that the Jones (1991) model 'provides the most comprehensive synthesis model of ethical decision-making'. Jones bases his model on a four-stage process of ethical decision-making introduced by James Rest (1986). According to this model, individuals move through a process whereby they:

(i) Recognize a moral issue.
(ii) Make some kind of moral judgement about that issue.
(iii) Establish an intention to act upon that judgement.
(iv) Act according to their intentions.

This is shown in **Figure 4.1.** As Jones (1991) suggests, these stages are intended to be conceptually distinct, such that although one might reach one stage in the model, this does not mean that one will necessarily move onto the next stage. Hence, the model distinguishes between *knowing* what the right thing to do is and actually *doing* something about it; or between *wanting* to do the right thing, and actually *knowing* what the best course of action is. So, for example, even though a salesperson might know that lying to customers is wrong (a moral judgement), for one reason or another—such as needing to meet aggressive sales targets—they might not actually always tell the truth (a moral behaviour). Similarly, although a purchasing manager may realize that receiving personal gifts from suppliers is ethically questionable (a moral recognition), they may defer making a judgement about the problem (a moral judgement) until someone actually questions them about it.

Relationship with normative theory

The role of normative theory (which is the type of theory we discussed in the previous chapter) in these stages of ethical decision-making is primarily in relation to *moral judgement.* Moral judgements can be made according to considerations of rights, duty, consequences, etc. Whilst there has been very little research actually examining the types of normative theories used by managers and employees, there is some evidence to suggest that commercial managers continue to rely primarily on consequentialist thinking (Premeaux and Mondy 1993). This is perhaps not surprising given that, as we saw in Chapter 3, much economic and business theory is itself largely predicated upon consequentialism (Desmond and Crane 2003).

An interesting example of this type of consequentialist reasoning is given by Joel Bakan (2004: 61–5) in his book, *The Corporation.* He describes the decision-making process at General Motors in the face of a design problem with its Chevrolet Malibu

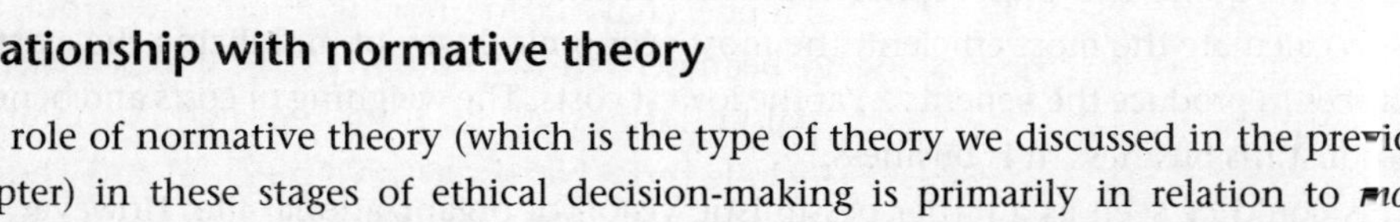

Figure 4.1. Ethical decision-making process

Source: Derived from Rost (1986), as cited in Jones, T. M. 1991. Ethical decision making by individuals in organizations: an issue-contingent model, *Academy of Management Review*, 16: 366–95. Reproduced with permission from the Academy of Management, conveyed through Copyright Clearance Center, Inc.

model. The company decided to reposition the fuel tank on the car, despite knowing that this would increase the possibility of passengers being harmed in fuel-fed fires if the car was involved in a rear collision. A 1970s report produced by a GM engineer had simply multiplied the 500 fatalities that such collisions caused each year by $200,000—an estimate of the cost to GM in legal damages for each potential fatality at the time. Then, by dividing that figure by the number of GM vehicles on the road (41m) the engineer concluded that each fatality cost GM $2.40 per car. In his report, the calculation appeared like this:

$$\frac{500 \text{ fatalities} \times \$200{,}000/\text{fatality}}{41{,}000{,}000 \text{ automobiles}} = \$2.40/\text{automobile}$$

Given that the cost to GM of preventing such fires was estimated to be $8.59 per car, the company reckoned it could save $6.19 ($8.59–$2.40) per car if it allowed people to die rather than changing the design—and so went ahead with the dangerous design anyway.

This type of cost-benefit analysis is extremely prevalent in organizational decision-making. Indeed, a subsequent court case against GM in the 1990s by Malibu fire victims received a crucial deposition from the US Chamber of Commerce that held up this type of cost-benefit analysis as a 'hallmark of corporate good behaviour'. Bakan (2004: 64) goes on to quote the philosopher Alasdair MacIntyre who argues that the executive 'has to calculate the most efficient, the most economical way of mobilizing the existing resources to produce the benefits . . . at the lowest costs. The weighing of costs and benefits is not just his business, it is business.'

This could be seen as a rather pessimistic vision of organizational life. However, the issue of *whether* and *how* normative theory is used by an individual decision-maker depends on a range of different factors that influence the decision-making process, as we shall now see.

? THINK THEORY

Think about the prevalence of consequentialist approaches to decision-making, such as cost-benefit analysis, in organizations that you've worked in. Is such reasoning as inevitable as Bakan and MacIntyre suggest or is it possible to invoke ethics of rights, duties, or justice, for example? Does it make any difference what type of organization you are considering—large or small, public or private, for-profit or not-for-profit?

VISIT THE WEBSITE for a short response to this feature

Influences on ethical decision-making

Models of ethical decision-making generally divide the factors which influence decisions into two broad categories: individual and situational (Ford and Richardson 1994).

- **Individual factors.** These are the unique characteristics of the individual actually making the relevant decision. These include factors that are given by birth (such as age and gender) and those acquired by experience and socialization (such as education, personality, and attitudes).

- **Situational factors.** These are the particular features of the context that influence whether the individual will make an ethical or an unethical decision. These include factors associated with the work context (such as reward systems, job roles, and organizational culture) and those associated with the issue itself (such as the intensity of the moral issue or the ethical framing of the issue).

Many versions of the ethical decision-making models attempt to link certain influences to certain stages in the decision process. However, in categorizing the factors into our two broad categories, we feel that this is neither feasible, nor particularly necessary. Attempts to isolate influences to one stage or another are often very reductive, whereas taken broadly, the two groups of factors actually help to explain why certain business decisions get made, and why people behave in ethical and unethical ways in business situations. From our point of view, it matters less at which stage in someone's decision process an influence occurs (after all, sometimes a person can go through the process in a matter of seconds!), and more whether it occurs at all, and what can be done about it. **Ethical Dilemma 4** provides a specific scenario where we might explore the impact of different influences on our decision-making.

For our purposes then, it is sufficient to present individual and situational factors as general influences on the ethical decision-making framework. This gives rise to the framework in **Figure 4.2**, which is the one that we shall use to structure our discussion in this chapter. During the rest of this chapter, we shall examine the two sets of factors in much more detail, with the intention of providing the basis for assessing their relative importance to ethical decision-making. Before we do, however, it is worth offering a brief word of warning about using a model such as this to structure our discussions.

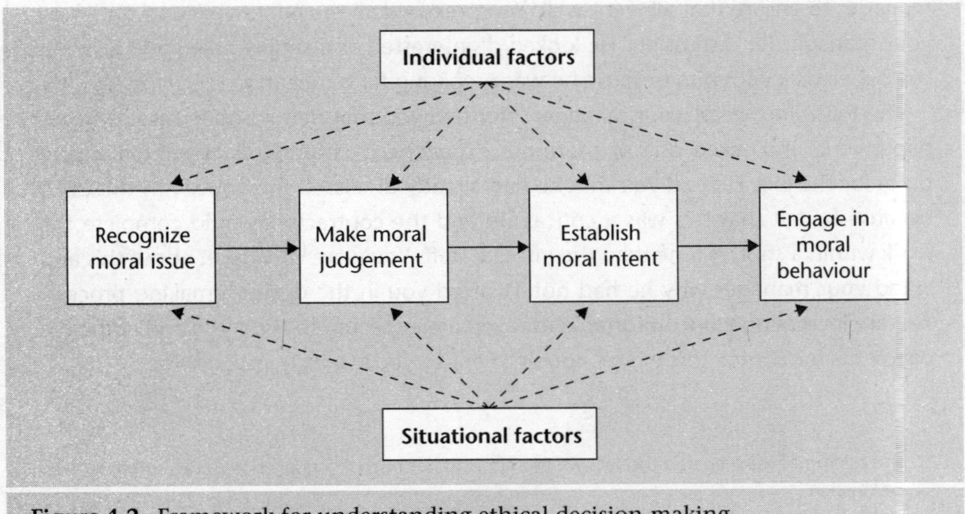

Figure 4.2. Framework for understanding ethical decision-making

AN ETHICAL DILEMMA 4

Stuck in the middle?*

You have recently been appointed to the position of civil engineer in a small town in a developing country. You are responsible for the maintenance of the town's infrastructure, such as public buildings and roads. You are one of the youngest members of the senior management team and report directly to the Director of Public Works. All the members of the management team have been working for the organization for a very long time, and you feel like something of an outsider. The Director of Public Works, the Human Resources Director, and the CEO often have lunch together, and it is generally felt that most important organizational decisions are taken over lunch.

Your position had been vacant for a long time prior to your appointment and the Director of Public Works had assumed responsibility for a number of your current responsibilities. On your appointment, your manager asked you to bounce off any major decisions with him before implementing them. He also retained the authority to approve major works.

After some time, you realized that despite having a full staff complement, a number of outside contractors were doing various jobs within the organization. When you queried this, the Director simply put it down to 'rusty skills', 'a significant backlog', and 'quality of work'. However, you have been impressed with the quality of work that your staff had produced on odd maintenance jobs that you have assigned. Recently, when you were complimenting one of your supervisors on the way he handled an emergency, he expressed his frustration at being given the 'boring, odd jobs' instead of the 'challenging' projects given to contractors.

You decided to utilize your own staff rather than contractors for the next project because you felt that you would be able to supervise the work better and ensure the right quality. You planned it meticulously and wanted to enlist the support of your manager to ensure that all went well. You prepared all the paperwork and took it to your manager for discussion. He looked disinterested and simply asked you to leave the paperwork with him because he was preparing for a meeting.

The following week, your manager informed you that he had gone through your paperwork, and asked one of the more experienced contractors to submit a proposal for the job. He told you that he had already discussed this issue with the CEO, because he felt that this was a critical job and the contractors would complete the work within a shorter time than the internal staff. You were very upset about this and asked your manager why he had not involved you in the decision-making process. You are increasingly uncomfortable that you are expected to supervise and authorize payments for contractors whose appointment to you seems questionable.

* This dilemma was prepared by Nelisiwe Dlamini and has been reproduced with the author's permission.

Questions

1 What is the right thing to do in this situation from an ethical point of view? What ethical theory supports your position?

2 If you were the civil engineer, what would you actually do? Is your response to this question different to your response to question 1? If so, why?

3 What are the factors that influenced your decision/action?

4 Do you think that everybody that reads this dilemma will make similar decisions? Why?

Limitations of ethical decision-making models

As we have said, the model depicted in Figure 4.2 is very useful for structuring our discussion and for seeing clearly the different elements that come into play within ethical decision-making. However, such an approach is not without its problems, and as we go through the chapter, you might notice that it is not always particularly straightforward (nor some would argue, sensible) to break down these various elements into discrete units. Many of the various stages and influences are, to differing degrees, related, perhaps even interdependent. It can thus seem quite optimistic at times to separate out an individual factor and attempt to identify its unique role in the process of ethical decision-making. Nonetheless, these are criticisms that can be levelled at *all* models of this type, and we feel that as long as one is aware that the model is intended not as a definitive representation of ethical decision-making, but as a relatively simple way to represent a complex process, such problems are not too serious. Finally, it is also worth mentioning that ethical decision-making models have largely originated in the US, and this can sometimes give a national or cultural bias to the types of issues and considerations that might be included. Let us just briefly then review the different international perspectives before continuing.

International perspectives on ethical decision-making

In Chapter 1, we discussed some of the global differences in business ethics (especially those between Europe, North America, and Asia), and we will again meet some of these in this chapter about ethical decision-making. As we mentioned in Chapter 1, in the US and Asia the central focus of the business ethics subject tends to be individual actors and their behaviour, whereas in Europe there is more interest in the design of economic institutions and how they function in a morally desirable way and/or encourage moral behaviour of business actors. This difference in perspective becomes quite visible with the topic of ethical decision-making since we could argue that research on *individual factors* influencing ethical decision-making has a strong North American bias, whilst *situational factors*, on the other hand, have been subject to a lengthy debate principally originated by European authors. The significance of this difference is that a focus on individual factors is consistent with the North American focus on choice *within* constraints, whilst a focus on situational factors reflects the more European concern with the *constraints* themselves.

To begin with, the very founders of modern organizational theory in Europe have stressed the influence of *social contexts* on ethical decision-making. For example, in the nineteenth century, the French sociologist Emile Durkheim (1993) discussed the emergence of, and necessity for, new work-related moral communities due to the effects of the industrial revolution on the erosion of traditional value systems that held societies together (Thompson and McHugh 2002). Similarly, the German sociologist Max Weber, to name another prominent example from the early twentieth century, shed a critical light on the ethical basis and influence of bureaucratic organizations (du Gay 2000). He distinguished between actions that were guided by an 'ethics of ultimate ends' and an 'ethics of responsibility'.[2] Whilst the first would represent an idealistic view of man, reflecting a person's real moral convictions rooted in social good, the latter is an ethics that sees responsibility for the pursuit of the organization's goals as the ultimate moral imperative (Parkin 1982).

We will discuss the influence of bureaucratic organizations on individual actors in more detail later in the chapter. However, along these lines, the Polish sociologist Zigmunt Bauman (1991) has more recently argued that there is not only an *influence* of bureaucratic organization on the morality of actors, but he regards the two as *mutually exclusive*. We have already come across Bauman in Chapter 2 as one of the key thinkers in postmodern ethics. As such, he contends that organizational dynamics act to neutralize the 'moral impulse' of the individual. Rational organizations require loyalty, discipline, and obedience, all of which, Bauman contends, stifle the personal and emotional aspects that are crucial for a sense of morality to exist (ten Bos and Willmott 2001). In contrast, US-based researchers have tended to focus more on the importance of individual agency in ethical decision-making. Although, as we shall see later in the chapter, important contributions to our understanding of the institutional basis of ethical decision-making have been made by American social psychologists such as Philip Zimbardo, business ethics researchers from the region have tended to focus on individual-level differences. Asian business ethics researchers, meanwhile, have also tended to replicate this approach by concentrating mainly on studies of managers and the cultural values that drive their ethical perception and choices (e.g. Christie et al. 2003; Nyaw and Ng 1994). We will explore some of these different influences on ethical decision-making later on in this chapter. We will start, though, with an examination of key individual influences.

■ Individual influences on ethical decision-making

What is it about you or your classmates that causes you to act in particular ways when confronted by ethical problems? Individual influences on ethical decision-making relate to these facets of the individual who is actually going through the decision-making process. Clearly all employees bring certain traits and characteristics with them into an organization, and these are likely to influence the way in which the employee thinks and behaves in response to ethical dilemmas. For example, evidence suggests that entrepreneurs and small business owners may think and act differently than others in response to ethical issues because they tend to be more achievement-oriented, autonomous, opportunistic, and risk-tolerant (Solymossy and Masters 2002). Although this could be taken to suggest that some people, such as small business owners, are simply more ethical than others, this is rather too simplistic a view. Individual factors can more readily account for why some people are perhaps more swayed than others into unethical conduct because of the influence of their colleagues. Similarly, individual factors can help explain why some people perceive particular actions to be unethical whilst others do not. Hence, the issue is not so much about determining the reasons why people might be more or less ethical, but about the factors influencing us to think, feel, act, and perceive in certain ways that are relevant to ethical decision-making. Over the years, researchers have surfaced a number of important individual influences, as we shall now see. The factors and their likely influence on ethical decision-making are summarized in **Figure 4.3.**

Age and gender

A good place to start in examining the individual influences on ethical decision-making is to consider some basic demographic factors, such as age and gender. For example, one common question is whether men or women are more ethical. This is no doubt an interesting question, and according to O'Fallon and Butterfield (2005), gender has been

Factor	Influence on ethical decision-making
Age and gender.	Very mixed evidence leading to unclear associations with ethical decision-making.
National and cultural characteristics.	Appear to have a significant effect on ethical beliefs, as well as views of what is deemed an acceptable approach to certain business issues
Education and employment.	Somewhat unclear, although some clear differences in ethical decision-making between those with different educational and professional experience seem to be present.
Psychological factors:	
Cognitive moral development.	Small but significant effect on ethical decision-making.
Locus of control.	At most a limited effect on decision-making, but can be important in predicting the apportioning of blame/approbation.
Personal values.	Significant influence—some empirical evidence citing positive relationship.
Personal integrity.	Significant influence likely, but lack of inclusion in models and empirical tests.
Moral imagination.	A new issue for inclusion with considerable explanatory potential.

Figure 4.3. Individual influences on ethical decision-making

the individual influence on ethical decision-making in business most often subjected to investigation. However, overall the results have been less than conclusive, with different studies offering contradictory results, and often no differences found at all (Loe et al. 2000; O'Fallon and Butterfield 2005). For example, half of the studies reported by Ford and Richardson (1994) conclude that women are more ethical than men, whilst half suggest no difference.

Perhaps, though, the problem is more with the studies themselves and the questions they seek to answer (Loe et al. 2000). As we have said, it is rather simplistic to assume that some people are just more ethical than others, and even if this could be claimed, there seems no obvious reason why gender would be an important determinant. However, as we saw when discussing feminist ethics in the previous chapter (which we shall return to shortly below), there is evidence to suggest that the way in which men and women think and act in response to ethical dilemmas might differ.

Another basic factor we might look at is whether age makes any difference to ethical decision-making. However, a similar problem is present with age as with gender. Empirical tests have tended to report very mixed results, with no clear picture emerging on the influence of age on ethical beliefs and action. Indeed, again it would seem to be too generalized to categorize certain age groups as 'more ethical' than others, although certain *experiences* might in themselves shape the way in which we recognize and respond to ethical problems.

National and cultural characteristics

Another basic demographic characteristic is nationality. When we meet people from different countries and cultures, either at home or overseas, it doesn't take long before we start to see certain differences in what they perceive as ethical or unethical, or how they might go about dealing with ethical issues. Issues of nationality, ethnicity, and religion have therefore been of increasing interest to researchers of ethical decision-making, as one might expect, given the trends towards globalization identified in Chapter 1.

As we argued previously, people from different cultural backgrounds are still likely to have different beliefs about right and wrong, different values, etc., and this will inevitably lead to variations in ethical decision-making across nations, religions, and cultures. There is again a problem here with assuming that people from particular nations, religions, or ethnic groups can simply be deemed to be 'more ethical' or 'less ethical' in their decision-making than others. Research has, however, suggested that nationality can have a significant effect on ethical beliefs, as well as views of what is deemed an acceptable approach to certain business issues.[3] These differences have been noted not just in the somewhat obvious cases of managers from developed and from less developed countries, but also between those from different countries within Europe, those from Europe and the US, or even between those from different ethnic groups in the same country.

Geert Hofstede's (1980, 1994) research has been extremely influential in shaping our understanding of these differences. Based primarily on surveys completed by IBM employees throughout the world, Hofstede suggests that differences in cultural knowledge and beliefs across countries—our 'mental programming'—can be explained in terms of five dimensions:

- **Individualism/collectivism.** This represents the degree to which one is autonomous and driven primarily to act for the benefit of one's self, contrasted with a more social orientation that emphasizes group working and community goals.
- **Power distance.** This represents the extent to which the unequal distribution of hierarchical power and status is accepted and respected.
- **Uncertainty avoidance.** This measures the extent of one's preference for certainty, rules, and absolute truths.
- **Masculinity/femininity.** The extent to which an emphasis is placed on valuing money and things (masculinity) versus valuing people and relationships (femininity).
- **Long-term/short-term orientation.** This addresses differences in attention to future rewards, where long-term-oriented cultures value perseverance and thrift, while short-term ones emphasize more preservation of 'face', short-term results, and fulfilment of social obligations.

Hofstede's dimensions can be seen to explain certain differences in ethical decision-making. For example, someone from an individualist culture, such as are found in northern Europe and America, might be more likely to reflect on ethical problems alone in order to make their own independent decision, whilst someone from a collectivist culture, such as are found in southern Europe and Latin America, might be more likely to consult with the wider group. Similarly, a high power distance culture (i.e. one that respects and accepts stratification in power and status) like Japan or China might be less willing to question the orders given by their superiors, even if they felt they were being asked to do something ethically questionable. Empirical work has generally tended to support these sorts of relationships (e.g. Vitell et al. 1993; Jackson 2001; Christie et al. 2003), although Hofstede's framework remains open to criticism (Baskerville-Morley 2005).

Clearly though, with the eroding of the territorial basis for business activities—exemplified by rising international trade, frequent international business travel, and growth in expatriate employment—the robustness and consistency of beliefs and values inherited simply from our cultural origin is likely to be increasingly weakened. For example, a Greek IT consultant with an MBA from Manchester University and five years' experience working for an American bank in Frankfurt might be expected to differ significantly from a Greek IT manager who has always lived and worked in Athens. This suggests that education and employment might also play a significant role in shaping our ethical beliefs and values.

? THINK THEORY

Think about Hofstede's 'mental programming' theory of culture in terms of its relevance for ethical decision-making. In the text, we have explained how the dimensions individualism/collectivism and power distance might influence decision-making. What are the likely influences of masculinity/femininity, uncertainty avoidance, and long-term orientation? Is this a helpful way of exploring the cultural influences on ethical decision-making?

VISIT THE WEBSITE for a short response to this feature

Education and employment

The type and quality of education received by individuals, as well as their professional training and experience, might also be considered to be important individual influences on ethical decision-making. For example, research reveals that business students not only rank lower in moral development than students in other subjects such as law, but are also more likely to engage in academic cheating, such as plagiarism (McCabe et al. 1991; McCabe and Treviño 1993)! Business students have also been found to be driven more by self-centred values than other students (McCabe et al. 1991). Similarly, individual values may shift as a result of exposure to particular working environments. During the financial crisis of the late 2000s, figures as diverse as US President Barack Obama, the Archbishop of Canterbury, Rowan Williams, and Rajan Zed, the President of the Universal Society of Hinduism, criticized the 'culture of greed' that many commentators suggested had allegedly 'poisoned' those working in the banking and finance industry.[4]

Clearly, business training devoid of ethics can reinforce the 'myth of amoral business' (De George 1999)—the idea that business is not expected to be concerned with questions of morality. Hence, although some aspects of individual morality may be developed through upbringing and general education, there is also a place for ethics training in enhancing people's ability to recognize and deal with ethics problems in the workplace (Treviño and Nelson 2007). Overall then, whilst the relationships between ethical decision-making and employment experience and education still remain somewhat unclear (Loe et al. 2000), some definite differences between those with different educational and professional experience seem to be present. Our hope is certainly that by studying business ethics in the critical and pluralistic fashion we advocate here, you might expand and refine your analytical skills in dealing with ethical issues and problems.

Psychological factors

Psychological factors are concerned with cognitive processes, in other words, how people actually think. From an ethical decision-making point of view, knowing about the differences in the cognitive processes of individuals can clearly help us to improve our understanding of how people decide what is the morally right or wrong course of action. We shall look at two of the most prominent psychological factors: cognitive moral development and locus of control.

Cognitive moral development

The most common theory to have been utilized to explain these cognitive processes comes from the psychology discipline, namely Lawrence Kohlberg's (1969) theory of cognitive moral development (CMD). In fact, virtually all models of ethical decision-making in business tend to utilize this theory, at least to some extent (Fraedrich et al. 1994).[5]

Kohlberg developed CMD theory to explain the different reasoning processes that individuals would use to make ethical judgements as they matured through childhood into adulthood. Hence:

Cognitive moral development refers to the different levels of reasoning that an individual can apply to ethical issues and problems.

Kohlberg suggested that three broad levels of moral development could be discerned, namely:

- **Level one.** The individual exhibits a concern with self-interest and external rewards and punishments.
- **Level two.** The individual does what is expected of them by others.
- **Level three.** The individual is developing more autonomous decision-making based on principles of rights and justice rather than external influences.

Kohlberg identified two specific stages within each of the three levels, giving six stages of moral development altogether. **Figure 4.4** sets out these six stages, providing an illustration of how each stage might be manifested in business ethics decisions.

CMD theory proposes that as one advances through the different stages, one is moving to a 'higher' level of moral reasoning. The important thing to remember about CMD theory, however, is that it is not so much *what* is decided that is at issue, but *how* the decision is reached in terms of the individual's reasoning process. Two people at different levels could conceivably make the same decision, but as a result of different ways of thinking. All the same, Kohlberg argued that the higher the stage of moral reasoning, the more 'ethical' the decision.

Empirical research by Kohlberg and others[6] has led to the conclusion that most people tend to think with level II reasoning (hence its 'conventional' tag). Research into the cognitive schema of business managers has also tended to place them at level II (e.g. Weber 1990). This means that most of us decide what is right according to *what we perceive others to believe*, and according to *what is expected of us by others*. As Treviño and Nelson (2007: 129) suggest, '[Most] individuals aren't autonomous decision-makers who strictly follow an internal moral compass. They look up and around to see what their superiors and their peers are doing and saying, and they use these cues as a guide to action.'

As we shall see shortly, this implies that the situational context in which employees might find themselves within their organization is likely to be very influential in shaping their ethical decision-making—although according to Kohlberg, this influence will vary according to whether employees are at stage 3 or 4 in moral development.

Although CMD theory has been very influential in the ethical decision-making literature, there have been numerous criticisms of the theory. It is worth remembering that the theory was initially developed in a non-business context, from interviews with young American males—hardly representative of the vast range of people in business across the globe! Hence, according to Fraedrich et al. (1994), the most notable criticisms of CMD are the following:

- **Gender bias.** Perhaps the most well known of Kohlberg's critics is one of his former students, Carol Gilligan, who claimed that the theory was gender biased due to its emphasis on the abstract principles esteemed by Kohlberg and his male subjects. As

Level	Stage	Explanation	Illustration
I Preconventional.	1 Obedience and punishment.	Individuals define right and wrong according to expected rewards and punishments from authority figures.	Whilst this type of moral reasoning is usually associated with small children, we can also see that business people frequently make unethical decisions because they think their company would either reward it or let it go unpunished (see Gellerman 1986).
	2 Instrumental purpose and exchange.	Individuals are concerned with their own immediate interests and define right according to whether there is fairness in the exchanges or deals they make to achieve those interests.	An employee might cover for the absence of a co-worker so that their own absences might subsequently be covered for in return—a 'you scratch my back, I'll scratch yours' reciprocity (Treviño and Nelson 2007).
II Conventional.	3 Interpersonal accord, conformity and mutual expectations.	Individuals live up to what is expected of them by their immediate peers and those close to them.	An employee might decide that using company resources such as the telephone, the internet and email for personal use whilst at work is acceptable because everyone else in their office does it.
	4 Social accord and system maintenance.	Individuals' consideration of the expectations of others broadens to social accord more generally, rather than just the specific people around them.	A factory manager may decide to provide employee benefits and salaries above the industry minimum in order to ensure that employees receive wages and conditions deemed acceptable by consumers, pressure groups and other social groups.
III Postconventional.	5 Social contract and individual rights.	Individuals go beyond identifying with others' expectations, and assesses right and wrong according to the upholding of basic rights, values and contracts of society.	The public affairs manager of a food manufacturer may decide to reveal which of the firm's products contain genetically modified ingredients out of respect for consumers' rights to know, even though they are not obliged to by law, and have not been pressurized into it by consumers or anyone else.
	6 Universal ethical principles.	Individuals will make decisions autonomously based on self-chosen universal ethical principles, such as justice, equality, and rights, which they believe everyone should follow.	A purchasing manager may decide that it would be wrong to continue to buy products or ingredients that were tested on animals because he believes this doesn't respect animal rights to be free from suffering.

Figure 4.4. Stages of cognitive moral development

Adapted from Ferrell et al. (2002); Kohlberg (1969); Treviño and Nelson (2007) we saw in Chapter 3, Gilligan (1982) argued that women tended to employ an 'ethic of care' in deciding what was morally right, emphasizing empathy, harmony, and the maintenance of interdependent relationships, rather than abstract principles. This work was subsequently influential in shaping *feminist ethics*, an approach to ethical theory that we discussed in the previous chapter.

- **Implicit value judgements.** Derry (1987) and others have expanded Gilligan's criticism to suggest that CMD privileges rights and justice above numerous other bases of morality, such as those discussed in the previous chapter. Kohlberg has thus interjected his own value judgements regarding the 'most ethical' way of reasoning into what is essentially supposed to be a descriptive theory of how people *actually* think.

- **Invariance of stages.** Kohlberg's contention that we sequentially pass through discrete stages of moral development can be criticized if we observe that people either regress in CMD or, more importantly, if they use different moral reasoning strategies at different times and in different situations. Studies by Fraedrich and Ferrell (1992) and Weber (1990), for example, both revealed cognitive inconsistency amongst managers across work and non-work situations when making ethical decisions. Essentially, we do not always use the same reasoning when we are at work as we do at home or on the sports field. This is the reason why in this chapter we highlight the context dependency of business people's reasoning about ethical problems (Jones 1991; Thompson 1995).

Despite these criticisms, CMD appears to be widely accepted as an important element in the individual influences on ethical decision-making. Various empirical studies have suggested that it at least plays some role in the decision-making process (e.g. Treviño and Youngblood 1990; Goolsby and Hunt 1992), although its influence appears to be rather more limited than that proposed by Kohlberg.

Locus of control

The second psychological factor commonly identified as an influence on ethical thinking is *locus of control*.

> **An individual's locus of control determines the extent to which he or she believes that they have control over the events in their life.**

So someone with a high *internal* locus of control believes that the events in their life can be shaped by their own efforts, whereas someone with a high *external* locus of control believes that events tend to be the result of the actions of others, or luck, or fate. You might think of this in terms of how you might respond if you received a grade for your business ethics exam that was lower than you expected. If you had an external locus of control, you might automatically blame your professor for setting a difficult test, or you might blame Crane and Matten's book for not preparing you properly. If you had an internal locus of control, however, your first thoughts would probably be more along the lines of questioning whether you had really done enough preparation for the exam.

In terms of ethical decision-making, Treviño and Nelson (2007) suggest that those with a strong internal locus of control might be expected to be more likely to consider the consequences of their actions for others, and may take more responsibility for their actions. Internals may also be more likely to stick to their own beliefs, and thus be more resistant to peer-group pressure to act in a way that violates those beliefs. However, there hasn't actually been a great deal of empirical research on the effects of locus of control on ethical decision-making in business. What research has been conducted, though, gives a generally mixed picture: whilst some studies have discerned no significant effect (e.g. Singhapakdi and Vitell 1990), others have identified a noticeable influence (e.g. Treviño and Youngblood 1990).

Overall, even among the individual factors, it would appear that locus of control has, at most, only a relatively limited effect on ethical decision-making. Nonetheless, understanding whether your co-workers have internal or external loci of control can be important for predicting how they will respond to business ethics problems, and particularly how they apportion blame or offer approbation when faced with the consequences of those decisions.

Ultimately, factors such as demographics, experience, psychological factors, and other personality factors can only ever tell us so much about ethical decision-making, perhaps because they only have a relatively indirect effect on how we might actually decide in any given situation. A more immediate relationship to decision-making is perhaps provided by our next three individual factors —values, integrity, and moral imagination.

Personal values

Conventionally speaking, personal values might be regarded as 'the moral principles or accepted standards of a person'.[7] This makes sense superficially, but such a view does not capture what is distinctive about values and sets them apart from, say, principles or standards. Sociologists, psychologists, philosophers, and others have therefore invested a great deal of work in defining, identifying, and even measuring the values that we have, giving rise to a diverse and multifaceted literature. Probably the most frequently cited definition from a psychological point of view comes from Milton Rokeach (1973: 5) who stated that:

> **A personal value is an 'enduring belief that a specific mode of conduct or end-state of existence is personally or socially preferable to an opposite or converse mode of conduct or end-state'.**

This means that values are about the behaviours and things that we deem important in life, but crucially, Rokeach identifies that values (i) persist over time (i.e. they are 'enduring'); (ii) that they influence behaviour (i.e. they are concerned with 'conduct' and 'end-states'); and (iii) are concerned with individual and/or collective well-being (i.e. 'personally or socially preferable'). Hence, common values include such examples as self-respect, freedom, equality, responsibility, and honesty.

Personal values have long been argued to be influential in the type of decisions we make in organizations (Agle and Caldwell 1999). This is particularly true of ethical decisions since values are key repositories of what we regard to be good/bad and right/wrong. However, knowing that values are important influences is one thing, but finding out exactly what values people have, and which ones influence which decisions, is fraught with difficulty and represents a tricky conceptual and empirical endeavour (Meglino and Ravlin 1998). After all, researchers such as Rokeach (1973) have suggested that people typically have more than 70 operative values, and even amongst these, some values will be more influential on behaviour than others. Moreover, there is a great deal of disagreement among researchers even over whether values can be relied upon to predict behaviour or whether environmental influences should be given greater emphasis (Meglino and Ravlin 1998).

Whatever the case, values are clearly an important aspect of ethical decision-making, and corporations are increasingly recognizing that they cannot simply ignore their employees' personal values in tackling ethical problems in their business. PIC, the biotechnology multinational whose business 'is the genetic improvement of pigs', puts it this way: 'personal values describe the way we operate as individuals—we expect them to guide the decisions and behaviour of our employees around the world'. The company has identified three personal values—integrity, respect, and innovation—that its employees should possess, stressing that 'we are honest and ethical in all aspects of our business'.[8]

This kind of attention to values has been particularly evident at the level of corporate or **organizational values.** Many companies have attempted to set out what values their organization has or stands for and, as we will see in the next chapter, values statements, and codes of conduct based on core organizational values, have been probably the most common approaches to managing business ethics over the years. Perhaps unsurprisingly, an alignment of personal and organizational values is typically seen as an ideal basis for developing good working relations, and for retaining and motivating staff. However, it is unclear whether such a situation is necessarily better for encouraging ethical decision-making. For example, employees in professions such as education, medicine, pharmacy, accountancy, and journalism might see dangers in aligning their professional ethics with the increasingly market-oriented values of their organizations. As such, employees are often called upon to exercise personal integrity in the face of such ethical challenges.

Personal integrity

Integrity is typically seen as one of the most important characteristics of an ethical person, or, as we saw in the last chapter, of a 'virtuous' decision-maker. As such, it is no surprise that integrity has increasingly surfaced in relation to ethical decision-making. Although there are a variety of meanings applied to integrity, the most common meaning refers to integrity as *consistency* (Brown 2005: 5). Hence, we might define integrity in the following way:

Integrity is defined as an adherence to moral principles or values.

The original meaning of the word is concerned with unity and wholeness, and we can see that an adherence to moral principles essentially means that one maintains a consistency

VISIT THE WEBSITE for links to useful sources of further information

ETHICS ONLINE 4

Ethics pledges

Making career choices can be hard when you want to make a difference. What if a potential employer seems to be offering you a great position but you're not convinced that it shares your values? One way that prospective graduates have been addressing this problem is by making an ethics pledge. Emanating originally from Bentley University in the US, the 'Graduation Pledge of Social and Environmental Responsibility' is perhaps the best known. It is based around a pledge to 'to explore and take into account the social and environmental consequences of any job' that signers might consider, and commits signers 'to try to improve these aspects of any organizations for which [they] work'. Although individuals cannot sign up online, the initiative's website enables potential organizers to learn about how to organize on-campus campaigns, and to download posters, wallet cards (see illustration), and other resources.

More than a hundred schools and colleges are using the pledge, but other initiatives have also emerged, including the 'Shanghai Consensus' pledge organized by the China-Europe International Business School (CEIBS) in Shanghai, and for business leaders, the 'Business Ethics Pledge', which begins 'I pledge allegiance, in my heart and soul, to the concepts of honesty, integrity, and quality in business'. Unlike the other alternatives, the Business Ethics Pledge even allows you to sign electronically and start advertising your business online as a signatory.

As might be expected, such pledges have been particularly popular in North America, and to a lesser extent China and Taiwan, reflecting perhaps the focus in such cultures on individual level agency in business ethics. Those who subscribe to such initiatives clearly believe in the importance of personal integrity and of the power of individuals to make a difference. As the Business Ethics Pledge founder, Shel Horowitz, says, 'This is about changing the world! About creating a climate where businesses are expected to behave ethically, and where executives who try to drag their companies into the unethical swamplands find that nobody's willing to carry out their orders.'

Sources

Anon. 2006. Shanghai consensus: CEIBS students pledge responsible corporate behavior. *China CSR*: http://www.chinacsr.com.

Business Ethics Pledge website: http://www.business-ethics-pledge.org.

Graduation Pledge Alliance website: http://www.graduationpledge.org.

or unity in one's beliefs and actions, regardless of any inducement or temptation to deviate from them. Another way of looking at this is to consider integrity as being a matter of 'walking the talk', i.e. being consistent in word and action (Brown 2005). An interesting example of how some students and businesses have tackled this issue is in signing some kind of integrity pledge, as discussed in **Ethics Online 4**.

Integrity frequently plays a central role in incidents of *whistleblowing*, which refers to acts by employees to expose their employers for perceived ethical violations. If, for instance, an engineer identifies a safety problem with one of her firm's products, she may decide to tell her work colleagues or her boss. As a result, the engineer may be encouraged to ignore the problem or desist from taking any further action as her superiors have taken on responsibility for the issue. However, if the problem persists, even after further warnings from the engineer, she may choose to reveal the problem—or 'blow the whistle'—by approaching an industry regulator, a journalist, or some other outside agency. Although there are clearly various other factors involved, such acts of external whistleblowing often require the employee to maintain their personal integrity, or commitment to a set of principles, despite being confronted with numerous difficulties, obstacles, and opposition. This is especially the case since whistleblowers have often subsequently been faced with a range of negative consequences for their actions. This includes victimization by colleagues or superiors as a result of their 'betrayal'; being passed over for promotion; job loss; even 'blacklisting' to prevent them getting another job in the same field (Rothschild and Miethe 1999).

Some acts of ethical decision-making are therefore strongly influenced by the degree of personal integrity held by the individual. Think, for example, of a situation where all of your work colleagues habitually steal small items of company property from the storeroom. A group can easily see this as 'acceptable' simply because 'everyone does it'. If this was something that you thought was wrong, it might require some degree of integrity—that is, adherence to your moral principles—to register your disapproval with your colleagues, and may need some courage to report it to a superior. Certainly then, the exercising of integrity also often requires some level of protection from possible recrimination. For example, in some countries, regulators have sought to provide legal protection for whistleblowers. In the US, Sarbanes–Oxley regulations require companies listed on US stock exchanges to adopt methods for anonymous reporting of ethical and legal violations to an audit committee of the board of directors. In Europe, companies listed in the US are also covered by this legislation, but overall the picture is somewhat confused, especially since some US companies found that their global whistleblower procedures actually contravened EU data protection law! Whilst in some countries there is an institutional structure which facilitates free disclosure by employees (e.g. 'openness laws' in Sweden, and workers' councils in Germany), others, such as Norway, Romania, and the UK, have specific whistleblower protection laws.

Despite increasing attention to the importance of the issue of integrity (e.g. Solomon 1999), most descriptive models of ethical decision-making have not tended to include it as a factor influencing how we decide in business ethics matters. Whilst it would appear that this might be likely to change as we start to learn more about its role and effects, for the moment, business ethics scholars seem to be largely uncertain as to how and why personal integrity affects the process of ethical decision-making.

Moral imagination

Finally, another individual factor which has been accorded increasing attention in business ethics over the past few years is *moral imagination*. Moral imagination is concerned less with whether one has, or sticks to, a set of moral values, but with whether one has 'a sense of the variety of possibilities and moral consequences of their decisions, the ability to imagine a wide range of possible issues, consequences, and solutions' (Werhane 1998: 76). This means that moral imagination is the creativity with which an individual is able to reflect about an ethical dilemma. Interest in moral imagination has been driven by the recognition that people often bracket their personal moralities and moral considerations whilst at work (Jackall 1988). According to Werhane (1998), higher levels of moral imagination can allow us to see beyond the rules of the game that seem to be operating in the workplace, and beyond the day-to-day supposed 'realities' of organizational life, so as to question prevailing ways of framing and addressing organizational problems. Thus, rather than accepting the usual organizational recipe for looking at, prioritizing, and dealing with things, those with greater moral imagination should be able to envisage a greater set of moral problems, perspectives, and outcomes.

VISIT THE WEBSITE for a short response to this feature

? THINK THEORY

Think about the notion of moral imagination from the perspective of our three different approaches to normative ethical theory: absolutism, relativism, and pluralism. Would you say that moral imagination would be of help or a hindrance to applying ethical theory in each of these approaches?

As with personal integrity, moral imagination has yet to be included in typical models of ethical decision-making, and has been subjected to little, if any, empirical testing. However, it holds significant potential for helping us to uncover why there is variation between individuals in the effect of work context on their ethical decision-making—a vital issue if we are to understand the relative influence of our two sets of factors, individual and situational. Hence, it would seem timely now to consider in more depth the second of our sets of factors, namely those dealing with the situation in which the decision is taking place.

■ Situational influences on decision-making

The proceeding section sought to examine the influence of various differences between individuals on the judgements and decisions they make when faced with ethical problems. However, as we saw, the judgements and decisions that people make in businesses, and perhaps more importantly, the things they actually do, cannot be successfully explained simply in terms of these individual traits. After all, many people appear to have 'multiple ethical selves' (Treviño and Nelson 2007: 180)—that is, they make different decisions in different situations. In fact, most evidence we have points to situational influences being at least equally, and probably *more* important, in shaping our ethical decision-making. **Ethics in Action 4.1** discusses the case of the 'rogue trader', Jérôme Kerviel, who ran up huge losses at the French bank Société Générale through covert trading activities in the financial market—and shows that even here, individual factors are not always the whole story.

There are a number of important factors to consider regarding situational influences. For a start, the decision process we go through will vary greatly according to what type of issue it is that we are dealing with. Some issues will be perceived as relatively unimportant, and will therefore prompt us into fairly limited ethical decision-making, whereas issues seen as more intense may well necessitate deeper, and perhaps somewhat different, moral reflection. For example, if you worked in a bar, you might think rather more deeply about the morality of taking €20 out of the cash register for yourself than you would pouring your friends a couple of unauthorized drinks 'on the house'. These differences in the importance we attach to ethical issues are what we call *issue-related factors*.

At another level, we must also remember that we are, after all, 'social animals'. Hence our beliefs and actions are largely shaped by what we see around us: the group norms, expectations, and roles we are faced with; the nature of the climate in which we work; and the rewards and punishments that we can expect as a consequence of our actions. After all, we have already seen that Kohlberg's theory of cognitive moral development suggests that the majority of us are at a conventional level of morality, which prompts us to seek guidance from those around us. These types of influences are called *context-related factors*.

Accordingly, we can identify two main types of situational influences:

- Issue-related factors.
- Context-related factors.

The principal factors in these two categories, and their likely influence on ethical decision-making, are presented in **Figure 4.5**, and are discussed in more detail in the following sections.

Type of factor	Factor	Influence on ethical decision-making
Issue-related.	Moral intensity.	Reasonably new factor, but evidence suggests significant effect on ethical decision-making.
	Moral framing.	Fairly limited evidence, but existing studies show strong influence on some aspects of the ethical decision-making process, most notably moral awareness.
Context-related.	Rewards.	Strong evidence of relationship between rewards/punishments and ethical behaviour, although other stages in ethical decision-making have been less investigated.
	Authority.	Good general support for a significant influence from immediate superiors and top management on ethical decision-making of subordinates.
	Bureaucracy.	Significant influence on ethical decision-making well documented, but actually exposed to only limited empirical research. Hence, specific consequences for ethical decision-making remain contested.
	Work roles.	Some influence likely, but lack of empirical evidence to date.
	Organizational culture.	Strong overall influence, although implications of relationship between culture and ethical decision-making remain contested.
	National context.	Limited empirical investigation, but some shifts in influence likely.

Figure 4.5. Situational influences on ethical decision-making

VISIT THE WEBSITE for links to useful sources of further information

ETHICS IN ACTION 4.1

Rogue trader, latest edition

When Ladbrokes (a UK chain of betting shops) started taking bets on who would play the role of Jérôme Kerviel in a movie, it marked a dubious honour for France's newest, 'most-wanted man'. Catapulted from obscurity to the front pages of the global media virtually overnight during January 2008, Kerviel was the young city trader whose covert trading at the French bank Société Générale racked up almost 5bn in losses—more than the entire capitalization of the company—and brought the bank to the brink of financial disaster.

Since the legendary rogue trader Nick Leeson, whose hidden trading in Singapore brought down Barings Bank in the 1990s, such cases have happened with a certain regularity. Leeson was eventually jailed, but continued to remain high on the public consciousness with the publication of an autobiography that was subsequently made into a film, *Rogue Trader*, starring Ewan McGregor as Leeson. He is now a football club executive and highly paid public speaker about business ethics!

What was different about the Kerviel case though was not only the magnitude of the losses (at the time, it was the biggest trading fraud ever recorded), but also the fact that Kerviel himself appeared to have made little, if any, direct personal gain from his unauthorized trades. According to his employer, the solitary 'Mr Average' was said to have been suffering from family problems, but Kerviel had no record of criminal behaviour or anything in his history that would have suggested that he would wind up as France's most wanted man. According to his university tutor, he was 'not a student who made an impression on his year, either in a good or bad way ... If he was a genius, then we didn't spot it.' He was a reasonably successful and appreciated employee of the bank, a junior trader whom colleagues described as 'shy', 'an introvert' and 'generally pretty ill at ease'. His combined salary and bonus in 2006, before the off-book trading began in earnest, was a relatively modest €100,000.

His own explanation for the spectacular losses is that he just wanted to show his superiors that he was better than his colleagues. According to the *Wall Street Journal*, 'he yearned to prove that he could match and even exceed better educated and more highly valued colleagues'. In the midst of his rogue trading, he was by some accounts in profit by €1.4bn by Christmas 2007 and had asked for a €600,000 bonus for the year—ten times what he had received in the previous year and a figure far in excess of what a trader at his level would normally receive. He actually received around €300,000.

It is unclear exactly how much the management at Société Générale actually knew about the secret deals. With ever more complex financial products, electronic systems, and multifaceted global markets, it is increasingly challenging for senior bank managers to keep up with the pace of innovation and to design effective oversight and control. However, Société Générale was known to be a leader in the more complex derivatives trading that Kerviel was involved with—and the bank was certainly very aware of the huge profits that Kerviel had started reeling in before his luck turned sour.

Kerviel himself claims that the bank itself was lax in its controls and missed even elementary signs that something was wrong. In his testimony to investigators, he pointed to the fact that he only took four days of holidays in 2007, suggesting that 'it is one of the first rules of internal controls: a trader who doesn't take holidays is a trader who doesn't want his books to be seen by others'. Kerviel appeared to have something of a point when an independent report from February 2008 revealed that Société Générale had missed 75 warning signs of his activities. The report found that although risk control procedures were followed correctly, compliance officers rarely went beyond routine checks and did not inform managers of anomalies, even when large sums were concerned.

Although Société Générale continued to maintain that the trader was acting alone, the bank was fined by France's banking commission for risk control failures and allowing alerts to go unheeded. Two senior managers also resigned in the wake of the scandal—the head of equities and derivatives and the head of trading. As for Kerviel, charges of fraud were dropped, and he was provisionally released on bail after 35 days in prison in March 2008. Further investigation by prosecutors on less serious charges of breach of trust, falsifying documents, and hacking into the bank's computers continued, with a trial eventually set for 2010. And although the terms of his release prevented Kerviel from seeking employment again in anything related to financial markets, he was quickly back in employment after his release—as a trainee at an IT consultancy specializing in computer security!

Sources

Chrisafis, Angelique. 2009. 'It was like playing a video game', says Kerviel. *Guardian*, 22 January: http://www.guardian.co.uk.

—— and Boyer, Emilie. 2008. Solitary 'Mr Average' perpetrated biggest trading fraud ever. *Guardian*, 26 January: http://www.guardian.co.uk.

Clark, Nicola. 2008. Kerviel starts new job at computer consulting firm. *International Herald Tribune*, 25 April: http://www.iht.com.

Gauthier-Villars, David and Mollenkamp, Carrick. 2008. How to lose $7.2 billion: a trader's tale. *Wall Street Journal*, 2 February: http://www.wsj.com.

Seib, Christine. 2008. Societe Generale missed 75 warnings on trader Kerviel, *The Times*, 21 February: http://www.timesonline.co.uk.

? THINK THEORY

Think about the Kerviel case in terms of the individual factors set out in models of ethical decision-making. How important do you think these are for explaining his actions, and which other factors might also be at play here?

VISIT THE WEBSITE for a short response to this feature

Issue-related factors

Although initially absent from many models of ethical decision-making, issue-related factors have been increasingly recognized as important influences on the decisions business people make when faced with ethical problems. At one level, we need to consider the nature of the ethical issue itself, and in particular its degree of *moral intensity*—that is, how important the issue is to the decision-maker. However, it is also evident that, regardless of the intensity of an issue, we need also to consider how that issue is actually represented within the organization, in that some issues will be presented as important ethical issues, whilst others may not. Hence, we need to also consider the issue's *moral framing.* Such issue-related factors have been shown to influence both whether an individual actually recognizes the moral nature of a problem in the first place (i.e. the moral recognition stage) and also the way that people actually think about and act upon the problem (the subsequent stages in the ethical decision-making process).

Moral intensity

The notion of moral intensity was initially proposed by Thomas Jones (1991) as a way of expanding ethical decision-making models to incorporate the idea that the relative importance of the ethical issue would itself have some bearing on the process that decision-makers go through when faced with ethical problems. Jones (1991: 374–8) proposes that the intensity of an issue will vary according to six factors:

- **Magnitude of consequences.** This is the expected sum of the harms (or benefits) for those impacted by the problem or action. Obviously, an issue will be felt more intensely if the consequences are significant, such as health problems or death as a result of a faulty product.
- **Social consensus.** This is the degree to which people are in agreement over the ethics of the problem or action. Moral intensity is likely to increase when it is certain that an act will be deemed unethical by others.
- **Probability of effect.** This refers to the likelihood that the harms (or benefits) are actually going to happen.
- **Temporal immediacy.** This is concerned with the speed with which the consequences are likely to occur. When outcomes are likely to take years to have much effect, decision-makers may perceive the moral intensity to be much lower—for example, in the case of the long-term effects of smoking or other 'unhealthy' products.
- **Proximity.** This factor deals with the feeling of nearness (social, cultural, psychological, or physical) the decision-maker has for those impacted by his or her decision. For example, poor working conditions in factories in one's own country might be experienced as a more intense moral issue than poor conditions in a developing world country.
- **Concentration of effect.** Here we are concerned with the extent to which the consequences of the action are concentrated heavily on a few, or lightly on many. For

example, many people may feel that cheating a person out of a hundred Euros is much more morally intense than cheating the same sum out of a large multinational with millions of shareholders.

Jones' (1991) original formulation of moral intensity is theoretical (based largely on social psychology), but we can see its relevance in real cases of business ethics. For example, the contaminated milk scandal that led to the deaths of six babies in China in 2008 represents a clear case of high moral intensity. There is considerable consensus about the moral unacceptability of deliberately producing toxic milk for infants, especially given the immediacy and magnitude of the consequences in terms of making babies ill. That the effects were on Chinese babies (rather than American children or pets, as in earlier toxic products emanating from China) also means that the cultural and temporal proximity in this incident was high. As such, it was unsurprising that the events were met with widespread protests and heavy sentences for the culprits, although perhaps only in China would such actions warrant a death sentence for two of the accused.[9]

Moral intensity's role in ethical decision-making has also been exposed to empirical testing, providing good support for Jones' original propositions. O'Fallon and Butterfield (2005), for example, reviewed 32 such studies and concluded that there was strong support for the influence of moral intensity on ethical decision-making, especially with respect to magnitude of consequences and social consensus. However, we would suggest that the intensity of an issue is not necessarily an objective, factual variable, but rather depends on how the issue and its intensity are understood and made meaningful within and around organizations. This is where moral framing comes in.

Moral framing

Whilst it may be possible to determine the degree of intensity a moral issue should have for decision-makers according to Jones' (1991) six variables, it is clear that people in different contexts are likely to perceive that intensity differently. The same problem or dilemma can be perceived very differently according to the way that the issue is framed. For example, imagine that a student talks about 'cutting and pasting some material from the internet' into their assignment. This may sound quite innocuous. But imagine that if instead the student says, 'I plagiarized something I found on the internet', or even 'I stole someone's ideas and passed them off as my own'! This would give a very different impression, and would make us sense a deeper moral importance about the student's actions. The way in which moral issues are framed is therefore a key influence on ethical decision-making.

As we can see from the example above, probably the most important aspect of moral framing is the language in which moral issues are couched. As Treviño and Nelson (2007: 123) state: 'Using moral language (positive words like integrity, honesty, fairness, propriety, or negative words such as lying, cheating, stealing) will more likely trigger moral thinking because these terms are attached to existing cognitive categories that have moral content'. The problem is that many people in business are reluctant to ascribe moral terms to their work, even if acting for moral reasons, or if their actions have obvious moral consequences. Bird and Waters (1989) describe this as *moral muteness*. In a widely cited research project based on interviews with managers, they found that groups of managers would tend to reframe moral actions and motives, and talk instead of doing things for reasons of practicality, organizational interests, and economic good sense. According to Bird and Waters (1989), managers would do this out of concerns regarding perceived threats to:

- **Harmony.** Managers tended to believe that moral talk would disturb organizational harmony by provoking confrontation, recrimination, and finger-pointing.
- **Efficiency.** Managers often felt that moral talk would cloud issues, making decision-making more difficult, time consuming, and inflexible.
- **Image of power and effectiveness.** Managers also felt that their own image might suffer since being associated with ethics could be seen as idealistic and utopian, and lacking sufficient robustness for effective management.

These are very real concerns for people employed at all levels in companies, and the dangers not only of moral talk, but of being seen as overly involved in business ethics, can impact negatively on employees working in organizations where such issues are viewed with suspicion. Andrew Crane's (2001) study of managers involved in environmental programmes highlights some of these concerns and problems, suggesting that fears of being marginalized can lead managers to engage in a process of *amoralization*. That is, they seek to distance themselves and their projects from being defined as ethically motivated or ethical in nature, and instead build a picture of corporate rationality suffused with justifications of corporate self-interest. On the positive side, this means that managers may well be able to make what they see as morally good decisions, even ones driven by a strong set of personal values, providing they couch the decision in business terms (Watson 2003). On the flip side, the process of amoralization may mean that even ostensibly 'intense' ethical issues may be seen by co-workers and others as simply a business problem rather than a moral one.

Moral framing can also occur after a decision has been made or an act carried out. It is important therefore to look not just at what people decide, but how they then justify their decisions to themselves and others. Anand, Ashforth, and Joshi (2004: 39) call these justifications, rationalization tactics—namely 'mental strategies that allow employees (and others around them) to view their corrupt acts as justified'. They identify six such strategies—denial of responsibility, denial of injury, denial of victim, social weighting, appeal to higher loyalties, and the metaphor of the ledger—which are described and illustrated in **Figure 4.6.** People in organizations tend to use these rationalizations in order to neutralize regrets and negative associations of unethical practices.

Again, one of the most important factors abetting this type of rationalizing is euphemistic language, 'which enables individuals engaging in corruption to describe their acts in ways that make them appear inoffensive' (Anand et al. 2004: 47). The authors give the example of Nazi doctors working at Auschwitz referring to execution by lethal injection as 'euthanasia' or 'preventative medicine', but it is easy to see in contemporary corporate terms such as 'corporate restructuring' (i.e. massive lay-offs), and 'facilitation payments' (i.e. bribes) that euphemistic language is prevalent in everyday business practice. In fact,

Strategy	Description	Examples
Denial of responsibility.	The actors engaged in corrupt behaviours perceive that they have no other choice than to participate in such activities.	'What can I do? My arm is being twisted.' 'It is none of my business what the corporation does in overseas bribery.'
Denial of injury.	The actors are convinced that no one is harmed by their actions; hence the actions are not really corrupt.	'No one was really harmed.' 'It could have been worse.'
Denial of victim.	The actors counter any blame for their actions by arguing that the violated party deserved whatever happened.	'They deserved it.' 'They chose to participate.'
Social weighting.	The actors assume two practices that moderate the salience of corrupt behaviour: 1. Condemn the condemner, 2. Selective social comparison.	'You have no right to criticize us.' 'Others are worse than we are.'
Appeal to higher loyalties.	The actors argue that their violation of norms is due to their attempt to realize a higher-order value.	'We answered to a more important cause.' 'I would not report it because of my loyalty to my boss.'
Metaphor of the ledger.	The actors argue that they are entitled to indulge in deviant behaviours because of their accrued credits (time and effort) in their jobs.	'It's all right for me to use the internet for personal reasons at work. After all, I do work overtime.'

Figure 4.6. Rationalizing unethical behaviour

Republished with permission of Academy of Management, from Anand, V., Ashforth, B.E., and Joshi, M. (2004). Business as usual: the acceptance and perpetuation of corruption in organizations. *Academy of Management Executive*, 18 (2): 39–53 (Table 1, p. 41); permission conveyed through Copyright Clearance Center, Inc

these sorts of framings easily become socialized within organizations over time, thereby creating a context that repeatedly shapes ethical decision-making, as we shall now see.

? THINK THEORY

Think about the theory of rationalizing tactics in the context of your own experience—can you recognize these having been used? Can you provide specific examples of the types of language that people have used to rationalize potentially unethical behaviour?

VISIT THE WEBSITE for a short response to this feature

Context-related factors

Our second group of situational influences are context-related factors. By context, we mean the organizational context in which an employee will be working—especially the expectations and demands placed on them within the work environment that are likely

VISIT THE WEBSITE for links to useful sources of further information

ETHICS ON SCREEN 4

Michael Clayton

A tale of greed, lies, and under-the-table violence—an exposé of what corporations do, and the way corporate law firms help them get away with it

Owen Gleiberman, *Entertainment Weekly*

Released in 2007 to widespread critical acclaim, the Oscar-nominated feature *Michael Clayton* stars George Clooney as the eponymous 'fixer' in a corporate law firm. The movie is set in classic business ethics territory—a cynical, down-on-his-luck character, who does the dirty work for his high profile corporate law firm, gets drawn into a messy legal case involving an agrichemical company, a series of apparently connected cancer deaths, and a colleague who looks to be ready to blow the whistle. As the *New York Times* put it, Clayton 'works in that rarefied gray zone where the barely legal meets the almost criminal'.

The plot revolves around Clayton's involvement in trying to clean up the mess when one of the law firm's most brilliant litigators, and a long-time friend of Clayton, Arthur Edens, has a breakdown. Edens (played by Tom Wilkinson), goes into meltdown in the middle of defending a multimillion dollar lawsuit being waged against the law firm's biggest client, the agricultural products conglomerate U-North. Clayton learns that Edens claims to have unearthed internal U-North documents that directly implicate the firm in trying to cover up known health problems associated with one of their herbicides, making it potentially responsible for hundreds of deaths. Rather than defending the firm, Edens is in the process of switching sides, thereby plunging himself into emotional and mental turmoil, and threatening to derail the case completely for his client. Clayton's job is to get to Eden, keep him quiet, and ensure that everything gets back on track smoothly for all concerned.

As the movie progresses, Clayton is increasingly faced with some tough moral choices. Although the moral ambiguities around his role as a fixer become ever more troubling, he is also beset by financial problems, a stalled career, and a set of expectations from everyone from his family to his boss that seem to offer him little room for manoeuvre. So although the movie portrays the corporate world in a stark and unforgiving light, with its carefully drawn, character-driven narrative, it succeeds in focusing our attention not simply on the evil that firms sometimes do, but on the effect this has on the ordinary people that work in them. The movie is peopled with a set of characters that occupy the murky world of business ethics, and shows the powerfully seductive forces of corruption that work upon them. Probably the most striking realization of this is the U-North corporate counsel, Karen Crowder, who does everything she can to save her firm from disaster. In an Oscar-winning performance by Tilda Swinton, Crowder is shown to be at once powerful and fearful—going from pulverizing the lives of anyone who crosses her to vomiting with fear at the prospect of losing the biggest battle of her career.

Castle Rock/Section Eight/The Kobal Collection

Ultimately, then, *Michael Clayton* is a compelling movie that explores the corrosive effects of corporate life on individual moral character. Thus, like many films before it, including movies such as *The Insider, Boiler Room*, and *Glengarry Glen Ross*, it is all about how our personal ethics intertwine with the harsh realities of corporate ethics, and the choices we sometimes have to make in navigating between them.

Sources

Dargis, Manohla. 2007. They call him the fixer in a world that's a mess. *New York Times*, 5 October: http://www.nytimes.com.

to influence their perceptions of what is the morally right course of action to take. These factors appear to be especially important in shaping ethical decision-making within organizations. In **Ethics on Screen 4**, for example, the depiction of the amoral world of corporate law in the movie *Michael Clayton* is discussed in relation to the ethical decision-making of the main characters in the film. Just as importantly for the management of business ethics, these contextual factors are also, as we shall see, probably the main factors that can be addressed in order to *improve* ethical decision-making in the workplace.

Systems of reward

We tend to take it for granted that people are likely to do what they are rewarded for—for example, many organizations offer commission or bonuses for salespeople in order to motivate them to achieve greater numbers of sales—yet it is easy to forget that this has implications for ethical conduct too. For example, if an organization rewards its salespeople for the number of sales they make, then those salespeople may be tempted to compromise ethical standards in their dealings with customers in order to earn more commission. This would particularly be the case if the organization did not appear to punish those salespeople who were seen to behave unethically towards their customers, for example by exaggerating a product's benefits, or misleading customers about a competitor's products. Quite simply, ethical violations that go unpunished are likely to be repeated.

Similarly, adherence to ethical principles and standards stands less chance of being repeated and spread throughout a company when it goes unnoticed and unrewarded—or still worse, when it is actually punished, as we saw with the example of whistleblowing above. In fact, survey evidence suggests that something like one in eight employees actually experiences some form of retaliation for reporting ethical misconduct—and as a result, more than 40% who observe misconduct do not report it (Ethics Resource Center 2007). Sometimes, however, the effects of rewards and punishments may not even be direct; employees may sense the prevailing approach to business ethics in their organization by looking at who gets promoted and who doesn't, or who seems to get the favour of the boss and who doesn't, and interpret 'correct' behaviour from the experiences of their more or less fortunate colleagues.

There is considerable evidence to suggest that employee's ethical decision-making is indeed influenced by the systems of reward they see operating in the workplace. We have already seen in the previous section how Crane's (2001) research revealed that fears of marginalization and lack of progression could influence managers to avoid the explicit moral framing of problems and issues. Robert Jackall's (1988) extensive research into managers' rules for success in the workplace further reveals that what is regarded as 'right' in the workplace is often that which gets rewarded. For instance, he reports a former vice-president of a large firm saying: 'What is right in the corporation is not what is right in a man's home or in his church. *What is right in the corporation is what the guy above you wants from you.* That's what morality is in the corporation' (Jackall 1988: 6).

Tony Watson (1998) contends that managers are actually more likely to take a balanced approach, whereby pragmatic concerns and instrumental rewards are consciously interwoven with moral considerations in management decision-making. Survey work, however, has certainly tended to support a strong relationship between rewards and ethical behaviour, with Loe et al. (2000) reporting that a majority of studies have revealed a significant correlation between the rewarding of unethical behaviour and the continuation of such behaviour.

Authority

This leads us to also consider the issue of authority. People don't just do what gets rewarded, they do what they are told to do—or perhaps more correctly, what they *think* they're being told to do. Sometimes this can be a direct instruction from a superior to do something that the subordinate does not necessarily question or refuse to do because of their lower status in the hierarchy. At other times, the manager may not be directly instructing the employee to do something unethical; however, their instructions to the employee may appear to leave little option but to act in a questionable manner. For example, a university professor may ask their PhD student to grade 200 undergraduate exam scripts in two days, leaving the PhD student insufficient time to even read all of the scripts, let alone mark them competently. As a result, the student might resort to grading the scripts in an arbitrary and unfair way.

Managers can also have an influence over their subordinates' ethical behaviour by setting a bad example. Many of us tend to look up to our superiors to determine what passes for ethical behaviour in the workplace. Significantly, however, employees sometimes seem to perceive their superiors as lacking in ethical integrity. For example, a recent survey of government employees revealed that (Ethics Resource Center 2008: 9):

- Around 20% think top leadership is not held accountable for their own violations of ethics standards.
- About 25% believe that top leadership tolerates retaliation against those who report ethical misconduct.
- About 30% do not believe their leaders keep promises and commitments.

Clearly, those in authority can influence their employees' ethical decision-making simply by looking the other way when confronted with potential problems. For example, Chhabara (2008) claims that the widespread prevalence of sexual harassment in the workplaces of domestic companies in Asia is at least partly due to lack of attention by managers. Fearing any escalation in complaints and lawsuits, managers avoid instituting the kinds of sexual harassment prevention programmes that may avoid unethical behaviour in the first place. However, with surveys suggesting that the proportion of women experiencing sexual harassment is as much as 40% (China), 47% (India), or even 78% (Pakistan), lack of attention clearly does little to curb the rate of incidence (Chhabara 2008).

Bureaucracy

Underlying the influence of rewards, punishments, and authority is the degree of bureaucracy in business organizations. Bureaucracy is a type of formal organization based on rational principles, and characterized by detailed rules and procedures, impersonal hierarchical relations, and a fixed division of tasks.

Based on the work of Max Weber (1947) regarding the bureaucratic form, as well as later discussions of bureaucracy in relation to morality by Robert Jackall (1988), Zigmunt Bauman (1989, 1993), and René ten Bos (1997), the bureaucratic dimension has been argued to have a number of negative effects on ethical decision-making:[10]

- **Suppression of moral autonomy.** Individual morality tends to be subjugated to the functionally specific rules and roles of the bureaucratic organization. Thus, effective bureaucracy essentially 'frees' the individual from moral reflection and decision-making since s/he needs only to follow the prescribed rules and procedures laid down to achieve organizational goals. This can cause employees to act as 'moral robots', simply following the rules, rather than thinking about why they are there or questioning their purpose.
- **Instrumental morality.** The bureaucratic dimension focuses organization members' attentions on the efficient achievement of organizational goals. Hence, morality will be made meaningful only in terms of conformity to established rules for achieving those goals—i.e. instrumentalized—rather than focusing attention on the moral substance of the goals themselves. Accordingly, ethical decision-making will centre around whether 'correct' procedures have been taken to achieve certain goals rather than whether the goals themselves are morally beneficial. Thus, loyalty rather than integrity ultimately becomes the hallmark of bureaucratic morality.
- **Distancing.** Bureaucracy serves to further suppress our own morality by distancing us from the consequences of our actions—for example, a supermarket purchasing manager in Lyon is rarely going to be faced with the effects of their supply negotiations on farm workers producing the supermarket's coffee beans in Columbia.
- **Denial of moral status.** Finally, bureaucracy has been argued to render moral objects, such as people or animals, as things, variables, or a collection of traits. Thus, employees become human 'resources' that are means to some organizational end; consumers are reduced to a collection of preferences on a marketing database; animals become units of production or output that can be processed in a factory. The point is that by dividing tasks and focusing on efficiency, the totality of individuals as moral beings is lost and they are ultimately denied true moral status.

VISIT THE WEBSITE for a short response to this feature

? THINK THEORY

Think about the theory proposed here—that bureaucracy suppresses morality. Consider a bureaucratic organization that you have had personal experience of and try to relate the four effects highlighted here to that organization. Does the theory seem to have much validity in this instance?

Work roles

As we have seen, the bureaucratic organization of work assigns people to specific specializations or tasks that represent work roles. These are patterns of behaviour expected by others from a person occupying a certain position in an organization (Buchanan and Huczynski 1997: 374). Work roles can be *functional*—for example, the role of an accountant, an engineer, or a shop assistant—or they can be *hierarchical*—the role of a director, manager, or supervisor for example. Roles can encapsulate a whole set of expectations about what to value, how to relate to others, and how to behave.

These expectations are built up during formal education, training, and through experience, and can have a strong influence on a person's behaviour. For example, think about when you are in the lecture theatre or seminar room of your university or college. Most of you probably naturally adopt the role of 'student' in the classroom—listening, taking notes, asking and answering questions when prompted—and the person taking the class will probably naturally adopt the role of 'teacher'. But it wouldn't take much for us to refuse to adopt those roles: for the students to stand up and walk out, or for the teacher to sit down and say nothing. The main reason we do not is the fact that, as a rule, we all seem to know how we are supposed to act and we stick to it fairly faithfully. We simply adopt our prescribed roles.

In the business ethics context, prescribed work roles, and the concomitant expectations placed on the person adopting the role, would appear to be significant influences on decision-making. Our individual morality, the values and beliefs we might normally hold, can be stifled by our adoption of the values and beliefs embedded in our work role. Perhaps the most vivid illustration of this is the Stanford prison experiment, which is the subject of **Ethics in Action 4.2.** This is about as powerful an example as you can get of how work roles can have substantial impacts on how we behave. However, whilst there is considerable evidence supporting a significant impact for work roles on organizational behaviour *generally*, there has been rather limited research to date that has specifically addressed the impact of roles on *ethical* decision-making and behaviour. Nonetheless, the important thing to remember is that many of us will adopt different roles in different contexts, reinforcing this idea of people having multiple ethical selves. For example, many people take on different roles when with their family compared with when they are at work, or with their friends, or in other social situations. Roles are therefore not constant traits or facets of our personality (as was the case with our individual factors), but are highly contextual influences on our decision-making and behaviour.

Organizational norms and culture

Another set of potentially powerful influences on ethical decision-making are the group norms that delineate acceptable standards of behaviour within the work community—be this at the level of a small team of workers, a department, or the entire organization. Group norms essentially express the way in which things are, or should be, done in a certain environment, and might relate to ways of acting, talking, justifying, dressing, even thinking and evaluating. Group norms may well conflict with the official rules or procedures laid down by the organization. For example, a group of office workers may agree amongst themselves that illegally pirating licensed software from work for home use is perfectly acceptable as an unofficial 'perk' of the job, even if it is officially prohibited. As such, group norms tend to be included within a more or less unofficial or informal set of characteristics, including shared values, beliefs, and behaviours that are captured by the notion of *organizational culture*.

Whilst there are numerous, often conflicting definitions of what organizational culture actually is, at a basic level we can say that it represents the overall environment or climate found within the organization (or certain parts of it). Culture is further said to constitute particular meanings, beliefs, and common-sense knowledge that are shared among the members of the organization, and which are represented in taken-for-granted assumptions, norms, and values. Organizational culture has been widely identified as a key issue in shaping ethical decision-making. Not only has it been frequently included in models of ethical decision-making (e.g. Ferrell et al. 1989), but it has also been widely examined in empirical investigations (O'Fallon and Butterfield 2005). This is not particularly surprising, for there is wide-ranging evidence, as well as strong conceptual support, for the proposition that culture and ethical decision-making are profoundly interwoven (e.g. Sinclair 1993; Dahler-Larsen 1994; Starkey 1998; Anand et al. 2004). Clearly, as employees become socialized into particular ways of seeing, interpreting, and acting, this will shape the kinds of decisions they make when confronted with ethical problems. Cultural expectations and values can provide a strong influence on what we think of as 'right' and 'wrong'. For example, the failed US energy giant Enron was shown to have developed a culture of dishonesty that culminated in the misleading accounting that brought down the firm in 2001 (Sims and Brinkmann 2003). Our cultural understandings and knowledge can thus act as both facilitators and barriers to ethical reflection and behaviour.

As a consequence of such reasoning, as well as compelling survey evidence (e.g. Ethics Resource Center 2007, 2008), many authors, such as Treviño and Nelson (2007) and Ferrell et al. (2008), thus speak of the need for an 'ethical culture' to enhance and reinforce ethical decision-making. However, as we shall see in the next chapter (when we move on to discuss ways of managing business ethics), there is considerable disagreement about how this should be done, or indeed, whether it is even possible or desirable. Certainly, it would appear that the deliberate management of culture is an extremely challenging undertaking, and one where many of the outcomes will be unpredictable. Nonetheless, even though it may be unclear how to deal with organizational culture's influence on ethical decision-making, the very fact that there is some kind of relationship between the two would appear almost irrefutable.

VISIT THE WEBSITE for links to useful sources of further information

ETHICS IN ACTION 4.2

The Stanford prison experiment

The Stanford Prison Experiment, co-ordinated by Dr Philip Zimbardo, took place in 1971. The experiment frequently features in discussions about human psychology, roles, and ethical behaviour—and has achieved an enduring place in popular culture. Not only has it served as the inspiration for a BBC TV Show called *The Experiment*, a German movie, *Das Experiment*, as well as a US movie release from Imprint Entertainment (the company behind the 2008 *Twilight* movie) slated for 2011, but it has also given its name to an American punk band, the *Stanford Prison Experiment*. So what accounts for the classic status of Zimbardo's experiment?

Zimbardo's plan was to take 24, average, healthy, middle-class, male college students and randomly assign them into one of two groups—one to play prisoners and the other to play prison guards—for a two-week period. His intention was to examine the psychology of prison life. The 'prisoners' were rounded up unexpectedly by a police squad car, blindfolded, handcuffed, and then locked in stark cells in the 'jail' in the basement of the Stanford University psychology building. While the prisoners were given smocks and nylon stocking caps to wear, the guards were given uniforms, reflector sunglasses, clubs, and handcuffs—all of which emphasized their roles, minimized their individuality, and reinforced the power differentials between the two groups. Prisoners had to refer to guards as 'Mr Correction Officer', and guards were given only minimal instructions in order to achieve their goal of 'maintaining law and order'. Although physical violence was forbidden, they were allowed to devise their own rules and ways of working.

Although planned to last two weeks, the experiment was dramatically halted after only six days. Some of the guards had begun to treat the prisoners with excessive aggression and clearly took pleasure in exercising their power and inflicting psychological cruelty. The prisoners quickly became servile, dependent, helpless, and depressed, thinking only of their own survival and their hatred of the guards. After only 36 hours, the first prisoner had to be released due to fits of rage, uncontrollable crying, and depression. More prisoners were released in the days that followed, suffering from similar symptoms.

Despite being randomly allocated to the two roles, the study's participants had almost immediately begun to think of themselves as their prisoner and guard roles. They rapidly adopted the ways of thinking and behaving associated with those roles, and the arbitrary rules of the new organizational environment into which they had been thrust were accepted as legitimate. The participants became so programmed to think of themselves as prisoners that they did not feel capable of just withdrawing from the experiment, and the researchers themselves even became so locked into their roles as prison authorities that the prisoners' deteriorating physical and mental conditions were initially interpreted as faked in order to 'con' their way out of the experiment! The distinction between the real self and the role had blurred to such an extent that nearly all aspects of the individual's thoughts, feelings, and behaviours, whether as participant or researcher, had experienced dramatic changes. Zimbardo concluded that the experiment supported the theory that individual behaviour is largely controlled by role and situation, rather than personal characteristics and traits.

Although it is clear that most workplaces are quite different to the prison environment, the Stanford experiment does show us that people very easily adopt the roles they are assigned to, and may quite readily fall into attitudes and behaviours that conflict significantly with those they have in 'normal' life. As Zimbardo himself said of the guards: 'These guys were all peaceniks. They became like Nazis.' Zimbardo later served as an expert witness in the defence of one of the prison guards at the notorious Abu Ghraib prison in Baghdad where guards had been involved in torture and degradation of prisoners in the aftermath of the 2003 invasion of Iraq. Zimbardo's subsequent book, *The Lucifer Effect: Understanding How Good People Turn Evil*, drew on similarities between his experiment and the events at Abu Ghraib to illustrate how perfectly decent individuals can be influenced by their environment to act unethically.

Sources

http://www.prisonexp.org.
http://www.lucifereffect.com.
Brockes, E. 2001. The experiment. *Guardian*, G2, 16 October: 2–3.
Buchanan, D. and Huczynski, A. 1997. *Organizational behaviour: an introductory text*. Hemel Hempstead: Prentice Hall: 380–1.
For more details, go to: http://www.prisonexp.org, which has a detailed description of the experiment, including a slide show and video clips. There are also links for further reading.

? THINK THEORY

Think about what this experiment says about roles and moral relativism. Is it reasonable to justify any kind of behaviour on the grounds that ethical evaluations may differ according to different contexts?

VISIT THE WEBSITE for a short response to this feature

National and cultural context

Finally, just as the culture of the organization or work group may influence ethical decision-making, so might the country or culture in which the individual's organization is located. This factor varies from the national and cultural characteristics discussed in pp. 150–11 on individual influences: at that time, we were looking at the nationality of the individual making the decision; now we are considering the nation in which the decision is actually taking place, regardless of the decision-maker's nationality. As we have discussed a number of times in the book so far, different cultures still to some extent maintain different views of what is right and wrong, and these differences have significant effects on whether a moral issue is recognized, and the kind of judgements and behaviours entered into by individuals. For example, a French office manager working in the US may start to become sensitized to different perceptions of what constitutes sexual harassment compared with their colleagues back in France. Or a Danish human resource manager might consider the issue of employment conditions quite differently should she be working in Indonesia rather than at home. However, with globalization eroding some of these national cultural differences, we might expect to see shifts in the influence of this factor, perhaps with more complex effects and interactions emerging.

Whilst some models have incorporated factors relating to the social and cultural environment (e.g. Hunt and Vitell 1986; Ferrell et al. 1989), there has been little empirical research investigating the effect of this on ethical decision-making. However, one key study suggests that the local national context does indeed have an effect on otherwise similar managers from a given country, but that its impact varies according to the type of situation faced by the manager (Spicer et al. 2004). That is, the local national culture impacts decision-makers where norms are ambiguous, but not, it would appear, where there is more broad cross-cultural consensus, such in the case of 'hypernorms' like basic human rights.

■ Summary

In this chapter, we have discussed the various stages and influences on ethical decision-making in business, so that by now you should have a reasonably clear picture of the overall process and its most important elements. The basic model presented in the chapter provides a clear outline of how these elements fit together, although as we mentioned earlier, this model should be regarded simply as an illustration of the relationships involved, not as a definitive causal model. Having discussed both individual and situational influences on ethical decision-making, we would suggest that some individual factors—such as cognitive moral development, nationality, personal values, and integrity—are clearly influential, particularly on the moral *judgements* made by individuals. However, in terms of *recognizing* ethical problems and actually *acting* in response to them, it is situational factors that appear to be the most influential. This is important because it means that it is situational factors that are likely to be the most promising levers for attempts to manage and improve ethical decision-making in organizations. In particular, the possibilities for addressing organizational culture as a route to managing ethics has been widely alluded to in the literature and will provide an important aspect of our discussions in the next chapter.

Study questions

1 What is the difference between descriptive and normative ethical theories?

2 Set out the four stages in Rest's (1986) ethical decision-making process. What are the relationships between each stage?

3 Is the prevalence of unethical behaviour in business due to a few 'bad apples' or is it more a case of good apples in bad barrels? How would your answer differ for government or civil society organizations?

4 Describe Kohlberg's theory of cognitive moral development and critically evaluate its contribution to our understanding of ethical decision-making in organizations. What are the main implications of the theory for business leaders?

5 What are the two main types of issue-related factors in ethical decision-making? What is the significance of these factors for managers seeking to prevent ethical violations in their organizations?

6 What are the main impacts of bureaucracy on ethical decision-making? How would you suggest that a highly bureaucratic organization could enhance its employees' ethical decision-making?

Research exercise

Ethics on Screen 4 described the events in the movie, *Michael Clayton*. If you can, get the movie out of the video store or library and watch it. Alternatively, select another movie that you know involves people having to make ethical decisions in organizations. Use the events in the movie to provide a critical appraisal of the ethical decision-making literature.

Key readings

VISIT THE WEBSITE for links to further key readings

1 **Bird, F.B. and Waters, J.A. 1989. The moral muteness of managers. *California Management Review*, Fall: 73–88.**

This is a classic article about the way in which managers often feel unable to express the moral dimensions of their activities. It is important to read it because it provides a good understanding of why organizational life can seem so devoid of moral talk even when ethical issues seem to be so important and widespread.

2 **Anand, V., Ashforth, B.E., and Joshi, M. 2004. Business as usual: the acceptance and perpetuation of corruption in organizations. *Academy of Management Executive*, 18 (2): 39–53.**

This article will help you to see why unethical practices persist in organizations, and provides a really helpful way of thinking about how people and organizations respond to corruption.

Case 4

VISIT THE WEBSITE for links to useful sources of further information

Siemens: Just breaking the eleventh commandment?

This case examines the circumstances that led to the highest ever fine paid by a firm in a bribery settlement. It looks closely at accusations of a long-standing, ingrained system of corruption at Germany's biggest conglomerate, the engineering firm Siemens. The case is an illustration of many of the individual and situational factors of ethical decision-making discussed in Chapter 4.

Founded in 1847, Siemens is not only one of the oldest and largest conglomerates in Germany, but counts among the top 30 companies worldwide in the Fortune 500 Index in terms of sales. The engineering giant produces a wide range of goods and services, from light bulbs to power stations, and has a leading position in many of its markets, which include white goods, rail transportation systems, healthcare technology, IT and financial services, to name just a few. It is a large, decentralized conglomerate operating in 190 countries globally.

One area where Siemens can claim to be a record holder is rather less prestigious. In December 2008, after a long-running bribery scandal, the company settled out of court with the US authorities and was landed with a record fine of US$800m—a figure far in excess of any previous penalty imposed under the US Foreign Corrupt Practices Act. Along with fines levied in Germany of around €600m, this brought the total paid by the company to more than US$1.6bn, roughly 35 times larger than any previous anti-corruption settlement. However, including lawyers' and accountants' fees charged to the company during the case, the full cost was ultimately even higher, at some US$2.5bn in total, not counting the various other smaller fines likely to result from investigations in other countries around the world.

The company had been investigated on multiple counts of bribery, adding up to more than $2.3bn in alleged payments during the 1990s and 2000s. This included allegations of $5m paid to the son of the Bangladeshi prime minister for a mobile phone contract, $22m to Chinese officials for a metro trains deal, and $40m worth of payments in Argentina for a $1bn contract to produce identity cards—just to name a few examples.

The scandal unfolds

The settlement was the final episode of a scandal which had been simmering for more than five years at the troubled engineering firm. The company's tribulations really began in the early 2000s when prosecutors in Germany and the US first started to investigate bribery allegations at the company. The firm and its leadership initially denied any knowledge of the payments. But with more incidents coming to light, the magnitude of the payments becoming ever higher, and trials of former company managers suggesting that bribery was common practice in the firm, this position became increasingly tenuous. As the scandal unfolded, it became clear that this was not simply a case of a few rogue managers acting alone and breaking the company rules to secure lucrative overseas contracts. Corruption looked to be endemic at Siemens, or, as one prosecutor put it, 'bribery was Siemens' business model'.

Facing increasing pressure from within, the CEO and nearly the entire board resigned in 2007, including long-time former CEO and then supervisory board chairman Heinrich von Pierer, a prominent and vocal member of the Christian Democratic Party in Germany. The firm decided to co-operate with the US authorities in its investigations and initiated an amnesty for any whistleblowers with knowledge of bribery in the company.

The various trials and investigations brought to the surface a murky picture of the payments made to public officials in a bid to win large overseas contracts for the company. Part of the problem is that many of Siemens' products, such as railway systems, mobile phone networks, or complex hospital equipment, are sold to governments. These projects are often of a very high value and are subject to complex decision-making processes in the respective countries. Moreover, given that many of these projects are located in developing countries with poor governance and a high prevalence of corruption, Siemens managers often found themselves in a competitive market, where other players were apparently willing to bribe, with 'customers' often willing to accept.

According to various witness statements, Siemens' employees often simply thought that bribery is how the game was played and that they had to engage in corruption in order to win business, keep jobs secure, and their company strong. As an organization dominated by employees with an engineering background, these things tended to be perceived as another technical exercise to get the job done, another trick of the trade to move the product. It would appear that corruption at Siemens was seen in rather amoral terms and as a victimless crime—if a crime at all. Furthermore, it did not exactly help that the German corporate tax code only made bribery technically illegal in the late 1990s. Until then, bribes paid in foreign countries were even tax deductible and were declared under the notorious label 'useful expenses' (in German: *nützliche Aufwendungen* (NA)).

Another important factor is that German multinationals like Siemens are typically very decentralized and compartmentalized. Compared with American or Japanese multinationals which often centralize key functions and use foreign subsidiaries just for a limited set of tasks, German multinationals tend to leave a lot of autonomy to local executives—the argument being that they usually sell complex technical products with a need for a high level of customer-specific local adaptation. The downside from an ethical perspective, however, appeared to be twofold. First, decisions about payments may be taken locally, without any real oversight or understanding from the headquarters. Second, once the leadership back home does become aware, the decentralized structure can make it difficult to implement effective ethics management across the firm's span of operations. For Siemens, when the first signs of the bribery allegations surfaced in 2005, the then newly appointed CEO announced that fighting corruption would be his top priority. However, he was forced to resign within two years because of the ongoing stream of bribery allegations that continued to plague the company.

A particular issue with Siemens also appears to be a strong corporate culture, deeply rooted within the 160-year-old firm, which made it particularly hard to initiate a major change in values and attitudes within the company. Many Siemens employees had been with the company for all their careers, leading to densely woven webs of contacts, informal relationships, and networks, in which problems like corruption (and its cover-up) can thrive. It is notable that it was only as a result of the crippling scandals engulfing the company that in 2007 Siemens made its first appointment of an outsider as CEO. Moreover, as the trial hearings revealed, the maintenance of corruption on the scale alleged at Siemens actually required a degree of loyalty from employees not always found in large multinationals. One of the more junior level executives in the telecoms section of the firm testified to the court that he was chosen to become the coordinator of the 'useful expenses' payments because his superiors trusted him and because he was a loyal worker who could be relied on not to simply direct some of the bribe money into his own pockets.

Corruption allegations at Volkswagen

The Siemens case occurred at a time when Germany had just gone through a number of corruption scandals, most notably at carmaker Volkswagen. There, the alleged bribery did not occur in bidding for contracts, but in relationships with the works council and trade union members. As with many German companies, works councils are very powerful and need to give their consent to all major strategic decisions of a company. In order to push through some painful cost-cutting measures, VW was alleged to have operated a slush fund to provide all sorts of perks to senior members of the works council. These included an illegal €2m bonus for the head of the works council, provision of prostitutes and mistresses to members of the council, and shopping trips to Paris for their wives.

The parallel with Siemens is that, according to the allegations, these were not one-off acts of corruption by lone individuals, but went on for a considerable length of time and were tolerated at all levels of the organization. At VW, the scandal led to the resignation of the most prominent member of the board, Peter Hartz, who, as the former head of personnel, was found guilty of endorsing the perks-and-prostitutes arrangement.

Siemens introduces anti-corruption initiatives

At Siemens, the corruption scandal has prompted a raft of new initiatives in the company. After forcing the board and chairman to resign, the new CEO hired an American law firm and spent millions on the internal investigation and co-operated fully with the courts—the only reason why the US fine was not even higher than the US$800 ultimately levied on the firm. The new chairman of the supervisory board, Gerhard Cromme, otherwise known for the latest German corporate governance code, has also implemented new measures to enhance transparency and accountability within the organization. Among other things, Siemens agreed to appoint a former German Finance Minister as an in-house monitor to help ensure that the company remains corruption free.

Although the nature of the final settlement in the US did not actually require the firm to admit to bribery (it was only required to admit to having inadequate controls and keeping improper accounts), the new Siemens' leadership has made it clear that the firm needs to change its ways. As the new CEO, Peter Löscher, said: 'We regret what happened in the past but we have learned from it and taken appropriate measures. Siemens is now a stronger company.' It will, however, be difficult to change the long-standing culture within the company. As one insider put it, many in the firm still secretly think that where Siemens went wrong in the scandal was not in its payment of bribes, but in breaking what Germans colloquially allude to as the 'eleventh commandment': don't get caught…

Questions

1. What are the main individual and situational factors encouraging the alleged bribery at Siemens? Which, in your opinion, are the most important?
2. Explore the corruption scandals in terms of the issue-related factors discussed in Chapter 4, namely moral intensity and moral framing. To what extent did the firms featured experience corruption as a morally intense issue and what impact did the moral framing of the activities involved have on this?
3. Critically evaluate the initiatives Siemens has implemented to address bribery problems across its operations. Are these sufficient or would you suggest further action?
4. Thinking of bribery from the perspective of wider society, do you think that a fine—however high—is an adequate response? What penalties, for instance, could you suggest to foster more ethical values at the company or higher personal integrity on the part of its employees?

Sources

Anon. 2007. Hit by an earthquake: how scandals have led to a crisis in German corporate governance. *Knowledge@Wharton*, 28 March: http://knowledge.wharton.upenn.edu.

Ewing, J. 2008. Siemens settlement: relief, but is it over? *Business Week*, 15 December: http://www.businessweek.com.

Gow, D. 2008. Record US fine ends Siemens bribery scandal. *Guardian*, 16 December: http://www.guardian.co.uk.

Schubert, S. and Christian Miller, T. 2008. At Siemens, bribery was just a line item. *New York Times*, 20 December: http://www.nyt.com.

Verschoor, C. 2007. Siemens AG is the latest fallen ethics idol. *Strategic Finance*, November: 11–12, 61.

Notes

1 See BP Sustainability Review 2007 (http://www.bp.com); Boxell, J. and Harvey, F. (2005). BP sacked 252 in corruption drive. *Financial Times*, 12 April: 22.

2 The English translations are quite misleading, as 'ethics of responsibility' ('Verantwortungsethik') sounds more positive than in its original German rendition, whereas 'ethics of ultimate ends' ('Gesinnungsethik') seems rather narrow for Weber's argument.

3 There are numerous studies that have examined this question, including: Becker and Fritzsche's (1987) study of French, German, and US managers; Lysonski and Gaidis' (1991) study of US, Danish, and New Zealand business students; Nyaw and Ng's (1994) study of Canadian, Japanese, Hong Kong, and Taiwanese business students; Jackson's (2000) study of French, German, British, Spanish, and US managers; and Jackson's (2001) ten-country study across four continents.

4 Gledhill, R. 2008. Rowan Williams says 'human greed' to blame for financial crisis. *The Times*, 15 October 2008: http://www.timesonline.co.uk; Stolberg, S.G. and Labaton, S. 2009. Obama calls Wall Street bonuses 'shameful'. *New York Times*, 29 January: http://www.nytimes.com; Anon. 2008. Hindus blame greed for current global financial crisis and suggest adopting 'spiritual economics'. *American Chronicle*, 7 October: http://www.americanchronicle.com.

5 For example, CMD is included in ethical decision-making models by Ferrell et al. (1989), Ferrell et al. (2002), Jones (1991), Treviño (1986), and Treviño and Nelson (2007), among others.

6 James Rest (1986), whose depiction of the stages of ethical decision-making we presented earlier in the chapter, has been a vigorous proponent of cognitive moral development and devised a widely used measuring instrument called the Defining Issues Test. A summary of some of the vast amount of empirical work carried out can be found in Rest (1986), some of which is also presented in Goolsby and Hunt (1992).

7 *Collins English Dictionary and Thesaurus*, standard edition. 1993. Glasgow: Harper Collins: 1287.

8 See the company website for more information: http://www.pic.com.

9 BBC. 2009. Chinese milk scam duo face death. *BBC News*, 22 January: http://www.news.bbc.co.uk.

10 Criticizing bureaucracy has been a popular pastime for organization scholars for a considerable time, and business ethics writers have also tended to offer largely negative evaluations of the effects of bureaucracy on ethical decision-making. However, for a powerful and eloquent critique of some of these ideas, see du Gay (2000).

5

Managing Business Ethics

TOOLS AND TECHNIQUES OF BUSINESS ETHICS MANAGEMENT

In this chapter we will:

- Discuss the nature, evolution, and scope of business ethics management.
- Identify why firms increasingly manage their overall social role rather than focus primarily on just managing the ethical behaviour of employees.
- Provide a critical review of arguments and evidence relating to the usefulness of introducing codes of ethics in order to manage the ethical behaviour of employees.
- Examine current theory and practice regarding the management of stakeholder relationships and partnerships.
- Describe the development of social accounting, auditing, and reporting tools, and analyse their contribution to managing and assessing ethical performance.
- Examine different ways of organizing for the management of business ethics, and critically assess the role of organization culture and leadership.

■ Introduction

It is being increasingly recognized by managers, policy-makers, and researchers that business ethics in the global economy is simply too important to be left merely to chance. Global corporations such as McDonald's, Shell, Nike, Nestlé, and others have realized to their cost the threat that perceived ethical violations can pose to their zealously guarded reputations. Stricter regulation has also had a significant impact. For instance, the 2002 US Sarbanes–Oxley legislation prompted companies listed in the US to introduce codes of conduct, ethics policies, and whistleblower hotlines, whilst legislation in countries such as Denmark, France, Japan, Malaysia, and the UK has required large firms to report on certain social and environmental factors relating to their business.

As a result, there have been numerous attempts, both theoretical and practical, to develop a more systematic and comprehensive approach to *managing* business ethics. Indeed, this has given rise to a multi-million Euro international business ethics 'industry' of ethics managers, consultants, auditors, and other experts available to advise and implement ethics management policies and programmes in corporations across the globe. This is all relatively recent. For instance, in 2005, *Business Ethics* magazine identified that corporations were 'rushing to learn ethics virtually overnight, and as they do so, a vast new industry of consultants and suppliers has emerged. The ethics industry has been born' (Hyatt 2005). Similarly, in 2006, Wal-Mart, the world's largest retailer advertised for a new Director of Global Ethics to lead the company's global ethics strategy and to oversee its ethics-related infrastructure, administration, and training. Even in 2009, some commentators still saw the global financial crisis as, at least in part, a failure of attention to managing ethics in large financial institutions.

But how can companies actually manage business ethics on a day-to-day basis across the various national and cultural contexts that they may be operating in? Is it possible to control the ethical behaviour of employees so that they make the right ethical decision every time? And what kinds of management programmes are necessary to produce the level of information and impacts that various stakeholders demand? These are the kinds of questions that we will deal with in this chapter. However, in this area in particular there are as yet few definite answers, not least because many of the questions themselves have only fairly recently been addressed at any length. Indeed, much of the theory and practice covered in this chapter is at the very forefront of current business ethics debates.

■ What is business ethics management?

Before we proceed any further, it is necessary to first establish what exactly it is that we mean by managing business ethics. Obviously, managing any area of business, whether it is production, marketing, accounting, human resources, or any other function, constitutes a whole range of activities covering formal and informal means of planning, implementation, and control. For our purposes though, the most relevant aspects of the management of business ethics are those that are clearly visible and directed specifically at resolving ethical problems and issues. Hence, we might offer the following definition:

Business ethics management is the direct attempt to formally or informally manage ethical issues or problems through specific policies, practices, and programmes.

This, as we shall now show, covers a whole range of different elements, each of which may be applied individually, or in combination, to address ethical issues in business.

Components of business ethics management

There are numerous management activities that could be regarded as aspects of business ethics management, some of which, such as codes of ethics, are fairly well established, whilst others, such as social auditing, are still in the relatively early stages of development and uptake. Without intending to be exhaustive, **Figure 5.1** sets out the main components currently in place today, at least within large multinational corporations. These are all explained briefly below. The most important of these components are described in fuller detail in the section, Setting standards of ethical behaviour (p. 191) onwards, when we look in depth at managing the ethical behaviour of employees, managing stakeholder relations, and managing and assessing ethical performance.

Mission or values statements

These are general statements of corporate aims, beliefs, and values. Such statements frequently include social goals of one kind or another (David 1989; Starkey 1998). For example, the global pharmaceutical company GSK has a mission 'to improve the

Typical components of business ethics management

- Mission or values statements.
- Codes of ethics.
- Reporting/advice channels.
- Risk analysis and management.
- Ethics managers, officers, and committees.
- Ethics consultants.
- Ethics education and training.
- Stakeholder consultation and partnership.
- Auditing, accounting, and reporting.

Figure 5.1. Business ethics management

quality of human life by enabling people to do more, feel better and live longer', whilst the UK smoothie producer Innocent Drinks aims 'to make drinks that taste good and do you good'. Virtually all large and many small- and medium-sized organizations now have a mission statement of some kind, and it is clear they are important in terms of setting out a broad vision for where the company is going. However, in terms of business ethics, they often fail to set out a very specific social purpose, and there is little evidence to suggest that they have much impact on employee behaviour (Bart 1997). Moreover, even a well-crafted, appropriate, and inspirational social mission is unlikely to be effective unless it is backed up by substantive ethics management throughout the organization.

Codes of ethics

These are explicit outlines of what type of conduct is desired and expected of employees from an ethical point of view within a certain organization, profession, or industry. As probably the most widespread approach to managing business ethics, we shall discuss codes of ethics in more detail in the section, Setting standards of ethical behaviour (pp. 191–201).

Reporting/advice channels

Gathering information on ethical matters is clearly an important input into effective management. Providing employees with appropriate channels for reporting or receiving advice regarding ethical dilemmas can also be a vital means of identifying potential problems, and resolving them before they escalate and/or become public. Some organizations have therefore introduced ethics hotlines or other forms of reporting channels specifically for employees to notify management of ethics abuses or problems and to seek help and guidance on solutions. UK survey evidence reports that something like 50% of large firms have instituted channels of this kind (Webley and Le Jeune 2005), although some EU countries such as Germany and France prohibit certain features of hotlines due to privacy restrictions.

Risk analysis and management

Managing and reducing risk has become one of the key components of business ethics management, not least because awareness of potential reputational and financial risks has been one of the key drivers of increased attention to business ethics in recent years. As Alejo Jose Sison (2000) suggests, the language of risk assessment has enabled business ethics to 'show its bite' by spelling out the risks that firms run by ignoring ethics, and measuring these risks in monetary terms, such as the fines, damages, and sanctions that courts can impose. This has been particularly prominent in the US, with the Foreign Corrupt Practices Act and the Sarbanes–Oxley Act providing a legal impetus for greater attention to unethical business practices such as bribery and accounting malpractice. In Europe and Asia too, such legislation is having a similar effect on the large number of non-US multinationals that are jointly listed in the US or that do business in the country.

Managing business ethics by identifying areas of risk, assessing the likelihood and scale of risks, and putting in place measures to mitigate or prevent such risks from harming the business has led to more sophisticated ways of managing business ethics, although as yet, most companies have not developed an integrated approach to risk and ethics. Perhaps inevitably, such risk management techniques tend to focus more on easily identifiable legal risks and more quantifiable ethical risks, such as those relating to pollution or product liability. However, this is an area of continual development, and a greater range of ethical problems such as human rights violations, corruption, and climate change impacts are beginning to be seen on the risk radar of major companies.

Ethics managers, officers, and committees

In some organizations, specific individuals or groups are appointed to co-ordinate and/or take responsibility for managing ethics in their organization. Designated ethics officers (under various titles) are now fairly prevalent, especially in the US where an Ethics and Compliance Officer Association (ECOA), set up in 1992, has grown to around 1,300 members, including representatives from more than half of the Fortune 100. This growth is at least partly due to the increasing emphasis on compliance in the US with the tightening in regulations that followed the Sarbanes–Oxley legislation. As one commentator put it, 'the structure of sentencing policy has driven the appointment of ethics officers and fuelled a boom in business ethics training. If an executive ends up in the dock for corporate wrongdoing, he or she will get a shorter time in the nick if they can demonstrate that they have hired an ethics officer and rolled out courses across the firm' (Reeves 2005).

In Europe, Asia, and elsewhere, such positions are less common, but the ECOA now boasts members across five continents and, in countries such as the UK and France, organizations such as the Institute of Business Ethics and the Cercle Européen des Déontologues (European Circle of Ethics Officers) provide membership services to ethics managers. A growing number of large corporations also now have an ethics committee, or a CSR committee, which oversees many aspects of the management of business ethics. For example, the UK supermarket J. Sainsbury plc has a board-level Corporate Responsibility Committee with responsibility for recommending corporate responsibility policy, and agreeing and approving the annual corporate responsibility report.

Ethics consultants

Business ethics consultants have also become a small, but firmly established fixture in the marketplace, and a wide range of companies have used external consultants rather than internal executives to manage certain areas of business ethics. The initial growth in this sector was driven by environmental consultants who tended to offer specialist technical advice, but as the social and ethical agenda facing companies has developed, the consultancy market has expanded to offer a broader portfolio of services including research, project management, strategic advice, social and environmental auditing and reporting, verification, stakeholder dialogue, and others. At present, whilst there are numerous small ethics consultancy firms, the market is dominated by large professional service firms such as Ernst & Young, KPMG, and Deloitte, which offer management, risk, fraud, reporting and assurance services, as well as leading niche specialists, such as AccountAbility, Bureau Veritas, SustainAbility, and Two Tomorrows.

Ethics education and training

With greater attention being placed on business ethics, education and training in the subject has also been on the rise. Provision might be offered either in-house, or externally through ethics consultants, universities and colleges, or corporate training specialists. Again, formal ethics training has tended to be more common in the US than elsewhere, with the US army even announcing a move to provide ethics training to its troops in Iraq in 2006 following the alleged murder of civilians.[1] However, a recent survey of large UK businesses revealed that ethics training was now being conducted at 71% of participating companies in the UK, a 50% increase in just three years (Webley 2008). In Asia, organizations such as CSR Asia also provide a wide range of training courses to meet growing demand in the region.

Many academic writers have stressed the need for more ethics education among business people, not only in terms of providing them with the tools to solve ethical dilemmas, but also to provide them with the ability to recognize and talk about ethical problems more accurately and easily (Thorne LeClair and Ferrell 2000). Diane Kirrane (1990) thus summarizes the goals for ethics training as: (a) identifying situations where ethical decision-making is involved; (b) understanding the culture and values of the organization; and (c) evaluating the impact of the ethical decision on the organization. Some companies have developed innovative approaches to achieving this, an example being Novartis, the Swiss healthcare multinational, where 'employees "play" their way to learning about the company's code of ethics in "Novartis Land", an online training program where employees interact online with 3D characters and have dialogues based on scenarios found within the company's corporate policies. They navigate through the dialogue, making decisions they may have to make in real life and answer a quiz style game show on company ethics' (Ethical Corporation 2009).

Stakeholder consultation, dialogue, and partnership programmes

There are various means of engaging an organization's stakeholders in ethics management, from surveying them to assess their views on specific issues to including them more fully in corporate decision-making. The more advanced forms may be central activities in the promotion of corporate accountability. Just as importantly though, it is evident that if 'good' business ethics is about doing the 'right' thing, then it is essential that organizations consult with relevant stakeholders in order to determine what other constituencies regard as 'right' in the first place. Either way, stakeholder consultation, dialogue, and partnership are increasingly becoming accepted—if still relatively new—ways of managing business ethics, and since they are issues that we will return to throughout the book, they will be afforded further elucidation in the section, Managing stakeholder relations (pp. 201–11), when we address the more general topic of managing stakeholder relationships. In the meantime, **Ethics Online 5** discusses the rather novel phenomenon of corporations communicating with their stakeholders about corporate responsibility issues through blogs.

Auditing, accounting, and reporting

Finally, we come to a set of closely related activities that are concerned with measuring, evaluating, and communicating the organization's impacts and performance on a range of social, ethical, and environmental issues of interest to their stakeholders. Unlike most of the previous developments, these aspects of business ethics management have not been pioneered in the US, but rather in Europe, with companies such as BT, the Co-operative Bank, Norsk Hydro, Traidcraft, the Body Shop, and Shell being at the forefront of innovation in this area. However, there is rapid development in this field across the globe, with KPMG's recent survey suggesting that 80% of the largest 250 companies worldwide now issue corporate responsibility reports, up from about 50% in 2005 (KPMG International 2008). According to the survey, national-level companies tend to trail the large multinationals (with only about 45% issuing reports), but this varies from more than 90% in Japan to under 20% in Mexico. This global diffusion is further evident in programmes such as SA 8000 and the Global Reporting Initiative (GRI) that—as we shall discuss in more detail later—seek to provide internationally comparative standards for aspects of auditing, accounting, and reporting. Indeed, although these elements of management are still in relatively early periods of experimentation and development, they can play a crucial role in enhancing corporate accountability in the era of corporate citizenship, as we suggested in Chapter 2. Accordingly, we will return to these developments in more detail below in the section, Assessing ethical performance (pp. 211–17).

Evolution of business ethics management

Before proceeding to discuss some of the most common components in more detail, we should stress that few, if any, businesses are likely to have *all* of these tools and techniques in place, and many may not even have *any* of them. This will particularly be the case with small- and medium-sized companies, which tend not to introduce the more formal elements of ethics management and reporting (Spence 1999). However, in general, the take-up of different components does appear to be increasing. For example, UK and US surveys over the last few years have tended to report escalating adoption of most, if not all, components (Ethics Resource Center 2007; Webley 2008).

Also, over the last decade or so, there appears to have been a change in emphasis concerning the purpose of business ethics management. Whereas previously, business ethics management tended to focus primarily on *managing employee behaviour* (through codes, etc.), there has been increasing attention to developing and implementing tools and techniques associated with the *management of broader social responsibilities*. These more externally focused components have typically involved the consideration of other stakeholder demands and considerations, such as in the development of social accounting tools and techniques.

Few would argue that these kinds of external components have an ethical dimension, yet business ethics as a management practice has historically had a tendency to focus primarily on the internal aspects of the business. Nonetheless, effective business ethics management needs to take account of both aspects—the internal and the external

VISIT THE WEBSITE for links to useful sources of further information

ETHICS ONLINE 5

Stakeholder communication through corporate CSR blogs

A notable development in recent years has been the emergence of corporate CSR (corporate social responsibility) blogs, typically written by a senior CSR executive or team to inform stakeholders of developments in their social and ethical initiatives through online media. Although still in its infancy, the phenomenon does seem to be gaining some momentum. Probably the most well known is the McDonald's blog 'Open for Discussion', which was launched back in 2006. But CSR blogs have probably been most conspicuous amongst technology companies, with the likes of Intel, Sun Microsystems, and Lawson Software all launching CSR blogs of one kind of another. Although IT companies may not be the most prominent in the business ethics world, especially compared with fast food companies like McDonald's, there is clearly a whole range of responsibility issues that the industry is having to deal with. The interesting thing though is that they are choosing to use their technology focus to develop new ways of engaging with stakeholders through the medium of blogs.

In many respects, the CSR blog is not a major breakthrough in the development of stakeholder communication, but it does represent an attempt to connect with people about responsibility issues in a potentially more personalized and interactive way than corporate reports, press releases, and TV commercials. As Intel claims, it is an 'intent to create greater transparency through open dialogue'. Or, as McDonald's puts it: 'Get personal perspectives on the issues, hear open assessments of the challenges we face, and engage in civil dialogue with the people behind the programs at the Golden Arches'.

Clearly the rhetorical emphasis here is on dialogue, although in reality most corporate CSR blogs do not seem to feature much in terms of real conversation with stakeholders. Typically, the blog is used as simply another channel of communication for presenting the corporate position on CSR issues, rather than as a venue for critical debate. The titles of McDonald's postings, such as 'What my little league days say to me about the root causes behind obesity' and 'An alternative perspective on larger-scale agriculture' probably won't leave anyone guessing about what positions the company is seeking to advocate—i.e. that fast food is not to blame for obesity and that big agriculture is good for society.

Other CSR blogs take a different approach—the law firm Addleshaw Goddard, for example, sets out 'the mental meanderings of our CSR Manager' as more of a diary for its CSR programme than anything else. The *Guardian* newspaper's sustainability blog, meanwhile, actively solicits input from stakeholders on, amongst other things, the role of online communication in developing better—and more interactive—social reporting.

On current evidence, there are clearly different ways of going about developing a corporate CSR blog. But it seems likely that with corporate transparency under question, the more corporations simply use CSR blogs as another vehicle to 'get their message out', the less successful they will be. Stakeholders are not just looking for more information, but to be engaged with in a different way—a way that treats their concerns seriously, that seeks to find common understandings and solutions, and that genuinely engages in dialogue. CSR blogs hold some potential for this, but most companies do not yet appear to have realized this effectively. A change in mindset is required, not simply a change in communication channel. As one commentator put it: 'Companies that try to connect with young people via web 2.0 sites dedicated to sustainability are like an embarrassing dad at a party'. But what certainly is refreshing and different about CSR blogs is that stakeholders get to identify with a real person, an individual with a name and a face, writing about a company's CSR activities. With personalization, with a 'moral face' even, there is greater potential for a meaningful ethical shift than with the bland, faceless messages of traditional corporate communications.

Sources
Knight, P. 2009. The web 2.0 cap doesn't fit. *Ethical Corporation*, January 2009: 22.
McDonald's CSR blog 'Open for Discussion': http://csr.blogs.mcdonalds.com/.
Intel blog 'CSR@Intel': http://blogs.intel.com/csr/.
Sun Microsystems 'Global citizenship' blog: http://blogs.sun.com/GlobalCitizenship/.
Guardian Sustainability blog: http://www.guardian.co.uk/sustainability/blog.
Addleshaw Goddard CSR blog: http://www.addleshawgoddard.com/csr.

dimensions. However, firms have tended to be slow in integrating their ethics and compliance functions with the CSR and sustainability areas of the business.

In the next three sections, we shall take a look at the three main areas where the management of business ethics might be particularly relevant:

- **Setting standards of ethical behaviour.** Here we shall mainly examine the role of ethical codes and their implementation.
- **Managing stakeholder relations.** Here we shall look mainly at how to assess stakeholders, different ways of managing them, and the benefits and problems of doing so.
- **Assessing ethical performance.** Here we shall consider the role of social accounting in contributing to the management and assessment of business ethics.

Setting standards of ethical behaviour: designing and implementing codes of ethics

Over the past couple of decades, many organizations have made efforts to set out specific standards of appropriate ethical conduct for their employees to follow. As we shall see later in the chapter, much of this standard-setting might well be done informally or even implicitly, such as through the example set by leaders. However, most attention in business ethics theory and practice has focused on *codes of ethics* (also called codes of conduct).

Codes of ethics are voluntary statements that commit organizations, industries, or professions to specific beliefs, values, and actions and/or that set out appropriate ethical behaviour for employees.

There are four main types of ethical codes:

- **Organizational or corporate codes of ethics.** These are specific to a single organization. Sometimes they are called codes of conduct or codes of business principles, but basically these codes seek to identify and encourage ethical behaviour at the level of the individual organization.
- **Professional codes of ethics.** Professional groups also often have their own guidelines for appropriate conduct for their members. Whilst most traditional professions such as medicine, law, and accountancy have long-standing codes of conduct, it is now also

increasingly common for other professions such as marketing, purchasing, or engineering to have their own codes.

- **Industry codes of ethics.** As well as specific professions, particular industries also sometimes have their own codes of ethics. For example, in many countries, the financial services industry will have a code of conduct for companies and/or employees operating in the industry. Similarly, at the international level, the electronics industry has developed a code of conduct 'to ensure that working conditions in the electronics industry supply chain are safe, that workers are treated with respect and dignity, and that manufacturing processes are environmentally responsible'.[2] The code was developed by a number of companies engaged in the manufacture of electronics products, including Dell, Hewlett Packard, IBM, and Celestica, the Toronto-based firm that manufactures Xbox 360 hardware. It has since been adopted by a range of multinationals, such as Apple, Cisco, Intel, Logitech, Microsoft, Samsung, and Sony.
- **Programme or group codes of ethics.** Finally, certain programmes, coalitions, or other sub-grouping of organizations also establish codes of ethics for those participating in specific programmes. For example, a collaboration of various business leaders from Europe, the US, and Japan resulted in the development of a global code of ethics for business called the CAUX Roundtable Principles for Business (http://www.cauxroundtable.org). Sometimes, conforming to a particular programme code is a prerequisite for using a particular label or mark of accreditation. For instance, companies wishing to use the Fairtrade Mark must meet international Fairtrade standards which are set by the FLO, the international certification body, Fairtrade Labelling Organisations International (see Chapter 9, pp. 423–6 for more details).

There has been a lot of research on codes of ethics over the past two decades, primarily focusing on four main issues:

- Prevalence of corporate codes of ethics.
- Content of codes of ethics.
- Effectiveness of codes of ethics.
- Possibilities for global codes of ethics.

Prevalence of codes of ethics

On the first point, codes of ethics are increasingly common, with a substantial rise in their usage identified during the 1990s and 2000s, particularly in large and medium-sized companies. Whilst studies have differed in their findings (usually due to different definitions of what constitutes a code of ethics), it is reasonable to conclude that something like two-thirds of large UK firms now have some kind of formal ethical code, whilst in the US, it has been suggested almost all large firms have a code of ethics of some kind (Weaver et al. 1999a; Webley and Le Jeune 2005). Evidence on their prevalence

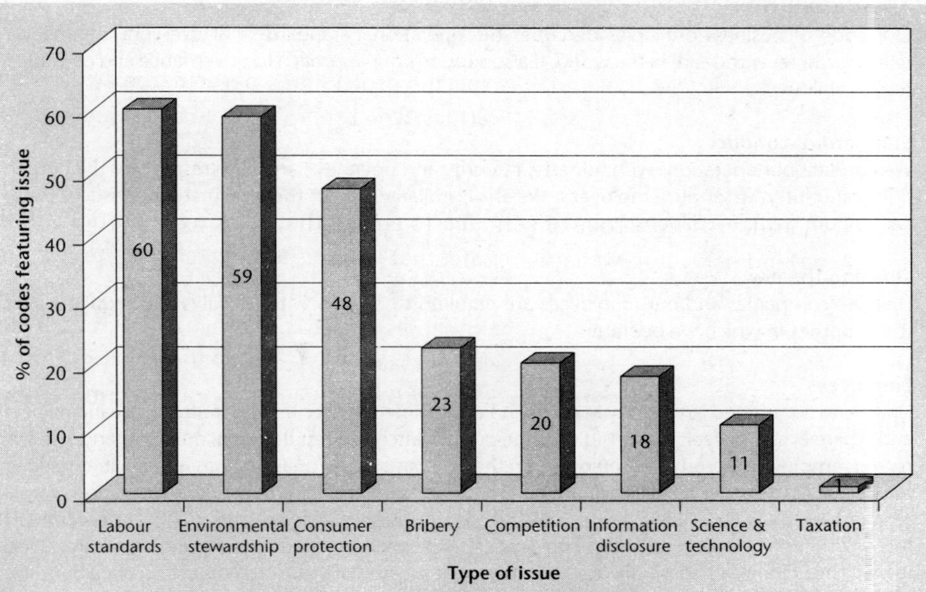

Figure 5.2. Prevalence of issues found in codes of conduct

Source: Derived from OECD (2001) *Codes of Corporate Conduct—An Expanded Review of Their Contents*. Paris: Organisation for Economic Co-Operation and Development: p.8. Data used with permission from the OECD.

elsewhere, and in SMEs, is fairly scant, but the general indication is of a much lower figure (Spence and Lozano 2000).

Content of codes of ethics

In terms of content, codes of ethics typically address a variety of issues, many of which appear to reflect industry factors and the prevailing concerns of the general public. As the OECD (2001: 2) reports, 'environmental management and labour standards dominate other issues in code texts, but consumer protection and bribery and corruption also receive extensive attention'. Perhaps unsurprisingly, codes from the apparel industry tend to focus more than others on labour issues, whilst codes from the extractive industry tend to feature environmental issues more than others. See **Figure 5.2** for an overview of the types of issue found in codes, and their prevalence.

In dealing with these issues, most codes attempt to achieve one or both of the following:

(a) Define principles or standards that the organization, profession, or industry believes in or wants to uphold.

(b) Set out practical guidelines for employee behaviour, either generally or in specific situations (such as accepting gifts, treating customers, etc.).

Our code of business principles describes the operational standards that everyone at Unilever follows, wherever they are in the world. It also supports our approach to governance and corporate responsibility.

Standard of conduct
We conduct our operations with honesty, integrity and openness, and with respect for the human rights and interests of our employees. We shall similarly respect the legitimate interests of those with whom we have relationships.

Obeying the law
Unilever companies and our employees are required to comply with the laws and regulations of the countries in which we operate.

Employees
Unilever is committed to diversity in a working environment where there is mutual trust and respect and where everyone feels responsible for the performance and reputation of our company. We will recruit, employ and promote employees on the sole basis of the qualifications and abilities needed for the work to be performed. We are committed to safe and healthy working conditions for all employees. We will not use any form of forced, compulsory or child labour. We are committed to working with employees to develop and enhance each individual's skills and capabilities. We respect the dignity of the individual and the right of employees to freedom of association. We will maintain good communications with employees through company based information and consultation procedures.

Consumers
Unilever is committed to providing branded products and services which consistently offer value in terms of price and quality, and which are safe for their intended use. Products and services will be accurately and properly labelled, advertised and communicated.

Shareholders
Unilever will conduct its operations in accordance with internationally accepted principles of good corporate governance. We will provide timely, regular and reliable information on our activities, structure, financial situation and performance to all shareholders.

Business partners
Unilever is committed to establishing mutually beneficial relations with our suppliers, customers and business partners. In our business dealings we expect our partners to adhere to business principles consistent with our own.

Community involvement
Unilever strives to be a trusted corporate citizen and, as an integral part of society, to fulfil our responsibilities to the societies and communities in which we operate.

Public activities
Unilever companies are encouraged to promote and defend their legitimate business interests. Unilever will co-operate with governments and other organizations, both directly and through bodies such as trade associations, in the development of proposed legislation and other regulations which may affect legitimate business interests. Unilever neither supports political parties nor contributes to the funds of groups whose activities are calculated to promote party interests.

Figure 5.3. Unilever's Code of Business Principles

Source: www.unilever.com. Reproduced with permission.

The environment
Unilever is committed to making continuous improvements in the management of our environmental impact and to the longer-term goal of developing a sustainable business. Unilever will work in partnership with others to promote environmental care, increase understanding of environmental issues and disseminate good practice.

Innovation
In our scientific innovation to meet consumer needs we will respect the concerns of our consumers and of society. We will work on the basis of sound science, applying rigorous standards of product safety.

Competition
Unilever believes in vigorous yet fair competition and supports the development of appropriate competition laws. Unilever companies and employees will conduct their operations in accordance with the principles of fair competition and all applicable regulations.

Business integrity
Unilever does not give or receive, whether directly or indirectly, bribes or other improper advantages for business or financial gain. No employee may offer, give or receive any gift or payment which is, or may be construed as being, a bribe. Any demand for, or offer of, a bribe must be rejected immediately and reported to management. Unilever accounting records and supporting documents must accurately describe and reflect the nature of the underlying transactions. No undisclosed or unrecorded account, fund or asset will be established or maintained.

Conflicts of interests
All Unilever employees are expected to avoid personal activities and financial interests which could conflict with their responsibilities to the company. Unilever employees must not seek gain for themselves or others through misuse of their positions.

Compliance – Monitoring – Reporting
Compliance with these principles is an essential element in our business success. The Unilever board is responsible for ensuring these principles are communicated to, and understood and observed by, all employees. Day-to-day responsibility is delegated to all senior management of the categories, functions, regions and operating companies. They are responsible for implementing these principles, if necessary through more detailed guidance tailored to local needs. Assurance of compliance is given and monitored each year. Compliance with the code is subject to review by the board supported by the audit committee of the board and the Unilever executive committee. Any breaches of the code must be reported in accordance with the procedures specified by the joint secretaries. The board of Unilever will not criticize management for any loss of business resulting from adherence to these principles and other mandatory policies and instructions. The board of Unilever expects employees to bring to their attention, or to that of senior management, any breach or suspected breach of these principles. Provision has been made for employees to be able to report in confidence and no employee will suffer as a consequence of doing so.

In this code the expressions 'Unilever' and 'Unilever companies' are used for convenience and mean the Unilever group of companies comprising Unilever N.V., Unilever PLC and their respective subsidiary companies. The board of Unilever means the directors of Unilever N.V. and Unilever PLC.

Figure 5.3. Continued

Figure 5.3 shows the code of ethics developed by Unilever for its business operations across the globe. As you can see, this mainly focuses on *general* principles, such as 'Unilever believes in vigorous yet fair competition', but also includes *specific* guidelines for behaviour in areas such as bribery. For instance, the code specifies that 'any demand for, or offer of, a bribe must be rejected immediately and reported to management'.

VISIT THE WEBSITE for a short response to this feature

> **? THINK THEORY**
>
> Think about the distinction between principles and guidelines, and see if you can identify further examples of each in the Unilever code. Evaluate these in terms of the degree of commitment from Unilever and the feasibility of their implementation, especially across national contexts. Do you consider the code to be a useful management tool?

According to Hoffman et al. (2001: 44), to be effective, codes should address *both* of these tasks: 'rules of conduct without a general values statement lack a framework of meaning and purpose; credos without rules of conduct lack specific content'. The question of exactly how codes can actually be crafted to achieve these ends is, however, a crucial one. Cassell et al. (1997), for example, argue that whilst clarity is obviously important, the desire for clear prescriptions for employees in specific situations can clash with needs for flexibility and applicability to multiple and/or novel situations. As we shall discuss in more detail shortly, this is particularly pertinent in the context of multinationals where employees are likely to be exposed to new dilemmas and differing cultural expectations (Donaldson 1996). Similarly, given that many ethical dilemmas are characterized by a clash of values or by conflicting stakeholder demands, ethical codes might be expected to identify which values or groups should take precedence—yet the need to avoid offending particular stakeholder groups often results in rather generalized statements of obligation (Hosmer 1987).

Such ambiguousness has unsurprisingly led many commentators to conclude that codes of ethics are primarily a rhetorical PR device that firms can offer as evidence of ethical commitment in order to pacify critics, whilst maintaining business as usual. Indeed, there is little empirical evidence to suggest that simply having a formal written code is either sufficient or even necessary for ensuring ethical behaviour (Kaptein and Schwartz 2008).

Effectiveness of codes of ethics

In many respects then, in terms of effectiveness, it is perhaps less important what a code says than how it is developed, implemented, and followed up. A code imposed on employees without clear communication about what it is trying to achieve and why might simply raise resentment. Similarly, a code that is written, launched, and then promptly forgotten is unlikely to promote enhanced ethical decision-making. Perhaps worst of all, a code that is introduced and then seen to be breached with impunity by senior managers or other members of staff is probably never going to achieve anything apart from raising employee cynicism.

So how to get the implementation right? Whilst there are few, if any, unequivocal answers to this question, a number of suggestions have been presented. Lisa Newton (1992), for example, has stressed the importance of maximizing the *participation* of organization members in the development stage in order to encourage commitment and 'buy-in' to the principles and rules of the code. Simon Webley (2001) further contends that in order for codes to have credibility, companies must be willing to *discipline* employees found in breach of them. Similarly, Treviño et al.'s (1999) survey revealed that *follow-through* (such as detection of violations, follow-up on notification of violations, and consistency between the policy and action) tended to be much more influential on employee behaviour than the mere presence of a code, regardless of how familiar employees might be with it.

Just consider the likely effect on employees of the experiences at Boeing, the US aerospace giant. The veteran CEO, Harry Stonecipher, was forced to resign in the mid-2000s following revelations that he was having an affair with a female executive of the company—a breach of the very ethics code that he had done so much to promote in his 15 months as chief executive. Although the affair itself was not prohibited by the code, Stonecipher's behaviour (allegedly including explicit email exchanges) was adjudged to have violated a section of the firm's code that stipulated that an employee 'will not engage in conduct or activity that may raise questions as to the company's honesty, impartiality, reputation or otherwise cause embarrassment to the company'. Stonecipher had been brought out of retirement to help restore the company's bruised reputation after a series of ethics scandals in the early 2000s, and had been successful in restoring trust and boosting the share price by 50%. However, his insistence that even minor violations of the code could not be tolerated ultimately let to his own ignominious exit.[3]

Follow-through of this nature sends an unambiguous message to employees. But how are organizations to ensure that such follow-through is established throughout its span of operations? For this to happen, it is imperative that violations are identified and procedures are put in place to deal with them. Sethi (2002) therefore suggests that codes need to be translated into a standardized and quantified *audit instrument* that lends itself to clear and consistent assessment, and that code compliance must be linked to managers' *performance evaluation*.

Unfortunately, clear research findings relating to the effect of codes and their implementation on employee decision-making and behaviour is still relatively limited (Cassell et al. 1997). Moreover, recent years have witnessed the emergence of a stream of literature more critical of ethical codes. Not only have codes been identified as questionable control mechanisms that potentially seek to exert influence over employee beliefs, values, and behaviours (Schwartz 2000), but as we saw in Chapter 3, there is a growing interest from postmodernists, feminists, and others in the possibility for codified ethical rules and principles to 'suppress' individual moral instincts, emotions, and empathy in order to ensure bureaucratic conformity and consistency. In **An Ethical Dilemma 5**, you can work through some of these issues in the context of a specific example.

AN ETHICAL DILEMMA 5

Clear codes for grey zones?

It's another Monday morning and after a weekend of celebrating the birthday of one of your friends, you sit in your office and sort out your diary for the week. As the IT manager of a small credit card company, you have to prepare for your staff meeting at 10am when all of your 15 team members will be present. You are planning to discuss the launch of your new promotion scheme, which is due to begin at the end of the week. Fortunately, Paul, who is the main market analyst for the company, was ready to do some extra work at home over the weekend in order to make sure the forecasts were ready for the meeting.

While sipping your first cup of coffee, someone knocks at the door. It is Fred, the hardware manager. He looks a bit embarrassed, and after a little stilted small talk, he tells you that 'a problem' has come up. He has just checked-in the laptop that Paul the market analyst had taken out of the company's pool and used at home over the weekend in order to finish the forecasts you had asked for. However, when completing the routine check of the laptop, Fred tells you he noticed links to various pornography sites in the history file of the laptop's internet browser. He tells you that they must have been accessed over the weekend that Paul had the laptop—the access dates refer to the last two days, and as is usual practice, the history file was emptied after the last person had borrowed it.

There is a strict company policy prohibiting employees from making personal use of company hardware, and access to sites containing 'material of an explicit nature' is tantamount to gross misconduct and may result in the immediate termination of the employee's contract. When your hardware manager leaves the office, you take a big breath and slowly finish your coffee.

After a few minutes thinking through the problem, you ask Paul to come into your office. You have a quick chat about his work and tell him that you are really pleased with the forecasts he put together over the weekend. Then, you bring up the problem with the laptop's history file. When you tell him what has surfaced in the history file, Paul is terribly embarrassed and assures you that he has absolutely no idea how this could have happened. After some thought, though, he tells you that he did allow a friend to use the laptop a couple of times over the weekend to check his email. Although Paul says that this is the only possible explanation for the mystery files, he does not volunteer any more information on the friend involved. As it happens, this does not actually make you feel much better about the situation: the company's code of conduct also prohibits use of IT equipment by anyone other than employees.

While driving home that evening, you turn the issue over and over in your head. Yes, there is a corporate code of conduct with regard to web access and personal use of company resources. And in principle you agree with this—after all you were part of the committee that issued the code in the first place. A company like yours has to be able to have clarity on such issues, and there have to be controls on what the company's equipment is used for—no doubt about that. You can't help thinking that Paul has been pretty stupid in breaking the rules—whether he visited the sites himself or not

On the other hand, you are also having a few problems with taking this further. Given the amount of embarrassment this has caused Paul already, isn't it likely to be just a one-off? Doesn't the company need Paul's experience and expertise, especially now with the big launch a few days off? Why make problems over the matter of a few websites? Couldn't you just forget about it for once? As soon as you start thinking this, though, you remember that Fred already knows about the problem—and given his good connections throughout the firm, you can imagine that the gossip has started circulating already. This looks set to be a tough call.

Questions

1 What are your main ethical problems in this case?
2 Set out the possible courses of action open to you.
3 Assess these alternatives according to a utilitarian perspective and a duty-based perspective. Which is the most convincing?
4 What would you do, and why?
5 Based on your answer, what are the apparent benefits and limitations of the code of conduct in this example?

Global codes of ethics

Finally, the issue of global codes of ethics has also received increasing attention from business, researchers, and others in recent years. Given the rise of multinational business, many organizations have found that codes of ethics developed for use in their home country may need to be revisited for their international operations. Are guidelines for domestic employees still relevant and applicable in overseas contexts? Can organizations devise one set of principles for all countries in which they operate?

Consider the issue of gift giving in business. This is an issue where cultural context has a distinct bearing on what might be regarded as acceptable ethical behaviour. Whilst many organizations have specific guidelines precluding the offer or acceptance of gifts and hospitality as part of their business operations, in some countries, such as Japan, not only is the offering of gifts considered to be a perfectly acceptable business activity, but the refusal to accept such offerings can be regarded as offensive. Similarly, questions of equal opportunity are somewhat more equivocal in a multinational context. European or US organizations with codes of practice relating to equal opportunities may find that these run counter to cultural norms, and even legal statutes overseas. For example, in many countries such as India, there is a cultural expectation that people should show preference for their close friends and family over strangers, even in business contexts such as recruitment. In many Islamic countries, the equal treatment of men and women is viewed very differently from how it is in the West, with countries such as Saudi Arabia still having major restrictions on women even entering the workforce (Murphy 2007).

According to Thomas Donaldson (1996), one of the leading writers on international business ethics, the key question for those working overseas is: when is different just different and when is different wrong? As such, the question of how multinationals should address cultural differences in drafting their ethical codes returns us to the discussion of relativist versus absolutist positions on ethics that we introduced in Chapter 3. A relativist would suggest that different codes should be developed for different contexts, whilst an absolutist would contend that one code can and should fit all. Donaldson's (1996) solution is to propose a middle ground between the two extremes, whereby the organization should be guided by three principles:

(a) Respect for core human values, which determine an absolute moral threshold.
(b) Respect for local traditions.
(c) The belief that context matters when deciding what is right and wrong.

What this means is that global codes should define minimum ethical standards according to core human values shared across countries, religions, and cultures, such as the need to respect human dignity and basic human rights. Beyond this, though, codes should also respect cultural or contextual difference in setting out appropriate behaviour in areas such as bribery or gift giving.

The search for core values or universal ethical principles as a basis for global business codes of ethics has given rise to a number of important initiatives:[4]

- In 1994, business and government leaders, theologians, and academics representing three religions—Christian, Jewish, and Islamic—devised the **Interfaith Declaration: A Code of Ethics on International Business for Christians, Muslims and Jews.** This sought to identify key principles shared by the three faiths that could guide international business behaviour. These principles are justice, mutual respect, stewardship, and honesty.

- The **CAUX Roundtable**, an international network of senior business leaders from Europe, the US, and Japan, launched its own set of principles in 1994, as a 'worldwide vision for ethical and responsible corporate behaviour'. The principles were guided by two broad ethical ideals—human dignity and *kyosei* (a belief of living and working together for the good of all), and were reformatted in 2009 in response to the global financial crisis.

- In 2000, the United Nations launched the **UN Global Compact,** a set of ten 'universally accepted' principles concerned with human rights, labour, the environment, and anti-corruption. By 2009, more than 4,700 businesses in 120 countries around the world had signed up to the compact. For an extended discussion of the global compact, see Ethics in Action 11.2 in Chapter 11 (pp. 532–3).

Whilst the necessity of developing globally acceptable and relevant principles means that such codes tend to be rather general in nature, these developments do at least show that some level of international agreement on appropriate standards of business behaviour is possible. And for multinationals, although establishing and implementing a global code of ethics represents a huge challenge, it is one that is increasingly expected in the contemporary business environment (Sethi 2002). This doesn't just go for those high-profile big brand companies on the high street, but also companies that are more frequently below the ethics radar. Consider, for example, the Swedish engineering group, Sandvik. The company launched its code across its global operations in the mid-2000s with a series of two-day seminars for all of its managers in some 130 countries. With the goal of rolling out the code to the firm's entire 50,000 employees, it is clear that multinationals such as Sandvik have to invest a great deal of time, energy, and resources into introducing a global code in a meaningful way.

Ultimately, however, it is important to realize that the drive for codes of ethics, whether national or international, is never going to 'solve' the management of business ethics. As we saw in the previous chapter, there is a vast array of influences on individual decision-makers within the organization, of which a written code is but one aspect. A code can rarely do more than set out the *minimum expectations* placed on organizations and their members, and cannot be expected to be a substitute for organizational contexts supportive of ethical reflection, debate, and decision-making, or decision-makers with strong personal integrity. Moreover, whilst the introduction of codes of ethics primarily represents an attempt to manage employee conduct, organizations have increasingly found that the management of business ethics also requires them to manage relationships with a wide range of stakeholders, as we shall now discuss.

? THINK THEORY

Think about the notion of a global code of ethics from the perspective of (i) rights and (ii) postmodern perspectives on ethics. What does each contribute and can they be reconciled?

VISIT THE WEBSITE for a short response to this feature

■ Managing stakeholder relations

In Chapter 2, we introduced stakeholder theory as one of the key theories in the debate on the role and responsibilities of business in society. Whilst our main concern there, and in the subsequent chapter, was to highlight the normative basis of stakeholder theory, it is important also to acknowledge the descriptive argument that managers do indeed appear to recognize distinct stakeholder groups and manage their companies accordingly (Clarkson 1995). Whilst in some countries this is institutionalized in corporate governance, such as in the German two-tier supervisory board, even in more shareholder-focused countries, many managers appear to have embraced at least some degree of recognition for stakeholder claims. A *McKinsey* (2006) survey found that four out of five executives from global companies agreed that generating high returns for investors should be balanced with other stakeholder interests, with Indian managers articulating the most positive response (90% endorsed a 'public-good' dimension) and executives based in China demonstrating the least commitment (25% said that investor returns should be the sole focus of corporate activity).

The recognition that not only businesses, but organizations of all kinds, including charities, schools, universities, and governments, have a range of stakeholders whose interests might need to be taken into account in making decisions has given rise to a significant body of research dealing with the management of stakeholder relations. Let us look at some of the main themes addressed in this literature.

Assessing stakeholder importance: an instrumental perspective

Much of the stakeholder management literature has tended to focus on the strategic aspects of identifying which stakeholders actually matter to the organization and how they should be dealt with in order for the organization to effectively achieve its goals. Thus, Hill and Jones (2007: 374–7), in one of the leading Strategic Management textbooks, suggest that: 'Balancing the needs of different stakeholder groups is in the long-run interests of the company's owners, its shareholders ... A company cannot always satisfy the claims of all stakeholders. The goals of different groups may conflict, and in practice few organizations have the resources to manage all stakeholders ... Often the company must make choices. To do so, it must identify the most important stakeholders and give highest priority to pursuing strategies that satisfy their needs'.

As Donaldson and Preston (1995) contend, it is important to distinguish this *instrumental* perspective on stakeholder theory from the *normative* perspective we developed in Chapters 2 and 3, and the *descriptive* perspective briefly mentioned above. Hill and Jones' (2007) argument is not so much that organizations have to rate the relative strength of the *ethical* claims of their various stakeholders, but rather that strategic objectives can best be realized by deciding which stakeholders are more likely to be able to *influence* the organization in some way. This is likely to be particularly important when organizations are in a position where they have to decide how to assign relative importance or priority to competing stakeholder claims.

Following a comprehensive review of the stakeholder management literature, Mitchell et al. (1997) suggest three key relationship attributes likely to determine the perceived importance or *salience* of stakeholders:

- **Power**. The perceived ability of a stakeholder to influence organizational action.
- **Legitimacy**. Whether the organization perceives the stakeholder's actions as desirable, proper, or appropriate.
- **Urgency**. The degree to which stakeholder claims are perceived to call for immediate attention.

According to Mitchell et al. (1997), managers are likely to assign greater salience to those stakeholders thought to possess greater power, legitimacy, and urgency. Thus, stakeholders thought to be in possession of only one of these attributes will be regarded as the least important and might be regarded as 'latent' stakeholders. Those in possession of two of the three qualities are moderately important and hence can be thought of as 'expectant' stakeholders. Finally, those in possession of all three will be seen as the most important constituencies and hence are termed 'definitive' stakeholders. For businesses, these definitive stakeholders often require active engagement in order to develop an effective and appropriate working relationship. Indeed, a variety of different relationships might be expected to emerge between businesses and their stakeholders, as we shall now see.

Types of stakeholder relationship

Until relatively recently, it had been generally assumed that relationships between businesses and their stakeholders tended to be somewhat antagonist, even confrontational in nature. For example, just as companies might exploit consumers or downsize employees, consumers might equally boycott company products, employees could initiate industrial action, suppliers withhold credit, competitors engage in industrial espionage, and pressure groups employ aggressive direct action campaigns against companies. **Ethics on Screen 5**, for example, discusses a movie on Wal-Mart that features a wealth of antagonistic relations between the company and its stakeholders.

Increasingly however, it has been recognized that there might also be a place for co-operation between stakeholders. To begin with, the 1990s witnessed an explosion in business–business collaboration, taking the form of joint ventures, strategic alliances, co-marketing initiatives, supplier partnership programmes, and other means of collaborative activity. This was followed by a dramatic increase in collaborations between businesses and other stakeholders, such as non-governmental organizations (NGOs), government bodies, and trade unions.

Much of this development in broader stakeholder collaboration was pioneered in the field of environmental management. For example, as we shall describe in more detail in Chapter 10, various partnerships between businesses and NGOs emerged across the globe during the 1990s and 2000s, aimed at tackling environmental problems such as packaging, deforestation, green product innovation, mining, and fishing (Bendell 2000a; Murphy and Bendell 1997). These have involved leading national and multinational companies such as AEG Hausgeräte, the Body Shop, Intergamma, McDonald's, and Unilever, as well as many well-known NGOs, including Greenpeace, Friends of the Earth, and WWF. Similarly, the Dutch covenant approach, initially pioneered in the 1980s and developed extensively since, has involved business and government in jointly setting up voluntary environmental agreements based on consensus and consultation between government and industry bodies (Elkington 1999: 236–7). Increasingly, these extended forms of stakeholder collaboration have also emerged in other areas of business too: various charities have joined with corporations in cause-related marketing campaigns; governments have worked with corporations to develop public-private partnerships for tackling social, educational, health, and transportation problems; and NGOs, trade unions, and government organizations have worked with businesses to develop initiatives aimed at improving working conditions, and stamping out child labour and other human rights abuses in developing countries.

VISIT THE WEBSITE for links to useful sources of furthur information

VISIT THE WEBSITE to see a trailer for 'Wal-Mart: The High Cost of Low Price'

ETHICS ON SCREEN 5

Wal-Mart: The High Cost of Low Price

An engrossing, muckraking documentary about the retail giant that's been called 'the world's largest, richest and probably meanest corporation.'

Kenneth Turan, *Los Angeles Times*

Named after its founder Sam Walton (but trading under the Asda brand name in the UK) the US-based Wal-Mart is the world's largest retailer, and America's biggest employer. But along with commercial success, inevitably comes a degree of criticism from those concerned about the social impacts that such a retail giant can have on the communities in which it operates. So perhaps it is no surprise that, as with McDonald's before it (in the movie *Supersize Me*), the supermarket giant eventually found itself the reluctant star of its very own movie.

Wal-Mart: The High Cost of Low Price is a feature-length documentary produced and directed by Robert Greenwald, the man behind the coruscating attack on Fox News, *Outfoxed: Rupert Murdoch's War on Journalism*, as well as a string of other documentaries and feature films. In the Wal-Mart film, Greenwald directs his fire at the company, using personal stories of the various people who have been affected by the company's policies and tactics. This includes employees compelled to turn to public assistance to provide healthcare for their families, workers who claimed to have been coerced into unpaid overtime, unions obstructed by powerful crack-downs, and the legions of small family businesses forced to close down after Wal-Mart took advantage of tax subsidies to open big new stores that wiped out the local competition. The point of the film is to take us behind the low prices that Wal-Mart offers us, and see the ethical impacts such prices can have on regular, hard-working people—in fact, exactly the same people that Wal-Mart targets as customers.

Courtesy Brave New Films

While the film itself is an interesting invective on the firm's supposed unwillingness or inability to manage ethically, what is perhaps most interesting is the way that Wal-Mart has responded to the film, and the changes that have begun to emerge in its practices. Whilst the company initially claimed that they would 'pretty much ignore' the film, its release in the US at the end of 2005 prompted a flurry of activity from Wal-Mart that sought to counter the claims made in the movie and question the integrity of its makers. In fact, even before the film itself was released, Wal-Mart attacked the film's three-minute trailer for being 'neither fair nor honest to his audience or the American people', and so released their own short video detailing the 'three errors in three minutes' made by Greenwald's trailer—which Greenwald in turn then 'remixed' to present a different picture entirely!

In addition to trashing the trailer, Wal-Mart developed a media strategy to attack the credibility of Greenwald and his film, and an internal management strategy to try and minimize the impact on its legions of employees across America—all of which is detailed on the film's website. The media strategy included sending out a comprehensive press kit criticizing Greenwald and detailing evidence about the film's 'inaccuracies', as well as a dossier of bad reviews from some of Greenwald's previous films. Characterizing the director as a 'failed fantasy filmmaker' and a 'Hollywood elitist', Wal-Mart's media team clearly decided to fight hard against the film they viewed as a 'sensationalized', 'fabricated', 'contorted vision'.

The filmmakers also provide evidence to show that the company sent a memo to every store manager in the US to warn them of the release of the film and to provide them with a script to read to employees in which key details of the film were refuted and the company's position was reinforced. As the script proclaims: 'You can hold your head high in knowing that Wal-Mart provides unrivalled value to America's working families. We offer 1.3 million hardworking men and women not only jobs, but careers. We offer families the opportunities to save significantly by shopping at Wal-Mart .... We urge you that if you feel as strongly as we do about these untruths directed at our company, please ensure that your friends, family and members of the community know the truth about our company.'

The truth or otherwise of the claims made by Greenwald in the movie, we will leave to the viewer to decide for themselves. But it is interesting that the film's contribution to mounting criticism of the company seems to have prompted more than just defensiveness from Wal-Mart. A range of initiatives including a commitment to sourcing all its fish from sustainable sources, and a move to introduce affordable organic produce into the stores, were launched late in 2005 and early 2006 following an unprecedented speech by then CEO Lee Scott that committed the company to an ambitious sustainability platform. The company now aims to achieve 100% renewable energy use, zero waste, and sustainable products in its stores. By 2009, the company had rewritten its company purpose to focus on 'saving people money so they can live better' and was proclaiming that sustainability was 'one of the most important opportunities for both the future of our business and the future of our world'. Whilst some critics have remained sceptical about Wal-Mart's ethical u-turn, the company has made significant strides in tackling a range of key social and environmental issues relevant to its business. Maybe, then, *Wal-Mart: The High Cost of Low Price* ended up doing more than just entertaining its audience, and actually had a tangible impact on the company's strategy.

Sources

http://www.walmartmovie.com.
http://www.walmart.com.

All of these developments and more will be discussed in greater detail in the second part of the book where we focus on business ethics and specific stakeholder groups. What is immediately clear, however, is that stakeholder relationships can take a variety of different forms, including the following:[5]

- **Challenge**—relationship based on mutual opposition and conflict.
- **Sparring partners**—relationship based on 'healthy conflict' and periodic bouts of conflict.
- **One-way support**—relationship based on philanthropy, sponsorship, or other forms of resource contribution from one party to the other.

- **Mutual support**—relationship based on formal or informal two-way support, such as derived from strategic philanthropy, or as formalized through a third-party association or body of some kind.
- **Endorsement**—relationship based on paid/unpaid public approval granted from one partner to the other in relation to a specific product or programme, such as in the case of labelling and accreditation schemes.
- **Project dialogue**—relationship based on discussion between partners regarding specific project or proposal, such as stakeholder dialogue accompanying major regeneration or construction projects.
- **Strategy dialogue**—relationship based on discussion between partners over longer-term issues and the development of overall strategy for organizations, industries, or regulatory regimes.
- **Task force**—relationship based on co-operation to achieve a specific task, such as a research project or new product/system development.
- **Joint venture or alliance**—relationship based on formal partnership involving significant mutual resource commitment to achieve specific goals.

Ethics in Action 5.1 describes a range of different types of 'social partnerships' that corporations have engaged in with their various stakeholders, including those with civil society organizations, public sector bodies, competitors, suppliers, and even customers. As this suggests, whilst it would appear that confrontational forms of relationship are still very much in evidence, there has certainly been a significant shift towards the more collaborative types of relationship, such as stakeholder dialogue and alliances (Selsky and Parker 2005).

Collaboration between stakeholders will certainly not always lead to beneficial ethical outcomes (consider, for example, the problems posed by two competitors collaborating over price setting). However, it is certainly an increasingly important tool for *managing* business ethics, primarily because closer forms of collaboration can bring to the surface stakeholder demands and interests, and thereby provide companies with a greater opportunity to satisfy their stakeholders in some way. Moreover, by involving stakeholders more, it can be argued that a greater degree of democratic governance is introduced into corporate decision-making, thus enhancing corporate accountability.

On the reverse side, it is also clear that despite their obvious benefits for the management of business ethics, developments towards closer stakeholder relationships are not without their problems.

Problems with stakeholder collaboration

Potential problems with stakeholder collaboration can arise at a number of different levels, but can be basically summarized as follows:

1 **Resource intensity.** Stakeholder collaboration can be extremely time-consuming and expensive compared with traditional forms of corporate decision-making. Not only may firms not have sufficient resources to engage in extensive stakeholder collaboration,

but by doing so, they may fail to meet the short-term financial goals expected of them by shareholders. Small businesses, in particular, may typically lack the time and financial resources necessary to develop partnerships, even though they often stand to benefit significantly due to the need for external expertise and support.

2 **Culture clash.** Companies and their stakeholders often exhibit very different values and goals, and this can lead to significant clashes in beliefs and ways of working, both between and within collaborating groups (Crane 1998).

3 **Schizophrenia.** At the same time as they are collaborating on one issue or project, companies and their stakeholders may also often be in conflict over another issue or project. This development of 'multiple identities' can result in apparently schizophrenic behaviour on either or both sides, which their partners may find hard to deal with (Crane and Livesey 2003; Elkington and Fennell 2000).

4 **Uncontrollability.** Even with the best intentions on the part of all parties, there is no guarantee with stakeholder collaboration that a mutually acceptable outcome can always be reached. However, not only can consensus be elusive, but by collaborating with many different partners, companies can lose control of both their strategic direction and their corporate image (Crane and Livesey 2003).

5 **Co-optation.** Some critics have raised the question of whether, by involving themselves more closely with corporations, some stakeholder groups are effectively just being co-opted by corporations to embrace a more business-friendly agenda rather than maintaining true independence. The UN's Global Compact initiative described earlier in the chapter was criticized by some NGOs for allowing corporations to 'bluewash' their questionable practices by aligning themselves with the blue flag (and humanitarian ideals) of the UN and thereby weakening the scope for the UN to hold companies accountable for addressing environmental, labour, and human rights issues.[6]

6 **Accountability.** Whilst stakeholder collaboration may partially redress problems with *corporate* accountability, there are also important concerns about the accountability of stakeholder organizations themselves (Bendell 2000b). Government bodies, quangos, trade unions, and NGOs, for example, can also be challenged on grounds of accountability to their members or the general public. Moreover, when stakeholders such as business and government collaborate 'behind closed doors', accountability to the public may be compromised.

7 **Resistance.** As a result of these and other concerns, organization members or external parties may try and resist the development of collaborative relationships, thus preventing the partners from fully achieving their goals (Selsky and Parker 2005).

Again, we shall revisit some of these questions and problems in more detail in the relevant chapters in the second part of the book. However, our general conclusion regarding the benefits or otherwise of closer business-stakeholder relationships is that, whilst the problems noted above need to be effectively thought through and dealt with, such

VISIT THE WEBSITE for links to useful sources of further information

ETHICS IN ACTION 5.1 http://www.ethicalcorp.com

Partnerships—working better together

EC Newsdesk, 5 September 2008

Ethical CORPORATION

Companies will always draw heavily on internal expertise to deliver community investment programmes. But in some instances there are clear advantages to partnering with other organisations. Forming partnerships goes far beyond simply sponsoring a charity; it involves the creation of new activities to which the company can contribute and add value.

In the past, companies would support a single global charity, such as UNICEF or Save the Children, through large regular donations, forming the central pillar of their community investment activity. As community investment aligns itself more closely with corporate objectives and companies become clearer about what they wish to achieve from their community investment, this model is looking outdated.

First, a company chooses an issue. Then it builds appropriate partnerships. For companies with global presence, single charity partnerships often do not make sense from a practical perspective. BP corporate responsibility director Sheldon Daniel explains: 'For a multinational with a diverse geographic portfolio, it's hard to have global partnerships which would be able to meet needs in such a variety of operating environments'.

In some instances, a company will choose to work with multiple charity partners in a single region. Social issues are often best addressed through collaboration, rather than competition. Vodafone UK Foundation head Sarah Shillito says: 'Now we say to charities you have to choose who else you're going to work with when you make a proposal to us. We think it's a good way of creating a deeper learning experience.'

Partnerships last longer

Companies are increasingly building partnerships for the long term, recognizing that this allows charities to budget and plan for the future. There are also business benefits to developing longer-term relationships, given how long it can take to build internal and external awareness of such partnerships. Changing partners annually is not an effective way to send a clear message about what you are doing.

The companies surveyed for this study tend to establish partnerships for at least three years. Some go much further. Royal Bank of Scotland head of community investment Stephen Moir describes the partnerships formed to deliver the bank's financial inclusion programmes as 'generational commitments'. He says: 'Our experience has shown that things like skills transfer and building the capacity of an organisation take much longer than three years. We will support them for an undetermined period, until such a point as it stops being sensible and we undertake another strategic review.'

Microsoft similarly has no set rules about the lifespan of partnerships and many have continued for more than 10 years. Ensuring that the objectives of a partnership stay fresh and relevant, whatever its lifespan, is most important, the company says.

Public sector partnerships

Tackling social issues through community investment increasingly means partnering with public sector organizations as well as traditional charity partners. These relationships reflect a growing willingness from both governments and companies to work together to achieve specific aims.

Working with a public or governmental body lends extra credibility to a company's activity and helps it develop closer links with other organizations. It can also be more efficient, as it ensures companies are not duplicating work being done by governments.

For its Children's Safe Drinking Water initiative, Procter & Gamble has worked with the US Centers for Disease Control and Prevention to develop low-cost technology for water purification sachets for use in developing countries. It now works to deliver this technology with a coalition of charities, with substantial support from the US Agency for International Development.

Both IBM and Microsoft run a number of global programmes to bring IT skills to children. The companies' primary partnerships are with the ministry of education or regional governments in each country. BP often works with government agencies to encourage enterprise—for example, collaborating with the UN Development Programme to train local people in Indonesia, home of its Tangguh gas project. And Microsoft's work on employability is designed to feed directly into the EU's Lisbon agenda with its aim to promote a more inclusive knowledge economy.

Rivals together

One of the most interesting developments in community investment is the growing number of business-to-business partnerships that are being formed to deliver community investment goals.

Microsoft has always been well aware of the limitations of what it can provide, and has a long history of encouraging its partners and other businesses to work with it on community initiatives. 'We know very well that we're a software company and that we bring certain competencies to the table, but not all of them,' says Sylvie Laffarge, community affairs director for Europe, the Middle East and Africa.

A good illustration is Microsoft's work in Europe with the Employability Alliance. This is a public-private initiative by Microsoft with partners including Cisco Systems, Randstad and State Street. These companies agreed that it makes sense for them to work together on building employability skills. The alliance's aim is to provide 20 million Europeans with access to technology, content, certification, and training in computer technology and other skills by 2010.

Microsoft also partners with other businesses to donate various products. TechSoup is an organization that provides a one-stop-shop for non-profit groups looking for technology donations, and gives businesses a platform for making donations. This is much more efficient than individual companies running their own programmes, and non-profits and charities applying to each one for donations. Microsoft has been instrumental in setting up and supporting TechSoup's international expansion through local NGO partners in collaboration with Microsoft subsidiaries and other industry partners.

Technology is one of the more obvious candidates for this kind of partnership, since each company will be able to provide part of the solution: software, hardware or training skills. But this is not the only industry where partnerships of this type are emerging. Very different companies may find synergies in their areas of interest. Vodafone UK is working on developing a mentoring project for former prisoners, which involves several other high profile companies from different industries. Shillito says: 'It's a really important message to convey if we're trying to encourage charities to work together with their competitors—we should be doing the same thing.'

Companies acknowledge that this development brings a number of challenges. It can be hard to find initiatives that fit equally well with the objectives of different businesses. There may also be concerns about losing distinctiveness. When reputation is a key driver of community investment, companies may be unwilling to risk what could be a key differentiator for their brand.

Client collaboration

Working with suppliers and clients is another option for creating business-to-business partnerships. This has been a route for IBM, which found that its clients were increasingly looking for opportunities to collaborate on community investment programmes. An example is KidSmart, an IBM programme that makes computers loaded with educational software available to preschool children. IBM has run joint team events with clients to install the computers at local kindergartens.

Microsoft regularly invites its business partners to provide inputs appropriate to a particular initiative. For example in working with Junior Achievement, a youth skills organization in Latvia, it was able to engage a local web-hosting firm to host a web services portal for the organisation.

Some of the most exciting developments in community investment are happening in this area of partnerships as varied expertise is brought together in new ways. The examples here are set to be replicated as companies see the benefits of delivering their community investment plans through partnerships with the non-profit, public and private sectors.

Sources

Ethical Corporation, 5 September 2008, http://www.ethicalcorp.com.

VISIT THE WEBSITE for a short response to this feature

? THINK THEORY

What type of stakeholder relationships are described here? What are the benefits and limitations of these approaches for managing business ethics?

developments should be cautiously welcomed and encouraged, given their considerable potential for enhancing the management of business ethics.

■ Assessing ethical performance

As with any other form of management, the effective management of business ethics relies to some extent on being able to assess and evaluate performance. Low or disappointing performance in business ethics might call for increased attention to ethical issues and problems; high performance might indicate an effective approach to the management of business ethics. Almost immediately, however, it is possible to identify some drawbacks with this whole notion of ethical performance. What exactly is ethical performance? How can it possibly be measured? What criteria can we use to determine how good or bad an organization's ethical performance is? What level of ethical performance is expected by, or acceptable to, stakeholders? These are all vitally important questions to answer if we are to make any progress at all towards the effective management of business ethics. Unfortunately, whilst there are impressive developments currently taking place in this area, we are still a long way from being able to provide a comprehensive response

At present, there is a whole patchwork of initiatives that we might include within the umbrella of assessing ethical performance. These include social auditing, environmental accounting, and sustainability reporting, as well as various other mixtures of terminology. With such a diversity of labels in use, there are obviously problems with distinguishing between different tools, techniques, and approaches. This is not helped by the fact that, at times, the distinctions between these terms are fairly illusory and there has been much inconsistency in the way that different terms have been applied and used. Whilst Toyota currently produces a 'sustainability report', Total produces a 'CSR report', Microsoft produces a 'citizenship report', and the Body Shop produces a 'values report'. Sometimes even the same company changes between the different labels from one year to the next! Here though are some general distinctions that tend to apply in most cases:

- Approaches prefaced 'ethical' often tend to focus on internal management systems, or individual-level aspects of the business, such as compliance with codes of ethics, incidences of bribery, legal violations, etc. For example, Ferrell et al. (2008: 233) suggest that an 'ethics audit is a systematic evaluation of an organization's ethics program and performance to determine whether it is effective'. A second common use of 'ethical' is found in approaches which tend to focus on stakeholder values, such as the 'ethical accounting' technique used by SbN Bank and Wøyen Mølle and the Body Shop's 'ethical audit' technique.[7]

- Approaches prefaced 'environmental' tend to focus exclusively on the organization's impact on the natural environment. Hence an environmental report will typically report on an organization's policies, programmes, and performance in various areas of environmental management, such as air and water pollution, resource efficiency, recycling, etc.

- Approaches prefaced 'social' tend to have a broader remit, covering a range of issues in addition to (or sometimes separate from) the environment, such as employee conditions, health and safety, equal opportunities, human rights, corporate giving, community relations. These approaches often incorporate impacts on a wide range of organizational stakeholders.

- Approaches prefaced 'sustainability' tend to be concerned with the triple bottom line of social, economic, and environmental considerations.

- Differences between the use of the terms 'auditing', 'accounting', and 'reporting' are still less clear cut, but essentially 'accounting' is an overall process or discipline which includes 'auditing' (i.e. a measurement or checking exercise) and 'reporting' (i.e. a means of communicating data).

Given these distinctions, we shall refer to **social accounting** as the generic term, which encapsulates the other tools and approaches. With its first usage dating back to the early 1970s, social accounting is also, according to Gray et al. (1997), the longest established and simplest term with which to work.

Defining social accounting

Probably the key factors that distinguish social accounting from conventional (financial) accounting are:

- Its focus on issues other than (but not necessarily excluding) financial data.
- The intended audience being stakeholders other than (but again not excluding) shareholders.
- Unlike financial accounting, social accounting is not (at least as yet) required by law in most jurisdictions.

Broadly defined, then, we regard social accounting as the following:

> **Social accounting is the voluntary process concerned with assessing and communicating organizational activities and impacts on social, ethical, and environmental issues relevant to stakeholders.**

So what does the process of social accounting involve? Again, there are no clear answers to this question. Unlike financial accounting, there are as yet no strict formal standards laying down the rules that determine which issues should be included, how performance on particular issues should be assessed, or on how the organization should communicate its assessments to its audience. In many ways, this is not surprising. After all, whilst it is reasonably straightforward to calculate how much wages an organization has paid, or how many sales it might have made, this is much more difficult with social, ethical, and environmental issues. True, some of the social activities of an organization can be reasonably accurately determined, such as how much effluent might have been discharged into local rivers, or how much money has been given away to charitable causes. But even here, this does not tell us what the actual impact of these activities has been—how polluted this makes the water, and what is the ultimate consequence for fish and other life. Or what were the actual effects of company donations on their recipients and how much happiness did they cause?

Much of the data collected and reported in social accounting is therefore inevitably qualitative in nature, particularly as organizations move away from an emphasis on environmental impacts towards more integrated social or sustainability reports. For example, *The Shell Sustainability Report 2008* includes a mixture of quantitative data, such as greenhouse gas emissions, safety statistics, and gender diversity, as well as more qualitative data in the form of case studies of specific projects, quotes from various stakeholders, and outlines of key social issues and Shell's position on them.

The problem though is not only one of how to assess social impacts, but also of which impacts to *account for* in the first place. Organizations have different aims, problems, and achievements, their stakeholders have different interests and concerns, and the reasons for even engaging in social accounting at all will vary between different organizations. Inevitably, then, the nature and process of social accounting adopted by any organization is to some extent a function of how the particular organization sees itself and its relationship with its stakeholders (Zadek et al. 1997). As such, the practice of social accounting to date has tended to be evolutionary in nature, with organizations not only developing and refining their techniques over time, but also building in adaptation within the development cycle of a given report or audit. For example, **Figure 5.4** shows a framework originally established by the Body Shop. This includes *stakeholder consultation* to identify issues regarded as salient or of particular interest to stakeholders, prior to the main collection of data. Similarly, it also includes a process of *stakeholder dialogue* following publication of the report in order to obtain feedback and set priorities for future action.

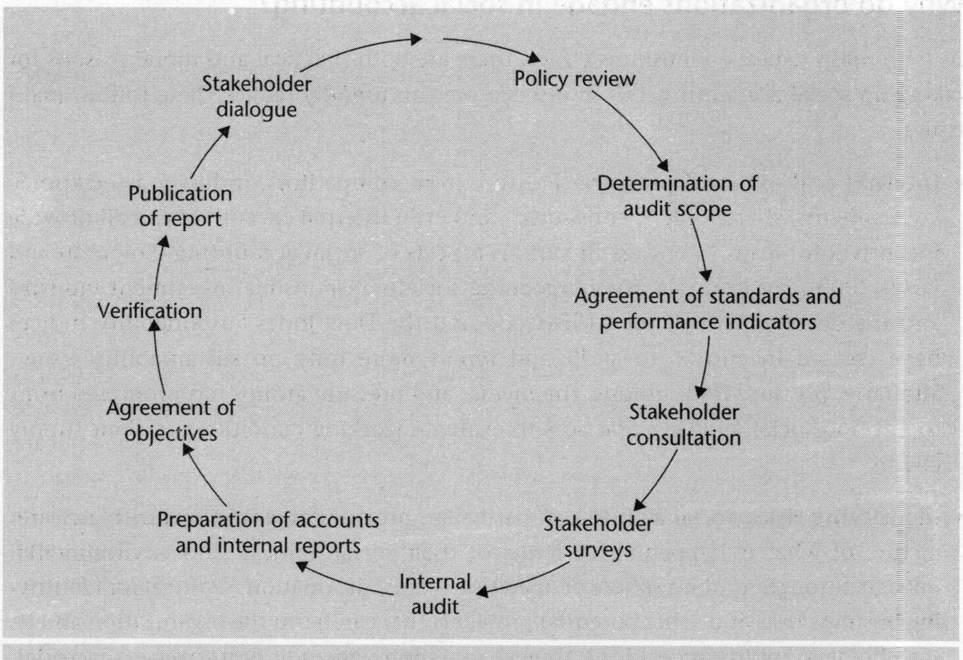

Figure 5.4. Framework for social accounting established by the Body Shop
Source: Derived from Sillanpää and Wheeler (1997) and Sillanpää (1998).

Much of the activity involved in social accounting has therefore tended to increasingly revolve around communicating with stakeholders and getting their views on what issues matter, and how they regard the organization's impact on areas of concern. *Stakeholder satisfaction surveys*—of employees, customers, and others—have therefore been extensively used, as have focus groups and other methods of communication and data collection. In recent years, there has also been a dramatic increase in *social auditing* and other forms of internal assessment to evaluate organizations' performance in relation to their codes of ethics. This has been particularly evident in the supply chains of multinationals, and is a subject that we shall discuss in more detail in Chapter 9.

What is clear is that in the absence of recognized standards for social accounting, organizations have had to (or been able to) develop their own particular approaches. Although this has resulted in some innovative, impressive, and genuinely useful methodologies and reports, it has also led to the production of some vague, self-serving, and rather disappointing efforts that have been useful neither to stakeholders nor to the organization's management. Thus, whilst early pioneers such as Traidcraft, BSO/Origin, Shell, SbN Bank, the Body Shop, Co-op Bank, Volvo, and others have won awards and plaudits for their social and environmental reports, many other companies (and even some of those we have just mentioned!) have simply been accused of trying to cynically 'greenwash' the public. This raises two important questions:

- Why do organizations take up social accounting in the first place?
- What makes for an effective approach to social accounting?

Why do organizations engage in social accounting?

As with many aspects of business ethics, there are both practical and moral reasons for taking up social accounting, but in essence, we can usefully reduce these to four main issues.

- **Internal and external pressure.** Pressure from competitors, industry associations, governments, shareholders, consumers, and even internal executives can all provide incentives for firms to engage in various aspects of social accounting (Solomon and Lewis 2002). For example, the burgeoning socially responsible investment industry and the development of the FTSE4Good and the Dow Jones Sustainability indices have created incentives to audit and report more fully on sustainability issues. Similarly, pressure from unions, the media, and pressure groups has prompted firms to develop social auditing practices to evaluate working conditions in their supply chains.

- **Identifying risks.** Social auditing, in particular, provides organizations with a clearer picture of what is happening in terms of their social, ethical, and environmental impacts throughout their sphere of operations. This information is critical for identifying business risks and other potential problems that can harm the organization and its stakeholders. For instance, in the absence of a thorough audit of its overseas factories, how can an organization know if it is potentially threatening the human rights of its employees or at risk of a major environmental problem?

- **Improved stakeholder management.** At the very least, social accounting provides a new channel of communication to stakeholders by which organizations might seek to improve their reputation. Indeed, consumers and other stakeholder tend to believe that concerns for marketing and enhancing the corporate image are the main reasons corporations engage in such processes (Solomon and Lewis 2002). At a more sophisticated level, though, it is evident that in order to manage their relationships with stakeholders effectively, organizations need to know *what* issues those stakeholders regard as important, and how well they think the organization is *performing* in those areas (Zadek et al. 1997). Social accounting can therefore give organizations a clearer picture of what they are trying to achieve, what they are actually doing, and what the implications are of their business activities (Zadek 1998).

- **Enhanced accountability and transparency.** Social accounting is not just about more effective management though. As we saw in Chapter 2, the need for corporations to make evident their social role and impacts (transparency) is a key requirement for ensuring that they are answerable in some way for the consequences of their actions (accountability). Clearly by reporting on social performance, social accounting can play a significant role in this drive for enhanced accountability and transparency (Gray 1992; Owen 2005; Zadek 1998). However, there are also limitations to the approach, particularly as it currently stands. Not only is social accounting voluntary, but also without adequate standards, organizations can effectively report on anything they want. As David Owen (2005: 26) concludes in reviewing leading-edge social reports, 'whilst the corporate lobby apparently espouses a commitment to stakeholder responsiveness, and even accountability, their claims are pitched at the level of mere rhetoric which ignores key issues such the establishment of rights and transfer of power to stakeholder groups'.

Given these reasons, there is a reasonably strong case for suggesting that corporations 'should' engage in improved social accounting, provided one believes that stakeholders have some intrinsic rights and legitimate claims on the corporation. Clearly, though, as yet most corporations do not practice any form of social accounting. It is notable, for instance, that the reporting element of social accounting is still almost exclusively a large firm phenomenon, with few small and medium enterprises producing standalone reports (Owen and O'Dwyer 2008). This suggests there are a number of important **disincentives for social accounting**. These include: perceived high costs; insufficient information; inadequate information systems; lack of standards; secrecy; and an unwillingness to disclose sensitive or confidential data.

? THINK THEORY

Should social accounting be advocated on a consequentialist or non-consequentialist argument? How would the two arguments differ?

VISIT THE WEBSITE for a short response to this feature

What makes for 'good' social accounting?

Clearly the question of what is 'good' social accounting will depend on what the initial purpose is, and which perspective—organizational, stakeholder, or other—you are asking the question from. However, it is evident that as the development of tools and techniques has evolved and been refined over time, there is some consensus emerging about standards of quality. The following eight issues have been proposed by three leading figures in social accounting as the key principles of quality (see Zadek et al. 1997):

- **Inclusivity.** Good social accounting will reflect the views and accounts of all principal stakeholders, and will involve two-way communication *with* them, rather than just one-way communication either *to* them or *from* them.
- **Comparability.** In order for assessment of social performance to be meaningful, social accounting should allow for comparisons across different periods, with other organizations, and relative to external standards or benchmarks.
- **Completeness.** All areas of the organization's activities should be included in the assessment, rather than just focusing on areas where a more positive impression might be realized.
- **Evolution.** In order to reflect changing stakeholder expectations, social accounting practices should also demonstrate a commitment to learning and change.
- **Management policies and systems.** To ensure effective institutionalization of the social accounting process, it should be consolidated within systems and procedures that allow it to be rigorously controlled and evaluated.
- **Disclosure.** The issue of accountability would suggest that good social accounting should involve clear disclosure of accounts and reports to all stakeholders, in a form that is appropriate to their needs.
- **External verification.** The extent to which audiences will have faith and confidence in a social account will depend to some extent on whether it has been verified as a true representation of reality by an external body trusted by that audience. The perceived independence of verifiers from the organization will also be critical in this respect.
- **Continuous improvement.** Finally, a good method of social accounting should be able to actively encourage the organization to continually improve its performance across the areas covered by the process, and to extend the process to areas currently unassessed, or assessed unsatisfactorily.

Existing evidence suggests that many of these principles are not currently integrated particularly well into most companies' social accounting procedures. As O'Dwyer and Owen (2005: 208) note, 'many academic researchers have been critical of key features of emerging practice, given its tendencies towards managerialism at the expense of accountability and transparency to stakeholder groups'. Analyses even of leading social reports suggest that whilst improvements are evident, significant deficiencies in some of these quality indicators persist (Belal 2002; O'Dwyer and Owen 2005; Owen and O'Dwyer 2008).

Nonetheless, the delineation of quality principles does represent an important step in a process towards developing adequate standards for social accounting—a process that is already well under way. Several important schemes are currently in place that seek to tackle specific aspects of social accounting. For example:

- **Auditing and certifying.** The social accountability standard, *SA 8000*, is a global workplace standard launched in 1997 that covers key labour rights such as working hours, forced labour, and discrimination, and crucially, certifies compliance through independent accredited auditors. Therefore, following inspection, production facilities can be certified as SA 8000 compliant, thus guaranteeing a widely accepted level of ethical performance. SA 8000 was developed through consultation with a broad range of stakeholders, including workers, employers, NGOs, and unions, and by 2003, had certified over 1,800 facilities in nearly 70 countries, amounting to almost 1 million workers (http://www.sa-intl.org).

- **Reporting.** The *Global Reporting Initiative* (*GRI*) is an international multi-stakeholder effort to create a common framework for reporting on the social, economic, and environmental triple bottom line of sustainability. **Ethics in Action 5.2** describes the challenges and achievements of the GRI in more detail.

- **Reporting assurance.** The *AA1000S Assurance Standard*, launched in 2002, is the first attempt to provide a coherent and robust basis for assuring a public report and its underlying processes, systems, and competencies against a concrete definition and principles of accountability and stakeholder engagement. The standard is specifically designed to be consistent with the GRI sustainability reporting guidelines (http://www.accountability21.net/).

Such programmes are still in the relatively early stages of development, yet they clearly offer considerable potential in providing more effective means for assessing, and ultimately improving, the sustainability and accountability of corporations through social accounting. Moreover, the ongoing efforts of the organizations leading the development of AA1000S, GRI, and SA 8000 to integrate their different systems and approaches means that corporations are gradually being offered a range of interlocking standards for some of the many different aspects of business ethics management. As we shall now see, in the next and last main section of this chapter, there are a number of different ways of organizing these various aspects within an overall approach to business ethics management.

■ Organizing for business ethics management

If businesses are going to directly manage business ethics, then at some stage they are likely to face the question of how best to organize the various components and integrate them into the company in order to achieve their goals. In the US, it has become commonplace for business ethics specialists and textbooks to advocate formal ethics or compliance programmes, and such an approach has been taken up by many leading US corporations. However, due to a different regulatory environment, as well as significantly different business cultures in Europe, Asia, and elsewhere, such a formal approach to business ethics management has been much more rarely promoted or adopted outside

VISIT THE WEBSITE for links to useful sources of further information

ETHICS IN ACTION 5.2

The Global Reporting Initiative

At present, several thousand companies around the world report information on their economic, environmental, and social policies, practices, and performance. However, this information is often inconsistent, incomplete, and unverified. Measurement and reporting practices vary widely according to industry, location, and regulatory requirements. A generally accepted framework for reporting is therefore regarded as vital if stakeholders are to be able to gauge the social performance of organizations and make meaningful comparisons with other organizations.

The Global Reporting Initiative (GRI) was established in 1997 by the Coalition for Environmentally Responsible Economies (CERES) in partnership with the United Nations Environment Programme (UNEP). Its mission was to create just such a common framework for voluntary reporting on economic, environmental, and social performance, i.e. the 'triple bottom line' of sustainability. The GRI is an international multi-stakeholder effort, involving dialogue and collaboration between corporations, non-governmental organizations (NGOs), accountancy organizations, business associations, and other stakeholders in order to develop and implement widely applicable sustainability reporting guidelines.

Following a lengthy consultation period and extensive pilot-testing in companies such as British Airways, the Body Shop, Electrolux, Norvo Nodisk, and Ford, the first GRI guidelines were released in 2000. These represented the first global framework for comprehensive sustainability reporting, and have been referred to, or followed by, hundreds of companies across the globe since their release. By 2009, there were more than 1,500 organizations using the GRI guidelines in developing their reports—a 100% increase since 2005.

Certainly, then, the GRI guidelines have taken an enormous step in the ongoing drive towards harmonization and enhancement of reporting procedures. Clearly, though, the path to widely accepted guidelines for reporting on something as complex and multifaceted as sustainability is likely to be a long and difficult one. The standardization sought by GRI, particularly given the impressive inclusivity of its consultation process, might easily become a recipe for dilution of standards towards the lowest common denominator.

GRI obviously recognizes the enormous challenge presented by its mission and adopts a process of continual learning and revision of its guidelines. Immediately following the release of the 2000 guidelines, the GRI initiated another extensive and wide-ranging consultation process involving hundreds of organizations and individuals, including both reporters and report users. The purpose of this was to develop the next draft of the guidelines, which were subsequently released in 2002. A similar process of consultation and feedback preceded the release of the third generation of GRI guidelines, known as G3, in 2006. Recent years have also seen the development of sector supplements for particular industries, national annexes for country-level information, training materials, and even the provision of specialist guidance for small- and medium-sized enterprises.

The GRI has come a long way towards its vision of becoming 'the generally accepted, broadly adopted worldwide framework for preparing, communicating, and requesting information about corporate performance'. In fact, the organization claims that its G3 Guidelines 'have become the de facto global standard for reporting'. Certainly, the guidelines appear to promote most of the key indicators of quality identified by reporting experts, including transparency, inclusiveness, completeness, relevance, auditability, and independent assurance. However, the GRI has understandably had to make compromises along the way. In fact, even its original aim of elevating sustainability reporting to the status enjoyed by financial reporting and to make sustainability reporting 'as routine and credible as financial reporting in terms of comparability, rigour, and verifiability' appears to have been dropped in favour of its more realistic new vision. Another issue on which GRI has been criticized is its concern only with establishing procedures for *voluntary* reporting, rather than having an explicit aim to promote *mandatory* reporting.

Nonetheless, the GRI has met with considerable success in making the critical first steps towards greater harmonization in sustainability reporting, and it represents an important and progressive attempt to wrestle with the enormous challenge of enhancing corporate accountability through social accounting.

Sources

http://www.globalreporting.org.

Laufer, W.S. 2003. Social accountability and corporate greenwashing. *Journal of Business Ethics*, 43 (3): 253–61.

? THINK THEORY

Think about the GRI in terms of Zadek et al.'s (1997) eight principles of quality in social accounting. To what extent would you say it conforms to and contributes to good practice?

VISIT THE WEBSITE for a short response to this feature

the US. However, the increasing attention being devoted to ethical codes, as well as to various accounting, auditing, and reporting standards, suggests that a more formal approach to ethics management is becoming more widespread, and can be expected to become more so in the future.

Formal ethics programmes

According to Treviño et al. (1999), there are four main ways of approaching the formal organization of business ethics management (see **Figure 5.5**):

- **Compliance orientation.** Under this approach, the main emphasis is on preventing, detecting, and punishing violations of the law. Employees are informed of the law and are motivated to do the right thing through fear of being caught. This is based on the assumption that, regardless of their own values, the competitive environment

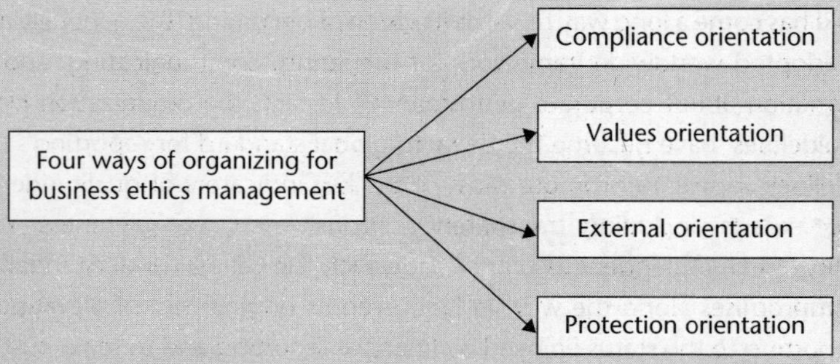

Figure 5.5. Organizing for business ethics management

may encourage employees to do whatever it takes to get a job done, including illegal or unethical activity (Hoffman et al. 2001). However, according to Lynne Sharpe Paine (1994), because a compliance approach defines ethics in terms of legal compliance rather than ethical aspirations, it implicitly endorses a 'a code of moral mediocrity'.

- **Values orientation.** This approach is based on defining organizational values and encouraging employee commitment to certain ethical aspirations (Paine 1994). According to Treviño et al. (1999: 135), the values approach is 'rooted in personal self-governance' and provides the means for ethical decision-making where no particular rules are in place.

- **External orientation.** An external orientation focuses less on company values, and more on satisfying external stakeholders such as customers, the community, and shareholders (Treviño et al. 1999). Here, what is regarded as right is what is expected, or at least acceptable, to key external constituencies.

- **Protection orientation.** Finally, Treviño et al. (1999) suggest that some programmes are primarily (or at least perceived to be) oriented towards protecting top management from blame for ethical problems or legal violations. Employees and other stakeholders may see the introduction of ethics management as little more than an attempt to create legal cover for managers in case of accidents or legal infractions of some sort. Indeed, it is not uncommon for regulators to impose lower fines on corporations with some kind of management system in place to prevent ethical, environmental, or legal violations.

In the US, compliance approaches appear to predominate (Weaver et al. 1999b), whereas in Europe and Asia, as we have seen, the emergence of ethics management has tended to be driven more by external and values-based approaches. However, the important thing to remember is that these four approaches are not mutually inconsistent, and most organizations are likely to combine two or more approaches (Weaver et al. 1999b). For example, earlier in the chapter, we explained that many ethical codes are based on core corporate values and principles (a values orientation), whereas the effectiveness of such codes also depended on appropriate implementation and follow-through, such as the disciplining of employees found in breach of them (compliance orientation). Similarly, rigorously policed ethical auditing processes based on stakeholder consultation and engagement might be said to combine values, external, and compliance orientations.

Although research on the effectiveness of different approaches (and combinations of approaches) is fairly scant, Treviño et al.'s (1999) survey of over 10,000 employees in six large American companies suggests that a values orientation is the most effective single orientation for encouraging ethical behaviour, although compliance and external orientations should also, to a lesser degree, be helpful. A protection approach was found to be a clearly harmful approach. Nonetheless, regardless of their importance, these formal elements are only one aspect of business ethics management. As Treviño and Brown (2004) argue, the idea that formal ethics codes and programmes are sufficient to manage ethics is no more than a commonly held myth. As we saw in the previous chapter, many authors suggest that the broader ethical context, embedded in the culture and climate of the organization, is highly influential in shaping ethical decision-making. So, without a supportive culture, formal programmes are unlikely to significantly influence behaviour. Hence, in organizing for business ethics management, it is important to also consider the ethical culture of the organization.

? THINK THEORY

Think about the growth in business ethics management, identified earlier in the chapter, that is due to the impact of Sarbanes–Oxley legislation and other governance reforms in the early/mid-2000s. Are these developments likely to initiate business ethics management that is characterized by a compliance, values, external, or protection orientation?

VISIT THE WEBSITE for a short response to this feature

Informal ethics management: ethical culture and climate

In Chapter 4, we saw how the culture and norms of an organization could have a profound effect on ethical decision-making. However, this does not necessarily mean that culture can be simply changed or made 'more ethical' to support enhanced business ethics. Nonetheless, this is exactly the argument that has been most commonly advocated in the business ethics literature. Improvements in ethical decision-making have been widely argued to require a managed transformation of the organization's values in order to create a 'more ethical' culture (Chen et al. 1997; Robin and Reidenbach 1987; Treviño and Nelson 2007). Thus, Treviño and Nelson (2007: 256), in their best-selling textbook, suggest that 'organizations can and should proactively develop an ethical organizational culture, and that organizations with "ethics problems" should take a culture change approach to solving them'. The US-based Ethics Resource Center (2007, p. v) even goes as far as to say that it 'has been able to show definitively that companies that move beyond a singular commitment to complying with laws and regulations and adopt an enterprise-wide ethical culture dramatically reduce misconduct'.

Despite the popularity of the **culture change** approach, there has been rather limited attention focused on establishing how such a transformation might take place, why it might occur, or even if it is possible at all. As the management and organizational studies literatures have so effectively demonstrated, the deliberate management of culture is a difficult, lengthy process, which is rarely successful, except at very superficial levels.[8] Indeed, there has been precious little empirical evidence in the literature that provides wholesale support for the claim that culture can indeed be managed in the realm of ethical behaviour. Existing cultural beliefs and values about what is right and wrong tend to be very resistant to change (Crane 2000; Desmond and Crane 2004).

Accordingly, the use of explicit culture change to improve corporate ethical behaviour has also been seriously questioned. Amanda Sinclair (1993: 68), for example, concludes that: 'the lessons from research are that you meddle with the organizational culture if you've got little choice, lots of resources, and lots of time—a combination of circumstances, some would argue, rare enough to render the approach irrelevant'. Peter Dahler-Larsen (1994) further contends that attempts to create 'ethical cultures' tend to reward conformity rather than the very autonomy that is crucial for a sense of morality to exist. Even the Ethics Resource Centre (2007), which is one of the most strident advocates of culture change approaches, acknowledges that despite heightened attention to ethics management, less than 10% of US companies have a strong ethical culture—and that this has remained more or less constant throughout the 2000s.

A somewhat different approach has therefore also been advocated that focuses more on **cultural learning**. Rather than seeking conformity to a single set of values, the learning approach focuses on smaller subcultural groups within the firm and enabling employees to make their own ethical decisions. By encouraging surveillance, dialogue, and critique between these subcultural groups (and with the firm's stakeholders), 'ethical discourse and dialectic as well as conflict' can be prompted, thus bringing to the surface and challenging commonplace assumptions and behaviours (Sinclair 1993: 69). Ken Starkey (1998) thus contends that moral development in organizations requires factionalism and dissent in order to promote learning. The role of management consequently becomes one of identifying conflicting values, unleashing the moral commitment of subcultures, and from this promoting *moral imagination* rather than imposing authoritarian *ideological control* (Stansbury and Barry 2007).

Clearly both approaches have their merits and problems. The culture change approach may have only limited potential to effect real change, but is considerably more attractive to many firms who not only may desire considerable control over the culture, but may also be worried about the potentially damaging effects of bringing out moral differences through the process of cultural learning. Moreover, both pose significant challenges for company leaders in shaping a more appropriate context for ethical decision-making.

Business ethics and leadership

Whatever approach an organization might have to managing business ethics, whether it is formal or informal, compliance-based or values-based, minimal or extensive, the role of the organization's leaders is going to be significant. Leaders are often said to set the ethical tone in organizations. If they are perceived as being ruthless and inconsiderate in their dealings with others, or if they seem to care only about the short-term bottom line, employees are likely to get that message too. When that happens, there would appear to be little prospect of ensuring ethical behaviour lower down the organizational hierarchy. Leaders can thus play a significant role in the contextual factors, such as authority, norms, and culture, which we have shown to be key influences on ethical and unethical decision-making (Sims and Brinkmann 2002).

Unfortunately, although leadership is one of the most widely discussed and researched areas of organizational behaviour, there is considerable disagreement about even the most elemental aspects of the subject (Gini 1997). However, the main starting point is usually to delineate leadership from management. According to Kotter (1990), whereas management is about *imposing order*—through planning, organizing, budgeting, and controlling—leadership is more about *coping with change*—setting direction and vision, motivating and inspiring people, and facilitating learning. For many writers then, leadership is an intrinsically moral terrain, for it is fundamentally entwined with a particular set of values or beliefs about what is the right thing to do. As Gini (1997: 325) argues: 'All leadership is value laden. All leadership, whether good or bad, is moral leadership ... The point is, all leadership claims a particular point of view or philosophical package of ideas it wishes to advocate and advance. All forms of leadership try to establish the guidelines, set the tone and control the manners and morals of the constituency of which they are a part.'

If one accepts this argument, then leaders clearly have a profound role in shaping the ethical decisions of their employees. However, as we saw above in relation to the management of culture, it is one thing to say that something—leadership, culture, etc.—*shapes* business ethics, but it is quite another to then suggest that one can simply *change* the culture or the leadership to ensure ethical behaviour. Nonetheless, it would appear reasonable to conclude that since leaders do appear to influence the actions of their employees, it is important to look at how best to develop ethical leadership.

If we return to our two approaches to managing for an ethical culture—*culture change* and *cultural learning*—it is possible to identify two very different modes of ethical leadership. Under the culture change approach, the leader's role is to articulate and personify the values and standards that the organization aspires to, and then to inspire and motivate employees to follow their lead. For example, Treviño et al. (2000) suggest that there are two pillars to developing a reputation for ethical leadership: to be perceived as a *moral person* and as a *moral manager*. According to the authors, for the executive to be perceived as a moral person, employees need to recognize genuine individual traits in them such as honesty and integrity; to be seen as a moral manager entails focusing the organization's attention on ethics and values and infusing the organization with principles that will guide the actions of all employees. This is a well-worn path for commentators on business ethics to go down, but it holds clear dangers if employees perceive a credibility gap between the public pronouncements of senior executives and the reality they experience according to their view 'from the trenches' (Badaracco and Webb 1995). As we saw earlier in the chapter, follow-through is often significantly more important in encouraging ethical behaviour than statements of beliefs or codes of ethics.

From the cultural learning perspective, the role of leadership is more one of participation and empowerment in order to foster moral imagination and autonomy. Thus, employees are encouraged 'to think independently, to be able to make reasoned, responsible evaluations and choices on their own; to be, in short, free moral agents' (Rosenthal and Buchholz 2000: 194). There are resonances here with those advocating both postmodern ethics and discourse ethics. Ethical behaviour is not to be promoted simply through the promulgation of specific beliefs and principles, but through facilitating personal moral engagement, dialogue, and choice (Crane et al. 2008). There are dangers here too though—such as shifting from encouraging individual choice to accepting moral relativism, or surrendering control over employees and their decisions.

Ultimately, given the controversy and debate that continues to rage in the leadership literature, there is unlikely to be any real consensus emerging in relation to ethical leadership. Clearly, though, it is an important area of business ethics management, and without top management support, most of the tools and techniques discussed in this chapter would be unlikely to contribute all that much to improving business ethics. However, there is always a slight danger of focusing too strongly on the few people at the top of the organization when many of the fundamentals of business ethics are about the day-to-day decisions that each and every one of us makes in our organizational lives.

VISIT THE WEBSITE for a short response to this feature

? THINK THEORY

Think about organizations you have been part of, either as an employee or as a member of some sort. To what extent would you say that the leaders of those organizations were ethical leaders in that they promoted ethical behaviour from you or your colleagues? Which model of ethical leadership, if any, did they fit into?

■ Summary

As this chapter has demonstrated, the area of business ethics management is evolving rapidly, and much of the literature we have covered here has been at the very forefront of contemporary business ethics theory and practice. As a result, much of what we have presented here is, by its very nature, somewhat partial and inconclusive. Nonetheless, we have shown that the nature of business ethics management increasingly emphasizes an external, socially-based orientation, rather than concentrating solely on ethical codes to ensure compliance. Indeed, we have shown that the effectiveness of codes of ethics has been seriously questioned, with current thinking stressing the importance of implementation over content. We have also set out a clear picture of developments in stakeholder management, social accounting, and organizing for the management of business ethics.

We will finish the chapter by addressing a more general criticism that has frequently been raised about business ethics management tools and techniques, particularly regarding how they have been implemented in business practice. Does the development and use of these practices represent a genuine commitment by companies to accept their social responsibilities, or does it merely represent an increasing sophistication in deflecting criticism through smart public relations?

At one level, dismissing these efforts as 'merely PR' does an injustice to both fields. Many of these techniques share a common goal with public relations in their emphasis on developing and maintaining good relationships with key stakeholder groups (Clark 2000). PR models suggest that sophisticated public relations involves two-way dialogue with relevant publics in order to build mutual understanding and consensus, as well as to understand emerging issues and pressures (Grunig and Hunt 1984). However, the accusation of 'merely PR' is distinctly pejorative, and is meant to suggest that business ethics management is largely a cosmetic exercise to make the company look more responsible that it actually is. Clearly, this is a very real concern, and one that is habitually raised by consumers, employees, and others in response to various developments in business ethics management.

Our view is that, whilst there may well be little substance behind many impressive sounding codes of ethics or glossy environmental reports, this doesn't mean that we should denounce *all* business ethics management as just cynical window-dressing. Each case should be assessed on its own merits. The key issue to address is how to determine what makes for best practice in each area, and how best to establish widely accepted frameworks and quality standards through which meaningful evaluations and comparisons can be made.

At another level, perhaps one of the reasons why some commentators are so often critical of the application of business ethics management tools and techniques is that those who promote or use them may simply be overstating their benefits. Suggesting that an organization's ethics problems will be solved simply by having an ethical code, an ethics officer, a marketing tie-up with a charity, or any of the other elements we have discussed in this chapter, is never going to bear up to scrutiny. The application of these tools can only ever assist in managing business ethics, and their success or failure rests not so much on the tool itself, but on the motivation for its use, the process of its development, and the manner in which it is implemented and followed up.

Study questions

1. What are the main elements of business ethics management? Discuss and account for the extent to which they are likely to be used in large versus small companies.
2. What are codes of ethics and how useful are they for the management of business ethics?
3. Set out the main types of relationship that corporations can have with their stakeholders. Are any of these types preferable? Explain your answer with reference to examples from current business practice.
4. What is social accounting, and why do companies engage in it?
5. Assess the relative benefits and drawbacks of different approaches to ethics management. Would you recommend that an organization emphasized a formal or an informal approach to business ethics management?
6. Identify a well-known business leader and critically examine the case that he or she is an ethical leader.

Research exercise

Search on the internet for examples of two companies that produce social reports where the two companies are either:

(a) From different industries but in the same country; or
(b) From the same industry but different countries.

1. What differences are evident between the two companies in terms of the range of issues dealt with in the reports and the depth of coverage on specific issues?
2. To what extent can these differences be explained by the country or industry differences? What other explanations might there be?
3. Assess the apparent quality of the social accounting approach utilized by each company according to Zadek et al.'s (1997) criteria.
4. How appropriate would it be for the two companies to use the same standardized approach?

VISIT THE WEBSITE for links to further key readings

Key readings

1. **Gray, R., Dey, C., Owen, D., Evans, R., and Zadek, S. 1997. Struggling with the praxis of social accounting: stakeholders, accountability, audits and procedures.** *Accoun ing, Au i ing an Accoun abili y Jou nal*, 10 (3): 325–64.

   This is a classic paper from some of the leading contributors to the social accounting literature. It offers a comprehensive analysis of the major challenges facing those engaged in the theory and practice of social accounting.

2. **Treviño, L.K., Hartman, L.P., and Brown, M. 2000. Moral person and moral manager: how executives develop a reputation for ethical leadership.** *Califo nia Manage en Re iew*, 42 (4): 128–42.

   This article addresses the question of what it means to be an ethical leader. Featuring the results of a survey of employees, it shows the importance of different dimensions of ethical leadership. A 'must-read' for anyone hoping to develop a reputation for ethical leadership!

VISIT THE WEBSITE for links to useful sources of further information

Case 5

Managing the ethics of internet censorship: where next for the Global Network Initiative?

This case examines how information and technology communication (ITC) firms have gone about managing ethical challenges around internet censorship. In particular, it focuses on the Global Network Initiative, an industry-led programme aimed at building a framework for effective protection of freedom of speech online. The case presents an opportunity to explore ways of managing business ethics, and to address the challenges associated with managing ethics in complex, cross-sector international issues.

In 2007, when the internet company Yahoo found itself at the receiving end of a dressing-down by the US authorities, the firm's founder was lambasted by the US House Foreign Affairs Committee chair who remarked caustically: 'Technically and financially, you are giants, but morally, you are pygmies.' A few days later, the company settled out of court a lawsuit from the World Organization for Human Rights that accused the company of complicity in human rights abuses for its part in the arrest and detention of a Chinese journalist. But Yahoo was not alone. Google had provoked a storm of controversy after it agreed to self-censorship in order to launch its China service, while the hardware company Cisco was roundly criticized by the internet community for selling large numbers of surveillance routers and switches used by the Chinese government in its rigid internet censorship regime, nicknamed the 'Great Firewall of China'.

Clearly, the ethical challenges faced by ITC firms around their alleged complicity in repression of basic entitlements had become a headache. What was needed was a clearer framework for action, and in November 2008 a major step was taken with the launch of the Global Network Initiative (GNI), a multi-stakeholder initiative aimed at 'protecting and advancing freedom of expression and privacy in information and communications technologies'. After several years of bad publicity concerning the censorship issue, it looked as though the industry was finally starting to get its management of business ethics in better shape. But a number of key critics remained unconvinced by the developments, and the GNI still has many challenges ahead before it proves to be an effective remedy to the censorship challenge.

The internet and censorship

The internet has been presented by many as a great force for connectivity, freedom of speech, and democracy. However, not all governments are quite as enamoured of the great freedoms that the web brings as others. In authoritarian regimes, the internet is often seen as a threat to the ruling authorities and therefore significant attempts are made to censor or monitor internet activity around politically sensitive subjects. Such restrictions can impede freedom of speech and expression by internet users—and by extension, that of consumers of internet service providers, search engines, and other technology services. In a 2009 report, the press freedom organization Reporters Without Borders identified 12 countries as 'enemies of the internet' for their efforts to prevent their populations from accessing 'undesirable' online information—Burma, China, Cuba, Egypt, Iran, North Korea, Saudi Arabia, Syria, Tunisia, Turkmenistan, Uzbekistan, and Vietnam. Suggesting that the authorities in these countries had effectively transformed their internet into an intranet, Reporters Without Borders claimed that 'all these countries distinguish themselves not only by their ability to censor online news and information but also by their virtually systematic persecution of troublesome Internet users'. The organization also placed ten other governments 'under surveillance' for adopting measures that could endanger online free expression, including democracies such as Australia and South Korea.

Much of the world's attention to internet censorship has focused thus far on China. The country now has the most internet users in the world—some 300 million—yet internet use is highly restricted and the government regularly blocks websites and blogs that it views as a threat to state security. Reporters Without Borders marks China out as 'the world's biggest prison for cyber-dissidents', with a total of 49 imprisoned bloggers in 2009. According to the organization, the state employs nearly 40,000 workers to monitor files circulating on the internet, and the authorities maintain strict enforcement of internet restrictions through sophisticated filtering technologies and regular instructions to news media and websites. Blackouts are also used during particularly sensitive events. For example, violent riots in Xinjiang Province in 2009 were accompanied by the closing down of service for several days on Twitter and Youtube, as well as the blocking of more than 50 internet forums.

Complicity of internet companies

Internet censorship is a difficult area for ITC companies to navigate. Whilst countries such as China offer huge potential for developing new markets, dealing with overseas governments can raise a host of problems that firms are ill prepared to deal with, especially when they are operating through a local subsidiary or joint venture. If they refuse to accept the demands of host governments, they won't be allowed to operate in the country. If they do accept them, they risk being complicit in human rights abuses. For a number of years, for example, the internet provider Google simply chose not to locate its Chinese language server within the Chinese firewall. The price, however, was slow service to customers and even temporary closures of access to their site, resulting in a dwindling share in the world's fastest-growing internet market. The Chinese company, Baidu, has therefore been able to establish a dominant position as the country's number one search engine. Google finally agreed to the government's rules and launched its censored China-based site 'google.cn' in 2006, arguing that providing restricted information was still better than no information.

Yahoo, on the other hand, had run into controversy when its Hong Kong office passed on a journalist's personal details to the Chinese government. He was subsequently sentenced to ten years in a labour camp simply for emailing his newspaper's reporting restrictions to an overseas colleague. Yahoo, at the time, claimed it had no choice but to cede to the demands of the Chinese authorities, but following a stinging rebuke from Congress back home, the firm changed course. As part of its settlement of the lawsuit from the World Organization for Human Rights, Yahoo offered to pay legal bills for imprisoned customers, set up a fund to support human rights, and even lobbied the US government to press for the release of political dissidents detained by the Chinese authorities as a result of Yahoo's release of user information. In 2008, Yahoo's chief executive, Jerry Yang, went so far as to write to the US secretary of state Condoleezza Rice before her visit to Beijing, arguing that 'it is essential for our government—led by the State Department—to actively pursue the release of Shi Tao, Wang Xiaoning and other Chinese dissidents who have been imprisoned for exercising internationally recognised human rights'.

A step forward for ITC companies and internet freedoms

Yahoo's change in direction in China suggested that ITC companies were still looking to find a way of effectively managing censorship issues in a clear and consistent way. A major breakthrough came with the launch of the 'Global Network Initiative' in 2008. Led by Yahoo, Microsoft, and Google, three of the companies most in the firing line on such issues, the GNI is a partnership between tech companies, human rights groups, academic institutions, and other institutions involved in media and communications freedoms. The initiative was established following 18 months of development among the participants. It commits firms to a set of principles on freedom of expression and privacy that make clear the firms' commitments to protecting the human rights of their users. Some of the key principles are as follows:

- 'Participating companies will respect and protect the freedom of expression of their users by seeking to avoid or minimize the impact of government restrictions on freedom of expression, including restrictions on the information available to users and the opportunities for users to create and communicate ideas and information, regardless of frontiers or media of communication.'
- 'Participating companies will respect and protect the freedom of expression rights of their users when confronted with government demands, laws and regulations to suppress freedom of expression, remove content or otherwise limit access to information and ideas in a manner inconsistent with internationally recognized laws and standards.'
- 'Participating companies will respect and protect the privacy rights of users when confronted with government demands, laws or regulations that compromise privacy in a manner inconsistent with internationally recognized laws and standards.'

Beyond the principles themselves, the initiative also includes guidelines on implementation, including a commitment to human rights impact assessments. These are important in that such assessments provide companies with the knowledge necessary to identify when freedom of expression and privacy might be at risk, and to enable appropriate risk management strategies to be put in place. The initiative also comprises a built-in review process, and crucially, there is a commitment to institute independent monitoring of companies' compliance with their commitments (albeit not until 2011), and to report publicly on progress every year.

The GNI establishes for technology firms a much clearer framework for action than the piecemeal approach that was generally taken before—and one approved by a number of key stakeholders in the area of freedom of expression and privacy. However, one of the main challenges going forward will be to bring in other relevant stakeholders that have either been excluded or that have chosen to remain outside the initiative so far. For instance, although involved in some of the earlier discussions around the initiative, Amnesty International chose to drop out before it was launched, citing what it saw as several weaknesses in the programme. Even more critically, in order to achieve its aim of becoming the global standard for the entire sector, other ITC firms beyond the big three US firms will need to be recruited. For example, in 2009, claims emerged that a monitoring system developed through a joint venture of Nokia and Siemens had been used by the Iranian authorities to increase its surveillance of the web in the face of political protests during the country's recent election. A year after its launch, however, the list of participating companies in the GNI had barely changed from its inception, with no new ICT firms added to the roster. Significantly, as of 2009, not a single European or Asian ICT company had joined.

More broadly, the success of the initiative will likely depend on how the principles espoused by the initiative will be realized in practice. Especially interesting in this respect are the commitments to actively lobby governments to shift their expectations and demands. For example, the GNI states that: 'Participants will also encourage government demands that are consistent with international laws and standards on freedom of expression. This includes engaging proactively with governments to reach a shared understanding of how government restrictions can be applied in a manner consistent with the Principles.' The intricacies of this one passage alone demonstrate how difficult it will be to put the principles into practice in a clear and consistent way. Google, for example, was again reminded of the difficulties it faced in managing its relationship with the Chinese government in 2009 when the authorities embarked on what the *Financial Times* referred to as a 'witch hunt' on Google China over censorship issues. As a result, Google.cn was forced to suspend its automated keywords service.

The GNI participants, however, appear to be aware of the challenges ahead. Recruitment of further companies is identified as a key priority in phase one of the initiative. And continuous learning, rather than detailed specifications at the outset, has been part of the overall design of the programme. As Sharon Hom, the executive director of Human Rights in China which helped develop the framework, said, 'The idea is that we believe the guidelines will need to be reviewed, and we will have to revise them as we take into account the actual experience ... It envisions an ongoing process of learning and sharing best practices.' So there is clearly still a lot to work out as the initiative unfolds, but it has at least been designed from the outset with an appropriate learning framework, drawing from the experience of initiatives such as the UN Global Compact. Even new companies joining the initiative will be given two years in which to establish appropriate ethics management capabilities before being submitted to independent assessment. But that, of course, depends on whether new members can be recruited. If not, the GNI may have to rein in its aims, but at the very least it looks set to provide its founding members with a new, if not yet fully formed, framework for managing some of their most important human rights issues.

Questions

1. What are the main challenges for ICT firms in protecting human rights in the area of freedom of expression and privacy?
2. How would you characterize the approach used by ICT firms to address these challenges prior to the establishment of the GNI?
3. Set out the main strengths and weaknesses of the GNI as a way of managing business ethics. How would you assess its likelihood of success given its current design, and what would enhance its potential for achieving its aims?
4. Looking forward, what should the key performance indicators be for GNI companies, and how should these be measured?
5. Assess the appropriateness of GNI as a model for use in managing other ethical issues for ICT firms, or for other sectors entirely.

Sources

Davis, P. 2008. Yahoo in China—censor turned freedom fighter. *Ethical Corporation,* 27 May: http://www.ethicalcorp.com.

Jacobs, A. 2009. Internet usage rises in China. *New York Times,* 14 January: http://www.nytimes.com.

Johnson, B. 2008. Amnesty criticises Global Network Initiative for online freedom of speech. *Guardian,* 30 October: http://www.guardian.co.uk.

Hille, K. 2009. Google has rude awakening in China. *Financial Times,* 19 June 2009: http://www.ft.com.

Reporters Without Borders. 2009. Internet enemies. *Reporters Without Borders,* 12 March: http://www.rsf.org.

Rhoads, C. and Chao, L. 2009. Iran's web spying aided by western technology. *Wall Street Journal,* 22 June: http://www.wsj.com.

Notes

1 BBC. 2006. Ethics lessons for US Iraq troops. *BBC News,* 1 June: http://www.bbc.co.uk/news.

2 See the website of the Electronic Industry Citizenship Coalition (EICC): http://www.eicc.info/.

3 See Daniel, C. 2005. Boeing chief ousted for having affair. *Financial Times,* 8 March: http://www.ft.com; Done, K. 2005. Stonecipher falls victim to own code of conduct. *Financial Times,* 8 March: http://www.ft.com.

4 For more information on these initiatives, there are further details on these (and other similar programmes) at the websites of the CAUX roundtable (http://www.cauxroundtable.org) and the global compact (http://www.unglobalcompact.org).

5 Adapted from Elkington and Fennell's (2000) and Hartman and Stafford's (1997) delineation of different forms of business-NGO relationship.

6 See, e.g. Nader, R. 2000. Corporations and the UN: Nike and others 'bluewash' their images. *San Francisco Bay Guardian,* 18 September. For more information: http://www.corpwatch.org/un.

7 For descriptions of these approaches, see chapters 5, 7, and 10 in Zadek et al. (1997).

8 This has been a recurring theme in the organizational and management studies literature. See, e.g. Ogbonna and Harris (1998).

PART B

Contextualizing Business Ethics

The Corporate Citizen and its Stakeholders

Introduction to Part B

The second part of the book looks in turn at the key individual stakeholder groups faced by the corporation—shareholders, employees, customers, suppliers, competitors, civil society, and government—and addresses business ethics within the specific context represented by each of these groups.

The structure of each chapter breaks down into five main parts reflecting some of the key themes developed in Part A of the book. So, following the introduction of each chapter there is:

(a) A brief explanation of how and why this particular constituency can and should be represented as a *stakeholder* for the corporation.

(b) An overview of the *ethical issues* and problems typically encountered in relation to this particular stakeholder, along with consideration of potential responses and solutions.

(c) A deepening discussion of those issues and problems in the light of *globalization*.

(d) An analysis of how these problems and issues can be reframed or responded to from the viewpoint of *corporate citizenship* thinking.

(e) An examination of the challenges thrown up by notions of *sustainability* in relation to this particular stakeholder group.

As we progress through Part B, we will also continue to raise the question of how theories relating to business ethics can be applied to address the problems faced by corporations with respect to stakeholder groups. To this end, the 'Think theory' comments and questions utilized in Part A will continue to be posed at relevant points in each chapter.

6

Shareholders and Business Ethics

In this chapter we will:

- Discuss the nature of shareholder relations to the corporation.
- Analyse the rights and the duties of shareholders in the context of corporate governance.
- Investigate specific ethical problems and dilemmas arising from the relation between companies and their shareholders.
- Discuss the ethical implications of globalization for shareholder relations.
- Explore the notion of shareholder democracy and the accountability of corporations to their shareholders and other stakeholders.
- Discover the differences in shareholder roles and corporate governance in various parts of the world.
- Develop perspectives on how shareholders can influence corporations towards sustainability.

■ Introduction: reassessing the importance of shareholders as stakeholders

For many people, corporations exist, and indeed act, solely for the benefit of shareholders. The pursuit of profitability in order to provide dividends, as well as the drive to increase share prices to satisfy financial markets, are major features of the dominant capitalist model of value creation—but have also been widely cited as crucial contributory factors influencing firms to play fast and loose with business ethics. Even if we adhere to this narrow view of shareholder dominance, nothing has brought ethical issues more attention than the financial crisis in the late 2000s. For instance, between October 2007 and October 2008 shareholders investing in companies traded on the New York Stock Exchange lost on average 40% of their investments (Nanto 2008)! As many of the reasons for this crisis have a strong ethical dimension (such as lending practices in the US mortgage industry), business ethics is now a core consideration for many investors and shareholders. Other people point to the expansion of ethical investment and the emergence of various indices of 'sustainable' or 'socially responsible' stocks to suggest that shareholders are interested in societal good as well as their own self-interest. Whichever way you look at it, the role of shareholders is fundamental to understanding business ethics, and as such, they are the first stakeholder group that we will focus on in this second part of the book.

We first discussed the role of shareholders in the corporation (albeit quite briefly) in Chapter 2. Our argument there was in favour of a broad perspective that acknowledged various constituencies with a stake in the corporation. This suggested that whilst shareholders clearly have a crucial stake in the corporation, this has to be understood within the range of other stakeholders, such as employees, consumers, and suppliers.

In this chapter, we will investigate the finer nuances of this perspective. Whilst maintaining support for a broad stakeholder perspective, we will examine the contention that shareholders in some way have a unique and superior claim upon the corporation. This relationship, as we shall see, confers certain crucial rights on shareholders, as well as imposing some quite important responsibilities in terms of the governance and control of corporations. By examining this relationship in some detail, we will provide the all-important context for discussing the various ethical issues that arise in shareholder relations, including insider trading, executive pay, and money laundering.

As we shall explain, both the impetus and the resolution of these issues and problems are shaped by certain national characteristics of corporate governance. We shall therefore go on to look at how shareholder relations vary quite significantly in different regional contexts. This will be followed by a further broadening of perspective to allow for a deepening understanding of the relationship between globalization and shareholder rights and responsibilities. Such issues have received a growing amount of attention due to the rapid global spread of the financial crisis in the late 2000s. We shall therefore move on to discuss the broader issues surrounding shareholder and stakeholder accountability before, finally, taking a look at how shareholders can use their unique position to address the question of sustainability of corporations.

■ Shareholders as stakeholders: understanding corporate governance

At the beginning of modern capitalism, and throughout the nineteenth century industrial revolution, the common pattern of governing companies was a very simple one. At that time, industrialists, such as the Cadburys in the UK or the Thyssens in Germany, both owned and managed their companies directly. Today, except in very small businesses, owner-mangers are considerably more rare. Some exceptions to this include Luciano Benetton (and family) in Italy, Richard Branson and his Virgin conglomerate in the UK, or the Tata family in India. However, the common pattern in large corporations is a separation of ownership and management functions. In fact, this separation is at the heart of modern capitalism: owners no longer have a personal relationship to 'their' corporation, but rather they buy a 'share' in the corporation, and expect the managers and employees of the company to run it in their (and other shareholders') interests.

The debate about the separation of ownership and control dates back at least to the 1930s and the landmark publication by Adolph Berle and Gardiner Means (1932). This debate essentially problematizes the notions of ownership when applied to corporations. In our everyday life, to own a bike or a car or even a house implies that we are able to do with our property pretty much whatever we like, and therefore can exert a considerable amount of control over it. After all, as we discussed in Chapter 2, the right to property is one of the fundamental rights of citizens. If I want to paint my bike green, ride it down the street, or even completely destroy it, then I can.

With regard to the ownership of corporations, there are, however, some crucial differences (see Parkinson 1993: 56–63; Monks and Minow 2004: 98–118):

- **Locus of control.** The control of the owned property no longer lies in the hands of the owner. The actual control lies in the hands of the directors, the board, or another committee. Shareholders thus have at best indirect and impersonal control over their property.
- **Fragmented ownership.** There are so many shareholders of a corporation that one individual could hardly consider themselves to be the owner in the same way that the plumber next door owns her own company.
- **Divided functions and interests.** Shareholders have interests that are not necessarily the same as the interests of those who control the company. Shareholders might seek profits, whilst managers seek growth. Furthermore, a shareholder has no real task and responsibility regarding their property apart from keeping a piece of paper that entitles them to a share in the company.

Given this somewhat modified relation between shareholders and directors of corporations we can analyse their relationship a bit more closely. Obviously the primary consideration for *shareholders* is the protection of their right to property which in the given context, amounts to certain specific *rights* (Monks and Minow 2004).

- The right to sell their stock.
- The right to vote in the general meeting.

- The right to certain information about the company.
- The right to sue the managers for (alleged) misconduct.
- Certain residual rights in case of the corporation's liquidation.

Most notably, these rights do not include the right to a certain amount of profit or dividend; this is not only subject to the effort and skill of the management but is also—even if the company is profitable—dependent on the decision of the other shareholders in the general meeting.

Managers are entrusted with the duty to run the company in the interest of shareholders (Moore 1999b). This general duty breaks down into various more specific duties (Parkinson 1993: 76–100):

- **Duty to act for the benefit of the company.** This obligation can be interpreted both in terms of short-term financial performance and long-term survival of the company. Principally, it is for the shareholders to decide at which level they want the company to perform; however, managers have a considerable amount of discretion in actually implementing this duty.
- **Duty of care and skill.** Living up to this duty implies that managers seek to achieve the most professional and effective way of running the company.
- **Duty of diligence.** This last duty is the most general one and, as a rather legally flavoured term, 'refers to the expected level of active engagement in company affairs' (Parkinson 1993: 98). Consequently, this is the broadest way of establishing pressure on managers to invest every possible effort in running the company in the most successful way.

Clearly, then, the duties of managers are rather broadly defined. After all, one of the main tasks of a manager is to manage the property of shareholders in their interests. This involves so many things that it is hard to pin it down to concrete activities and initiatives: which strategies, which products, which international investment projects will add to the success of the corporation? These questions are already hard to tackle for an insider, let alone for a shareholder who has only a little knowledge about the internal workings of the corporation and the finer specifics of its products, markets, and competitors.

The relationship between shareholders and the company is therefore defined by relatively narrow, but well-defined, *rights for the shareholder* and far-reaching, but rather ill-defined, *duties for managers* or for the firm in general. It is no wonder that this situation has always been a delicate one and that conflicts continue to plague the relationship between managers and shareholders. Such conflicts focus on the key phrase of 'corporate governance'. In the light of the above, this can be defined along the following lines (Parkinson 1993: 157):

Corporate governance describes the process by which shareholders seek to ensure that 'their' corporation is run according to their intentions. It includes processes of goal definition, supervision, control, and sanctioning. In the narrow sense, it includes shareholders and the management of a corporation as the main actors; in a broader sense, it includes all actors who contribute to the achievement of stakeholder goals inside and outside the corporation.

Corporate governance: a principal-agent relation

When looking at recent scandals and problems in corporate governance, one might ask why the relationship seems to be so delicate. Let us have a look at some examples that have grabbed the headlines recently:

- When Sir Fred Goodwin, CEO of the Royal Bank of Scotland, was fired after the collapse of the bank in 2009, he had no reason to worry about his future. However, the £16.9m pension he was awarded not only outraged many in the wider public but was also voted down later by 90% of RBS shareholders. All this though could not prevent 'Fred the Shred' from taking home his bonus despite the destruction of his shareholders' wealth. In a similar vein, why is it that shareholders could not prevent Wall Street bankers cashing in a combined $18.4bn in bonuses in 2008 despite the fact that these same bankers had helped wipe out large chunks of their shareholders' wealth?
- For more than five years between 1998 and 2003, the management of the Dutch retail conglomerate Ahold systematically overstated the earnings of its US operations in order to inflate the profits of the company. This resulted in one of the biggest accounting scandals in Europe in recent years, and led to court prosecutions on both sides of the Atlantic (Teather 2005). Why were the shareholders of Ahold unable to detect this problem for more than five years?
- Over his 15-year tenure as CEO of Porsche, the sports car manufacturer, Wendelin Wiedeking made Porsche the most profitable car company in the world by 2008. Few people knew though that most of the profits actually came from speculative investments by its finance department. When some of the speculative assets, including a botched takeover attempt of Volkswagen, went sour in May 2009 it suddenly became clear that the company was only days away from bankruptcy (Schneider and Buchenau 2009). Why were the owners of Porsche, which is still family controlled, unable to discover that the company they 'owned' was in such a dangerous situation?

? THINK THEORY

Think of the duties of managers to their shareholders from the perspective of ethics of duty (Kant's theory). Apply this theoretical lens to the three incidents described above.

VISIT THE WEBSITE for a short response to this feature

The problem is obviously that firm-shareholder relations cannot be that easily framed in a contract that neatly states rights and responsibilities. As authors like Jensen and Meckling (1976) have shown, the relation is a so-called *agency relation*. This means that the shareholder is a *principal* who contracts management as an *agent* to act in their interest within the boundary of the firm. **Figure 6.1** shows a very basic view on the relationship between firm, manager, and shareholder using this framework.

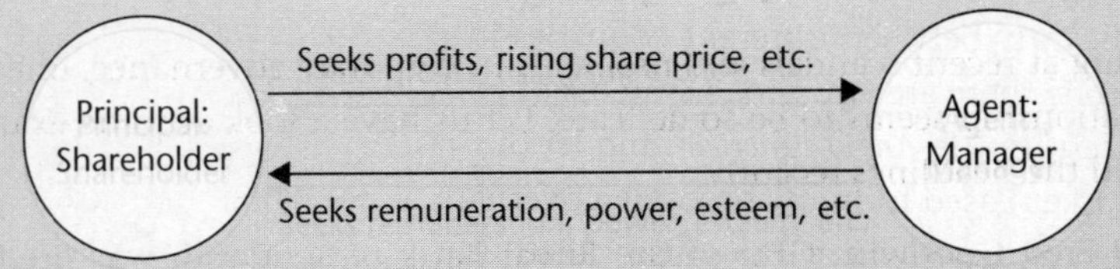

Figure 6.1. Agency relation between the manager and shareholder

Shareholders want the managers in the firm to perform a certain task for them. As a principal, they want managers to do certain things with their property. Managers as agents, on the other side, have certain interests as well, and the figure gives some examples from a potentially long list of such interests. Agency relations, however, are special relations due to two features that are by no means necessarily common for all other manager-stakeholder relations (Shankman 1999):

1. There is an inherent *conflict of interest* between shareholders and managers. Shareholders want profits and increases in share price, which require major effort on the part of managers, and may suggest low salaries. Managers want to have high salaries and might pursue power and prestige to the detriment of shareholder value. For instance, the evidence that acquisition and merger lead to higher returns for shareholders is at best equivocal, and at worst indicates that they often erode shareholder value (Johnson and Scholes 2002: 332–40). Why then do managers continue to create mega-mergers which put them at the head of enormous corporations?
2. The principal has only limited knowledge and insight into the qualifications, actions, and goals of the agent, something economists refer to as an *informational asymmetry*. Porsche shareholders in our example above might have been happy with the profitability of the company, yet they only had limited insight into the actual running of their company and the risks associated with it. RBS shareholders might have hated to see Sir Fred taking his 'golden parachute', but they had limited knowledge of the details of his pay package agreed with the board years ago.

It is the combination of these two characteristics that makes shareholder relations with managers, and the whole issue of corporate governance, so precarious. Indeed, conflicts of interest and informational asymmetry can be seen to underlie a host of ethical problems and dilemmas for either side to deal with in the area of corporate governance, as we shall see in a moment. Before we move on to the main ethical issues pertaining to shareholders, though, we need first to clarify the position of shareholders in relation to other stakeholders. Specifically, it is important to recognize that there are different models of corporate governance in different parts of the world.

Shareholders' relations with other stakeholders: different frameworks of corporate governance globally

The corporate governance framework 'describes whom the organization is there to serve and how the purposes and priorities of the organization should be decided' (Johnson and Scholes 2002: 195). The role of shareholders in the governance framework varies quite significantly between different countries internationally (Clarke 2007). For many commentators, there are two broad systems of corporate governance. On the one hand, we could identify the *Anglo-American* model of capitalism (Aguilera et al. 2006) that is chiefly a market-based form of corporate governance. On the other hand, there is a *continental European model*, sometimes also called 'Rhenish Capitalism' (Albert 1991). This model is more a network-based form of corporate governance of which the European model is the oldest and widely known. However, a similar *relationship* (rather than market) based approach can also be found in many countries, in particular in the developing world. **Figure 6.2** provides an overview of the relevant differences from the perspective of corporate governance.

Within Europe, the Anglo-American model is predominantly in evidence in the UK and Ireland. Crucially, though, it is also strongly represented in the US, as well as a few other countries such as Australia. In a similar vein, the Anglo-American model has started to influence many emerging economies, particularly in Latin America and Asia (Reed 2002). The continental European model is evident throughout most of the rest of Europe, most notably France, Italy, Germany, and Spain as the largest economies on the continent. When simplifying the corporate governance frameworks within Europe along these lines, it is important to take into account some important qualifications. First, there are considerable pressures towards convergence of national business systems, so that the continental European model appears to be gradually taking on elements of the Anglo-American model. Secondly, this process is even more manifest in smaller countries such as Sweden or the Netherlands, so that the alleged dichotomy of systems is clearly an oversimplification in such cases (Coffee 2001). Finally, different countries characterized under one system may actually differ quite considerably. This goes not only for the diverse countries captured by the continental European umbrella, but also, as Aguilera et al. (2006) show, for the approaches evident in the UK and the US.

The *Anglo-American model* focuses on the stock market as the central element of the system of governance. Most of the larger, publicly owned, companies source their capital on the market, and in these countries, shareholding is largely in the hands of smaller shareholders with the result that shares are broadly dispersed, ownership is frequently changed, and goals emphasize profitability and shareholder value (Aguilera et al. 2006; Becht and Röell 1999). With the stock market being the most important source of capital, corporations have to provide a high degree of transparency and accountability to shareholders and investors. Executives are in turn increasingly remunerated with regard to their corporation's performance on the stock market.

In this model, ethical concerns from the shareholder's perspective arise mainly around the proper functioning of market mechanisms and the market-related patterns of corporate governance. Typical ethical problems would be insider trading or manipulated accounting statements. In a broader perspective, the Anglo-American model clearly assigns a dominant role to shareholders and consequently, all major criticisms of the shareholder-oriented model of managerial capitalism discussed in Chapter 2 would apply to this approach.

	USA, UK (Anglo-American Model)	France, Germany, Italy ('Rhenish Capitalism')	Russia	India	China	Brazil
Ownership structure	Dispersed	Concentrated, interlocking pattern of ownership between banks, insurance companies, and corporations	Concentrated in either the hands of owner-mangers or the wider circle of employees in joint-stock corporations	Highly concentrated; recent tendency to more dispersed ownership	Highly concentrated in state-owned companies; fairly concentrated in private enterprises	Highly concentrated ownership by family owned business groups; wave of privatization since 1990 has reduced state ownership
Ownership identity	• Individuals • Pension and mutual funds	• Banks • Corporations • State	• Owner-managers • Employees • State	• Families • Foreign investors • Banks	• State • Families • Corporations	• Family owned business groups • State
Changes in ownership	Frequent	Rare	Frequent, but decreasing tendency	Traditionally extreme rare, but recently changing	• Rare, but increasingly dynamic	• Rare • Increasing influence of foreign investors
Goals of ownership	• Shareholder value • Short-term profits	• Sales, market share, headcount • Long-term ownership	• Profit for owners • Long-term ownership	• Long-term ownership • Growth of market shares	• Long-term ownership • Sales, market share	• Long-term ownership • Profit for owners
Board controlled by	• Executives • Shareholders	• Shareholders • Employees	• Owner-managers • Other insiders	• Owners • Other insiders	• Owners • Party/the state	• Owners/shareholders
Key stakeholders	• Shareholder	• Owners • Employees (trade unions, works councils)	• Owners • State	• Owners • Customers in overseas markets	• Owners • Guanxi-network of suppliers, competitors and customers (mostly) in overseas markets	• Owners • Customers in overseas markets

Figure 6.2. Comparison of corporate governance regimes globally

In the *continental European model* of governance, corporations tend to be embedded in a network of a small number of large investors, among which banks play a major role. Within this network of mutually interlocking owners, the central focus is typically the long-term preservation of influence and power. For the purpose of sourcing capital, banks and their loans (rather than just the market) are of major importance for continental European corporations. Next to shareholder value, the expansion of market share, retention of employees, and other goals not directly profit-oriented are important for owners. Executive pay is usually less directly performance-related, and has historically been regarded as an issue between the boards of corporations and managers, without any perceived relevance or need to disclose this to the general public. More recently, this practice has begun to change, mostly due to the increasing influence of global investors in Europe.

Perhaps most significantly from an ethical point of view, within the continental European model, stakeholders other than shareholders also play an important role, sometimes even equivalent to or above that of shareholders (Fiss and Zajac 2004). For instance, in German companies, up to half of the members of a corporation's supervisory board (which oversees the management of the firm) have to be appointed by the employees of the corporation. In contrast, in the Anglo-American model, employees have no say at all in the control of the firm. From an ethical perspective, then, one could argue that the continental model of capitalism is to some extent a European manifestation of the stakeholder theory of the firm. With the most important stakeholder next to shareholders in this model being employees, corporations in continental Europe are seen more as a member of a certain community which has to serve wider goals than just those of investors. From the perspective of a single shareholder, however, major ethical concerns derive from the fact that the system of ownership prefers the interests of big, mostly corporate shareholders and the interests of many other actors who have no direct ownership rights in the corporation.

In some ways, the continental European model of governance is similar to the approach to *corporate governance in Asia* (Claessens and Fan 2002), which by some is referred to as a *relationship-based approach* to corporate governance (Clarke 2007). The economic structures of countries such as Korea with its large, mostly family-owned conglomerates (*chaebol*) or Japan with its mostly bank-financed *keiretsu* organizations are close to the European approach in that they do not rely predominantly on the stock market for sourcing capital and investment. The Japanese *keiretsu* model often consists of a large multinational company, such as Toyota or Hitachi, and can include their suppliers, customers, and other related firms in the supply chain.

As a consequence, the interests pursued by these companies are not predominantly the maximization of shareholder value, but include a host of other considerations, especially when they are also state-owned, such as in China and Taiwan. These considerations include securing employment, market share, and wider societal interests, such as education, social security (through life-time employment), and others. From a corporate governance perspective, the situation of minority shareholders or foreign investors in these systems is particularly precarious as reporting, transparency, and accountability among these organizations are still fairly underdeveloped, particularly in comparison with the Anglo-American model.

As Figure 6.2 shows, the BRIC countries (Brazil, Russia, India, and China) tend in one way or another to follow what is akin to a relationship-based approach, according to their specific economic and political heritage. In all of these countries, however, we see recent pushes and reform towards more market-based mechanisms. An interesting example of how these different trends blend into each other can be found in the Indian approach to corporate governance (Sarkar and Sarkar 2000), which on the one hand is similar to the continental European and Japanese model (as it is based on large block holdings of majority investors), but on the other hand also demonstrates elements characteristic of the Anglo-American approach (since many of these investors are actually companies and senior executives). Partly due to its colonial past, this development is particularly encouraged by comparatively large numbers of foreign investors. Similar hybrid forms of governance can be found in many emerging economies such as Brazil, where it is only in the last few decades that companies have tried to attract more foreign capital and therefore adopted elements of the Anglo-American model (Rabelo and Vasconcelos 2002). The Russian case, furthermore, is interesting in particular for the phenomenon of 'owner managers', often referred to as 'oligarchs', who amassed large parts of privatized former state-owned industries in the Boris Yeltsin era of the 1990s. With owners being managers at the same time, we can envisage considerable conflicts of interest here.

VISIT THE WEBSITE for a short response to this feature

? THINK THEORY

Thinking of different corporate governance practices around the world, are these just 'different' (i.e. reflecting different cultural and customary practices) or would you argue that some of them are clearly more or less ethical from a moral perspective?

■ Ethical issues in corporate governance

Corporate governance has been a topic high on the agenda of all major economies in recent years. Partly this has been the result of various scandals that have hit the headlines during the last decade or so. This started with the 'dot-com bubble' and the financial scandals of the early 2000s, which saw the spectacular bankruptcy of companies such as Enron, Tyco, and WorldCom in the US, and shocking revelations of financial irregularities at Parmalat in Italy and Ahold in The Netherlands, amongst others. Recent attention has turned to the collapse of many banks and financial institutions in the financial crisis in 2008, where managers took on major financial risks unbeknown to shareholders, and there have been criticisms of the huge bonuses of bankers and 'fat cat' CEOs. Such phenomena have resulted in unprecedented interest in the ethical dimensions of corporate governance. In the following sections, we will examine the main issues arising here, focusing specifically on those that primarily affect shareholders. **Ethics on Screen 6** provides a discussion of several of these issues in the context of the classic business ethics movie, Wall Street, and provides some interesting historical context for the current debate.

Executive accountability and control

Looking at corporate governance, there are certain core elements that need to be present in order for the principal-agent relationship to be managed effectively. The most important element is a separate body of people that supervises and controls management on behalf of principals, namely a board of directors. In practice, this tends to result in a dual structure of the leadership of a publicly owned corporation. On the one hand, there are *executive directors* who are actually responsible for running the corporation. On the other, there are *non-executive directors* who are supposed to ensure that the corporation is being run in the interests of principals, usually shareholders.

The different governance frameworks globally come with important differences in how this board is structured and composed. There are basically two extremes. In the *Anglo-American* model, there is usually a single-tier board that comprises both executive and non-executive directors. In *continental Europe*, however, a two-tier board is more common. The upper tier is composed of non-executive directors and the lower tier of executive directors. The upper tier, often also called a *supervisory board*, effectively oversees the lower tier, which is more concerned with the day-to-day running of the company. As we have already said, the supervisory board commonly includes representatives of stakeholders other than just shareholders, including banks and employees.

Regardless of the structure, the central ethical issue here is clearly the independence of the supervisory, non-executive board members. They will only be able to reasonably act in the principal's interest if they have no directly conflicting interests. In order to achieve this, a number of points are important (see Nader 1984; Boyd 1996):

- Non-executive directors should be largely drawn from outside the corporation.
- They should not have a personal financial interest in the corporation other than the interests of shareholders. This includes the fact that the remuneration for the non-executive director role must not significantly exceed a reasonable compensation for time and other expenses.
- They should be appointed for a limited period in order to prevent them from getting too close to the company.
- They should be competent to judge the business of the company. This would require, and to some degree allow, a limited number of insiders, such as former executives or even works council members (such as in certain parts of Europe).
- They should have sufficient resources to get information or commission research into the corporation.
- They should be appointed independently. This would be either by the shareholders directly in the annual general meeting, or through appointment by the supervisory board.

A further element of supervision comes from an independent auditor who audits the work of the executive board—normally the main aspect of their role—and also of the non-executive board. We will discuss the role of auditors and the ethical issues involved a little later.

VISIT THE WEBSITE for links to useful sources of further information

ETHICS ON SCREEN 6

Wall Street

An upscale morality tale to entertain achievers who don't want to lose touch with their moral centers, but still have it all.

Vincent Canby, *New York Times*

20th Century Fox/The Kobal Collection

Wall Street is one of the best-known movies to have brought the dilemmas and challenges of business ethics to mainstream Hollywood cinema. Released in 1987, it has become a classic—mostly due to its powerful storyline, great writing and directing by Oliver Stone, and an Oscar-winning performance by Michael Douglas. It is considered by many to be the ultimate 1980s portrait, reflecting the rise of liberalized financial markets and the stock-market boom during that decade.

The core story is about a young stockbroker Bud Fox (Charlie Sheen) who in his quest for the success and glamour of a rich Wall Street banker's life gets under the spell, and later the auspices, of corporate raider Gordon Gekko (Douglas). The moral maze that Bud finds himself in focuses on a deal regarding the takeover of an airline company, which he can recommend to Gekko based on insider information gathered through his father. The latter, played by Sheen's own father Martin, is an airline mechanic and union member—and as such, highly suspicious of the dealings of his son. Ultimately, the Securities and Exchange Commission (SEC) gets wind of the deal and after being arrested, Brad ends up saving his own neck by providing evidence about Gekko's role as the true villain in the game.

Besides being a highly entertaining, funny, and intelligently scripted piece of cinematography, the film has become a classic for a number of reasons. Certainly, it is full of witty and thought-provoking dialogue. Michael Douglas delivers killer lines such as 'lunch is for wimps', 'I create nothing. I own' and 'rich' isn't '$450,000 a year, but rich enough to have your own jet'. Unforgettable too is his notorious 'greed is good' speech in the film, which he makes to the shareholders of a company he wants to buy out. These scenes remind us of how closely the film is modelled on some of the real-world insider scandals on Wall Street at that time. One of those Wall Street icons, Ivan Boesky, later sentenced for insider trading, gave a nearly identical speech to a business school audience months before.

The film also explores the factors which cause individuals to commit unethical acts in business. Certainly, the Charlie Sheen character of a slightly stiff, awkward young broker getting lured into and seduced by the promises of quick success, not least to keep his posh interior designer girlfriend happy, showcases many of the aspects we discussed in Chapter 4.

The film is a good watch for today's students of business ethics since Wall Street (the place) has once more gained attention, if not notoriety, in the recent global financial crisis. And to add an extra incentive, there is currently a film project under way which will be a sequel, after 23 years, to the movie *Wall Street*. Under the project name 'Money Doesn't Sleep', Michael Douglas is set to reprise his role as Gordon Gekko (now recently released from jail), and Oliver Stone is installed as director again to provide us with a new critique of the world of American corporate finance. Planned for release in 2010, the film promises to be an exciting take on all that has not changed on Wall Street, as well as the personal fate and struggles which hide behind a glamorous, high-powered world of easily earned billions.

Sources
Canby, V. 1987. Film: Stone's Wall Street. *New York Times*, 11 December.
Shoard, C. 2009. Shia LaBoeuf likely to join Michael Douglas on Wall Street 2. *Guardian*, 29 April.
http://www.rottentomatoes.com/m/wall_street.

Despite the guidelines above, the independence of non-executive directors remains a delicate issue. Often they belong to the same peer group as executive directors, or are themselves in executive roles elsewhere, or have been in such role in the past. This means that a completely neutral and independent approach will always be quite difficult to achieve (Gordon 2002).

Executive remuneration

The financial crisis of the late 2000s brought the issue of executive pay centre stage in an unprecedented fashion, given that executives of bankrupt or failing companies continued to earn millions in salaries and billions in bonuses. 'Shameful' and 'the height of irresponsibility' were President Obama's comments in January 2009 on what continued to be common practice not only in the US, but in many other countries globally. The general trend towards million dollar salaries has been fuelled by the revitalization of the shareholder value ideology, combined with the massive privatization move in the late 1980s and early 1990s, which saw the remuneration enjoyed by bosses of formerly public companies skyrocket.

Probably the key element in the continuing escalation in executive pay actually derives from an attempt to address the core of the agency problem: in order to align the interests of both parties, the perfect solution appeared to be to pay executives in the same 'currency' that matters to shareholders, namely dividends and rises in share price. The logical conclusion then is to pay executives in shares—or more commonly, in options that allow executives to buy shares on a future date. In order to make the incentives work, it would not be sufficient to pay them with just a few shares or options but to a degree that substantially impacts on their wealth. As a consequence, the US in particular has led the way in rewarding senior managers with massive stock option deals. This approach of performance-related pay has particularly spread in the financial industry, resulting in high salaries and bonuses even for mid-level executives in financial services and banking.

Europe's highest earning CEO in 2008 was Porsche CEO Wiedeking, with an estimated whopping €77m (Focus 2009)—eclipsing even the highest earner in the US, Oracle CEO

Ellison, with $84m. According to a 2008 survey, executives such as Sir Martin Sorrell, CEO of the advertising and communications group WPP, earned 550 times more than their average employee, whilst the highest ratio was 790 at mining conglomerate Lonmin (*Guardian* 2008). The same survey identified the average rise in salary of the top earners to be 125% in the past year. However, while the financial crisis of the late 2000s has exposed the stark contrast between the performance of many managers and their pay, the link between executive remuneration and stock market performance has always been somewhat tenuous (Walsh 2008).

Examples such as these unveil many of the ethical problems with executive pay in firm–shareholder relations:

- First, there is the issue of designing appropriate *performance-related pay* in a world of reinvigorated shareholder value (Koslowski 2000). In order to tackle the problem of divergent interests, most executive salaries nowadays contain a significant amount of shares and share options to align shareholder and manager's interest. The first problem here, however, is that by including these elements, salary levels have exploded, often leading to considerable unrest within companies. Furthermore, this pay model does not always result in the desired effect on share prices, as these are of course linked to other factors as well.
- Secondly, these shifts in remuneration show the influence of *globalization* on executive pay: the market for executive talent is a global one and so the standards of the highest level of pay seem to be applicable across the board. This means that in regions such as Europe, where the introduction of performance-related pay has entered the executive suite quite recently, further significant rises in pay can still be expected. This domination of the Anglo-American shareholder value orientation has also had its influence in newly privatized companies in public transport, telecommunication, and utilities, where salaries have rocketed during the last 15 years (*Guardian* 2008).
- Thirdly, this case also illustrates that the *influence of the board* is limited, and often fails to reflect shareholder (or other stakeholder) interests. Why would shareholders want to reward a CEO who had overseen a period of poor performance?

Such problems show few, if any, signs of diminishing, and indeed may be expected to occupy shareholders (not to mention the general public) for sometime yet. Conspicuously, US President Barack Obama announced in February 2009 his intention to introduce a salary cap of $500,000 on all companies receiving federal support funds (TARP). Similar discussions are currently under way in many European countries (Anderson et al. 2009). Although, as we shall see at the end of this section, corporate governance reforms have been proposed in many countries, the issue of executive remuneration touches an ethical chord. This is not actually so much because the public feels sorry for shareholders, but because the pay differentials between those at the top and those at the bottom appear to be so inequitable. We shall pick up this issue again in the next chapter when we address the question of fair pay for employees.

> **? THINK THEORY**
>
> Assess the pay packages of chief executives from the perspective of justice theories. Is the main objection one of distributive justice (executives get more than they deserve or are rewarded when other deserving parties are not), or procedural justice (in that the mechanism for executive remuneration is not fair)?

VISIT THE WEBSITE for a short response to this feature

Ethical aspects of mergers and acquisitions

From a societal point of view, mergers and acquisitions might be encouraged if they involve the transfer of assets to an owner who will use them more productively and thereby create wealth. The alternative is to leave the assets in the hands of a less effective management, with higher costs, less innovation, and other costs to society. However, there are a number of ethical issues that might arise, as many examples of unsuccessful mergers demonstrate—the failed and finally reversed merger of Daimler-Benz and Chrysler being just one recent manifestation. The central source of ethical concern in this context is that managers may pursue interests that are not congruent with the shareholder's interests. Basically, the conflict is around executive prestige on the one hand, and profit and share price interests of shareholders on the other.

There is in particular a wealth of discussion in the American business ethics literature on this issue, mainly since the US business system very much encourages these types of transactions—more so than is the case in tightly regulated Europe or in BRIC countries with more narrowly held stock ownership. However, with an increasing deterritorialization of financial markets, these practices have also become more common across the globe in recent years, as the recent example of mergers of French, German, or Swedish companies in the telecommunication and utility industries illustrates. In the following, we will have a look at the main issues that have arisen or are likely to arise.

Next to 'normal' mergers: there are particular ethical problems involved in so-called *hostile takeovers*. Here, an investor, or a group of investors, intends to purchase a majority stake in a corporation (often secretly) against the wishes of its board. Without going into a detailed philosophical debate, there are basically two lines of argument here (see De George 1999: 462–4). On the one side, it could be argued that hostile takeovers are ultimately possible only because shareholders want to sell their stocks; otherwise they would keep them anyway. On the other side, an ethical concern may arise with the remaining shareholders that do not want to sell. If the company is taken over by someone who has different ideas about the corporation—for instance, an 'asset stripper' that wants to split the company and sell off certain parts—a hostile takeover might interfere quite significantly with the property rights of those remaining shareholders.

A particularly interesting role is played by the executives of the corporation to be taken over. According to Carroll and Buchholtz (2008: 132-4), they basically have two main options in this situation:

- First, they could be seduced into agreeing to the takeover, for example by being offered a '*golden parachute*', i.e. a large sum of money to be paid if they agree to the merger and their own redundancy. Their 'agreement', of course, does not mean that they actually have an active role in selling or buying shares, but in past cases, the role of the CEO has been quite crucial in recommending the merger to the supervisory board and to shareholders.

- The second type of reaction of management is just the opposite. In order not to lose their job after the takeover, managers could secretly send '*greenmail*' (as opposed to blackmail) to the potential hostile party and offer to buy back the shares for the company at a price higher than the present market price. By this, managers secure their jobs using corporate money. This raises a significant ethical problem regarding whether such a move is actually in the company's interest or not. Sometimes it may be, but in other instances, greenmail appears to be primarily used because the CEO does not want to lose their lofty position.

A particular ethical line of conflict opens if we have a look at the intentions and consequences of mergers and acquisitions. Jack Welch, the well-known former CEO of General Electric (GE) acquired his nickname 'Neutron Jack' because he turned GE into one of the best-performing conglomerates on Wall Street through the acquisition of all sorts of corporations, and significantly *restructuring* and *downsizing* them immediately after takeover. The buildings and assets remained; only the people had to leave—similar to the effect of a neutron bomb. Very often acquisitions only target the profitable parts of the bought-up corporation, while at the same time the other parts will be liquidated. Sometimes these acquisitions even focus only on the brand value or certain patents and technologies of the bought-up firm, with the consequence that other stakeholder interests, such as those of employees or local communities, are seriously disregarded.

The role of financial markets and insider trading

There has been a remarkable silence in the literature on financial markets with regard to ethical issues (Rudolph 1999). A simple justification for this would be the following: financial markets, especially the stock market, are based on shareholders expecting a future dividend and/or a rise in share prices as a basis for their decision to buy or sell stocks. As long as the rules of the market are fairly set and every player plays according to these rules, there is no ethical dilemma to be expected. Issues such as mergers, acquisitions, or executive pay then are not so very much the object of ethical consideration as a simple part of the economic calculation of the shareholder: if she does not agree to the CEO's remuneration demands, she is fully entitled to sell the stock. It might be presumptuous to demand more pay, or the merger might be problematic, but ultimately the shareholder can take a fully informed decision and could sell their stock.

Behind this argument, there is the assumption of a perfect market, and in particular the assumption that, ultimately, all publicly available information about the company is reflected by the stock price. However, we all know that this simple rationale of 'the stock market never lies' is only part of the truth. Sometimes, the alleged 'information efficiency' of stock markets is quite flawed, as the following issues show.

Speculative 'faith stocks'

An often-discussed problem is the speculative nature of share prices. This not only became evident in the financial crisis of the late 2000s but also during one of its predecessors, the burst of the 'dot-com' bubble in the late 1990s. Start-ups that had not made a single cent in profit but were valued at billions of dollars on the Nasdaq in New York or the Neuer Markt in Frankfurt then took this speculative element to an extreme. These stocks were not so much built on solidly calculated profit expectations, but were more like 'faith stocks' (Gordon 2002), built on little more than blind faith. Even a company such as Amazon.com, which is one of the successful survivors of that crisis, needed more than seven years to make even a dollar in profit. When it finally cleared the hurdle in 2002, it had amassed some $2.2bn in long-term debt, despite once being valued at more than $30bn (Hof and Green 2002).

In some sense, the latest financial crisis has similar roots. The complex structured finance products that mortgage lenders and other financial institutions traded to manage the risk of sub-prime mortgages were all based on 'faith' that the real estate market would continue to rise. As long as this 'faith' was in the market, most actors involved thrived. When the downturn set in, however, it not only turned out that the optimism was misplaced, but also that the products were way too complex for the managers involved to foresee the likely consequences.

One problem here is that many pensioners whose funds had invested in these bonds lost large parts of their income. The ethical issue clearly lies in the fact that while stock prices always contain an element of speculation, stock markets do not always fully reveal the amount of uncertainty. This might be somewhat trivial for brokers or other stock-market professionals; however, with large institutional investors investing other people's money in these stocks, the fact that these bonds may be based entirely on speculation can be said to be close to an abuse of trust. This also questions the role of analysts and accountants (see below) who, among others, are responsible for ensuring *informed* transactions on the stock market.

Insider trading

Almost the opposite problem exists with the phenomenon of insider trading, namely that some investors might have superior knowledge in the market. Insider trading occurs when securities are bought or sold on the basis of material *non-public* information (Moore 1990). The executives of a corporation and other insiders know the company well and so might easily know about events that are likely to have a significant impact on the company's share price well in advance of other potential traders. Consequently, insiders are privileged over other players in the market in terms of knowledge, a privilege that they could take advantage of to reap a questionable profit.

In the long run, insider trading can undermine investors' trust in the market—a problem that has led most stock markets to forbid the practice (Carroll and Buchholtz 2008: 134–5).

However, concerns around insider training persist, as the high-profile examples of George Soros and American life-style guru Martha Stewart demonstrate. While in 2002 Soros was fined for insider trading, Stewart even went to jail for five months in 2004 for lying to government investigators about selling stock in a pharmaceutical company after having been allegedly tipped off about the failure of one of the company's new drugs to gain governmental approval.

The ethical assessment of insider trading is still quite controversial, but there appear to be a number of possible routes. Jennifer Moore (1990) for instance, discusses four main ethical arguments that have been used against insider trading:

- **Fairness.** There are inequalities in the access to relevant information about companies, leading to a situation where one party has an unfair advantage over the other. Moore (1990) argues that this is the weakest, but most common argument that tends to be used against insider trading.
- **Misappropriation of property.** Insider traders use valuable information that is essentially the property of the firm involved, and to which they have no right of access. According to Moore (1990), this has become a common basis for legal cases involving insider trading.
- **Harm to investors and the market.** Insider traders might benefit to the cost of 'ordinary' investors, making the market riskier, and threatening confidence in the market.
- **Undermining of fiduciary relationship.** The relationships of trust and dependence among shareholders and corporate managers (and employees) are based on managers acting in the interests of shareholders, yet insider trading is fuelled by self-interest on the part of insiders rather than obligation to their 'principal'. Moore (1990) argues that this is the strongest argument against insider trading.

VISIT THE WEBSITE for a short response to this feature

? THINK THEORY

How do these four arguments correspond to the traditional ethical theories set out in Chapter 3?

Whichever way we look at it, the central problem here seems to lie in the question of where to define the boundaries. After all, every investor tries to receive as much knowledge about a company as possible and analysts of major investment banks would by no means treat their knowledge necessarily as publicly available. A particular problem has arisen from the aforementioned fact that many companies remunerate their executives and staff with share options or shares. These people may use their inside knowledge of the company to decide when to exercise their options or sell their shares (and, arguably, it could be irrational to expect them to do otherwise). As a result, such 'acceptable' incentives are difficult to distinguish from 'unacceptable' insider trading. **Ethical Dilemma 6** presents a typical situation where the boundaries of insider trading might be very difficult to draw clearly.

The role of financial professionals and market intermediaries

One of the main institutions to bridge the asymmetric distribution of information between shareholders and corporate actors is that of financial professionals and market intermediaries. Among the two single most important professions here are *accountants* and *credit-rating agencies* (CRAs). The task of these organizations is to provide a 'true and fair view'—as they say in accounting—of a company's financial situation or a judgement of the trustworthiness of an investment opportunity. While the three major CRAs (Fitch Ratings, Moody's Corporation, and Standard & Poor's) are a global oligopoly, the role of accountants varies from country to country. In the Anglo-American sphere, for instance, accountants are most heavily involved in the actual accounting process, whereas in continental Europe they have more of a supervisory role and primarily verify whether the company's accounts give a realistic picture of the company's actual financial situation.

With shareholder value orientation becoming more and more popular over the last few years, the nature of the accounting profession has undergone substantial changes (Mellahi and Wood 2002). Rather than certifying the quality of published accounts, today's audits target the actual or potential shareholder, and therefore focus a great deal not only on statements of past periods but on the future potential of the corporation. This process, sometimes pejoratively termed 'creative accounting' (Pijper 1994), mirrors the demands of a major group of addressees of corporate statements. However, the risk inherent in this process is evident: the discretionary element of auditing existing figures is already quite significant; this is even more the case for projections based on these figures. To take up the expression used above, the ethical challenge for audit firms lies in the fine line between presenting a share as a 'faith stock' or repackaging what one would normally simply call a dud or a 'lemon' (Gordon 2002: 1236).

Issues of a similar nature have occurred with CRAs, which are seen by some experts as one of the main culprits in the financial crisis of the late 2000s. The primary role of the CRA is to provide a credible assessment of financial products, so that investors have a better idea about what a fair price for the product would be and what the risks associated with that product are. From that perspective, CRAs are a pivotal element of the largely deregulated infrastructure of global financial markets, where only a few governments still decide on which products should be traded or not. The main contention then is whether the assessment of the CRA is trustworthy. For many, this is all but proven: as of writing, all three of the main CRAs have been sued in the US because they rated the majority (of mortgage-based securities) as triple A, the best possible rating (Bahena 2009). Even Lehman Brothers had at least an 'A' rating from all three agencies up to the very day before it collapsed (Evans and Salas 2009).

It is therefore no wonder that accountancy firms and CRAs increasingly find themselves in the ethical spotlight. Ballwieser and Clemm (1999) identify five main problematic aspects of the financial intermediary's job:

- **Power and influence in markets.** Auditors and other intermediaries do not necessarily make a judgement about the economic viability of a corporation—they often simply make a judgement about whether the accounts of the corporation provide a realistic

AN ETHICAL DILEMMA 6

Who cares whose shares?

Friday nights out drinking with your friends have become something of an institution since you started working with PharmChemCo (PCC) five years ago. And it has been a great five years. The company is one of the biggest pharmaceutical and chemical companies in the world, and working there has not only brought you career success and a very healthy bank balance, but it has also made you a successful player in the stock market. Since you were promoted to regional marketing director for the North East, PCC has paid a large chunk of your bonuses in stock options. Even with a dipping market, this has proved to be an extremely lucrative package, given your success in meeting sales targets and, of course, shrewd investment over the last two and a half years.

But this Friday night, however, you are not feeling so relaxed. Yes, you have an expensive bottle of imported beer in your hand; yes, you have some of your best mates with you, all totally up for a big night out; and yes, Freddie, your best friend from college, will be arriving any minute. However, the last week in the office has been a nightmare. A special meeting had been called by one of the vice presidents for all of the senior managers. At the meeting, it had been announced that scientists in a leading research lab at SFW University in the US had discovered some potentially lethal side-effects associated with of one PCC's best-selling herbicides. The report had been confidential to the board of PCC, but an article containing the research was going to be published in *Big Science* magazine next week on Thursday. The purpose of the meeting was to inform everybody and to discuss potential strategies to tackle the problem. Consequently, you were urged to be absolutely silent about the research findings, particularly as the likelihood was that this would turn out to be a major news story.

Knowing about this makes you uneasy now. It is pretty certain that this information will have a major effect on the share price of PCC, as court cases in the US with huge damages are a certainty. Digesting the news in your office after lunch, you had already decided to sell your shares in PCC first thing on Monday—as it is almost certain that the value of your stocks will never be the same in the foreseeable future once this news is out. However, you are certain that Freddie, your friend from college, is also going to be very much affected by the news once it gets out. He is now an account manager for a major investment bank. And not only has he invested heavily in PCC shares himself, but he has also advised many of his clients—among them managers of major funds—to invest in PCC.

You are quite uneasy now about what to do. Freddie is an old mate, and you want to help him. You know he will hear of the news soon anyway, and maybe given his contacts, before it is even published next Thursday. But if you tell him now, you are certain that he will not only sell his own shares (which you really would not mind), but as he is measured by the performance of his advice to his clients, you can be pretty certain that he will also advise his clients to sell. The effect on the share price before the publication of the article could be substantial.

Questions

1 What are the main ethical issues in this case?

2 Who are the main stakeholders here, and how would you compare the relative importance of their stakes?

3 Explain how you would ultimately decide and why.

4 Is there a difference between acting yourself on the information you were given and passing this information on to Freddie?

picture of the real situation. This means though that they have to make an assessment of whether the company is legitimately putting a good light on the figures or presenting a deceptive account. If an auditor is too outspoken about a company presently sailing in rougher waters, this might actually have detrimental effects on the firm and thus potentially add to its difficulties. On the other hand, the presentation of a deceptive account is a risk mainly incurred by the auditor itself. Even though there are fairly well-defined rules, regulations, or codes of practice for the auditing process, there remains discretion in valuing assets, foreign currency transactions, goodwill assets, etc. Just how much market power intermediaries wield became especially evident in the financial crisis in 2008. The bankruptcy of American International Group (AIG) and its subsequent bailout of $85bn by the US Treasury were precipitated by the fact that CRAs downgraded AIG's double A score by two to three points in September 2008. As many of AIG's contracts with other banks worldwide were predicated on a double A rating for AIG, the company suddenly had to hand back many collaterals to their partners—but was not able to come up with the cash needed for these transactions (Evans and Salas 2009). In some ways, then, CRAs were at the centre of a pivotal event in the worst financial crisis since the Great Depression of the 1930s. This power of CRAs can even have a political dimension as they also rate government-issued bonds. This became a delicate political issue for the UK government in May 2009 when Standard & Poor's downgraded the UK from 'stable' to 'negative' due to high levels of governmental debt following the rescue of several British banks (BBC 2009).

- **Conflict of interest.** Intermediaries necessarily get a very close insight into the corporation. Auditing firms, for example, especially the big global firms such as Deloitte, PriceWaterhouseCoopers, and KPMG, have a large pool of expertise as they get to see so many companies. It is only natural then that they use this insight and experience to develop an extra source of income by providing management consultancy and other business services to their clients. The crucial problem, however, is that this involvement with a corporation puts an end to the necessary neutrality of the auditor. The same problem exists with CRAs, since 98% of ratings are paid for by the issuers of financial products—not the investors in whose interest the ratings should be. Consequently, CRAs have strong incentives to provide good ratings to their clients in order to secure business and prevent them from switching to a competing CRA to get better results. In many cases, CRAs even 'consult' their clients about how to structure and design a financial product only to give them the 'promised' ranking once the advice is taken (Bahena 2009).We will discuss the ethical issues involved here in more detail in Chapter 9 (p. 401) when we discuss conflicts of interest in company-supplier relations.

- **Long-term relationships with clients.** Financial intermediaries and their individual representatives enter a position of confidentiality with their clients and therefore the tendency is to look for long-term relationships. Although this is restricted by the accounting laws in some countries, the general problem persists. Having such a confidential position of trust with clients often creates long-term personal relationships that can threaten independence.

- **Size of the firms.** CRAs, such as Moody's or Standard & Poor's, and many accounting firms, such as KPMG or PriceWaterhouseCooper, are large multinational companies. The bigger the firm is, the more economies of scale it can realize in terms of staff training, standardization of auditing procedures, and rating tools, and the better it can specialize in different tasks. However, the more a firm grows, the harder it may become to maintain a constant standard of diligence. Standardized procedures of auditing may also diminish the diligence of the individual auditor, who might lose the personal sense of responsibility for the task. This distancing effect of bureaucracy was something we first discussed in Chapter 4 (pp. 171–2).

- **Competition between firms.** With intensifying competition between financial intermediaries over the last few years, there is an inherent danger that corners will be cut to reduce costs, raising the prospect of less diligence and scrutiny by these firms.

VISIT THE WEBSITE for a short response to this feature

? THINK THEORY

Explain the ethical dilemmas and conflicts for an accounting firm and CRAs by applying the theoretical framework of situational influences on ethical decision-making discussed in Chapter 4.

The ethics of private equity and hedge funds

The broad ethical concerns we have discussed already around issues of transparency and shareholder control have been recently exacerbated through the rise of *private equity* (PE) firms and *hedge funds* (HFs). PE firms usually invest money from institutional investors and wealthy individuals to reach a majority stake in a public company. After then taking the company private for a couple of years, these PE firms restructure the companies with the goal of reaching the highest possible value for the company or the parts of it.

There are a host of ethical issues raised with PE (see Nielsen 2008). The most general concern is that in most jurisdictions, once the company is taken private, there are no longer many obligations for public information about the company. While this entails ethical problems in itself, there are also other concerns around their lack of consideration for other stakeholders, most notably employees and earlier investors.

Hedge funds are one specific form of PE firm—initially for investing in complex structured financial products for 'hedging' risks from other investments, but now operating in a diverse array of financial investments—which have also raised a number of specific ethical concerns, most notably around their 'emblematic' opacity (Donaldson 2008). Transparency issues are particularly pronounced with HFs, since these highly specialized funds are structured in such a way that they do not have to report to regulators in the same way as other investment firms, and do not even fully disclose their strategies to their own investors. Despite fairly good returns—and fairy-tale salaries for their managers—HFs have become notorious because of their high risks, unusually low taxes, huge fees for investors, and an obvious potential for misleading potential investors about their performance (Donaldson 2008). It has also been suggested that their lack of transparency has a broader social cost because it hides systemic risk (Donaldson 2008). Some commentators have identified them as playing a key role in bringing about the financial crisis of the late 2000s. Moreover, their influence in restructuring many companies at the expense of jobs and employees' interests has prompted for instance the German Federal Minster for Labour, Franz Müntefering, to coin the pejorative term of 'locusts' to describe their ethical reputation during the mid-2000s.

■ Shareholders and globalization

Globalization has had a crucial impact on the role of shareholders, the nature of their ownership, and the scope of their activities. With global equity and finance markets being probably the most globalized, or *deterritorialized* markets, the consequences of this reformed role for shareholders have become increasingly visible. We might think of shareholders becoming players in the global arena in four different ways:

- Shareholders might become *directly* involved abroad by buying shares of companies in other countries. Typically, this would mean, for example, that French or Spanish investors would buy shares at the London Stock Exchange for a UK company.

- Shareholders might be involved *indirectly* by buying shares in a domestic (or international) company that operates globally by selling goods and services worldwide. Even the shareholders of a corporation such as Porsche, which avowedly wants to remain a 'German' company (by refusing to invest anywhere other than at home), are nevertheless involved in the globalization process given that the corporation has the majority of its sales abroad. This aspect has particular consequences for many European or Asian countries where the capital markets are still very nationally focused.

- Similar to this indirect involvement, but more pronounced, is the role of shareholders in explicitly *multinational corporations* (MNCs). Investing in such companies makes shareholders indirect players in global capital markets, especially if these companies are heavily involved in foreign direct investment activities in other countries.

- Finally, shareholders may become *direct players* in international capital market by investing in funds that explicitly direct their money to global capital markets. Significant players in this category are the so-called 'sovereign wealth funds' which we will discuss in more detail below.

This differentiation helps us to recognize the particular effects of globalization on the ethical issues confronting firm relationships with shareholders. The first two instances involve stakeholders as actors in certain well-defined national capital markets. The ethical issues of corporate governance as discussed above are therefore similarly relevant for these instances. The two latter cases, however, are special since they involve shareholders in the context of global financial markets. We would define these markets along the following lines:

Global financial markets are the total of all physical and virtual (electronic) places where financial titles in the broadest sense (capital, shares, currency, options, etc.) are traded worldwide.

If we just recall our definition of globalization in Chapter 1, global financial markets can perhaps be presently regarded as the most globalized markets since they are the least dependent on a certain territorial basis. The main factors leading to globalization that we mentioned in Chapter 1 are clearly at play here: *technological advances* mean that via electronic trading, financial markets today are confined neither to certain locations nor to certain time slots (Parker 1998: 267–72); the key *political development* is the high degree of deregulation of financial markets, which makes it possible to talk about one global market rather than many individual places of financial trade.

From an ethical point of view, these developments raise some serious issues, among the most important of which are the following:

- **Governance and control.** Deterritorialized markets impose the problem that no national government is entitled to govern these markets (Becker and Westbrook 1998). With regard to financial markets, this means that the allocation of a fundamentally important resource for modern industrialized economies takes place without any serious normative rules other than the 'laws' of supply and demand (Koch 2000: 189–209). This might not sound too much of a problem but it becomes immediately clear if we have a look at the sometimes negative consequences of global financial market transactions. The most recent example of this is certainly the financial crisis of the late 2000s. What initially started in the US very quickly became a global problem for many international banks since many of the mortgage-based securities were traded globally and assets based on these investments came under pressure all over the world. The spectacular effect of these rapid movements of capital around the globe became most visible in Iceland in 2009—a country that initially attracted large numbers of investors in the mid-2000s. When the rapid devaluation of mortgage-based securities occurred (in which many of the Icelandic banks were heavily invested), it caused the country to undergo one of the most severe financial crises ever experienced by a single economy.

- **National security and protectionism.** A specific governance issue has recently arisen with a particular group of investors often referred to as *sovereign wealth funds*. These are government-owned funds of countries which invest their budget surpluses—three-quarters of which comes from oil and gas revenues—in capital markets worldwide. Among the countries with large funds, apart from Norway, none is governed by a liberal democracy. These include funds held by the United Arab Emirates ($875bn), Singapore ($489bn), Saudi Arabia ($300bn), Kuwait ($250bn), and China ($200bn) (see *The Economist* 2008b). What if these funds invest in companies in North America or Europe for motives beyond the sheer maximization of their value? This became a subject of debate in the US when a Dubai-based investor was interested in buying a company that—among other things—owned strategic assets such as the ports of New York and New Jersey. Similar concerns were raised when capital from sovereign wealth funds was used in the rescue of many banks in Europe and North America, giving those funds some degree of strategic control over major financial institutions. One of the potential results of the rise of these funds then might be new forms of protectionism, by which governments in the West might want to avoid countries such as China or Venezuela gaining control of key industries, such as banking, telecommunications, and utilities.

- **International speculation.** Global financial markets encourage speculation. This is not an ethical problem as such, and in fact, speculation is one of the key principles underlying why financial markets exist in the first place. However, speculative movement of capital may have quite significant impacts on real-life situations. In the UK, many people still remember 'Black Wednesday' in 1995, where the plans of the British government to realign the currency rate of the pound to the European Currency System were undermined by speculative trading on both sides of the Atlantic. The result was serious damage to the government finances which, by some accounts, cost every British citizen £12, and contributed to the end of the Conservative government (McGrew 1997a). Many activists have pointed out, however, that large speculative movements of financial assets can have particularly detrimental effects on the poor in developing economies (Birchfield and Freyberg-Inan 2005). One much touted route for reform is via an instrument called the '*Tobin Tax*', which makes transactions less attractive to speculative traders due to a marginal tax imposed on international currency transactions (see Cassimon 2001). The other benefit of this 'Robin Hood Tax', as some call it, would be that the money generated by the tax could be used for poverty reduction. Although world leaders such as President Lula of Brazil and Prime Minister Zapatero of Spain have pronounced that 'a tax on foreign exchange transactions is technically feasible',[1] the momentum behind such reform appears to have dissipated in recent years.

- **Unfair competition with developing countries.** A number of economic crises in developing countries during the 1990s, such as in Mexico, Brazil, or most notably East Asia, were mainly triggered by speculative moves of capital out of the country. Investors had been attracted to invest there in boom phases, but as soon as it turned out that much of the boom was speculative, capital was withdrawn with disastrous effects for local economies and people. One of the main problems here is that while global financial markets are strongly deregulated and thus capital can flow easily in and out of the countries, this is not the case for the markets for goods and services (Hauskrecht 1999).

- **Space for illegal transactions.** As these markets are not fully controlled by national governments, they can easily be used for transactions that would be illegal in most countries. Terrorism, money laundering, international drug trafficking, and the illegal trade of weapons are all substantially aided by global financial markets in their present shape. The problem of tax evasion and fraud through international capital flows to so-called 'tax-havens', such as Luxembourg, the Channel Islands, or the Cayman Islands has also risen to prominence in recent years, with the G20 Summit in 2009 making a first serious attempt at addressing the issue. However, there are clearly major obstacles to reform in this arena, given the persistence of national idiosyncrasies in culture and regulation. For example, secrecy has been a major ingredient in the success of Switzerland as a global banking hub, and so implementing tougher global rules about the identity and origin of deposits in banks potentially threatens the very basis of the Swiss finance industry. Nonetheless, in 2009 the Swiss government made limited concessions on bank secrecy to avoid being added to a global blacklist of uncooperative tax havens.[2]

Reforming corporate governance around the globe

With the rise of global financial markets and the subsequent spread of Anglo-American forms of more market-oriented corporate governance, we have seen a flurry of attempts to reform this aspect of economic life in most countries in the world. Usually these reforms follow corporate scandals such as the introduction of the Sarbanes–Oxley Act in July 2002 in the US—leading to significant changes in the practices of corporate America (Wagner and Lee 2006). In contrast to many reforms discussed further in this section, this is a mandatory piece of legislation attempting to reform corporate governance through the improvement of internal controls and external reporting mechanisms—the main focus being the avoidance of criminal misconduct. Given that many European and Asian companies have substantial business activities in the US, the Sarbanes–Oxley Act has had palpable knock-on effects on the rest of the world, as well as in the US (Webb 2006).

In Europe, probably the main way that reform has been addressed is through the definition and implementation of new corporate governance codes—since 1998 more than 50 national corporate governance codes have been introduced in the region—and reform continues unabated (Clarke 2007). Such codes have also been increasingly common in other parts of world, especially in Asia (Webb 2006). Reforms of corporate governance have also taken place in the developing world, in particular in emerging economies, such as Brazil and South Africa (Rabelo and Vasconcelos 2002; Rossouw 2005). In particular, South Africa's 1994 'King Report on Corporate Governance in South Africa' (the 'King Code') has been influential as a template for corporate governance for the entire continent. Subsequently, then, we have seen the emergence of new governance codes in at least 15 countries on the African continent during the last decade (Rossouw 2005).

The idea of codes is to prescribe 'best practice' standards for corporations so as to help ensure that certain minimal standards of corporate behaviour are met. Typical issues dealt with in codes of corporate governance are:

- Size and structure of the board.
- Independence of supervisory or non-executive directors.
- Frequency of supervisory body meetings.
- Rights and influence of employees in corporate governance.
- Disclosure of executive remuneration.
- General meeting participation and proxy voting.
- Role of other supervising and auditing bodies.

The legal basis and the power of these codes vary significantly: while governments and the general public would ideally like to make codes legally binding, industry tends to adopt a more cautious stance. On the one hand, the general implementation and enforcement of codes is desirable; on the other hand, extra regulation makes business more inflexible and extends bureaucracy and 'red tape'. In practice, then, most of these codes have been voluntary, while some have implemented mandatory frameworks for disclosure that follow the rule 'comply or explain'. Although corporate governance codes are now an established element of most developed economies, their role is still therefore somewhat ambivalent. In developing countries, for example, the advantages gained by reform towards more market-oriented Anglo-American style governance—such as attracting foreign investment, increasing competitiveness, and reducing corruption—have to be balanced against the threats of 'crowding out' indigenous businesses through the influx of foreign companies and the shift towards a more globally homogeneous shareholder-oriented governance model (Reed 2002). This debate becomes even more pronounced as the financial crisis of the late 2000s has raised serious concerns about the viability of the 'tarnished' Anglo-American model of capitalism (Whitley 2009). While the jury is still out on the full impacts of the crisis, we have definitely seen in most Western economies a deeper involvement of the state, be it as direct owner or more active regulator, both of which point to the expectation of slightly more regulated markets for capital, and through this also for corporate control and governance (Cappelli 2009).

In the context of the financial crisis and the debate on alternative forms of capitalism and governance, the model of Islamic finance has been increasingly discussed. As a matter of fact, countries heavily governed by principles of Islamic finance have been much less affected by the economic crisis of the late 2000s, so that the system has therefore been hailed by some as a real alternative to the contemporary Anglo-Saxon model of capitalism.[3] **Ethics in Action 6.1** provides an overview of the specifics and the growth of Islamic finance in recent years.

VISIT THE WEBSITE for a short response to this feature

THINK THEORY

Think about the development of corporate governance codes from the perspective of postmodern ethics. Do you think that this is an area where codes of practice are a good way of dealing with ethical problems, or do you agree with those postmodernists who argue that codes tend to squeeze out a sense of morality from our relationships with others and that a more relativistic approach is necessary? What role do you think such codes can play in ensuring more ethical relations between managers, shareholders, and other stakeholders?

Shareholders as citizens of the corporation

In Chapter 1, we briefly mentioned the fact that globalization weakens national governments, while at the same time MNCs are becoming increasingly powerful. This idea was developed in Chapter 2 (pp. 69–70) with the broader notion of the firm as a *political actor* replacing some of government's role in governing citizenship. We also discussed the growing demand for transparency and accountability to the general public that results from this gradual shift in state–business relations. In this section, we take up these ideas and explore whether the constituency of shareholders could at least be a starting point to regain some control over corporations. The idea is to show that shareholders have a particularly powerful position from which to hold the company accountable on a variety of issues that involve the governance of citizenship.

Shareholder democracy

The notion of shareholder democracy is a commonly discussed topic in corporate governance (Parkinson 1993: 160–6). The basic idea behind the term is that a shareholder of a company is entitled to have a say in corporate decisions. Analogous to the political realm, shareholder democracy describes a community of people that own the company and are therefore able to influence it in some way. The idea here is that in comparison with other stakeholders, shareholders, by dint of their property rights, have a legally protected claim on the corporation.

Given the vast number of shares in dispersed ownership forms of governance, the influence of the single shareholder is rather small; however, with institutional investors, or holders of larger share packages, the situation looks considerably different. We need only look at the defeat the board of Shell suffered, when 60% of its shareholders voted down its remuneration report at its 2009 AGM, to see that organized blocks of shareholders can discipline managers they perceive as being out of line. Nevertheless, the actual ways of influencing the board of the corporation and the institutions of proxy differ across the globe. Furthermore, since the crucial occasion where shareholders vote is the annual meeting, their power is mainly focused retrospectively. They may or may not approve of the company's activities during the last year, whereas their influence on *future* plans is somewhat limited. This is because in most cases management will be reluctant to publish too much about their plans in advance.

Clearly though, these limitations and qualifications do not exclude corporations from being *accountable* to their shareholders. You may remember that we suggested in Chapter 2 that 'corporate accountability refers to whether a corporation is answerable in some way for the consequences of its actions'. Corporations and their managers are then (at least in principle) answerable to their shareholders, mainly through the AGM, but also through the shareholders' representatives on the board of directors. In empowering shareholders to exert power over the corporation, a crucial role also falls to the annual report. This is the main vehicle through which shareholders learn about 'their' company, and is the main resource they have by which to make decisions regarding how they will vote at AGMs.

Now this is all well and good, and our discussion would probably end just there if our interest were just in corporations being accountable for the financial performance reported on in their annual reports. However, our concern is more with whether shareholders can be a force for wider *social* accountability and performance. For this, we need to consider three further issues.

- **Scope of activities.** First, we have to consider the scope of activities for which a corporation has to assume accountability to shareholders. It is one thing to say that corporations need to answer for their financial performance, but it is quite another to suggest that they need to also be accountable for all sorts of other ethical decisions and social and environmental impacts. Are shareholders interested in such issues or do they just look for a decent return on their money? However, even if shareholders do have a conscience about where their money goes, are they even able to assess company performance in these areas?
- **Adequate information.** This leads on to the second issue, namely that if shareholders are to decide on the ethical performance of the corporation, they have to be provided with adequate information on such issues. This is where *social accounting* comes in. In Chapter 5 in the section, Assessing ethical performance (pp. 211–17), we discussed different ways of social accounting and outlined some indications of 'good' social accounting. Social accounting usually results in the production of a social report or sustainability report of some kind. This can be used by shareholders for making informed decisions, just as the annual report can. Therefore, this instrument can play an important role in empowering stakeholders to exert their 'democratic' rights over the corporation.
- **Mechanism for change.** Finally, we have to think about the mechanism for change that shareholders can use in order to communicate their ethical choices and influence the corporations they own stock in. One way of doing this is for family owners of corporations to use their powerful positions to encourage attention to business ethics. This was actually one of the first ways that ethical criteria were integrated into shareholders' decisions, beginning with the first capitalists, such as the Cadburys or Rowntrees in UK, who integrated philanthropic and paternalistic elements into the way they invested in their companies (Taylor 2000). However, our interests are mainly with situations characterized by a division of ownership of control. The role of shareholders here with respect to the ethical performance of corporations broadly falls into

VISIT THE WEBSITE for links to useful sources of further information

ETHICS IN ACTION 6.1 http://www.ethicalcorp.com

Islamic finance—London banks on sharia law

Locust, 15 July 2008

Ethical CORPORATION

The cutting edge of finance is usually associated with the likes of ever-more complex derivatives instruments or ultra-fast trading systems. Yet with the rise of modern Islamic finance, bankers the world over may soon find that knowledge of thousand-year-old religious principles is as much an asset as the ability to write clever algorithms. Islamic finance consists of financial products or services that adhere to Islamic, or sharia, law. Islamic financial services include banking, the issuing of Islamic bonds (sukuk), insurance and fund management. For a financial service to be certified as sharia-compliant, it needs to meet a number of criteria. These include that no interest be paid on any financial product, that all financial products be backed by a tangible asset, and that the service or product not be linked with anything incompatible with sharia law, such as alcohol, tobacco or gambling. While these principles have guided commerce in the Islamic world for a millennium, the last decade in particular has seen a surge in both the demand for and supply of Islamic financial instruments.

Surprisingly, alongside the likes of Bahrain, Saudi Arabia and the United Arab Emirates in the Middle East, and Kuala Lumpur and Singapore in south-east Asia, London is also looking to take advantage of the modern wave of sharia-compliant banking by positioning itself as a centre of Islamic finance. The UK now has three fully-sharia-compliant banks, founded in 2004, 2006, and 2007. In addition there are over 20 major western banks—four times more than in any other European country—that can offer customers in the UK an 'Islamic window' through which to buy Islamic financial products and services. Many UK-based law firms also offer services relating to Islamic finance.

Regulatory support

The UK's large Muslim population, along with London's status as a global centre of finance and its relatively much closer financial ties with the Middle East than, for example, New York, are driving the organic growth of Islamic finance. But Islamic finance has another great advantage in the UK, namely the support of the government. The UK has adapted its financial regulations to accommodate the requirements of sharia-compliant banking.

This support has a number of objectives. For example, it contributes to the government's effort to combat the social exclusion of minorities (especially young Muslim men), which is further backed up by the relatively large number of courses and qualifications in Islamic finance offered by UK institutions. The support also has a clear financial rationale in that, if the City of London is able to establish itself as the west's main port of call for financial banking, then the UK will be in a better position to benefit from international flows of sharia-compliant investment.

These flows are increasing at a staggering rate. International Financial Services London estimates, in a report released in January 2008, that the market for sharia-compliant financial services grew from $150 billion in the mid-1990s to $531 billion by the end of 2006. And a report released in May by Damac Capital International says that the global market for sukuk more than doubled between 2006 and 2007, hitting $62 billion from $27 billion a year earlier, and that it will reach $200 billion by the end of the decade. The Damac report suggests also that the entire Islamic banking and finance market is itself growing at 15–20 per cent annually. The UK has, since 2007, been expressing a determination to be the first western government to issue an Islamic bond. So far, the only western issuers of sukuk have been the Texas-based oil company East Cameron Partners, the German state of Saxony-Anhalt and the World Bank.

The SRI factor

There is another, less obvious way in which London is suitable as a home for Islamic finance: its experience and leadership in the field of socially responsible investing (SRI). For with its injunctions against investing in financial products linked with alcohol or tobacco, and, more generally, with its use of criteria and rules at odds with standard western practices, Islamic finance bears a striking resemblance to SRI. The fact that SRI managed to make a home for itself in the City of London augurs well for this new wave of investors who once again call for some outside-the-box thinking by the mainstream of UK investment professionals. What is more, the growth in Islamic finance in the west may in turn serve to break down more barriers for SRI advocates pushing for the greater use of non-financial investment criteria by western investors.

Sources

Ethical Corporation, 15 July 2008, http://www.ethicalcorp.com.

? THINK THEORY

Think about Islamic finance as an alternative form of governance. Would you agree as some argue, that in a financial system based on Islamic principles, the financial crisis of the late 2000s would not have been possible in the same way?

VISIT THE WEBSITE for a short response to this feature

two categories: *shareholder activism* and socially *responsible investment* (Sparkes 2001). In the following, we will have a look at both approaches to supposedly 'ethical' shareholding, an overview of which is provided in **Figure 6.3**.

Shareholder activism

One of the potential levers with which to make corporations accountable for their ethical behaviour is to buy shares in that company. The motive for doing so in this case is not so much to make a profit or to speculate on the market, but to make positive use of the rights of shareholder democracy. The most important right here is the right to speak

Stakeholder activism	Ethical investment
Single-issue focus	Multi-issue concerns
No financial concerns	Strong financial interest
Seeks confrontation	Seeks engagement
Seeks publicity	Avoids publicity

Figure 6.3. Two approaches to 'ethical' shareholding

Source: derived from Sparkes, R. 2001. Ethical investment: whose ethics, which investment? *Business Ethics: A European Review*, 10 (3): 194–205.

at the AGM and on other occasions where shareholders (and usually only shareholders) are allowed to voice their opinions on the company's policies.

Normally, these forums would be used by investors to take on the company on performance issues and other typical shareholder concerns. These rights, however, also open the possibility for other stakeholders to voice their concerns and challenge the company on allegedly unethical practices. Perhaps even more importantly, they also open up the possibility to get broad media attention for these issues by 'disrupting' the meeting from its usual course of action. In this situation, what we essentially have is a stakeholder group that adopts the role of a shareholder, but does so in a way that potentially provides it with greater leverage.

Shareholder activism has been taking place for decades, most notably in the US, where resolutions have addressed a range of social issues over the years, including product safety, labour issues, and climate change (O'Rourke 2003). In the first half of 2009 alone, more than 200 shareholder resolutions on ethical issues were recorded by the Interfaith Center on Corporate Responsibility.[4] In other countries, however, it can be quite difficult to raise issues at the AGM since this would need the involvement of larger institutional investors (Taylor 2000: 174). However, there are examples of shareholder activism in other parts of the globe in recent years where NGOs such as Greenpeace or Partizans, a London-based human rights group, have used shareholdings, or the influence of large institutional investors, to challenge corporations such as Shell, BP, Rio Tinto, and Huntingdon Life Sciences on issues such as treatment of indigenous populations, pollution, or animal testing. Embedded in larger campaigns, the filing of shareholder resolutions, talking at annual meetings, or even filing law suits as a shareholder can be very effective ways of making corporations change their behaviour—or at least of informing a broader range of constituencies (especially shareholders) about critical ethical issues.

On the downside, in buying shares of a corporation, the particular shareholder group gets involved with 'the enemy' and in the long run there might be certain integrity problems involved. Furthermore, for activists, shareholder resolutions are costly and resource intensive, and can impact negatively upon their other campaign tactics (O'Rourke 2003).

Socially responsible investment (SRI)

The second main mechanism, socially responsible or ethical investment, is further removed from the corporation and certainly less active than confronting managers head-on at AGMs. However, with the general public apparently getting increasingly concerned about corporate accountability, a large and rapidly growing body of shareholders has emerged who specifically include ethical concerns in their investment decisions (Rivoli 1995; Taylor 2001). In some ways, the US is the leading country here, with a market volume in 2008 of some $2.7trillion,[5] although the UK (with a market volume in 2008 of £6.8bn[6]) and continental Europe have shown remarkable growth in the last decade (Hill et al. 2007). The most recent development in the SRI world, however, is the growing interest among investors in emerging markets, though one could argue that among the chief selection motives for investors here are issues of good governance, rather than environmental or social criteria of their set of 'ESG' (Environmental, Social, and Governance) criteria, as they are commonly referred to as (EIRIS 2009).

In contrast to shareholder activism, socially responsible investors do not directly use their investment to make companies listen to their concerns and subsequently change their behaviour. Rather, they look for a profitable investment that at the same time complies with certain ethical standards. We could define SRI along the following lines (Cowton 1994):

> **Socially responsible investment is the use of ethical, social, and environmental criteria in the selection and management of investment portfolios, generally consisting of company shares.**

The criteria for choosing an investment can either be negative or positive. Investors can choose to exclude certain companies with undesired features (negative screening) or adopt companies with certain desired features (positive screening). **Figure 6.4** provides an overview of the most common issues for both types of criteria. Besides investment brokers and portfolio management companies, the key actors in ethical investment are funds that offer investment opportunities in company shares complying with certain defined ethical criteria.

> **? THINK THEORY**
>
> How could the ethical theories set out in Chapter 3 help an investment fund manager to determine positive and negative criteria? Take an example from Figure 6.4 and make your case by using some of the normative ethical theories.

VISIT THE WEBSITE for a short response to this feature

In addition to the normative motivations for SRI, some commentators (and indeed investors) have also argued that choosing according to ethical criteria makes sense from an economic perspective too. The risks of public boycott of products or the risk linked to environmental disasters can also influence the performance of shares, making ostensibly 'ethical' companies less risky investments. In a similar vein, the potential market success

Negative criteria

- Abortion, birth control
- Alcoholic beverages production and retail
- Animal rights violation
- Child labour
- Companies producing or trading with oppressive regimes
- Environmentally hazardous products or processes
- Genetic engineering
- Nuclear power
- Poor employment practices
- Pornography
- Tobacco products
- Weapons

Positive criteria

- Conservation and environmental protection
- Equal opportunities and ethical employment practices
- Public transport
- Inner city renovation and community development programmes
- Environmental performance
- Green technologies

Figure 6.4. Examples of positive and negative criteria for ethical investment
Source: Derived from McEwan (2001: 298–300)

of ethical products or environmental innovation might prove an ethical investment to be a very profitable one. So, for instance, the share price of the world's two largest wind-power companies, the Denmark-based Vestas and Spain's Gamesa, rose by 50% and 45%, respectively, in 2006 (Kelleher 2006). In a recent survey, 78% of European fund managers said that compliance with SRI criteria enhances the long-term value of an investment (Sullivan et al. 2006).

Among SRI funds, there are two broad types (Mackenzie 1998). *Market-led funds* are funds that choose the companies to invest in following the indication of the market. These gather data about the social and ethical performance of corporations from various research agencies. Among the most reputed institutions here is the London-based Ethical Investment Research Service (EIRIS), which provides regular research on 2,800 companies against various criteria, organized into four clusters—social, environmental, governance, and 'areas of specific ethical concern' (www.eiris.org.uk). The market though is not to

Position	Company	Industry
1	Petrobras (*Brazil*)	Oil and gas
2	Samsung Electronics (*South Korea*)	Consumer electronics
3	China Mobile (*China*)	Mobile phone provider
4	Taiwan Semiconductor (*Taiwan*)	Electronics
5	Teva (*Israel*)	Pharmaceuticals
6	Vale Do Rio Doce (*Brazil*)	Mining
7	America Movil (*Mexico*)	Mobile phone provider
8	Gazprom (*Russia*)	Oil and gas
9	Posco (*Korea*)	Steel
10	Ambev (*Brazil*)	Alcoholic beverages (e.g. Brahma)

Figure 6.5. Top 10 stocks held in SRI funds invested in companies in emerging markets 2009

Source: Data extracted and re-tabulated from EIRIS, 2009. *Emerging Markets Investor Survey Report: An analysis of responsible investment in emerging markets*. London: EIRIS. Data reproduced with permission.

everyone's tastes. For example, **Figure 6.5** below lists the companies most commonly held in SRI funds in emerging markets, and these might not necessarily feature on everyone's list of 'ethical' companies.

In contrast to market-led funds, *deliberative funds* base their portfolio decisions on their own ethical criteria. This involves more research and forces the fund's management to regularly assess companies and practices. The difference in practice is that deliberative funds provide investors with detailed ethical criteria, whereas market-based funds just provide a list of companies regarded as ethical by the market.

In practice, the choice of the right criteria and companies proves to be not always clear-cut (Cowton 1999b; Sparkes 2001; Entine 2003). So, for instance, many electronic corporations may well produce components for household appliances as well as military technology. Some investors would also object to investing in bank shares, as banks fund industries across the board, including probably a number of companies that do not comply with ethical norms of investors. These processes involve fund management in constant updating of their criteria and company research, encouraging a more flexible and less bureaucratic approach over time (Cowton 1999).

SRI is quite a striking example of what we referred to at the beginning of this section as shareholder democracy. By allocating their investment to corporations which comply with certain ethical standards, investors not only have some influence on the company's policy, but they also set incentives for other companies to review their policies. Increasingly, the internet has served as a boost to this process of providing information and transparency with regard to crucial SRI issues. **Ethics Online 6** provides an overview of the web-based forums and sources of information for the SRI community. Increasingly, analysts and investment firms question companies on their ethical policies, as the existence of ethical funds has proven to be not just simply a new niche in the market, but has raised awareness of a previously ignored issue. A particular example of this 'mainstreaming' process of ethical criteria in investment decisions is the growing number of efforts by banks and investors to include such criteria in decisions on large infrastructure projects, such as dams and pipelines in the developing world (Goff 2006). Examples include the 'Safeguard Policies' of the International Finance Corporation (the private sector arm of the World Bank) and the 'Equator Principles', a set of guidelines for commercial banks.[7] The latest development in this arena is the United Nations 'Principles of Responsible Investment', which were launched in 2005 and boast more than 557 signatories from the global investment industry.[8] They contain six basic principles committing signatories to the integration of environmental, social, and governance issues into investment decisions and ownership practices, as well as promoting the principles and reporting on progress.

Despite these initiatives, the jury remains out on the actual impact of SRI on improved ethical performance of companies. While there are numerous examples of companies responding to ethical demands from their investors, critics, in particular from the NGO community, have not been so enthusiastic. As Peter Frankental (2006) from Amnesty International argues, the impact of SRI itself has been rather limited since in practice fund managers are still predominantly occupied with financial performance and only when, for instance, human rights issues threaten the latter, are companies actually willing to change their practices. Certainly, the reaction of Rio Tinto, when de-listed by one of the world's biggest SRI funds, points to this problem (see **Ethics in Action 6.2**). More systematically, David Vogel (2005: 37–8) has summarized the main concerns regarding the contemporary SRI movement:

- **Quality of information.** Most of the information on social and ethical performance, on which funds base their decisions, is based on data provided by the companies themselves. While this in itself may not be a major problem, the main concern is that the sources, ways of verifying, and comparability of the data is rather heterogeneous, unregulated, and unstandardized. This makes the data somewhat questionable as a base of sound investment decision.

- **Dubious criteria.** Looking at the criteria SRI funds use (see **Figure 6.4**), some of them often reflect very specific ideological or political views. As Vogel argues, many ethical fund managers might actually enjoy a glass of wine, but during the working day they treat the companies who sell it to them as 'irresponsible'. In a similar vein, not everybody will find companies using genetic engineering to treat diseases or companies providing the technology for legitimate national defence purposes as 'socially irresponsible' per se.

- **Too inclusive.** Citing a study of 600 SRI funds, Vogel points at the fact that 90% of the Fortune 500 companies are held by at least one SRI fund. Not only were notorious

ETHICS ONLINE 6

Keeping up with the world of SRI

While socially responsible investment (SRI) has now clearly moved into the mainstream of the investment community, the range of web-based information forums on SRI still largely reflects its activist origins. One of the oldest players in the movement, the UK-based Ethical Investment Research Services (EIRIS) was set up by charities and churches back in 1983 which then were concerned about the ethical quality of the businesses they were investing in. Today EIRIS, though still a non-for profit foundation, boasts an impressive list of institutional investors as clients and counts among the most respected research providers on SRI. Its website features information for consumers, charities, and asset advisers, as well as various free downloadable research publications of use to students and academics.

The more the field of SRI has matured, the more we have seen national and regional organizations being set up with the goal of providing a broad range of stakeholders (most prominently of course investors) with information about the ethical practices of corporations as a basis for decisions on SRI. These Social Investment Forums (SIF) exist in Asia, Australia, Canada, Europe, and the USA. SIFs are professional not-for-profit associations of, as in the case of Eurosif, pension funds, financial service providers, academic institutes, research associations, and NGOs. The websites of these organizations are a rich source on information not just on SRI, but on a wide range of ethical issues in business. While the SIFs showcase how far the institutionalization of SRI has come, the activist nature of the movement still comes through: the National Ethical Investment Week in the UK (which ran from 8–14 November in 2009) is just one example of how SRI enthusiasts in business, academia, and civil society see their campaign as far from over and understand themselves as change agents for the wider business community and society at large.

The web provides a unique opportunity to communicate on SRI-related issues, many of which are global in nature. The most global platform here might be the website of the United Nations Principles of Responsible Investment (PRI), an initiative linked to the now decade-old activities of the United Nations Global Compact. But there is also movement at the grassroots: SocialFunds.com, for instance, is an organization in the US attempting to empower in particular 'the regular guy' to be able to make informed choices when it comes to being a responsible investor. In this respect, the SRI movement shows no signs of slowing down, and the web offers a great way of connecting up SRI information providers and activists with investors and other concerned stakeholders.

Sources

EIRIS: http://www.eiris.org
National Ethical Investment Week: http://www.neiw.org
SocialFunds: http://www.socialfunds.com/
United Nations Principles of Responsible Investment: http://www.unpri.org.
Social Investment Forum Websites:
Asia: http://www.asria.org
Australia: http://www.responsibleinvestment.org
Canada: http://www.socialinvestment.ca
Europe: http://www.eurosif.org (for further country websites click 'Mission')
USA: http://www.socialinvest.org

VISIT THE WEBSITE for links to useful sources of further information

companies such as Enron held by SRI funds, but so too were many of the overleveraged banks and mortgage houses that were involved in the financial crisis of the late 2000s. Companies such as Fanny Mae, AIG, Bank of America, and Citigroup were all involved in rather irresponsible approaches to risk management and lending practices, yet remained a major part of SRI portfolios (Entine 2008a).

- **Strong emphasis on returns.** Usually, fund managers in the SRI industry screen companies in terms of performance first, and then select among the good performers due to their social, ethical, or environmental criteria. A company that deliberately invests in a long-term strategy, for instance in green technology, and focuses on the achievement of ethical criteria at the expense of short-term profitability would therefore not stand a chance of being included in most SRI portfolios. So some of the more socially responsible companies may never make it onto the list of responsible companies in the world of SRI.

■ Shareholding for sustainability

With shareholders having the potential to use their power and ownership rights to encourage companies to live up to their role as corporate citizens, they might be said to contribute to one of the major goals of business ethics: the triple bottom line of environmental, economic, and social sustainability. In this last section, we will have a look at two selected aspects where shareholders become directly involved in contributing to sustainable corporate behaviour. The first area is closely linked to our discussion in the previous section and looks to shareholders aligning their investment decisions to the criterion of sustainability. While this first approach uses the market to achieve sustainability, the second approach focuses on corporate structure and will have a look at alternative ways of linking ownership, work, and community involvement.

The Dow Jones Sustainability Group Index

During the last decade, there have been several attempts to construct share indexes that rate corporations according to their performance towards the broader goal of sustainability. The more long-standing tradition emerges from the US, where the Dow Jones Sustainability Index (DJSI) has become the leading index in this respect since its inception in 1999. Subsequent developments in Europe led to the launch in October 2001 of the 'FTSE4Good' in London. This includes a family of indices that embrace companies which meet certain social, environmental, and ethical standards (Oulton 2006). Since 1990, we have witnessed the launch of more than 23 of such indices, mostly in Europe and North America, many of which focus on either smaller markets or different investor interests (Louche and Lydenberg 2006). A particular group of these are 'Cleantech Indexes',[9] which specifically include companies employing clean, environmentally friendly technology solutions. However, as the DJSI has been the first of these to be based on one of the major financial markets in the world, we will focus mainly on this.[10]

The DJSI follows a 'best-in-class approach', comprising those identified as the sustainability leaders in each industry. Companies are assessed in line with general and industry-specific criteria, which means that they are compared against their peers and ranked accordingly. The companies accepted into the index are chosen along the following criteria:

- **Environmental sustainability.** For example, environmental reporting, eco-design, environmental management systems, executive commitment to environmental issues.
- **Economic sustainability.** For example, strategic planning, quality and knowledge management, supply-chain management, corporate governance mechanisms.
- **Social sustainability.** For example, employment policies, management development, stakeholder dialogue, affirmative action and human rights policies, anti-corruption policies.

The data that form the basis for the judgements are based on questionnaires, submitted documentation, corporate policies, and reports, and finally, public information as far as it is available. The DJSI is in fact a family of indexes which comprise different markets and regions, adding a specific Asia-Pacific sub-index as of 2009.[1] The DJS World Index, for instance, comprised in 2009 the top 10% of the best social and environmental performers among the world's largest 2500 companies, spread over 57 industries.

According to its proponents, by focusing on sustainability, the index identifies those companies with future-oriented and innovative management. Interestingly, since its inception, the DJSI has slightly outperformed the mainstream Dow Jones Index, although it should be noted that financial robustness also forms an important part of the DJSI. It has also attracted significant interest from the investment community. In June 2009, 70 DJSI licences were held by asset managers in 16 countries to manage a variety of financial products, representing some $7.4 billion in total.

There are, however, a number of criticisms of the index, some of which focus on the technicalities of the index, and some of which actually concentrate on the ethical credentials of the companies chosen.

- The biggest criticism is that the data on which a company is accepted into the index depends largely on data provided by the corporation itself. Although the data are analysed by the Swiss consultancy firm, SAM Sustainability Group, and verified by an independent auditor, the assessment is basically an inside-out provision of data.
- This coincides with criticisms over the questionable criteria used by the index. Some critics have asked how it could be that corporations with massive ethical credibility problems, such as large oil companies, are included in the index. Similarly, the entry of the cigarette manufacturer, British American Tobacco, into the

VISIT THE WEBSITE for links to useful sources of further information

ETHICS IN ACTION 6.2 http://www.ethicalcorp.com

Ethical CORPORATION

Norway's oil fund—can divestment make a difference?

EC Newsdesk, 17 November 2008

Rio Tinto says conditions at the notorious Grasberg gold and copper mine, now condemned by one of the world's most powerful investors, are not likely to change as environmental best practice occurs there already. The Anglo-Australian miner was accused in September 2008 of being 'directly responsible for severe environmental damage' at the mine in the Indonesia-controlled Papuan highlands in New Guinea. The world's second-largest pension fund, Norway's Government Pension Fund Global, which owns about 1% of Europe's listed shares or about $375bn of assets, dumped its entire Rio Tinto holdings—worth an estimated $880m—and slapped the firm on an investment blacklist. About 30 companies, including Boeing, Wal-Mart, EADS, Safran and BAE Systems, are on the list of companies the fund will not invest in because it believes they are involved in human rights violations, corruption, environmental pollution or making 'particularly inhumane' weapons.

The Grasberg mine is owned by US-based Freeport McMoRan Copper & Gold, but Rio Tinto is a crucial partner in the huge open-pit mine's expansion. Rio and Freeport are now gearing up for the 2015 start of underground operations at the world's largest single gold reserve.

The Norwegian fund—known as the 'oil fund' because it invests Norway's oil and gas revenue for future generations—is famous for excluding companies from investment that do not meet its ethical standards. In 2006 the fund ditched its Freeport shares after concluding the US company's mine waste disposal methods at Grasberg were causing 'extensive, long-term and irreversible' environmental damage.

No dominos

The oil fund's decision to dump Rio shares came after unsatisfactory responses to concerns the fund raised in 2007 over the environmental damage from Grasberg. But will its decision to divest improve conditions at the mine or have a knock-on effect on Rio's ability to raise capital? 'We are now seeing the influence that responsible investors can have, not just through engagement, but also through divestment,' says Duncan Paterson, chief executive and founder of the Centre for Australian Ethical Research and director of Hong Kong-based Association for Sustainable and Responsible Investment in Asia. 'The Norway pension fund is highly influential. It published a list of companies it divested from on the grounds of the cost of carbon emissions. I have experience of several investment houses taking direct notice of information the fund made public,' Paterson says.

But Rio Tinto says the oil fund's exit will not change the way it runs the Grasberg mine. Company spokesman Nick Cobban says: 'The decision they took … is not going to have a direct impact, because we already take our responsibilities very, very seriously wherever we operate.'

Sensitive environment

Freeport McMoRan operates Grasberg through its 90.6%-owned subsidiary PT Freeport Indonesia, in which the Indonesian government, which controversially controls

Papua, owns 9.4%. The mine is environmentally sensitive as it borders Lorentz National Park, a Unesco heritage site. It also enriches the Indonesian government whose military, along with Freeport-employed mine security, have been accused of racist killings of local Papuans. A report by the Australian Council on Overseas Aid, an NGO umbrella group, found that in 1994 and 1995 the Indonesian military, aided by Grasberg mine security, was responsible for the death or disappearance of 22 civilians, as well as 15 people the Indonesian government described as rebels.

Rio Tinto came on board at Grasberg in 1996 and has since ploughed an estimated $1bn into its expansion. After 2021, Rio will get 40% of the whole output of the Grasberg mine. Freeport says Rio also has the option to participate in 40% of any of Freeport's other future exploration projects in Papua. 'It's not a hands-off involvement. We are regularly there, working with the Freeport people both in terms of the operations and in terms of the environmental and community activities. We are very closely working with them,' Cobban says.

The oil fund believes Rio Tinto has been either playing down or ignoring its concerns over environmental havoc caused by the mine. The company has not addressed the risk of 'severe and irreversible' environmental damage from the mine, the fund says, explaining its decision to divest from Rio in September. The fund says 230,000 tonnes of mine tailings are being dumped each day into a river that feeds an estuary that eventually flows into the Arafura Sea. The discharge into the river system is set to rise as Grasberg enters its new expansion phase, bringing a risk heavy metals will enter the food chain and cause long-term harm to ecosystems far from the mine site. Once the process of acid water containing heavy metals starts to pollute groundwater and water systems, the process is irreversible and may last for centuries, the Norwegian oil fund says. Mine waste-rock stockpiles now cover an eight-square-kilometre area. The fund drew upon facts from company statements, an International Institute for Environment and Development case study, as well as US media reports

Responsible divestment?

The fund perhaps wants Rio Tinto to walk away from Grasberg. But some say it has not considered the effect of such an exit on local Papuans. 'What matters is the sustainability of the Papuan people being affected by the mine's operations. They're the ones with the least power yet are the most damaged by the mine and its activities,' says Francis Grey, research manager at Sustainable Asset Management Australia. 'The fund perhaps should have considered if the Papuan people are better off with at least one party at the table who can try to influence the Indonesian military on the one hand and Freeport on the other. Or are they better off without having anybody there interested in these issues,' Grey says. He suggests Rio Tinto takes it upon itself to be more transparent with investors on the true environmental and social situation in the mine area. And that it allocates a portion of mine-related profits to be returned to local tribespeople, perhaps invested until there is reduced risk of funds flowing back to Indonesia's military.

Sources

Ethical Corporation, 17 November 2008, http://www.ethicalcorp.com.

VISIT THE WEBSITE for a short response to this feature

? THINK THEORY

Think about the difference between the strategies of socially responsible investment and shareholder activism. What are the advantages and disadvantages of each of them for the Norwegian Oil Fund in seeking to improve conditions at the mine?

index in 2002 was greeted with considerable controversy. The index does not, however, exclude on the basis of industry. Despite the obvious problems for sustainability of the tobacco industry (as well as armaments, alcohol, energy, and others), SAM argues that industry leaders should be identified and rewarded in order to stimulate progress towards sustainability. Other indexes, such as the FTSE4Good, would use negative criteria; for instance, currently the tobacco industry is excluded from it.

- The sustainability assessment focuses mainly on management processes rather than on the actual sustainability of the company or its products. Evidence of policies and management tools features more prominently than concrete emission data or resource consumption figures. Again, SAM argues that the index does not identify sustainable companies, but those making progress towards addressing the issues.

Overall, then, the DJSI has to be regarded as an important step in linking investors' interests in financial performance with the broader goal of sustainability. However, the development towards sustainable investment ratings is still relatively recent and hopefully we will see concerted progress towards more in-depth indexes and investment tools in the near future. Nonetheless, while criticisms that it is simply a case of 'greenwashing' without any substantial performance implications are probably a little overwrought, developments such as the DJSI are never likely to be sufficient to encourage firms towards fully sustainable practice. Indeed, another rather more fundamental way of addressing sustainability from the perspective of shareholders is to completely re-think the whole notion of corporate ownership.

Rethinking sustainable corporate ownership: alternative models of ownership?

For some advocates of sustainability thinking, one of the crucial limitations of corporations that are effectively 'owned' by shareholders is that whatever their attention to other stakeholders, the ownership model simply precludes an entirely just allocation of rewards. In passing, we have already discussed alternative ways of ownership of corporations. First, we may think of governments owning corporations, which in many countries prior to the 1980s was the case with postal and telecommunication services, utilities, or healthcare. Recently, in the aftermath of the financial crisis of the late 2000s, government ownership has resurfaced again in the US, UK, Germany, and other countries, in particular in the banking and car industries. In some respects, the 'bailout' of banks and car companies by governments is due to the fact that a potential failure of these companies would hurt too many other stakeholders beyond shareholders, in particular employees, suppliers, and local communities. It is interesting to see that many commentators are cautiously optimistic about this ownership approach (Wong 2009), partly because government bureaucrats are hardly able to do a worse job at governing these companies than the managers who ran them into trouble in the first place.

State-ownership also still thrives in other parts of the world. French and German governments, for instance, still own controlling stakes in Renault and Volkswagen, not to mention countries such as China, where the 'state-owned enterprise' (SOE) is still the dominant pattern of economic organization. It is, however, not clear whether governmental ownership is automatically a step to higher ethical standards or a more inclusive approach for all stakeholders. On the opposite side of the coin, corruption, inefficiencies, and rent-seeking are often dominant traits in government involvement (Wong 2004).

Another alternative ownership model of course is family ownership. The main feature of this approach from an ethical perspective would be that families often have longer-term goals for their companies, rather than short-term profit maximization. This said, though, it is not a given that families automatically will show more concern for other stakeholders. Nonetheless, many family-owned companies have shown quite a significant commitment to philanthropy and social responsibility, a prime example being the Tata Group in India, now fourth generation family-owned and run (Elankumaran et al. 2005).

A common hybrid form of ownership are co-operatives, which are businesses that are owned neither by investors nor by their managers (such as the first capitalist entrepreneurs) but they are owned and democratically controlled by their workers or their customers. Co-operatives are businesses that are not set up to make profit, but to meet the needs of their members. The reasons for founding co-operatives therefore can be quite different. For example, consider the following cases (http://www.coop.org):

- Retail co-operatives are set up to meet retailing needs: for example, in remote parts of Sweden, consumers founded the Kooperativa Forbundet to provide them with shopping facilities. Crédit Mutuel, nowadays the number four bank in France, was initially founded to supply its members with capital.
- Producer co-operatives are set up to meet production needs: for example, many agricultural co-operatives, today most notably in developing countries, were founded to share tools, supplies, and know-how.
- Purchasing co-operatives are set up to meet buying needs: for example, the German Dachdeckereinkaufis a co-operative of small companies in the roof-laying industry that use co-operation to increase purchasing power.

Worldwide, there are some 750,000 co-operatives, with 760m members in 100 countries. They are based on the principles of voluntary membership, democratic control through the members, and concern for the community. **Figure 6.6** provides an overview of the fundamental principles of co-operation.

Originally established in 1844 by the Rochdale Pioneers (a group of British social reformers who set up the first formal co-operative movement), the principles of co-operation have since been developed into an internationally agreed set of principles governing the co-operative movement across the globe. The principles as set out by the International Co-operative Alliance are as follows (cited in Butcher 1996):

1 Education of the membership, staff and general public.
2 Co-operation among co-operatives.
3 Voluntary and open membership.
4 Democratically based control.
5 Equitable use of profit/surplus.
6 Limits on the participation of capital.

Beyond these basic principles, underlying social ideals have been important in guiding the movement. The biographer of the UK co-operative union Arnold Bonner (1961: 292) described these ideals as 'an economic system based upon common ownership and mutual aid ... in which equity, individual freedom and a strong sense of fellowship would be the basis of social relations ... i.e. a system conducive to good character and consequent happiness.'

Figure 6.6. Principles of co-operation

Sources: Bonner, A. 1961. *British Co-operation*. Stockport: Co-operative Union Ltd
Butcher, M. 1996. The co-operative movement: business relic or a model for the future? *Business Studies*, December: 25–8

Cooperatives are common in countries with a more collectivist tradition, most notably southern Europe and in particular Italy (Thomas 2004). One of the well-studied examples of a co-operative is the Spanish Mondragon Corporacion Cooperativa based in the Basque region of Spain (see Cheney 1995). It was founded in 1956 by five engineers and a catholic priest, after having been built up over 15 years prior to that date. Today the co-operative is one of Spain's largest business groups and consists of 250 companies, about half of them also co-operatives, employing more than 100,000 people. It includes large companies such as the Eroski supermarket chain, as well as smaller companies in the manufacturing and finance sectors, and a training and education arm. Each co-operative has its own general assembly meetings where all workers have the same vote and decide on the corporate policies. On top of that, each company has a vote in the general assembly of the Mondragon co-operative as a whole. The co-operative has remained highly profitable, with some of the highest worker productivity in the country. Around 50% of the profit flows back to owner-member-workers, with the rest reinvested or allocated to community schemes (some €40m in 2007).

VISIT THE WEBSITE for a short response to this feature

? THINK THEORY

Evaluate the approach of Mondragon from the perspective of stakeholder theory. Does it represent a fairer balance of stakeholder interests than Anglo-American governance or does it simply replace the dominance of shareholders with the dominance of employees?

The contribution to sustainability of the Mondragon co-operative is striking:

- **Economic sustainability.** The principle of solidarity between the different parts means that they mutually support each other in years of economic downturn in one industry. This leads to long-term survival and growth of the co-operative as a whole. Furthermore, the workers will always have an interest in the long-term survival of the corporation, as they personally own it.
- **Social sustainability.** Tremendous job security, embeddedness in the local communities and active support for social projects such as education, housing, and drug prevention make Mondragon an active supporter of a socially stable and supportive environment. With workplace democracy as the guiding principle, the individual worker enjoys relatively high protection of the rights that we will discuss in detail in the following chapter.
- **Environmental sustainability.** Although the literature is not too explicit about this aspect, it is clear that with local ownership of the corporation, the group of people who would be directly affected by polluted air, water, or soil is at the same time the very constituency to decide about these issues. This at least ensures attention to environmentally friendly working conditions and production processes. By 2008, around a fifth of the Mondragon companies had ISO 14000 environmental certification in place.

However successful Mondragon has been in the past, it nevertheless faces some challenges in the age of globalization. The typical cultural fabric of the Basque region has increasingly eroded over the years, and the co-operative faces growing international competition. With greater mobility of workers, wage solidarity in the co-operative has also come under threat. From an initial ratio of 3:1 between the highest and lowest earners, the average figure across the Mondragon companies is now around 5:1—with a ratio in some cases as high as 9:1 (Herrera 2004). Although this represents a slight dilution of economic solidarity, it is still remarkable by international standards. Insiders expect further modifications towards more market orientation, but there is great optimism that Mondragon will continue to be a successful example of a 'third way' in corporate governance.

■ Summary

In business ethics texts, shareholders are normally a somewhat neglected species. This is perhaps not surprising, given that since they are prioritized so much in virtually all other areas of management education and practice, business ethics is usually considered the area where a counterpoint can be developed. However, our view is that since they are such an important corporate constituency, it is simply inappropriate to sideline them in this way. This chapter has then, in a way, tried to achieve a more balanced view on shareholders, and thereby afford them at least equal status with the other stakeholders discussed in the second part of the book.

We started by looking at the peculiarity of the principal-agent relation that defines the relationship between managers and shareholders, and provides the basis for our understanding of corporate governance. We showed here how divergent interests and an unequal distribution of information between the two parties effectively institutionalize some fundamental ethical conflicts in governance. This led us to examine the different models of governance evident across the globe, followed by the various ethical issues pertinent to shareholder relations, such as executive control, remuneration, insider trading, etc. Furthermore, the peculiar situation of shareholders also shone through in the three main issues that reframed the contemporary challenge for ethical business—globalization, citizenship, and sustainability.

Globalization, we have shown, has thrown up new challenges in the governance of international financial markets and has driven a range of reforms in corporate governance across the globe. We also discovered that shareholder democracy enables investors to use their critical role in the supply of capital to influence corporations to behave more ethically. Finally, we showed how shareholders could also play a role in driving corporations towards enhanced sustainability by their investment decisions on the stock market, as well as examining more unconventional patterns of ownership.

Study questions

1 Why is the ownership of corporations different from that of other forms of 'property'? What implications does this have for the nature of shareholder rights?

2 Define corporate governance. What are the main ethical problems that arise in the area of corporate governance?

3 'Executive pay is not an ethical issue—it is just a question of paying people a market rate.' Critically evaluate this statement using examples from contemporary business practice.

4 In this chapter, we have mentioned a number of times the financial crisis of the late 2000s. In your view, what are the main reasons from an ethical perspective for the occurrence of this crisis? Also, what potential solutions would you see to prevent such problems occurring again?

5 Define insider trading. What are the main ethical arguments against insider trading?

6 Compare the effectiveness of SRI and shareholder activism in ensuring ethical conduct in corporations.

Research exercise

Go to the university library or check on the web to do some research on the nature of corporate governance in your home country. You might find details in a corporate governance or corporate finance textbook, or on a website dealing with national governance codes or governance reform.

1 Set out as clearly as you can the system of corporate governance that operates in your home country.

2 To what extent is the system you have set out in accordance with the Anglo-American or the continental European governance model? How can you explain any differences?

3 What priority does this system appear to afford to different stakeholders?
4 Do you think that the governance system in your country provides a fair basis for corporate activity?

Key Readings

VISIT THE WEBSITE for links to further key readings

1 **Aguilera, R.V., Williams, C.A., Conley, J.M., and Rupp, D.E. 2006. Corporate governance and social responsibility: a comparative analysis of the UK and the US. *Co po a e Go e nance*, 14 (3): 147–58.**

This article provides a broad overview of the differences in corporate governance between the US and the UK, highlighting in particular the different roles played by institutional investors. It highlights the issues discussed in the first half of the chapter and exposes key characteristics of corporate governance from an ethical perspective.

2 **Donaldson, T. 2008. Hedge fund ethics. *Business hics Qua e ly*, 18 (3): 405–16.**

This article provides an interesting and very readable account of some of the key ethical issues involved in corporation-shareholder relations by focusing on one particularly controversial form of financial institution, the hedge fund. It highlights the critical role of transparency in effective governance, and suggests possible routes for ethical reform of hedge funds through regulation and self-regulation. This latter discussion provides a good introduction to some of the debates to be covered in Chapter 11 of the book.

Case 6

VISIT THE WEBSITE for links to useful sources of further information

Corporate governance of professional football clubs: for profit or for glory?

This case describes the corporate governance issues that have arisen from the professionalization of modern football clubs in Europe. The case discusses the ethical issues surrounding the transformation of football clubs into modern, multi-million business enterprises. It explores alternative forms of ownership of football clubs and provides an opportunity to understand the tensions between shareholding and stakeholding.

'United not for sale'—proclaimed the banners at Manchester United's home stadium Old Trafford, in response to plans announced by the American millionaire Malcolm Glazer to buy a 75% controlling stake in the club. Ultimately, though, the fans were wrong, and by May 2005 the club had been taken over by Glazer in a move that crystallized the movement from football as a community sport to a multi-million pound international industry much like any other.

The changing face of the football 'industry'

The commercialization of football has been a significant trend over the past few decades—and one that has transformed the way the sport is organized, controlled, marketed and financed almost beyond recognition. Long gone are the days of England's 1966 heroes, most of whom played for clubs paying them wages not much different from what a factory worker next door would earn. Players' wages at the time were largely paid for by gate ticket revenues, and football was chiefly a matter of entertaining local fans. Being a supporter or member of a football club was a life-long commitment, part of one's personal identity, and often handed down for generations within a family.

One of the key changes, of course, came through the involvement and growth of commercial television in the game. This led not only to vast increases in income for the clubs themselves, but also to a larger, global audience and fan base for clubs. It is by now commonplace to find fans of Europe's top clubs, such as Manchester United, Real Madrid, or AC Milan, in Africa, Asia, and Latin America. Parallel to these vast TV contracts, opportunities for generating revenue from merchandising club paraphernalia and advertising contracts have increasingly helped to fill the clubs' coffers. In 2009, Real Madrid was named as Europe's richest club with a turnover of around €330m, followed by Manchester United (€294m), Barcelona (€279m), and Bayern Munich (€266m). For many investors, football has proved to be a lucrative deal: for example, one of the early investors in Manchester United was able to increase his wealth from an initial £840,000 investment to a whopping £93m in just a few years. Combined with fairytale salaries for players—Real Madrid's recent signing Cristiano Ronaldo now makes €13m a year—today's football landscape is hardly any more the world of ordinary working men and women's weekend entertainment.

In recent years, however, the ownership and investment model of football club owners has begun to change, particularly among the English Premiership elite. In numerous cases, wealthy individuals have taken over top clubs and treated them more and more like an investment, in particular by leveraging the investment through massive accumulation of debt. In 2009, Manchester United had debts in excess of £750m, Chelsea owed £736m, and other clubs such as Manchester City, taken over by investors from the United Arab Emirates in 2008, are going in the same direction. These developments have had significant impacts on how the sport is organized. Although a number of clubs in the UK were floated as public limited companies (PLCs), and listed on the stock exchange, many have now been effectively brought into private ownership again through private equity.

Governance challenges

With these developments towards commercialization and high-level capital investment, significant challenges await the football 'industry'. With roots in what was a simple local institution for fans and communities, many football clubs have struggled to enter the world of professional business. Not only in the UK but all over Europe, spectacular bankruptcies such as the one of Borussia Dortmund in Germany, or corruption scandals, such as the one involving Juventus that saw the Italian club relegated to Serie B and stripped of two titles in 2006, have put in serious doubt whether football clubs have really accomplished a smooth transition into the professional business world.

Another serious issue concerns the role of fans in the running of football clubs. After all, at the end of the day, clubs depend on their fans for their livelihood, as either spectators, TV audiences, or consumers of merchandise. Yet, over the past decade, average attendances at English Premier League matches have stagnated and young people, in particular, have simply been priced out of the game: in 2009, only 7% of spectators in the UK were under 24—compared with around 25% in the 1980s. Fans appear to feel increasingly alienated by players' wages, and by the high cost of tickets for games. For example, the cheapest season ticket for Arsenal in 2008/9 cost £925, with the more expensive seats running into several thousands of pounds.

Frequent changes in traditional kick-off times due to programming demands from TV stations has further fuelled the feeling that football is no longer the fans' game but simply a business oriented to generating revenue for their owners. In a 2005 survey by Michie and Oughton, 60% of the fans who responded said that the dialogue between them and their club was ineffective, and nearly half said that their club was not protecting and promoting their interests as fans.

Ironically, it is particularly from the business angle where these developments have caused concerns. After all, a dwindling fan base threatens the very basis of the business success. And even with supporters shifting from attendance in the stadium to TV—who wants to watch a game that takes place in front of empty seats in the stadium? Between 1996 and 2006, the 72 clubs in the English Football League made a pre-tax loss of £981m. This is in stark contrast to other leagues where clubs are predominantly owned by fans, such as the German Bundesliga, where clubs made £210m operating profit in 2006/7—mainly through higher attendance of supporters at lower ticket prices.

Fans regain some control

In recent years, several initiatives have been taken to address fans' interests more directly, as two examples from the UK illustrate. A government-funded initiative, Supporters Direct, has initiated the creation of supporters' trusts, which organize collective shareholding for fans in their clubs. The aim of these trusts is 'to bring about responsible, democratic representation at spectator sports clubs, and so help promote the highest standards of governance, accountability and embed those clubs deeper into their communities'. The trusts have grown in popularity amongst supporters, and in 2009, nearly 70% of clubs in the UK had a supporters' trust. About one-third of these trusts had a director on the club's board of directors, although only a handful of small teams were actually owned directly by the trusts.

Another initiative by the clubs themselves has been the Football in the Community scheme. This involves the clubs in various social projects, generally targeted at embedding the club in the local community and addressing social exclusion, unemployment, or anti-social behaviour in the immediate vicinity of the clubs. Corporate social responsibility programmes have become more widespread in the world of football, especially amongst large clubs, where teams such as Arsenal and Chelsea now have initiatives, reports, and websites dedicated to social responsibility. Even smaller clubs, such as Charlton and Brentford, have initiated a host of award-winning community schemes, often in partnership with fans, the police, and local councils.

While these philanthropic initiatives appear laudable, the tension about the core purpose of a football club remains: is it just another business which can 'give back' to the community some of its commercial success, or is the actual primary purpose of clubs to provide value to fans? Perhaps the most striking alternative is illustrated by clubs such as Real Madrid and FC Barcelona, which are member-owned, democratic, not-for-profit organizations. Here, the club leadership is accountable to the people who watch and pay, and the primary rationale for the club is to play football. Members at

Barcelona, for example, can vote on the election of the club's president and the governing board, and have a right to participate in key decisions.

Unsurprisingly, unlike their English counterparts, these clubs have seen a steady surge in membership. By 2009, Barcelona could lay claim to being the club with the most official members in the world—some 175,000—an increase of around 15% over the past three years.

Back in the UK, governance issues remained high on the agenda, particularly in the face of the unfolding global financial crisis. In 2009, the All Party Parliamentary Football Group published a number of recommendations to improve governance in the 'industry'. They included:

- **A 'fit and proper persons test' for the management and ownership of clubs.** This reflected concerns around owners such as Thaksin Shinawatra, a convicted criminal in his native Thailand, who bought Manchester City in 2007.

- **Supporter-led governance.** Suggestions here included more supporters' representatives on the board of football clubs, affordable ticket prices, and more facilities and access for disabled supporters.

- **Nurturing domestic talent.** Rather than being a xenophobic effort, this idea reflected a belief that football clubs should represent the local communities in which they operated and therefore should concentrate on supporting young players from the local community. In England at the time, there was an average of 2.64 English players out of every 11 players in the team (compared with 7 out of 11 in Italy or Spain).

Another interesting development was the launch in 2009 of the Stewardship Scorecard developed by the CSR think-tank Tomorrow's Company. The scorecard ranks clubs according to criteria such as: 'putting the club first', 'long-termism', 'engagement with fans and the community', and 'passion, commitment, and conviction' of owners and the board. Top of the league in terms of stewardship among premiership teams were Aston Villa, Arsenal, and Wigan, whilst poor performers included West Ham, Liverpool, and Tottenham. Positions at the bottom of the league tended to reflect problems with financial mismanagement, debt problems, and ownership upheavals. Ultimately, though, while the stewardship scorecard may seek to reflect similar qualities to corporate CSR rankings, such as the Dow Jones Sustainability Index, the fact remains that football fans, compared with typical investors or consumers, are far less likely to switch allegiance due to poor performance.

Questions

1. Set out the main stakeholders of football clubs. Describe their 'stake' in the organization and assess the legitimacy of their interests.
2. What are the key governance issues each of these stakeholder groups might have?
3. The case describes a number of approaches that offer potential solutions to the governance issues raised. Set out these approaches and evaluate their likely effectiveness in dealing with governance challenges in football clubs.
4. Ultimately, who 'should' own football clubs and what should their priorities be in managing the enterprise?

Sources

All Parliamentary Football Group. 2009. English football and its governance, April: http://www.allpartyfootball.com.

Bland, B. 2008. Listed football clubs score own goals. *Daily Telegraph*, 7 April: http://www.telegraph.co.uk.

Holt, M., Michie, J., Oughton, C., Tacon, R., and Walters, G. 2005. *The state of the game: The corporate governance of Football Clubs 2005*. London: Football Governance Research Centre, Birkbeck, University of London.

Kelson, P. 2009. Manchester United will become first British club to break the £300 million turnover barrier. *Daily Telegraph*, 11 February: http://www.telegraph.co.uk.

McMahon, B. and Buckley, K. 2006. Scandal hits Italy World Cup plans. *Observer*, 14 May: http://www.guardian.co.uk.

Michie, J. and Oughton, C. 2005. The corporate governance of professional football clubs in England. *Corporate Governance: An International Review*, 13 (4): 517–31.

Northcroft, J. 2005. Stand by your fan. *Sunday Times*, 25 September: 7.

Shore, B. 2009. Football clubs must 'think long term'. *BBC News*, 20 August: http://www.bbc.co.uk/news.

Supporters Direct website: http://www.supporters-direct.org.

Tomorrow's Company website: http://www.tomorrowscompany.com.

Walters, G. and Chadwick, S. 2009. Corporate citizenship in football: delivering strategic benefits through stakeholder engagement. *Management Decision*, 47 (1): 51–66.

Notes

1 See http://www.stampoutpoverty.org.

2 BBC 2009. Switzerland eases banking secrecy. *BBC* News, 13 March 2009: http://www.bbc.co.uk/news.

3 See the various statements made at the World Islamic Economic Form 2009 at http://www.wief.org.

4 See http://www.iccr.org.

5 See http://www.socialinvest.org.

6 See http://www.eiris.org.

7 See http://www.ifc.org; http://www.equator-principles.com.

8 See http://www.unpri.org.

9 See http://cleantech.com/index/.

10 This section draws on the following articles, each of which might be referred to for further details and discussion: Barkawi (2002); Knoepfel (2001); Cerin and Dobers (2001a, 2001b).

11 See http://www.sustainability-indexes.com/djsi.

7

Employees and Business Ethics

In this chapter we will:

- Discuss the specific role of employees among the various stakeholder groups and identify issues of concern for corporations.
- Identify the core ethical topics of employees' rights and duties.
- Outline the ethical issues and problems faced in human resource management, by focusing particularly on the different rights of employees.
- Analyse the duties of employees and the company's involvement in enabling employees to live up to their duties.
- Examine basic issues and problems of managing employees in the different cultural and national contexts necessitated by globalization.
- Explore the notion of corporate citizenship in relation to employees by examining the influence of different national contexts on corporate accountability for protecting employee rights.
- Discuss the implications of sustainability for workplaces and for specific working conditions.

Introduction

Dealing with employees is probably the area where all of us at some stage are most likely to encounter ethical issues and dilemmas. Whether it is a question of fair wages and conditions, sexual harassment in the workplace, or simply taking advantage of company resources such as the phone or internet for personal use, employee-related ethical problems are unavoidable for most contemporary managers. Such problems can run from the most everyday questions of how to treat disabled workers appropriately to fundamental questions of human rights.

In a certain sense, one could argue that ethical issues with regard to employees have been a consideration for corporations long before the topic of 'business ethics' was even on the agenda of business schools, let alone of corporations. When we look to the first wave of the industrial revolution in the nineteenth century, the fair and proper treatment of employees was a controversial issue right from the outset. Famous writers, such as Charles Dickens in his novel *Hard Times*, explored the exploitation and poor working conditions of the masses during this era. In a more positive vein, this period also saw various examples of industrialists setting an example by looking after their workers' housing, healthcare, and diet, just to name a few examples (Cannon 1994: 7–29). As some have argued, this paternalistic involvement of employers with the working and living conditions of their employees was often motivated by what we referred to earlier as 'enlightened' self-interest: only if workers live in halfway decent living circumstances are they likely to be productive and committed to the firm's economic success (Fitzgerald 1999).

One could in fact argue that the major political divide of the twentieth century—between capitalism on the one hand and socialism or communism on the other—originally focused on the function of employees in the working process. Karl Marx, Lenin, and even Mao developed their ideas ostensibly with the improvement of workers' living conditions in mind. On a smaller scale, the political agendas of traditional 'labour', 'socialist', or 'social democratic' parties were targeted at changing legislation, implementing a so-called 'welfare state', and providing the masses with an entitlement to decent working conditions. By the end of the last century, however, with socialism and communism in retreat, and even most left-wing governments under heavy budget pressures to cut back on the welfare state and reduce regulation, ethical issues in employment have regained their position on the business ethics agenda.

These days, however, such issues are treated somewhat differently than in the past. Crucially, there are still problems similar to those faced by workers in the nineteenth century, albeit less so in industrialized countries, but certainly in developing countries. MNCs from the global North are confronted with issues such as the protection of workers' human rights in their factories in China or Cambodia, while at home, a variety of different ethical questions arise from the usage of new technologies such as the internet, and the introduction of new work environments such as call centres. A crucial development here seems to be that fewer and fewer issues are directly addressed through governmental legislation compared with a hundred, or even fifty, years ago. Increasingly, we witness a growing tendency to leave the solution of these issues to corporations themselves. Consequently, the discussion of ethical issues in firm–employee relations is a matter of growing interest and concern.

■ Employees as stakeholders

Like shareholders, employees take on a peculiar role among stakeholders as they are closely integrated into the firm. Whereas shareholders basically 'own' all material and immaterial assets of the firm, employees, in many cases even physically, 'constitute' the corporation. They are perhaps the most important production factor or 'resource' of the corporation, they represent the company towards most other stakeholders, and act in the name of the corporation towards them. This essential contribution, as well as the fact that employees benefit from the existence of their employers, and are quite clearly affected by the success or otherwise of their company, are widely regarded as giving employees some kind of definite stake in the organization.

> **? THINK THEORY**
>
> In Chapter 2, we discussed different models of the firm, notably the managerial view and the stakeholder view. The managerial view puts shareholders' interests first, while the stakeholder perspective would consider other groups' interests as legitimate as well. Try to construct an ethical argument in favour of employees as legitimate (maybe even dominant) stakeholders of the firm.

VISIT THE WEBSITE for a short response to this feature

Referring back to our definition of stakeholders in Chapter 2, both the legal and the economic side of the relation between employees and the corporation are worthy of examination. On the *legal* level, there is normally some sort of contract between the corporation that stipulates the rights and duties of the two parties. This legal relationship, furthermore, is quite strongly embedded in a rather dense network of legislation that provides a legally codified solution to a large number of issues between companies and employees. Although there is certainly, to a varying degree, a fair amount of legal rules pertinent to all other stakeholder relationships, the relation between corporations and employees is peculiar in that it has traditionally been the subject of governmental regulation in most countries, from the very beginning of the industrial revolution onwards.

This characteristic has strong implication also for the *economic* aspect of firm-stakeholder relationships. The relation between firms and employees is characterized by certain externalities on both sides—by which we mean that there are costs to each that are not included in the employment contract. These hidden costs can lead to situations of 'asset specificity'—that is, employees 'invest' time and effort in developing 'assets' specific to a particular employer, and vice versa. Such costs of specificity can create what we call a *moral hazard* for both parties, opening up a wide range of ethical issues. Examples from the perspective of the *employee* include investing in a new job by moving to a new town, including things like shaking up the circle of friends, finding new schools for kids, etc. Another aspect is hidden in the familiar English synonym of 'making a living' for having a job. Much of our waking life is committed to our job. As a result, it is often the place where friends and social relationships are made, and where the human need for self-actualization is met. All this results in a considerable amount of dependence by an employee on his or her employer.

Employers, on the other hand, also face similar elements of moral hazard from their employees. A spectacular example is the French trader Jérôme Kerviel (discussed in Ethics in Action 4.1, pp. 162–3), who brought down Société Générale in 2008: companies do not have complete control of their employees, and can sometimes find out only by hindsight whether they actually do their job properly. Especially in IT or other knowledge-intensive industries, employees have considerable power due to their specialized knowledge and employers face the risk that some of their most valuable assets might remain underused or even be poached by a competitor.

As mentioned above, many of these moral hazards in the employer–employee relation have been subject to legislation. As the moral hazard is normally greater for the employee (since they are the more dependent and weaker party), most of this legislation focuses around workers' rights. However, as we have discussed in Chapter 1, there are clear limits to the legal trajectory in settling ethical issues. Furthermore, the nature of the relation between employer and employees often makes the sheer application of existing law (and the exploitation or otherwise of legal loopholes) an object of ethical considerations, which is one of the reasons why we discussed 'legal responsibility' as one of the four key elements of corporate social responsibility in Chapter 2. In the following, we will have a look at the issues involved in the relations of the company to the stakeholder group of employees.

■ Ethical issues in the firm–employee relation

Management of human 'resources'—an ethical problem between rights and duties

Employees are, in principle, managed by the human resources department—a term which already indicates a first problem from an ethical perspective. As it is, the term 'human resource management' and its implications have been a subject of some debate in business ethics (Hart 1993; Torrington 1993; Barrett 1999; Greenwood 2002). If we recall Kantian theory, the second maxim requires us to treat humanity 'always as an end and never as a means only'. Human resources management (HRM), however, does exactly this: we as humans are constituted as an important *resource* and in most cases, the most costly resource as well. Consequently, employees are subject to a strict managerial rationale of minimizing costs and maximizing the efficiency of the 'resource'. In fact, one could argue that the core ethical dilemma in HRM lies in the fact that people in the firm, under economic criteria, are nothing more than a resource, next to and often competing with other resources, most notably new technology, or cheaper resources from overseas.

Ultimately, though, the management of human 'resources' implies more than just the application of economic criteria. In other words, human beings within the firm are, of course, a means to an end as they are employed to perform certain functions. However,

Rhetoric	Reality
'New working patterns'.	Part-time instead of full-time jobs.
'Flexibility'.	Management can do what it wants.
'Empowerment'.	Making someone else take the risk and responsibility.
'Training and development'.	Manipulation.
'Recognizing the contribution of the individual'.	Undermining the trade union and collective bargaining.
'Teamworking'.	Reducing the individual's discretion.

Figure 7.1. Rhetoric and reality in HRM
Source: Based on Legge (1998).

from an ethical perspective, they should not be treated as a 'means *only*', and it is this restriction that makes all the difference in terms of business ethics. **Ethics on Screen 7** provides a contemporary example of an industry where employees face the very real risk of just being treated as a commodity. This distinction becomes fairly visible when looking at the gap between the rhetoric of HRM policies and the reality often hidden behind it. Some common examples are given in **Figure 7.1.**

According to Kantian thinking, it is human dignity that forbids treating employees as a means only, and it is exactly this duty that posits the main ethical boundary for the management of employees. As we have argued earlier, Kantian duties have their equivalent in the rights of the individual. Human beings deserve respect, and on the other side of the coin, are entitled to certain basic rights. It is therefore no surprise that the central ethical issues in HRM can be framed around the issue of rights and duties of employees (van Gerwen 1994; Schwarzer et al. 1995; Rowan 2000).

? THINK THEORY

Think about what it means to talk about employees in terms of 'human resources'. Compare Kant's theory with the feminist approach to business ethics in relation to human resource management. Do you think the term HRM is adequately chosen? What are the implications of this terminology from both perspectives?

VISIT THE WEBSITE for a short response to this feature

In the following, we will have a look at the basic rights and duties of employees and discuss the major issues involved. **Figure 7.2** provides a selection of the most important right ands duties, and the main ethical problems commonly associated with them in the day-to-day reality of business.

We should stress that these rights are all more or less directly deduced from the general notion of human rights, and most of them are in some way or other codified in various acts and laws. The codification of workers' rights is particularly advanced in Europe (Ferner and Hyman 1998) so that corporations in most cases should simply have to obey

VISIT THE WEBSITE for links to useful sources of further information

VISIT THE WEBSITE to see a trailer for 'Picture Me'

ETHICS ON SCREEN 7

Picture Me

A rare and unsettling look at what must be one of the few unregulated industries in the western world

Louise France, Observer

The fashion industry is probably one of the most pervasive in the world, from huge billboards featuring the world's most beautiful models, to the lifestyle magazines filled with glamorous adverts for the latest designer collections, perfumes, and jewellery. There is even an international television station, Fashion TV, broadcasting 24/7 on all the latest fashion shows, designers, models, parties, and gossip.

Yet despite its ubiquity, it is rare that we actually see behind the glitz and the glamour of the catwalk. The real world of those who make a living in the fashion industry remains for most of us pretty much unknown. Outside of the well-publicized supermodel tantrum, or the occasional rumour of drug taking, the working lives of models are essentially offstage and out of sight. Most of us probably assume that the fantastic clothes, the famous faces, the glamorous locations, and the stratospheric salaries make modelling one of the best jobs in the world.

However, the release of the documentary *Picture Me* onto the festival circuit in 2009 looked set to lift the lid on the darker side of the modelling world. Made by Sara Ziff, a model, and her former boyfriend, filmmaker Ole Schell, the intimate film chronicles the high pressure, exploitative, and sometimes abusive environment faced by professional models, and the highly sexualized, predatory pressures they experience, even as young teenagers. Ziff is a true industry insider, having been discovered on the street by a photographer when she was 14, and then going on to become the face of numerous global brands such as Calvin Klein, Tommy Hilfiger, Dolce & Gabbana, and Gap. For almost five years, Schell followed Ziff with a small video camera as she worked for top designers, including Marc Jacobs, Stella McCartney, Louis Vuitton, Gucci, and Chanel. These experiences provided her and Schell with extraordinary

Courtesy Ole Schell

access to life behind the scenes of the fashion industry. And, by putting cameras in the hands of the models themselves, they were able to give voice to those who, as the film's MySpace page puts it, 'are often seen, but rarely heard'. As such, the film presents a sincere and engaging look inside the working life of models, documenting both the rewards and sacrifices that young women have to make.

In addition to Ziff and her fellow models, the film also features appearances and in-depth interviews with noted photographers and designers, including Gilles Bensimon, Karl Lagerfeld, Nicole Miller. By stitching these various accounts together, Schell and Ziff create a frank account of various ethical issues confronting the industry, such as age, anorexia, working conditions ... and of course the exorbitant salaries earned by top models. It also brings to light the surprising lack of regulation and protection governing the industry. In fact, the film itself is part of a nascent attempt by some models to bring greater visibility and protection into modelling. A handful have started writing behind-the-scene blogs chronicling their daily lives in intimate detail, whilst a successful 2007 campaign by two models, Victoria Keon-Cohen and Dunja Knezevic, led to the opening up of the actor's union Equity to catwalk and photographic models for the first time.

Sources

Campbell, D. 2007. Models reveal why they need union. *Guardian*, 16 Dec.: http://www.guardian.co.uk.

France, L. 2009. 'We might need to see you without your bra, he told me. I was 14. I didn't even have breasts yet'. *Observer*, 7 June 2009: http://www.guardian.co.uk.

http://www.myspace.com/picturemefilm.

Employee rights	Issues involved
Right to freedom from discrimination.	• Equal opportunities. • Affirmative action. • Reverse discrimination. • Sexual and racial harassment.
Right to privacy.	• Health and drug testing. • Work-life balance. • Presenteeism. • Electronic privacy and data protection.
Right to due process.	• Promotion. • Firing. • Disciplinary proceedings.
Right to participation and association.	• Organization of workers in works councils and trade unions. • Participation in the company's decisions.
Right to healthy and safe working conditions.	• Working conditions. • Occupational health and safety.
Right to fair wages.	• Pay. • Industrial action. • New forms of work.
Right to freedom of conscience and speech.	• Whistleblowing.
Right to work.	• Fair treatment in the interview. • Non-discriminatory rules for recruitment.
Employee duties	**Issues involved**
Duty to comply with labour contract.	• Acceptable level of performance. • Work quality. • Loyalty to the firm.
Duty to comply with the law.	• Bribery.
Duty to respect the employer's property.	• Working time. • Unauthorized use of company resources for private purposes. • Fraud, theft, embezzlement.

Figure 7.2. Rights and duties of employees as stakeholders of the firm

the existing law in the country. From this perspective, the density of codified employee rights would suggest little necessity for ethical reasoning in firm–employee relations. As discussed in Chapter 1 though, there is a widening 'grey zone' of ethical issues beyond those covered by the law, and the area of employee stakeholders is probably one of the fastest-growing parts of this zone.

This is chiefly due to globalization and its effect on nation states' abilities and willingness to regulate and enforce the protection of employees. Consequently, we have seen a massive surge in business involvement in ethical issues in HRM, mostly under the broader label of 'business and human rights' (Sullivan 2003; United Nations 2008). Almost all the rights of employees we have set out in Figure 7.2 are derived from some human right as enshrined in the Universal Declaration of Human Rights (UDHR) by the United Nations in 1948.[1] At the same time, the UDHR is considered to be probably the broadest common baseline on basic human entitlements globally, and is accepted across diverse culture and religions. It is therefore no surprise that global companies especially, for lack of other 'harder' standards, have begun to align their employment policies more in line with human rights. This has led to a number of global codes of conduct, many of which govern in particular the treatment of employees. Major codes here are, for instance, the various codes of the International Labor Organization (ILO)[2] or the SA 8000[3] standard, which predominantly focus on human rights from a labour perspective.

In the following sections, we shall therefore discuss each of the eight employee rights set out in the top half of Figure 7.2, before proceeding to examine the three main employee duties to the firm that are depicted in the bottom half of the figure.

Discrimination

Discrimination in the business context occurs when employees receive preferential (or less preferential) treatment on grounds that are not directly related to their qualifications and performance in the job.[4] The most common bases for discrimination in the workplace are race, gender, age, religion, disability, and nationality. However, any factor that is unrelated to job performance might be used to discriminate against employees, including marital status, physical appearance, sexual orientation, or even gender reassignment. Accordingly, many organizations are now having to come to terms with the fact that their employees increasingly come from a range of different religious, racial, national, and cultural groups, making the whole issue of *managing diversity* a prominent feature of contemporary business discourse as **Ethics Online 7** demonstrates.

The majority of diversity issues have been subject to extensive legislative efforts in most industrialized countries. Consequently, the mere issue of discrimination in most cases should just involve the application of existing legislation to a particular business situation. However, the question of whether a factor such as one's appearance, ethnic background, or marital status is related to one's job performance is sometimes not as clear as we might suppose.

Discrimination in essence is a violation of the second principle of Rawls' *Theory of Justice*, as outlined in Chapter 3, that 'social and economic inequalities are to be arranged so that they are attached to offices and positions open to all under conditions of fair equality of opportunity'. There are inequalities between individuals, but the reasons for

ETHICS ONLINE 7

Diversity about diversity on the web

VISIT THE WEBSITE for links to useful sources of further information

The history of tackling discrimination and advancing diversity at the workplace has long been a struggle for under-represented groups. A lot like the Tom Hanks character in the movie *Philadelphia*, many advances, changes in the law or in the general values of the public have been the result of individuals fighting against discrimination. Though, today, much progress has been made, much still needs to be done.

The internet has increasingly emerged as a space where people struggling with issues of diversity and discrimination in the workplace can find a host of resources. Be it as a source of information, a place to find like-minded people, a way of expressing oneself, or as a platform for discussion—there is a wide range of sites dealing with these issues.

It is remarkable to see how 'diverse' the world of diversity in fact is. You can find sites dedicated to general issues of fairness in the workplace, and in particular in a time of economic crisis, those concerned with job security and unfair dismissal. There are a number of sites dedicated to race, sexual orientation, and gender, of course, but also some rather specific ones: 'Women for Women', for instance, is a website which looks particularly at gender issues for women in post-conflict areas such as Afghanistan, Ruanda, Congo, or Bosnia. Another site is specifically dedicated to the discrimination issues transgendered people face in the workplace.

The nature of the sites is equally diverse. We find information portals, offers of training programmes, and blogs, just to name a few. The rise of social networking sites has led to a number of online groups where people with similar concerns meet and share information. On the professional network site Linked-In, there are more than 600 groups concerned with diversity issues. Similarly on Facebook, the search term 'equal opportunities' returns thousands of groups, some of which, though, such as the 'Equal Opportunities Sluts', apply a fairly creative interpretation of the topic!

Sources

http://transworkplace.blogspot.com/.
http://www.diversityworking.com.
http://www.dtui.com/diversityblog.html.
http://www.opportunitynow.org.uk/.
http://www.womenforwomen.org/.
http://www.workplacediversity.com.
http://www.workplacefairness.org/.

choosing one person over another should be based on qualifications that in principle could be fulfilled by anyone. Making gender or race a criterion for a particular position would exclude certain people right from the start, and would clearly constitute an act of discrimination. However, say for instance, the owner of an Indian supermarket in Rotterdam was looking for a manager who spoke Hindi or Urdu fluently, who had a reasonable knowledge of Indian culture, and had knowledge of current consumer preferences in the Dutch Asian products market. Although one might reasonably consider that this would mean that it would be perfectly acceptable to advertise specifically for an Indian manager, this would in fact be discriminatory. Certainly, these criteria might be *most likely* met by a certain ethnic group, but it is in principle possible for *all* potential applicants to attain these qualifications, and so they should have equal opportunity to apply.

Although the most overt forms of discrimination have by now been addressed reasonably successfully through regulation, problems of this nature persist. In the summer of 2009, the clothes retailer Abercrombie & Fitch lost a lawsuit filed by a female employee of their London flagship store (Topping 2009). The 22-year-old woman, who wore an arm prosthesis that she covered by wearing a cardigan, was removed from working on the shop floor as her dress style allegedly violated the 'good looks' policy of the company. The reason she won the case, however, was not that she was treated differently but that the company did not make an exception from their policy to take account of her disability.

In fact, issues of disability, as well as other concerns such as age discrimination, are among the most recent diversity issues in developed countries. The first of these includes some unique issues, in that the physical environment and systems of the company itself might prove to be discriminatory for disabled employees (and any other disabled visitors for that matter). The location of stairs can impair the ability of the physically disabled to do their job, the use of hard-to-read signs and documents can negatively impact those with sight disability or dyslexia, and failure to incorporate induction loop technology can seriously impede those with hearing impairment. Employees across the world with health problems such as HIV/AIDS have also faced considerable discrimination and harassment from their colleagues and bosses.

In the case of age discrimination, workers both old and young have suffered. For example, the trade union Amicus reported a number of cases in the UK where companies had laid off staff between the ages of 45 to 49 because pension rights make it far more costly to lay off workers beyond the age of 50. Some companies even run the risk of an employment tribunal, given that the fine for unfair dismissal can be considerably cheaper than paying redundancies for older workers (Wylie and Ball 2006).

Another as yet unresolved issue is gender discrimination. Women still, on average, receive lower wages for the same jobs as their male equivalents. Women are also still severely under-represented in top management positions, despite success lower down the ranks, and often outperforming men educationally. **Figure 7.3** sets out some recent statistics underlining that although some progress has been made, the problem of female under-representation in the boardroom persists. This picture varies dramatically across Europe, with 40% of Norwegian boardroom seats held by women, compared to 21% in Sweden, 13% in Germany, 2% in Italy, and 1% in Portugal![5]

The point is that no matter how good the legislation, many forms of discrimination are deeply embedded in business. In 2004, the investment bank Morgan Stanley agreed to a settlement for $54m after a female employee took the firm to court in the US over accusations of unequal pay and unequal career opportunities. Among other things, the allegation was that key client meetings were held in strip clubs and female employees were barred from these venues.[6] Sometimes this is referred to as *institutional discrimination*, namely that the very culture of the organization is prejudiced against certain groups. For example, one could suggest that in a company where there was an informal understanding amongst the staff that in order to get on, one had to stay late at the office and work far in excess of 'normal' office hours, certain groups, such as single parents (who might be unable to commit such time over and above their contractual obligations), would face an institutionalized barrier to progression.

	2000	2004	2008
Female held directorships (in % of total directorships)	69 (5.8%)	110 (9.7%)	131 (11 7%)
Female executive directors	11	17	17
Female non-executive directors	60	93	114
Companies with 2 women directors	14	19	39
Companies with no women director	42	31	22

Figure 7.3. Women in top management positions. Female directions in FTSE 100 companies 2000–2008. (FTSE 100: largest 100 companies on the Financial Times Stock Exchange Index).

Source: Sealy, R., Singh, V. and Vinnicombe, S. 2007. *The Female FTSE Report 2007*. International Centre for Women Leaders, Cranfield School of Management.

Sealy, R., Vinnicombe, S. and Singh, V. 2008. *The Female FTSE Report 2008*. International Centre for Women Leaders, Cranfield School of Management.

? THINK THEORY

Although we have suggested that employees have a *right* to be free from discrimination, it is clear that it still occurs. Is this just because employers haven't recognized that discrimination is wrong, or is it possible to establish a defence of discrimination from the perspective of other ethical theories? Which theory provides the most convincing defence?

@ VISIT THE WEBSITE for a short response to this feature

Sexual and racial harassment

As well as discrimination occurring in the areas of promotion, pay, and job opportunities, diversity considerations also have to take account of physical, verbal, and emotional harassment. In the case of sexual harassment, a problem might even be that certain sexual favours are requested for promotion or other rewards that would normally be a result of successful work (see also **Ethics in Action 7.2**). 'Mild' forms of harassment would be jokes or comments about a person's gender, race, sexual orientation, etc., that could lead to significant effects on working relations.

Regulators still tend to be quite reluctant to take up these issues. The main reason for this seems to be that the line between harassment on the one hand and 'office romance', 'joking', or other forms of 'harmless' harassment are pretty much blurred and often defined by a number of contextual factors such as character, personality, and national culture. So, for instance, in certain Latin American countries men might get away with patterns of behaviour that in other places would be regarded as overtly 'macho' behaviour, and vice versa. Companies increasingly have introduced codes of practice and diversity programmes in order to tackle these issues and to define for the specific context of the company the borders of harassment (Crain and Heischmidt 1995).

Equal opportunities and affirmative action

So how should organizations respond to problems of unfair discrimination? In one sense, they could simply look to legislation to tackle the problem, particularly as many industrialized countries have a reasonably well-established legal framework of anti-discriminatory laws and statutes. However, as we have already seen, even the existence of clearly specified laws hasn't prevented discrimination from occurring. Moreover, most legal approaches do not specify exactly how discrimination should be avoided, leaving many decisions open to the discretion of management. As a result, many companies have sought to tackle discrimination through the introduction of so-called equal opportunity or affirmative action programmes. These programmes establish policies and procedures that aim to avoid discrimination, and may even go so far as to attempt to redress inequity in the workforce.

The most basic and conservative approach is usually referred to as an *equal opportunity programme*. These have been widely introduced in business, and it is now common to see job adverts and company websites proclaiming that an organization is an 'equal opportunity employer'. Of course, many countries legally require that companies are equal opportunity employers, but the label is usually intended to signify that the organization has gone beyond the normal expectations.

Equal opportunity programmes mainly involve the introduction of procedures that ensure that employees and prospective employees are dealt with equally and fairly. For example, one way of ensuring equal opportunity to jobs is by ensuring that they are advertised in such a way that all potential applicants can reasonably learn of the vacancy and apply—as opposed to, say, simply selecting someone through informal channels. Similarly, by setting out specific criteria for jobs, and ensuring that interview panels use structured assessment of candidates against those criteria, factors unrelated to the job such as gender or race can be excluded from the formal appraisal of candidates. As such, equal opportunities programmes are generally targeted at ensuring that *procedural justice* is promoted, i.e. the key issue is ensuring that the procedures are fair to all.

Some equal opportunities programmes go further than merely introducing non-discriminatory procedures. Often referred to as *affirmative action* **(AA)** programmes, these approaches deliberately attempt to target those who might be currently under-represented in the workforce, for instance by trying to increase the proportion of women, disabled, or racial minorities in senior management positions. Four main areas of affirmative action can be distinguished (De George 1999: 431–5):

- **Recruitment policies.** In order to enhance the proportion of under-represented groups, AA programmes might look at actively recruiting these groups, for example, by deliberately targeting job ads in media with a wide circulation amongst under-represented groups, or dispatching outreach recruitment staff to areas or schools where under-represented groups might predominate. Barclays Bank, for instance, offers bonuses to headhunters who come up with more diverse candidates (L. Smith 2005). Peugeot, since 2005, has operated a system of online application that allows for 'anonymous CVs' as a basis for recruitment decisions in order to encourage the employment of a more diverse workforce.[7] In the UK, employers displaying the government-initiated 'disability symbol' guarantee a job interview to all applicants with a disability who meet the minimum criteria for a job vacancy.

- **Fair job criteria.** Discrimination can often surface in an ostensibly 'objective' form through the definition of job criteria in such a fashion that they automatically make the job beyond the reach of a great number of potential applicants. In many cases, these job criteria might not necessarily be crucial to the achievement of the job role, yet they disadvantage certain parts of the population more than others. For example, those from low income or immigrant communities may not have had the same educational opportunities as others. This will often mean that regardless of intelligence, experience, or ability to do the job, they may be less likely to have the formal qualifications required by potential employers. Similarly, given that it is usually mothers rather than fathers who most frequently take on childcare and other household roles, inflexibility in employees' working times can discriminate against women. Ensuring that job criteria are fair to all is often a major task for AA programmes to tackle.

- **Training programmes for discriminated minorities.** Even following the revision of job criteria to ensure some degree of fairness, it is very possible that they will still include certain special skills, qualifications, and experience that particular under-represented groups are simply unlikely, from a statistical point of view, to have. This might be because of discrimination earlier in life, historical or cultural precedents, or just the plain realities of certain groups' socio-economic situation. In principle, ethnic Algerians might be accepted by a French *Grand Ecole*, but in practice, the social situation of these families does not encourage the children to pursue such an academic option compared with certain other groups in French society. Not all possible remedies here are within the company's scope of action—no one is expecting them to eradicate discrimination throughout the whole of society—but targeted pre-recruitment training programmes for under-represented groups can boost their eligibility for vacant positions.
- **Promotion to senior positions.** Women and ethnic minorities are severely under-represented on boards of directors. For instance, in the UK, the average board consists of 8.7 white members and 0.2 minority members, whilst minorites occupy only 1.7% of directorships in Canada despite representing over 16% of the population (Dhir 2009). The fact that senior management positions in virtually all industries in Europe and North America are dominated by white males might also be tackled by specific leadership training for women and minorities once they are already within the organization. For example, the German automotive company Volkswagen AG operates a 'Women Driving Award', which awards achievement of women engineers in the company and is specifically designed to encourage career advancement of women in a profession that is still largely male dominated.[1]

Reverse discrimination

Affirmative action targets the remediation of long-standing discriminatory tendencies in the workplace: people of a certain gender, sexual orientation, or ethnic background become the subject of policies or regulations that provide supposedly fairer conditions for these groups. In many cases, this does not simply intend to provide equal opportunities for these groups, but AA in many cases focuses on the correcting of past injustices by, for instance, attempting to enhance the percentage of women in executive positions. One of the best-known examples of this approach in recent years has been the Black Economic Empowerment (BEE) laws in South Africa that seek to install a fairer representation of black workers after apartheid. **Ethics in Action 7.1**, however, also points to some of the risks and limits of the BEE laws. One common side-effect of such robust

VISIT THE WEBSITE for links to useful sources of further information

ETHICS IN ACTION 7.1 http://www.ethicalcorp.com

Black empowerment—slaying South Africa's sacred cow

Ethical CORPORATION

Markus Reichart, 14 July 2008

Enfranchising the black population through the policy of Black Economic Empowerment was going to be part of the new South Africa's bright future. But the policy designed to right the wrongs committed against the country's black majority during apartheid is working only for a few. This is the verdict of a group of top development economists from Harvard University that were asked by South African finance minister Trevor Manuel to recommend ways to reform the country's economy.

The group has made some unremarkable recommendations about abolishing the remnants of exchange control, making the labour market more flexible, and simplifying the tariff system to promote trade. But on BEE they argue that the policy in its present form has benefited 'a narrow elite and that this has had no noticeable impact on inequality in general'. This has stirred substantial controversy. The Harvard academics observe that the problem with many BEE deals to date is that they have tended to involve one or two members of a small group with excellent political connections but without the business experience to match.

A key problem lies in the way early BEE deals were financed. Between 1993 and 1998 many of the larger white-owned companies sold a proportion of their un-issued equity to black investors. Often the finance for the purchase of the shares came from using future earnings flows of the company itself as collateral. Many of those early BEE deals, the Harvard academics conclude, unravelled when markets turned in 1998 because they were structured in a way that only worked when economic times were good.

AngloAmerican, the mining giant, did some of the first BEE deals, convinced that creating black entrepreneurs would dilute the ruling party's interest in nationalisation. The Harvard study points out that while this worked in the short-term, 'enduring property rights security certainly requires a broader base than can be provided by such a policy'.

Get real

Another problem the Harvard academics identified with BEE is the targets it has imposed on different industries, under the so-called sector charters. These cover direct ownership, percentage of black executives, percentage of black management, procurement from black-owned business and community development. For example, the mining charter targeted 15 per cent direct black ownership by 2009 and 26 per cent by 2015.

But the political imperatives that drove the charters' targets often ignored economic realities. The mining sector sets a target of 10 per cent of employees being women by 2009. Historically women have had such low representation in the mining industry that this target cannot be achieved for all companies, even with substantial poaching from other sectors. And platinum mining company Lonmin admits as much in its annual report. Ricardo Hausmann, co-author of the Harvard report, argues that the charters, through their targets, are redirecting company attention to competing for scarce black skills instead of investing in the creation of new ones. He says that if BEE is to reach beyond a small elite, charter targets should be amended to allow firms to decide where to focus their empowerment efforts.

Focusing development

Former department of trade and industry official Polo Radebe says the government must look at 'how we give opportunities to small business'. This means caring less about targets for black ownership and instead emphasising enterprise and skills development, he says. The Harvard report's reception has been mixed. It was rejected by COSATU, South Africa's major trade union federation. Secretary-general Zwelinzima Vavi, says: 'We do not take instructions from the Harvard group.'

Others are more supportive. Brian Molefe, head of the Public Investment Corporation which administers most public sector pension funds, agrees with the Harvard assessment that BEE has been too focused on equity ownership, something he himself has aggressively championed at corporate AGMs. While big business is still too white, he now sees the real challenge of transformation as 'one of growth rather than re-arranging of equity'. Some BEE consortia have created 'broad-based' BEE structures to address these concerns. For example, Wiphold says it represents 18,000 indirect women beneficiaries, while Lonmin's empowerment partner Incwala represents 30,000 community members and 20,000 employees. While this is technically true, the familiar faces are the key shareholders or executives exercising control.

Some South African companies have attempted to outmanoeuvre BEE businessmen who already have more directorships than they can credibly service. Food retailer Woolworths and chemical giant Sasol have done BEE deals centred on employee shareholder schemes for their non-white staff. These schemes help bind staff to employers that need to retain their skills and experience. This way BEE does add real value for shareholders. The consequences of empowerment that is too narrow was evident recently when some townships erupted in xenophobic violence against migrants, killing 56 people and displacing 50,000 foreigners accused of taking local jobs. Xenophobia has a simple cause: competition for housing, water and education not delivered by the elite of new South African state who have used BEE to grow wealthy over the first 14 years of liberation.

BEE different

A high-profile BEE beneficiary is Patrice Motsepe, chairman and major shareholder of African Rainbow Minerals. Motsepe became the first of South Africa's new black billionaires thanks to snapping up mines from rival AngloAmerican for virtually nothing, and in the process has become a role model for the next generation of young black graduates. Yet executive management at ARM is still very white and investment in training and corporate responsibility is minimal. But Motsepe's considerable personal ownership stake helps the company meet BEE charter targets. Mvela Resources, a holding company run by former provincial premier Tokyo Sexwale, uses a similar business model to position itself as a BEE partner for many mining majors in the gold and platinum sector.

Sources

Ethical Corporation, Markus Reichart, 14 July 2008, http://www.ethicalcorp.com.

VISIT THE WEBSITE for a short response to this feature

? THINK THEORY

Using the theories of rights and justice discussed in Chapter 3, how would you justify the BEE policies? What suggestions would you make to improve the current state of the BEE success?

attempts at affirmative action is that at some point AA can itself be deemed discriminatory because it disadvantages those thought to already be in an 'advantaged' position. In some countries, it is deemed acceptable to 'tip the scales' to favour under-represented groups if candidates are thought to be equal on all other criteria. For example, if you are a white, Canadian man applying for a job in a Canadian university, the employment ad might inform you that in the case of equal qualification, a female aboriginal or racial minority applicant will be preferred. The situation is taken a step further if minorities are preferred to mainstream candidates when the minority candidate is *less qualified* for the job or promotion. For instance, some countries allow for certain jobs to be subject to quotas that specify that a proportion of a certain minority group must be selected for interview, or even for the job itself, regardless of whether they are less qualified than over-represented groups. In these cases, people suffer *reverse discrimination* exactly because AA policies prefer certain minorities.

The justification of 'reverse discrimination' is somewhat ambiguous. On the one hand, companies could argue that, for instance, women have been discriminated for such a long time and are so badly under-represented that it is time to reverse this development and consequently women deserve preferential treatment. This argument could be based on the notion of *retributive justice*—i.e. that past injustices have to be 'paid for'. On the other hand, there is the problem that the individual applicant, say a white male, is not responsible for the misconduct of his race or gender in previous occasions and so should not be made responsible by being the subject of reverse discrimination.

More defensible are arguments based on *distributive justice*—i.e. that rewards such as job and pay should be allocated fairly among all groups (Beauchamp 1997). These arguments tend to be underlined by the observation that many male executives have been promoted not necessarily because of their objective qualifications but because of their membership in 'old boys networks' or similar groups. Even objective 'merit' can be difficult to determine when certain roles and industries have been for so long dominated by certain genders or races. Women and racial minorities, it might be argued, require role models in professions they have been excluded from, and those professions in turn might need to acquire new ideas about what a 'normal' professional would look or sound like. How many of us, for instance, automatically assume that a company director will be a white man in his fifties or sixties, rather than, say, a young black man or a woman? For most advocates of reverse discrimination, then, cultural arguments such as these suggest that fair outcomes rather than fair procedures should be paramount.

Opponents of reverse discrimination tend to marshal a number of fairly compelling arguments criticizing the practice, not least the basic notion that discrimination is wrong per se and that procedural justice should be paramount. Moreover, it can be argued that someone promoted on the basis of their gender or colour may well be discredited amongst their peers, and if they are not the best person for the job, this can even harm business efficiency (Pojman 1997). Heilman (1997) has further shown that decisions made on the basis of race, gender, or any other characteristic unrelated to merit can actually serve to promote stereotyping and reinforce existing prejudices. Burke and Black (1997) go so far as to suggest that reverse discrimination can prompt a 'male backlash' against the perceived injustice.

For reasons such as these, stronger forms of reverse discrimination tend to be illegal in many countries. For example, whilst it may be acceptable for companies to have 'targets' or 'aims' of how many women or minorities they would like in certain roles or levels, they may be prevented from having an explicit quota that has to be fulfilled.

Employee privacy

Let us begin this next section with a short test. Answer each of the following questions True or False:

1 I feel sure there is only one true religion.

2 My soul sometimes leaves my body.

3 I believe in the second coming of Christ.

4 I wish I were not bothered by thoughts of sex.

5 I am very strongly attracted by members of my own sex.

6 I have never indulged in any unusual sexual practices.

You may be relieved to know that we're not going to ask you to announce your answers to these questions in class! However, these are actual questions from a pre-employment test administered by Dayton Hudson Corporation for the position of security guard at one of its Target stores in California in 1989 (Boatright 2009). The company eventually conceded in court that asking such intimate questions constituted an invasion of privacy, but the prospect of companies invading employees' privacy has become an increasingly pressing issue in the contemporary workplace. The escalation in health, drug, alcohol, even genetic testing of employees, coupled with the possibilities for more and better surveillance through advances in information and communication technologies, has meant that employee privacy has never been so much under attack.

The fundamental right to privacy consists of an individual's right to control information about oneself, and to control situations where such information could be gleaned (Cranford 1998). According to Michele Simms (1994), there are four different types of privacy we might want to protect:

- **Physical privacy.** Physical inaccessibility to others and the right to 'one's own space'. For example, organizations that place surveillance cameras in employees' private rest areas might be said to compromise physical privacy.
- **Social privacy.** Freedom to interact with other people and in whichever way we choose. For instance, some employers will threaten social privacy by suggesting that employees should not bring their firm into 'disrepute' by behaving in an 'unacceptable', 'immoral', or illegal way during their social lives.
- **Informational privacy.** Determining how, when, and to what extent private data about us are released to others. This can be breached, for example, when employers hire private security firms to make investigations about employees without due cause.
- **Psychological privacy.** Controlling emotional and cognitive inputs and outputs, and not being compelled to share private thoughts and feelings. For instance, psychological privacy is threatened when retailers introduce programmes aimed at making sure employers smile and appear happy in front of customers.

Obviously, not all social interactions or information about ourselves can be deemed private. Employers have a right to know about our qualifications and work experience, just as they have a right to know if we have had a meeting with one of the company's clients. The key issue is whether some certain aspects of our life are *relevant* to the relationship we have with our employer (Simms 1994). Let us take a look at this question in the main areas where employee privacy appears to be challenged.

VISIT THE WEBSITE for a short response to this feature

? THINK THEORY

Analyse the degree of employer surveillance of employee emails and internet use from a perspective of rights and justice. Which rights on both sides are involved and what would be a fair balance in addressing these issues?

Health and drug testing

In 2008, the Toronto Transport Commission (TTC), which operates the buses and subway lines in Canada's largest city, introduced drug testing for their employees (Kalinowski 2008). After an incident where an employee was killed under the influence of marijuana (and some further 39 cases of employees under the influence of drugs in the previous two years), management argued that for the safe operation of public transport they should be allowed to introduce drug testing. However, this was rather controversial with the union, who saw it as an intrusion into employee privacy. Although the initial proposal of random tests was ultimately not pursued, management argued that to guarantee safety to customers and co-workers, drug testing would take place in cases where there was reason to suspect that employees were under the influence of drugs. Beyond this example, other arguments brought forward in favour of these tests focus on the employer's right to know about future costs due to absenteeism and loss of productivity. So, for instance, proponents of drug testing point to the huge costs that drug abuse causes for companies (Cranford 1998). This latter aspect gets a further significance given the ever-increasing scope of information that could be gained by genetic testing in the workplace. This can provide far-reaching insights into an employee's future health prospects.

Health and drug testing, however, remains a highly contested issue in business ethics. The central objection seems to be that these tests make available far more information on the employee than the employer actually needs. Des Jardins and Duska (1997) highlight three main aspects here.

- **Potential to do harm.** There are only a few jobs where information on health and drug use is really vitally important for the safety of the job or for the protection of customers. An AIDS test might conceivably make sense for a nurse or a chef, but it is certainly not an issue for a software specialist or a lorry driver. The key issue for Des Jardins and Duska is whether the job involves *a clear and present danger to do harm.*
- **Causes of employee's performance.** Des Jardins and Duska also argue that an employer is entitled to information about the employee's performance, but not necessarily about the *causes of that performance*. Given that employees are expected to produce a certain level of performance, employers are well within their rights to determine whether their employees are performing at a satisfactory level. If an employee is found to be under-performing, then equally the employer is entitled to take action against the employee, perhaps by issuing a warning. However, we must question whether the employer has a legitimate right to know about all the factors influencing whether the employee is, or is not, performing at the required level. Suppose we are depressed, or suffering from bereavement, or have just stayed up drinking too much the night before—this may affect our performance, but then again it may not. It would be quite difficult to accept that we should reveal this information on arriving at the office in the morning unless there is a clear, ongoing problem with our performance. The fact is that it is the performance that is at issue, not the reason behind it, at least in the first instance.
- **Level of performance.** Finally, Des Jardins and Duska further claim that an employer is only entitled to an *acceptable* level of performance from their employees, not their *optimal* performance. Most drug, alcohol, and health tests aim to identify factors that *potentially* might prevent the employee from functioning in the most optimal fashion. Again, the key issue is whether we are performing at an acceptable level in the first place, not whether we could be made to perform better. This particularly questions AIDS tests and genetically-based tests, as in most cases they provide the employer with information about the employee far beyond what is necessary for the day-to-day performance of their job.

Despite these criticisms, such tests have become increasingly common in the modern workplace, particularly in the US. The particular cultural context of the US may help to explain this, in particular the strong legalistic approach that makes employers vulnerable to litigation from customers and others employees if members of staff are found to have put them at risk when unfit for work due to sickness, drugs, or alcohol. However, testing programmes are most certainly on the rise in Europe, Asia, and Australasia too, occasioned perhaps by the global spread of US business practices (Eaglesham 2000). Nonetheless, despite these developments, probably the biggest threat to employee privacy at present comes from the increasing use of electronic surveillance.

Electronic privacy and data protection

Surveillance and control of workers has a long legacy in management practice. However, as Ottensmayer and Heroux (1991) suggest, the escalation in usage of new technologies in business has added a new dimension to the issue of privacy.

First, there is the fact that the computer as a work tool enables new forms of surveillance (Ottensmeyer and Heroux 1991). The computer makes possible a detailed overview of the time and pace of work carried out, particularly since every strike of the keyboard can now easily be monitored. This means that the employer is not only in a position to judge the result of the employee's work, but they can also trace in every detail the process of its coming into existence. Similarly, many employers now routinely place cameras and other recording devices in work areas to monitor employees (Hartman 1998). Whilst this might be justified to assess performance or to prevent thefts and other misdemeanours, it is clearly an entry into the physical privacy of employees, particularly when it intrudes on ostensibly private areas such as changing rooms, bathrooms, and staff rooms. It remains a highly contested issue as to how far this breach of privacy is legitimate.

This control does not only extend to the work process, but it pertains also to the usage of employees' time for private reasons, such as when using email or the internet. This includes fairly straightforward issues such as the downloading of pornography, but also extends to all sorts of other usage of communication technologies for private purposes. Should companies be allowed to monitor and check their employee's email, or their private conversations on the phone? With regard to conventional mail, there are extensive regulations in place safeguarding privacy, which are simply not applicable to electronic mail in the same way. Most companies meanwhile have established codes of conduct that at least provide the employee with some knowledge of the boundaries to privacy established by the firm. However, globally, there are different standards in legislation that determine the extent to which privacy could be restricted in these areas. In the US, for example, employees have considerably less regulatory protection of their electronic privacy compared with their European and Canadian counterparts (Lasprogata et al. 2004).

While the abuse of company time is a perfectly legitimate complaint of companies, we might ask whether policing to prevent or identify such an abuse legitimates such a far-reaching incursion into workers' privacy. As with drug and alcohol tests, the invasion of privacy here is often based on the threat of *potential* harm to the company, rather than *actual* harm. However, the harm to both employees and the firm itself can be very real when implementing such extensive surveillance. After all, for employees such as call centre operatives, who spend most of their work time on the telephone, not only is almost every thing they say during the day open to surveillance, but employers often also enforce a way of talking and behaving to clients that potentially threatens psychological privacy also. In the long run, employers may also suffer by eroding trust within the organization and failing to capitalize on employee discretion.

Finally, the issue of privacy occurs in situations where data are saved and processed electronically (De George 1999: 346–53). The relation between an employee and the company's doctor is one of privacy, and if the doctor enters the data of the employee into his PC system, this is not a breach of patient–doctor confidentiality. But as soon as this database could be linked with the company's other systems, the employee's privacy would clearly be broken. The problem here is that it might not be a problem if companies are in possession of their client's or employee's data per se. The problem occurs where, for instance, the phone company is taken over by the credit card company and both clients' databases are matched: such an operation suddenly provides access to a wide range of information posing a far more potent breach of privacy. This issue is exacerbated by new social networking sites, such as MySpace or Facebook and **Ethical Dilemma 7** provides an opportunity to explore how this can typically pose an ethical problem in today's business world.

With advances in information and communication technologies accelerating at an unprecedented rate, we might expect threats to privacy such as these to intensify. However, legislation is often relatively slow to catch up with these changes, and since employee surveillance is so ingrained in management, managers often do not even recognize privacy as an ethical issue (Ottensmeyer and Heroux 1991). Therefore, we might at the very least question whether 'spying' on employees is counterproductive to fostering trust and integrity in the workplace.

> **? THINK THEORY**
>
> Think about electronic surveillance in terms of utilitarianism. What are the costs and benefits involved? Is this likely to offer a reasonable justification for incursions into employee privacy?

VISIT THE WEBSITE for a short response to this feature

Due process and lay-offs

As anyone who has ever worked in kitchens, bars, and restaurants will be able to vouch, many employees are constantly at risk of arbitrarily losing their jobs for relatively minor indiscretions, personality clashes, or simply because their face 'doesn't fit'. The right to due process though has a long history in working practices and can be deduced from the notion of procedural justice. As we saw with discrimination, this form of justice requires the application of rules and procedures to people in a consistent and even-handed way, avoiding arbitrary decision-making, and without discrimination on bases other than merit (Chryssides and Kaler 1996: 45). Promotion, disciplinary proceedings, and firing are the most common processes where the right to due process is particularly important.

AN ETHICAL DILEMMA 7

Off your face on Facebook?

You are the personnel manager of AllCure Pharmaceuticals. It's a busy time and the guys in the product approval department have called you up because they desperately need to hire a new team member to assist them with the clinical tests of what could become the next blockbuster drug for the company. You get to work and within a week have actually managed to get three well-qualified applicants for the job. The interviews went well and there are two really good applicants. Both are women, recent college graduates, and you find it hard to decide among them.

The clinical trials that the new hire will work on are very important. They require a very reliable, meticulous work attitude, but also good social skills to manage the different relations between the clinics, the approving authorities, and various departments in the company. A colleague suggests you check the two finalists out on MySpace, Facebook, or any other social networking site. Later at home, you go on Facebook, and yes, one of them is there! Surfing through the posts and her photos you see a very sociable, obviously well-travelled individual. The other candidate is a bit more difficult to locate. This is too bad, as she already has some work experience and is the slightly better candidate of the two. Her details are only available to friends, but browsing through her list of some 400 friends, you find that one of your current interns is actually on her list. Next morning you ask your intern, who it turns out briefly met this second candidate on a course they took together at college years ago, whether you could have a look at the Facebook page of the second candidate. Doing so, you make some interesting discoveries: not only do you find a number of photos of her at parties with precious few clothes on, but there are even two pictures where she enjoys what undoubtedly looks like a line of cocaine.

You thank your intern for her help and walk back to your office wondering what to do. You certainly do not want to hire someone who has this kind of reputation or where patients in trials or people from approving bodies say: 'Heard about Dr. X? You really have to see these pictures…'.

Questions

1 What are the main ethical issues in this case?

2 What are the main ethical arguments for and against the use of social network sites for potential employers in this situation?

3 Think of how you use Facebook or similar sites. Does this case influence the way you might use these sites in the future?

4 How would you finally decide as the personnel manager in this situation?

Source

Based on a real case published on http://www.msnbc.msn.com/id/20202935/from/ET/ (Wei Du. 2007. Job candidates getting tripped up by Facebook. 14 Aug.).

Promotion is typically a decision that is particularly reliant on the discretion of the employer. However, as with discrimination issues, an employee also can be said to have a right to be subject to the same promotion criteria as their colleagues, and for criteria to be clearly job-related. Some companies, and especially public bodies and authorities, even operate specific codes for promotion, linking criteria to certain positions in order to establish transparency in the process. This is even more necessary in the case of disciplinary procedures. Employees should only be subject to these if a clear and objective neglect of their duties, and a breach of their contractual obligations has occurred (van Gerwen 1994).

In case of firing and redundancies, the same procedures have to apply. Normally, the legal framework of many countries, certainly in places such as Europe and Japan provides detailed codification of employee and employer rights in these circumstances—even if some industries and countries tend not to respect these as fully as others. This is less clear-cut in the area of redundancies and downsizing of corporations. Following the concept of CSR (corporate social responsibility) as outlined in Chapter 2, the 'economic responsibility' as the first element of CSR might well ask for firms to cut back on labour costs to remain competitive and in business. In 2008 alone, 2.6m workers in the US lost their jobs due to the economic downturn, with some companies such as Citigroup planning to make 50,000 employees redundant in 2009 (Roner 2009). There are, however, certain ethical considerations in the process of downsizing.

- **Involvement.** A first important area is the information policy of the corporation (Hopkins and Hopkins 1999). It can be contended that employees have a *right to know* well ahead of the actual point of redundancy that their job is on the line. This issue of timing is closely connected to the method of announcement. For example, when General Motors and Peugeot downsized their operations in the UK in spring 2006, most of the employees only learned about the decisions when they were already at a fairly advanced stage. Furthermore, it is sometimes contended that employees have a right to know about the causes for the downsizing, as this will provide them with the possibility of judging the fairness of the downsizing process (Hopkins and Hopkins 1999).

- **Remuneration.** A second important area is the compensation package of redundancy payments and other benefits employees receive when laid off (Hopkins and Hopkins 1999). These typically should include enough money to bridge the time for finding a new job. Some firms tend to have quite a generous approach to these issues, and many also provide social schemes for redundant workers including early retirement options for those workers whose chances of finding another job are lower due to advanced age.

With increasing moves towards restructuring and flexibilization, however, the needs of employees in lay-off situations have moved beyond merely involvement and remuneration to retraining and re-integration into the workforce. Over the past decade, many employees have increasingly been exposed to the need for *occupational transitions*—i.e. having to find work in completely new industries rather than just switching employers. This has obviously meant that employees have experienced escalating insecurity, whilst also facing greater challenges in developing their *employability* (Kieselbach and Mader 2002).

Such developments have potentially raised new expectations on corporations, particularly in respect to developing 'outplacement' strategies to help employees find work following lay-offs. In the Netherlands, for example, most companies offer employability training, and restructuring is often supported with career counselling; in Belgium and Italy, companies are legally obliged to offer outplacement counselling in the case of lay-offs (Kieselbach and Mader 2002). Although in other countries, such as Spain and the UK, employment is primarily regarded as an individual or governmental responsibility, there is clearly a case for suggesting that some form of outplacement process might be a 'fairer' approach to lay-offs.

VISIT THE WEBSITE for a short response to this feature

? THINK THEORY

Think about outplacement strategies from the perspective of justice and fairness. See if you can set outplacement in the context of Rawls' theory of justice.

The right to due process is mainly concerned then with establishing appropriate procedures for treating workers, particularly in the case of lay-offs and dismissals. Some proponents of employee rights though make a somewhat stronger claim by suggesting that workers should also be involved in all company decisions that affect them. This is called the right to participation.

Employee participation and association

The recognition that employees might be more than just human 'resources' in the production process has given rise to the claim that employees should also have a certain degree of influence on their tasks, their job environments, and their company's goals—i.e. a *right to participation*. There are quite a number of ethical justifications for this claim (see Cludts 1999; Claydon 2000). Apart from references to human rights, some grounding can be derived from Kant's thinking. Specifically, participation implies that people are not treated only as a means to another's end. Employees have their own goals, and their own view of which ends should be served, and so might be said to have some rights to determine the modalities of their involvement in the corporation. Other justifications can be based on egoism, namely that an employee can only freely pursue their own interests or desires with some degree of participation at the workplace.

Questions over the right to participation continue unabated, not least because such a right often clashes with management's duty to determine how best to protect the interests of owners. However, the key issue at a practical level now is not so much whether employees should have a right to participate in decisions, but rather to what degree this should take place. There are two main areas to which a right to participation expands (Kaler 1999):

Financial participation allows employees a share in the ownership or income of the corporation. Some recent initiatives predicated on (partly) remunerating employees with shares or share options have tried to work in this direction. In Chapter 5, we discussed the example of the co-operative firm, which is the most common pattern of financial participation.

Operational participation occurs at a more practical level, and can include a number of different dimensions:

- **Delegation.** Employees might take control of a wider range of individual decisions relevant to their own jobs. Efforts of this kind have often been labelled as 'job enrichment' or 'job enlargement' schemes and have been practised successfully, for instance, in the automotive industry. Several European companies, such as Volvo and Porsche, have in part stopped their line production and reorganized their workforce in semi-autonomous teams. By this, many decisions about how to actually manufacture a car have been taken away from the formal control of line management and put into the sphere of the individual employee (Woywode 2002).
- **Information.** Employees might also receive information about crucial decisions that have an effect on their work. This concerns particularly information about the actual performance of the corporation, the security of jobs and pensions, etc. This form of participation is in many respects wider than just participation through delegation, since it may also pertain to issues that are not directly necessary for the fulfilment of the employee's own immediate task.
- **Consultation.** Employees are allowed to express their views on decision taken by the employer. This form of delegation is stronger still, since it opens up the opportunity to potentially influence the decision taken by the employer.
- **Co-determination.** Here employees have a full and codified right to determine major decisions in the company. This is the strongest form of participation and would include decisions about the strategic future of the corporation, such as mergers or diversification into new markets (Ferner and Hyman 1998).

In a global context, there is still quite a variety with regard to the degree of participation allocated to employees. Whereas employees in the US, for instance, mostly learn from the papers if their jobs are on the line, Swedish or French companies usually cannot take these measures without detailed communication, consultation, and agreement with employees. In many such countries, there is a quite extensive body of legislation that focuses on the representative organization of the workforce. Consequently, many of these participatory rights are not practised by employees directly but by their representatives in works councils, trade unions, or other bodies.

Given the important role for works councils and trade unions in facilitating the right to participation, we must also consider here the underlying question of whether employees have a 'right' to join together in such organizations. This is usually framed in terms of a *right to association*. The crucial factor here is that without a right to associate, employees often lack an effective form of representation of their interests to employers, leaving them in a far weaker position than management in bargaining over pay and conditions. Still, even where rights to associate are legally protected, companies may seek to obstruct or avoid them. For example, Royle (2005) vividly illustrates how, in the fast food industry, companies with a strong 'anti-union' stance, such as McDonald's, have been able to tame, neutralize, or subvert systems of employee representation, especially at a workplace level. In Germany, for instance, he argues that the company has 'been fighting the establishment of German work's councils for over 30 years' (p. 48). **Figure 7.4** provides an overview of how membership in trade unions has developed over the last four decades (Visser 2006). The figures not only reflect different legal frameworks and traditions in industrial relations—for example, if we compare the United States to Canada, Sweden, or Australia—but this table also provides a flavour of the general trend that union membership (with the exception of Sweden) has declined in most countries.

Despite this decline in the importance of unions, the underlying rights to participate and associate therefore remain crucial issues for corporations, especially when moving to countries where the legislative framework is different from at home. The motivation, however, does not only have to come from concerns about compliance with legislation or issues of fairness and equity. Increasingly, in modern organizations, participation at least has been identified as a means to enhance worker's efficiency, especially when jobs ask for flexibility and creativity on behalf of the employee (Collier and Esteban 1999). Ultimately, though, the rights to participation and association within a company follows a similar line of argument to that concerning participation of citizens in the political process (Ellerman 1999). Corporations have power over one of the most important areas of an employee's life, namely their economic survival. Consequently, the principles of a democratic society necessarily ask for some rights to participation in the firm, usually

	1970	2003	Absolute change in %
Australia	50.2	22.9	−27.3
Canada	31.6	28.4	−6.5
Germany	32.0	22.6	−9.5
Italy	37.0	33.7	−3.3
Japan	35.1	19.7	−15.4
Sweden	67.7	78.0	+10.3
United Kingdom	44.8	29.3	−15.5
United States	23.5	12.4	−11.1

Figure 7.4. Union density (percentage of union member of the total workforce) in selected countries worldwide

Source: Based on Visser 2006: 45.

through a representative body of some kind such as a trade union. Trade unions, however, also play an important role in other employee rights, including those of due process, fair wages, and as we shall now see, working conditions.

Working conditions

The right to healthy and safe working conditions has been one of the very first ethical concerns for employees, right from the early part of the industrial revolution. Novelists such as Charles Dickens and various social reformers such as Robert Owen, who pioneered the co-operative movement, sought to shed light on the appalling conditions faced by those working in mines, factories, and mills at the time. Consequently, a considerable number of issues concerned with working conditions were initially addressed as far back as the early nineteenth century, either by way of legislation (such as Bismarck's social laws in Germany) or by voluntary initiatives of paternalistic, often religiously motivated entrepreneurs (Fitzgerald 1999).

Today most industrialized countries have implemented a dense network of health, safety, and environmental (HSE) regulation that companies have to abide by. Consequently, such issues are either already regulated by existing laws or become an object of court proceedings, rather than necessarily being ethical issues that have to be resolved within the boundaries of the firm. The main issue, however, often becomes the *enforcement and implementation of existing regulation*. In practice, some companies may cut corners on health and safety through negligence or in contempt of regulators. Similarly, many of these regulations, such as wearing a safety helmet or ear plugs, may be disliked by workers themselves. This imposes a responsibility on employers to actually 'police' workers' compliance with regulations. A common example is the signs, typically found in the bathrooms of pubs and restaurants, which instruct members of staff to wash their hands (or 'wash your hands NOW!') after using the toilet. HSE requirements may also become a more pressing issue in developing countries, where corporations are not forced by law to heed tight standards. However, many of these issues, as mentioned earlier, actually occur in their suppliers' operations rather than their own, and as such will be discussed in more detail in Chapter 9.

However advanced protection measures and HSE regulation might be, there will always be certain jobs that include a high risk to health and life. Working on an oilrig, doing research in nuclear technology, or working as a stunt person in action films are all inextricably linked to certain hazards. As a general rule, one could adopt the *principle of informed consent:* no worker should be exposed to these factors without precise information about the risks involved. Consequently, any damage to the worker's health is the result of his or her deliberate decisions—perhaps to effectively 'trade' exposure to health risks for the higher compensation that is often linked to such jobs.

HSE issues though become increasingly relevant in the context of new risks, most commonly in the form of *new diseases* and *new technologies*. In fact, some diseases even owe their name to the company where they first occurred, such as 'Pseudo-Krupp', a lung disease first discovered among workers and neighbours of the German steel mill 'Krupp'. More recent examples of new diseases include the rise of the AIDS epidemic (McEwan 2001: 187–9). Employers see themselves as facing the dilemma that, on the one hand, they want to provide their employees with a reasonable level of protection, while on the other hand, a company does not want to discriminate against employees or customers (e.g. patients) infected with the disease.

A similar problem occurs in the context of new technologies. When asbestos was first developed for use as a fire retardant, nobody was yet aware of its inherent health risks. Given that asbestosis—the debilitating, often fatal condition caused by exposure to asbestos—can take up to twenty or thirty years to surface after exposure, enormous numbers of production and installation workers handling the substance were placed at serious health risk (Treviño and Nelson 2007). The long-term consequences of extended computer work for eyes and other parts of the body are also only now beginning to emerge. The dilemma for corporations lies in the fact that the more sophisticated certain technologies are, such as genetic engineering, the greater their potential benefits, but also the greater their potential risks. The principle of informed consent we mentioned earlier can only very partially be applied because the very nature of those risks lies in the fact that the potential consequences, let alone their likelihood, are simply not known. Some therefore suggest the necessity for something more akin to the *precautionary principle* that, in acknowledging scientific uncertainty about many processes and impacts, imposes the *burden of proof of harmlessness* on those introducing a technology.

Work-life balance

We briefly discussed the threat of unemployment above. However, many workers face exactly the opposite problem, namely the increasing incursion of working hours into their social life. There has been a growing pressure for longer hours in (and travelling to) the workplace. This is most notable amongst professionals, such as doctors or accountants, but it has been evident in other jobs too. Low pay and job insecurity, for example, can equally prompt people to exchange social time for employment time in order to guarantee certain standards of living. These problems are even more pronounced in developing countries, as with the dormitory labour system in China, where many workers from the western provinces leave their families there and move to work in factories in the East and live in dormitories under pretty dismal conditions (Smith and Pun 2006).

Clearly, a 'healthy' balance between work and private life—or 'work-life balance'—is difficult to maintain. Parents may face difficulty with childcare and/or hardly see their children, couples may face the delicate task of maintaining a long-distance or weekend relationship, and many employees might find that their life is completely absorbed by work without any time or energy left to maintain or build up meaningful social relationships (Simpson 1998; Collier 2001). In the following, we will discuss two of the most pressing issues in work-life balance, namely:

- Excessive working hours and presenteeism.
- Flexible working patterns.

Excessive working hours and presenteeism

An increasing threat to employee health and well-being that is receiving considerable attention now is excessive work hours. In particular, excessive hours are thought to impact on the employee's overall state of physical and mental health. For example one survey found that 84% of managers claimed to work in excess of their official working hours, with the average being between 50 to 60 hours a week (Simpson 2000).

'Presenteeism', as in the phenomenon of being at work when you should be at home due to illness or even just at rest and recreation (Cooper 1996), is a common cultural force in many organizations. The implicit assumption is that only those putting in long hours will be rewarded with career progression and other company rewards. Presenteeism appears to especially affect the middle and upper levels of management, and in particular is likely to disadvantage women's career progression since they tend to have more responsibilities for childcare, etc. at home (Simpson 1998). As such, the whole issue of *work-life* balance has come very much more to the fore in recent years.

Flexible working patterns

Changes in working patterns have also led to more 'flexibility' in working arrangements. Greater flexibility can enhance opportunities for women and other disadvantaged groups, but it can also have a major downside for those marginalized from 'standard' work and working conditions. As Karen Legge (1998) suggests in Figure 7.1, flexibility can just be another way of saying that management can do what it wants.

Pressures towards the deregulation of labour markets brought on by intensification of global competition, and rapid market changes, have led to the emergence of a large constituency of workers in 'non-standard' work relationships, including part-time work, temporary work, self-employment, and teleworking (Stanworth 2000). The legal status of such workers on the 'periphery' of the organization is often less secure than that of those at the 'core', giving rise to the potential for poorer working conditions, increased insecurity, lower pay, exclusion from training and other employment benefits, as well as a whole raft of other possible disadvantages.

These problems are particularly acute in low-skill service industries such as retailing, the hospitality industry, industrial cleaning, and in call centres—areas that have actually seen some of the greatest growth in jobs in recent years. Such workers are often expected to work 'unsocial' hours, with working hours often unpredictable and changed at short notice. Royle (2005: 46), for instance, claims that fast food companies in Europe commonly insist that workers clock off during quiet times and are even 'persuaded to compete in all-night cleaning "parties"'. Work intensification in such service industries is common, as are significant levels of surveillance and control. Perhaps the ultimate in flexible working patterns though is exemplified by some retailers that have used 'zero-hours' contracts. These guarantee no minimum hours, no stable level of earnings, and prevent workers from planning even the basic elements of their lives (Stanworth 2000).

Of course, there are good arguments for why flexibility can boost competitiveness and provide for a strong economy (Hayman 2009), as well as providing new opportunities for women and other groups traditionally excluded from 'standard' working patterns by dint of home responsibilities, etc. (Robinson 2005). However, the problem comes when flexibility erodes basic protections for employee rights, and/or where one group of workers on part-time, temporary, or otherwise 'flexible' contracts is treated unfairly compared with the core workforce.

The ethical problems here are quite difficult to resolve. From the individual's perspective, any demands for better work-life balance may ultimately be counterproductive to one's career aspirations or even a danger to one's job security. Furthermore, some jobs, especially where they involve a high level of specialized skill, are not easily reducible or sharable. Nonetheless, some companies have also discovered that employees with poor work-life balance might not be as effective in the long run, and that different work patterns might need to be encouraged. We will come back to some of the solutions when we discuss more sustainable working places later on.

Fair wages

As with most rights in this section, the right to a fair wage is to some extent protected through regulation in many countries. This certainly applies to lower incomes—for example, with the establishment of a statutory minimum wage, which is by now common in many countries. However, our assessment of what is a 'fair' wage becomes more complex when we place wage levels of those at the bottom of the organizational hierarchy in comparison with those at the top.

The basis for determining fair wages is commonly the *expectations* placed on the employee and their *performance* towards goals, measured by hours worked, prior training, risks involved, responsibility for assets, meeting of targets, etc. However, jobs are valued very differently in some employment markets compared to others. When football player Cristiano Ronaldo signed for Real Madrid in 2009, his reported annual salary was in the region of €13m. While one would certainly concede that being a professional footballer can be hard work and disciplined at times, this also applies to mining workers who are paid a fraction of Ronaldo's salary. Similar discussions about excessive compensation for executives came up when the US president suggested salary caps for CEOs of companies who had received governmental funding in the aftermath of the stock-market collapse of 2008. Athletes and CEOs are both examples where the measure for assigning compensation is related to the consequences of the employee's activities on relevant markets: if we put Cristiano Ronaldo's salary in relation to what his club earns from television and other media deals, one could potentially argue that his salary is acceptable. Similarly, some CEOs earn so much money because they get paid in relation to how the stock market values their company, and what the prevailing labour market for CEOs dictates is a 'reasonable' sum (see Chapter 6, pp. 248–9 for more discussion on the ethics of executive pay).

For corporations, the increasing influence of markets on various aspects of their business has brought about a difficult dilemma. On the one hand, traditional pay schemes are increasingly under threat, with serious consequences for the distribution of income within the firm and the perceived injustice of remuneration within the company. On the other hand, firms have to compete for talent, and if the market for managers is governed by these rules, there are ultimately few alternatives to paying the market rate. After all, it could be argued that in some cases, one of the reasons why public services are so badly run is that capable managerial talent has been siphoned off into private sector jobs because of the higher levels of remuneration found there. A tentative solution to the widening gap between executive and 'normal' staff pay is the effort by some companies to provide part of their salary to *all* their employees in stock options so that all groups can participate to some extent in the company's performance on the stock market.

This, however leads us on to the broader issue here of *performance-related pay* (PRP) and other contingent systems of reward. It is one thing rewarding those at the top for good performance, but when such procedures are introduced for those at lower levels, further ethical problems can arise. Edmund Heery (2000) suggests that this raises two main issues:

- **Risk.** First, PRP introduces greater risk into remuneration, meaning that salaries and benefits for employees become less secure, and potentially open more to arbitrary and subjective management decision-making.
- **Representation.** Secondly, PRP also tends to individualize employee pay bargaining, restricting the influence of collective representation of employee interests, and thereby weakening employee power.

Of course, there are also good arguments in support of PRP, but as Heery (2000) indicates, the ethical appeal of such payment systems often depends on how they are developed and implemented. Such arguments typically depend upon notions of justice, in that fair processes and outcomes should accompany pay schemes, regardless of the mechanism used.

An area of increasing ethical contestation is employee benefits, most notably health insurance and pension plans, where many employees have recently faced rather severe cuts. In the UK, for example, membership in occupational pension plans paid for by employers fell some 40% between 1967 and 2004 (B. Cooper 2009). In a similar vein, many companies in times of economic downturn consider their employees' pensions as a legitimate source of capital to cover for other losses. In the area of healthcare, especially in countries without public healthcare, similar ethical issues have arrived. Most notably, these issues have arisen in the US or in some developing countries, where health insurance is typically paid by employers rather than guaranteed by the public welfare system. This makes employees highly dependent on the company and may easily lead to a situation where employees are willing to put up with many demands just so as not to lose their health coverage. This represents a clear moral hazard, as we discussed in the early part of this chapter.

? THINK THEORY

Think about PRP from the perspectives of utilitarianism and ethics of justice. How would each approach determine a fair wage? Can the two approaches be reconciled?

VISIT THE WEBSITE for a short response to this feature

Freedom of conscience and freedom of speech in the workplace

Normally, the right to freedom of conscience and speech is guaranteed by governments, and so individuals can usually count on the government to protect these rights. However, within the boundaries of the firm, there might also occur situations where these rights, especially the freedom of speech, might face certain restrictions. This is the case with regard to, for example, speaking about 'confidential' matters regarding to the firm's R&D, marketing, or accounting plans that might be of interest for competitors, shareholders, or other stakeholders. In almost all cases, this restriction of the freedom of speech is unproblematic, since most rational employees would find it in their own best interests to comply with company policy, and there is little reason to suggest that most corporate decisions need to be made public.

There are, however, some cases where those restrictions could be regarded as a restriction of employee's rights. Imagine, for example, that a manager asks you to take part in activities that are of contestable moral status, such as some 'creative accounting' for the organization. The problem for you is that you cannot ask third parties outside of the organization for help in this situation without risking serious embarrassment, disruption, and even possibly financial harm to your company. As we said in Chapter 4, if employees decide to inform third parties about alleged malpractice within the firm, this behaviour is normally called 'whistleblowing' (see pp. 157–9). The main problem for employees with whistleblowing is the fact that it involves a considerable risk for them. As they violate the confidentiality that would normally be part of their duty of loyalty towards the firm, they put their job and thus their economic security at risk. This risk can be very high, and even if the allegations are right, the individual worker might find themselves in a critical situation until any whistleblowing activity is finally vindicated. Various regulatory efforts have been undertaken in a number of countries to secure the whistleblower's position, at least when there are issues of public interest at stake. These include efforts of self-regulation where companies work out a code of practice for whistleblowing, up to formal regulation such as the UK's 1998 Public Interest Disclosure at Work Act.

The right to work

Established in the Declaration of Human Rights and more recently in the European Charter of Human Rights, the right to work has been codified as a fundamental entitlement of human beings. As such, the right to work is derived from other basic human rights (De George 1999: 359–65), namely: it is linked to the *right to life*, since work normally provides the basis for subsistence; and it reflects the *right to human respect*, as the ability to create goods and services by working represents a major source for self-respect for human beings.

In the context of modern economies, however, there has been considerable debate whether a right to work automatically translates into a right to employment (van Gerwen 1994). On a macroeconomic level, one might argue that governments have the responsibility to create economic conditions that protect the right to work of every citizen. Nevertheless, as the efforts of the Obama administration and other governments in the course of 2009 to protect banks and car companies demonstrated, governments in most (capitalist) economies will normally only ever be able to provide this right indirectly, since they do not take the employment decisions themselves. So does this mean that individuals have a right to demand employment from corporations, since they are the ones who directly provide jobs?

The answer from an ethical perspective would be to ask if this right of the employee collides with the rights of the employer, and most notably the shareholders of the company. Employing and, most notably, paying people a salary, is only possible if the company is able to sell a reasonable amount of goods and services. If this condition is not fulfilled, a one-sided focus on the right to work would clearly violate the right to own property, and the right to free engagement in markets. Therefore, the right to work in a business context cannot mean that every individual has a right to be employed.

Is the right to work then completely irrelevant? Certainly not, but rather than granting everybody employment, the right to work should result in the claim that every individual should face the same equal conditions in exerting this right. If every individual has the same right to be employed, they are all entitled to the same rights in the process of exerting this fundamental right. Consequently, the right to work chiefly results in equal and fair conditions in hiring and firing. Thus, most notably the right to freedom from discrimination particularly has to be applied in the process of employing people as well as making people redundant (Spence 2000).

Relevant duties of employees in a business context

So far in this chapter, we have focused exclusively on employee rights. However these rights also of course need to be considered in the context of a set of duties that are expected of employees (van Gerwen 1994). You might wonder why we have given so much attention to employees' rights here. However, in the context of business ethics, the main focus has to be on the rights of employees, as these are the main considerations in determining ethical behaviour towards employees. The rights of employees are more endangered than the rights of employers, primarily since employees are more dependent on the employer and face a greater risk of sacrificing or bargaining away their rights in order to secure or keep a job, or face other undesired consequences. Consequently, even when talking about employee duties, our main focus will be the consequences of those duties for employers.

Among the most important duties of employees are the duty to comply with the labour contract and the duty to respect the employer's property. Among these duties count the obligation to provide an acceptable level of performance, make appropriate use of working time and company resources, and to refrain from illegal activities such as fraud, theft, and embezzlement. As research in employee theft has shown, the propensity of employees to commit crimes is highly dependent on the organizational climate in the organization (Gross-Schaefer et al. 2000). This leads to an important question when discussing employees' duties: what is the employer's responsibility with regard to ensuring that employees live up to their duties? Normally these duties are codified in the employment contract and other legal frameworks. Ethically delicate issues arise when looking at how the employer will enforce these duties and monitor employee compliance. Is the employer allowed to check emails and phone calls? Should they be allowed to monitor which websites employees are accessing? What measures are allowed to control working time and work quality? Most of these kinds of issues ultimately touch on the employee's right to privacy, which we have discussed already earlier on in this chapter.

There are, however, a few issues where corporations are actually responsible to some degree for ensuring that their employees live up to a particular duty. This is particularly the case with the duty to comply with the law, since this duty often asks for some 'help' from the side of the employer. We discussed in Ethics in Action 4.1 the example of the French 'rogue trader' Jérôme Kerviel at Société Générale. Many people argued that it was his employer's responsibility to put effective mechanisms in place that would have prevented him from his speculative deals. Similar issues occur, for instance, in the area of bribery: winning a contract by bribes does not only benefit the individual salesperson, but ultimately the corporation as well. Consequently, corporations might, on one hand, provide a context that to some extent encourages behaviour that is of dubious legality, and on the other, be expected to ensure that employees fulfil their legal obligations.

The most common tools for corporations to take up this responsibility are codes of conduct and employee training (Gordon and Miyake 2001; Somers 2001). In establishing such a code, corporations have to make sure that employees know about corporate policy with regard to the legal framework of its operations. However, such codes, and other forms of documenting and establishing policy, do not necessarily ensure that employees actually comply with their duties. From a corporate perspective, though, the main point is often to document that they have done everything they can to prevent illegality. In practice, then, many of these codes of conduct are more symbolic 'red tape' than they are real substance, and have been shown to have had mixed results on the actual ethical and legal behaviour of employees (Higgs-Kleyn and Kapelianis 1999). For further discussion on such codes and their impact, you might want to review Chapter 5 (pp. 191–201).

■ Employing people worldwide: the ethical challenges of globalization

Globalization of business practices has had a significant impact on the question of the ethical treatment of employees. The move towards international expansion, and global supply chains, has resulted in many companies operating subsidiaries or sourcing products from 'low-wage' countries in the developing world. While the simple explanation for this is obviously the lower costs associated with production in these countries, these 'favourable' conditions for companies are often accompanied by questionable working conditions for workers: low wages, high risks for health and safety, inhumane working conditions, just to name a few (Legge 2000).

This, however, is part of a broader question about the universality of employee rights. Issues such as discrimination, fair treatment, acceptable working conditions, fair wages, and the necessity for freedom of speech are interpreted and made meaningful in different ways in different cultures. For example, a conception of racial, sexual, or religious discrimination in Iceland might be different from that in Italy, India, Israel, or Indonesia. Similarly, freedom of speech might be conceived differently in Belgium than in Burma. In the following, we will look at some of the underlying issues involved here, namely:

- National culture and moral values.
- The race to the bottom.
- Migrant labour and illegal immigration.

National culture and moral values

As we discussed in Chapter 4, there is a connection between national cultures and moral values across the globe. We introduced at that stage the Hofstede (1980, 1994) model with its five dimensions characterizing different cultural values: individualism/collectivism, power distance, masculinity/femininity, uncertainty avoidance, and long-term/short-term orientation. These dimensions implicitly focus on some of the key aspects underpinning the moral values than govern employer–employee relations. For example, consider the dimension of individualism/collectivism, which represents the degree to which people think of themselves as independent autonomous actors or acting for the good of the group. Individualist cultures will tend to regard it as more acceptable for each worker to be individually responsible to their employer, whereas collectivist cultures will tend to emphasize the necessity of association and collective participation. Similarly, in collectivist societies, a person's ability to work well with others and make collaborative decisions might be just as much prized as educational and professional qualifications. As Treviño and Nelson (2007) suggest, this might mean that in a collectivist culture, the extent to which an applicant and their family are known, trusted, and liked by the employer will be considered an important qualification, whereas in individualist countries such 'nepotism' may be considered to be biased and discriminatory.

The point is that different cultures will view employee rights and responsibilities differently. This means that managers dealing with employees overseas, or even critics of business who look to business practices overseas, need to first understand the cultural basis of morality in that country. Of course, this then begs the question as to whether it is fair to treat people differently, and to what we in the developed world might regard as a 'lower' standard, just because they happen to live in Lagos and not in Lisbon. Do Vietnamese employees not have the same needs for health protection as workers in Venice? This raises the problem of relativism versus absolutism.

> **? THINK THEORY**
>
> We have just looked at one of Hofstede's five dimensions and its implications for understanding employee–employer relations. Think about the other four dimensions and set out how each may affect one's view of employee rights and duties. Go back to Chapter 4 (pp. 150–1) if you need to review Hofstede's theory.

VISIT THE WEBSITE for a short response to this feature

Absolutism versus relativism

We first discussed the issue of absolutism versus relativism in Chapter 3. Absolutism, we suggested, represented the idea that if an ethical principle were to be considered valid, it had to be applicable anywhere. Relativism, by contrast, suggests that no one view of ethics can be said to be right since it must always be relative to the historical, social, and cultural context. An example of how vast differences in ethical values between countries can be and how important these issues can become for business success is presented in **Ethics in Action 7.2.** We contended in Chapter 3 that both extremes of ethical absolutism and relativism do not give a sufficient answer to the different conditions evident in countries across the globe.

- *Relativists* would finish the argument quite easily by dismissing the necessity for moral judgement from the West about foreign cultural contexts. If Pakistani culture is permissive of a 14-hour working day, or harassment of women, who are we to judge by imposing our Western standards? Relativism ultimately would deny any ethical problem around exploitation and poor working conditions as long as such conditions comply with the standards of the respective country or culture.
- At the other end of the spectrum, *absolutists* would say that if our moral standards are right, they are right everywhere around the globe. Consequently, companies should respect employee rights equally, wherever it is that they are actually contracted to work.

Obviously, these two sides are never likely to reach a common solution. Therefore, if we are to find a practical way forward, we need to look at this a little differently, and a little more carefully. Far from having reached a consensus, the debate has nevertheless highlighted some yardsticks that might be useful for establishing guidelines for behaviour (Donaldson 1996).

The most general rule would be to start with *human rights* as a basic compass for providing direction (Frankental 2002). The Universal Declaration of Human Rights, ratified in 1948 through the UN, is the most widely accepted set of principles pertaining to the rights of others. If a certain practice violates human rights, there is fairly broad acceptance that it is ethically wrong and unacceptable.

Beyond considerations of human rights, ethical considerations circle around the fact that differences in the treatment of employees on a global scale are not necessarily ethically wrong per se, but depend on the relative *economic development* of the country in which the practice is taking place. The basic ethical question then is to ask whether the differences in wages and labour conditions are due to the economic development of the developing country (Donaldson 1989: 101–6). For example, would the 14-hour day that the French MNC imposes on its workers in Pakistan be acceptable if France had the same economic conditions?

The 'race to the bottom'

Apart from adapting or not adapting to *existing* employment standards in foreign cultures, Scherer and Smid (2000) among others argue that MNCs also play a role in *changing* standards in those countries. Globalization clearly enables corporations to have a fairly broad range of choice for the location of plants and offices. The deterritorialization of economic space has meant that when you pick up the phone in London and dial the customer service department of your bank, you could just as well be connected to an operative in Dublin or Delhi, Manchester or Mumbai. Consequently, developing countries compete against each other to attract the foreign investment represented by such relocation decisions.

Many critics of globalization have contended that among the key factors in this competition for investment are the costs incurred by MNCs through environmental regulation, taxes, and tariffs, social welfare for employees, and health and safety regulations. As a result, large investors may well choose the country that offers the most 'preferable' conditions, which often means the lowest level of regulation and social provision for employees. This competition therefore can lead to a 'downward spiral' of protection, or what is often called a 'race to the bottom' in environmental and social standards (Rudra 2008). MNCs in particular have been accused of being the key actors in propelling this race (Spar and Yoffie 1999).

The logic here is straightforward and compelling. Not surprisingly, though, it has also been hotly contested, not least because of the political and ethical ramifications of such an argument. Those advocating unfettered free trade tend to see the race to the bottom argument as not only fallacious, but opposed in principle to free trade and deregulated global markets. Still, evidence of the reality or otherwise of such a race is difficult to discern, not least because of the complexity of the equation, given the range of variables and motives involved (Spar and Yoffie 1999).

This leads to a broader potential responsibility for MNCs in the context of globalization. Rather than being concerned with ethical standards solely within the premises of their own company, MNCs, as perhaps the most powerful actors in such countries, are also in a position to assume a key role in building up so-called 'background institutions' (Spar and Yoffie 1999; Scherer and Smid 2000). This includes institutions such as trade unions, health and safety standards, and various other rules, regulations, and standards that help to protect workers' rights. Nien-hê Hsieh (2009), for instance, contends that MNEs have a responsibility because of their duty to avoid causing harm to promote minimally just social and political institutions in countries where they operate that lack them.

Migrant labour and illegal immigration

A more recent phenomenon of globalization has been the growing mobility of workers globally (Binford 2009; Wickramasekara 2008). This can typically occur in the form of South-to-North immigration, such as the influx of immigrants from Latin America to the US and Canada or from Africa into the European Union. But it also occurs in many other regions globally, such as in Southern Africa or the United Arab Emirates, the latter drawing a large workforce from Pakistan, India, and Bangladesh. Migrant labour can also be a phenomenon attracted by certain industries, such as the mining industry which often operates in geographic locations where there is no immediate workforce to recruit (Jeschke 2007).

VISIT THE WEBSITE for links to useful sources of further information

ETHICS IN ACTION 7.2 http://www.ethicalcorp.com

Workplace equality—putting harassment on notice

Ethical CORPORATION

Rajesh Chhabara, 22 October 2008

Sexual harassment at work has come under the spotlight in Asia in the past few years with growing pressure from human rights groups and increased media interest. More women are joining the urban workforce in fast-growing Asian economies, changing the gender landscape in companies. Worker rights groups say women are getting a raw deal in the workplace. Studies also indicate that a growing number of men are being sexually harassed by their female bosses.

Recent surveys across Asia have found widespread prevalence of sexual harassment at work, prompting calls for governments and companies to do more to protect staff. Companies that do nothing risk losing workers or potential recruits to multinational companies that tend to look after staff better. 'Western multinational companies attract the best talent in Asia because of better working conditions and clear human resource policies that almost always include issues of discrimination, sexual harassment and work-life balance and corporate social responsibility,' says Harminder Singh Soni, head of New Delhi-based recruitment firm Unitell. He adds: 'Asian companies have a long way to go.'

So far only Hong Kong, the Philippines and Japan have specific laws banning workplace sexual harassment. Even they are limited in scope. The Philippine law does not cover harassment among employees of equal rank, and Japan's only protects female workers. China amended its law on the protection of women's rights in 2005 after surveys reported widespread sexual harassment in factories and other workplaces. Critics said the amendment was vague as it did not define sexual harassment and employers could not be held responsible. Malaysia introduced a voluntary code of practice for the prevention of workplace sexual harassment in 1999. Observers say that while multinational companies generally adopted the code, local companies largely ignored it—a common complaint from equal rights campaigners in the region. Soma Sen Gupta, director of a Kolkata-based human rights group, which recently launched a handbook on prevention of workplace sexual harassment, says: 'Greater political will is required to create a culture of gender equality.'

Duty of care

India's largest business lobby, the Confederation of Indian Industries, says it is raising awareness among members on how to protect employees from discrimination. It has given companies a toolkit and handbook on preventing sexual harassment of staff, with the help of the UN Fund for Women. 'Seeing the increase in the participation of women in the workplace, it is important for all Indian companies to have a sexual harassment policy in place,' says Supriya Banerji, deputy director-general at the social development unit of the CII.

Campaigners are unimpressed. 'Only a handful of Indian companies have appointed sexual harassment committees as required by the Supreme Court guidelines,' says Mumbai-based lawyer and human rights activist Mihir Desai.

Pressure is rising on companies across the region to make their companies better places to work. In Malaysia, the government is considering mandatory sexual harassment prevention training for human resource managers. In July, the Women, Family and Community Development minister, Ng Yen Yen, said: 'Only a small number of employers have procedures in place to deal with sexual harassment complaints, and most victims fear losing their jobs if they report sexual harassment.'

In March, a government-appointed advisory panel in China, comprising the China Law Society, Chinese Academy of Social Sciences and the anti-workplace sexual harassment project team, recommended that employers should be held responsible for sexual harassment at work. New laws may help, but changing workplace cultures will require more than tougher rules from government, say observers. Desai says many HR managers fear that sexual harassment prevention programmes will create a surge in complaints and lawsuits. It seems that many companies would rather staff did not know their rights.

As Asian companies themselves go global, they will have to put in place strict measures against sexual harassment to avoid potential lawsuits in foreign lands and loss of reputation. Observers point to Indian IT giant Infosys, which had to fire Phaneesh Murthy, its US-based global head of sales and a board member, in 2003 after his secretary filed a sexual harassment lawsuit in a California court. The company reached an out-of-court settlement with the complainant. Japanese carmaker Toyota had to remove its North America president and chief executive Hideaki Otaka in 2006 after a $190m sexual harassment lawsuit by his secretary. The case followed one of the largest sexual harassment lawsuits in the US in the mid-1990s, when another Japanese carmaker, Mitsubishi, eventually agreed in 1998 to pay $34m in compensation to 300 female staff.

Apart from litigation, companies also risk decreased productivity if they fail to check sexual harassment. The International Labour Organization says the cost of sexual harassment includes decreased productivity among staff because of impaired judgment, compromised teamwork, demotivation and absenteeism. Asian companies that aspire to match western rivals in terms of being good employers will have to take bold steps to address workplace sexual harassment. Some firms now recognise the problem, say campaigners, but much more needs to be done to change the attitudes of bosses and staff regarding respect for their colleagues.

Harassment trends

- In China, 40% of women working for private and foreign companies have suffered sexual harassment, compared with 18% in state-owned companies.

- In Hong Kong, 45% of office workers say sexual harassment takes place at their workplace; 25% have suffered sexual harassment themselves. One-third of victims are men.
- In India, 47% of women say they have been sexually harassed at work.
- In Singapore, 54% of employees say they have been sexually harassed at work; 58% of the victims were women.
- In Pakistan, 78% of women face sexual harassment at work.

Sources

Ethical Corporation, Rajesh Chhabara, 22 October 2008, http://www.ethicalcorp.com.

VISIT THE WEBSITE for a short response to this feature

? THINK THEORY

Think about the difference between absolutism and relativism. To what extent are Asian attitudes towards sexual harassment simply a reflection of different cultural values or can the right to be free from sexual harassment be universalized? Consider what practical tools firms might use for dealing with sexual harassment in Asia.

Ethical issues around this phenomenon are manifold. To start with, migrant labour often results in questionable social phenomena, such as drug abuse or prostitution, and has put corporations in a position to provide a host of social infrastructure, such as housing, transport, healthcare, or education, in place. As migrant workers often come from poor countries, a crucial issue is that they are often willing to accept working conditions and salary levels that would normally be considered unacceptable. In Ethics on Screen 3, we saw a vivid illustration of these phenomena in a European context. A key issue, however, is that these workers often enter countries illegally. To employ migrant workers then in many places is against the law, however much businesses or even whole sectors may rely on such a pool of workers. In particular, the fact that, for instance, the US and the EU from time to time grant legal residency to these workers if they can prove that they are employed and pay taxes, puts companies in a grey zone: while it is illegal to employ these workers, the very fact that businesses employ them provides the basis for them to become legal residents. Thus, the contradictions and ambiguities concerning immigration policies on the political level reflect directly on corporations and confront them with a host of ethical issues.

The US-based clothing company American Apparel has taken a particularly interesting approach here. Having eschewed the more common approach of outsourcing its production and stitching to overseas contractors, the company focuses production in-house in its downtown Los Angeles facilities, where it makes extensive use of the city's pool of largely Hispanic migrant labour. Notably, the company offers its workforce generous working conditions, including decent wages, healthcare, subsidized lunches, English language classes, and employment security, that stand in stark contrast to conditions in most overseas contractors. Perhaps most unusual though is the company's active engagement in promoting progressive immigration reform in the US with its 'Legalize LA' campaign.[9]

■ The corporate citizen and employee relations

As we have discussed in some detail earlier in the chapter, ethical issues in employee relations are primarily framed in terms of a collection of rights. As such, these issues have a close relation to the notion of corporate citizenship: corporations govern a good deal of the social and civil rights of citizens in the workplace. They need to protect privacy of information, provide humane working conditions, ensure fair wages, and allocate sufficient pensions and health benefits. Looking across the globe, however, we discover that the extent to which corporations take over this role, as well as the degree to which corporations are held accountable for the governance of these rights, varies quite a lot.

A first aspect here is how far different legal and governance systems in various countries push companies to respect the rights of their employees. As we have discussed in Chapter 6, there are some quite substantial differences between the various regional approaches to corporate governance. Arguably, the area where legal frameworks are thickest is continental Europe, often referred to as 'Rhenish Capitalism', following the French author Michel Albert (1991). This alludes to the fact that the heartland of this approach lies particularly in those countries bordering the river Rhine: France, Germany, the Netherlands, Switzerland, Austria, but in a broader sense also the Scandinavian countries and Italy, Spain, and Portugal. The main difference in the context of this chapter is that capitalism in continental Europe has tended to take into account the interests of employees to a greater degree than the Anglo-Saxon model (which includes the UK, the US, and to some degree Canada). This has given rise to a variety of legal, educational, and financial institutions that focus particularly on the rights of employees.

The key concept in this context is the idea of *co-determination*, which describes the relationship between labour (employees) and capital (shareholders) in Europe, namely that both parties have an equal say in governing the company (Ferner and Hyman 1998). In Germany and France, in particular, this has resulted in a very strong legal position for workers, works councils, and trade unions. So, for instance, in German companies in the metal industry, half of the supervisory board consists of employee representatives and the executive board member for personnel has to be appointed by the workers directly. Consequently, the employees and their rights tend to be far better protected than in the Anglo-American model, where shareholders are regarded as the most important group.

Beyond the developed world context, it is fair to argue that generally the level of regulation (or at least enforcement of regulation) protecting employees is rather low in developing countries. Hence, many of the issues discussed here fall into the realm of voluntary 'good citizenship' from corporations which, as we discussed in Chapter 2, often assigns to companies a role in respecting, protecting, and implementing basic human rights in the workplace. This said, however, we see that in many emerging economies, governments have, over time, tended to strengthen the protection and implementation of employees' legal rights. A prime example here is perhaps China, which for a long time has made headlines for the fairly poor labour standards prevailing in much of its industrial system. In 2008, though, the Chinese government implemented a new Labor Contract Law which represented a sea change in its approach to these issues by better protecting workers rights, for instance by committing all employers to providing employment contracts (Wang et al. 2009). While there are still clear possibilities for circumventing such regulation, it has been seen to have had a significant impact on worker protection—albeit by also increasing costs for firms (Adams 2008).

These regional differences and shifts in legal protections over time make it difficult for corporations to determine the scope of their responsibilities for protecting employee rights, especially in relation to the government responsibility for doing so. A notable development seeking to address this problem in recent years has come from the work of the UN and its special representative on business and human rights, John Ruggie. Following extensive consultation and research, Ruggie (2008) has developed a framework for understanding business responsibilities in the area of human rights. This framework of 'protect, respect and remedy' offers an important starting point for delineating corporate and governmental responsibilities in this controversial area:

- **Protect.** Under international law, states have a duty to protect against human rights abuses by non-state actors, such as corporations. This might be when such abuses have affected people within the state's jurisdiction or, in some circumstances, when the corporation is within the jurisdiction of the state even if the abuse happens overseas (for example, in the case of the Swedish government protecting against abuse by a Swedish company in another country).
- **Respect.** Corporations have a responsibility to respect human rights in that they are expected to obey laws on human rights even if these are not enforced, and should respect the relevant international principles of human rights even if national law is absent. Firms are therefore required to undertake due diligence in identifying areas where there are potential threats to human rights and managing these risks accordingly with tools such as impact assessments and performance tracking.
- **Remedy.** Finally, given that disputes over human rights impacts are inevitable, firms and governments need to put in place formal grievance procedures and systems for investigation and punishment of abuses.

Although clearly still at a relatively early stage of development, such a framework offers some important clarifications about the different responsibilities of business and government for protecting employees' (and other stakeholders') rights. Much work still needs to be done, but the protect, respect, and remedy framework looks set to become a standard reference point for firms seeking to tackle human rights issues in the coming years.

■ Towards sustainable employment

In this chapter, we have talked a great deal about respecting and guaranteeing employee rights in the workplace. On the one hand, this inevitably suggests certain tensions when we think in terms of sustainability. Sometimes protection of wages and conditions for workers may have to be sacrificed to encourage sustainable economic development and maintain employment. Expansion of environmentally damaging industries such as the airline industry can often be seen to be good for job creation. Looking at it this way, there usually have to be some sacrifices or trade-offs between protecting employees and promoting various aspects of sustainability.

On the other hand, it is also possible to discern certain links with the intention to protect employee rights and the notion of sustainability. Only if we are gainfully employed in useful work, and feel respected as human beings, are we actively contributing to long-term sustainability in the *economic* sense. A workplace that puts us under stress or makes us want to forget the day as soon as possible will have long-term effects on our lifestyles, health, and well-being. This aspect is closely linked to the *social* dimension of sustainability: organizations should treat the community of workers in a way that stabilizes social relationships and supports employees to maintain meaningful social relationships with their families, neighbours, and friends. Sustainability, finally, is also an issue here in the *ecological* sense. The modern corporation has in many ways created workplaces that are ecologically unsustainable. Employing fewer and fewer people in a highly mechanized and energy-intensive technological environment, while at the same time making no use at all of something like 10–15% of the potential workforce, could be seen as a major waste of material and energy.

In this section, we shall look at three main ways in which these problems and tensions have been addressed, both in theory and in practice:

- Re-humanized workplaces.
- Wider employment.
- Green jobs.

Re-humanized workplaces

The 'alienation' of the individual worker in the era of industrialized mass production has been discussed at least since the time of Karl Marx. The suggestion is that the impact of technology, rationalized work processes, and the division of labour has meant that many employees simply repeat the same monotonous and stupefying actions over and over again, resulting in there being little real meaning, satisfaction, or involvement in their work (Braverman 1974; Schumacher 1974). Whether in factories, fast food restaurants, or call centres, much employment has been reduced to a series of meaningless 'McJobs' subject to intense management control, and with little chance of real engagement or job satisfaction. Even a shift towards more 'white collar' work in offices can be argued to have created a legion of cubicle dwellers, tirelessly tapping away at computers rather than enjoying active, creative, meaningful work.

Therefore, although our 'rational' ways of organizing work can, and have, brought us tremendous efficiencies and material wealth, they have also created the prospect of a dehumanized and de-skilled workplace. The relationship between technology and the quality of working life is, however, actually a much-contested one (see Buchanan and Huczynski 1997: 549–87). The impacts on the workplace are at the very least contingent on a variety of factors, including work organization, managerial motivation, and employee involvement (Wallace 1989).

There have been numerous attempts over the years to re-humanize the workplace in some way, for example by 'empowering' the employee (Lee and Koh 2001). This might include 'job enlargement' (giving employees a wider range of tasks to do) and 'job enrichment' (giving employees a larger scope for deciding how to organize their work). Many of these ideas attempt a completely different pattern of production. Rather than mass production in a Fordist style (after the inventor of the production line, Henry Ford), the idea is to create smaller-scale units where workers can be engaged in more creative and meaningful work, utilizing 'human-centred' technology (Schumacher 1974). Some car manufacturers (most notably the Swedish firms Saab and Volvo) have experimented with replacing the production line with small, partly autonomous, team-based working groups. Again, though, the success of such schemes has been contested, suggesting that the 'humanized' approach might be more appropriate and effective in some cultures (e.g. Scandinavia) than others (Sandberg 1995).

Wider employment

The mechanization of work has led to the situation where a large proportion of unemployed people has become a normality in many countries, threatening not only the right to work, but the social fabric of communities. It has been argued that efforts by politicians to change job markets or re-invigorate their economies will only ever partly solve the problem, since the increasing level of mechanization and computerization of working processes has meant that we simply do not require as many workers to provide the population with its needs (Gorz 1975). Authors such as Jeremy Rifkin (1995) have even gone so far as to suggest that new technologies herald the 'end of work'.

From a sustainability perspective, the problem is essentially one of ensuring that meaningful work is available to all. Modern employment patterns have tended to create a cleavage between those who have the highly skilled jobs which require long hours of work for high returns, and those who are reduced to unemployment or at best a succession of low-skilled, poorly paid, temporary jobs. In recent years, there have been a number of interesting efforts to tackle this problem of creating a society of 'haves' and 'have-nots'. One recent attempt from the French government was the introduction of a 35-hour week. By legally reducing the working time for the individual, the idea was that organizations would be forced to employ more people to maintain the same level of output. Attractive as the idea may have been to some, it nevertheless had an ambiguous effect. For certain industries, the number of workers employed clearly rose, while in others the relative increase in the cost of labour prompted a tendency to replace labour with technology (Milner 2002).

Another initiative at the corporate level has been discussed in the global automotive industry. Rather than laying off large parts of the workforce, an alternative approach has been to reduce working time for all workers and keep a larger number of workers employed. This approach has been practised in the past, for instance by Volkswagen who set up its '5000 × 5000' model in the early 2000s. This allowed Volkswagen to keep 5,000 workers with a reduced working time and fixed pay of DM 5,000 (Schmidt and Williams 2002).

Green jobs

In the context of the economic downturn of the late 2000s and the debate on how to restructure the economy in a more sustainable fashion, many politicians and business leaders put specific attention on the idea of creating more 'green jobs' (Gopal 2009) One aspect of these green jobs is of course that they are in industries producing environmentally friendly products (such as Hybrid cars or solar panels) and services (such as recycling or car sharing). Another aspect of this movement toward green jobs is that the job itself, the workplace, the way labour is organized, become more environmentally sustainable (Forstater 2006; Gnuschke 2008).

There are a number of approaches companies have taken to achieve the goal of a greener workplace. Incentivizing car pooling, introducing the paperless office, substituting business travel by videoconferencing, increasing recycling, moving into low energy use office space are just some examples of the types of initiatives organizations have explored to green the workplace. Another widely advocated solution is home-based teleworking. Although, as we discussed previously, this can be used as an excuse for poorer working conditions, teleworking can also, for example, help those with families to carry out their jobs whilst at the same time still being able to look after children and fulfil other important family roles (Sullivan and Lewis 2001). Apart from the *social* benefits for the employee that teleworking can potentially bring, there may also be *economic* benefits for the company, and even *ecological* advantages too. For instance, rather than commuting into work and adding to road congestion and air pollution, teleworkers are likely to use far fewer resources by staying at home and communicating remotely.

? THINK THEORY

To what extent is the role of the company in providing a sustainable workplace an expression of the extended view of corporate citizenship? What are the specific areas where corporations are replacing traditional features of the welfare state here?

VISIT THE WEBSITE for a short response to this feature

■ Summary

In this chapter, we have discussed the specific stake that employees hold in their organizations, and suggested that although this stake is partially regulated by the employment contract, employees are also exposed to further moral hazards as a result of the employee–employer relationship. We have also discovered how deep the involvement of corporations with employees' rights can be. Nearly the entire spectrum of human rights is touched upon by the modern corporation, including issues of discrimination, privacy, fair wages, working conditions, participation, association, due process, and freedom of speech.

The corporate responsibility for protection and facilitation of these rights is particularly complex and contestable when their operations become more globalized, thus committing them to involvement with employees whose expectations and protections for rights may differ considerably. Indeed, we explained that the governmental role of issuing legislation in favour of, and aimed at the protection of, employees' rights has to some extent retracted. With the removal of such certainties, corporations would appear to have gained a good deal more flexibility with respect to employee relations. This has its downside in that corporations are left with a far larger degree of responsibility and discretion regarding the protection of employee rights, making ethical decision-making far more complex and challenging—and more ripe for abuse.

We suggested that corporations in different parts of the globe face different regulatory environments, making it sometimes easier, sometimes more difficult, to live up to ethical expectations. While some of the issues, such as human rights or the role of trade unions, are more long-standing, we also discussed recent challenges such as illegal immigration or migrant labour. We also saw that the corporate role in relation to employees quite often puts them in fact in a position very similar to the responsibilities governments have towards their citizens. This role also became visible when we discussed the recent challenges coming from the call for more sustainable workplaces. This aspect is sure to be of increasing ethical interest in the firm's relation to its employees.

Study questions

1 What rights do employees have in a business context? To what extent are employee rights protected by:

(a) The employment contract.

(b) Legislation.

2 Do firms have an ethical obligation to increase diversity in the workplace? Provide arguments for and against, providing examples where relevant.

3 What is reverse discrimination? What are the main ethical arguments for and against reverse discrimination?

4 What are the four main types of privacy that employees might expect? Provide examples where each type of privacy might potentially be violated in a business context.

5 To what extent is it possible to accept that a Western multinational corporation will offer lower standards of wages and conditions in less developed countries? What implications does your answer have for the proposition that when in Rome, we should do as the Romans do?

6 What responsibility should employers have for ensuring that their employees maintain an appropriate work-life balance? Set out some practical steps that employers could take to improve work-life balance and ensure a sustainable workplace environment for employees.

Research exercise

The American clothing company American Apparel has developed an unusual approach to labour rights with its vertically integrated manufacturing model and its Legalize LA campaign on immigration reform. Review the firm's website and answer the following questions:

1 Set out the main elements of American Apparel's approach to labour rights.
2 Evaluate this approach in relation to one or more of American Apparel's competitors. What are the strengths and weaknesses of the firm's approach in relation to these competitors?
3 In which ways are these practices likely to impact upon the economic sustainability and prosperity of the firm?
4 Should the company be involved in campaigning for immigration reform? What value does this create for the firm and for its stakeholders?
5 How would you advise the company to go forward with its labour rights strategy?

Key readings

VISIT THE WEBSITE for links to further key readings

1 Ruggie, J. 2008. Protect, respect and remedy: a framework for business and human rights. *Inno a ions* (Spring): 189–212.

This publicly available paper from the UN provides a helpful introduction to the problems of allocating responsibilities between business and government in the area of human rights. It offers a clear description of the increasingly influential 'protect, respect and remedy' framework that has been developed by Ruggie and promoted by the UN.

2 Royle, T. 2005. Realism or idealism? Corporate social responsibility and the employee stakeholder in the global fast-food industry. *Business hics: A u opean Re iew*, 14 (1): 42–55.

This article illustrates employee-related ethical issues in one of the world's most controversial industries. It also provides an interesting backdrop for understanding differences in managing employees in a US-European comparative perspective.

Case 7

VISIT THE WEBSITE for links to useful sources of further information

Uzbek cotton: a new spin on child labour in the clothing industry?

This case describes the controversy surrounding the use of cotton sourced from Uzbekistan by high street clothing brands and retailers. It sets out the allegations of poor working conditions in the industry, most notably around child and forced labour, and traces the subsequent response by major companies. It offers an opportunity to examine questions of human rights in the supply chain, specifically in the context of an oppressive regime, and prompts consideration of the extent of corporate responsibilities for protecting workers' rights.

Most clothing brands and retailers have become accustomed to dealing with problems of child labour in their supply chains. Codes of conduct banning the most unsavoury sweatshop practices, regular factory audits, and other measures are now largely standard practice in the industry. But these initiatives usually just start and finish at the gates of the factories making the clothes. What about the raw materials, such as cotton, which are used to make the clothes in the first place? Cotton is the indispensable element in most of the clothes we wear. Shirts, T-shirts, jeans, dresses, underwear—you name it, cotton goes into it. The question of who grows that cotton, however, and under what kind of conditions they work, is rarely one that we think too much about. But all that started to change when revelations started emerging in 2005 that Uzbekistan, the world's second largest cotton exporter, made extensive use of forced child labour in harvesting its annual cotton crop. With a 2007 BBC programme exposing how classrooms were emptied across the country every year to pick the harvest, child labour, it seemed, was once again set to become a major ethical problem for major clothing brands.

The Uzbek cotton industry

The Central Asian Republic of Uzbekistan, a former part of the Soviet Union, is one of five countries dominating global cotton production, the others being China, the US, India, and Pakistan. Uzbekistan is widely regarded as being an oppressive regime, led by President Islam Karimov, who has been in power since 1991. The country has limited media freedoms, low levels of democracy, high corruption, and a poor record of human rights violations. The Uzbek government rigidly controls cotton production, using a Soviet-style quota system. This involves compulsory state purchase, and various forms of pressure to ensure that targets are met.

According to the Environmental Justice Foundation, 'cotton production in the Central Asian Republic of Uzbekistan represents one of the most exploitative enterprises in the world'. Due to the low, centrally set prices paid to farmers for their quota, a large proportion of the profits generated by cotton exports are retained by regional governors and the state. Cotton farmers typically persist on low pay with poor working conditions. Reports from the foreign media and NGOs have identified a range of human rights violations in the industry, the most serious of which concern the use of forced and child labour.

Child labour accusations

According to many independent observers, child labour has long been rife in the Uzbek cotton industry, and it has been actively condoned and even facilitated by the state. Due to underinvestment in technology, some 90% of Uzbek cotton is harvested by hand rather than by machine, as it is in most other countries. It is alleged that the need for labour during the cotton harvest is so acute, and cost pressures from regional governors are so heavy, that much of the harvesting ends up being carried out by children. Reports suggest that during the harvesting season (typically from September to November), schools are closed and tens of thousands of children are compulsorily transported to the fields to help with the harvest. Younger children are returned home by bus or truck every day, but older children often spend the season living in barrack-style accommodation in local farm or school buildings, sometimes without water or electricity. During this time, child cotton workers can miss up to three months of school, usually toiling all day at strenuous manual work. The children are poorly paid (around 40 cents a day), and have to pay for their own food and transport, sometimes even leaving them with next to nothing for their work after deductions have been made.

This desultory picture of the Uzbek cotton industry was first exposed in detail in a comprehensive 2005 report from the Environmental Justice Foundation. Running to some 45 pages, the report, *White Gold: The True Cost of Cotton*, set the child labour allegations within the broader context of the authoritarian nature of the Uzbek regime and the complex cotton trading system. In addition to child labour and other human rights abuses, the report also detailed a swathe of environmental problems associated with the cotton industry in Uzbekistan. Concluding that 'cotton production in Uzbekistan occurs within a framework of systematic exploitation, human rights violations, and environmental destruction', the report argued that 'clothing manufacturers and retailers have an obligation to look beyond the "sweatshops" and into the cotton fields ... Corporate enterprises must make a critical assessment of their role in driving the problems ... and demonstrate that their supply chain does not exacerbate the chronic situation within Uzbekistan.'

At first, the response from the international business community was muted. As the Executive Director of the Environmental Justice Foundation put it: 'EJF has lobbied clothing retailers and manufacturers, using testimonies from children who are forcibly enlisted into an underpaid, overworked army of cotton pickers in Uzbekistan ... EJF has been repeatedly told, "we can't tell where the cotton comes from, our supply chain is too complicated and so we can't boycott Uzbek cotton, even if we wanted to". Case closed, so to speak.'

To some extent the corporations had a point. Because of the complexity of international supply chains, the provenance of the cotton used in any particular garment is very difficult to determine. Countries such as Uzbekistan sell their cotton to international commodities-trading companies, who then sell it on to a chain of processors, manufacturers, and stitchers, before it arrives as a complete garment on the shelves of retailers. The commodity nature of cotton means that a final product will typically consist of cotton from a variety of sources. So, whilst clothes usually feature a label stating where the product was made, the source of its raw materials usually remains invisible to buyers.

As the pressure increased on firms though, the message started to change. Further NGO reports, a series of articles in *Ethical Corporation* magazine, and a corporate workshop held by the Ethical Trading Initiative all helped to push home the seriousness of the situation. Then, in 2007, a BBC documentary screened nationally in the UK brought the issues to the wider public's attention, and quickly the tide began to turn. First, in a joint venture with EJN launched in September 2007, the UK-based T-shirt manufacturer, Continental Clothing, started labeling all its garments with the country of origin of the cotton in order to assure consumers that the firm's cotton did not originate from Uzbekistan. Then the Finnish clothing design company, Marimekko, and the Estonian textile producer, Krenholm, both announced a boycott of Uzbek cotton in November 2007. By 2008 a string of clothing brands and retailers had signed up to the boycott, including the UK retailers Asda, Tesco, and Marks and Spencer, the Swedish chain H&M, and the US brands, Gap and Levi's. Suddenly the impossible was possible.

The boycott marked a major victory for campaigners. The question that remained though was whether it would have any tangible impact on the lives of forced child labourers in Uzbekistan. If companies simply stopped purchasing Uzbek cotton, their customers' consciences might become clearer, but farmers could end up in even harsher economic conditions. Further compounding the problem was the realization that even if retailers switched to cotton sourced from other countries, labour problems might still be prevalent. For example, neighbouring Turkmenistan and Tajikistan also produce cotton and have less repressive regimes than Uzbekistan—but remain of concern to campaigners for their apparent disregard for international labour standards.

On the other hand, it was evident that the boycott could just push the Uzbekis to target other markets less concerned about their exploitative labour practices. Indeed, despite the ban by large Western companies, Uzbekistan continued to expand its other markets for exported cotton in the late 2000s, particularly in Asia. For example, at the 2008 International Uzbek Cotton Fair, officials signed export deals worth about $1bn, amounting to some 950,000 tonnes of cotton fibre. Among the chief purchasers were China, India, Pakistan, Bangladesh, South Korea, and the United Arab Emirates.

The boycott, it seemed, looked set to solve some of the retailers' immediate problems, but was not necessarily going to address all of the deeper underlying problems for Uzbek workers. A major turning point was reached, however, in September 2008 when the Uzbekistan government announced that it would ban children under 16 from picking cotton and signed ILO conventions committing the country to stop using child labour. This had the potential to really make a difference in the cotton fields for those most at risk. Nonetheless, campaigners remained unconvinced that much would change, given the poor record of the Uzbek authorities. As one industry expert commented: 'There is a distinct lack of trust among many observers as to whether the measures will be implemented'. Further reports of exploitation from NGOs seemed to back up these initial doubts. With options running out, some commentators even suggested that Western companies might need to expand beyond a boycott to an engagement-type strategy with the government to lobby for deeper change and help develop the state's capacity for robust enforcement procedures. But with their products no longer tainted by the spectre of Uzbek child labour, the incentives for corporations to take further action seemed to be on the wane.

Questions

1 Which human or employee rights are at stake in this case, and who are the key stakeholders?

2 Apply John Ruggie's framework for business and human rights of 'protect, respect and remedy' to this situation. What does this suggest about the relative responsibilities of corporations and governments in this case?

3 Should Western companies consider further action to help protect child cotton workers, or have they already effectively discharged their ethical responsibility by instituting a boycott of Uzbek cotton?

4 If you were working for a group dedicated to eradicating child labour, what would your strategy be now?

Sources

Ansett, S. 2009. Uzbek cotton and forced child labour—is the Government serious? *Ethical Corporation*, 21 Sept.: http://www.ethicalcorp.com.

BBC. 2007. Child labour and the High Street. *BBC News*, 30 Oct.: http://www.bbc.co.uk/news.

Davis, P. 2009. Politics diary: Cotton's child labour shame. *Ethical Corporation*, 16 Feb.: http://www.ethicalcorp.com.

Environmental Justice Foundation. 2005. *White gold: the true cost of cotton*. London: Environmental Justice Foundation.

Mathiason, N. 2009. Uzbekistan forced to stop child labour. *Observer*, 24 May: http://www.guardian.co.uk.

Webb, T. 2008. Corporate action on Uzbeki white gold. *Ethical Corporation*, Mar.: http://www.ethicalcorp.com.

Notes

1 For more details on the UN Declaration of Human Rights, see http://www.un.org.
2 Full details on these codes (or protocols, as the ILO calls them), can be found at http://www.ilo.org.
3 For more details on SA 8000, see Chapter 5, p. 217 or the Social Accountability website, at http://www.sa-intl.org.
4 The word 'discrimination' in the proper sense just means 'to make distinctions'. However, in the context of employment issues, people nearly always talk of 'discrimination' when in fact they mean 'unfair' or 'unjust discrimination'. For simplicity reasons, we use the term in this normative sense as well.
5 Statistics from 2007, reported in Reier, S. 2008. Women take their place on corporate boards. *New York Times*, 21 March 2008: http://www.nytimes.com.
6 Business Legal Reports. 2004. Morgan Stanley settles landmark discrimination case for $54m. http://learnmoreabouthr.blr.com, 13 July.
7 See http://www.sustainability.psa-peugeot-citroen.com.
8 See http://www.vw-personal.de.
9 See the website of American Apparel for more details: http://americanapparel.net/.

8

Consumers and Business Ethics

In this chapter we will:

- Identify the stake that consumers have in corporate activity, specify consumer rights, and explore where consumer interests converge on and diverge from those of firms.
- Outline the ethical issues and problems faced in business–consumer relations, paying particular attention to the criticisms commonly raised against questionable marketing practices.
- Examine these issues in the context of globalization.
- Analyse the arguments for more responsible marketing practices.
- Further develop the notion of corporate citizenship in relation to consumers by exploring the role of ethical consumption in effecting positive social change.
- Examine the challenges posed by sustainable consumption.

■ Introduction

Consumers are obviously one of the most important stakeholders for any organization, since without the support of customers of some sort, such as through the demand for or purchase of goods and services, most organizations would be unlikely to survive for very long. By consumers, though, we do not just mean the end consumers who ultimately buy finished products in the shops. All of the organizations that purchase or otherwise contract for the provision of goods and services from other organizations can be regarded as consumers. Your university, for example, is just as much a consumer as you or we are, in that it buys furniture, stationery, books, journals, cleaning services, and various other products and services in order to go about its business of providing teaching and research. It has also become increasingly common for people to refer to departments serviced in some way by other departments within the *same* organization as internal customers. Hence, whilst our main focus will be on private individual consumers such as you or us, we will also at times refer to the broader category that includes the whole chain of internal and external constituencies that receive goods or services through exchange.

Given the importance of consumer support for the ongoing success of an organization, it is no surprise that being ethical in dealing with consumers is generally regarded as one of the most crucial areas of business ethics. Moreover, since consumers are primarily outside the organization, ethical problems in this area are often some of the most visible and most difficult to hide of ethical violations. This can lead to potentially damaging public relations problems, media exposés, and other threats to the reputation of the corporation that might be more easily avoided in the context of employees, shareholders, and other stakeholders.

In this chapter, we shall examine the challenges faced by corporations in dealing ethically with consumers in the global economy. The main corporate functions responsible for dealing with consumers are sales and marketing, and it is evident that these professions have long been subjected to a great deal of ethical criticism. Many writers on marketing ethics have highlighted the lack of public trust in the advertising, public relations, and sales professions (e.g. Assael 1995; Laczniak and Murphy 1993; Larsson 2007), and marketing has long been perceived as among the least ethical of business functions (Baumhart 1961; Tsalikis and Fritzsche 1989).

However, although ethics does not appear to have traditionally been a central concern of marketing professionals and academics, there is some evidence of moral considerations entering marketing thought for as long as marketing has existed as a distinct field in its own right (Desmond 1998). After all, it does not take someone with an MBA to work out that there are likely to be certain benefits in having customers that feel they have been treated honestly and ethically, rather than just feeling like the victims of a cynical rip-off operation! More recently, though, there has been a surge in interest from the public, practitioners, and academics alike regarding ethical marketing, ethical consumption, and the like. As we shall see, this has led to a fascinating, yet still unresolved debate about the nature of ethical marketing, and in particular about the role of consumers in shaping the social impact of corporations through their purchase decisions. In order to address such questions, though, we first have to establish the nature and scope of the stakeholder role played by consumers.

■ Consumers as stakeholders

It is by now largely commonplace to hear the argument that businesses are best served by treating their customers well. Indeed, this is essentially one of the core tenets of business strategy—that organizations succeed by outperforming their competitors in providing superior value to their customers. Those companies that prosper in the marketplace are those that pay close and continuous attention to satisfying their customers. Indeed, in many ways, it is hard to argue against the logic of this argument. Of course, an organization will seek to satisfy its customers, for if it does not, then those customers will defect to competitors, thus resulting in loss of market share, and ultimately, profitability.

However, one might also ask why is it, if the interests of producers and consumers are so closely aligned, that ethical abuses of consumers continue to hit the headlines and that the reputation of the marketing and sales professions remains so poor? For example, in recent years, there have been numerous examples of firms being accused of treating their customers in a questionable manner:

- Multinational drug companies have been accused of exploiting the sick and poor in developing countries by maintaining high prices for treatments for diseases such as HIV/AIDS and malaria, and preventing the sale of cheaper generic drugs.
- Fast food and soft drinks companies have been condemned for targeting children with unhealthy, high sugar, low nutrition products.
- Banks and credit card companies have put their customers, and even their own businesses, at risk of financial ruin by offering easy credit to people already in serious debt.
- Mobile phone companies have been condemned for overcharging their customers with expensive call rates, and restrictive contracts.
- Technology companies have raised concerns about consumer privacy by enabling the tracking of web use by marketing research firms.
- Schools have been criticized for offering pupils a diet of cheap processed food at lunchtimes rather than serving appropriately nutritional meals.

These are just a few of the many examples that are regularly revealed by the media and by consumer groups and other 'watchdog' organizations. Clearly, such incidents are cause for concern, but what does this tell us about the nature of the stake held by consumers? The first point to make here is that we must question whether the satisfaction of consumer stakeholders is necessarily always consistent with the best interests of the firm. Whilst such an assumption of aligned interests may well be legitimate in some contexts, or where certain conditions are met, there may also be situations where the interests of buyers and sellers *diverge* (N.C. Smith 1995).

We shall examine some of these contexts and conditions as we proceed through the chapter, but at the most basic level, the co-alignment of interests between the two groups depends on the availability of alternative choices that the consumer might reasonably be able to switch to. Secondly, in the absence of a clear mutual interest in all contexts, we also need a normative conception of the stake held by consumers in order to determine what constitutes (un)ethical behaviour towards them. Typically, this normative basis has been established on notions of **consumer rights.**

Given the notion of rights that was introduced in Chapter 3, consumer rights can be regarded as follows:

> **Consumer rights are inalienable entitlements to fair treatment when entering into exchanges with sellers. They rest upon the assumption that consumer dignity should be respected, and that sellers have a duty to treat consumers as ends in themselves, and not only as means to the end of the seller.**

What constitutes *fair treatment* is, however, open to considerable debate. In the past, consumers were adjudged to have few if any clear rights in this respect, and the legal framework for market exchange was largely predicated on the notion of *caveat emptor*, or 'buyer beware' (see N.C. Smith 1995). Under *caveat emptor*, the consumer's sole right was to veto purchase and decide not to purchase something (Boatright 2009: 274). The burden for protecting the consumer's interest, should they have wanted to go ahead with purchase, therefore lay with the consumer, not with the party making the sale. So, under the rule of buyer beware, providing producers abided by the law, it was the consumer's responsibility to show due diligence in avoiding questionable products. If they were subsequently harmed or dissatisfied with a product or service, it was regarded as their own fault.

The limits of *caveat emptor*

During the latter part of the twentieth century, this notion of *caveat emptor* was gradually eroded by changing societal expectations and the introduction of consumer protection laws in most developed countries (N.C. Smith 1995). Consequently, protection of various consumer rights, such as the right to safe and efficacious products (i.e. effective in doing what they are supposed to do) and the right to truthful measurements and labelling, is now enshrined in UN guidelines, as well as in EU regulations and various national laws. **Figure 8.1**, for example, shows the main objectives and principles of the UN Guidelines on Consumer Protection, which set out the consumer needs that governments are expected to meet. As we have restated a number of times in this book, though, business ethics often begins where the law ends. So, it is frequently in the context of the more ill-defined or questionable rights of consumers, and those that are not legally protected, that the most important ethical questions arise.

For example, we might reasonably suggest that consumers have a right to truthful information about products, and legislation usually proscribes the deliberate falsification of product information on packaging and in advertisements. However, certain claims made by manufacturers and advertisers might not be factually untrue, but may end up

Objectives

Taking into account the interests and needs of consumers in all countries, particularly those in developing countries; recognizing that consumers often face imbalances in economic terms, educational levels and bargaining power; and bearing in mind that consumers should have the right of access to non-hazardous products, as well as the right to promote just, equitable and sustainable economic and social development and environmental protection, these guidelines for consumer protection have the following objectives:

(*a*) To assist countries in achieving or maintaining adequate protection for their population as consumers.
(*b*) To facilitate production and distribution patterns responsive to the needs and desires of consumers.
(*c*) To encourage high levels of ethical conduct for those engaged in the production and distribution of goods and services to consumers.
(*d*) To assist countries in curbing abusive business practices by all enterprises at the national and international levels which adversely affect consumers.
(*e*) To facilitate the development of independent consumer groups.
(*f*) To further international cooperation in the field of consumer protection.
(*g*) To encourage the development of market conditions which provide consumers with greater choice at lower prices.
(*h*) To promote sustainable consumption.

General principles

Governments should develop or maintain a strong consumer protection policy, taking into account the guidelines set out below and relevant international agreements. In so doing, each Government should set its own priorities for the protection of consumers in accordance with the economic, social and environmental circumstances of the country and the needs of its population, bearing in mind the costs and benefits of proposed measures.

The legitimate needs which the guidelines are intended to meet are the following:

(a) The protection of consumers from hazards to their health and safety.
(b) The promotion and protection of the economic interests of consumers.
(c) Access of consumers to adequate information to enable them to make informed choices according to individual wishes and needs.
(d) Consumer education, including education on the environmental, social, and economic impacts of consumer choice.
(e) Availability of effective consumer redress.
(f) Freedom to form consumer and other relevant groups or organizations and the opportunity of such organizations to present their views in decision-making processes affecting them.
(g) The promotion of sustainable consumption patterns.

Figure 8.1. UN guidelines on consumer protection

Source: United Nations. 2003. United Nations Guidelines for Consumer Protection (as expanded in 1999). New York: United Nations Department of Economic and Social Affairs: 2–3. www.un.org

misleading consumers about potential benefits. For instance, in many countries, claims that a food product is 'low fat' are permissible providing the product is lower in fat than an alternative, such as a competing product or another of the company's product line. This means that even a product with 80% fat can be labelled 'low fat' providing the company also markets an alternative with 85% fat. For customers seeking a healthy diet, the 'low fat' product may seem attractive, but might not actually provide the genuinely healthy benefits suggested by the labelling. Indeed, evidence suggests that low fat labels lead people, especially those who are already overweight, to actually increase their calorie intake (Wansink and Chandon 2006). So we might reasonably question whether the consumer purchasing such a product has been treated fairly by the seller. It is in such grey areas of consumers' rights that questionable marketing practices arise. In the following section, we will review the most common and controversial of these ethical problems and issues.

Before we go on to discuss these practices, though, it is important to mention at this stage that the stake consumers hold in corporations does not only provide them with certain rights, but also entrusts them with certain responsibilities too. At one level, we can think of this just in terms of the expectations we might have for consumers themselves to act ethically in dealing with the producers of products. Customers might sometimes be in a position where they can take an unfair advantage of those who supply them with products, particularly if we think about the situation where customers are actually other firms. For instance, powerful retailers may exert excessive pressure on their suppliers in order to squeeze the lowest possible prices out of them for their products. Even at the level of individual consumers like you or us, there are certain expectations placed on us to desist from lying, stealing, or otherwise acting unethically in our dealings with retailers, insurance companies, and other companies. For instance, illegal file sharing on the web has prompted record companies to combat music downloaders, for instance through legal proceedings against individual consumers, and via new arrangements with internet service providers. One recent case resulted in a woman being fined nearly $2m for wilfully violating the copyright of 24 songs through illegal peer-to-peer file sharing (Swash 2009).

At a different level though, and probably more importantly, various writers have also suggested that there are certain responsibilities placed on us as consumers for controlling corporations in some way, or for avoiding environmental problems, through our purchase decisions. If we don't like the way that Adidas treats its third world labour force, or the way that ExxonMobil has responded to global warming, is it not also up to us to make a stand and avoid buying their products in order to get the message across? If we really want to achieve sustainability, don't we have to accept certain curbs on our own personal consumption? These are vital questions in the context of corporate citizenship and sustainability, and we will discuss these problems in more depth towards the end of the chapter.

■ Ethical issues, marketing, and the consumer

The question of dealing ethically with consumers crosses a wide range of issues and problems. Generally speaking, these fall within one or another of the three main areas of marketing activity, as summarized in **Figure 8.2**. We shall look at each of these in turn, and explore the different perspectives typically applied to such problems in order to reach some kind of ethical decision or resolution.

Ethical issues in marketing management

Most ethical issues concerning business–consumer relations refer to the main tools of marketing management, commonly known as the 'marketing mix'—product policies, marketing communications, pricing approaches, and distribution practices.

Area of marketing		Some common ethical problems	Main rights involved
Marketing management.	Product policy.	Product safety. Fitness for purpose.	Right to safe and efficacious products.
	Marketing communications.	Deception. Misleading claims. Intrusiveness. Promotion of materialism. Creation of artificial wants. Perpetuating dissatisfaction. Reinforcing stereotypes.	Right to honest and fair communications. Right to privacy.
	Pricing.	Excessive pricing. Price fixing. Predatory pricing. Deceptive pricing.	Right to fair prices.
	Distribution.	Buyer–seller relationships. Gifts and bribes. Slotting fees.	Right to engage in markets. Right to make a free choice.
Marketing strategy.		Targeting vulnerable consumers. Consumer exclusion.	Right to be free from discrimination. Right to basic freedoms and amenities.
Market research.		Privacy issues.	Right to privacy.

Figure 8.2. Ethical issues, marketing, and the consumer

Ethical issues in product policy

At the most basic level, consumers have a right to—and in most countries, organizations are legally obliged to supply—products and services which are safe, efficacious, and fit for the purpose for which they are intended. In many respects, it is in both the buyer's and the seller's interest that this is the case, since a producer of shoddy or unsafe products is generally unlikely to prosper in a competitive marketplace. Indeed, the vast majority of exchanges are conducted to the entire satisfaction of both parties. However, many everyday products that are bought or used can potentially harm, injure, or even kill people, especially if they are used improperly. This goes not only for products such as alcohol and cigarettes, but also for cars, bicycles, tools, medicines, public transport, investment services, catering services—in fact almost no area of consumption is free from at least the potential to inflict some form of physical, emotional, financial, or psychological harm upon consumers. The questions that arise then are:

(i) To what lengths should the producers of goods and services go to make them safe for the consumer's use?
(ii) To what extent are producers responsible for the consequences of the consumer's use of their products?

One way in which to look at this is to argue that manufacturers ought to exercise **due care** in ensuring that all reasonable steps are taken to ensure that their products are free from defects and safe to use (Boatright 2009: 295). The question of what exactly constitutes due care is of course rather difficult to define, but this assessment tends to rest on some notion of negligence and whether the manufacturer has knowingly, or even unwittingly, been negligent in their efforts to ensure consumer protection. Such presumptions go well beyond the moral minimum typically presented by the notion of *caveat emptor*. Rather, here the suggestion is that it is the producer's responsibility to ensure that products are fit and safe for use, and if they are not, then producers are liable for any adverse consequences caused by the use of these products.

Ultimately, though, safety is also a function of the consumer and their actions and precautions. Providing a producer has exercised due care in ensuring consumers are protected under expected conditions (or perhaps even extreme or emergency situations), consumers themselves must take some responsibility for acting hazardously or misusing the product. For example, surely we can't blame a manufacturer of ice cream if a consumer eats so many tubs in one go that they make themselves sick from (over)consuming the product (providing at least that such practices have not been advocated by the firm in its advertising).

If we think about the example of cars, we can see that the consumer's right to a safe product is not an *unlimited right*. Whilst they might certainly expect that a manufacturer has ensured that the vehicle meets 'reasonable' safety standards, any given cars could obviously have been made safer yet—though at some cost, and in all likelihood with some compromise on other features such as performance or styling. Because these improvements are possible, it does not mean that consumers have a right to them. However, as **Ethics in Action 8.1** demonstrates, firms marketing inherently risky products (such as tobacco or unhealthy food), or products which are especially prone to misuse (such as alcohol), might still exercise responsibility in ensuring that consumers properly understand the risks involved in consuming their products.

Ethical issues in marketing communications

In all of the areas of business ethics pertaining to marketing and consumption, probably no other issue has been discussed in so much depth and for so long as has advertising. Advertising, though, is just one aspect of marketing communications, and whilst much less attention has been afforded to other aspects, ethical problems and issues also arise in respect to personal selling, sales promotion, direct marketing, public relations and other means of communicating to consumers (see Smith and Quelch 1993). Criticisms of these practices have been extensive and varied, but can be usefully broken down into two levels: individual and social. At the level of the individual consumer, critics have been mainly concerned with the use of *misleading or deceptive practices* that seek to create false beliefs about specific products or companies in the consumer's mind, primarily in order to increase the propensity to purchase. At the social level, the main concern is with the *aggregate social and cultural impacts* of marketing communications on everyday life, in particular their role in promoting materialism and reifying consumption.

Looking first at **misleading and deceptive practices** affecting individual consumers, marketing communications are typically said to fulfil two main functions:

(i) To *inform* consumers about goods and services; and

(ii) To *persuade* consumers to actually go ahead and purchase products.

If such communications were just about providing consumers with information, then it could be suggested that the question of misleading practices is essentially one of assessing whether a particular claim is factually true or not. However, this perspective suffers from a number of shortcomings, most notably that: first, marketing (along with much human communication) does not only deal with straightforward declarative sentences of literal fact; and secondly, that it is possible to mislead even when making statements of fact (De George 1999: 278).

The first shortcoming is evident if we think about some typical advertisements. Consider, for example, the ad campaign for the soft drink Red Bull which claims 'Red Bull gives you wings'. Obviously, the advertiser is not claiming that by drinking Red Bull the consumer will literally sprout a pair of wings, simply that the high caffeine drink can give you a bit of an energy boost. Similarly, the 'global warming ready' slogan used by the Italian clothing company Diesel in its controversial Life's a Beach ad campaign in the late 2000s was not meant to deceive us that Diesel clothes would literally prepare us for climate change, but was rather meant as an ironic statement about their cool summer collection. Such claims are not misleading because we don't expect them to be telling us a literal truth.

The second shortcoming of this perspective is clear if we look at some cases where manufacturers have been criticized for making factually true, yet somewhat misleading claims. For example, when firms claim that only 'natural' flavourings and colours are used in a product, this may veil the true provenance of the additives used. For example, Eric Schlosser's (2001) book *Fast Food Nation* calls attention to the very unnatural processes that

VISIT THE WEBSITE for links to useful sources of further information

ETHICS IN ACTION 8.1 http://www.ethicalcorp.com

Diageo—marketing to remember

Ben Cooper, 7 July 2008

Ethical CORPORATION

Drinks companies are used to dealing with bad publicity about the negative effects of their products on public health, the rise of binge drinking and alcohol-related violence. In recent years the industry has made significant strides in terms of responsible marketing, notably in the UK through the work of the Drinkaware Trust and the Portman Group. Drinks companies have started to tone down contentious forms of advertising, such as linking alcohol consumption with sexual success. But with its 'Choices' responsible drinking advertising campaign, global market leader Diageo has taken a bold step to communicate alcohol's harmful effects to consumers.

Rather than simply adding a responsibility message at the end of a branded commercial, the Choices campaign makes that message the subject of the advertisement. Some of the prime Diageo brands—Guinness, Smirnoff and Bells—appear at the end of the ad as small icons. Otherwise, it has more of the appearance of a generic public information film. Aimed at the 18-to-24 age group, the new campaign has already been seen in the UK, Germany and Spain. Other markets will follow, possibly with different ads, the company says.

The campaign comprises two ads, one targeted at men and the other at women. Each represents two possible scenarios for an enjoyable evening out, one in which alcohol is enjoyed responsibly and contributes to a fun evening, and another where excessive consumption has the opposite effect. The viewer is finally asked the question: 'A night to remember? Or one to forget? The choice is yours.'

Behind the scenes, Diageo has made Attitudes to Alcohol a brand unit with its own global marketing director, Pamela Bower-Nye, an experienced marketer who has headed up its flagship Smirnoff brand in both the UK and the US. She says: 'We believe that we are the first drinks company to run a CSR programme from within our marketing function. As a company we know that our strengths lie in our in-depth knowledge of consumers and in creating fantastic marketing campaigns so we want to use this strength to create a positive change in people's attitudes to alcohol.'

Getting serious

While it may seem an awkward transition from marketing Smirnoff as glamorous and aspirational to communicating the risks of alcohol misuse, Bower-Nye maintains the two tasks are closer than they appear. 'The common ground is that responsibility is at the heart of all our marketing,' she says. What the two tasks patently have in common is the target consumer. Diageo stresses that it knows these consumers well and has a proven record of successfully marketing to them. 'We have a unique opportunity, through our consumer insights into the behaviour of 18-to-24 year-olds, to really get under the skin of this age group and understand what makes them behave in the way that they do,' Bower-Nye says. 'By knowing this we can develop a campaign that we believe will really make them change their attitude to alcohol.'

Diageo claims some success in achieving this. In a survey it commissioned after the campaign's initial burst in November 2007, 62 per cent of the 300 viewers in its sample said they were more likely to consider drinking responsibly as a result of seeing the adverts, while some 92 per cent said the ads and website were the kind 'that make you think about drinking responsibly'.

Dr Andrew McNeill, director of the Institute of Alcohol Studies, remains sceptical of corporate involvement in health education. 'One of the golden rules of public education is that the education must be coming from a credible source and I'm not sure how credible Diageo or any other company is in giving health messages.' He sees Diageo's move as predominantly a response to political pressure and the threat of tighter regulation and higher taxation. 'It's a response to perceived pressure and that pressure will increase, not just in the UK but it is certainly increasing in Europe and it will increase globally,' McNeill says.

Bower-Nye concedes that retaining market freedoms is important to Diageo, but insists this is not the prime motivation behind her work. 'We promote responsible drinking because first and foremost it is the right thing to do. By doing so, it also allows us the freedom to operate.'

Inside knowledge

Notwithstanding his misgivings, McNeill accepts that Diageo's insights into the mindset of 18 to 24-year-olds are undeniable. 'If the question is of the two different groups, health education on one side and drinks companies on the other, which has been more adept at understanding what consumers, particularly younger consumers, want, it's no contest.' McNeill adds that the campaign could be seen as a positive move if it is part of 'a changing culture' in the industry.

UK alcohol charity Alcohol Concern also believes it is important that Diageo's lead is followed by other companies. 'Diageo has always taken a position of leadership when it comes to corporate social responsibility issues and it would be great if they were to inspire other companies to make more of a contribution,' says Frank Soodeen, head of public affairs at Alcohol Concern. 'However, I think we could achieve more in this area if there were greater distance between the people who pay for these campaigns and those who execute them.'

This also relates to the question of credibility, but there seems to be a genuine dichotomy here. Diageo's closeness to the consumer provides something that public health agencies may lack, but there remain concerns about an alcohol marketer being so directly engaged in what is ostensibly a public education task. How Diageo goes about reconciling this is not clear. Bower-Nye sees Diageo's work as complementary to government campaigns that are appropriately more 'hard-hitting'. Diageo communicates a different message, Bower-Nye adds, 'which is about everyone having a choice on a night out.'

By setting up a brand unit for promoting responsible drinking, assigning one of its most experienced brand marketers to head it, and devising a new style of responsible drinking campaign, Diageo is pledging to lead by example on responsible drinks marketing. But how effective corporate advertising can be to improve standards of public health education, however, remains open to further scrutiny.

Sources

Ethical Corporation, Ben Cooper, 7 July 2008, http://www.ethicalcorp.com.

VISIT THE WEBSITE for a short response to this feature

? THINK THEORY

Consider the notion of due care in the context of Diageo's campaign. How far do drinks companies have to go to exercise due care? Are company ads the best way of ensuring that consumers are appropriately educated about the dangers of excessive drinking?

sometimes lurk behind the all-natural claims. One example he gives is of cochineal extract (also known as carmine or carminic acid, or simply hidden by the phrase 'colour added') which 'is made from the desiccated bodies of female *Dactylopius coccus* Costa, a small insect harvested mainly in Peru and the Canary Islands. The bug feeds on red cactus berries, and colour from the berries accumulates in the females and their unhatched larvae. The insects are collected, dried, and ground into a pigment. It takes about 70,000 of them to produce a pound of carmine, which is used to make processed foods look pink, red, or purple.' As Schlosser claims, carmine is used in many frozen fruit bars, sweets, and fruit fillings, as well as Ocean Spray pink-grapefruit juice drink and Danone strawberry yoghurt—yet few customers (including vegetarians!) would have any idea where the products got their colour from.

The situation, then, is not so clear-cut that we can simply limit our discussion to factual truth. The persuasive nature of most marketing communications means that we expect them to exaggerate, overclaim, boast, and make playful, if sometimes outlandish, allusions—and indeed often enjoy them for these very same reasons (Levitt 1970). When Honda claims that it has 'The Power of Dreams', we are not evaluating this as a factual statement but as a typically exaggerated claim that seeks to convince us of the superior quality of the company's products.

It is important to recognize, then, that persuasion in itself is not inherently wrong. We all attempt to persuade people to do or believe certain things at various times: your lecturer might try and persuade you about the benefits of reading your Crane and Matten, *Business Ethics* text; your friends might try and persuade you to forget about studying and join them for a night of drinking and partying. The problem comes when persuasion involves deception of some sort.

Deception is somewhat difficult to define in this respect, but is largely concerned with acts where companies deliberately create false impressions on the part of consumers to satisfy their own ends. It is one thing to put a good gloss on something—after all, much marketing communications activity, such as public relations and advertising, is intended to show organizations and their goods and services in the best possible light. However, when this involves creating or taking advantage of a belief that is actually *untrue*, then we start to move into the field of deception.

The following definition, derived from Boatright (2009: 285), should help us then to clarify the nature of deception in the context of marketing communications:

> **Deception occurs when a marketing communication either creates, or takes advantage of, a false belief that substantially interferes with the ability of people to make rational consumer choices.**

For example, if your lecturer chose to persuade you to read Crane and Matten's book by suggesting that by doing so you would automatically get better marks in the end of semester examination, then we might consider that she had attempted to create a false belief in your mind. If a person of reasonable intelligence would be likely to believe her claim, then it could be suggested that this might impair your rational judgement about whether to read the book or to go out with your friends, and thus would constitute an act of deception. However, it is important to recognize that deception is not just about telling lies, or even just about verbal claims. Consumers can also be deceived by advertisements that appear to intimate that using a certain product will make them more attractive, more popular, or more successful. They also might be deceived by images that give a false impression of a product's qualities. For example, in 2009, the Costa Brava Tourist Board was criticized for misleading consumers in using a photograph of a Caribbean beach thousands of kilometres away in its advertisements for the quintessential Spanish holiday destination (Tremlett 2009). By focusing on consumers' ability to make rational choices as a result of their exposure to marketing communications, we are essentially concerned with consumers' rights to make independent decisions free from undue influence or coercion.

Potential violations of such rights occur fairly frequently in the field of marketing communications, not least because the line that needs to be drawn between honest persuasion and outright deception becomes somewhat hazy where certain practices are concerned. For instance, some manufacturers have chosen to veil price increases by making small, unannounced reductions in package sizes whilst keeping prices constant, thus creating the impression that prices have remained stable. Should we expect them to issue us with announcements of any size changes, or given that weights and volumes have to be legally identified on packaging anyway, is it not up to us as consumers to check sizes? **Ethical Dilemma 8** presents another typical situation where questions of deception might arise.

Practices such as these are usually perfectly legal, particularly as the advertising industry continues to push for self-regulation rather than governmental regulation of its members. The European Advertising Standards Alliance (EASA), for example, brings together self-regulatory organizations and advertising industry representatives throughout Europe to promote self-regulation and to set and apply ethical rules and guidelines for good practice.[1] Even so, many marketing communications continue to push the ethical boundaries in terms of customer deception. For example, in 2008, Apple iPhone adverts were criticized for deceiving consumers by exaggerating the phone's operating speed with unrealistic depictions of the iPhone in action. A UK ad was ultimately banned following a ruling by the Advertising Standards Authority (Sweney 2008). Ultimately,

AN ETHICAL DILEMMA 8

A fitting approach to shoe selling?

You are the manager of an independent high street shoe store, specializing in trendy shoes for men and women. Your staff comprises a small team of eight salespeople who all take part in selling shoes, checking and maintaining stock, and processing sales and orders. You run a pretty successful operation, but there is intense competition in the city where you are located from major shoe-store chains, as well as one or two other independent stores. To motivate your staff, a couple of years ago you introduced an incentive scheme that gives employees 5% commission on everything they sell. This has worked pretty well—the store has maintained profitability and the employees are all fairly well paid.

You have recently hired a new salesperson, Lola, who has made quite an impact on sales. And she not only seems to be enjoying a great deal of success selling shoes, but she also has proved to be popular with everyone in the store, including the customers. Since she has arrived, though, Lola has also been giving you some cause for concern. Although no one has complained about her, you have noticed that, at times, some of her successful sales techniques sometimes do not always rely too much on the truth.

For example, on one occasion last week you noticed that she was serving a customer who was plainly unsure whether to purchase a particular pair of shoes. Lola obviously thought the shoes suited the woman, but to create a little more urgency, she said that the model the woman was interested in was the last pair in stock and that she didn't think the store would be able to get any more for another month. However, you knew for certain that there were a good five or six pairs in the stockroom, and that re-ordering when they were sold out should only take a week. Still, the customer eventually decided to buy the shoes and once she had made the decision, seemed delighted with them.

Then yesterday, Lola was serving a man who obviously wanted a particular pair of shoes that he'd seen in the window. She asked him his size (which was 43) but when she got to the storeroom, discovered that there was only a 42 and a 44 in stock. She asked you if you knew whether there was a 43 anywhere but you had to tell her no—you'd sold the last one yourself only the day before. Undeterred, Lola picked up both the 42 and the 44 and took the shoes back out to the man. Giving him the 42 first, she said to him that the company didn't sell 'odd' sizes and they only came in 42 and 44. The customer tried on the 42, but obviously found them too small. While he was doing this though, Lola took out the 44 and carefully placed an additional insole in the bottom of the shoe. 'Give this a go,' she said handing the shoes to the man, 'this should do the trick'. To his delight, they fitted fine and he said he'd take them. At this point, Lola mentioned that because the manufacturer didn't do 'odd' sizes, she'd put insoles into the shoes, which would cost an additional €3. Still pleased with the shoes, the man said fine and paid for both the shoes and the insoles.

You were unsure what to do about the situation. Although the customers seemed pleased with their purchases, Lola was clearly lying to them. Would there be any long-term repercussions of such practices? And what would the rest of the team think about it? Would they start copying Lola's successful sales techniques too?

Questions

1 What are the arguments for and against Lola's actions?

2 Do you think such practices are common in sales situations? What would you think if you were a co-worker or a customer of Lola's?

3 To what extent do you think your incentive scheme has contributed to Lola's actions?

4 How would you approach this situation as Lola's manager?

any assessment of consumer deception will depend critically on what degree of interference in consumers' rational decision-making we decide is acceptable, how well consumers can delineate between fact and fiction, and whether by getting this wrong they will be significantly harmed. After all, as Boatright (2009: 285) contends: 'claims in life insurance advertising, for example, ought to be held to a higher standard than those for chewing gum'.

The second level at which criticisms of marketing communications have been raised concerns their **social and cultural impact on society**. For instance, the UK self-regulatory body, the Advertising Standards Authority (ASA), suggests that advertisements should be 'legal, decent, honest & truthful' in that they:

- Should not cause serious or widespread offence.
- Should not cause undue harm or distress.
- Should contain nothing that might provoke anti-social or violent behaviour.
- Should contain nothing that is likely to result in the physical, mental or moral harm of children.[2]

Most of the complaints received by the ASA refer to advertisements that have caused offence, such as those featuring nudity, or shocking images of one sort or another. However, the argument about social and cultural impacts also concerns the aggregate impact of marketing communications in society rather than just being specifically focused on particular campaigns or techniques. There are a number of strands to this argument, but the main objections appear to be that marketing communications:

- **Are intrusive and unavoidable.** We are exposed to hundreds of adverts every day, on the television and radio, in newspapers and magazines, on the internet, in stores, on billboards, on the side of buses, at concerts, on tickets and programmes, on athletes and footballers, to the extent that almost no public space is free from the reach of corporate branding, sponsorship, or promotion. In her bestselling book about the ubiquity of branding, *No Logo*, Naomi Klein (2000) highlights the increasing incursion of brands into previously unbranded space including schools, towns, streets, politics, even people (think, for example, about the popularity of the Nike 'swoosh' logo as a template for tattoos).

- **Create artificial wants.** The persuasive nature of advertising has long been argued to make us want things that we do not particularly need (e.g. Packard 1957). The economist John Kenneth Galbraith has perhaps been the most popular advocate of this argument, suggesting that firms generate artificial wants in order to create demand for their products (Galbraith 1974). For example, one might question whether we really felt a need for products such as personal computers, mobile phones, or cars that talk to us before companies developed the technology and set out to create a demand for them. The problem here, though, is in defining what are 'real' wants and needs and what are 'artificial' or 'false' ones. Jean Baudrillard (1997), for example, condemns Galbraith's 'moralizing idealism' and his depiction of the individual as a passive victim of the system, suggesting instead that the consumer is an active participant seeking to satisfy very real needs for social identity and differentiation through consumption.

- **Reinforce consumerism and materialism.** More broadly then, the saturation of everyday life under a deluge of marketing communications has been argued to generate and perpetuate an ideology of materialism in society, and to institute in our culture an identification of consumption with happiness (Pollay 1986). Contemporary cultural studies authors, as well as the popular press, now commonly depict modern Western society as being a 'consumer society', where not only is consumption the principal site of meaning and identity, but it also increasingly dominates other arenas of life such as politics, education, health, and personal relations (e.g. Baudrillard 1997; Featherstone 1991). Thus, emotional or psychological ills, such as a broken relationship, depression, or low self-esteem, might be more readily addressed through 'retail therapy' or 'compensatory consumption' than through other more traditional or professionalized channels (Woodruffe 1997).

- **Create insecurity and perpetual dissatisfaction.** Ashamed of your mobile phone? Embarrassed by your cheap brand of coffee? Guilty that your baby isn't clothed in the most advanced and effective (and expensive) diapers? Worried that your feminine sanitary products will let you down? These are all typical worries and insecurities that ad campaigns identify and perpetuate in order to enhance demand. Hence, critics of advertising have further contended that by presenting glorified, often unattainable images of 'the good life' for us to aspire to, marketing communications create (and indeed rely on creating) constant dissatisfaction with our lives and institute a pervading sense of insecurity and inadequacy (Pollay 1986).

- **Perpetuate social stereotypes.** Finally, marketing communications have also been argued to spread socially undesirable stereotypes of certain categories of person and lifestyle (see Pollay 1986), such that women are always either housewives or sex objects; health, beauty, and happiness are only possible with 'perfect' body shapes; 'nuclear' families become associated with 'normality'; and racial minorities, the disabled, and gays and lesbians become excluded from the picture of 'normal' life. Whilst the usual defence to this argument is that marketers no more than reflect the social norms of target audiences (Greyser 1972), it is clear that it is in companies' own interest to depict images desired by their customers. For example, a few years ago an Indian television commercial for the best-selling skin whitener 'Fair & Lovely' produced by Hindustan Lever (a subsidiary of Unilever) caused a great deal of controversy because it suggested that fairer skinned women could find better husbands and jobs than those with darker skins. Whilst the Indian broadcasting minister called it a 'repellent' advertisement, the company pointed to research that showed that 90% of Indians wanted to use whiteners because fair skin is seen as an aspirational step up the social and economic ladder (Luce and Merchant 2003).

Such criticisms have been common for at least the last 30 years. **Ethics on Screen 8**, however, gives a very contemporary account of some of the major critiques of marketing in respect to the race to develop products to treat 'female sexual dysfunction'. Nonetheless, many social commentators also contend that, as a society, we have never been so informed and educated about the role of advertising, promotion, and branding as we are today, and that it provides us with much needed enjoyment and escapism (Holbrook 1987). Accordingly, it would appear that consumers now are much more media literate and less likely to be the 'victims' of marketing communications than when these criticisms were first raised. To some extent, then, the wider ethical case against marketing communication as a social phenomenon is fairly difficult to uphold, not least because many of the criticisms often essentially boil down to criticisms of capitalism (Phillips 1997).

However, this is not to deny that these problems with marketing communications are significant, more that if we accept capitalism, we must also to some extent accept these problems. The question remains, though, given such drawbacks, to what extent should marketers be held responsible for the consequences. Moreover, we must also question how far marketing communications should increasingly be allowed to advance into hitherto ad-free social spaces. As the success of Klein's (2000) book attests, this is perhaps one of the most popular criticisms currently raised against marketing communications today, and as we will discuss later in the chapter, this is particularly pertinent when considering the global context of marketing and consumption.

? THINK THEORY

Think about the question of whether marketers should be responsible for the aggregate consequences of their actions. Which ethical theories do you think would typically be used to argue either for or against this proposition?

VISIT THE WEBSITE for a short response to this feature

Ethical issues in pricing

It is perhaps unsurprising that issues of pricing are often among the criticisms levelled at companies, for it is in pricing that we most clearly see the potential for the interests of producers and consumers to diverge. Whilst consumers may desire to exchange the goods and services they require for as little cost as possible, producers are likely to want to maximize the amount of revenue they can extract from the consumer. Pricing issues are thus central to the notion of a fair exchange between the two parties, and the **right to a fair price** might typically be regarded as one of the key rights of consumers as stakeholders.

VISIT THE WEBSITE for links to useful sources of further information

VISIT THE WEBSITE to see a trailer for 'Orgasm Inc'

ETHICS ON SCREEN 8

Orgasm Inc

A sexy feature-length indictment of big pharma

Antonia Zerbisias, *Toronto Star*

Orgasm Inc, which premiered in 2009 at the Toronto Hot Docs Canadian International Film Festival, is a humorous and revealing documentary about what director Liz Canner calls 'the strange science of female pleasure'.

The film is the result of a nine-year journey by Canner chronicling the attempt by the pharmaceutical industry to medicalize so-called 'female sexual dysfunction' (FSD) and devise a potentially billion dollar 'cure'. Having first been drawn into the project during an assignment to edit erotic videos used in drug trials for a pharmaceutical company, she sets out to research and record the commodification of female sexuality, and the female orgasm in particular, by the medial industry. Along the way, she meets a colourful cast of characters, including a doctor who is testing an Orgasmatron (which involves having electrodes inserted into the spine and activated at the press of a button), a sex shop owner who gatecrashes pharmaceutical conferences to educate the attendees, and a vintage vibrator collector who provides insight into the history of female 'hysteria'.

Orgasm Inc. movie poster. Documentary produced and directed by Liz Canner, 2009. To purchase the DVD go to www.orgasminc.org.

Orgasm Inc is well researched and provocative in its exploration of the development of new markets and products to treat FSD. It is also striking in the way that it really shows the depth of the corporate world's reach into the most intimate areas of our lives. After the tremendous commercial success of Viagra, many pharmaceutical companies sought to discover whether similar products could be developed for women. The problem though is that while problems in bed with many men are clearly, say, a 'mechanical' dysfunction, the alleged absence of sexual satisfaction with women is a much more complex phenomenon. However, the firm shows that by carefully funding research, paying celebrity sex columnists and TV presenters, and influencing a whole host of other players, the pharmaceutical industry has provided considerable momentum for the development of FSD as a medically recognized and treatable condition.

Once that had been achieved, the next step is obvious: create a pill, a patch, a lotion, an implant—in short, a profitable product to 'cure' women of FSD. As the film demonstrates though, the industry faces considerable problems in developing a safe and efficacious product. More fundamentally, numerous experts deny that FSD is even a real condition that can be pharmaceutically treated. Rather, they suggest, difficulties in experiencing a pleasurable and satisfying sex life for women depend less on basic physical factors, and more on a whole host of social, psychological, economic, and relational conditions.

Ultimately, the goal of the film is to help protect women from being deceived into undergoing unnecessary and possibly unsafe medical treatments, but it is also a remarkably insightful look at the role of marketing and product development in reshaping our everyday assumptions about health and illness, sex and desire.

Sources
http://www.orgasminc.org.
Gopaul, S. 2009. Orgasm Inc. *Popjournalism*, 6 May: http://www.popjournalism.ca
Zerbisias, A. 2009. Female 'desire drug' a real turnoff. *Toronto Star*, 29 Apr.: http://www.thestar.com

The concept of a fair price is open to a number of different views, but typically is thought of as the result of a mutual agreement by the buyer and seller under competitive conditions. Thus, under neoclassical economics, prices should be set at the market equilibrium, where marginal cost equals marginal revenue. However, the assumption here is that buyers and sellers can leave the market at any time, and that there are a number of competing offerings in the market. Problems of fairness arise then when prevailing market conditions allow companies to exploit an advantageous market position, such as a monopoly, or where consumers are unable to leave the market, perhaps because they have an irrevocable need for a product, such as for housing, food, or medicine.

In most countries, there are regulatory agencies in place to police market distortions of this kind. In Europe, for instance, organizations, such as the Bundeskartellamt in Germany and the Nederlandse Mededingingsautoriteit in the Netherlands, provide national protection, whilst the Competition Directorate of the European Commission deals with pan-European issues. In Japan, a Fair Trade Commission deals with such issues, whilst in China, enforcement is handled through the Ministry of Commerce. However, ethical problems still arise in different countries, either because the distortions are opaque, or because market conditions fail to explain the perceived unfairness of prices.

There are four main types of pricing practices where ethical problems are likely to arise:

- **Excessive pricing.** Sometimes known as *price gouging*, the charge of excessive pricing rests on the assumption that the fair price for goods and services has been exceeded. Whilst this may well be due to prevailing market conditions, as discussed above, the perceived fairness of a price may also depend on other factors, such as the relative costs of the producer, or the price charged to other consumers. For example, accusations of overcharging of car customers in certain parts of Europe has followed publication of price differentials by the European Commission, a sample of which is given in **Figure 8.3.** These figures show that Germany is typically the most expensive market overall in the EU, whilst Finland and Denmark are among the cheapest.

- **Price fixing.** The problem of excessive pricing is probably most difficult to address when, rather than being the actions of one single firm, it occurs as a result of collusion between competing firms to fix prices above the market rate. This is illegal in Europe, the US, and most other parts of the world, but difficulties in detection and conviction mean that many instances of price fixing go unnoticed. However, the last few

Make and model	Approx. Price in Euros (000s excluding tax)				
	Germany	Finland	Italy	Denmark	UK
Audi A3	19.0	16.9	18.4	16	16.3
Ford Focus	15.3	12	13.7	12.2	15.9
Nissan Almera	13.5	11.4	12.1	10.9	13.9
Peugeot 207	12.2	10.5	10.9	9.5	10.5
Renault Laguna	23.4	26	26.4	25.5	20.2
VW Golf	13.6	11.1	12.8	10.9	12.9

Figure 8.3. Price differentials in car prices across Europe
Source: Based on figures from 'Car prices within the European Union at 1/01/2008', European Commission, Competition DG, http://ec.europa.eu/competition/sectors/motor_vehicles/prices/2008_04_full.pdf/

years have seen an intensification of investigations into price fixing, leading to recent convictions of big brand companies such as British Airways, LG, Sharp, Hitachi, and Nintendo.

- **Predatory pricing.** A further problem of anti-competitive practice can occur when a firm adopts the opposite course of action, and rather than charging *above* market rate, sets price significantly *below* the market rate in order to force out competition. Known as predatory pricing, this practice allows firms with a size or other advantage to use their power to eliminate competitors from the market so that more favourable market conditions can be exploited. For example, in 2009 the European Court of Justice confirmed that Wanadoo, a subsidiary of France Télécom, should be fined €10m for predatory pricing of its broadband Internet services during the early 2000s. Following a European Commission investigation, Wanadoo, the clear market leader at the time, was found to have set retail prices below cost, which restricted market entry and the development potential for competitors, thus harming consumers. In welcoming the Court's decision, the European Commission noted that since the original investigation and conviction, more providers have been able to enter the French market and prices for internet access in France had fallen substantially. In fact, by 2009, French broadband prices were the second cheapest among OECD countries (Japan being the lowest).[3]

- **Deceptive pricing.** Finally, unfair pricing can also occur when firms price in such a way that the true cost to consumers is deliberately obscured. For example, many airlines have been criticized in the past by advertising watchdogs for misleading consumers over the price of budget air tickets. Advertised prices that were often only available for a small percentage of flights, with substantial booking restrictions, and with no acknowledgement of the additional taxes and fees that would be levied, were argued to have deceived consumers into thinking prices were lower than they actually were. Given that advertised prices represent a claim on the part of producers, deceptive pricing can be assessed in the same way as deception in marketing communications.

Clearly, the issue of pricing is a crucial one when it comes to assessing and protecting the relative rights and responsibilities of consumers and companies. As we can see here, much of the activity associated with ethical practice in this area actually also concerns the relationships between firms and their competitors. This we shall examine in more depth in the next chapter.

> **? THINK THEORY**
>
> Fairness in pricing will obviously depend on how we define fairness. One way we can do this is by using Rawls' theory of justice (p. 113). How would the practices outlined here be assessed according to this theory?

VISIT THE WEBSITE for a short response to this feature

Ethical issues in channels of distribution

In the final area of marketing management, channels of distribution, we are concerned with the ethical issues and problems that occur in the relations between manufacturers and the firms which deliver their products to market, such as wholesalers, logistics firms, and retailers. This is often referred to as the *product supply chain*. Given that we shall be devoting most of the next chapter to such relationships between firms and their suppliers, we shall do no more than mention here that ethical problems clearly arise in this context—for example, when retailers demand 'slotting fees' from manufacturers in order to stock their products, or when assessing the environmental impact of different logistics systems—and reserve a fuller discussion until the following chapter.

Ethical issues in marketing strategy

Marketing strategy is primarily concerned with the decisions of market selection and targeting. The targeting of markets is central to marketing theory and practice, and the choice of specific groups of consumers (or market segments) to target has been carefully refined over the years by companies eager to focus their efforts on 'attractive' segments, characterized by factors such as high profitability, low competition, or strong potential for growth. As marketers have become more adept at targeting specific groups of consumers—and even sometimes individual consumers—important criticisms have emerged. In particular, critics tend to be concerned over potential violations of the consumer's **right to be treated fairly**. This violation can happen in two main ways:

- **Vulnerability**. Some target markets are composed of consumers who are deemed 'vulnerable' in some way, such as children, the elderly, the poor, or the sick, and marketers may unfairly take advantage of this vulnerability to satisfy their own ends.

- **Exclusion**. Certain groups of consumers may be discriminated against and excluded from being able to gain access to products that are necessary for them to achieve a reasonable quality of life.

Targeting vulnerable consumers

If we begin with the targeting of vulnerable consumers, it is evident that this concern rests largely on this perceived right to fair treatment for consumers, which imposes certain duties on sellers. Specifically, arguments criticizing unfair targeting practices are based on the degree of *vulnerability of the target*, and on the *perceived harmfulness of the product* to those consumers (N.C. Smith and Cooper-Martin 1997).

Vulnerability of the target is somewhat difficult to determine here, and to some extent will be contextually defined. Clearly, though, there is a case for saying that some consumers are less capable than others of making an informed, reasoned decision about whether to purchase a product. There are a number of reasons why consumers might be vulnerable, such as because they:

- Lack sufficient education or information to use products safely or to fully understand the consequences of their actions.
- Are easily confused or manipulated due to old age or senility.
- Are in exceptional physical or emotional need due to illness, bereavement, or some other unfortunate circumstance.
- Lack the necessary income to competently maintain a reasonable quality for life for themselves and their dependants.
- Are too young to make competent independent decisions.

In the case of customers perceived to be vulnerable in some way, the idea that consumers should be treated as ends in themselves is often said to give rise to a **duty of care** on the part of sellers. Where it is possible for a seller to exploit the vulnerability of a potential customer—for example, where a drug company might be in a position to charge an excessively high price for life-saving medications, or an insurance salesperson might consider exploiting the illiteracy of a potential investor by misrepresenting the terms and conditions of the investment—it can be argued that the seller has an inherent duty to act in such a way as to respect the interests of the consumer, as well as the interests of themselves and their company.

For example, one of the main groups typically agreed to be vulnerable in some way are young children. A child of 4 or 5 might reasonably be said to lack the cognitive skills necessary to make entirely rational choices. Therefore, it is perhaps not surprising that the direct targeting of young children, especially for toys, has been the subject of much criticism over the years (see E.S. Moore 2004; Sharp Paine 1993). It is not so much that the children themselves purchase the products targeted at them, but that advertisers seek to encourage and take advantage of the 'pester power' that children have towards their parents. Practices such as daytime television advertising for toys, as well as merchandising tie-ups with children's movies and computer games like *Harry Potter* and *Shrek*, might be said to take advantage of young children, who are highly impressionable, incapable of distinguishing the persuasive intent of advertising, and cannot understand the usual limitations of family purchasing budgets. The development of commercially sponsored websites containing games, promotions, and contests designed for children (often with brands as an integral element of the game as a game piece, prize, or secret treasure) has raised further concerns about the blurring of advertising and entertainment directed at children (E.S. Moore 2004). Whilst one could maintain that it is the responsibility of parents as the ultimate purchasers to resist the pestering of their children, this does not detract from the criticism that by directly targeting a vulnerable group, advertisers might be guilty of violating consumer rights through deliberate manipulation and treating children only as means to their own ends (De George 1999: 283).

Still there is the difficulty here in deciding at what age children can be legitimately regarded as able to make a rational, informed decision. Although there is considerable controversy over research results, it is apparent that even very young children tend to recognize and recall advertising very well, but it would appear that they do not have a good understanding of its persuasive intent until they are around 8 years old (Gunter et al. 2005)—but even then may not invoke that understanding when forming judgements (E.S. Moore 2004). Many countries have actually introduced legislation restricting advertising to children, although these restrictions vary enormously between countries, even within a single continent such as Europe (see **Figure 8.4**). Greece, for example, bans toy advertising on television until after 11pm, Norway does not permit advertising during children's programmes, and Sweden bans all advertising to children under 12.

Specific advertising restriction	Country or area
Advertising to children under the age of 12 years is banned.	Norway, Sweden.
Advertising before and after children's programmes is prohibited.	Austria, Belgium (Flemish part only), Luxembourg, Norway.
Advertising of toys to children between 7 am and 11 pm is prohibited; advertising of war toys is prohibited at all times.	Greece.
Advertisements during cartoons are prohibited; advertisements using cartoon characters before and after the programmes in which they appear are also prohibited.	Italy.
Advertisements that attempt to persuade a child to buy a product through a direct offer are prohibited.	Finland, Germany.
Advertisements in which sales pitches are delivered by familiar cartoon characters or children are prohibited.	Finland.
Figures and puppets that appear in children's programmes are prohibited from appearing in advertisements.	Denmark.
Children's television personalities are prohibited from appearing in any advertisements before 9 pm; merchandise based on children's television programmes must not be advertised within 2 hours preceeding or succeeding the programme concerned.	United Kingdom.

Figure 8.4. Restrictions on television advertising to children in selected European countries

Source: Reproduced with permission of the World Health Organization from Corinna Hawkes 2004. *Marketing food to children: the global regulatory environment.* Geneva: World Health Organization: Table 4, p. 19. http://whqlibdoc.who.int/publications/2004/9241591579.pdf

In other countries, such as Spain and France, governments have desisted from regulation, insisting that not only is exposure to advertising necessary preparation for life in consumer society, but also that firms have a democratic right to inform potential consumers about products which, in the final analysis, are not likely to pose any real harm to them. Nonetheless, concerns about escalating obesity and other health problems among children have prompted considerable debate about advertising of food and drink products to children, which in turn has led to an escalation in *industry self-regulation*. In a comprehensive review of regulatory efforts across more than 70 countries, Corinna Hawkes (2007) showed that recent efforts to curb food advertising to children have mainly focused on self-regulation from business rather than new government restrictions, with more than a 100% increase in just two years. One prominent example of industry self-regulation in this arena has been the 2008 commitment by the global soft drinks industry, including Coca-Cola and PepsiCo, to cease advertising of soft drinks to children under the age of 12 across all print, TV, internet, SMS, and other media.[4]

The issue of the **perceived harmfulness of the product** is also a critical one in assessing the ethics of particular targeting approaches. Although there is evidence of a general social unease with the targeting of vulnerable groups, whatever the harmfulness of the product, it is perhaps unsurprising that much of the literature dealing with ethics and targeting has focused on products with a clear and present potential to do harm, such as cigarettes and alcohol (N.C. Smith and Cooper-Martin 1997). By focusing on such products, the ethical arguments shift somewhat from a focus on rights and duties towards a greater focus on consequences. Hence, the argument is less that taking advantage of consumer vulnerability is wrong in and of itself, but that it is primarily wrong only if the consumer might be expected to suffer in some way. For instance, the issue of selling 'sub-prime' mortgages really came to prominence in the wake of the financial crisis in 2008. The devastating consequence of people losing their homes brought to the fore ongoing questions about the ethics of targeting home purchasers who could not really afford the mortgages they were being sold.

Consumer exclusion

Some criticisms of marketing strategy focus not on who *is* targeted but on who *is not* included in the target market. In some cases, this can lead to accidental or even deliberate exclusion of certain groups of consumers from accessing particular goods and services that might be deemed necessary for them to maintain a reasonable quality of life, thus exacerbating social exclusion and other problems. This problem has come to particular prominence in recent years with widespread debates around, for example, financial exclusion of poor families, lack of access to affordable water and other amenities in undeveloped regions, and the exclusion of low-income neighbourhoods from access to fresh and healthy food. As Kempson and Whyley (1999) show, exclusion can take a variety of forms, including:

- **Access exclusion**—where lack of appropriate distribution outlets and channels may prevent people from accessing essential goods and services such as postal and health services, utilities, and food.

- **Condition exclusion**—where restrictive conditions on product offerings such as financial service products may prevent certain groups from being able to qualify for purchasing them.
- **Price exclusion**—where the price of a product is simply too expensive for consumers to be able to purchase it in sufficient quantities for a reasonable standard of living.
- **Marketing exclusion**—where firms deliberately exclude certain groups from their target marketing and sales activities.
- **Self-exclusion**—where people may decide that there is little point applying for or trying to access a product because they believe they would be refused, either due to previous negative experiences, or because of a belief that 'they don't accept people who live round here'.

In the case of financial products, evidence suggests that in countries such as the UK something like 7% of households have no financial services, 6–9% of adults have no bank account, and almost 30% have no access to credit from conventional providers (Devlin 2005). At least some of this is due to the spread of the practice of 'redlining', whereby particular areas in towns and cities where the populace predominantly has low incomes and very poor credit ratings are denied access to financial products, primarily through marketing and condition exclusion. By effectively drawing a red line around particular geographical no-go zones, critics charge that companies can be said either to be discriminating against consumers (by judging them on their residential location rather than individual merit) or to be treating them unfairly by preventing them from participating in normal market activity. This practice can be particularly problematic when consumers are subsequently forced to enter into arrangements with unscrupulous, sometimes illegal, substitute providers of these products, such as loan sharks and unregistered moneylenders. In the huge Dharavi slum in Mumbai, for example, the cost of credit is over 50 times more than in a rich neighbourhood of the city, whilst potable water is almost 40 times more expensive (Prahalad and Hammond 2002).

Ethical issues in market research

The final area where we need to examine the rights of consumers is in relation to market research. The main issue here is one of the possible threats posed to the consumer's **right to privacy**. Market research involves the systematic collection and analysis of enormous amounts of data pertaining to individual consumers, including much information that consumers may not know that researchers have in their possession, and much that they might not wish to have shared with a third party. Surveys suggest that most consumers are concerned about the type, accuracy, and deployment of information held about them, but it appears that many are also unaware of the regulations in place to protect them, and make only limited use of strategies to avoid infringement of privacy (Dommeyer and Gross 2003).

Many of the most pressing issues of consumer privacy are related to dangers posed by developments in information and communication technology, especially with regard to **online privacy**. As Milne and Culnan (2004) suggest, the online environment in particular makes it possible to collect new forms of personal information, such as clickstream data or location data that go beyond traditional market research information. Hence, 'disclosing information to an online organization requires a degree of trust because of information asymmetries that limit the consumer's knowledge about the organization's information practices and whether their personal information may be used in ways that could result in harm to the consumer, or lead to unwanted future solicitations, credit card theft, or even a hijacking of one's online identity' (Milne and Culnan 2004: 16). For instance, the advertising targeting service marketed by Phorm (which enables companies to build up profiles of their customers based on their browsing history and then target adverts at them) stirred up considerable controversy in the late 2000s, particularly after it was revealed that the telecoms company BT had secretly trialled the software on consumers without seeking their consent (Arthur 2008).

Another major area of pressing concern that has arisen recently is the use of **genetic testing** results by insurance companies. Whilst there are various advantages to the emergence of tests which can predict the likelihood of an individual's genetic predisposition to certain conditions and illnesses, there are fears that insurance companies might use the information to increase premiums or deny cover altogether for those with high susceptibility. Whilst one might argue that such information is private, particularly if it might be used to create a 'genetic underclass' unable to obtain health or life cover, it can also be argued that premiums are 'fairest' when based on the best available information. The case for such 'genetic discrimination' has yet to be fully resolved, and in the UK, for example, the government has an agreement with the Association of British Insurers to maintain a moratorium on the use of predictive genetic tests results in assessing applications for life insurance policies until 2011.[5]

■ Globalization and consumers: the ethical challenges of the global marketplace

Convergence in consumer needs across different countries has been widely identified as one of the key drivers of globalization in business, not least because brands such as Coca-Cola, McDonald's, Microsoft, Sony, and Toyota among others have been able to expand into multiple international markets, often necessitating little if any adaptation in their products to local tastes and preferences.

At one level, these developments have clearly extended many of the issues identified in the previous section to an international context, and indeed have made a number of the problems more acute. The problem of 'acceptable' levels of safety, for example, is accentuated where the lack of even basic products and services might mean that even partially defective products may be better than none. For example, it might be deemed appropriate for a Western pharmaceutical company to supply drugs that tackle dysentery in a country such as India, where the incidence of such a condition is extremely high, even though sale may be banned or delayed in Europe because of side-effects (Donaldson 1996).

At another level, globalization has also brought with it a new set of problems and issues relevant to consumer stakeholders (Witkowski 2005). Broadly speaking, these expanded, reframed, and/or new issues can be explained in relation to three main considerations:

- Different standards of consumer protection.
- Exporting consumerism and cultural homogenization.
- The role of markets in addressing poverty and development.

Different standards of consumer protection

As we saw at the beginning of the chapter, international organizations such as the UN recognize a set of global rights for consumers. However, the fact remains that the level of protection offered to consumers varies considerably across the globe, in terms of both government regulation, and the standards offered by companies. Globalization therefore offers firms the opportunity to exploit these differences, especially where the provision of higher standards of protection, such as may be offered in developed countries, may be seen as an added cost burden that can be avoided in developing countries.

A good example is provided by the global tobacco industry. With markets in decline in most developed countries, tobacco firms have increasingly looked to developing countries for continued growth. Restrictions on the marketing of tobacco in Africa, Asia, and Latin America have frequently been less stringent than in North America and parts of Europe, giving companies more opportunity for concerted marketing campaigns direct to customers. Sales of cigarettes in developing countries have therefore escalated enormously, with China now representing the largest market globally for tobacco sales—some 37% of all cigarettes sold in 2007—and countries such as Russia and Indonesia among the top five consumers of cigarettes.[6] Unsurprisingly, tobacco companies have been increasingly criticized for targeting cigarettes at customers in developing countries, especially as such customers might have less knowledge of health problems, be more susceptible to inducements to purchase such goods as free gifts, and less likely to be protected through regulations on advertising.[7] A major response to this situation emerged with the development of the World Health Organization Framework Convention on Tobacco Control (FCTC), which went into force in 2005. This commits signatory countries to a range of measures designed to reduce tobacco demand and supply, including a ban on tobacco advertising, promotion, and sponsorship. As of 2009, 164 countries had signed up to the framework, making it one of the most widely embraced treaties in UN history.[8] Such a concerted international response is rare, however, and for products such as food and drink, medicines, and automotives, substantial differences persist across countries.

Exporting consumerism and cultural homogenization

A second problem associated with the drive by companies to expand into new international markets with brands already successful at home is that they frequently run up against the accusation that they are not only exporting products, but are also ultimately exporting a whole set of cultural values too. A prominent focus of debate here is the potential for mass marketing of global products and brands to contribute to the erosion of local cultures and the expansion of **cultural homogenization** (Baughn and Buchanan 2001; Witkowski 2005). Whilst colonialism and global trade have long provided a context for cultural exchange or imposition, the unprecedented international success of global brands has led to increasing concerns over rising standardization and uniformity (Klein 2000). There are few high streets in the cities of Europe, Asia, or North America now without the ubiquitous McDonald's, KFC, or Starbucks outlets, or where the shops do not stock the same global products, such as the Apple iPod, Diesel jeans, Heineken beer, or L'Oréal cosmetics. Even in the entertainment and media industries, Hollywood movies, recording artists such as Beyonce, and even sports stars like David Beckham or Tiger Woods have become global brands that have driven out interest in local cultural products. In their defence, of course, global marketers point to the fact that they have never forced consumers to buy their products, and that their success is simply based on giving people what they want. However, as we shall examine in more detail in the next chapter, some have argued that the tactics of many such multinationals include the deliberate and aggressive removal of incumbent domestic rivals.

Whatever the intentions behind international marketing efforts, the drive for global dominance has meant an intensification of marketing activity in countries once largely immunized from mass marketing activities. Expansion in global communications technologies such as satellite TV and the internet has meant that the promotion and glorification of consumerist lifestyles now takes place not just within national borders but on a global scale (Sklair 1991). The increasing predominance of **consumerist ideologies** in emerging and transitional economies such as China and the countries of Central Europe has therefore raised considerable debate, particularly around the role of advertising in promoting consumerism (e.g. Zhao and Belk 2008).

These developments raise a number of complex ethical problems, particularly at a time when Western modes of consumption are increasingly subject to criticism due to their role in fostering socially and environmentally undesirable consequences. By promoting products and brands that are beyond the purchasing possibilities of the majority of consumers in developing countries, are multinationals simply reproducing dissatisfaction on an even greater scale than previously possible? Should emerging economies countries be 'protected' from potentially making the same mistakes or do they also have a right to the same 'opportunities' in terms of raising consumption levels? Are indigenous patterns of consumption in less developed countries inherently better, fairer, or more sustainable than Western patterns or are they even more inequitable and destructive? Whose responsibility is it, if anyone's, to police consumption activities?

The launch of the Tata Motors 'Nano' car in 2009 brought many of these ethical questions to the surface. By targeting a price of 1 lakh or 100,000 rupees (approx. €1500), the so-called 'People's Car' utilized cost-saving innovations to offer millions of Indians a once unimaginable opportunity for car ownership. On the one side, advocates argued that the fuel-efficient car would revolutionize mobility, drive economic growth, and offer a safer and more environmentally friendly alternative to motor rickshaws and other common forms of transport in developing countries. On the other hand, critics have argued that the Nano's likely impact on an already expanding car market in developing countries could be socially and environmentally disastrous and bring countries like India to gridlock.

? THINK THEORY

Compare arguments based on consequences with arguments based on rights and justice in assessing the impact of a product such as the Tata Nano in India. What recommendations do you think proponents of these theories would have for responsible marketing practice in such a context?

VISIT THE WEBSITE for a short response to this feature

The role of markets in addressing poverty and development

Finally, as the Tata Nano example suggests, globalization also raises the prospect of firms potentially targeting their products at a much wider, but far poorer, market of low-income consumers in developing countries. This issue has received considerable impetus in recent years with the introduction of the **bottom of the pyramid** concept. Developed mainly by C.K. Prahalad and his colleagues, the concept essentially urges multinationals to tap into the 'fortune at the bottom of the pyramid' of economic development by offering innovative products and services to the world's poorest people in Africa, Asia, and Latin America. As Prahalad and Hammond (2002: 48) put it: 'By stimulating commerce and development at the bottom of the economic pyramid, MNCs could radically improve the lives of billions of people and help bring into being a more stable, less dangerous world. Achieving this goal does not require multinationals to spearhead global social development initiatives for charitable purposes. They need only act in their own self-interest, for there are enormous business benefits to be gained by entering developing markets.'

In the global marketplace, this idea has gained significant attention and there is clearly a case to be made for advancing poverty reduction by developing what the United Nations Development Programme (UNDP) calls 'inclusive markets' in less developed countries and regions. Examples of successful initiatives include the provision of microcredit services for poor entrepreneurs in the informal sector in Brazil by Banco Real (owned by the Spanish multinational bank, Santander), the launch of a high nutrition yoghurt product for poor children in rural Bangladesh by the French food company Danone, and the development of a low-cost laptop for school children in developing countries by the American microchip manufacturer Intel.

Despite garnering considerable enthusiasm, the bottom of the pyramid concept has also met with some important criticism. For example, Aneel Karnani (2007) has identified what he terms the 'mirage' of marketing to the bottom of the pyramid, suggesting that the profit opportunities are actually quite limited, and that firms looking to tackle poverty should focus on the poor primarily as producers rather than as consumers. As he contends, 'the only way to alleviate poverty is to raise the real income of the poor' (2007: 91). Certainly, there are few examples of firms actually generating anything like the 'fortune' that Prahalad promises, leading us to conclude that the drive towards more inclusive markets in developing countries probably relies as much on social purpose and corporate responsibility as it does on naked profit motivation—a point underscored by the relatively high proportion of non-profit social enterprises that have flourished in this niche (Karnani 2007).

■ Consumers and corporate citizenship: consumer sovereignty and the politics of purchasing

We said at the beginning of this chapter that changing expectations and improved protection of consumer rights had moved us away from the traditional conception of *caveat emptor* or buyer beware. More now is expected of firms in terms of how they treat their customers. But what exactly would constitute truly ethical marketing in this sense? According to Craig Smith (1995), the most effective way to answer this question is by drawing on the notion of *consumer sovereignty*.

Consumer sovereignty

Consumer sovereignty is a key concept within neoclassical economics. It essentially suggests that under perfect competition, consumers drive the market; they express their needs and desires as a demand, which firms subsequently respond to by supplying them with the goods and services that they require. This gives rise to the idea that the customer is king—or, to put it another way, that consumers are sovereign in the market.

Real markets, however, are rarely characterized by perfect competition: consumers may not know enough about competing offerings to find out exactly where they can get the best deals (what economists call informational asymmetries); there may be very few competitors in some markets, thus limiting consumer choice; some firms may be able to take advantage of monopolistic positions to exploit consumers with high prices; and so on. Hence, in practice, there are clearly some limitations to the power and sovereignty of consumers. In many situations, they simply cannot exercise informed choice.

These limitations in making informed choices are an ethical problem on two counts. First, it may well mean that individual transactions will be unfair in some way to certain consumers. And secondly, that without consumer sovereignty, the economic system itself does not work efficiently and allocate resources fairly (see N.C. Smith 1990). In basic terms, this would imply that the economy serves business interests rather than those of consumers. By the same token, then, enhanced consumer sovereignty would therefore shift the balance of power *away* from business and *towards* the consumer. It is for this reason that Smith (1995) argues that consumer sovereignty represents a suitable ideal for marketing ethics to aspire to, and to be evaluated against. According to this argument, the greater the degree of sovereignty in a specific exchange or market, the more ethical the transaction should be regarded as. But how is consumer sovereignty to be assessed? For this, Smith (1995) proposes the **consumer sovereignty test** (CST).

According to Smith (1995), consumer sovereignty is comprised of three factors:

- **Consumer capability.** The degree of freedom from limitations in rational decision-making enjoyed by the consumer, for example, from vulnerability or coercion.
- **Information.** The availability and quality of relevant data pertaining to a purchase decision.
- **Choice.** The extent of the opportunity available to freely switch to another supplier.

	Dimension	Definition	Sample criteria for establishing adequacy
	Consumer capability.	Freedom from limitations in rational decision-making.	Vulnerability factors, e.g. age, education, health.
Consumer Sovereignty Test.	**Information.**	Availability and quality of relevant data.	Quantity, comparability and complexity of information; degree of bias or deception.
	Choice.	Opportunity for switching.	Number of competitors and level of competition; switching costs.

Figure 8.5. Consumer sovereignty test
Source: Derived from Smith. 1995.

The CST therefore is a test of the extent to which consumers are capable, informed, and free to choose when confronted with a potential purchase situation. If sovereignty is substantially restricted—say if the consumer's capability is reduced through vulnerability, or the option of switching is precluded due to high switching costs—then we might suggest that any exchange that happens may well be, at the very least, open to ethical question.

How exactly one defines what is an adequate level of sovereignty is of course rather hard to define. Sovereignty is a relative, rather than an absolute, concept. However, some of the ways in which adequacy can be established for each factor in the CST are presented in **Figure 8.5**, along with a summary of the main elements of the CST.

Ultimately, as with many business ethics tools, the CST cannot really be expected to tell us exactly where consumers have been treated unethically. However, it does provide us with a relatively simple and practical framework with which to identify possible ethics violations, and even to suggest potential areas for remediation. This is particularly important from the corporate citizenship perspective. If, as we have argued, corporations, just as much as governments and other social actors, have come to be responsible for protecting consumers' rights, then they need clear ways of assessing ethical situations. Nonetheless, as Smith (1995) suggests, the application of the CST by managers not only requires some kind of moral impulse or conscience on their part, but also leaves consumers relying on the marketer's paternalism for their protection.

Finally, consumer sovereignty also has a yet more profound role to play in the citizenship perspective on consumer stakeholders. This relates to the emergence of what has become known as ethical consumption.

Ethical consumption

Whilst forms of ethical consumption of one sort or another have been around for centuries, the phenomenon has risen to considerable prominence in the last ten to fifteen years. Ethical consumption covers a range of different activities, including boycotting certain companies in response to a poor social, ethical, or environmental record, buying non-animal-tested products, avoiding products made by sweatshop or child labour, choosing fair trade or organic products, re-using or recycling products, etc. It is difficult to sum up the full range of activities that could potentially be included under the umbrella of ethical consumption, but a reasonable definition that captures the main essence of the concept might be as follows:

Ethical consumption is the conscious and deliberate choice to make certain consumption choices due to personal moral beliefs and values.

What makes a consumption decision driven by moral beliefs different from one that isn't is open to debate, but arguably one of the key characteristics here is that the decision is about considering others—i.e. ethical consumption is about decisions beyond self-interest. The main form of ethical consumption we are concerned with here is where the consumer's personal moral beliefs and values refer to the specific actions of businesses, such as a decision to deliberately boycott Esso over its approach to global warming, or a decision to deliberately seek out detergents low in bleach because of environmental considerations.

There is much evidence to suggest that many consumers do indeed include ethical considerations in their evaluations of businesses and the products they sell. For example, one recent UK survey suggested that almost 60% of consumers had bought a product because of the company's responsible reputation in the last year.[9] Whilst few consumers have been found to be completely consistent in their selection of ethical features over the alternatives (Auger et al. 2006), such findings do imply that ethical consumerism can no longer be dismissed as simply a few disparate pockets of extremists. Taken together, the ethical market for products is now said to be worth something like £35bn in the UK, which although representing only a tiny fraction of the overall market spend of approximately £600bn, indicates that the market share of ethical products is growing by something like 15% a year.[10] Much of this growth has come from 'ethical finance' products such as ethical investments, which we explored in some detail in Chapter 6 (pp. 268–73). Other major areas of growth include ethical food and drink, such as organic and fair trade products, which we will discuss in more detail in the following chapter (pp. 423–46). Similar findings have appeared across much of the rest of the world. According to a recent survey of nearly 30,000 online consumers in 51 markets, over 80% of consumers thought it was very or somewhat important that companies implement programmes to improve the environment (88%) and/or society (84%), whilst almost 70% of global consumers claimed that their purchase decision could be influenced by whether or not a product supported a worthy cause.[11]

Such findings obviously have significant implications for businesses—although survey results of this kind have to be treated with caution, given that respondents tend to provide socially desirable answers that do not necessarily closely match with their purchasing behaviour (Auger and Devinney 2007). Nonetheless, there seems little doubt that a small, but significant, proportion of purchases are influenced by ethical considerations—and that this occurs across the globe, from Europe to the US to Asia (Auger et al. 2006).

Ethical consumers have therefore been increasingly seen as playing an important role in prompting businesses to address ethics more enthusiastically, either through marketing specifically ethical products, or through developing a more ethical approach to business in general (Crane 2001). As such, firms can adopt either an *ethical niche* orientation or a *mainstream* orientation to the ethical market (Crane 2005). Whilst the former is concerned with offering specialist ethical products to a committed minority, the latter involves firms in integrating ethical considerations into conventional product offerings for broader market segments. **Ethics in Action 8.2** provides an illustration of how these two orientations have played out in the travel industry.

If we draw the connection here with consumer sovereignty, what this means is that consumers to some extent can act as a social control on business (Smith 1990). If consumers demand improved business ethics through the market, then business might be expected to listen and respond. Hence, the consumer is effectively using their purchases as 'votes' to support or criticize certain business practices rather than using the ballot box to vote for political solutions through government and regulation. Dickinson and Carsky (2005: 36) refer to this as *consumer citizenship*. This, as we initially mentioned in Chapter 2, is significant for the notion of corporate citizenship since the corporation may then act as a form of conduit for the exercise of consumers' political entitlements and aspirations as a citizen.

As Noreena Hertz (2001b) has noted, increased political apathy has taken hold in many European countries, the US, and elsewhere, yet consumer activism appears to be on the increase. As she contends (Hertz 2001a: 190), '. . . instead of showing up at the voting booth to register their demands and wants, people are turning to corporations. The most effective way to be political today is not to cast your vote at the ballot box but to do so at the supermarket or at a shareholder's meeting. Why? Because corporations respond.' For example:

- As we saw in case 7, when concerns about child labour in the Uzbekistan cotton industry escalated in the late 2000s, it was clothing retailers such as Wal-Mart, Tesco, Levi's that stepped in to deal with the problem by boycotting Uzbek cotton and forcing a change in labour legislation in the country.[12]
- While governments across the world stalled on applying sanctions to Burma, consumers applied their own sanctions—the threat of a consumer boycott, orchestrated by the Free Burma Coalition, encouraged major multinationals such as Philips, Heineken, C&A, and Carlsberg to pull out of the country.

Child welfare and oppressive regimes have traditionally been issues dealt with by politicians. In Hertz's words, such issues have undergone a 'silent takeover' by corporations, with consumers using the lever of the all-important corporate reputation to effect social change. These developments take ethical consumption away from merely being a way for consumers to assuage their consciences, towards active participation in making social and political choices.

In the absence of better ways to make their views heard, ethical consumption is certainly a positive phenomenon. However, it does have its downside. For example:

- However socially responsible they may be, the motives of corporations will always be primarily financial rather than moral. Hence, their attention to social concerns will always be driven by market appeal. Minority interests or unattractive causes are likely to be ignored or pushed aside.

VISIT THE WEBSITE for links to useful sources of further information

ETHICS IN ACTION 8.2

A take-off for responsible travel? Responsible travel.com targets a growing niche of 'ethical tourists'

With air travel representing the fastest growing source of carbon dioxide emissions, it is clear that the rapidly growing numbers of people that are flocking to tourist destinations across the globe are becoming unsustainable. The social, ethical, and environmental impacts of a sustained rise in tourism over the past century are becoming evident almost everywhere. Whether it is a Thai fishing village, a Mediterranean beach, or a London monument, concerns regarding overdevelopment of all kinds of tourist destinations have become very real. Air and road traffic have mounted, local resources such as water and sanitation have been overstretched, natural attractions have become blighted by overcrowding and littering, and local communities have seen few of the rewards being reaped by what is now the world's largest industry.

At the same time, consumers, the hotel and leisure industry, airlines, travel agents, as well as local and national governments, are pressing for yet more expansion of the tourist trade. In defence of their negative impact on local habitats, proponents of the tourist industry stress the importance of the revenues generated by tourism for economic development. Countries in the developed world, just as much as in the developing world, are keen to enjoy the benefits that a growing influx of tourists brings.

For some people though, the delights of mass tourism are beginning to pale against the negative side-effects. Consumers wishing to have a more positive impact on their host environments are beginning to seek out alternative holiday offerings that minimize their social and environmental impacts, and maximize the economic benefits for local people. One such company is responsibletravel.com, an online travel agent based in the UK that caters for 'those who've had enough of mass tourism'. Launched in 2001 by Justin Francis and Harold Goodwin in Brighton, the company offers holidays for the concerned traveller from over 300 tour operators and 600 lodges and small hotels. It claims to have been the world's first dedicated travel agent for responsible holidays, and purports to offer the largest selection of such holidays on the web.

Responsibletravel.com doesn't organize holidays itself, but pre-screens holidays from tour companies to ensure that they benefit local communities and minimize any negative social and environmental impacts. Screening is conducted against the firm's criteria for responsible travel, which are published in full on its website. These are a set of minimum standards, developed by NGOs and academics, covering a range of social, environmental, and economic issues. This includes requirements that holiday firms request destination suppliers to employ local people and make use of local produce, manufacturers, and other services wherever possible. Travellers must also be provided with suggestions on how to reduce water use in their destinations and how to minimize damage to the environment, wildlife, and marine ecosystems. Another essential requirement is that companies must provide evidence that they offer suggestions for destination visits to local projects with direct or indirect benefits to the host community.

Site visitors can review full holiday details and make booking enquiries through the site. They can also read suppliers' responsible tourism policies and unedited, independent reviews from fellow tourists. The company claims that it is unique in that 'it encourages a dialogue between travellers and suppliers, providing a framework for travellers to comment on tour operators' and accommodation owners' stated practices. With our members' permission, we independently contact travellers who have experienced members' trips or accommodation, and then publish their feedback on the site—warts and all—to help inform future travellers and enable our members to assess and improve their products.'

Whilst the company is clearly providing a valuable service to concerned travellers in the ethical niche, it also seeks to have an impact on the mainstream tourist industry. For example, in 2004, its campaign to pressurize major UK tour operators to develop policies on responsible tourism culminated in major policy commitments from the market leaders, Thomson, Thomas Cook, and MyTravel. And in 2008, the company conducted and published a ranking of 40 of the UK's top travel companies for the *Telegraph* national newspaper in order to keep up the pressure on industry laggards and reward the leaders.

All this is undoubtedly good news for an industry that has such a major impact on people and places across the globe. However, for the critics, the only really responsible travel is staying at home—or close to it. With air travel being the single most significant environmental impact of any holiday, the marketing of long-haul destinations in Asia, Australasia, Latin America, and Africa, even by companies such as responsibletravel.com, may ring a little hollow for proponents of more sustainable tourism. Friends of the Earth have even gone so far as to demonstrate at major airports, waving placards and demanding travellers to think about whether their trip is really necessary. Responsible travel companies may counter this by arguing for the positive social and economic benefits that engagement with distant communities can bring, but the industry clearly indicates some of the limitations, as well as the benefits, that ethical consumption can deliver.

Sources

http://www.responsibletravel.com

? THINK THEORY

Think about the difference between a niche and a mainstream orientation to the ethical tourism market. What are the advantages and disadvantages of both?

VISIT THE WEBSITE for a short response to this feature

- Market choices are predicated on an ability and willingness to pay. If consumers decide they no longer want to pay extra for these ethical 'accessories', or if they can no longer afford them, will they just be dropped?
- If purchases are 'votes', then the rich get far more voting power than the poor. The market is hardly democratic in the same way that elections are.

For all its benefits, then, ethical consumption is never going to be an adequate replacement for political action—even if the latter appears to be falling out of favour as the former becomes more mainstream. It does, however, show us that consumers are now important actors in the regulation and shaping of business ethics—and that whether we like it or not, corporations are increasingly becoming the most viable channel through which moral choices can be expressed. And if the value of ethical consumption is subject to challenge, the question of sustainability contests the whole practice of consumption itself.

■ Sustainable consumption

As we noted earlier in the chapter, it is now commonplace to refer to the contemporary world as a consumer society. Not only are levels of consumption ever-increasing, but we increasingly define ourselves by what and how we consume; we use consumption as a site for social, cultural, and, as we saw above, political activity; and consumption of products and services increasingly pervades new areas of our lives, such as the movement away from active participation in sporting activities to consumption of sports products such as TV programmes, computer games, and replica shirts, or the replacement of home cooking with pre-packaged 'ready meals'.

Consumption is ultimately the reason why anything gets produced. Without doubt, the massive growth in consumption in the latter part of the twentieth century and the beginning of the twenty-first has placed enormous strains on the natural environment. After all, consumer society is built on two very problematic assumptions: that consumption can continue to increase because there are no finite resource limits, and that the by-products and wastes created by consumption can be disposed off indefinitely. Hence, it is not unreasonable to suggest that high (and ever increasing) levels of consumption pose enormous barriers to the development of sustainable business (Kilbourne et al. 1997; Schaefer and Crane 2005)—and that consumers can be held responsible for much of the social and environmental degradation that their spiralling demands for products and services inevitably seems to bring (Heiskanen and Pantzar 1997). This is particularly true in the developed world, where consumption is, on average, about 32 times more per person than in the developing world (Diamond 2008). Even in China, which has seen such sustained economic growth over the past two decades, per capita consumption is about 11 times lower than in the developed countries of Europe and North America (Diamond 2008).

What is sustainable consumption?

Whilst current levels of consumption may indeed be unsustainable, the question of how to move towards a more sustainable form of consumption is a vexed one, but also a vital one. As we saw at the beginning of the chapter, even the UN now regards the promotion of sustainable consumption as a basic element of consumer protection (see Figure 8.1). So what would constitute a sustainable level of consumption? One reasonable definition which is used by the European Environment Agency and a number of other organizations comes from the 1994 Oslo Symposium:

Sustainable consumption is: 'the use of goods and services that respond to basic needs and bring a better quality of life, while minimising the use of natural resources, toxic materials and emissions of waste and pollutants over the life-cycle, so as not to jeopardise the needs of future generations'.

However, it would be a mistake to assume that people can, or will, readily give up current levels of consumption, given that it is widely regarded as enjoyable, liberatory, and expressive activity in modern society (Borgmann 2000). Indeed, the whole notion of ensuring that the satisfaction of needs does not compromise the satisfaction of future generations' needs is extremely problematic if the 'needs' satisfied by contemporary consumption are those of sustaining our self-image, our identity, and even our social relationships and culture (Schaefer and Crane 2005). This goes back to Galbraith and Baudrillard's debate about 'real' versus 'artificial' needs that we raised on p. 354. Nevertheless, whatever our normative position on whether people *should* have needs for products simply for social status or self-image, it is clear that consumption *does* serve such functions in contemporary society. Let us look a little closer at what kind of challenge this presents for sustainability.

The challenge of sustainable consumption

Rogene Buchholz (1998) suggests that a move towards more sustainable consumption needs to be seen in the light of changes in the ethics governing our societies (see **Figure 8.6**). Returning to the work of Max Weber, Buchholz argues that the Protestant ethic of self-discipline and moral sense of duty that held sway during the establishment of market systems in much of Europe encouraged people to engage in productive labour for the pursuit of gain, but to desist from immediate pleasure in order to accumulate capital and wealth (ostensibly for the glory of God). However, the advancement of secularization,

Ethic	Imposes limits to	Promotes
Protestant ethic	Consumption.	Investment in productive capacity.
Consumerism ethic	Saving.	Instant gratification and consumption.
Environmental ethic	Consumption.	Alternative meanings of growth and investment in the environment.

Figure 8.6. Changing social ethics and consumption
Source: Derived from Buchholz. 1998.

and in particular the ethic of consumerism that has gradually replaced these traditional values, have served to promote instant gratification and hedonism, and have downgraded the value of saving and durability.

To move towards sustainability, Buchholz suggests, we need a new environmental ethic that again provides moral limits to consumption. Of course, reducing consumption is problematic, both politically and practically, for it also has serious implications for employment, income, investment, and other aspects crucial to economic well-being and growth. The culture of consumption is deeply embedded in the dominant organizing framework of modern societies—a framework which is beneficial to, and sustained by, powerful social, economic, and political actors (Kilbourne et al. 1997; Schaefer and Crane 2005). However, as we said in Chapter 7, by redirecting growth towards more socially beneficial ends—such as environmental products, green jobs, clean technologies, etc.—growth *could* still occur. Ultimately though, the real challenge of sustainable consumption is to introduce alternative meanings of growth into society so that we can learn to cultivate deeper non-material sources of fulfilment. You don't need us to tell you that this is an immense challenge in the consumer culture of the twenty-first century.

Such changes in values can only ever happen gradually, and usually imperceptibly. In terms of real actions to promote more sustainable consumption on a day-to-day level, we need to look at the more practical solutions that are emerging from businesses, government, and consumers.

VISIT THE WEBSITE for a short response to this feature

? THINK THEORY

Think about the challenge of sustainable consumption from a consequentialist point of view. This is the main approach to justifying increased consumption, but can it also provide the basis for moving towards a more sustainable level of consumption?

Steps towards sustainable consumption

On a practical level, there is much that business, government, and consumers *can* do to seek more sustainable modes of consumption. **Ethics Online 8** provides an illustration of some of the practical tools available to individual consumers to measure and modify their consumption choices with respect to environmental impacts. As yet, however, progress towards more sustainable consumption has been slow, though signs of change are emerging, primarily in the following areas:

Producing environmentally responsible products

Perhaps the most obvious way for firms to respond to the challenge of sustainable consumption is to develop and market products that impact less harmfully on the environment. This has been an area of activity for some 25 years or so, and has led to the development of a vast array of products, including recycled and unbleached paper, 'green' detergents, low-energy light bulbs, non-toxic toys, and energy-efficient

ETHICS ONLINE 8

Tracking sustainable consumption

VISIT THE WEBSITE for links to useful sources of further information

Few would argue that we need to move towards more sustainable consumption patterns, but most of us are not exactly sure who among us really needs to change, by how much, and how. In recent years, though, a number of online tools and indices have been launched which help us to track how our personal consumption choices impact on the environment, and how they compare with those of our fellow citizens.

Zerofootprint, for example, is 'an organization dedicated to the mass reduction of global environmental impact' and provides free online tools for individuals and organizations to measure and manage their carbon footprints, including 'one minute calculators' and a 'personal carbon management' tool that also enables users to connect and collaborate with others sharing similar environmental goals. Zerofootprint's personal carbon management tool also helps users see the kind of difference their individual consumption choices can make by aggregating the pledged carbon reductions of its users and showing how individual small changes can make a big difference when combined with everyone else's in a given community.

National Geographic also provides a free online tool for consumers to measure their environmental impact with its *Greendex* system, developed in collaboration with Globescan, the international polling firm. More than this, though, the Greendex project is based on an annual survey of consumer progress towards environmentally sustainable consumption in 17 countries around the world. As a result, it provides a rating of consumers across different countries over time, and shows which countries have the most environmentally responsible consumers and which are making the greatest or least progress towards reducing their environmental impact. In the 2008 results, for example, the top three rated countries in the Greendex were India, Brazil, and China, whilst bottom of the list were Japan, Canada, and America. As the website suggests, 'the results reminded us that consumers in wealthy countries have a proportionately greater impact on the environment than others—and that they can and should make more sustainable choices'.

Sources

National Geographic Greendex: http://www.nationalgeographic.com/greendex.

Zerofootprint website: http://www.zerofootprint.net.

appliances. Even the car market has begun to see genuine innovations towards more environmentally responsible products. The Toyota Prius, for example, boasts a hybrid petrol and electric motor. As a result, it has low emissions, high fuel efficiency, and is about 90% recyclable—making it one of Japan's most popular cars, and one of Toyota's top-selling lines in North America. A number of companies have also now released zero-emission electric cars, including Canada's Zenn Motor Company, Tesla Motors, based in California, and General Motors' long-anticipated Chevy Volt. Competition is also escalating from emerging economies such as India and China, where companies are seeking to be global leaders in electric vehicles by leapfrogging existing petrol-based technologies.[13]

Developing new products is a key element of any movement towards sustainable consumption, but consumers also have to want to use them. Green product development should therefore be seen within a broader context of *sustainable marketing*, whereby firms develop and promote sustainable solutions for consumers. A key element of sustainable marketing is the development of appropriate **eco-labels** that communicate to consumers a product's environmental features.

Eco-labels are important because, as we saw above, consumer sovereignty demands that consumers have appropriate information with which to make informed choices between competing offerings. However, a recent survey of products in the US, Canada, UK, and Australia revealed that although environmental claims and information were becoming significantly more common, most of them committed at least one 'sin' of greenwashing—namely 'the act of misleading consumers regarding the environmental practices of a company or the environmental benefits of a product or service' (Terrachoice 2009). Eco-labels, therefore, need to act as a trusted guarantee that a product genuinely delivers the environmental benefits that it claims. Effective and successful eco-labels tend to be operated or verified by independent third parties (rather than simply being a company's self-declared stamp of greenness); they should be easy to recognize and understand, comparable, and focused on criteria that matter to consumers.

Growing public concern about climate change, for example, has prompted the development of a carbon label in the UK under the auspices of the Carbon Trust.[14] This shows the amount of carbon dioxide emitted in the production, distribution, use, and disposal of a given product (its 'carbon footprint'), with a view to enabling more climate-friendly consumer choices. However, although the label is now being applied to a range of products, including food, fashion, and electrical items, it will be some time yet before the list is extensive enough for consumers to be able to make meaningful comparisons among competing products.

More broadly, progress towards sustainability will also require a willingness to change markets as well as changing products (Peattie and Crane 2005). Hence, rather than just considering the introduction of new products and labels, attention is beginning to focus more on **product service systems**—i.e. constellations of products, services, supporting networks, and infrastructure that provide benefits to consumers in ways that impact less on the environment (Mont 2004). These include product-recapture systems, service replacements for products, product sharing, and other innovative ways of re-engineering markets.

Product recapture

Current business systems of production tend to operate on a linear model where materials are used to make products, which are then consumed and disposed of (see **Figure 8.7**). And that is the last that we see of them. However, moving towards a circular use of resources—ensuring that so-called 'waste' is recaptured and brought back into productive use—not only minimizes waste, but means that less 'virgin' material is needed at source (Fuller 1999). Reconstructing products in this way (by recycling, refurbishing, or

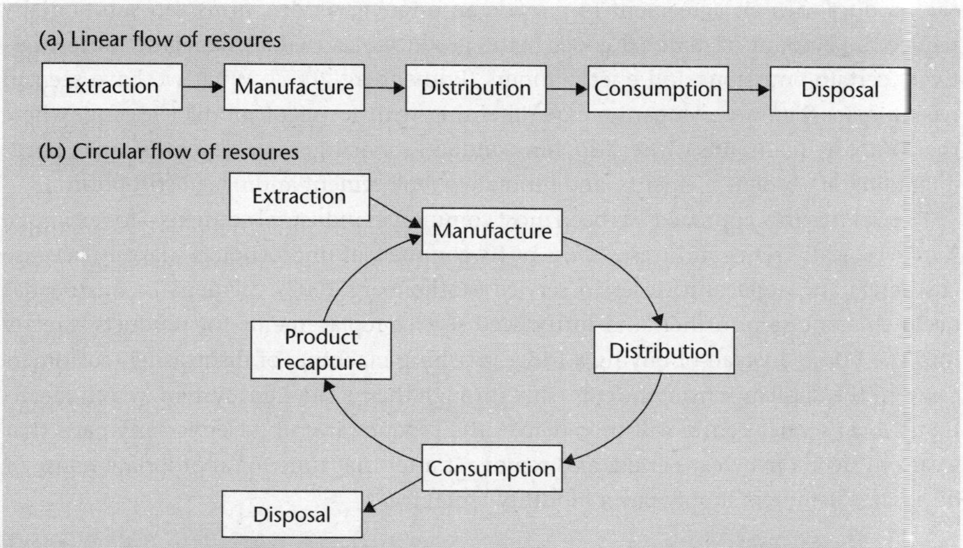

Figure 8.7. From a linear to a circular flow of resources

re-manufacturing) can also help to bring prices down because the cost of material inputs is often lower (Pearce 2009). As we shall see in the next chapter, this often relies on close collaboration between businesses to be truly effective, but product recapture can also be introduced within a single company. The challenge for companies is to design for recycling, re-use, and repair and to establish channels that facilitate the flow of product recapture.

Such considerations were brought into sharp focus in Europe with the EC Directive on Waste Electrical and Electronic Equipment (WEEE), which came into force in 2004. This aims to minimize the impacts of electrical and electronic equipment on the environment by encouraging and setting criteria for the collection, treatment, recycling, and recovery of waste equipment. Controversially, it makes producers directly responsible for financing most of the activities involved in taking back and recycling electrical and electronic equipment, at no cost to the consumer. However, by 2008, only a third of such waste was being treated in line with the directive, with the rest going to landfill and sub-standard treatment sites. This prompted the EC to announce revised laws with higher targets, but ostensibly lower administrative costs.[15]

Service replacements for products

If this thinking is taken a little further, there is no reason for the consumer to own the product in the first place. After all, what we are often seeking when we buy products is their performance—the ability to wash clothes for example—not necessarily the ownership of the physical product itself—a washing machine. By replacing the sale of the product with an agreement to provide an ongoing service, firms can substantially reduce the amount of material goods being produced, as well as managing more effectively certain emissions and energy inputs (Rothenberg 2007). What we have seen in recent years then are companies experimenting with forms of product leasing, where the company maintains ownership, but conducts servicing, replacement of worn parts, upgrading of obsolete elements, and ultimately replacement and/or redistribution.

The 'servicizing' approach has been most common in industrial contexts—for example, Xerox typically rents and leases most of its commercial photocopiers—largely because customers are larger and easier to service (Rothenberg 2007). Siemens in Austria has taken this one step further, and introduced service replacements for products directly into the home. Instead of buying a fridge, washing machine, or dishwasher, customers can rent the appliance from the company through their Extra-Rent system, which means that a local service centre will then deliver the product, install it, service any parts that wear out over a five-year period, and remove it after that time for appropriate re-use or disposal. Customers simply pay a monthly rental fee.[16]

Product sharing

Another similar way of reducing consumption is for products to be shared by groups of consumers, thereby getting more use out of the same resources. This way of increasing eco-efficiency has been fairly successful in certain parts of Europe, such as Germany and the Netherlands, with products such as cars, washing machines, and certain tools being found to be particularly suitable for sharing (Schrader 1999). Although inconvenience is a major disadvantage, studies suggest that consumers welcome the savings in storage space, money, and the hassle of repairs and maintenance—not to mention benefiting the environment. One area where this idea has particularly caught on is in car sharing, which now operates in more than a thousand cities across the globe.[17] One of Europe's largest and longest-running car-sharing companies is the Swiss co-operative Mobility. Created following a merger in 1997, Mobility now boasts an impressive 84,000 members. The world's largest car-sharing company, however, can now be found in North America. Although car sharing is relatively new to the continent, Zipcar has imported the European car-sharing idea to attract almost 300,000 members, who can drive away their signature minis, hybrids, and other models from locations in more than 50 cities and over 100 universities across the US, Canada, and even London in the UK.

Reducing demand

Ultimately, though, the challenge of sustainability can only really be met if society accepts that people simply have to buy less stuff. It doesn't take much intelligence to work out that this idea tends not to be too popular with business—nor for that matter with customers or governments either! However, there are some areas where deliberate reduction of demand has been actively encouraged. For example, in 2008, China instituted a complete ban on free plastic bags in order to reduce pollution—and within a year had saved an equivalent of 1.6 million tonnes of oil (Watts 2009). Where excessive consumption can even mar consumer enjoyment and threaten business—such as in the tourism industry—demand reduction can be particularly pertinent (see Ethics in Action 8.2 for further discussion of some of these issues in the tourism industry).

Demand reduction can also come from consumers themselves. As a slightly different form of ethical consumption (as described earlier in the chapter), consumers choosing to go down the route of 'voluntary simplicity' or 'downshifting' go beyond registering their approval or disapproval of certain companies or practices and actively attempt to consume less overall. Indeed, as Shaw and Newholm's (2001) study of voluntary simplifiers makes clear, some degree of reflection on restraint is almost inevitable once consumers begin to take ethical stances on consumption. Instead of buying a shirt guaranteed to be sweatshop free, why not do without completely? Just as car sharing might seem more sustainable than owning your own, the decision to cut down on making journeys altogether probably represents a yet more sustainable option. For many people, such decisions will probably be taking things just a step too far. But if modern society is to tackle sustainability seriously, we may just find that reducing consumption is simply a bitter pill that just has to be swallowed.

■ Summary

In this chapter, we have discussed the specific stake held by consumers and outlined some of the main rights of consumers, including rights to safe products, honest and truthful communications, fair prices, fair treatment, and privacy. That firms still sometimes fail to respect these rights suggests that the interests of producers and consumers are not always seen by firms to be as aligned as stakeholder theory might imply. These problems simply wouldn't occur if firms really saw their own interests to be best served by looking after their consumer's best interests. Of course, in many of the problems and examples we have traced in this chapter, there are quite complex ethical arguments at stake. And doing the right thing by customers and potential customers may not always seem particularly attractive when one thinks that they are, for most companies, the single source of revenue to keep the business going. Still, consumers appear to be demanding better treatment, and we suggested that tools such as the consumer sovereignty test might at least provide some guidance on what should constitute ethical practice.

What we have also shown in this chapter, though, is that as the expectations placed on business have grown, so too have the possibilities for consumers to assume certain responsibilities in the control of business. The rise of ethical consumption places consumers in the role of policing companies, and even exercising their political rights as citizens through corporations. Notwithstanding the problems and dangers of such a situation, the challenge of sustainability pushes this yet further. In the consumer society that we currently live in, it appears that consumers might be expected to shoulder increased responsibilities, as well being afforded certain rights.

Study questions

1 'Of course, corporations should avoid treating their customers in an unethical manner. After all, in the long run, unethical behaviour towards customers only serves to harm firms' own interests.' Critically evaluate this statement with reference to examples from the following:

(a) Mobile phone companies.

(b) Holiday companies.

(c) Chemical companies.

How does your answer differ for each type of company? Explain your answer.

2 What is deception in marketing communications? Give examples of marketing practices that you believe are deceptive.

3 Set out and explain the four main pricing practices where ethical problems are likely to arise.

4 How is it possible to determine consumer vulnerability? Whose responsibility is it to prevent exploitation of vulnerable consumers? Explain, using examples from contemporary business practice.

5 What are the arguments for and against firms extending their marketing strategies to poor consumers in developing countries? Should firms have a responsibility to serve those at the bottom of the pyramid?

6 What is the difference between ethical and sustainable consumption—and how should firms respond to either challenge?

Research exercise

Food companies have often been accused of targeting children with adverts for unhealthy products such as fast food, confectionery, and snacks. Your task is to determine the extent of such targeting, and its appropriateness.

1 Review the websites of three major food companies serving these markets in your country (for example, one fast food, one confectionery, and one snacks), and collect examples of communications to customers.

2 Record three hours of TV programming on Saturday morning and note the details of all the adverts—the product, the advertiser, and the target.

3 Assess the extent of advertising of 'unhealthy food' to children based on this evidence—is it more or less than other products? Are children targeted more than adults?

4 Analyse the way that children are communicated to in these marketing communications. To what extent are advertisers taking advantage of the vulnerability of children?

Key readings

VISIT THE WEBSITE for links to further key readings

1 **Smith, N.C. 1995. Marketing strategies for the ethics era. *Sloan Manage en Re iew*, 36 (4): 85–97.**

This is an easy-to-read article that explores a number of interesting cases in order to take a close look at changes in expectations about marketing ethics. It then presents a powerful way of thinking about what should constitute an ethical exchange in today's marketplace.

2 Prahalad, C.K. and Hammond, A. 2002. Serving the world's poor, profitably. *Ha a Business Re iew*, 80 (9): 48–57.

A ground-breaking article offering a new perspective on marketing to the world's poorest people. It doesn't really deal with all of the ethical issues involved, but it provides a great introduction to the debates about the role of corporations in poverty reduction and social inclusion.

Case 8

VISIT THE WEBSITE for links to useful sources of further information

Targeting the poor with microfinance: hype or hope for poverty reduction?

This case discusses the phenomenon of microfinance, whereby small-scale financial services are targeted directly at poor consumers in developing countries that have been excluded from the mainstream banking sector. It explains the different forms and providers of microfinance, the challenges faced in using microfinance as a strategy for addressing poverty, and raises questions over the rates of interest charged to borrowers. The case provides an opportunity to explore questions of consumer exclusion, fair pricing, and 'bottom of the pyramid' marketing strategies.

Microfinance refers to the range of financial services targeted directly at poor customers who are normally unable to access traditional banking services. The reasons for the exclusion of the poor from mainstream banking are many. This includes their lack of formal employment, little access to collateral for loans, a perceived lack of creditworthiness, limited banking infrastructure in poor areas, and the unwillingness of banks to service small ticket financial services (because of the high cost ratio involved). According to most reliable estimates, somewhere in the region of 40–80% of the population of most developing countries lack access to formal banking services.

Microfinance seeks to open the doors to poor consumers by developing financial services specially suited to their circumstances. The types of services offered range from small-scale loans (often referred to as 'microcredit'), to savings vehicles, insurance services, and money transfer services. It is microcredit, though, that has garnered the most attention to date, not least because lending services have been the longest and most well-developed form of microfinance. Pioneered in Bangladesh in the 1970s by the Grameen Bank and its founder, Muhammad Yunus (who together won the 2006 Nobel Peace Prize), microcredit can work in a number of ways. The main characteristic, however, is that it is not based on collateral, or even necessarily any legally enforceable contracts, but rather on a system of 'group lending'. That is, rather than covering the lender's risk with assets of the borrower and/or the threat of legal proceedings, borrowers are formed into small groups where they either monitor one another through mutual trust or are required to guarantee each other's loans. Repayment is typically organized into instalments with relatively short spacing (often weekly or semi-weekly), the amounts lent are relatively modest (averaging around

€100, hence the 'micro' label), and services are often targeted predominantly at women in order to address gender inequality issues.

Despite the scepticism of traditional lenders, microcredit has proved to be an extremely successful lending model. By 2009, there were more than 3,500 microcredit institutions, lending to over 150 million customers who otherwise would have been simply unable to access financial services—or forced to rely on unscrupulous moneylenders in the informal economy. The default rates, on average, have been considerably lower than for conventional loans. Globally, microcredit repayment rates average around 97%, according to the Microfinance Information Exchange which records data on some 1,500 microfinance institutions across the developing world. Grameen Bank, for example, boasts a loan recovery rate of 98% across almost 8 million borrowers—a full 97% of whom are women.

Microcredit institutions have also managed to generate good returns from lending to the poor, with an average rate of return of around 6% per year. The best performers can generate three or four times that amount. For instance, the Mexican microfinance institution, Compartamos, regularly yields a return on assets of around 20%, and profit margins of 40%.

Beyond microcredit, microfinance providers have increasingly offered a wide array of other services. As well as savings and loans, some microfinance institutions also offer education on financial issues and even social services. In recent years, attention has particularly focused on the introduction of innovative services provided through new information and communication technologies. In 2007, for instance, Vodafone's Kenyan subsidiary, Safaricom Kenya, launched a mobile banking service, M-Pesa. In a country where only 2 million of the 32 million residents have a bank account, M-Pesa seeks to provide financial services for Safaricom's more than 11 million subscribers, using a system of money transfer based on text messaging. The system allows customers to use mobile phones like debit cards, so that they can transfer money between virtual accounts. This enables users to make a range of financial transactions, including the withdrawal and deposit of cash with registered outlets, paying for goods, and even repaying microcredit loans—all simply by sending a text message.

Building a path to poverty reduction?

In many respects, then, the development of microfinance is clearly a success story. Microfinance has been particularly successful in Asia (which accounts for 70% of the global microfinance market), with countries such as India, Bangladesh, and Indonesia among the largest national markets. Latin America and Africa too have increasingly embraced microfinance practices, and even developed countries such as the US have a small number of providers.

Such financial inclusion has enabled those towards the bottom of the economic pyramid to participate more fully in the formal economy, develop financial literacy and independence, evade the risks and uncertainty of informal saving and lending, and build credit histories that can in turn lead to further accumulation of assets. Some evidence also suggests that microfinance has led to greater consumption (which in turn drives local economic growth), and by extension, can provide greater opportunities for education of borrowers and their families. Although the evidence supporting such claims remains somewhat inconclusive, it does appear fairly certain that if nothing else, microfinance has helped borrowers to smooth their consumption levels so that they are less vulnerable to seasonal variations, such as the vagaries of crop success or failure, or to personal emergencies and natural disasters.

Another impact frequently claimed for microfinance is that it has a positive effect on alleviating poverty. Indeed, for many of its advocates, poverty reduction is essentially the *raison d'être* of microfinance. This is because many microfinance institutions specifically target small-scale microbusinesses, offering financial and other support to create self-employment opportunities for the poor. That is, rather than providing funds for consumption, microfinance is often directed towards small business start-ups to fuel income generation. These businesses include: cottage industries such as weaving, crafts, embroidery, and jewellery making; microretail businesses such as street stalls, kiosks, and small shops; agricultural and farming businesses; and a range of small-scale trading operations. By supporting the establishment of these businesses, microfinance providers offer their clients the opportunity to help themselves rather than rely on charity or government handouts. It views the poor as empowered producers rather than exploited workers or passive consumers.

To date, though, despite the claims of its many enthusiastic supporters, the evidence on the impact of microfinance on poverty alleviation is limited. In part, this is simply due to the relative youth of the industry, as well as the very real problem of providing any definitive correlations, given the range of variables involved in determining poverty levels. Despite numerous case studies of successful initiatives, hard empirical evidence is lacking. At best, the existing evidence seems to suggest that, on average, microfinance reduces vulnerability and dependence among client groups, even if it doesn't necessarily make them richer. And certainly many small businesses supported by microcredit have thrived, even at times bringing new and much needed new goods and services to poor areas. A good example is provided by the Grameen 'telephone-ladies' who use Grameen Bank loans to buy mobile phones and offer phone services in Bangladeshi villages previously without accessible telecommunications. As of 2009, some 360,000 telephone-ladies had started businesses in this way, most of which have proved to be profitable.

Some critics though, such as Aneel Karnani, a Professor at the University of Michigan, have raised a more fundamental criticism of microfinance and its impacts on poverty reduction. According to Karnani and other critics, microfinance can actually hinder efforts to reduce poverty because it diverts attention and resources away from other more proven ways of promoting economic development such as the creation of employment through small and medium-sized enterprises (as opposed to microbusinesses and self-employment). As he argues, 'rather than giving microloans of $200 each to 500 women so that each can buy a sewing machine and set up a microenterprise manufacturing garments, it is much better to lend $100,000 to an entrepreneur with managerial capabilities and business acumen and help her to set up a garment manufacturing business employing 500 people … Microcredit, at best, does not help to reduce poverty, and probably makes the situation worse by hindering more effective approaches to poverty reduction.' One need only look to China to see how poverty reduction can also be achieved through supporting the introduction of larger-scale industry.

Amongst the supporters of microfinance, such views are contested, not least because the innovativeness of the model means it has the potential to offer a more organic, inclusive, bottom-up approach to poverty alleviation than traditional models. That said, even the most ardent supporters recognize that more work needs to be done to refine the model, and to evaluate real impacts on poverty levels.

Balancing the books

Another challenge facing microfinance is its underlying business model, and the degree to which microfinance institutions can (or should) balance business success with explicit social goals. At one end are microfinance organizations operated by civil society organizations, or those directly funded by government or charities, which put a premium on poverty reduction and other social goals. At the other extreme are commercial banks, which have increasingly entered the microfinance market as a result of the model's proven results in generating returns and keeping default rates down—as well as its relative immunity to the recent global financial turmoil.

Among the banks involved in microfinance are major multinationals such as Standard Chartered, HSBC, and Deutsche Bank, as well as numerous smaller, local players. These providers typically operate microfinance as a niche offering among their broader portfolio of products and services, and emphasize the need for it to demonstrate its commercial viability. To date, commercial banks have tended to fluctuate in their interest in microfinance, depending on the financial results they have generated. However, in the past few years, there has been a significant hike in uptake. For example, in Latin America and the Caribbean, banks provide something like 20% of all microfinance loans, whilst in India domestic banks are required by law to set aside 40% of their reservable funds for the 'priority sector', which includes microfinance.

In between these two extremes is a large swathe of dedicated microfinance institutions, ranging from those, like Grameen, that are set up with a distinct social mission, to those, like Compartamos in Mexico, that have a more explicit commercial orientation—but all seek to operate on a secure financial footing. Wherever they might fall on this continuum, then, the aim of almost all microfinance institutions is to marry pro-poor business models with some degree of economic viability. The problem comes with determining how the right balance should be reached. Providing financial services to the poor may not be as risky as once thought, but it remains expensive because of the large numbers of small transactions that need to be processed and the considerable resources that need to go into developing education and outreach services. For this reason, many microfinance organizations continue to rely on donors.

However, among those like Grameen and Compartamos that have proved they can become sustainable without additional funding, there remain unresolved questions about what kind of pricing model they should adopt. When Compartamos, one of the largest microfinance institutions in Latin America, held a public offering of its stock in 2007, the sale was oversubscribed by 13 times, and the bank's valuation shot to $1.6 billion, making millions for its owners. The bank's financial success, however, rested on an aggressive business development strategy that had seen the company reap high profits from its microcredit business. At the time of the stock offering, Compartamos' borrowers were paying interest rates of more than 90%, a quarter of which went straight into profit. Whilst this certainly demonstrated once and for all that microfinance had the clear potential to attract the private investment necessary to expand rapidly and service more clients, critics suggested that the bank's practices were tantamount to 'microloan-sharking'. The levying of high interest rates on the poor, the argument went, was against the very purpose of the movement: microfinance companies were supposed to be social businesses, not cynical moneylenders. 'Microfinance', one commentator noted at the time, 'has lost its innocence'.

The debate over fair pricing has continued. Some, such as Muhammad Yunus, have advocated a legal cap on interest rates to prevent exploitation by microlenders. To date, though, the legal route has not been widely followed, although government pressure, market dynamics, and company priorities have led to a substantial variation in interest rates across countries and companies. The global average is currently around 35%, which is considerably higher than for conventional lending (around 12% in the US, for example). This, most commentators agree, can be justified to some extent by the higher costs involved in servicing small loans. Nonetheless, many lenders charge considerably more even than this, with the average in Mexico, for example, exceeding 60%. By way of comparison, the average in Bolivia is only 17%. Perhaps, though, given the aim of many in the microfinance community to prove its commercial credentials, this should not come as too much of a surprise. As one leading figure in the industry remarked, 'To attract the money they need, microfinance institutions have to play by the rules of the market. Those rules often have messy results.'

Questions

1. Consider the market for financial services in developing countries in terms of consumer exclusion. What forms of financial exclusion are being practised by mainstream financial institutions, and how legitimate is this practice?
2. In what ways might microfinance improve the lives of poor consumers?
3. To what extent is microfinance likely to have a significant impact on poverty alleviation? Where, in your opinion, should governments, civil society, and business be focusing their attention in addressing poverty?
4. Are microcredit lenders justified in charging high rates of interest to poor borrowers? What exactly is a fair price in this context?
5. Consider the case for regulation of microfinance pricing. Would this help or hinder the plight of the poor?

References

Chhabara, R. 2008. Banking on the poor. *Ethical Corporation*, 15 Dec.: http://www.ethicalcorp.com.

Cull, R., Demirgüç-Kunt, A., and Morduch, J. 2009. Microfinance meets the market. *Journal of Economic Perspectives*, 23 (1): 167–92.

Karnani, A. and Santos, F. 2009. Is microfinance helping to reduce poverty? *Ethical Corporation*, 11 Aug.: http://www.ethicalcorp.com.

Lewis, J. C. 2007. What would Leland Stanford Do? An editorial commentary submitted to the microfinance community about the Compartamos IPO. *Microcredit Summit E-News*, 5 (1), July 2007: http://www.microcreditsummit.org.

Rosenberg, R. 2008. Why do microcredit interest rates vary so dramatically around the world? *CGAP Microfinance Blog*, 20 June: http://microfinance.cgap.org.

Von Stauffenberg, D. 2007. Remarks by Damian von Stauffenberg, Executive Director, MicroRate. *Microcredit Summit E-News*, 5 (1), July: http://www.microcreditsummit.org.

Growing inclusive markets website: http://www.growinginclusivemarkets.org.

Mixmarket website: http://www.mixmarket.org.

Notes

1 For more information, see http://www.easa-alliance.org.
2 See http://www.asa.org.uk.
3 European Commission. 2009. *Antitrust: Commission welcomes judgment of the Court of Justice in French broadband case*. Press release, 2 Apr.: http://europa.eu. European Commission. 2003. *High-speed internet: the Commission imposes a fine on Wanadoo for abuse of a dominant position*. Press release, 16 July: http://europa.eu.
4 For more information, see the website of the International Council of Beverages Associations (ICBA) at http://www.icba-net.org.
5 See HM Government/Association of British Insurers. 2005. Concordat and moratorium on genetics and insurance. London: Department of Health. http://www.abi.org.uk.
6 For data on global tobacco consumption, see http://www.tobaccoatlas.com.
7 *Guardian*. 1999. Exporting addiction. *Guardian*, 13 Jan.: 17; BBC. 2000. UK tobacco firm targets African youth. *BBC News*, 20 Sept.; BBC. 2000. A global smoking battle. *BBC News*, 2 Aug.: http://www.news.bbc.co.uk.
8 See http://www.who.int/fctc for more details.
9 Co-operative Bank. 2008. *The ethical consumerism report 2008*. Manchester: Co-operative Bank. http://www.goodwithmoney.co.uk/ethicalconsumerismreport.
10 ibid.
11 Nielson. 2008. Corporate Ethics and Fair Trading: A Nielsen Global Consumer Report. Downloaded from: http://tr.nielsen.com/site/documents/CSR_Fairtrade_global_reportOctober08.pdf.
12 See Ansett, A. 2008. Uzbek cotton and forced child labour—is the Government serious? *Ethical Corporation*, 21 Sept. 2008: http://www.ethicalcorp.com.
13 Anon. 2009. Electric car to hit roads in Sept: Ratan Tata, *The Times of India*, 4 June: http://www.timesofindia.com; Bradsher, K. 2009. China vies to be world's leader in electric cars. *The New York Times*, 1 Apr.: http://www.nytimes.com.
14 For more information, see http://www.carbon-label.com.
15 For more information on the WEEE, see http://ec.europa.eu/environment/waste/weee/index_en.htm.
16 For details, see Adams, G., Hafkesbrink, J. and Steiner, S. 2005. Ecolife II: new business models. Centre for Sustainable Design, Sept. http://www.cfsd.org.uk.
17 See the World Carshare Consortium at http://ecoplan.org/carshare/cs_index.htm.

9

Suppliers, Competitors, and Business Ethics

In this chapter we will:

- Show how suppliers and competitors exist in mutual interdependence with an organization, raising the prospect that they too can legitimately claim a stake in the firm.
- Describe the ethical issues and problems that arise in an organization's dealings with its suppliers and competitors, including bribery and gift giving, negotiation, intelligence gathering, and abuses of power.
- Outline how globalization reframes these problems, and in particular examine the effect of MNC actions on overseas suppliers and competitors.
- Discuss whether corporations should assume some degree of extended responsibility for the ethics of their suppliers, and analyse the role of corporations in influencing the social and environmental choices of suppliers and competitors through their business relationships.
- Assess the arguments suggesting that attention to business interrelationships and the network economy may contribute to more sustainable business models.

■ Introduction

The relationships between different businesses—as opposed to relationships between a firm and its non-business stakeholders—have probably been among the most commonly overlooked aspects of business ethics. This is perhaps not so very surprising when we stop to consider that ethical problems in dealing with consumers, employees, pressure groups, or the local community tend to be quite public and visible, and frequently enjoy the spotlight of media attention. Ethical problems between businesses, however, tend to stay relatively hidden from public view, and violations of one sort or another are rather less easy to uncover and scrutinize when they do not emerge from behind the screen of the business world. More recently, though, responsibility issues in the supply chain have come much more to the fore, due in part to revelations of poor social and environmental conditions in supplier factories, as well as recognition that ethical reputations depend as much on what happens in an organization's business partners as it does within the organization itself.

In this chapter, we shall examine these inter-organizational relationships in the context of two types of businesses—suppliers and competitors. The issue of other businesses that are customers is something we have already dealt with in the previous chapter. What, though, of an organization's behaviour or responsibilities towards those who supply it with the goods and services necessary to conduct its day-to-day business? There are clearly many, many of these suppliers, whether they are providing raw materials for making products, stationery for the office, cleaning services for the plant, or consultancy services to help improve competitiveness—just to name a few examples. Contracts between businesses and their suppliers often involve substantial sums of money, which can even mean the difference between business survival and failure. Hence there is always the possibility for relationships with suppliers to give rise to ethical problems, for instance when procurement staff are offered bribes or kickbacks to encourage them to select a particular supplier. Likewise, we have already seen that relationships between competitors in the same industry can lead to ethical problems if consumers get short-changed—for example, because of collusion over pricing. Such anti-competitive practices are only half the story though. Some of the main ethical problems that arise in relations with competitors are as a result of arch-rivals employing 'dirty tricks' tactics in order to outdo one another.

What will soon become clear, then, as we go through this chapter is that the relationships between businesses can raise ethical problems both by being too adversarial as well as by being too cosy. Ultimately, though, whatever the nature of a specific relationship between two businesses, our interests in business ethics among suppliers and competitors are best framed in a somewhat broader context that takes account of the network of relationships and interdependencies that constitute the business community. It is, after all, membership in this wider community that not only helps give credence to a notion of the corporation as a citizen of some sort, but also serves as a launch pad to explore the possibilities of addressing sustainability through business–business relationships. It is also, as we shall now see, the basis for defining other businesses such as suppliers and competitors as organizational stakeholders.

■ Suppliers and competitors as stakeholders

Models of organizational stakeholders, from Freeman's (1984) original formulation onwards, have tended to vary somewhat in their definitions of what constitutes a stakeholder and which constituencies should be included or excluded. Many conceptualizations even discriminate between primary (mainly economic) stakeholders and secondary (non-economic) stakeholders (see Carroll and Buchholtz 2009: 85–7). All formulations, however, tend to include suppliers and most, if not all, tend to exclude competitors (Spence et al. 2001). Although there are very good reasons for this, in our view, such a distinction is not entirely useful or appropriate. Let us briefly have a look at some of the arguments.

Suppliers as stakeholders

In Chapter 2, we used Evan and Freeman's (1993) definition as a way of clarifying what a stakeholder is. A stakeholder of a corporation is an individual or a group that either is *harmed by or benefits from the corporation* or whose *rights can be violated*, or *have to be respected*, by the corporation.

It is clear without much further argument that suppliers are stakeholders—they can benefit from the success of the corporation by receiving orders for products and services and they can be harmed by losing orders. Similarly, we might easily suggest that suppliers have certain rights that might need to be respected by corporations, such as the right to a contract, to a fair deal, or to some level of fair treatment or loyalty. Indeed, organizations and their suppliers can be seen to be *mutually dependent* on each other for their own success: just as suppliers rely on their customers for the orders which keep them in business, so too do the purchasing firms rely on their suppliers to provide them with the products and services they need to carry on their operations. Nonetheless, as we saw with consumers in the previous chapter, though, by saying that organizations and their suppliers are interdependent does not necessarily imply that their interests are always convergent. For example, whilst the buying company may wish to reduce costs by sourcing cheaper products, the supplier will usually seek to obtain the best possible deal and maximize revenue. We shall examine a number of such problems in the next section.

Competitors as stakeholders

Competitors, on the other hand, are rarely referred to as stakeholders—certainly not in academic treatments of business ethics, nor, it would seem, in most business communications by corporations and their leaders. As Spence et al. (2001) suggest, competitors are very much the 'forgotten stakeholders'. Why? Well, competitors are, to begin with, typically seen as being in an ongoing, zero-sum battle with each other for customers, resources, and other rewards. Why should organizations accord their competitors any specific ethical claim when these are the very businesses that they are vying with for such rewards? What rights could, say, Nokia possibly have in its competition for mobile phone customers with Motorola?

This is not actually as simple, or as redundant, a question as it might at first seem. Nokia certainly has a number of *legal rights* that are more or less protected by national and international trade agreements that Motorola must respect. These include the right to freely enter and leave the market, the right to set their own prices free from influence or coercion, and the right to inform potential customers about their products. For instance, it would be illegal for Nokia to try and influence the price that Motorola sets for its handsets.

It is a relatively short step from these legal rights to claim that a competitor also has some form of *moral claims* on an organization which go beyond those codified in law—for example, some form of right to privacy, or a right to 'fair play'. Certainly, few would contend that the mere fact of a competitive situation bestows upon an organization *carte blanche* to act in any way they choose in order to beat their competitors, including lying, deception, poaching staff, and other such questionable practices that we shall examine as we proceed through the chapter—not to mention outright illegal activities such as theft and extortion.

In addition to these claims, if we look at the first condition of being a stakeholder given above, there is little doubt that competitors most certainly can be *harmed by* or *benefit from* the organization (Spence et al. 2001). Competitors can experience a loss or gain of market share as a result of the actions of their rivals, they can experience a change in trading conditions (for example, their suppliers might switch to a competitor offering higher prices), or they can face changes in the perception of their industry by customers, regulators, or other stakeholders as a result of the behaviour of their competitors.

To sum up then, businesses should not be seen as isolated islands of economic activity, but as actors operating within a web of other businesses, bound by mutual interests and interlinked flows of resources and rewards. This suggests that firms are probably best understood as part of an **industrial network**, rather than just as part of a simple exchange between two parties (Easton 1992; Håkansson and Snehota 2006). An illustration of such a network is shown in **Figure 9.1**, with the focal relationship between a corporation and its supplier highlighted, and put into context with other relationships amongst competing companies, suppliers, and their suppliers.

According to the industrial network model, notable decisions about how the firm deals with any single other firm (such as one of its suppliers) can have a significant effect on numerous other members of the business network, including other suppliers, potential suppliers, and competitors. Whilst the ethical obligations the firm has to these other network members might vary, this does not deny the fact that they all have some form of stake in the decisions made—and may act upon that stake in ways that are of consequence to the organization.

These interrelationships give rise to a number of potential ethical problems. In the following two sections, we shall look at the specific issues that arise with respect to dealings with suppliers and competitors, before moving on to examine the impact of globalization on the ethics of these business relationships.

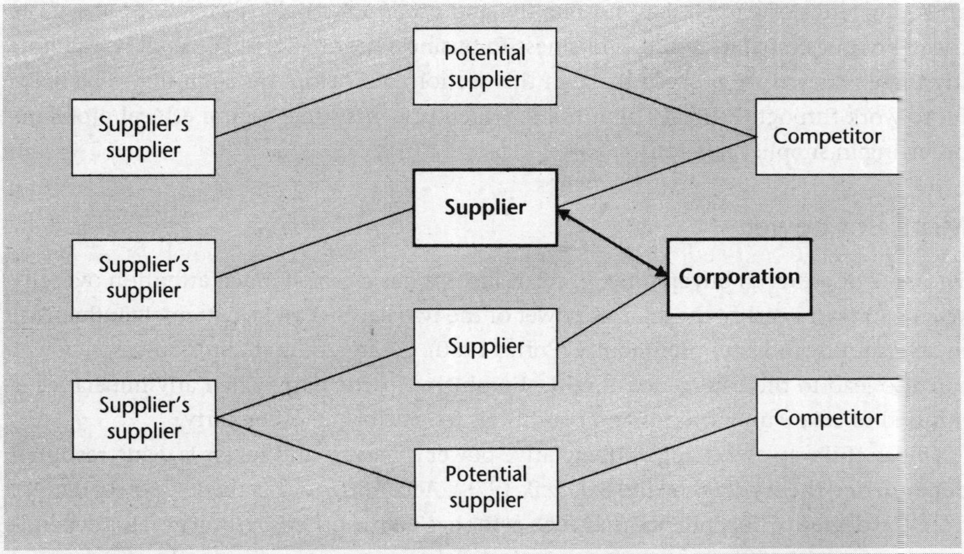

Figure 9.1. Supplier relationship as part of an industrial network

■ Ethical issues and suppliers

On reading a typical contemporary text on supplier management, one might wonder how ethical problems could possibly arise in relations with suppliers. Close relationships have been widely touted as an effective business strategy for improving performance and achieving win-win solutions for organizations and their suppliers (Anderson and Jap 2005; Lemke et al. 2003; Lambert 2008). Thus, firms have continued to increasingly move away from traditional adversarial relationships with suppliers (based upon short-termist, transactional arrangements with large numbers of supply firms) towards more partnership-based approaches that emphasize long-term relationships with core supply firms based upon mutual trust and collaboration (Durán and Sánchez 1999).

The attention afforded to partnership sourcing is significant for our understanding of business ethics because it very much reinforces the notion of suppliers as stakeholders in the firm. In fact, though, the partnership approach is certainly not representative of all, or probably even the majority, of business–supplier relationships. Evidence suggests that whilst many progressive firms have indeed moved towards more collaborative approaches, much so-called 'partnership' sourcing actually involves problematic power relations and troublesome intra-firm tensions (Hingley 2005; New 1998). This 'dark side' of close relationships (Anderson and Jap 2005), as we shall see, can quite easily reveal a number of ethical issues.

It is also important to recognize that regardless of the overall approach to business–supplier relations that is adopted by an organization, the individuals who actually conduct these relationships—namely the purchasing and sales staff—are often confronted with a whole host of ethical dilemmas on a day-to-day level. This can include the giving and acceptance of gifts, bribes, hospitality, and other potential inducements, as well as the use of questionable tactics in business-to-business negotiations. We shall be examining these issues as we proceed through this section, but before we do, it might be helpful to work through **Ethical Dilemma 9**, which presents some typical ethical problems occurring in supplier relations.

Misuse of power

The issue of power in buyer–supplier relationships has received much attention over the years, not least because the relative power of the two parties can be extremely influential in determining industry profitability (Porter 1980). Clearly, though, imbalances in power can also lead to the emergence of ethical problems, particularly when any imbalance is misused to create unfair terms and conditions for one or the other party.

One useful way of looking at the relative power of buyers and sellers is using **resource dependence theory** (Pfeffer and Salancik 1978). According to this theory, power derives from the degree of dependence that each actor has on the other's resources. This dependence is a function of how scarce an organization's resources are—i.e. the level of *resource scarcity*—and how useful they are to the other party—i.e. the *resource utility* (Cox et al. 2000). Therefore, the buyer is likely to be able to wield considerable power over the supplier when:

(a) The supplier's resources are relatively plentiful and not highly important to the buyer; and/or

(b) The buyer's resources are relatively scarce and highly important to the supplier.

This situation has been a major feature of the relationship between major European supermarkets and their suppliers. With a handful of very large supermarket chains dominating each national market—such as Aldi and Metro in Germany, Carrefour and Intermarché in France, and Tesco, Sainsbury, and Asda in the UK—their resources, in terms of purchase potential and access to markets, have become relatively scarce but extremely important for food suppliers. At the same time, the suppliers' resources have become less scarce and important to the supermarkets, since they increasingly source on a global basis from a vast array of suppliers and manage to stock an impressive range of products which, except in a very few cases, would hardly suffer from the removal of one supplier's products. It is perhaps not surprising, then, that Europe's supermarkets have often been criticized for abusing their power over suppliers. For instance, in 2008, the European Parliament declared that 'evidence from across the EU suggests large supermarkets are abusing their buying power to force down prices paid to suppliers (based both within and outside the EU) to unsustainable levels and impose unfair conditions upon them'.[1]

Such practices can be criticized from a **deontological** perspective—in that those with power might be said to have a duty not to abuse it. More interesting, however, is a **consequentialist** position: the problems caused by abuse of supply-chain power are not just of consequence to the weaker partner. Using the example of the suppliers of UK clothing retailers, Jones and Pollitt (1998) show that an opportunistic abuse of power by

AN ETHICAL DILEMMA 9

A beautiful deal?

You work as a purchasing manager for a large European retailing company that is in the process of revamping its line of own-label cosmetics. This line is important to your business, and as your company has expanded, own-label cosmetics have gradually occupied an increasingly prominent role in the product mix in stores.

Your existing supplier of own-label products, *Beauty To Go*, has supplied your company for ten years and over two-thirds of their business is accounted for by your company's orders. You have a good relationship with the Account Manager of *Beauty To Go* who, like yourself, has been in her role for a number of years, and has become a good friend.

As you are considering how to proceed with the revamp, a competing supplier, *Real Cosmetics*, also contacts you, offering virtually identical products to *Beauty To Go*, with what appears to be equivalent supply arrangements, but at a slightly lower price per unit. Over a year this would work out to approximately €200,000 savings—not a huge sum for your company, but quite a substantial saving of about 2% on your costs. In addition, *Real Cosmetics* also highlights in its sales pitch that they go well beyond the industry standard for non-animal testing of their products' ingredients—again, a significant improvement over what *Beauty To Go* has been offering you.

Questions

1 What are the ethical issues at stake in this situation?
2 Which ethical theories do you think might be of help in deciding an appropriate course of action?
3 What are the main considerations that these theories raise?
4 How would you proceed in this situation?

retailers can lead to reductions in quality, lack of investment, lack of innovation, and even job losses and industry decline. In this case, the overexposure to risk may result in an underperformance of suppliers. Ultimately, excessive abuse of power may eventually even harm the powerful partner, particularly if their supplier relations become so dysfunctional as to jeopardize product quality and industry growth—thereby reducing long-term profitability.

Given such a set of possible negative outcomes, one might wonder why abuse of power would ever happen. Jones and Pollitt (1998) suggest that:

- In the short term, there may well be profit advantages to be gained by exercising excess power.
- Many firms will view the situation from a relatively narrow perspective and fail to see the broader cumulative industry effects that may ultimately harm them.

However, abuse of market power may also be somewhat more subtle and far less destructive at the macro level than envisaged by Jones and Pollitt (1998). Although market conditions can disadvantage suppliers, purchasing firms may choose to exploit their power differentials in some areas of business—for example, by forcing down prices—but offer support and investment in others—for example, by contributing market knowledge, financial support, and other management resources. This more variegated picture may well offer a more realistic picture of some industries (Bloom and Perry 2001; Ogbonna and Wilkinson 1996), but it makes any conclusive ethical evaluation difficult. Whilst individual actions may seem unethical, when put in the context of a longer-term interaction, the action may be more acceptable.

The question of loyalty

Related to the issue of power is the question of loyalty. The fair treatment expected by suppliers can be viewed in terms of a given deal struck between the two parties, but as we have just intimated, where those parties have been involved in a long series of exchanges over some time, we might also include further considerations. In particular, one might start to consider whether such an arrangement also confers some kind of expectation for loyalty on the part of the organizations. After all, if a company has been reliably supplying another for many years, should this not entitle them to some kind of stability and commitment from their partner in terms of ongoing orders and support? From an ethical point of view, though, does it make sense to suggest that firms have some kind of moral obligation of loyalty to their suppliers—and if so, how do we determine which suppliers can legitimately expect loyalty, and what exactly does an obligation of loyalty entail?

Loyalty is one of the virtues often prized in business, but loyalty to suppliers does not easily fit with an *economic view of the firm* that stresses the importance of free competition in order to achieve the most beneficial outcomes. According to this view, if a retailer such as Carrefour is 'encumbered' by loyalty from selecting new suppliers which offer higher quality or lower costs, then the retailer will become less competitive and its final consumers will have to face higher prices and/or poorer quality products.

It is possible to question these assumptions on several grounds:

- First, loyalty does not necessarily imply slavish acceptance of any conditions offered by the supplier. It can perhaps be better interpreted as the establishment of a long-term commitment, from which the two partners can potentially seek mutually beneficial outcomes. So rather than accepting a poorer deal from its supplier, the firm might work with their supplier to ensure that it remains as competitive as its rivals.

- Secondly, a long-term commitment can provide the opportunity to take advantage of reduced transaction costs through less switching of suppliers and contracts, as well as enabling more complex and customized ways of working together that benefit both partners, but are not easily replicable by other industry players (Artz 1999).

These arguments can be used to construct a fairly robust defence of intra-organizational loyalty from a consequentialist point of view, provided the area of business involved is one in which benefits can accrue through longer-term working relationships. The UK retailer, Marks and Spencer, for example, has long enjoyed a reputation for long-term, even paternalistic, supplier relationships. In areas such as food retailing, this has provided the basis for the firm to develop competitive differentiation with respect to its competitors by enabling it to develop premium quality products. However, a restructuring of its food operations, aimed at matching some of the tougher terms of its competitors (dubbed Project Genocide by its critics), led some commentators to suggest that the firm was risking the unique differences that had made it so successful in the first place (Braithwaite and Urry 2008).

Some industries, however, appear to rely almost exclusively on short-term transactional supplier relationships. This is particularly the case where the products being exchanged are commodities with little potential for adding value through the supply arrangement, such as basic manufacturing components or simple foodstuffs like rice and sugar. In this case, the ethical case for loyalty to suppliers would have to rely on deontological or virtue-based reasoning.

? THINK THEORY

How would you apply deontological reasoning to the question of supplier loyalty? Does this offer, in conjunction with the consequentialist argument above, a sufficient rationale for judging the actions of companies such as Marks and Spencer to be ethical or unethical?

VISIT THE WEBSITE for a short response to this feature

One situation where the presumption of the need for loyalty is particularly strong is where a single buyer represents a significant proportion of the supplier's total business—and hence, is effectively keeping them in business. In an era of long-term partnership supplying, this is not exactly an unusual situation, but clearly creates a situation ripe for exploitation, and might be said to place a heftier responsibility on the purchasing company. **Ethics in Action 9.1**, for example, describes some of the ways that brand-name companies in the apparel industry have been helping some of their major suppliers respond to a sudden loss of business through 'responsible exit' strategies. Nonetheless, the issue of supplier loyalty becomes considerably more complex when we look at the situation from the point of view of other potential suppliers. What may seem like loyalty to the two partners involved may seem more like unfair preferential treatment to other suppliers, as we shall now see.

Preferential treatment

The giving of preferential treatment to favoured suppliers is widely identified as one of the main ethical issues faced by purchasing staff—and one of the most complex challenges (Rudelius and Buchholz 1979). Where does an obligation to be loyal end and the granting of an unfair advantage begin? For example, is it acceptable for a firm to give a valued supplier information about its competitors' quotations so that the supplier can have a better chance of offering the best quotation?

VISIT THE WEBSITE for links to useful sources of further information

ETHICS IN ACTION 9.1 http://www.ethicalcorp.com

Ethical CORPORATION

Factory closures—breaking up is hard to do

Sean Ansett, 3 May 2009

The economic crisis is creating new dilemmas for brands, suppliers and workers in global supply chains. When the tills stop ringing on the high street, suppliers that make products for these brands face diminished cash flows, fewer orders and job cuts. The textile industry has been hit particularly hard. In January 2009, according to trade magazine Just Style, textile imports into the US were down 23% year-on-year. In autumn 2008, Hanesbrands announced nine factory closures in five central American countries, affecting roughly 8,000 workers. In March 2009, Nike announced cuts in shoe orders of 10% from four countries. Buyers are fighting for survival by cutting orders, reducing inventory, renegotiating terms of contracts and seeking to sell lower volumes at higher margins. Suppliers are faced with freezing credit, payment delays from their clients, and severe cash flow problems, making wage payments and required government contributions difficult.

Two scenarios can cause factory closures: situations when brands reduce or cancel orders. The degree of the impact will vary depending on the amount of production the brand had with the supplier and if the supplier has other clients. In some cases, workers have arrived at the factory to start a shift only to find the gates locked, machines gone, and owners who have fled the country, leaving workers without their wages and other benefits. If the workers are migrants, they may not even be able to get back to their country of origin, making them economic refugees. So what are the responsibilities of brands in these situations? What is the responsibility of the factory owner and government? What can be reasonably expected?

Painful transition

Nike has formulated a responsible transition policy. According to Nike's 2005–06 corporate responsibility report, the company will dedicate more time to assessing the financial health of suppliers and provide sufficient notification of any change of terms. Nike will also send an integrated response team, including compliance, sourcing, communications and government affairs experts to assess impacts on workers should there be production changes.

The MFA (Multi-Fiber Arrangement) Forum is a multi-stakeholder initiative set up to mitigate the negative impacts and production changes caused by the end of the Multi-Fiber Arrangement. It has formed a responsible transitions working group, which has been working full speed during the financial crisis. The forum has developed guidance related to responsible exits, particularly when the brand is responsible for more than 30% of production. Expectations regarding company behaviour include the following:

- Conduct a risk assessment of the impact of a decision to withdraw orders from the factory in question.
- Where a decision to reduce orders is likely to result in substantial retrenchment and/or closure, evaluate this business decision against its social impact.
- Give the contractor sufficient notice of the ending of the business relationship to allow for a retrenchment consultation procedure with the workforce, and monitor the consultation process.
- Where workers are retrenched as a result of a decision to reduce orders, monitor supplier adherence to national laws in order to ensure that workers are compensated in line with national law.
- Where migrant workers are involved, work with the supplier and the governments concerned to ensure that the workers enjoy equality of treatment with national workers and are redeployed within the country where possible, or if that is not possible, repatriated with all costs covered.

Gap's senior manager of social responsibility, Darryl Knudsen, says working through the forum can help make the transition to lower production in the clothing supply chain as painless as possible. He explains: 'The potentially enormous impact that widespread closures across industries and geographies could have on workers and communities demands collective action among global and local stakeholders. The needs of governments, brands, suppliers and workers must all be incorporated to translate policy debates into operational reality.'

While the MFA Forum's guidance is welcome and helpful, Lynda Yanz, executive director of the Maquiladora Solidarity Network, adds: 'Brands should ensure that factory management is also consulting workers or their representatives during a reduction in orders or exit process to explore options to stay or plan for an orderly exit process. Additionally, more transparency is needed from brands regarding their internal policies related to closures and sourcing decisions.'

Clearly, factory closure is an issue that one brand cannot solve on its own. Government has an important role to play too. 'Even large companies are limited in their ability to control international economic issues due to the crisis. Governments are increasingly going to need to play a strong role in ensuring that they have sufficient safety nets for impacted workers,' says Eileen Kaufman, executive director of Social Accountability International. Brands should seriously consider the potential damage to their licence to operate if factory exits and closures become commonplace. Will governments be as welcoming to these firms if they acted irresponsibly in bad times when the global economy improves? Neil Kearney, secretary-general of the International Textile, Garment and Leather Workers Federation, says: 'In cases, where factories fail to pay severance and other benefits to their workers, brands—which are in essence secondary employers—should arrange to pay the outstanding payments owed to workers.'

Actions taken today by companies in the economic downturn will impact their stakeholder relationships in the future. This crisis may just serve as the acid test to determine if ethical sourcing programmes are truly embedded in corporate strategy or merely words. Just as in a divorce, business exits should be managed skillfully and with great care.

Sources

Ethical Corporation, Sean Ansett, 3 May 2009, http://www.ethicalcorp.com.

VISIT THE WEBSITE for a short response to this feature

? THINK THEORY

Think about the case of responsible exits in terms of the conflicting duties that companies such as Gap and Nike have to their various stakeholders. Who are these stakeholders and how would you assess the strength of their rights in this situation?

One way of addressing the problem of preferential treatment is to apply the notion of **procedural justice**. Procedural justice is concerned with the fairness of the processes through which decisions are made. You may remember that in Chapter 7 (pp. 297–303), we discussed equal opportunities policies in relation to procedural justice. In the context of avoiding unduly preferential treatment for suppliers, we would be concerned about whether the contracting processes applied to different suppliers were equitable, such that all suppliers had equal opportunity to bid for business, their bids were assessed in the same way, and the assessment criteria used were non-discriminatory. As we have already said, it may very well be that a long-standing supply relationship is a criterion pertinent to the awarding of a contract, and this can legitimately be used to assess relative bids. But according to the tenets of procedural justice, this does not mean that valued suppliers can be advantaged by going through a process that discriminates against their competitors. This, however, is the case in the example given above because only the valued supplier gets to glean information about their opponents' quotes.

Of course, many cases of preferential treatment of suppliers occur when the individual purchasing officer is offered personal gifts or other inducements to sway their opinion. This can interject a **conflict of interest** into the supply relationship, since the interests of the purchasing officer might diverge from the interests of their company. As we shall see in a moment, this is one of the main ethical problems facing business–supplier relations. Before we look at this, though, we shall first briefly consider the more general issue of conflict of interest.

Conflicts of interest

Conflicts of interest are critical factors in causing various ethical problems, not just in relation to suppliers. However, purchasing and supply-chain management are areas where conflict of interest is particularly likely to surface (Handfield and Baumer 2006). A conflict of interest occurs when a decision has to be made about whose interests to advance. However, the key element in a conflict of interest situation that distinguishes it from a normal decision about whose interests to advance—for example, where a decision has to be made about which employee to promote—is that it involves an explicit obligation to act in another's interest (Boatright 2009: 124). Using this as a starting point, we can define conflict of interest as follows:

> **A conflict of interest occurs when a person's or organization's obligation to act in the interests of another is interfered with by a competing interest that may obstruct the fulfilment of that obligation.**

Organizational conflicts of interest typically occur when a firm is employed as a supplier of professional services of one sort or another—and hence would be expected to act in their client's interest—but this arrangement clashes with another interest of the supplier—perhaps an arrangement with a competitor to the first client, or even a desire to gain more work from the same client. Accounting firms, marketing agencies, law firms, and investment bankers are all organizations that might face conflicts of interest of this sort (Boatright 2009). For example, a market research agency might be employed to do a pilot study for a consumer products company to investigate the market potential for a new product. In expectation that positive results will lead to the client contracting further, more lucrative, market analysis, the market research company might be tempted to put an overly optimistic spin on its findings and thereby commit its client to an imprudent course of action. In Chapter 6 (pp. 255–7), we also described how rating agencies, as suppliers of financial information to investors, experience conflicts of interest because they are dependent on income from investment providers. Whilst conflicts of interest such as these are clearly of major importance, most problems of this type actually pertain to conflicts of interest between individuals, especially in the giving and receiving of gifts, bribes, and hospitality, as we shall now see.

Gifts, bribes, and hospitality

Gifts, gratuities, hospitality, bribes, kickbacks, bungs, sweeteners—there is seemingly no end to the variety of terms that are used to describe the official and unofficial 'perks' that purchasing staff might be offered in the course of their interactions with salespeople. Some of these offers might be innocent and quite genuine expressions of gratitude; some might be part and parcel of maintaining a decent buyer–seller relationship; some, however, will simply be inducements to get business that would not otherwise have been earned by more legitimate means. The offering of personal inducements is regularly identified by purchasing staff as one of the main ethical issues confronting their profession (Rudelius and Buchholz 1979; Cooper et al. 2000). The key question is where to draw the line between acceptable and unacceptable practice.

We have already discussed some of the main issues involved in this problem—inducements usually are made in order to secure some form of *preferential treatment* for the supplying company, and typically involve purchasing staff in a *conflict of interest* between their own personal gain and the best interests of their firm (Fisher 2007). As employees of the firm, purchasers are expected to fulfil an obligation to act in the firm's interest—namely getting the best deal, whether in terms of price, quality, support services, or whatever else best achieves the company's goals. When a purchaser receives a personal benefit from the seller—such as a bottle of whisky, a trip to a sports event, or an envelope stuffed with money—the problem is that the purchaser may be swayed to make a decision that does not fulfil this obligation to their employer.

Of course, many of us could probably quite easily rationalize that the gift did not affect our decision, particularly if it was unsolicited, or it was received after the actual transaction took place. How could one be influenced by something that hadn't even happened when the decision was made? There are a number of ways of looking at this.

- One is to consider the **intention of the gift-giver**. If their intention is to gain an additional advantage (as opposed to merely offering thanks for a job well done), then we might question the action.
- Another way is to look at the **impact on the receiver**. If their evaluation of the gift giver is enhanced after receiving the gift, then again we might start to raise some doubts about its ethicality. This is pertinent even when the gift is received after a deal has been concluded, since it might be seen to prejudice future evaluations.
- Finally, we might focus on the **perception of other parties**. If a competing supplier might interpret the giving of the gift as a deliberate bribe, then again we should probably question the action.

The raising of the issue of perception by others is significant here because it suggests that the resolution of ethical dilemmas does not just depend on those who are directly involved in them. Bribery in particular is a problem that, when its occurrence is perceived by others, can erode trust and reinforce a culture of dishonesty. For instance, imagine if you heard that your class professor had received a Christmas present of an expensive bottle of cognac from one of your class members. Regardless of the intention of the student, or its impact on the professor, if the student's grades were anything other than terrible then you might well start questioning the integrity of your professor, and even maybe consider the possibility of purchasing a small gift yourself!

As we saw in Chapter 4 (p. 173), once a culture of dishonesty has been created, the prevailing ethic in the workplace can be difficult to dislodge and can be profoundly influential on subsequent behaviour. Although many large organizations have a formal **purchasing code of ethics** in place, and guidelines for appropriate behaviour on issues such as gifts and hospitality are provided by professional bodies such as the Chartered Institute of Purchasing and Supply (see **Figure 9.2**), the purchasing function is widely regarded (by other company personnel and outsiders) to be largely unconcerned with ethics and very commercially minded (Drumwright 1994). Indeed, the purchasing environment seems to suffer more than most other organizational functions in relation to

As a member of the Chartered Institute of Purchasing & Supply, I will:

- Maintain the highest standard of integrity in all my business relationships
- Reject any business practice which might reasonably be deemed improper
- Never use my authority or position for my own personal gain
- Enhance the proficiency and stature of the profession by acquiring and applying knowledge in the most appropriate way
- Foster the highest standards of professional competence amongst those for whom I am responsible
- Optimise the use of resources which I have influence over for the benefit of my organisation
- Comply with both the letter and the intent of:
  - the law of countries in which I practise
  - agreed contractual obligations
  - CIPS guidance on professional practice
- Declare any personal interest that might affect, or be seen by others to affect, my impartiality or decision making
- Ensure that the information I give in the course of my work is accurate
- Respect the confidentiality of information I receive and never use it for personal gain
- Strive for genuine, fair and transparent competition
- Not accept inducements or gifts, other than items of small value such as business diaries or calendars
- Always to declare the offer or acceptance of hospitality and never allow hospitality to influence a business decision
- Remain impartial in all business dealing and not be influenced by those with vested interests

Use of the Code

Members of CIPS are required to uphold this code and to seek commitment to it by all those with whom they engage in their professional practice.

Members are expected to encourage their organisation to adopt an ethical purchasing policy based on the principles of this code and to raise any matter of concern relating to business ethics at an appropriate level.

The Institute's Royal Charter sets out a disciplinary procedure which enables the CIPS Council to investigate complaints against any of our members and, if it is found that they have breached the Code of Ethics to take appropriate action. Advice on any aspect of the Code of Ethics is available from CIPS.

Figure 9.2. Chartered Institute of Purchasing and Supply's Code of Professional Ethics

Source: Chartered Institute of Purchasing and Supply, March 2009: www.cips.org
Reproduced with permission from the Chartered Institute of Purchasing and Supply

the conditions that might foster ethical abuse. As Badenhorst (1994: 741) has argued: 'The purchasing environment creates a climate which promotes unethical behaviour ... Often sales representatives have little concern for ethical behaviour, and purchasers are tempted to obtain some personal gain from a transaction, often with the approval of the representative's employer. The management often encourages its sales representatives to act in a manner which they would find entirely unacceptable in their purchasing department. These double standards create a climate of dishonesty in a company, and tempt everyone, especially the purchaser.'

Given this pervading influence of culture, it is not surprising that some industries are more prone to problems of bribes, gifts, and hospitality than others. The construction industry, for example, has a long history of unofficial payments of one sort or another. In recent years, professional sport has also been rocked by a number of cases of bribes and kickbacks, such as the 2006 conviction of the Italian football club Juventus for match-fixing, resulting in their demotion to Serie B and the stripping of their Serie A titles. In fact, the growing threat of corruption in sport has seen sports governing bodies such as the International Cricket Council and the Association of Tennis Professionals spending more than €1m a year on their anti-corruption units.[2]

Ethics in negotiation

Finally, any discussion of ethics in supplier relationships is not complete without addressing the issue of business–supplier negotiation. As we said at the start of this section, many commentators have identified a shift away from adversarial supplier relationships towards something closer to a partnership model, suggesting that negotiation might be less subject to questionable ethics than in the past. Although to some extent this may well be true, the whole process of negotiation between buyer and supplier inevitably raises some ethical tensions, given that the situation itself is often characterized as one of two combatants coming together to do battle (Badenhorst 1994). As Reitz et al. (1998) suggest, to many people ethics and negotiation are like oil and water: they just don't mix. To illustrate their point, they list ten popular negotiating tactics, all of which they contend can be challenged on ethical grounds:

- Lies—about something material to the negotiation.
- Puffery—i.e. exaggerating the value of something.
- Deception—including misleading promises or threats and misstatements of facts.
- Weakening the opponent—by directly undermining the strengths or alliances of the opponent.
- Strengthening one's own position—for example, by means not available to the opponent.
- Non-disclosure—deliberately withholding pertinent information that would be of benefit to the opponent.
- Information exploitation—misusing information provided by the opponent in ways not intended by them.
- Change of mind—engaging in behaviours contrary to previous statements or positions.
- Distraction—deliberately attempting to lure opponent into ignoring information or alternatives that might benefit them.
- Maximization—exploiting a situation to one's own fullest possible benefit without concern for the effects on the other.

According to Reitz et al. (1998), although there are certain risks in doing so, a more ethical approach to negotiation can, and should, steer clear of such tactics. This is not only because it is the right thing to do, but also because such practices can incur costs on the negotiator. Specifically, these costs are:

- **Rigid negotiating**. Unethical tactics can draw negotiators into a narrow view of the tactics available to them, especially if they are perceived as having been successful in the past. However, in longer-term relationships, a more flexible and open approach may help to yield more advantageous win-win solutions.
- **Damaged relationships**. Customers and suppliers rarely cease to rely on each other once a deal has been negotiated. Even when the negotiation is a single event, implementation of the deal may be marred as a result of perceived ethical infractions. Where negotiations are part of a longer-term cycle, the costs of unethical negotiation may mount, as negotiators turn into embittered enemies rather than mutually supportive partners.
- **Sullied reputation.** Unethical negotiation can have a negative influence on the individual's or their company's image, making future bargaining more troublesome.
- **Lost opportunities.** Unethical negotiation not only undermines the negotiators' capabilities to reach mutually beneficial win-win agreements, but it also tends to prevent any progressive discussions which could bring new, profitable issues to the table.

Whilst this undoubtedly presents an overly positive perspective on ethics in negotiation between buyers and sellers, it is useful in helping us to view negotiation not so much as a zero-sum game, but as a chance to build towards a more mutually beneficial relationship. Firms' dealings with their suppliers do not always have to be characterized as a tussle between warring combatants. Somewhat more challenging, however, is the idea that this can also be true of their relationships with their competitors. Let us now look at this in more detail.

Ethical issues and competitors

As we have already mentioned, whilst there is some disagreement in the literature as to whether competitors are actually legitimate stakeholders in an organization, there does seem to be a reasonable case for suggesting that we can expect a certain level of ethical behaviour between competitors. Of course, this certainly does not preclude active, or even quite aggressive, competitive behaviour between rivals. In fact, as we saw in the previous chapter (and shall elucidate on below), the deliberate avoidance of competitive behaviour is itself a cause for ethical concern should consumers and other stakeholders be disadvantaged as a result.

The point is then that there appears to be a need to establish some kind of parameters regarding the limits to competition at either end of the scale. This means that ethical issues in dealing with competitors can relate to two distinct problems:

- **Overly aggressive competition**—where a company goes beyond acceptable behaviour in its direct relationship with a competitor, thereby harming the competitor in a way that is seen as unethical.
- **Insufficient competition**—where the actions of one of more companies acts to restrict competition in a market, thereby harming consumers in a way that is seen as unethical.

In the following, we shall examine the main issues and dilemmas that arise in both areas.

Problems of overly aggressive competition

In a competitive global marketplace, firms are expected to act aggressively in trying to secure a competitive advantage against their competitors. However, sometimes, this behaviour goes beyond the ethical boundaries of acceptable competitive behaviour—for instance, when competitors engage in spying, dirty tricks, and anti-competitive practices, as we shall now see.

Intelligence gathering and industrial espionage

All organizations collect and make use of some kind of information about their competitors. Just as your university or college will typically investigate the courses offered by their main competitors, so too will companies take a keen interest in the products, policies, and processes undertaken by their rivals. Indeed, such intelligence-gathering activities are very much a standard aspect of conventional market research and competitor benchmarking, and make for effective competitive behaviour. As Andrew Crane (2005) suggests, though, ethical questions arise when one or more of the following are deemed to have occurred:

(a) The *tactics* used to secure information about competitors are questionable since they appear to go beyond what might be deemed acceptable, ethical, or legal business practice.

(b) The *nature* of the information sought can itself be regarded as in some way private or confidential.

(c) The *purposes* for which the information is to be used are against the public interest.

Questionable tactics may take many forms, from the clearly illegal, such as breaking and entering a competitor's offices to steal information and installing tapping devices, to rather more grey areas. These grey areas include eavesdropping, searching through a competitor's rubbish, hacking, hiring private detectives, covert surveillance through spy cameras or electronic 'spyware', misrepresenting oneself by posing as a potential customer or employer, pressuring competitors' employees to reveal sensitive information about their operations—or even simply being accidently exposed to sensitive data by misdirected faxes or emails (Hallaq and Steinhorst 1994; Crane and Spence 2008). **Figure 9.3** provides examples of some common grey areas encountered by competitive intelligence professionals—and what they deem to be an appropriate response.

Some of these tactics are doubtful from an ethical point of view primarily because they violate a duty to be honest and truthful in business dealings (Boatright 2009: 120),

How do you match up to professional competitive intelligence gatherers? Here are two scenarios that were put to experienced industry insiders to explore their perspectives on the ethics of different tactics for generating competitive intelligence.

An eavesdropping scenario

You are a competitive intelligence professional seated on a long-haul airplane. Your neighbour opens a document that is entitled "Marketing Strategy for Product X," which is directly competitive with one of your firm's major products. After reading a few pages, he gets up to go to the bathroom on the plane. You have four options for your next action.

- **Option A:** I will take the copy of the marketing plan and hide it in my bag. When he returns and asks me if I saw his report, I'll tell him I don't know what he's talking about.
- **Option B:** While he's gone, I'll just take notes on the key elements of the competitor's strategy. Then I'll return the document to the exact place he left it and won't say anything.
- **Option C:** While he's gone, I will ask the flight attendant to find me a new seat on the plane. I will just move to a new seat to avoid the risk of potential unethical behaviour.
- **Option D:** I won't look at the document while he's gone. When he returns, I'll advise him that I work for a competing firm, and tell him that if he chooses to keep reading, it is at his own risk that he does so.

What would you do in this situation? Most industry professionals suggested that they would select Option D. When presented at a competitive intelligence industry conference, the majority of respondents (60%) selected this option, which is typically regarded as appropriate professional conduct. Only 1% selected Option A, the outright theft. However, a full 30% selected Option B, which, from an ethical and a legal point of view, could be considered highly questionable.

A misrepresentation scenario

You are attending a trade show. You take off the badge that identifies you as a competitor, and you then approach a booth at the exhibition. You tell the representative you have an interest in the product.

In your assessment, is this behaviour either:

- **Option A:** Normal competitive intelligence gathering practice
- **Option B:** Ethical, but aggressive competitive intelligence gathering practice
- **Option C:** Unethical competitive intelligence gathering practice
- **Option D:** Illegal competitive intelligence gathering practice

If industry insiders are anything to go by, your response to this may have reflected your country of origin. In a survey of more than 100 competitive intelligence professionals in the US and Europe, most North Americans thought this action was either unethical (48%) or illegal (44%), probably reflecting the strict legal enforcement of industrial espionage in the US. Europeans, in contrast, saw the action as either aggressive (39%) or unethical (55%), but only 6% viewed it as illegal.

Figure 9.3. Ethics in the grey areas of competitive intelligence

Sources: Fuld, L. M. 2006. Cultural effects on legal and ethical competitive intelligence. In D. Fehringer and B. Hohhof, *Competitive Intelligence Ethics: Navigating the Gray Zone*, Alexandria, VA: Competitive Intelligence Foundation: 51–5; Sapia-Bosch, A. and Tancer, R.S. 1998. 'Navigating through the Legal/ Ethical Gray Zone: What Would You do?' *CI Magazine*, vol.1 (1), April-June: 1–13.

and might easily be criticized from the perspective of deontological precepts such as the 'golden rule'—do unto others as you would have them do unto you—or Kant's categorical imperative. Moreover, once such methods become accepted into business practice—or to use Kant's words, they become 'universal law'—all firms tend to lose out: (a) because the industry is likely to suffer from a loss of trust; and (b) because it becomes necessary for all industry players to commit resources to institute procedures guarding against the loss of trade secrets to unscrupulous competitors (Boatright 2009: 120).

Private or confidential information may refer to any kind of information which the organization feels should not be freely available to outsiders and which therefore should have some kind of moral or legal protection. Whilst in principle this seems quite reasonable, it is rather more difficult to establish a corporation's right to privacy than it is an individual's—and certainly, the enforcement of privacy is considerably trickier. Specifically:

- Corporations are to some extent 'boundary-less'—they have fewer clear boundaries to define the private 'corporate space' compared with private individuals.
- Corporations consist of, and deal with, multiple individuals making control of information difficult.
- Much corporate activity takes place in public and quasi-public spaces such as shops, offices, hospitals, colleges, etc., and via shared infrastructure such as roads, railways, seas, telephone lines, fibre-optic cables, etc. These are easily and usually quite legitimately observed, infiltrated, or tracked.

However, even if it is difficult to fully ascribe a right to privacy to corporations, it is relatively more straightforward to suggest that certain information that corporations have is a form of property and is thus subject to *property rights* (Boatright 2009: 114). This particularly tends to apply to trade secrets, patents, copyrights, and trademarks—all of which are to some extent legally enforceable **intellectual property** that is said to belong to the organization.

Intellectual property rights can be assigned to many intangible forms of property, including product formulations, theories, inventions, software, music, formulae, recipes, processing techniques, designs, and so on. The development of such 'information' frequently involves organizations in millions of Euros investment in R&D costs. Unsurprisingly, then, corporations often go to great lengths and invest substantial resources in trying to keep this information secret from their competitors, so that they may reap the rewards of their investment. However, with improvements in information and communication technologies, the ease of replication of digital information, as well as the refinement of 'reverse-engineering' techniques (where competitors' products are stripped down and analysed in order to copy them), the unauthorized accessing and exploitation of intellectual property has been on the rise (Picard 2004; Shapiro 1998). In the pharmaceutical industry, for example, the protection of intellectual copyright through patents has been critical in providing firms with incentives to invest in research for new drugs. However, the lack of attention to providing affordable treatments for infectious diseases such as HIV/Aids, tuberculosis, and malaria in the developing world has generated a huge ethical and legal debate, especially with the rise of generic drug producers in countries such as Brazil and India who have made unauthorized copies of 'Big Pharma's' drugs and sold them at greatly reduced prices. In 2009, the British-based pharmaceutical giant GlaxoSmithKline announced a major shift in strategy in respect of such issues, marked by a commitment to low prices for developing countries, and most significantly of all, a pledge to set up a 'patent pool' so that drug companies can share intellectual property on neglected diseases (Balch 2009).

Public interest issues can arise when the information gleaned through espionage is put to purposes such as anti-competitive behaviour, including the deliberate removal or ruin of competitors, price hikes, or entrenchment of a monopoly position. Public interest issues may also arise when intelligence germane to national or international security or domestic economic performance is secured. With corporations involved in designing, producing, and servicing military hardware and software, governmental data storage, and other security-related products and services, the accessing of company data by competitors (especially from overseas), or even foreign governmental agencies can lead to threats to the public interest.

Unsurprisingly, public interest issues usually rest on *consequentialist* reasoning, namely that the action can be said to cause an overall aggregate reduction in happiness for affected members of society. Should competition be reduced as a result of industrial espionage, then the public may suffer because of increased prices and lower innovation over the long term. Spying related to military or other sensitive information may harm the public through increased exposure to risks of various kinds. For instance, in December 2007, *The Times* reported that the Director-General of the UK Security Service, MI5, had sent a confidential letter to 300 chief executives and security chiefs at banks, accountants, and legal firms, warning them that they were under attack from Chinese state organizations. The newspaper suggested that MI5 was effectively accusing China of carrying out 'state-sponsored espionage against vital parts of Britain's economy, including the computer systems of big banks and financial services firms' (Blakely et al. 2007).

'Dirty tricks'

Overly intense competition can also lead to questionable tactics beyond just stealing secrets and spying on competitors. A more generic term often used in the business world to describe the range of morally dubious practices that competitors occasionally turn to in order to outdo their rivals is 'dirty tricks'. In addition to industrial espionage, dirty tricks can include various tactics, among them:

- **Negative advertising**: where the firm deliberately sets out to publicly criticize their competitors, their products, or any product or performance claims the competitor may have made.
- **Stealing customers**: where a rival's customers are specifically approached in order to encourage them to switch suppliers, often using underhand methods such as misrepresentation, providing false information, bribery, or impersonating the competitor's staff.
- **Predatory pricing**: as we saw in the previous chapter, this involves the deliberate setting of prices below cost in order to initiate a price war and force weaker competitors out of the market.
- **Sabotage**: this can take many forms, but basically involves direct interference in a competitor's business in order to obstruct, slow down, or otherwise derail their plans.

While some of these tactics may seem a little extreme, they are not all that uncommon in contemporary business practice, and with new technologies emerging, the range of potential techniques is expanding. 'Malware', such as internet viruses, worms, and Trojan horses, may be covertly used by firms to sabotage their competitors' systems, or to divert customers from their intended website onto a competitor's.

Anti-competitive behaviour

Putting rival firms out of business can be about more than just intense competition between two industry rivals. In many cases, the stakes are considerably higher, since the action can signal an attempt to deliberately restrict competition in an industry in order to reap longer-term profitability. As we argued in the previous chapter, such anti-competitive practices usually contravene competition law, which is in place to ensure fair competition and protect consumers and other firms from monopolistic behaviour. However, such charges can be extremely difficult to prove.

One recent case that did lead to a major victory for regulators, however, came in 2009 when Intel the microchip manufacturer was handed a record fine of more than €1bn by the European Commission for offering hidden rebates to retailers if they sold only Intel products. Despite holding a substantially dominant position (80% of the market), it was Intel's abuse of this position in restricting competition that the EC criticized, not the monopolistic position itself. As the Competition Commissioner Neelie Kroes said at the time of the announcement, 'Intel has harmed millions of European consumers by deliberately acting to keep competitors out of the market for computer chips for many years'.[3]

Problems of insufficient competition

Anti-competitive behaviour can obviously also hurt consumers, particularly when it results in companies being able to abuse their dominance in a market to exploit customers through higher prices. Sometimes, though, ethical problems arise here not so much because rivals are overly competitive with each other, but because competition is reduced by rivals being insufficiently competitive with each other. Most of such behaviours are precluded by competition law, but the problems of determining when firms have colluded or abused a position can be difficult to determine.

Collusion and cartels

At the other end of the scale from such intense rivalry, then, is where select groups of competitors band together in a cartel or trading group to fix prices and other trading arrangements for their own mutual benefit. Again, we briefly discussed this issue of collusion in the previous chapter (p. 357), since it mainly results in a potential threat to consumer interests.

Abuse of dominant position

Finally, some markets may already be dominated by a single large competitor, which then has the opportunity to use its extra muscle to disadvantage consumers and smaller competitors alike. The European Commission, for example, ruled in 2004 that Microsoft's move into the market for low-end servers (i.e. the hubs of computer networks) abused the dominant position of its Windows operating system and that its bundling of Media Player software with Windows gave it an unfair advantage over competing audio and video software. Microsoft was ordered to pay a landmark €497m fine and to make Windows available to the market without Media Player software (Buck and Morrison 2005). The company was then slapped with further fines of €280m in 2006, and a record-breaking €899m in 2008 for failing to comply with the anti-trust ruling.[4] Further EC investigations into Microsoft's alleged abuse of its dominance of the PC market were also launched in 2008.

Globalization, suppliers, and competitors: the ethical challenges of global business networks

Deterritorialization of the corporate value chain can be identified as an important influence contributing to the process of globalization. George Yip (1995), for example, identifies the key forces driving globalization in business to be:

- Convergence of markets.
- Global competition.
- Cost advantages.
- Government influence.

Convergence of markets has meant that firms have increasingly sold their products across the world, thereby bringing them into direct competition with firms in, and from, different countries. This move towards *global competition* means that competitors may now hail from cultures with different understandings and expectations of business and of the nature of competition. Moreover, the impact of foreign competition in many countries might well have significant effects on the local economy.

The potential for *cost advantages* overseas has involved business in a fundamental restructuring of supply chains in the pursuit of lower-cost sites for production. This has seen vast numbers of multinational corporations shifting the sourcing and production of their products, components, and labour to less developed countries—a move that has been expedited by *government influence* in these countries. Again, this has involved corporations in business relationships with organizations operating under a different set of cultural practices and assumptions, and where standards of working practices, and health, safety, and environmental protection may differ markedly from at home.

What we have seen, then, is a dramatic reshaping of ethical considerations and problems when dealing with suppliers and competitors in a global, as opposed to a purely locally based, business network. This reshaping brings to the fore four main considerations:

- Different ways of doing business.
- Impacts on indigenous businesses.
- Differing labour and environmental standards.
- Extended chain of responsibility.

Different ways of doing business

By coming into contact with overseas suppliers and competitors, corporate managers are often confronted with very different ways of thinking about and evaluating business ethics. As we have already seen in earlier chapters dealing with employees and consumers, it is clear that certain practices which may be morally questionable at home might be seen as perfectly legitimate in a different cultural environment, just as some practices which are perfectly acceptable in one's own country may raise questions overseas. For example, Jerold Muskin (2000) suggests that for *competitors*, differences in national culture and law give rise to different notions of *intellectual property*. Whilst European, and even more so US, companies might expect the granting of exclusive rights to any novel technologies they develop, in Asia innovation is often seen as a public good to be used for the advance of technology by all.

In the main, though, different ways of doing business are primarily important for corporations' dealings with their *suppliers*, particularly in relation to **gift giving, bribery, and corruption**. Different countries tend to exhibit differing attitudes towards the appropriateness of gift giving between customers and suppliers. As we saw in Chapter 1, in Chinese cultures the widespread practice of *guanxi*—namely, 'a system of personal connections that carry long-term social obligations'—places considerable emphasis on the desirability and acceptability of reciprocal favours and gift giving to develop and maintain relationships (Millington et al. 2005: 255). This establishes different cultural expectations around gift giving in buyer-seller relationships. Whilst a European purchasing officer might easily interpret the gift as an attempt at bribery rather than simple courtesy, if they refused to accept the gift, they might risk causing offence, thus harming the business relationship and jeopardizing the deal.

Thomas Donaldson (1996) suggests that, in consequence, as Western firms have become more familiar with such traditions, they have increasingly tolerated gift-giving practices and even applied different limits on gift giving and receiving in countries such as China and Japan than elsewhere. This, he argues, is not so much a matter of *ethical relativism* (which he claims, as we have, is a highly problematic approach to business ethics), but is simply a matter of respect for local tradition.

Going back to our different ways of evaluating gift giving above (p. 402), if the act is without an *intent* to gain undeserved favour, if it does not have the *effect* of doing so, and if it is not *perceived* as doing so, then probably it should be regarded as acceptable when consistent with a broader social norm. This is especially the case when the norm also dictates that the giving is an *exchange*. There is, it would seem to us, a significant difference between a buyer and a seller exchanging gifts, and a salesperson simply offering the buyer a long line of presents with the expectation that the reciprocity would come in the form of extra business rather than a gift in return. The latter offers a lot more potential for conflict of interest than the former.

The main problem here, though, is that people all too often regard this kind of respect for tradition as a signal that all local customs should be accepted and adapted to, regardless of their ethical implications. If we accept gifts from suppliers, then why should we blanch at taking or giving bribes to oil the wheels of business? The issue of corruption is a major problem in many countries, especially in less developed or developing economies.

However, evidence suggests that managers in such cultures often draw a clear distinction between gift giving within a culturally accepted framework, such as *guanxi*, which is designed to build business relationships, and illicit payments that serve the purpose of lining people's pockets at the expense of their organization (Millington et al. 2005).

However, the problem is not simply with those accepting bribes, but also with those willing to pay them. For example, the *Bribe Payers Index*, produced by the not-for-profit organization Transparency International, provides an illuminating picture of the propensity for bribe paying by MNCs from various countries. The index, based on responses from almost 3,000 senior business executives in 26 countries, shows that companies based in large emerging economies such as Russia, China, and India are widely seen as likely to use bribery to gain business abroad. At the other end of the scale, Belgium, Canadian, and Dutch companies are seen as the least likely to bribe (see **Figure 9.4**). The survey on which the index is based also shows that the public works, construction, and real estate sectors are seen to be more likely to bribe officials in their business dealings than others **(see Figure 9.5)**.

Rank	Country	Score
1	Belgium	8.8
1	Canada	8.8
3	Netherlands	8.7
5	Germany	8.6
5	United Kingdom	8.6
5	Japan	8.6
8	Australia	8.5
9	Singapore	8.1
9	USA	8.1
12	Spain	7.9
14	South Africa	6.5
14	South Korea	6.5
17	Italy	7.4
17	Brazil	7.4
19	India	6.8
20	Mexico	6.6
21	China	6.5
22	Russia	5.9

Figure 9.4. Bribe paying by multinational companies abroad according to country of origin

Scores based on 0 to 10, where a perfect score, indicating zero perceived propensity to pay bribes, is 10. Thus, companies headquartered in those countries with a lower score have a higher perceived propensity to bribe.

Source: adapted from 2008 Bribe Payers Survey. Copyright 2008 Transparency International: the global coalition against corruption. Used with permission. For more information, visit http://www.transparency.org.

Business Sector	Score
Public works/construction	5.2
Real estate/property development	5.7
Oil and gas	5.9
Heavy manufacturing	6.0
Mining	6.0
Pharmaceuticals/medical care	6.2
Utilities	6.3
Civilian aerospace	6.4
Power generation and transmission	6.4
Forestry	6.5

Figure 9.5. Top ten sectors for bribe paying

The scores range from 0 to 10, where 0 represents the view that 'bribes are almost always paid' and 10 that 'bribes are never paid' by a sector.

Source: adapted from 2008 Bribe Payers Survey. Copyright 2008 Transparency International: the global coalition against corruption. Used with permission. For more information, visit http://www.transparency.org.

Why is bribery so endemic to international business? The answer to some extent seems to be that multinational businesses are promulgating the practice because it is 'normal', 'expected', or 'customary' in the host country. Unless we are going to slip into relativism though, this does not necessarily condone the practice. Just to say something is 'normal' does not imply that it is 'right'. Thirty-eight states across the world have now signed up to the OECD Anti-Bribery Convention. The convention is aimed at stamping out corruption in international business, and the broad range of signatories suggests a gathering international consensus over the undesirability of corruption, and a commitment to dealing with it. Nonetheless, enforcement of the convention remains a challenge for most states, with one recent report suggesting that there was little or no enforcement in at least 21 of the signatory countries to the convention.[5]

In fact, though, for the individual manager, the question is not always one of whether bribery is right or wrong, but whether doing business in certain countries is even *possible* without such practices. Regardless of whether an individual firm has a code prohibiting bribery, or whether one's country has signed up to the OECD convention, if a reasonable level of business cannot go ahead without bribery, how is the individual going to proceed? Many MNC staff seem to be caught between the ethical commitments of their code, and the realities of everyday business. One way that some firms have responded to this problem is to amend their codes of conduct so that employees are not penalized for any loss of business due to avoidance of bribery. For instance, if you go back to Unilever's code of business principles in **Figure 5.3**, this categorically suggests that 'the board of Unilever will not criticise management for any loss of business resulting from adherence to these principles'.

Impacts on indigenous businesses

The role of MNCs in corruption is often one of perpetuating extant problems. However, they can often bring new problems too. The size, power, and political influence of MNCs often means that they enjoy considerable cost and other advantages compared with local competitors. As Jennifer Spencer (2008: 341) suggests, multinationals 'can harm indigenous firms by posing strong competition in product, labour, and financial markets and by offering employment alternatives to individuals who would otherwise found their own business'. This can mean that the exposure to the competition of a major multinational such as Starbucks, IKEA, Microsoft, or Monsanto can 'crowd out' local enterprises and severely threaten the business of indigenous competitors (Klein 2000).

Of course, the introduction of more and better competition can often be a force for innovation, better products, lower prices, and economic growth. Multinationals can build value-enhancing partnerships with local firms, expose local entrepreneurs to new practices, and contribute to the human capital of local workers (Spencer 2008). This is why international organizations such as the WTO promote global trade, and why even humanitarian organizations such as the UN promote the desirability of market development for underdeveloped countries. However, such competition can also result in the matching of unequal rivals, where the ultimate consequence can be the elimination of local competition, and as we saw in the previous chapter, a homogenization of the high street.

The key point here is that MNCs may often be able to negotiate far more attractive trading arrangements than their weaker indigenous competitors; they may bring specialized management knowledge, economies of scale, advanced technology, powerful brands, and a host of other advantages (Dawar and Frost 1999). Similarly, they may be able to force local suppliers into accepting terms and conditions which barely keep them in business. There are clearly issues of fairness to be considered here, as well as questions of whether local competitors should be protected in some way—particularly if MNCs themselves are benefiting from certain protections. For example, the interests of large MNCs are often promoted by their own national governments (because their success is vital to economic growth), and even by host governments overseas (since the influx of jobs and investment can be highly beneficial).

This problem of unfair competition from MNCs is a particular cause for concern when it threatens the viability of an entire local industry as this can lead to more fundamental social and economic decay. For example, the so-called 'banana wars' (between the EU and the Caribbean on one side and the US and Latin American countries on the other) have turned into the World Trade Organization's longest running dispute. The clash is a result of European attempts to protect small-scale Caribbean banana growers against cheaper imports from US MNCs, such as Dole foods, Del Monte, and Chiquita International. Many Caribbean countries have been reliant on the banana industry, but with costs up to double those of Latin American-based producers, the sustainability of the Caribbean industry has long been dependent on a special trading relationship with the EU, coupled with restrictions and tariffs on Latin American imports. The US, Ecuador, and other Latin American countries, partly driven by lobbying from American multinationals, have lodged a series of complaints against the EU's 'discriminatory' system with the WTO. Over the course of the dispute, the US imposed sanctions valued at nearly €200m on certain European imports, whilst in 2001 the EU agreed to change its rules, providing for the phasing out of protection for Caribbean bananas by 2006. In a further blow to the EU, though, the WTO ruled in 2008 that EU import duties on bananas continued to flout global trade rules.[6]

VISIT THE WEBSITE for a short response to this feature

? THINK THEORY

To what extent is it appropriate to protect local businesses from 'unfair' competition from MNCs? Consider this situation from the perspectives of theories of justice and utilitarianism.

Differing labour and environmental standards

As firms from industrialized countries have increasingly sourced through global supply chains, probably the most prominent ethical problem to have come under the spotlight is the labour and environmental conditions under which their suppliers operate. You may remember that back in Chapter 7 we looked at the 'race to the bottom' occasioned by the demand by MNCs for lower-cost production in developing countries such as China, Indonesia, Vietnam, India, and Bangladesh. This raises substantial ethical problems for companies that source their products in lower-cost countries, for it is often the case that lower costs are accompanied by poorer labour conditions, less environmental protection, and lower attention to health and safety protection. These, as we have already mentioned a number of times in the book so far, can, and frequently have, led to human rights and other abuses.

The number of high-profile media exposés of such incidents since the beginning of the 1990s has been phenomenal. Clothing and sportswear producers have frequently been the most affected, with accusations of sweatshop conditions being launched at major European brands such as Adidas, C&A, Marks and Spencer, and Reebok, as well as high-profile US brands such as Disney, Gap, Levi's, Nike, Tommy Hilfiger, and Wal-Mart. Other industries that have been the subject of media, trade union, and pressure group attention include toy assembly, rug and carpet making, and food production.

Typically, the debate has mainly centred on pay, working conditions, and child labour. The fundamental conventions of the International Labour Organization (ILO), however (which are probably the most widely recognized and influential agreements on labour rights), also refer to broader issues, such as freedom of association, equality, abolition of forced labour, etc. Many companies have discovered (or their critics have discovered for them) that in their suppliers' factories, workers have been paid below a living wage, subjected to physical and verbal abuse, worked compulsory overtime, failed to have statutory rights to time off recognized, and even engaged in child labour.

We have seen in Chapter 3 that different ethical theories provide a range of arguments for and against issues such as child labour. However, these conditions have been seen as all the more inequitable because of the startling comparison that they make with the prices paid by consumers in Europe and the US for the products they make, as well as the pay and conditions earned by staff in the company's head office—in particular, the stellar remuneration packages of the companies' CEOs. For example, one widely quoted statistic is that while ex-Disney CEO Michael Eisner was earning $9,783 an hour in the 1990s, a Haitian worker sewing Disney pyjamas earned just 28 cents an hour. This means it would have taken a Haitian worker 16.8 years to earn Eisner's hourly income (Klein 2000: 352). Such disparities are alarming, and to many appear unjustifiable when the total costs of labour in producing, for example clothes, typically only amount to something like 1% of the final retail price (compared with 25% for brand profit, overheads, and promotion) (Robins and Humphrey 2000). **Ethics on Screen 9** presents a vivid portrayal of these issues as they relate to the global supply chain for coffee.

> **? THINK THEORY**
>
> In Chapter 7, we discussed Thomas Donaldson's argument that many problems of poor wages and conditions were problems of relative development rather than simply differences in ethics (p. 322). How would you compare Donaldson's argument with that of the justice-based argument above?

VISIT THE WEBSITE for a short response to this feature

Different environmental and health and safety standards in suppliers' countries can also provide a loophole through which firms can potentially secure lower-cost supplies by bypassing the stringent standards in their country of origin. For example, the recycling of 'end-of-life' electronic waste (see p. 379 in the previous chapter) has increasingly been outsourced to developing countries in Asia and Africa. Despite international laws banning the export of hazardous waste to developing countries, the combination of spiralling amounts of waste, lax regulation, and a thriving and lucrative informal economy in countries such as China, India, Ghana, and Nigeria has led to a growing problem of unregulated reprocessing, where the release of lead, mercury, and other dangerous chemicals poses serious threats to human and environmental health. With millions of tonnes of electronic waste being illegally shipped by companies in the developed world to unscrupulous processors in developing countries, the problem of 'digital cemeteries' of e-waste has become a major ethical issue for manufacturers and recyclers alike. In response to growing criticism, the US computer producer Dell announced in 2009 that it would ban all exports of e-waste to developing countries.[7]

Extended chain of responsibility

Ultimately, the implication of these shifts towards global supply and competition is that individual firms appear to be faced with the prospect of an extended chain of responsibility. Where once it may have been perfectly acceptable to argue that the ethics of a firm's suppliers, or a firm's impact on its competitors, was simply not any of its business, this is no longer the case (see Emmelhainz and Adams 1999). The different social and economic conditions present in other countries, as well as the sheer inequalities brought to the surface by international trade, have meant that the relatively level playing field constituted by national business has been replaced with the sloping and bumpy playing surface of globalization.

VISIT THE WEBSITE for links to useful sources of further information

VISIT THE WEBSITE to see a trailer for 'Black Gold'

ETHICS ON SCREEN 9

Black Gold

It shows with haunting clarity the discrepancy between the paltry amounts farmers receive and the gargantuan profits made in the West.

Adam Forrest, *Sunday Herald*

Drinking your morning cappuccino, you may have little idea about how the coffee beans with which it has been made came to get there. The investigative documentary, *Black Gold*, however, lifts the lid on the global coffee industry and shows us exactly where they come from and who the winners and losers have been along the length of the global supply chain. In particular, it seeks to demonstrate how trade in the world's most popular drink operates to enrich a few large multinational food and beverage companies, whilst impoverishing farmers in the global South.

Speak-it Productions Docfactory

The film tells the story of Tadesse Meskela, the manager of the Oromia Coffee Farmers Co-operative Union in Ethiopia. Ethiopia is actually the birthplace of coffee, having been the original location for the coffee plant that is now cultivated in numerous countries worldwide. The film follows Meskela, as he goes on a mission to save the thousands of struggling small-scale coffee farmers in his co-operative. With low coffee prices pushing many of his farmers into bankruptcy, Meskela attempts to find buyers willing to pay a higher (and, the film argues, fairer) price for his highly regarded, and high quality Ethiopian beans.

The film travels from the coffee farms in Ethiopia to the World Trade Organization conference in Cancun, Mexico, and from the Seattle home of Starbucks to the trading floors of international coffee exchanges. In so doing, it explores the complex economics of global commodity chains, and demonstrates how a €2 cappuccino in the West may deliver only 2 cents to the grower in Africa. The message is that despite much of the value of coffee residing in the quality of the beans, most of the economic value is captured by the companies who act as middlemen between the farmers and the consumer. As a result, it is the global corporations that dominate the international coffee industry, namely Nestlé, Kraft, Proctor and Gamble, Sara Lee, and especially Starbucks, that the film targets as the main culprits for causing the Ethiopian farmers' misery.

Despite a relatively limited theatrical release, the film showed at over 60 international film festivals and has been widely seen on DVD and national TV. It has even had special screenings at 10 Downing Street in the UK, the UN in New York, and the EU in Brussels. As a result, it has generated a substantial amount of publicity, and no shortage of attention from the companies it targets in the movie, most notably Starbucks. In response to the film, the company rolled out a PR offensive, including emailing employees to emphasize the good work the company was doing, sending representatives to screenings to offer a more positive spin on the coffee-growing story, and putting a clear message on its website saying Black Gold 'incompletely represents the work Starbucks is doing'.

The film has clearly helped educate a growing number of people about social and economic conditions in the coffee supply chain. It offers an entertaining and hard-hitting critique that also manages to be visually impressive, and at times quite poetic. That it is perhaps somewhat overly strident in its castigation of corporations is understandable given the filmmakers' closeness to its main protagonist. Nonetheless, its critics have questioned the easy shots it takes at big corporations, when the problems with the coffee supply chain remain somewhat more complex. As Mark Pendergrast, the American author and independent historian, said: 'Black Gold is very good in terms of raising issues, but it's a very unfair film because the implication is that Starbucks is starving people in Ethiopia. That's a very black-and-white way of looking at an issue with many shades of grey. Starbucks have one of the best sustainable practices in the world, although they do a bad job of communicating it. Yes, they could do more, but if you want to pick a bad guy in coffee, Starbucks is not it.'

Sources

Forrest, A. 2007. Grounds for complaint? *Sunday Herald*, 26 May: http://www.sundayherald.com.
Seager, A. 2007. Starbucks stirred by fair trade film. *Guardian*, 29 Jan.: http://www.guardian.co.uk.
Smith, D. 2007. British film-makers ask: what is the hidden cost of your £2 latte? *Observer*, 27 May: http://www.guardian.co.uk.
http://www.blackgoldmovie.com.

What we see, then, is that relations with other businesses are no longer only conducted within a national community with legislation and broadly agreed rules of the game that are considered to be fair to all. Hence, corporations now have to consider their ethical responsibilities much more broadly, not least because pressure groups have discovered that the best way to focus attention on practices and conditions in anonymous factories in far-off places is not to target the factory itself, but to target the big brand multinational which sources its products from them. This, as we shall now see, has led to the supply chain being used as a conduit for ethics management and regulation.

■ The corporate citizen in the business community: ethical sourcing and fair trade

We stated in Chapter 2 that one of the most crucial areas where corporations enter the realm of citizenship and begin to take over the role of governments is in the regulation and control of other businesses. This can be mainly seen to happen through the supply chain, via a process known as *ethical sourcing*.

Ethical sourcing

Ethical sourcing (also known as ethical trade or responsible supply-chain management) occurs when a supply-chain member introduces social and environmental criteria into their purchase decisions in order to support certain practices and/or suppliers. Therefore, whilst it can actually take a variety of forms, ethical sourcing can be broadly defined as follows:

Ethical sourcing is the inclusion of explicit social, ethical, and/or environmental criteria into supply chain management policies, procedures, and programmes.

Although far from comprehensive, increasing numbers of large companies now include some kind of criteria of this kind in their purchasing policies and agreements (Hughes 2005). One of the forerunners of this practice was the UK DIY retailer B&Q which, since 1991, has required all of its suppliers to provide information on environment performance as part of its Supplier Environmental Audit. More recently, various firms such as Adidas, Nike, Reebok, and Puma have introduced ethical codes of conduct intended to prevent labour and human rights abuses in their suppliers' operations, whilst companies such as the Body Shop, Chiquita, Fat Face, Fyffes, and Marks and Spencer have joined the Ethical Trading Initiative to improve their implementation of such codes (Emmelhainz and Adams 1999; ETI 2009; Frenkel and Scott 2002). **Ethics Online 9** discusses some of the online resources that have emerged to help firms deal with responsibility issues in the supply chain.

It has been increasingly common for firms engaged in ethical sourcing to introduce some kind of social auditing approach in order to ensure compliance with their sourcing guidelines in supplier factories, farms, and other production units. This practice was discussed in detail in Chapter 5 (pp. 211–17). Of course, the mere inclusion of ethical sourcing criteria in supply-chain management is no guarantee that they will be especially germane to the continuation of supply relationships. However, studies have shown that supply-chain pressure has been a key factor in prompting firms to seek various social and environmental certifications of one sort or another, even if they are not necessarily perceived as intrinsically valuable. These include accreditations such as the staff training and development award, *Investors in People* (Ram 2000) and the environmental quality standard *ISO 14001* (Delmas and Montiel 2009). For example, in the early 2000s, all of the American 'big three' carmakers—Ford, GM, and Chrysler—requested their suppliers to adopt ISO 14001 accreditation—although only about 25% actually did so before the deadline set by the companies. As Delmas and Montiel (2009) demonstrate, the willingness of suppliers to comply with or resist such initiatives is strongly determined by the type of relationship they have with the companies that purchase from them. Specifically, those suppliers with a high dependence on their customers are more likely to comply (because their assets cannot easily be deployed in supplying other firms), as are those which are relatively new entrants to the industry (because they need to build up their reputation). For suppliers, the public act of gaining ethical certification can therefore act as a way of reducing *information asymmetries* between themselves and potential buyers (King et al. 2005).

Ethical sourcing as business–business regulation

In the absence of specific or sufficient legislation in suppliers' countries, or more usually, where there is simply weak enforcement of existing legislation, this kind of supply-chain pressure can be the most effective form of regulation for these companies. Although this is not regulation in the formal sense of ensuring compliance with government legislation, the pressure exerted by powerful corporate customers to comply with ethical sourcing guidelines and criteria does constitute some form of a regulatory intervention in the supply chain (Cashore 2002; Hughes 2001, 2005; Locke and Romis 2007). The threat of losing business or being de-listed by a major customer can act as a powerful force for

ETHICS ONLINE 9

Practical resources for managing supply chain ethics

VISIT THE WEBSITE for links to useful sources of further information

For most companies, the challenge of tackling ethics in the supply chain is a daunting task. It is one thing to manage business ethics internally, but where do you start in dealing with all your suppliers, and their suppliers, and so on? Even companies with lots of experience in one area of supply chain ethics may lack expertise in important new areas such as supply-chain sustainability. Suppliers too need help in developing ethical relationships with their corporate customers.

In the last few years, pressing demands for improved supply-chain ethics have led to the emergence of numerous online practical resources to help managers get to grips with some of these challenges. The *Portal for Responsible Supply Chain Management*, for example, was developed by a consortium of businesses and support organizations, including Hewlett Packard, Titan, Volkswagen, and L'Oréal to provide hands-on tools and information to both producers and buyers. The site features advice on the key steps in developing responsible supply-chain management from either side of the exchange relationship and includes various resources in the form of company guidelines, sourcing standards, and other reference materials.

Another site with lots of practical advice and guidance is provided by *Business and the Community* under their 'Marketplace' programme on responsible supply chains. A notable feature of this site is the interesting assortment of case studies of successful company initiatives from British American Tobacco's work with tobacco growers, the office equipment company Ricoh's green procurement initiative, and Sainsbury's programme to develop sustainable fish sourcing for their UK supermarket business.

Of course, if you're a manager looking for practical help with supply-chain ethics, then you are already probably fairly well convinced that your company needs to take the issue seriously. But what about other people in the organization—the marketing, purchasing, or operations staff who remain uncommitted to ethical practices—or the suppliers or customers that will need to come on board to make any new initiatives successful? The *Ethical Trading Initiative* site provides resources for managers facing these challenges, with factsheets, leaflets, DVDs, and video clips laying out the case for ethical trade, and how to secure buy-in from key stakeholders. The site also offers access to codes of conduct, workbooks, guidelines, and other useful materials for practitioners.

Online resources such as these offer managers—and students of business ethics—plenty of insights into the practicalities of ethical supply-chain management. And for those looking for further support and assistance, they also offer paid consultancy, membership, advisory services, and conferences along with the freely available materials. After all, the organizations behind the websites are also potential suppliers (and we might hope ethical ones) of business services for the corporate community.

Sources

Business in the Community website: http://www.bitc.org.uk.
Ethical Trading Initiative website: http://www.ethicaltrade.org.
Portal for Responsible Supply Chain Management: http://www.csr-supplychain.org.

change, particularly when the threat is shown to be more than just an idle one. In particular, when *competitors* within an industry collaborate to introduce ethical guidelines for suppliers, it is often difficult for suppliers to avoid compliance.

This kind of pressure on suppliers can effect further change through the supply chain, and even in the wider business network. This is because not only are suppliers' own suppliers often involved in any progress towards compliance with ethical sourcing guidelines (and in turn *their* suppliers, and so on), but competing suppliers also have a chance to gain business if they have the right ethical policies or accreditations. Hence, a purchasing 'multiplier effect' can be set in motion which has the potential to achieve social change more quickly and thoroughly than any other single activity that a particular firm could undertake (Preuss 2005).

The mechanism by which ethical sourcing works is very much the same as the process of ethical consumption discussed in the previous chapter—except that here it is a corporation (or group of corporations) that is the customer, not an individual person. This obviously constitutes a concentration of buying power far in excess of that wielded by individual consumers, implying that ethical sourcing is a very potent source of corporate citizenship. As Sarah Roberts (2003) explains, though, the success of ethical sourcing initiatives depends on a number of factors in addition to the power of the corporate buyers. This includes the power of suppliers, the reputational vulnerability of network members, the diffuseness of the supply base, and the length of the supply chain between the corporate buyer and the companies where the ethical issues are most pronounced. This, she suggests, explains why ethical sourcing initiatives in the forestry products and apparel industries have been more successful than those in the confectionery industry.

Another factor to consider is whether ethical sourcing is attempted by individual firms alone, or whether whole groups of competing firms join together in a coalition to address the problem. Such industry alliances can take a number of forms, from setting up supplier codes of conduct, to systems of supplier auditing and evaluation. Frequently, they also involve pressure groups or government agencies as advisers or even managers of the programme. We shall be looking at some examples of these types of multi-actor initiatives in the next two chapters, but in the meantime, let us consider the types of strategies that firms or alliances might use in ethical sourcing.

Strategies of business–business regulation

There are two main ways in which firms can effect ethical sourcing through the supply chain (see Winstanley et al. 2002):

- **Disengagement**. This involves the setting of clear standards for suppliers (e.g. a code of conduct), coupled with a means for assessing compliance with those standards (such as an ethics audit). Failure to meet standards in the short to medium term will result in disengagement by the company in order to do business elsewhere. The toy company Mattel's 'zero tolerance' policy on violations of its supplier code of conduct is illustrative of this approach (Iwata 2006). This *compliance pattern* 'is characterized by global firm domination: the global firm develops and introduces the code, communicates its importance, and is responsible for its enforcement' (Frenkel and Scott 2002: 33).

- **Engagement**. This too involves setting standards and compliance procedures but tends to rely on longer-term 'aims', together with incremental 'targets', in order to foster a step-by-step approach to improving standards. Here, the firm is likely to work with their suppliers to achieve improvements, utilizing a *collaboration pattern* based on partnership (though not power equality) (Frenkel and Scott 2002). The German sporting good company Adidas is an example of a company that emphasizes an engagement approach (Frenkel and Scott 2002).

Whichever strategy an organization adopts, an ethics code or supplier code of conduct is likely to play an important role. We saw in Chapter 5 that there were four types of codes, any of which might be used in this context. This includes corporate codes, a professional code (such as the UK Institute of Purchasing code of conduct in Figure 9.2), industry codes (e.g. the Apparel Industry Partnership's Workplace Code of Conduct—see van Tulder and Kolk 2001), or a programme code (such as the Ethical Trading Initiative base code—see Chapter 10).

However, we also noted in Chapter 5 that simply having a code was insufficient for ensuring ethical behaviour. According to Emmelhainz and Adams (1999), to be successful in practice, ethical sourcing of this kind actually requires three things:

- A workable code of conduct.
- A system of monitoring supplier compliance with the code.
- Enforcement policies which establish the penalties for violation.

Whilst many companies have been relatively quick to introduce supplier codes of conduct, the introduction of effective monitoring and enforcement has proved to be less common (Emmelhainz and Adams 1999). This no doubt is at least partially due to the complexity and expense of doing so. Moreover, an effective collaborative approach requires that the firm does more than set compliance targets but engages over the long term in supplier development. One area where a more comprehensive and participative system has been successfully introduced is in the fair trade industry.

Fair trade

So far, we have discussed ethical sourcing as a form of regulation through the supply chain. This tends to give the impression that ethical sourcing is always a way of controlling suppliers. However, in some cases, ethical sourcing can actually be more developmental, where suppliers that are seen to be socially beneficial in some way are protected, rewarded, and assisted in achieving development goals (Blowfield 1999; Hughes 2005). For example, we saw earlier in the chapter (pp. 415–16) how the so-called 'banana wars' represented an attempt to apply a form of ethical sourcing to protect the interests of Caribbean farmers. Similarly, the Body Shop has for some years operated a 'Trade Not Aid' programme, which seeks to assist small-scale, indigenous communities in enhancing their standard of living through supposedly 'fair' supply contracts with the retailer.

Approaches to ethical sourcing that focus on equitable trade arrangements, small-scale producers, and supplier empowerment are usually referred to as *fair trade*. As

Smith and Barrientos (2005) suggest, the two types of approach—ethical sourcing and fair trade—have traditionally been quite different. The former has mainly been driven and implemented by big brand multinationals, whilst the latter has been more relational in approach and led by alternative trading organizations. Although recent years have witnessed growing convergence of the two approaches (Smith and Barrientos 2005), fair trade retains a distinctive flavour, or what some refer to as an 'ethical value-added' to conventional trading arrangements (McMurtry 2009). Thus, fair trade might be usefully defined as follows (Nicholls and Opal 2005: 6):

> **Fair trade is a system aimed at offering 'the most disadvantaged producers in developing countries the opportunity to move out of poverty through creating market access under beneficial rather than exploitative terms. The objective is to empower producers to develop their own business and wider communities through international trade'.**

Many of the growers of everyday products such as coffee, tea, rice, and fruit live in poverty, and are faced with poor working conditions, exploitation, and limited health, safety, and environmental protection. At the heart of this problem are international commodity markets, which often set prices that fail to provide the growers even with a living wage. The aim of the fair trade movement is to foster the protection and empowerment of growers, as well as to encourage community development by guaranteeing minimum prices and conditions (Brown 1993; Nicholls and Opal 2005). This is achieved through the application, monitoring, and enforcement of a fair trade supply agreement and code of conduct, typically verified by an independent social auditing system operated by a national body such as the Fairtrade Foundation (in the UK), Max Havelaar (in the Netherlands), Reilun Kaupan (in Finland), or Transfair (in the US and Canada). Common international standards are set by the Fairtrade Labelling Organization (FLO).[8]

The systems put in place by fair trade organizations ensure that whatever price the market may allocate to goods such as cocoa and tea, the growers involved are guaranteed a minimum price by the purchaser. And, if market prices exceed this minimum, fair trade farmers receive a premium in order to finance development goals. As a result, growers are not only prevented from sinking into poverty at the whim of commodity markets, but can also plan and implement community initiatives. **Figure 9.6** provides an illustration from the cocoa market of how the guaranteed price offered by Fairtrade has compared with market prices over time.

Products such as filter coffee, chocolate bars, and bananas sourced and produced according to the strict Fairtrade conditions are permitted to use the 'FAIRTRADE Mark' (see **Figure 9.7**), indicating to consumers that growers have received a fair price and been afforded decent conditions and community support. Many growers involved in the fair trade system organize into local co-ops in order to ensure that the benefits are shared appropriately and so that community development can be promoted (Brown 1993).

The fair trade movement initially operated through charitable organizations such as Oxfam, and alternative trade organizations (ATOs) such as Traidcraft. For many years now, though, fair trade products have also been sold through mainstream supermarkets, and other high street stores such as the Body Shop have introduced their own operations outside of the established international framework for fair trade accreditation. Over the past

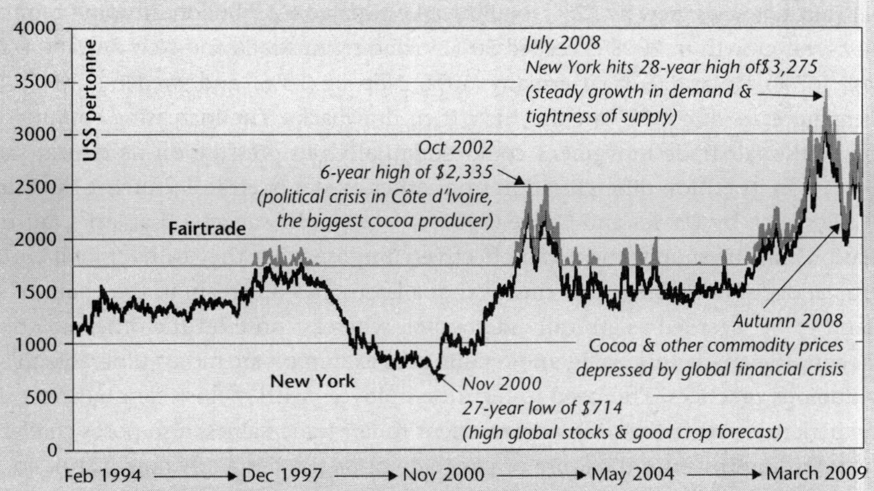

NB Fairtrade price = Fairtrade minimum price of $1600/tonne + $150/tonne Fairtrade premium
When the New York price is $1600 or above, then the Fairtrade price = New York price + $150 premium. *The NY price is the daily closing price of the second position Cocoa contract at ICE Futures US (New York Board of Trade)*
© Fairtrade Foundation

Figure 9.6. The cocoa market 1994-2009: comparison of Fairtrade and New York prices
Reproduced with permission from the Fairtrade Foundation

Figure 9.7. The FAIRTRADE Mark
The FAIRTRADE Mark is a registered independent product certification label. It represents an alternative system of international trade and is owned by Fairtrade Labelling Organizations International, the umbrella organization for Fairtrade. Look for this Mark on Fairtrade products.

Source: www.fairtrade.net (Reprinted with permission)

decade there has therefore been a move within the established fair trade movement away from its charity-supported background towards a more commercial position (Nicholls and Opal 2005; Davies 2007). This has given rise to the emergence of private sector for-profit fair trade companies, such as Divine Chocolate, which markets chocolate products in the UK and US. This greater commercialization has been accompanied by a steady growth in penetration of fair trade products. For example, despite an economic downturn in 2008, global Fairtrade sales grew by 22%, totalling an estimated €2.9 billion. In some countries, year-on-year growth in 2008 exceeded 50%, including Australia and New Zealand (72%), Canada (67%), Finland (57%), Germany (50%), Norway (73%), and Sweden (75%).[9]

Such successes of course can also have their drawbacks. The increasing commercialization of the fair trade movement could potentially put pressure on its ethical standards—and on its ethical differentiation from other modes of ethical sourcing (McMurtry 2009). Research by Davies and Crane (2003), for example, suggests that strict fair trade regulations on the supply chain can effectively impose what they call a 'moral curtain' on ethical decision-making. This means that all activities upstream in the chain of supply tend to be regarded as ethically sacrosanct, whereas those on the other side of the moral curtain—marketing, sales, and retailing for example—are more vulnerable to ethically dubious practices. The need to recruit employees with mainstream business skills and experience (rather than just commitment to fair trade values) also poses challenges for maintaining the ethical culture of fair trade firms (Davies and Crane 2010). For the growers, though, the continued success of fair trade is clearly still providing a positive force for change—and has generated increasing interest from more mainstream industry players. This is discussed in more detail in **Case 9** at the end of this chapter.

VISIT THE WEBSITE for a short response to this feature

? THINK THEORY

Fair trade is presented as a fairer means of doing business—benefits are distributed more equally, and basic rights are protected. However, some critics have argued that such schemes might be deemed unethical. What arguments might there be against fair trade practices and which theoretical bases do you think they are derived from?

■ Sustainability and business relationships: towards industrial ecosystems?

Finally, then, we need to look at the corporation's relationships with other companies in the context of sustainability. What does it mean to think of a sustainable supply chain, or more broadly, a sustainable business community? We shall look at three key levels here: sustaining the supply chain; turning supply chains into supply loops; and building industrial ecosystems.

Sustaining the supply chain

As we have just seen, approaches such as fair trade are one way in which notions of sustainability can be addressed through business–business relationships. The mixture of economic, social, and environmental goals associated with fair trade programmes are very much within the spirit of sustainability thinking. For example, Fairtrade standards stipulate, amongst other things, that traders must:

- Ensure a guaranteed minimum price which is agreed with producers.
- Pay a 'premium' that producers can invest in social, economic, and environmental development.

- Enable pre-financing for producers who require it.
- Set clear minimum and progressive criteria to ensure that the conditions for the production and trade of a product are socially and economically fair and environmentally responsible.[10]

Fair trade is therefore concerned with more than just the fairness of exchange relationships in a narrow economic sense. It is just as much concerned with sustaining an organization's suppliers and the communities and environments where these suppliers are located. Indeed, it is increasingly recognised that one of the critical best practices in sustainable supply-chain management is a focus on *supply-chain continuity*—that is, ensuring the stability and capability of one's suppliers at every level in the supply chain (Pagell and Wu 2009). Firms that ignore threats to the continuity of their supply chain risk being unable to develop effective sustainability initiatives since these are heavily reliant on the actions and investments of supply-chain members. For example, what would it mean to be a sustainable hamburger restaurant if the social, economic and environmental stability of cattle farming could not be assured?

Sustaining the supply chain requires firms to engage in a variety of initiatives, from training and financing of suppliers to enable them to switch over to more sustainable production methods, to investing in local community development. **Ethics in Action 9.2** discusses the challenges faced by the confectionery company, Cadbury, in sustaining its cocoa supply in Ghana in the face of a widespread decline in the country's cocoa-growing sector. More broadly, investments in supply-chain continuity are also critical for developing greater linkages among the various firms in the supply chain—and even for turning such chains into more sustainable 'closed loop' systems.

Turning supply chains into supply loops

As we proposed in Chapter 1, sustainability encourages us to think about the long-term maintenance of systems, raising issues of resource efficiency, pollution prevention, and waste minimization. In the previous chapter, we introduced the notion of product recapture—i.e. bringing 'waste' products back into the supply chain as resources—as a way of developing more sustainable consumption. As we suggested, such a development shifts our thinking about supply relationships away from a linear view towards a more circular perspective. If wastes are to be recaptured and brought back into productive use, we need to think not of supply chains, but of supply loops that create a circular flow of resources (we illustrated this in Figure 8.7 in the last chapter).

According to Geyer and Jackson (2004), supply loops are product end-of-life management strategies that fulfil two criteria:

- They divert end-of-life products from landfill or incineration by collecting them for economic value recovery.
- The reprocessing of these end-of-life products produces secondary resources that replace primary resources in forward supply chains.

In this respect, supply loops address sustainability issues at both the front and the back end of linear supply-chain systems. To their proponents, such **closed-loop supply-chain** models have therefore been promoted as not only waste reducing, but even eliminating

VISIT THE WEBSITE for links to useful sources of further information

ETHICS IN ACTION 9.2 http://www.ethicalcorp.com

Cadbury invests in flaking supply chain

John Russell, 6 October 2008

Ethical CORPORATION

Cadbury has been sourcing from Ghana for 100 years and today buys 70% of its cocoa, a key ingredient in chocolate, from the west African country. All Cadbury chocolate sold in the UK—in brands such as Dairy Milk, Flake and Creme Egg—is made using cocoa beans grown in Ghana. This gives Cadbury a 'unique position' when it comes to helping Ghana's cocoa farmers improve their lives, says the company's conformance and sustainability director, David Croft. One in seven Ghanaian cocoa farmers, or 100,000 individuals, supply Cadbury through the Ghana Cocoa Board, the state body that controls Ghana's cocoa industry.

Cadbury sources from Ghana because of the country's high quality cocoa beans—for which farmers are paid a 10% premium on the world market price. But in recent years, productivity in Ghana's cocoa sector has dipped, putting the secure supply of Cadbury's main source of quality cocoa at risk. The UK Institute for Development Studies and the University of Ghana warned in August that cocoa farms in the country were generating just 40% of their yield potential. The research, commissioned by Cadbury, found that cocoa output was falling as farmers got older and their children turned down farm work for jobs in cities. Report author Dr Stephanie Barrientos explains: 'The whole sector is stuck in more traditional ways and young farmers are wanting to move on.'

To secure supply of quality cocoa from Ghana, Cadbury is to invest £30m in rural development in the country over the next 10 years. The money forms the bulk of the £45m Cadbury Cocoa Partnership, a decade-long commitment launched in January to invest in communities that grow cocoa for Cadbury. Apart from Ghana, the partnership covers India, Indonesia and the Caribbean. Croft says Cadbury has worked with other chocolate companies on building cocoa farming capacity, but 'there was a need to scale up and reach more farmers more quickly'. Cadbury aims to help farmers increase their incomes through the partnership. It will, for example, fund work to teach cocoa farmers about the benefits of pest-resistant hybrid trees, and how they can get hold of them. The company is considering giving farmers microfinance loans to help them grow other crops such as mangoes and sweet potatoes that will offer new sources of income. The goal, says Cadbury, is to support 'community-led development' that puts the views of rural villagers at the heart of development plans.

Powerful partnerships

Kate Nicholas of World Vision, the NGO whose Ghana chapter is working with Cadbury on the cocoa project, says: 'It is the real understanding of community needs and ability to empower people to tackle poverty that is essential to ensure that these kinds of partnerships and the schemes they create are sustainable.'

In September 2008, Cadbury started asking farmers in 100 villages in Ghana's cocoa-growing regions what they needed to improve their lives, a process the company says will take four months. Apart from World Vision Ghana, the company is consulting cocoa farmers through two other NGO partners, Voluntary Service Overseas and Care. All three sit on the Cocoa Partnership Board in Ghana, which includes representatives from the Ghanaian government, the UN Development Programme, and the UK Department for International Development.

Cadbury is aware of the tensions that will arise from putting 'community-led development' into practice. For example, its Ghanaian NGO partners are keen to encourage farmers to foster organic farming in the cocoa sector, where farmers rely on pesticides provided by the cocoa board. Cocoa farmers are upset that the government can only manage to give farmers two of the six pest-control products they have been promised. Croft says: 'We are finding that the government is struggling to meet that responsibility.' Cadbury's head of corporate responsibility, Alison Ward, adds: 'With a lot of villagers you talk to, the first thing they say they want is pesticides.'

Depending on what feedback it gets from cocoa farmers, Cadbury will have to decide how much of the £3m slated as part of the partnership in 2009 will fund projects to promote farming methods that reduce reliance on pesticides. It will have to manage the potential conflict between what farmers say they want and what NGO partners and other development experts say is best. Barrientos points out that Cadbury has started work with the Ghana Cocoa Board on a project to extend traceability in the cocoa supply chain back to individual farms—a prerequisite for being able to certify farms as organic.

While Cadbury has made a clear commitment to improve the incomes of Ghana's cocoa farmers, it is up against a powerful demographic shift. In a sector where farmers survive on less than $1 a day, the cocoa partnership may find it easier to listen to what young farmers want than persuade them to unpack their bags and decide not to quit for the city.

Sources

Ethical Corporation, John Russell, 6 October 2008, http://www.ethicalcorp.com.

the very concept of waste (Lovins et al. 1999). Moreover, although typically seen as an additional cost burden on firms (e.g. as a result of product take-back legislation), they have also been shown to be important potential sources of value recovery (Guide and Wassenhove 2006). That is, rather than disposing of 'used' resources, organizations can transform waste into valuable materials that can be deployed productively.

Closing supply loops to increase resource efficiency and minimize waste places a considerably larger burden on inter-firm relationships than is the case with more traditional modes of supply. Effective stewardship of a product requires attention throughout its entire lifecycle, thus necessitating active collaboration between value-chain participants (Roy and Whelan 1992). To achieve ongoing product recapture, re-use, recycling, and re-manufacture, firms have to communicate, exchange information, develop joint-proposals, co-design, and conclude stable exchange relationships. In many instances, firms have to seek out, develop, and institutionalize new markets for recaptured components. For example, Nike's 'Reuse-A-Shoe' programme turns used sports shoes into 'Nike grind', a material used by surfacing companies in sports surfaces such as gym flooring, basketball courts, and soccer fields (Kumar and Malegeant 2006). Since 1990, some 23 million shoes have been collected as part of the initiative.[11]

Industrial ecosystems

Supply loops begin to shift our way of conceiving organizations away from an atomistic view, where each organization is seen as a separate entity with its own inputs and outputs, towards a more system-oriented view, where groups of firms are seen as interdependent entities that share resources and produce a shared environmental burden. Sustainability urges us to take such thinking still further though. Taken beyond the context of a single product supply and recapture loop, we can begin to also conceive of wider communities of organizations bound by interdependence of all kinds of resources and wastes. These are called **industrial ecosystems** (Allenby 1993).

According to Paul Shrivastava (1995), the concept of industrial ecosystems parallels that of natural ecosystems: just as natural ecosystems comprise a balanced network of interdependent organisms and their environments, which feed off each other and give and take resources off each other to maintain equilibrium and survive, so too can businesses use each other's waste and by-products to minimize the use of natural resources.

Shrivastava (1995) uses the example of a much cited network of companies in Kalundborg in Denmark to illustrate the concept of an industrial ecosystem (see **Figure 9.8**). It consists of a power plant, an enzyme plant, a refinery, a chemical plant, a cement plant, a wallboard plant, and some farms. These different companies all use one another's wastes and by-products as raw materials, co-ordinating their use of energy, water, raw materials, and waste management. For example, instead of dumping it, the power plant sells its used steam to the enzyme plant and refinery, hands over its waste ash to the cement factory, and its surplus heat to the city for domestic heating. It also warms a fishery—which in turn provides its waste to local farms as fertilizer. Additional fertilizer comes from the enzyme plant's waste.

Industrial eco-systems such as the one in Kalundborg are relatively rare, but a number of similar examples have gradually emerged, often without any deliberate formal planning or organization. Examples of such 'self-organizing' networks include the city of Jyväskylä in Finland, the network clustered around the Guitang Group sugar refinery in China, and the mineral-processing area of Kwinana, Australia (Chertow 2007). One of the most complex and diverse examples yet uncovered is the industrial recycling network in the Austrian province of Styria, which includes a network of exchanges among over 50 facilities.

More formal, planned projects have also been developed, often to be found in so-called 'eco-parks', or even 'eco-cities'. This includes initiatives in the US, Europe, and Asia—although to date these have met with mixed success (Chertow 2007). One of the most high profile and ambitious of these projects is the mooted eco-city of Dongtan near Shanghai in China. Designed by the UK engineering firm Arup, Dongtan was hailed as a landmark in sustainable urban design and industrial ecosystem thinking, but has failed so far to get past the planning stage (Moore 2008).

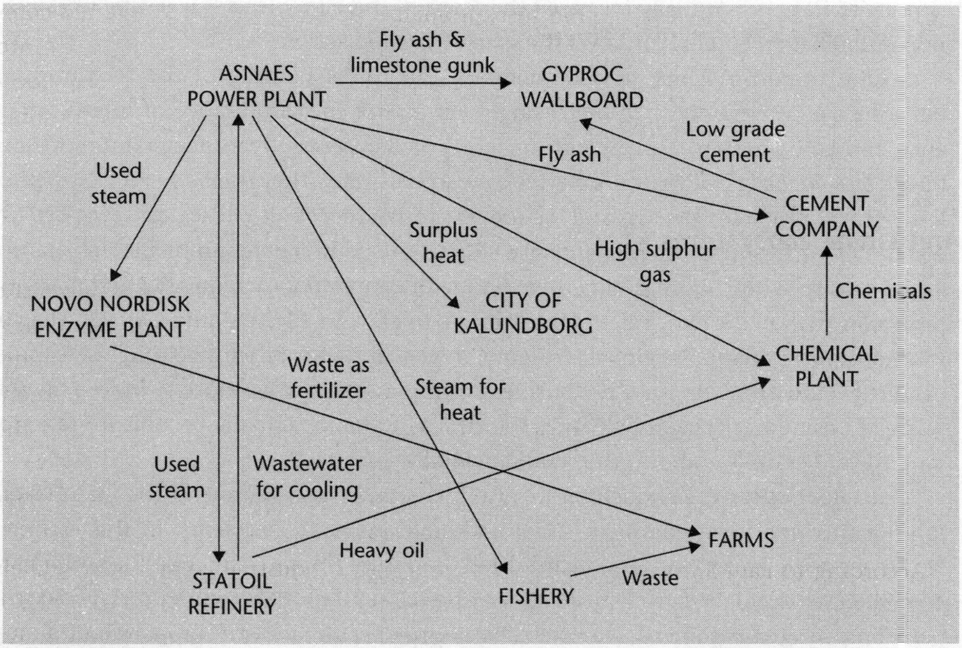

Figure 9.8. Kalundborg industrial ecosystem

Republished with permission of Academy of Management, from Shrivastava, P. 1995. Ecocentric management for a risk society. Academy of Management Review, 20 (1): 118–37; permission conveyed through Copyright Clearance Center, Inc.

Whether industrial eco-systems will ever become more than an interesting, perhaps even utopian, vision of how industry could be organized remains to be seen. Much will no doubt rest on how local and national governments go about supporting, encouraging, and planning such initiatives. However, with the general shift towards more collaborative business activity identified at the outset of this chapter, and the drive for more climate-friendly approaches intensifying, closed-loop business models of various levels of complexity will undoubtedly become an increasingly important, if challenging, component of the industrial mix of the future.

■ Summary

In this chapter, we have discussed the stake held by other companies in a corporation, focusing on both suppliers and the somewhat more contestable role of competitors. Our argument was that there were certainly issues of an ethical nature that arose in both groups of companies that went well beyond the legal protections of fair competition. These included: misuse of power, loyalty, preferential treatment, conflicts of interest, bribery, and negotiation with suppliers; and intelligence gathering, industrial espionage, dirty tricks, anti-competitive behaviour, and abuse of a dominant position in the context of competitors. Globalization appears to have substantially increased the scope of these problems, suggesting expanded responsibilities for corporations over the span of their operations.

Despite these problems, developments in our understanding of the relationships between businesses appear to increasingly emphasize the importance of interdependence and co-operation. This is both in terms of our descriptive understandings (how businesses *do* relate) and our normative assessments (how they *should* relate). Nonetheless, ethical problems persist, and we are left to wonder if all parties can ever benefit equally from business interdependence. Many of the apparent problems are mainly raised simply by the highly competitive nature of contemporary industries and markets, particularly when the basic rules of the game do not favour all companies equally. Hence, it would appear that in the global economy, there will always be winners and losers—and justice, even within the so-called business 'community', can be elusive. Indeed, as the scope of business operations expands, the ethical problems actually become more wide-ranging and complex, and so the stakes inevitably increase.

That said, business relationships are also increasingly seen as one of the main levers for effecting greater attention to social and environmental problems. In this chapter, we have mainly looked at intra-organizational pressure through the supply chain. However, such self-regulation from business can also happen amongst competitors. For example, competing companies have often developed specific industry programmes aimed at addressing social or environmental issues, such as the chemical industry's Responsible Care programme. Here, competing firms, including ICI, Aventis, or Bayer via their global association ICCA (International Council of Chemical Associations), have banded together to develop a common response to environmental issues in the industry. Failure to meet specified standards or targets can result in pressure from competitors to comply, or even the issuing of sanctions. There are numerous other examples of self-regulation amongst groups of companies, ranging from those with little or no power to those that are able to wield considerable influence. The point is that government is certainly not the only source of business regulation, and that much informal and formal control actually takes place within the business community itself. As we shall see in the next chapter, we should not even stop there. In addition to government and business, we also need to think about another sector involved in business regulation, namely pressure groups, or what have become known as 'third sector' or 'civil society' organizations.

Study questions

1. Compare the case for (a) suppliers and (b) competitors to be regarded as stakeholders of a corporation. How convincing are the arguments proposing that each group is a legitimate stakeholder?
2. What is a conflict of interest? Outline the conflicts of interest that might typically arise in firm–supplier relations.
3. Should firms accept gifts from overseas suppliers? How can a firm ensure that its relationships with suppliers are strictly ethical if gift giving is allowed?

4 'Competition between rival firms is like a battle. You play to win and anything goes.' Critically assess this statement in the context of Western multinationals competing with domestic firms in developing countries.

5 What is ethical sourcing? What factors are likely to influence the success of ethical sourcing in changing supplier practices?

6 Explain the following:

(a) Closed-loop supply chains.

(b) Industrial ecosystems.

What are the main differences between the two concepts and why are they considered to be important components of sustainable business?

Research exercise

Select a high street retailer of food, clothes, or electronics and conduct some research on their ethical sourcing practices so that you can answer the following questions:

1 Describe the supply-chain infrastructure that the firm uses—for example, does it have few or many suppliers, where are they based, etc?

2 How would you describe your selected company's approach to ethical sourcing—for example, is there an overall strategy in place, what are the different components of the system, and how far down the supply chain does the initiative go?

3 What other organizations, if any, does the firm work with in managing its ethical sourcing programme? Can you explain why these organizations are involved?

4 To what extent does the firm report on the outcomes of its ethical sourcing initiatives?

Key readings

VISIT THE WEBSITE for links to further key readings

1 Jones, I.W. and Pollitt, M.G. 1998. Ethical and unethical competition: establishing the rules of engagement. ***Long Range Planning***, **31 (5): 703–10.**

This is one of the few articles that considers ethical issues with respect to both suppliers and competitors—and does so within an economic framework that illuminates the crucial competitive elements in inter-firm relationships. The use of short case studies of different industries helps to show why certain ethical and unethical practices might be more or less likely to arise in particular contexts.

2 Hughes, A. 2005. Corporate strategy and the management of ethical trade: the case of the UK food and clothing retailers. ***n i on en an Planning*** **A, 37: 1145–63.**

This is a great primer on ethical sourcing, and provides a useful insight into the strategies of retailers involved in such initiatives. It features some fascinating interview material from discussions with ethical trading managers, social auditors, and consultants.

VISIT THE WEBSITE for links to useful sources of further information

Case 9

Fair enough? Big business embraces fair trade

This case examines the rise of fair trade, and in particular the challenges associated with its uptake by big business. The case provides an opportunity to address issues relating to ethical sourcing and buyer–seller relationships, as well as considerations raised in the previous chapter about ethical consumption and fair pricing.

Not so long ago, fair trade was seen by many as a minority concern, of interest only to the 'alternative trade' of charities, co-operatives, wholefood shops, and the ethical consumer fringe. Now, it appears, fair trade is seen as having major mass-market appeal. In recent years, leading supermarket brands, such as Sainsbury and Marks and Spencer, have made high profile commitments to selling fair trade products in their stores, whilst the world's largest coffee roaster, Nestlé, launched its first fair trade coffee brand in 2005—after years of denying that fair trade actually helped suppliers. When the UK's best-selling chocolate bar Cadbury's Dairy Milk went fair trade in 2009, it appeared incontrovertible that fair trade had indeed become big business. Although on the face of it, this is a great achievement for the fair trade movement, this move into the mainstream also brings with it a number of critical challenges.

Fair trade is a form of ethical sourcing that delivers a guaranteed price to growers in developing countries. With many at risk from the fluctuating prices of international commodity markets, growers in the fair trade system are offered income stability at a liveable wage, and benefit from a 'social premium' to fund development projects. Fair trade also emphasizes direct purchasing from producers (rather than using agents and brokers), co-operative trade relations, long-term relationships, and sustainable production, amongst other things. An international fair trade labelling system provides product accreditation to participating firms that enables them to use the 'Fairtrade' mark on packaging and promotional material.

The growth in fair trade has been spectacular in recent years, most notably in Europe, but also to a lesser extent in North America, Australasia, and Japan. The first fair trade-labelled product was launched by the Max Havelaar Foundation in the Netherlands in 1988 on coffee sourced from Mexico. Since then, the range of products has expanded considerably to now include fruit, tea, wine, sugar, flowers, clothes, footballs, and a whole host of other products. In the UK, which has the largest fair trade market, there were over 3,000 certified products in 2009—a 100% rise since 2006. Worldwide, there were some 6,000 certified products on the market altogether. Similarly, figures from the Fairtrade Foundation suggest that retail sales have also rocketed in recent years. In the UK, for instance, sales of many products have recorded exponential growth (see **Figure C9.1**).

Fair trade figures also show that sales across the globe have been growing at a remarkable rate, with an annual growth rate for 2008 in excess of 70% in Australia, Sweden, and Norway. Perhaps most significantly in terms of the movement of fair trade out of the fringe and into the mainstream, products can now be found in thousands of supermarkets all over Europe, including 23,000 stores in Germany, 10,000 in France, and about 3,000 in the UK, Finland, and the Netherlands. This has led to some significant overall market shares for fair trade products. For instance, in 2008, 52% of all bananas, and 17% of the sugar sold in Switzerland were fair trade labelled. Even high street clothing retailers such as Top Shop, and the global coffee chain Starbucks, now sell fair trade alternatives.

	Estimated retail value (£ million)			
	2000	**2003**	**2005**	**2008**
Coffee	15.5	34.3	65.8	137.3
Tea	5.1	9.5	16.6	64.8
Chocolate/cocoa	3.6	10.9	21.9	26.8
Bananas	7.8	24.3	47.7	184.6

Figure C9.1. Sales of fair trade products in the UK
Source: Fairtrade Foundation. 2009. Sales of Fairtrade products in the UK. www.fairtrade.org.uk

Such a success story has undoubtedly provided significant benefits for the suppliers of these products. The social premium has helped thousands of farmers fund education, healthcare and training projects, among other things, that simply would not have been possible under the old exploitative trading relations. However, critics have raised question marks over the uptake of fair trade by large global businesses. For example, when Nestlé launched its fair trade coffee, 'Partners Blend', some campaigners boycotted the product out of concerns that the company's conversion to fair trade was a cynical attempt to cash in on the growing market, rather than a genuine commitment to the fair trade ideals—even though the product had complied with the rigorous international fair trade certification scheme. As the director of one of the UK's 'alternative trading' pioneers, Twin Trading, put it 'the real worry is that these guys are coming in just to grab the current growth. When that's done and chewed up, they'll walk away from it and we'll be in a worse position to continue the momentum.' Some small producers have expressed fears that the power of multinationals will marginalize those who the system was originally set up to protect.

Another challenge raised by the move into the mainstream is simply the sheer quantity of product needed to supply major brands and supermarkets. Whilst fair trade has its roots in small-scale co-operative farms, market growth has necessitated the certification of huge privately held plantations as well. For example, in the US, 98% of Fairtrade tea comes from plantations. Critics argue that this threatens the fair trade goals of producer power and waters down the founding principles of the movement. The president of one fair trade company, Equal Exchange, put it simply: 'plantations do not belong in the Fair Trade system in the first place'. Others suggest that rapid growth has contributed to a compromise in monitoring and enforcement of standards—a claim that fair trade organizations vehemently refute. Nonetheless, increased scrutiny of working conditions at fair trade-certified producers seems certain given the greater public profile of the movement as it goes mainstream.

A further criticism faced by the movement is that the inclusion of big brands does little to change large corporations' core business. For example, for many supermarkets, fair trade makes up only a small proportion of their sales, whilst 'unfair trade' prevails in their main product lines. As Friends of the Earth said of the UK supermarket, Tesco, whilst fair trade banana producers are guaranteed a fair wage, other 'banana plantation workers are paid just a penny for every pound's worth of bananas sold in Tesco, not enough to feed their families. Tesco takes 40p. The UK importer/ripener is barely breaking even just to stay as a Tesco supplier.'

It is not only campaigning groups and fair trade diehards that have criticized the entry of big business into the fair trade movement, though. A 2006 BBC programme suggested that much of the higher prices paid by consumers for fair trade products was going into the hands of supermarkets, while a 2009 article in *The Times* suggested that workers on fair trade-certified tea plantations had yet to benefit from the premium. Even the *Wall Street Journal* ran a story arguing that 'Europe's experience shows that the biggest winners aren't always the farmers—but can be retailers that sometimes charge huge mark-ups on fair trade goods while promoting themselves as good corporate citizens'. Citing evidence that the British supermarket chains Sainsbury's and Tesco sold fair trade products at big ticket prices that gave the companies sizeable margins that were not passed on to growers, the newspaper claimed that the supermarkets were mainly exploiting fair trade products for their own advantage—and that growers and consumers alike were losing out.

Naturally, the big players entering the fair trade market have refuted the criticisms, arguing for the positive social benefits they have delivered to their suppliers, and pointing to the growing numbers of satisfied consumers who were swelling the market—which in turn would help to bring prices down. However, whether the criticisms are justified or not, it seems likely that the fair trade industry is reaching a critical point in its development. On one level it points to a potentially progressive model of firm–supplier relationships that seems to emphasize more equitable relationships, but it also requires firms to embrace a set of values that might be counter to those engrained in its typical supply-chain management model. Some critics are doubtful that big business can genuinely embrace the transformation necessary to make fair trade more than a tokenistic exercise, yet many in the fair trade movement are keenly aware that without the global players, the incredible momentum of the movement over the past decade may be lost, leaving fair trade products back on the margins of the market again. Ultimately, the rise of fair trade provides a powerful success story that could act as a catalyst for broader change, or could simply be a sideshow in the relentless drive towards cost minimization through global supply chains. As the executive director of the Fairtrade Foundation put it: 'the public are leading the way at the moment, and they want companies and governments to follow. We need all world trade to be made fair, but in the meantime we can get on and show how it might be done.'

Questions

1. Set out the main arguments for and against the involvement of big business in fair trade. Consider the arguments from the point of view of customers, supermarkets, and suppliers.
2. Are the critics justified in condemning the involvement of major brands in the fair trade movement? On what ethical basis have you made this decision?
3. To what extent is the price paid by consumers relevant for determining whether growers are being treated fairly?
4. Ultimately, whose responsibility is it to ensure that growers' interests are protected—the growers themselves, product manufacturers, retailers, or consumers? Do these different constituencies in the supply chain have different responsibilities towards growers? What are these?

Sources

Bahra, P. 2009. Tea workers still waiting to reap Fairtrade benefits. *The Times*, 2 Jan.: http:// www.timeonline.co.uk.

Equal Exchange. 2009. *Equal Exchange Joins Critique of Fair Trade Plantations*, Equal Exchange Press Release, 13 Jan. 2009: http://www.csrwire.com.

Friends of the Earth. 2003. *Media briefing—Tesco: exposed*. Friends of the Earth Press Release. http://www.foe.org.uk.

Krier, J.-M. 2005. *Fair trade in Europe 2005: facts and figures on fair trade in 25 European countries*. Brussels: Fair Trade Advocacy Office.

Moreton, C. 2006. News analysis: shopping with a conscience—Fairtrade. *Independent on Sunday*, 5 Mar.: 28–9.

Purvis, A. 2006. This new school in El Salvador was paid for in coffee beans—by the Kraft corporation. Is global business hijacking the Fairtrade bandwagon? *Observer Food Monthly*, Jan.: 30–7.

Stecklow, S. and White, E. 2004. What price virtue? At some retailers, 'fair trade' carries a very high cost. *Wall Street Journal*, 8 June

Tucker, A. 2006. Fair enough? Big business, mass markets and fretting farmers. *New Internationalist*, Nov.: http://www.newint.org.

http://www.fairtrade.org.uk.

Notes

1 For the full text, see 'Declaration of the European Parliament on investigating and remedying abuse of power by large supermarkets operating in the European Union' (P6_TA(2008)0054). Text adopted 19 Feb. 2008: http://www.europarl.europa.eu.

2 See Vulliamy, E. 2007. The long road to redemption. *Observer*, 1 Apr.: http://www.guardian.co.uk; Scott, M. 2009. Sports want help to fund anti-corruption units. *Guardian*, 10 Feb.: http://www.guardian.co.uk.

3 BBC. 2009. EU slaps a record fine on Intel. *BBC News*, 13 May: http://www.bbc.co.uk/news; Nuttall, C. and Tait, N. 2009. Intel looks beyond EU litigation. *Financial Times*, 13 May: http://www.ft.com.

4 BBC. 2006. Microsoft hit with 280m euro fine. *BBC News*, 12 July: http://www.bbc.co.uk/news; BBC 2008. EU fines Microsoft record $1.4bn. *BBC News*, 27 Feb.: http://www.bbc.co.uk/news.

5 See Heimann, F. and Dell, G. 2009. OECD Anti-bribery Convention Progress Report 2009. Berlin: Transparency International. Available at http://www.transparency.org.

6 BBC. 2008. EU suffers defeat in banana wars. *BBC News*, 7 Apr.: http://www.bbc.co.uk/news; Lister, D. 2001. US group sues European Union over banana war. *The Times*, 26 Jan.; Lister, D. 2001. Europe and the US end 8-year war over bananas. *The Times*, 12 Apr.

7 Wray, R. 2008. Breeding toxins from dead PCs. *Guardian*, 6 May: http://www.guardian.co.uk; Mintz, J. 2009. Dell bans e-waste export to developing countries. *Associated Press*, 12 May: http://www.abcnews.com; Greenpeace 'Greener Electronics' campaign: http://www.greenpeace.org/international/campaigns/toxics/electronics.

8 'Fairtrade' (one word, capital F) relates exclusively to the work of FLO International and its partners. 'Fair Trade' or 'fair trade' relates to the wider movement of organisations working to promote fairer trade policy and practice and includes fairly traded products which do not carry the FAIRTRADE Mark.

9 See 'Global Fairtrade sales increase by 22%'. FLO International press release, 4 June 2009: http://www.fairtrade.net.

10 See http://www.fairtrade.org.uk.

11 See the iniative website at http://www.nikereuseashoe.com.

10

Civil Society and Business Ethics

In this chapter we will:

- Show how the role played by various types of civil society organizations in society constitutes them as important stakeholders of corporations, both directly and indirectly.
- Examine the tactics that such groups might employ towards corporations to achieve their purposes, as well as the ethical problems and issues that typically accompany civil society action.
- Discuss the impacts of globalization on the nature and extent of the role played by civil society towards corporations.
- Discuss the appropriate relationships between business and civil society, identifying a significant shift from a conflictual mode of engagement to a more collaborative or blended approach.
- Assess the role of civil society in providing for enhanced corporate sustainability.

Introduction: what is civil society?

So far in this book, we have looked at business ethics in relation to the corporation's four main economic stakeholders—i.e. those vital constituencies that provide firms with the resources they need merely to exist. Shareholders supply capital, employees provide labour, consumers provide income, and suppliers provide the materials necessary to produce products and services. In the next two chapters, we shall broaden our scope to consider other stakeholders outside the immediate economic realm of the corporation—in this chapter, civil society, and in the next, government. These constituencies, as we shall see, also have important stakes in the corporation, and various ethical problems and issues can arise in the corporation's dealings with such actors.

To some readers, though, the notion of civil society might be unfamiliar. Although civil society as a concept has long been in use, it has only returned to popular use in the last decade or so (Bendell 2000a; Doh and Teegen 2003; Reece 2001). Previous to this resurgence, social and political theorists tended to model a two-sector world, comprising the market or economic sector (business) and the state sector (government). Therefore, it was assumed that issues such as social welfare and environmental protection would be looked after either through labour and product markets, state provision, or else corporate philanthropy. More recently, though, considerable attention has focused on the role of other types of organizations such as pressure groups, charities, non-government organizations (NGOs), local community groups, religious organizations, etc., in attending to these issues. There are a number of reasons to explain this renewed attention, including a failure of the state or the market to ensure effective provision of social welfare, and scepticism among certain sectors of the public that the traditional two-sector institutions actively listened to and served their interests (see Beck 1992).

This has opened up space to consider a third type of institutional actor in society, namely what has become known as civil society. As such, civil society is often said to comprise a *third sector* after the market and the state. This is illustrated in **Figure 10.1**. As a third sector, civil society is usually regarded as a counterbalance to the state (and more recently also to business), guarding against the abuse of power and ensuring that the people's best interests are served (Reece 2001). Hence, the supposed role of civil society is to ensure a degree of social and political pluralism that provides for a more civilized society. More recently, as a response to globalization, it has become popular to talk of *global civil society*, as many of the issues dealt with in this context are indeed transcending the scope of just national communities, as we will explore later in this chapter (e.g. Baker and Chandler 2005; Keane 2003).

Civil society is made concrete and meaningful for corporations through specific **civil society organizations** (CSOs). Only very rarely do corporations actually deal with individual citizens who are not their workers or customers. It is therefore CSOs as the tangible manifestation of civil society that we shall mainly be concerned with in this chapter. However, there is considerable confusion, contradiction, and overlap in the definition of CSOs and related organizational types such as NGOs, non-profit organizations, pressure groups, and the like (McIntosh and Thomas 2002; Yaziji and Doh 2009). We shall use

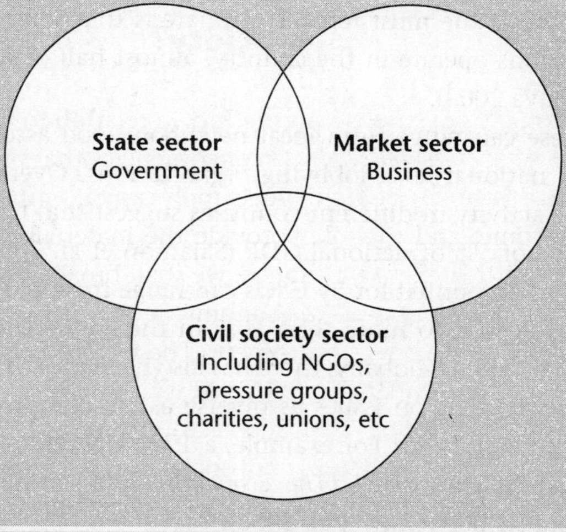

Figure 10.1. Civil Society as the 'third sector'

CSO as an umbrella term for the different types of organization that might be considered to be civil society actors. Although NGOs tend to be the most visible actors in the literature dealing with business and civil society, organizations such as labour unions, consumer associations, religious groups, community groups, etc., are also important CSOs, yet are typically not thought of as NGOs.

Essentially, then, we are using the term CSO to describe all of these voluntary, non-profit bodies outside of business and government that represent a particular group or cause which brings them into contact with corporations. As such, for the sake of simplicity, we might reasonably suggest the following basic definition:[1]

> **Civil society organizations include pressure groups, non-governmental organizations, charities, religious groups and other private, non-profit distributing, organizational actors that are neither business nor government institutions, and which are involved in the promotion of societal interests, causes and/or goals.**

Clearly, there are any number of interests, causes, and goals that CSOs might be involved with, from environmental protection, to animal rights, social welfare, urban regeneration, child protection, development, famine relief, or health promotion—all of which, it would appear, could easily pertain to business ethics in some way.

Many of the larger international CSOs are at least as well known as large multinational corporations: the Red Cross, Greenpeace, Friends of the Earth, WWF, Amnesty International, and Oxfam, for example, are just some of the most widely recognized civil society organizations. However, although many of us may be aware of little more than a handful of the major CSO actors, the number and scope of CSOs are actually quite staggering. Given such a heterogeneous collection of organizational types, getting accurate estimates of the number of CSOs in operation is extremely difficult, but the consensus amongst most experts is that the number is huge and growing (Yaziji and Doh 2009). For example, in the US alone, there are now around 1.8 million domestic civil society organizations with tax-exempt charitable status, whilst even in the UK there are some 180,000 registered charities.[2] In India, the most reliable estimate is that something like 1.2 million non-profit organizations operate in the country, almost half of which are unregistered (Tandon and Srivastava 2003).

CSOs such as these can range from local neighbourhood associations and religious groups to powerful national level lobbying organizations. Overall, estimations of the scale of civil society activity in different countries suggest that CSOs account for something like an average of 5% of national GDP (Salamon et al. 2007). The proportion of national employment accounted for by CSOs can range from less than 1% in countries such as Mexico and Poland to more than 10% in the Netherlands, Canada, Belgium, and Ireland (Hall et al. 2005). Globally, there has also been an explosion of international CSOs working across borders on issues as diverse as climate protection, international development, and human rights. For example, a 1995 UN report suggested that nearly 29,000 international NGOs existed (*The Economist* 2000), whilst this figure is now estimated to be about 91,000 (Gray et al. 2006).

It is evident, then, that there is an enormous heterogeneity and diversity amongst these millions of CSOs. Not only might they be different in terms of the issues they focus on and their scope of operations, but they also take different forms and structures and are involved in a varied mixture of activities. **Figure 10.2** illustrates this breadth of diversity in more detail.

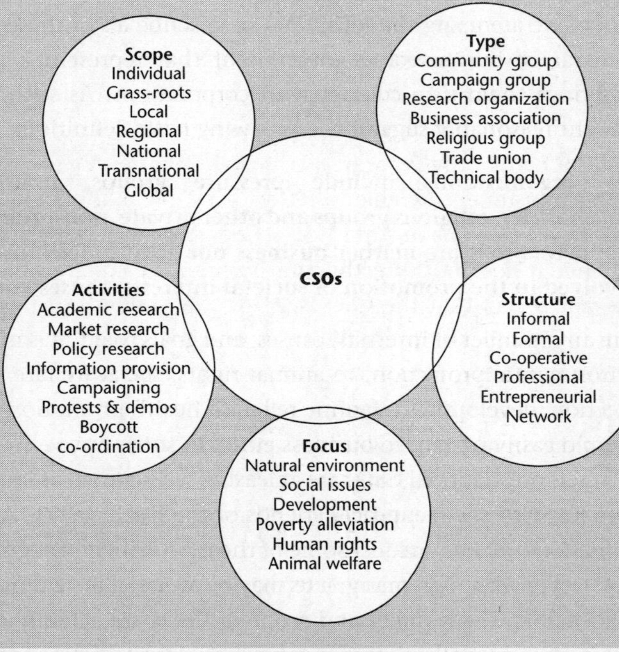

Figure 10.2. Diversity in CSO characteristics

Source: adapted from McIntosh and Thomas (2002: 31)

In this chapter, we shall examine the relationships that CSOs have with corporations, exploring the specific stake that they have and the ways in which they seek to influence corporate action. Whether through media campaigns, boycotts, or actively working together with corporations and governments, it is clear that now, perhaps more than ever, CSOs have a vital role to play in enhancing and ensuring ethical behaviour in business. Indeed, as we shall see as the chapter progresses, the global reach of many CSOs, coupled with their successes in working with businesses and governments, has meant that they are now often seen as an integral part of the global governance regime that shapes and regulates corporate practice.

■ Civil society organizations as stakeholders

It is clear that CSOs of one sort or another have long been involved in the activities of corporations. Whether it is receiving corporate donations, organizing employee resistance to labour practices, leading consumer boycotts of particular products, or more violent action, such as firebombing animal-testing laboratories, various CSOs have over the years been very much involved in the business ethics field. In recent years, this has escalated enormously. As Yaziji and Doh (2009: 16) state, the 'growth in the number, power and influence of NGOs represents one of the most important societal developments in the past twenty years, in terms of how the dynamics of public debates and government policies concerning corporate behaviour are changing'.

In many respects though, the stake held by CSOs is quite different from that held by other stakeholder groups. Employees, consumers, and shareholders, for example, all contribute something directly to the corporation in the form of labour, income, or capital. Likewise, as we shall see in the next chapter, governments provide corporations with a licence to operate in a particular territory.

CSOs, on the other hand, only very rarely contribute any resources directly to corporations. Hence, while consumers are able to retract their purchases from an oil company seeking to expand its operations in Antartica, a CSO does not really have anything tangible to retract, since it does not directly contribute to the company in the first place. However, this is not to say that the CSO is not a stakeholder in this situation. As an organization with a mission, for example, to protect the environment on behalf of its members, the CSO certainly might have a stake in the decision contemplated by the company. And as an actor organizing a consumer boycott or other action against the company, the CSO has an important role to play on behalf of those consumers and other citizens who disagree with the oil company's decision.

Looking at it this way, the stake held by CSOs is largely one of **representing the interests of individual stakeholders**. By organizing together into a CSO, individual stakeholders of whatever kind can gain greater voice and influence than they have alone. If a local resident of Heathrow or Frankfurt wanted to voice their concern about the development of a new runway, they would have little effect alone. However, by joining a local association, or even a national or international lobby group dedicated to preventing air and noise pollution from air traffic, they would be much more likely to have their views heard. Similarly, we can also see this illustrated by trade unions and other labour organizations: they represent the interests of individual employee stakeholders, both inside the workplace and on the political stage.

If we look at the oil company–CSO situation another way, though, a slightly different form of representation effected by CSOs becomes evident. Rather than its members, or the wider public, the CSO could be argued to representing the environment itself. As a non-human entity, the environment clearly cannot speak for itself—and therefore CSOs step in essentially as proxy stakeholders. A similar case can be made for animal welfare CSOs such as the RSPCA (Royal Society for the Protection of Animals) or PETA (People for the Ethical Treatment of Animals). Hence, another potential CSO role is **representing the interests of non-human stakeholders**.

VISIT THE WEBSITE for a short response to this feature

? THINK THEORY

Think about the stakes of non-human stakeholders such as animals or the environment from the perspective of utilitarianism. Would a non-human stake be given a lower valuation in cost-benefit analysis than a human stake? Think through this problem in the context of animal testing or the building of a new road in an area of high biodiversity.

Whichever of these two ways of conceptualizing the stakeholder role of CSOs is relevant, it is clear that the stake of CSOs is *indirect* and *representative*. CSOs are mainly delineated as stakeholders on the grounds that they represent some broader, if less tangible, constituency of civil society itself. Corporations tend not to deal with civil society as a group of innumerable individual citizens, but as a more discrete collection of representative CSOs. As such, CSOs form part of the *licence to operate* for companies.

The literature on pressure groups suggests that, depending on whom exactly they are representing, CSOs tend as a result to fall into two main types—*sectional groups* and *promotional groups* (see N.C. Smith 1990: 104–13; Whawell 1998). Some of the key differences between these types are summarized in **Figure 10.3**:

- **Sectional groups** include trade unions, professional associations, student bodies, neighbourhood groups, parent associations, etc. They are member-based and primarily seek to represent the interests of their members (who are deemed to be a particular 'section' of society). The membership of sectional CSOs is only open to those fulfilling certain objective criteria that put them within the specific section to be represented, for example, that they are part of a particular workplace, profession, or geographical region. The CSO will above all else pursue the self-interest of this membership.
- **Promotional groups** in contrast are focused on promoting specific causes or issues. Environmental groups, anti-smoking groups, and pro-life groups are all examples of promotional CSOs. These organizations represent those with a common ideology or shared attitudes about an issue. Membership is usually open to all, although only those with similar subjective viewpoints are effectively represented. These groups are less concerned with the self-interest of their members and more focused on seeking to achieve wider social aims.

	Sectional groups	Promotional groups
Membership	Closed	Open
Represent	Specific section of society	Issues or causes
Aims	Self-interest	Social goals
Traditional status	Insider	Outsider
Main approach	Consultation	Argument
Pressure exerted through	Threat of withdrawal	Mass media publicity

Figure 10.3. Different types of CSOs

Traditionally, sectional groups have been said to enjoy insider status, whilst promotional groups have largely been outsiders (Whawell 1998). What this means is that because sectional groups are regarded as the legitimate representative of a specific, identifiable constituency—say electricians, farmers, Muslims, or students—their views are actively solicited (or at least readily accepted as legitimate) on issues relevant to the constituency. For example, if the government were developing agricultural policies, then it would typically engage in some kind of consultation with farming unions.

Promotional groups, however, have tended to have less easy access to governmental or corporate policy-making. Since they do not represent a readily identifiable constituency, it is not obvious whom exactly they are speaking for. As a result, promotional groups have tended to need to mobilize mass public opinion before they are heard or involved in any kind of decision-making. For this reason, promotional groups have needed to be very active and visible in the promotion of the issues they are concerned with (hence the label promotional group). This has typically involved them in articulating vigorous arguments, demonstrations, and/or provocative media stunts in order to get their message across. One need only think of Greenpeace's dramatic confrontations over the years with its adversaries in the whaling, oil, and nuclear industries to see the importance of a provocative and media-friendly argument to many promotional groups.

More recently, the various successes of promotional CSOs such as Greenpeace, Amnesty, WWF, Friends of the Earth, etc., in establishing themselves as credible and legitimate contributors to major social and environmental debates in society have given them much more of an insider status than they were once afforded (Whawell 1998). As **Figure 10.4** shows, NGOs such as these enjoy more trust from the public than business or the government in most parts of the world, especially in Europe, where trust in business continues to be low. Even in Asia Pacific, where trust in NGOs is still lower than for other actors, overall trust in civil society has been growing steadily over the years (Edelman 2009).

? THINK THEORY

In the light of fundamental differences between Europe, the US, Asia, and Latin America in business ethics, how can you explain some of the differences illustrated in Figure 10.4?

VISIT THE WEBSITE for a short response to this feature

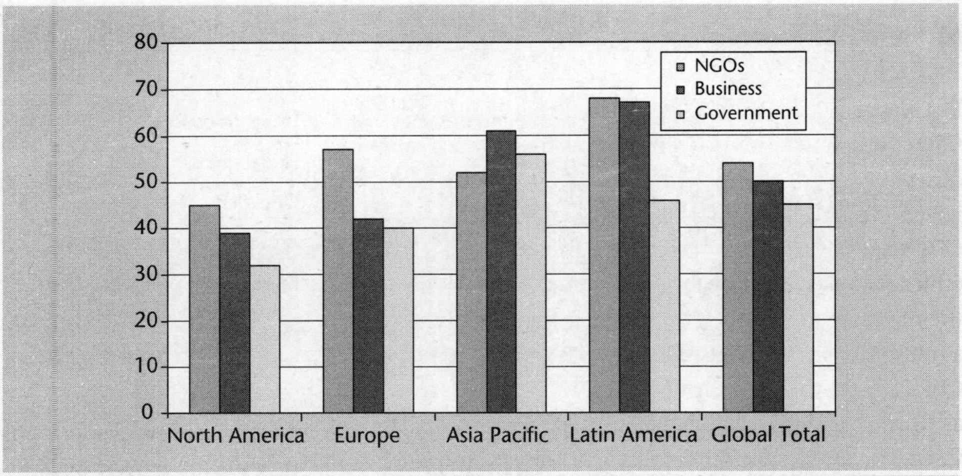

Figure 10.4. Degrees of trust in different types of organization in selected global regions

Source: original figures extracted and re-tabulated from Edelman 2009. *2009 Edelman Trust Barmoter*: www.edelman.com

Although survey evidence of this type—based on the opinions of relatively small samples of key informants—does not provide conclusive evidence, the favourability and trust apparently enjoyed by CSOs give a clear indication that they demand some degree of attention from corporations (see also Doh and Guay 2006). In the past, this attention was typically gained through a situation of often quite intense conflict—CSOs would exert pressure on companies through strikes, boycotts, demonstrations, media campaigns, etc. in order to achieve their ends. Whilst this was particularly true of promotional groups, it was often the case even with sectional groups, such as unions, whose most potent weapon has often been the threat of disruption and withdrawal. More recently, though, as the insider status of CSOs has expanded to include previous adversaries of corporations, we have also seen a move towards a more consensual and collaborative approach in business–CSO relations (Murphy and Bendell 1997; Selsky and Parker 2005; Yaziji and Doh 2009)—a point we first introduced in Chapter 5 and one that we shall develop further later on in this chapter.

It is clear, then, that in many ways, CSOs have become just as much an accepted part of the debate over business ethics as other more conventional 'economic' or 'primary' stakeholders. Although their claim is often an indirect one, since it is a claim to represent individual stakeholders or even causes themselves, it would be hard to refute the argument that CSOs are legitimate claimants of stakeholder status—albeit less clear-cut ones. Indeed, questions of exactly *which* CSOs are legitimate stakeholders of a corporation, and *how* exactly they should go about claiming or exercising their stake, are certainly not straightforward. As we shall now see, such questions are in fact at the root of a bundle of interrelated ethical problems and issues that underlie the emergence of CSOs as significant stakeholders in the corporation.

■ Ethical issues and CSOs

In Chapter 1 (pp. 15–17), we showed that despite their mission to address societal issues, CSOs were not immune from ethical problems. Those working in civil society appear to observe similar types of misconduct, and at similar intensities, as those in business and government.[3] But beyond these normal ethical problems, what of the specific problems in CSO relationships with business? Given the growing importance of CSOs to the business ethics field, it is perhaps surprising that only rather limited attention has yet been paid in the literature to these ethical issues surrounding corporate engagement. However, there are a number of significant issues that arise from the somewhat less tangible stake held by CSOs. Chief among these are the decisions by corporations about which CSOs might be recognized as worthy of attention, the tactics used by CSOs to gain attention, and the degree to which CSOs are genuinely representative of, and accountable to, their intended beneficiaries.

Recognizing CSO stakes

If we take any given corporation—say, BP—it is fairly straightforward to objectively determine who their consumers, suppliers, employees, shareholders, and competitors are. Once we acknowledge that inclusion within any of these groups confers some kind of stake in the company, it is a short step to very clearly defining who BP's main stakeholders are. With civil society stakeholders, however, this question is considerably more muddied. With BP's diverse interests in the energy sector, it is possible to think of hundreds, probably even thousands, of CSOs that might potentially claim a stake in the company's activities. From Azerbaijan farmers, to UK transport organizations, to Saharan desert communities, or fishing community groups in Trinidad, BP has been involved in debates about its operations with an extensive array of CSOs across the globe. But how does a company such as BP determine which of these groups are legitimate stakeholders and which are not? And who is to determine legitimacy here? Just because, hypothetically speaking, BP may decide that a radical Inuit land rights group has no legitimate cause to pursue regarding the company's drilling operations in Alaska, does this necessarily mean that it is not a stakeholder?

These are taxing problems to resolve, but they go to the heart of what it means to be a stakeholder. If we look back to Chapter 5 (pp. 202–3), when we discussed how corporations might manage their stakeholders, we suggested that one way of assessing which stakeholders were worthy of attention that was popular in the strategy literature was the *instrumental* approach. Here, the *relative salience* of stakeholders would be assessed according to, for example, their power, influence, and urgency (Mitchell et al. 1997). However, we also suggested that such an approach ignores the fact that even though some stakeholders might lack much salience to the corporation, they might reasonably claim to have an *ethical right* to be involved in a particular decision or process (Hummels 1998).

What this comes down to is that in any given company (or any other organization for that matter), the definition of 'who our stakeholders are' is not simply a matter of objective observation. Rather, this decision is influenced by the *subjective interpretations* of managers and their value judgements of what constitutes a legitimate claim (Fineman and Clarke 1996). This issue is particularly pronounced in the case of promotional CSOs, since they cannot usually call on any specific constituency as the source of their inherent rights to claim stakeholder status. Of course, many of these groups tend to 'self-declare' themselves as stakeholders in a particular issue (Wheeler et al. 2002). This they accomplish by issuing statements, launching campaigns, or initiating some kind of action towards the corporation. For example, in 2008, McDonald's suddenly found itself confronted by the anti-gay organization, the American Family Association (AFA), which self-declared itself as a stakeholder to protest at the firm for 'promoting the homosexual agenda, including homosexual marriage'. In instigating a publicity campaign and boycott against the firm, the AFA sought to pressure McDonald's to cease its membership of the US-based National Gay and Lesbian Chamber of Commerce (NGLCC).[4]

Self-declaring does not, however, necessarily lead to *recognition*. For instance, Wheeler et al. (2002) illustrate how, for a number of years, Shell failed to recognize the CSO called the Movement for the Survival of the Ogoni People (MOSOP) as a legitimate stakeholder in its Nigerian operations. Initially, the company referred to 'the Ogoni community' in its literature on the issue without identifying specific stakeholder CSOs. Then, as the situation intensified, and MOSOP's figurehead, Ken Saro-Wiwa, starting gaining greater attention, Shell sought to represent MOSOP as illegitimate, and questioned the CSO's authority to represent the Ogoni. Instead, the company began dealing with what became known as 'Shell Chiefs'—namely, conservative Ogoni leaders who were more compliant with the company's position, but who had little mandate to represent the majority of the Ogoni. As Wheeler et al. (2002) demonstrate, it was only when Saro-Wiwa and MOSOP gained third-party legitimation through international NGOs such as Amnesty International and Greenpeace that MOSOP was granted stakeholder status by Shell. By this time, however, a gulf had opened up between the company and the Ogoni nation in general (and MOSOP in particular), leading to persistent problems in achieving subsequent reconciliation. In 2009, Shell was even forced to agree a €10m out-of-court settlement with relatives of Saro-Wiwa and the other executed MOSOP campaigners for alleged human rights violations.[5] This is not to say that MOSOP was the only CSO that Shell should or could have recognized as a stakeholder in Ogoniland, but it does illustrate quite powerfully some of the complexities involved in identifying CSOs as stakeholders.

So the question remains: which CSOs should corporations recognize as legitimate stakeholders? On the one side, there is certainly a case for arguing that companies cannot be expected to listen and engage with every organization that decides to take issue with their policies. Simon Zadek (2001: 156), the former Director of AccountAbility, for example, reports the following discussion with one exasperated British utility manager:

> **As a water utility we are a major landowner. We have been approached by representatives from the anti-hunting league and asked to stop renting out a parcel of land for use by sports-hunters. To be honest, we don't particularly have a corporate view on hunting, and do not particularly want to have one. Where does this all end? If there is a church but no mosque on our land, will we eventually have to have a view on God?**

However, even though many CSOs and their demands may seem peripheral, illegitimate, or just simply unrelated to the corporate sphere of activity, this does not mean they can merely be ignored. As soon as a CSO starts to direct its attentions towards a corporation, the stakes begin to rise, and the potential impact on the corporation and its reputation becomes more hazardous. Whilst ignoring ostensibly 'irrelevant' CSOs and hoping they will go away may be a typical corporate response to such 'irritants', it may have detrimental long-term consequences. Zadek (2001: 163), therefore, goes so far as to say that 'it is simply not really the company's choice who is and is not a stakeholder'. Clearly, as he suggests, the boundaries defining which CSOs can reasonably be defined as stakeholders are permeable and evolving, rather than concrete and fixed.

Certainly, though, managers have to make important decisions as to how to best respond to CSO demands for inclusion, and where to draw the boundaries of their responsibilities to such groups (Zadek 2001). After all, there is usually only a limited allocation of time and resources available for managing relations with CSOs. At present, it would appear that there is typically, though not unsurprisingly, still a strong element of instrumental logic embedded in such decisions within corporations (Cragg and Greenbaum 2002). Firms are more likely to recognize and respond to CSOs that are known, trusted, and not too critical. Typically, they will distinguish between campaigners who are regarded as 'reasonable' and those deemed 'unreasonable', and between those who are thought to have 'sound' or supposedly 'suspect' intentions in raising an issue (Fineman and Clarke 1996).

Normative stakeholder theory is not at its most helpful in determining specific boundaries of responsibility to civil society groups (Banerjee 2000). Although it may help us to identify that most affected groups have *some* claim on the firm, the nature of this claim is difficult to determine very precisely. Ultimately, though, there would seem a reasonable case to be made for at least *listening* to all those who feel they have a stake in the firm—even the critics. Harry Hummels (1998) suggests that managers have much to gain from listening to the alternative realities of critical voices—and in a complex, multifaceted, global economy, there are likely to be many sides to any major corporate action which impacts significantly on society. Listening to critics can raise awareness of potential problems, help to define priorities, and aid in setting out more informed visions of the future.

Of course, simply listening to what CSOs have to say is not always going to be a sufficient level of involvement, but it represents a good place to start. Hart and Sharma (2004: 7) go further to suggest that corporations should 'systematically identify, explore, and integrate the views of stakeholders "on the fringe"—the poor, weak, isolated, non-legitimate, and even non-human—for the express purpose of managing disruptive change and building imagination about future competitive business models'. Whilst this type of strategic reorientation would pose quite a challenge for most corporations, it certainly suggests that there appear to be both ethical *and* instrumental arguments to support an acknowledgement of at least a limited stake in the company for such fringe groups. **Ethical Dilemma 10** gives you the opportunity to think about and apply some of these ideas in a specific situation.

AN ETHICAL DILEMMA 10

Where's the beef?

As the public affairs manager of U-Buy, the country's leading supermarket chain, things have been fairly busy this last year. Still, having successfully dealt with the media response to the company's plans to close a number of unprofitable rural branches, you feel that the latest incident shouldn't be causing you quite as much trouble as it is.

It all started when you received an email from *Gay Men for Equality* (GAME), an activist group in the US. Although you had never even heard of GAME before, the group wrote to you asking about your company's position on BigBeef Corporation, a large US food company that supplies much of your processed meat products. Thinking it a strange request, but having no idea of any problems that GAME might be concerned about, you replied by saying simply that U-Buy had always enjoyed a good commercial relationship with BigBeef.

Thinking that this would be the last you would hear of GAME, you were surprised then to get back a much more stridently worded email that asked why U-Buy was supporting a company that had recently been convicted after a string of accusations about discrimination and harassment of gay employees, and whose chief executive Buck Leghorn was an outspoken critic of the gay and lesbian equality movement.

You decided to do some research on the accusations, and it appeared that GAME was pretty accurate in its claims about BigBeef and Leghorn. And from the press coverage in the US, it looked like BigBeef wasn't going to back down too much on this one. It appeared that GAME had been campaigning for some time against the company, but had yet to force a change of policy.

Although you could have done without the association between discrimination and U-Buy, this was BigBeef's business, and you felt it did not have much to do with your company. In the meantime, though, you had starting receiving several emails a day from GAME demanding a response, so you decided to write to them again. This time you reiterated that U-Buy had always enjoyed a good working relationship with BigBeef, but added that U-Buy deplored discrimination of any kind and itself actively complied with all relevant legislation.

GAME refused to be pacified by your response and started intensifying its demands, claiming that U-Buy should demand a complete apology and change of policy at BigBeef or else cease trading with them. When you got this email from GAME you almost laughed, thinking what a crazy suggestion this seemed to be. What did this have to do with you and U-Buy? It wasn't your fault that BigBeef had been prosecuted. And it certainly wasn't up to you what their chief executive Buck Leghorn decided to pronounce upon in the papers.

Still, you thought you'd mention the problem to the Head of Purchasing and let him know what was happening. When you did so, he made it extremely clear that there was no way he was willing to risk the good relations that U-Buy had with BigBeef. The company was one of U-Buy's most important suppliers, and the company had a lot of influence in the global food industry. 'This will soon blow over,' he told you, 'just lie low and don't say anything that will get us into trouble.'

Despite the Head of Purchasing's forecast, GAME's campaign seemed to be gaining a bit of steam, and even your own national press had somehow got hold of the story. It looked like GAME had turned its attention to some of BigBeef's main customers in the public eye (such as U-Buy) to try and force some changes at the company. And to your dismay, it now appeared that a local chapter of GAME had even been set up specifically to target U-Buy—and were said to be planning a demonstration outside your flagship store in the capital. Things were certainly escalating to a level that needed dealing with. You didn't want to risk threatening U-Buy's good relations with your powerful American supplier, but at the same time, you didn't want to be associated with discrimination, however indirectly. You could just see the placards now: 'U-Buy supports gay harassment' or some such thing. How come this minor little problem was causing you such a major headache?

Questions

1 Which are the legitimate stakeholders in this situation? Give reasons as to why you think they are legitimate and establish some kind of priority ranking.

2 How would you proceed in this situation?

3 How would you try and prevent similar problems from occurring in the future?

CSO tactics

Obviously CSOs are not passive actors in the process through which corporations confer (or do not confer) legitimacy upon their stake in a situation or issue. CSOs are frequently very active in promoting their causes and in seeking corporate recognition, engagement, and response. However, some of the tactics used by CSOs to do this can be challenged on ethical grounds (Whawell 1998). Is it acceptable, for example, for animal rights activists to break into animal-testing labs to release animals, or even to threaten the staff of testing companies? Is it possible to defend the occupation of oil platforms, the vandalism of fast food restaurants, or the deliberate destruction of GM crops?

There is, in fact, a whole range of tactics that CSOs might call on in seeking to achieve their aims. One set of tactics is through *indirect* forms of action, such as provision of data, research reports, and policy briefings, etc. (N.C. Smith 1990). At a more advanced level, though, we must also question how exactly CSOs pressure corporations in more *direct* forms of action. Craig Smith (1990) classifies the main approaches as violent direct action and non-violent direct action.

Indirect action

At the most basic level, indirect action will tend to involve research and communication about the issues of relevance to the organization. For promotional groups in particular, the

VISIT THE WEBSITE for links to useful sources of further information

ETHICS IN ACTION 10.1 http//:www.ethicalcorp.com

Ethical CORPORATION

NGO campaigns—campaigners scrutinized but unrepentant

Nick Jones, 5 June 2007

Campaigners have been a major force in the rise of the corporate responsibility agenda through bringing companies' actions to public attention. In turn they have become more powerful themselves, growing in size and international reach, which has brought their own working methods under the spotlight. Campaign groups are facing criticism from companies and commentators for a lack of professional care and competence in some of their reports.

Documents released by members of the Core Coalition face particular scrutiny. The Core Coalition is an alliance set up in 2001 by several NGOs to campaign for tougher regulation of the private sector by the UK government. Its three broad principles are by now a commonly heard refrain for big companies. Campaigners demand transparency through reporting, accountability through directors' duties, and rights of redress through some sort of foreign direct liability. A large number of reports are collated on Core's website, targeting individual firms ranging from Unilever to Royal Bank of Scotland and sectors ranging from retail to mining, and presented as 'case studies' to support the call for binding legislation.

Core complaints

Some Core members' reports, particularly those from ActionAid and Friends of the Earth, have drawn harsh criticism from companies. Objections concern these reports' conclusions, which all call for the same three changes to UK law as proposed by the Core coalition since its foundation. The accusation is that the conclusions were reached before the research was carried out. To some observers this is comparable to finding a defendant guilty before the trial begins, and casts doubts over whether a company will ever receive a fair hearing.

Reports in the ActionAid 'Stop Corporate Abuse' campaign are a good example. Reports in this series target an individual sector, link a well-known company to social problems witnessed by the group's researchers, and end by calling for the Core coalition's three company law reforms. The suspicion is that the verdicts were decided well in advance, and that the researchers cast around to find facts that backed up overarching Core Coalition demands rather than giving each company a fair hearing. ActionAid's head of trade and corporates, Claire Melamed, responds: 'We do not seek objectivity, but see it as our role to give a voice to the poorest and most powerless.'

Some NGOs have been criticized for not allowing companies a chance to respond to the accusations against them. In a letter of October 2006, AngloGoldAshanti rebuked the head of policy at ActionAid for denying it a chance to answer allegations made in a report about mining in Ghana. And campaigners' reports have garnered frustration for being inflexibly dismissive of companies' voluntary initiatives. Sainsbury's response to an ActionAid report about women workers in poor countries draws attention to what the firm calls its industry-leading efforts on fair trade products, which were not considered in the NGO's account.

More broadly, some have come under fire for perceived weakness in their research methods. The accusations include thin and selective use of evidence, failure to demonstrate a convincing link between the company's actions and the social problems they are accused of causing, short and cursory methodology sections, and a lack of competence in business and economics when tackling issues that call for these.

Necessary pressure?

Questions are also being asked over the motivation behind such reports. While the public generally sees the motives of NGOs as beyond reproach—compared with the perceived self-interest of politicians and business leaders—a number of organizational interests may actually be coming into play.

Some NGOs may benefit from playing the anti-corporate card through the Core campaign, energizing their supporters by provoking indignation at a well-known brand. This can effectively grab headlines and pull in donations, without the need to engage directly with the company, since the campaign is targeted at members of parliament. One man who has suffered stinging criticism from NGOs is Dan Rees, director of the Ethical Trading Initiative. Some NGOs participate in ETI, addressing labour standards in UK supply chains in partnership with companies and trade unions, while others keep their freedom to criticize from the sidelines. 'We take any criticism on the chin,' Rees says. 'We know we're not perfect and we don't say we are—otherwise we wouldn't have published a warts-and-all account of the impact of ETI members' activities last year.'

A War on Want report entitled 'Fashion Victims' says the initiative has failed to improve conditions for Bangladeshi workers, while a Core/Save the Children report, 'Why CSR harms children', describes it as inadequate at best and harmful at worst. Rees responds: 'Voluntary initiatives like ours work. The recent independent impact assessment of our members' ethical trade activities carried out by the Institute of Development Studies showed that factories and other workplaces are now safer for millions of workers.' But Rees refuses to hit back at his critics too strongly. 'It may be true that some recent reports have been a bit weak methodologically,' Rees says, 'but the main accountability of these organizations is to the workers whose issues they raise. Campaigners are doing a necessary job and they keep us all on our toes.'

These mixed feelings are shared by others who, like staff at the ETI, carry out work that is driven by the public indignation that such reports fuel. Corporate social responsibility departments also take an indulgent view towards their critics, and hold a store of good will for campaigners that keep them in the spotlight. But, campaigners themselves are unabashed. War on Want campaigns director John Hilary says: 'We stand by our research and the concerns raised in the reports which we have published. These reports are based on the testimonies of workers who have first-hand experience of exploitation at the sharp end of the supply chain.'

But those in the firing line are increasingly distinguishing between reports that are constructive and competent, and those that are weak on logic and evidence. For the latter, the goodwill may be running out—as dubious methods and a suspected vested interest in bashing industry leave a sour taste.

Sources

Ethical Corporation, Nick Jones, 5 June 2007, http://www.ethicalcorp.com.

VISIT THE WEBSITE for a short response to this feature

? THINK THEORY

Consider this example from the perspective of stakeholder theory. Who are the legitimate stakeholders of CSOs such as War on Want or ActionAid and what intrinsic rights do they have? What obligations do CSOs have to the companies they target?

need to compete for public attention and approval often requires that they first establish a sound basis of research in order to develop credible arguments (Smith 1990: 123). Sometimes, though, the need to raise interest and convince a sceptical or apathetic public can lead CSOs into potential misrepresentation and overclaiming on the basis of their evidence. One area where CSOs have typically been open to ethical criticism is therefore in relation to the **provision of misleading information** (Whawell 1998). For example, in 2009, a row ensued in India after the London-based tribal people CSO, Survival International, was accused of 'bullying' and providing 'grossly incorrect' information in its campaign to halt the construction of a resort on the Andaman Islands by the Barefoot Group. Survival's accusation that the company was potentially going to be responsible for 'genocide' of the Jarawa people of the Andamans prompted some of Barefoot's fellow 'responsible travel' companies to mount a concerted counter-attack challenging the irresponsibility of NGO campaigners.[6] **Ethics in Action 10.1** discusses key elements of the broader debate on CSO responsibilities in producing research and reports.

Overall, although there is growing attention to CSO duties to be honest and truthful in their communications, the provision of misleading information does not seem to be as much of an ethical problem for CSOs as it does for corporations (see Chapter 8). As we have already said, many CSOs have been extremely successful in establishing themselves as credible and authoritative institutions, and many are now more trusted sources of information on social issues in business than the businesses themselves. More marginal CSOs involved in anti-business communication, as well as other clearly partisan civil society actors, may not of course enjoy the same degree of overall trust from the public. However, their specific slant is usually reasonably well understood, with the result that their information is often seen more as subjective interpretation than objective fact.

Violent direct action

Violent direct action is often illegal, although as Smith (1990) notes, it frequently generates the most publicity. Because of the publicity it raises, violent action also raises awareness of the issues that the CSO is promoting very quickly. For example, it was when the 1999 anti-globalization protests at Seattle degenerated into street riots that the issue of anti-globalization was assured front-page coverage across much of the world. **Ethics on Screen 10** discusses the dramatization of these events in the recent movie *Battle in Seattle*. Similarly, the often violent campaign against animal cruelty at Huntingdon Life Sciences, led by SHAC (Stop Huntingdon Animal Cruelty) and others, has led to extensive media publicity and a series of damaging set-backs for the company, its suppliers, customers, and investors.

Nonetheless, it is difficult to condone the more violent protest by CSOs—although the destruction of property and violence towards people would seem to be on somewhat different moral planes. For one thing, it calls into question whether such action can really be deemed 'civil' at all. Perhaps in the interests of attempting to create a more civil society in the long run (for example, one where animals were not used for tests of cosmetic ingredients), we could begin to see a defence of violent action on consequentialist grounds. However, the perceived illegitimacy of such tactics by the public, government, and business tends to make them largely unsuccessful at gaining CSO members access to decision-makers and the decision-making process—which is often a major goal of such campaigns. Sometimes, even fairly legitimate protests can be denigrated when associated with violent protest. Overall, then, violent direct action remains an important, if highly controversial, tactic for CSOs. We would suggest that it seems to be particularly attractive for those who are (or who feel they are) largely excluded from any other means of engagement with decision-makers, and who feel that their ends justify their means. In a liberal, pluralistic society, though, such means have to be severely questioned.

Non-violent direct action

Non-violent direct action is a far more common approach for CSOs to use (Smith 1990). With the rise of the internet and social media, it has become far easier for even small CSOs to organize campaigns and other forms of activism aimed at corporations, as illustrated in **Ethics Online 10 p. 459**. Non-violent direct action, whether online or on the ground, can take a variety of forms including:

- Demonstrations and marches.
- Protests.
- Letter, email or social media campaigns.
- Boycotts.
- Occupations.
- Non-violent sabotage and disruption.
- Stunts.
- Picketing.

VISIT THE WEBSITE for links to useful sources of further information

VISIT THE WEBSITE to see a trailer for 'Battle in Seattle'

ETHICS ON SCREEN 10

Battle in Seattle

A film that leaves bruises.

Stephen Holden, *The New York Times*

The meeting of the World Trade Organization (WTO) 1999 in Seattle was a landmark event in the global civil society movement. Forty thousand protesters turned up in Seattle and basically shut the city down, preventing many delegates from even getting to the meeting sites in downtown hotels. It resulted ultimately in a breakdown of the talks and the WTO delegates had to leave town without results.

The film *Battle in Seattle* is a drama which follows the main actors, groups, and organizations involved in the events in that November week in 1999: campaigners (both peaceful and violent), the police, the mayor of Seattle, WTO delegates (conservatives and critics), and the media. The main thread along which the storyline evolves is the life of policeman Dale (Woody Harrelson) and his pregnant wife Ella (Charlize Theron) whose lives get changed forever in the course of events during the 'Battle in Seattle'. While Dale is part of the Seattle police's riot squad and is right in the middle of the 'battle', his wife's shopping trip meets a tragic halt when the city's shops close down and, on her way to a friend's apartment downtown, she gets randomly struck in the stomach by a police baton.

Linked into this story are the lives of many other characters that illustrate the complex and multifaceted issues and events that constitute contemporary civil society action. The major of Seattle, Paul Schell (played by *Goodfellas* star Ray Liotta), for example, represents well the clash of activism versus conservatism. Himself an ex-anti Vietnam protestor, Schell is sympathetic to the cause of the peaceful demonstrators. At the same time, he comes under pressure from the (Clinton-era) White House to make sure that the WTO consultations can go ahead, and from his own police chiefs, who are getting increasingly worried about the unravelling violence on the streets of Seattle.

Courtesy Hyde Park International

The film opened to mixed reviews—earning a meagre 52% score on the film review website 'Rotten Tomatoes', for instance. However, it certainly provides a great illustration of the issues surrounding a growing and increasingly powerful civil society movement which corporations and governments can no longer simply ignore. It also shows how the internet and modern technologies such as mobile phones have empowered ordinary citizens in organizing a powerful political movement. At the same time, it also shows that the NGO world is, in itself, a political arena full of contest, controversy, and debate. If anything, the film is a kaleidoscope of the different tactics, approaches, and agendas of the many groups commonly lumped together under the 'civil society' label. It also highlights in particular the close and vital link this movement has to the media and how it depends on the media in achieving success.

Though the film clearly leaves little doubt that it sides politically with the civil society movement, it still offers a rather differentiated picture, for instance, of the role of the police and the mayor and lets the viewer share their constraints, struggles, and conflicting pressures. And with a high profile cast, a well-told story, and high-paced cinematography, it is an entirely watchable and enjoyable way to learn more about the intersection of civil society and business ethics.

Sources

Holden, S. 2008. When worlds collided by Puget Sound. *The New York Times*, 19 Sept.
http://www.battleinseattlemovie.com
http://www.rottentomatoes.com/m/battle_in_seattle/.

Sometimes these may cross the line into illegality, such as when road protestors trespass on private land in order to prevent clearing and construction work from commencing on infrastructure projects. In the main, though, direct action of this sort tends to remain quite legal. As a result, there are often considerably fewer ethical problems arising with non-violent direct action. However, supposedly non-violent actions can lead to intimidation, and can even tacitly encourage action that is more violent. Moreover, tactics such as boycotts can also raise some concerns, and sometimes the very choice of companies to target can be a point of contention. We won't go into detail on all of the non-violent direct action tactics open to CSOs, but it seems worthwhile to focus a little more attention on the latter two points since boycotts are such an important part of the CSO 'tool box'.

Boycotts

Boycotts are probably the most commonly recognized, and most widely used, form of non-violent direct action. Research suggests that something like 30% of people claim to have boycotted, or are willing to boycott, a product for ethical reasons.[7] As such, they represent an organized form of *ethical consumption*—a subject we first discussed in Chapter 8. Essentially, whilst ethical consumption is often an individual activity or choice, a boycott is usually a co-ordinated endeavour that seeks to achieve some impact on corporations through *collective action* (Smith 1990). Boycotts can thus be defined as follows (from Friedman 1999: 4):

> **A boycott is an attempt by one or more parties to achieve certain objectives by urging individual consumers to refrain from making selected purchases in the marketplace.**

CSOs of one sort or another are usually the parties behind most boycotts of corporations and products. Some CSOs, in fact, even come into existence simply to organize boycott activity, such as the various pro-Palestinian organizations that have sprung up to support and co-ordinate efforts to boycott Israeli products and companies operating in, or supporting, Israel in some way. These include the *Boycott Israeli Goods* (BIG) campaign, *Boycott Israel Now*, and the Innovative Minds organization's *Boycott Israel* campaign.

Target company	CSO Organizer	Dates	Main issues	Outcomes
ExxonMobil (Esso)	Greenpeace, Friends of the Earth, People, and Planet	2001–4	Anti-climate change position, including active lobbying against Kyoto global warming treaty; lack of investment in renewable energy	Raised awareness and brought (unsuccessful) shareholder resolutions to the AGM. ExxonMobil has since shifted to a more accomodating climate change position
Triumph International	Burma Campaign	2001–2	Manufacturing operations in Burma	Announced withdrawal from the country in 2002
KFC	People for the Ethical Treatment of Animals (PETA)	2003–	Cruelty towards chickens in the KFC supply chain	Some improvements in practices. Campaign called off in Canada due to new animal welfare plan but continues in US, UK, and several other countries.
PG Tips Tea	Captive Animals' Protection Society (CAPS)	2004	Use of performing chimpanzees in advertisements—claimed to reduce animals to ridicule, and to involve taking young chimps from their mothers, and potential physical punishment	Removed advertisements featuring the chimpanzees in 2004, having used the image for 45 years. Now uses animated animals.
Body Shop	Naturewatch	2006–	Sale of Body Shop to L'Oreal, which is part owned by Nestlé. Main issues involved L'Oreal's use of animal testing	A Naturewatch press release claimed that the Body Shop had lost millions in revenue in just one year due to the campaign. No change in policy at L'Oreal.
Guess	The Coalition to Abolish the Fur Trade (CAFT)	2007–8	The international clothes retailer Guess sells products made with real fur.	Following an international campaign, Guess announced that it would not buy fur after September 2007, and would stop selling fur in their 800 shops worldwide by April 2008.
Heinz	Stonewall	2008	Company accused of discrimination against homosexuals after it dropped a UK advert featuring two men kissing following the receipt of more than 200 customer complaints	Ad is investigated by Advertising Standards Authority. Heinz sticks to decision not to reinstate ad despite a motion being filed in Parliament condemning decision.

Figure 10.5. Some well-known boycotts

Sources: www.ethicalconsumer.org.uk; www.caft.org.uk; www.greenpeace.org.uk; www.stopanimalcruelty.co.uk/bodyshop; www.captiveanimals.org

ETHICS ONLINE 10 http://www.ethicalcorp.com

Ethical CORPORATION

VISIT THE WEBSITE for links to useful sources of further information

Campaigns 2.0

It reads like a spoof text message. 'London, 14 January, 7pm, Heathrow. Deeds not words! Bring picnic blankets.' It's no joke though. More than 1,000 environmental protestors took up the call and held a mass sit-in at Heathrow's Terminal 1. The message daubed over their blankets, 'Climate Chaos—It's no picnic', was splashed over the next day's newspapers.

Climate Rush is symbolic of where activism is at these days. Campaigners are slick, smart and, above all, new media savvy. Styling themselves as modern-day suffragettes, climate rushers liaise through a basic, low-cost website. The tone is direct and no-nonsense. No flash graphics. No PR speak. Action alerts wing their way out by email. Word is spread further via social media tools such as Facebook and Bebo. And so a street protest is born.

It is not hard to work out why social media appeals so much to the campaign community. The latest generation information technologies are cheap, fast and almost infinite in reach. Little wonder the signature collectors of old have swapped pens for PCs. 'Online campaigning is a hugely powerful tool ... as it enables you to start from nowhere,' says Ben Stewart, a spokesman for environmental campaign group Greenpeace. He should know. Greenpeace's propulsion onto the world stage came in the mid-1990s, just as new media technologies were taking off. The television news beamed live video footage from its campaign ship Rainbow Warrior to millions of viewers around the world. Boycotts followed and Greenpeace's membership numbers shot up.

Greenpeace's recent campaign to prevent an extension to Heathrow airport shows just how quickly things are developing in cyberspace. The placards and press releases are still in place. But leading the charge is a cutting-edge website. All users need to do is click on and sign up to become 'beneficial owners' of the land earmarked for the proposed new runway. About 10,000 people did so in the first 24 hours that airplot.org went live.

The main corporate website of BAA, the operator of Heathrow airport, hosts a single page on the issue. The dry text, written in small grey font, reads blandly by comparison. Users are encouraged to check out the company's corporate social responsibility report for more information. A temptation most would pass.

BAA's response highlights the difficulty for companies operating in an age of virtual activism. Responding directly to every web critic is impractical. The average large consumer brand is the subject of thousands of websites, MySpace pages, email strings and chatrooms around the globe. The first challenge is simply to monitor what is out there. The job has become easier since the introduction of powerful search engines, but keeping track of what's being said on the web remains a labour-intensive job. Google, for example, is great for indexing text-based content but not video or other new social media.

Working out who is who in cyberspace presents its difficulties as well. Historically, companies would chart the potential influence of a stakeholder against the potential reputational risk of the issue at hand. A high registry on both would set the alarm bells ringing. Online activism is not quite so simple. Financial resources, political clout, moral authority and media presence used to determine a stakeholder's influence. They still do. But into the mix must go the exponential power of the internet.

That leaves companies with the tricky conundrum of when, and indeed whether, to respond. Careful judgment is required on both counts. Act too quickly, and a company can give too much weight to an unsubstantiated complaint. Leave it too long and an online campaign can snowball out into the street and onto the shop-front. As online campaigners become more interactive, the impulse is on companies to keep pace.

Sources

Extracted from Balch, O. 2009. Campaigns 2.0. *Ethical Corporation*, May: 18–21. http://www.ethicalcorp.com. Reproduced with permission.

Consumer boycotts have been targeted at numerous companies over the years. At any given time, the *Ethical Consumer* website typically lists more than 50 current boycott actions, while the *Boycott Israel* campaign alone lists more than 30 so-called 'guilty companies' to boycott.[8] **Figure 10.5** lists some more well-known boycotts that have occurred over the years.

The arguments for and against whether to boycott companies are rarely as clear as their proponents suggest. Some boycotts are clearly more controversial than others. The questions of **which companies should be targeted** (and the reasons why) are critical ethical choices for CSOs to make. For a start, whilst CSOs often try to occupy the moral high ground, the values and causes they promote are obviously not going to be to everyone's taste. For example, boycotts of companies operating in Israel have often been met with considerable controversy given the contentious politics of the Middle East. In the US, companies participating in anti-Israel boycotts can even be fined.[9]

Slightly less controversial, perhaps, has been the boycotting of companies operating in Burma, whose repressive regime has been implicated in human rights abuses. Protestors argue that firms investing in Burma provide support for the country's military dictatorship, and a number of companies have even been argued to have utilized forced labour provided by the authorities. Boycotts have been initiated against firms such as Triumph, Pepsico, Arco, and Texaco, all of which have now left the country. However, many companies retain business links with the country, and in 2009, the International Confederation of Free Trade Unions (ICFTU) listed more than 400 multinational companies with business links to the Burmese dictatorship.[10] This included:

- Lonely Planet Publications, the Australian guidebook publisher now owned by BBC Worldwide, which markets a holiday guide to Burma.
- Harrods, the UK high-end retailer, which sells rubies sourced in Burma.
- Petronas, the Malaysian national oil company, which operates a wholly owned subsidiary with exploration interests in Burma.
- Caterpillar, the US machinery and work-wear company, that sells tractors and other equipment through dealers in Burma.

However, not everyone is in agreement about the morality of boycotting firms with links to Burma. For example, some companies targeted by campaigners have argued that by remaining in Burma, and abiding by established codes of ethics, they can raise awareness about human rights and protect workers from forced labour and other such abuses. If they left the country, the companies argue, these problems would only worsen. Similar debates arose in the past about the presence of multinationals in South Africa during the apartheid era (De George 1999: 542–8). Such issues illustrate that arguments can be made both for and against corporations having a more positive role in promoting civil rights in countries with poor human rights records. However, boycotts against firms remaining in both South Africa and Burma have already shown that organized campaigns can put firms in the ethical spotlight, leading to potentially major (and costly) publicity problems.

VISIT THE WEBSITE for a short response to this feature

? THINK THEORY

Think about the arguments for and against the presence of companies in Burma. Which ethical principles and theories would you say these arguments primarily rely on?

Of course, the reasons for boycotts can vary. Friedman (1999), in fact, suggests that CSOs might actually have four different purposes for boycotts:

- **Instrumental boycotts** aim to force the target to change a specific policy. Goals may be very clear, such as the repudiation of the challenged policy, the introduction of better conditions, etc.
- **Catalytic boycotts** seek to raise awareness about the company's actions and policies. The boycott itself is more of a means to generate publicity, either for the CSO or for a broader campaign of action against the company.
- **Expressive boycotts** are more general forms of protest that effectively just communicate a general displeasure about the target company. This form tends to be characterized by more vague goals, since their focus is more on the CSO and consumers registering their disapproval.
- **Punitive boycotts** seek to punish the target company for its actions. Therefore, rather than communicating displeasure, the boycotters actively seek to cause the firm harm, usually by aiming for significant erosions of sales.

Regardless of the purpose of CSOs in calling a boycott, it is often the extent and intensity of consumer participation that determines whether such goals are met. Clearly, a number of factors can affect whether consumers join and maintain boycotts, including the degree of effort involved in switching to an alternative, the appeal of the boycotted product to the consumer, social pressure, and the likelihood of success (Sen et al. 2001). In practice, though, many, many more boycotts are called than are successful and many are never even brought to the notice of the general public. This, then, of course starts to raise the question of which constituencies exactly are CSOs supposed to be representing—and perhaps more importantly, in what way are they answerable to those whose interests they are supposed to be advancing? These are essentially questions of CSO accountability, the last of our main ethical issues confronting business relations with CSOs.

? THINK THEORY

Investigate the boycotts in Figure 10.5 and categorize them in terms of instrumental, catalytic, expressive, and punitive boycotts. What explains the difference in objectives for CSOs?

VISIT THE WEBSITE for a short response to this feature

CSO accountability

In recent years, the issue of CSO accountability has been raised with increasing regularity (Bendell 2005; Unerman and O'Dwyer 2006). This is perhaps not surprising when one considers that they have often been the parties most vociferously questioning the accountability of corporations. We might reasonably expect critics of corporate accountability to 'have their own house in order' first (Hilhorst 2002).

Indeed, it is interesting to note that questions about CSO accountability have largely mirrored the same questions that have been raised in relation to corporations. For example, who exactly is an organization such as Greenpeace supposed to be serving? Are the interests of its managers aligned with those of its principal constituents? To what extent and to whom are Greenpeace responsible for the consequences of their actions? We have asked almost exactly the same questions in discussing issues of corporate responsibility and accountability in Chapter 2, and issues of ownership, control, and governance in Chapter 6. This suggests that we can conceptualize CSO managers as 'agents' for a broader collective of civil society 'principals' in the same way as we do for corporate managers and shareholders (see Doh and Teegen 2002). Likewise, we can model CSOs as representative of different stakeholder interests just as we can with corporations (e.g. Hilhorst 2002).

Specifically, **CSO stakeholders** might be said to include:

- Beneficiaries.
- Donors.
- Members.
- Employees.
- Governmental organizations.
- Other CSOs.
- General public (especially those who support their ideals).

Significantly, though, there is also very clearly a case for saying that CSOs represent some notion of *civil society itself*—a largely indefinable stakeholder, but one that is nonetheless central to the notion of the third sector. Interestingly, a growing number of organizations very similar to CSOs have been initiated recently, with *business* itself as a main stakeholder, examples being the World Business Council for Sustainable Development (WBCSD), the Global Business Coalition on HIV/AIDS (GBC), and the Global Climate Coalition (GCC). In contrast to real grassroots organizations, these are sometimes dubbed 'astroturf NGOs' (Gray et al. 2006), as they pick up typical issues of CSOs, but address them from the rather narrow angle of business interests.

Given such a range of stakeholders, issues of accountability and responsibility in CSOs are clearly quite complex. Different stakeholders might have different expectations of CSO performance, and of how that performance is reported. Similarly, different stakeholders might have very different expectations about how much say they should have in the affairs of the organization. Whilst we might, as the general public, support the work of Oxfam in providing famine relief, we do not expect to have much meaningful input into how they go about providing this. Perhaps our interest in this respect grows if we donate significant sums of money to the organization, but even so, we would generally be less concerned about how they spent our money than the intended beneficiaries would be.

Unsurprisingly, then, it is the accountability of CSOs to their *supposed beneficiaries* that tends to raise the most debate. A number of problems are evident here (see Ali 2000; Bendell 2000b, 2005; Edwards and Fowler 2002; Hilhorst 2002), including:

- CSOs in developed countries purporting to represent the interests of those in developing countries have been accused of imposing their own agendas on local people without adequately understanding their situations and needs.
- The involvement of beneficiaries in agenda setting, defining priorities, and making strategic decisions is often limited.
- The need for financial support and other resources can focus CSOs' interests on donors' priorities rather than those of their intended beneficiaries.
- Beneficiaries typically lack effective mechanisms to voice approval or disapproval of CSO performance.

In some ways, it would appear that many CSOs have tended to be equally as inattentive to certain issues of accountability and democracy as many corporations have. Given their largely positive impact on society, as well as their values-based stance, it could be argued, though, that perhaps the issue of accountability is less crucial in respect to CSOs. Indeed, *formal accountability* (in the form of public accounts and performance metrics) might be said to be less important for CSOs than a more *informal accountability* based on the more complex and closer ties between CSOs and their stakeholders (Gray et al. 2006). However, given the growing importance of their role in society in general, as well as their involvement in business specifically, the question of CSO accountability is only really likely to gain in significance. A recent landmark in the debate was the launch in 2006 by a group of international NGOs, including Oxfam, Amnesty International, and Greenpeace, of a new 'Accountability Charter' intended to serve as a code of conduct for NGOs on the international stage (Russell 2006). As we saw in Chapter 5, simply having a code does not ensure ethical behaviour; effective implementation, employee buy-in, and credible enforcement and follow-through are critical for ensuring a code's success.

For corporations, the main questions around CSO accountability are: (i) how they should assess the legitimacy of any CSO contribution to the debate about business ethics; and (ii) what this means in terms of how they should respond to particular CSO challenges. At one extreme, they could choose to play CSOs at their own game and refuse to take seriously the views of unelected, unaccountable ideologues. At the other, they could seek to work together to develop enhanced mechanisms of governance and accountability for both types of organizations. The reality, however, is likely to be somewhere in the middle—with all the ambiguity and ambivalence that such a situation brings.

? THINK THEORY

Think about the relevance of stakeholder theory for CSOs compared with corporations. In which aspects is it more or less relevant or applicable for either category of organization?

VISIT THE WEBSITE for a short response to this feature

■ Globalization and civil society organizations

Globalization has brought a number of significant changes to CSOs that are relevant for our understanding of business ethics. First, globalization has brought MNCs into confrontation with an extended community of CSOs, including a whole new set of local CSOs in other countries that they did not have to deal with before. Second, we have seen the emergence of new global issues for CSOs to engage with. Indeed, even the very contestability of the benefits or otherwise of globalization has led to the formation of new 'anti-globalization' CSOs. Finally, we have also seen CSOs themselves increasingly globalize in terms of scale and/or scope. Clearly, it is not only corporations that organize across borders, and CSOs have often been extremely effective at galvanizing a transnational community of constituents to support their campaigns aimed at corporations.

In summary, it is possible to discern three main areas where globalization is reshaping the relations between corporations and CSOs.

- Engagement with overseas CSOs.
- Global issues and causes.
- Globalization of CSOs.

Let us look at each of these in a little more detail.

Engagement with overseas CSOs

For corporations acting solely within the domestic sphere, the notion of civil society tends to be quite naturally framed simply in terms of national or even regional constituencies. Just as an Italian corporation, such as the construction giant Impregilo, might typically have been mainly involved in dealing with Italian labour and environmental groups (such as Campagna per la Riforma della Banca Mondiale), so might an Indian corporation such as Tata Tea, the largest tea company in the subcontinent, typically have dealt with just Indian CSOs. However, the increasingly deterritorialized nature of business activity inevitably puts corporations with international operations into a number of different civil societies across the globe. MNCs are therefore confronted with a whole new set of unfamiliar CSOs in overseas countries.

For example, BP's involvement in extracting, refining, and transporting oil in hundreds of projects around the globe exposes the company to the attention of various local environmental and community groups in each of the countries involved. These can amount to hundreds of different groups, not just of local origin, but also local subsidiaries of global CSOs, such as Save the Children, the Refugee Council, and others.

It should be noted here that in countries like India, the CSO population is huge, whilst in others, such as China, the local CSO population is very limited. Indeed, CSOs hardly existed in China prior to the mid-1990s, since which time their number has escalated quite rapidly. Some CSOs are now developing greater independence from the government and a variety of grassroots CSOs 'have grown up between the cracks in the legislative pavement' (Young 2002: 36). Nonetheless, Chinese CSOs still face substantial political constraints, and they typically have little choice but to employ non-confrontational methods that emphasize co-operation and participation (Gadsden 2008; Yang 2005). In fact, many developing and transitional economies tend to lack a strong and institutionalized civil society, with international CSOs often taking up the slack. On the one hand, a lack of local CSOs can be a plus for corporations in that it means they can either engage with international organizations, or even conduct their business relatively unhindered by CSO activism. On the other hand, international groups may lack legitimate representation of local communities, and the absence of an effective third sector can reinforce welfare and democracy deficits in countries where corporations would benefit from greater societal governance.

Global issues and causes

In addition to bringing corporations into contact with an extended community of CSOs overseas, it is evident that many of the problems now dealt with by CSOs in their relations with corporations are global in nature and/or emerging as a consequence of globalization in other areas of business. Many of the issues championed by CSOs such as climate change, pollution, and human rights, are **problems that transcend national boundaries**. We won't go into these in any more detail here, as most such issues are covered elsewhere in the chapters dealing with the specific stakeholders involved, but it is important to recognize that campaigns addressing such issues often have to be scaled up from a local to an international level to be truly effective. For instance, WWF's commitment to water conservation led to the striking of a major global partnership with Coca-Cola in 2007. As part of the initiative, WWF and Coke are tackling the conservation of seven of the world's most critical freshwater river basins in China, South East Asia, North America, Eastern Europe, and East Africa.[11] This shows how global issues such as water security, raise the prospect of coordinated global attention from international CSOs and multinational corporations.

Given this attention to global problems, though, it is perhaps unsurprising that much of the currently popular **critique of globalization** itself has been initiated, sustained, and popularized by civil society actors (Eschle and Maiguashca 2005). At one level, this has involved existing CSOs incorporating messages critical of certain aspects of globalization into their campaigns. For example, in the 2000s, Friends of the Earth, which is mainly known for its environmental activism, initiated a campaign targeting 'corporate globalization', and now campaigns on other 'anti-global' issues, such as 'food security' and 'resisting neoliberalism'.[12] Moreover, many groups with a more directly political orientation, such as anarchist cells and Marxist action groups, have maintained a position of resistance to global capitalism for many years—although many of these might be more correctly regarded as political organizations rather than CSOs.

On another level, there have been the new groups that have sprung up specifically to protest against aspects of globalization (Heartfield 2005). Most notable in their demonstrations at the various meetings of economic and political leaders including the World Economic Forum, WTO, and G8 summits, the civil society challenge to globalization has seen the emergence of a myriad of new groups dedicated to a range of causes which mainly relate to the taming of global corporations, global capitalism, international finance, free trade, and various other aspects of globalization. Again, which of these groups and organizations should actually be regarded as civil society actors is somewhat debatable, but certainly those which advance a specific cause that is primarily outside the political or market sector would seem to fall within a broad definition of civil society.

The CSOs tackling globalization have taken many forms—and it is evident that some of them are more civil than others! One of the main European CSOs involved in this movement (arguably at the more intellectual end of the scale) is ATTAC.[13] It consists of a network of around a 1,000 independent national and local groups in 40 countries, including by 2009 some 4,000 Facebook members. The aim of the group is to work towards social, environmental, and democratic rules in the globalization process. Some of its core campaigns have been around the promotion of an international tax on currency speculation (the Tobin Tax), as well as campaigns to end tax havens, replace pension funds with state pensions, cancel third world debt, and reform of the WTO (Birchfield and Freyberg-Inan 2005).

At the other end of the scale are groups that claim to focus more on pranks and spectacle. This includes the Biotic Baking Brigade, whose approach relies on throwing pies at leading advocates of globalization (including former Microsoft CEO Bill Gates and the right-wing economist Milton Friedman whom we first discussed in Chapter 2), and the UK-based Reclaim the Streets, which organized dance parties and 'guerrilla' tree plantings on public roads in the 1990s (see Klein 2000: 311–26).

We can see here echoes of the *postmodern* take on ethics that we introduced in Chapter 3: individuals forming loose, fragmented coalitions in order to stake out temporary zones of autonomy where they can challenge the 'grand narratives' of society (capitalism, globalization, progress, etc.) and make active choices about how to act (Desmond et al. 2000). There is much to be said for such tactics, not least because they can result in tremendous publicity for the 'cause' (Higgins and Tadajewski 2002). Clearly, though, there is the danger that, as a consequence, serious questioning may be dismissed as a mere media stunt, devoid of commitment and moral force (Gabriel and Lang 2006).

This leads us on to perhaps one of the most interesting aspects of the protests: the way that the CSOs involved have tended to make use of many of the phenomena that they themselves criticize (Higgins and Tadajewski 2002). For example, consider Adbusters, the Canadian organization which seeks to promote an 'anti-marketing', 'anti-corporate' agenda through creative media and advertising, or even the popularizer of the anti-globalization movement, Naomi Klein herself, who not only registered the 'No Logo' logo on the front of her book as a trademark, but even published the book in the UK through an arm of Rupert Murdoch's global publishing empire (Higgins and Tadajewski 2002). Whichever way we look at it, there are a number of intriguing parallels, interlinkages, and commonalities between the anti-globalization protestors and their targets. Perhaps, though, the most visible aspect of these is the increasingly globalized nature of civil society itself.

Globalization of CSOs

'The resistance will be as transnational as capital.' So goes one of the main rallying calls of the protest movement. And as this suggests, the so-called anti-globalization movement is as much reliant on, and a by-product of, globalization, as are Gap stores in every high street and the ubiquity of McDonald's hamburgers. In particular, the mobilization of anti-corporate sentiment across the world has only been realized on such a scale because of the supra-territorial scope of the internet (Harding 2001a). With the ability to co-ordinate international protests and boycotts, to use sophisticated technology to transmit media-friendly images to the world press, not to mention the possibility of travelling across the globe as a result of cheaper air fares it is clear that the travelling circus of protestors has been considerably expedited by certain aspects of globalization (Harding 2001b, 2001c).

Significantly, though, this is not only true of the anti-globalization protestors, but of much of contemporary civil society. Rather than just engaging with multiple local civil societies (as we suggested in the section 'Engagement with overseas CSOs' above), some corporations have been faced with something more akin to a *global civil society*. Talk of a global civil society to describe such developments first began to spread in the 1990s and has now become fairly commonplace in social and political debates (Baker and Chandler 2005; Kaldor et al. 2002; Keane 2003). From giant NGOs such as WWF, Greenpeace, and Friends of the Earth, to international union bodies such as the International Confederation of Free Trade Unions (ICFTU), and fringe activist outfits such as SHAC, there are innumerable civil actors engaged in the debate about corporate practices which are organized on a transnational basis. Just as corporations have increasingly gone global, so too have CSOs.

However, this position as global institutions, on a similar (de)territorialized basis as corporations, potentially brings with it new roles and responsibilities for CSOs. Given that most regulation of business activity was formerly in the province of local and national governments, the movement of both corporations and CSOs (but less so governments) to a global level means that CSOs might be expected to take on some of these responsibilities that were formerly held by government. As we have said a number of times, business ethics tends to begin where the law ends. And with a dearth of global laws, global CSOs have found themselves involved in (and at times, have pushed themselves into) the process whereby global regulation of business is debated, decided, and implemented (Doh and Teegen 2002, 2003; Zadek 2001). As we shall discuss in more detail in the next section, this potentially has significant implications for our understanding of corporate citizenship (CC) with respect to civil society.

? THINK THEORY

Think about the notion of globalization as deterritorialization. Which aspects of CSOs are, or could be, deterritorialized? How does the degree of deterritorialization of CSOs and CSO protests compare with that of corporations?

VISIT THE WEBSITE for a short response to this feature

■ Corporate citizenship and civil society: charity, collaboration, enterprise, or regulation?

So far in this chapter, we have mainly discussed corporate and civil society actors as though they were dedicated adversaries in a perpetual state of conflict. However, recognition by firms that 'good' citizenship might entail a positive response to civil society challenges has for some time now brought them into more constructive contact with civil actors Traditionally, this has mainly centred on **charitable giving** and other philanthropic acts intended to benefit community groups and other civil actors. More recently, though, we have also witnessed an increasing incidence of more intensive **business–CSO collaboration**, seeking to provide more partnership-based solutions to social and environmental problems (McIntosh and Thomas 2002; Murphy and Bendell 1997; Selsky and Parker 2005; Warner and Sullivan 2004). At times, CSOs have even eschewed partnership with corporations and developed their own businesses, namely **social enterprises**. Finally, looking at the nature and purpose of CSO involvement in the business sector, a number of authors have also advanced the proposition, raised in the previous section, that CSOs might even go beyond collaborating with business to actually forming some kind of '**civil regulation**' of corporate action (e.g. Bendell 2000b; Zadek 2001).

These tighter interrelationships should come as no surprise, particularly when we stop to think about the implications of talking about citizenship in the context of corporations. After all, civil society is typically thought of as an important arena where individual citizens can express and pursue their particular values and interests. Whether we think of corporations as fellow citizens in this society (as the *limited* and *equivalent views* of CC suggest) or as governors of citizenship for individuals (as our preferred *extended view* proposes), corporations must almost inevitably at some time become involved in civil society. In this section, we will look at these ways in which corporations and civil society have become more tightly interrelated, and consider the question of what role CSOs can play in making corporations more responsible and accountable within society.

VISIT THE WEBSITE for a short response to this feature

> **? THINK THEORY**
>
> Think about our competing definitions of CC in Chapter 2 (go back and read the chapter if you are unsure of them). Which of these definitions do you think would be most acceptable to the CSOs that we have discussed in this chapter? Why do you think this is?

Charity and community involvement

The main starting point for a consideration of business involvement in civil society is inevitably charitable giving and other forms of corporate philanthropy and community involvement. As we have suggested a number of times already in the book, corporations have long been involved in philanthropic behaviour towards local communities, charities, the arts, and various other aspects of civil society. Based on the notion of 'putting something back', many large corporations have now set up separate units or **corporate foundations** to strategically manage philanthropic activities—or 'social investments', as they are often referred to—on a global scale (Kotler and Lee 2005). For instance, the foundation of the mobile phone company Vodafone coordinates more than 20 local national foundations, as well as a global Vodaphone Group Foundation. Between 2002 and 2008, it had invested more than £100m in social projects, involving CSOs such as Common Purpose, MapAction, Oxfam, Télécoms sans Frontières and the United Nations Foundation.[14]

Employees are also often involved in philanthropy schemes with CSOs, such as through **employee volunteering**. Although volunteering for charities has traditionally been part of a citizen's private civil engagement, companies have also increasingly offered their employees the opportunity to volunteer on company time. By enabling employees to commit their time and efforts to social initiatives in this way, firms may be able to achieve a number of aims, including (Muthuri et al. 2009; Peloza and Hassay 2006):

- Making a meaningful social contribution
- Contributing to the development of their human resources
- Enhancing the firm's reputation
- Increasing employee morale
- Building 'social capital' within the community.

However, as a recent national survey of employee volunteering in Canada revealed, 'passive' forms of company support for employee volunteering (such as unpaid leave and provision of access to company facilities) are far more common than 'active' forms (such as paid leave and formal integration with training and development programmes) (Basil et al. 2009). This suggests that, despite its prevalence, many firms have yet to deploy a strategic or proactive approach to employee involvement, but rather rely on employees to take the initiative.

Many firms tend to regard employee involvement and charitable donations and the like as the mainstay of their 'corporate citizenship' programmes, and clearly some corporations have made significant contributions to civic life through such activities. The scale and form of corporate giving, however, varies significantly between companies and between different regions. In general, US firms tend to exhibit the highest levels of corporate giving. European firms have tended to lag behind those from the US, but typically outstrip donations from Asian firms (Brammer and Pavelin 2005; Muller and Whiteman 2009). Such differences reflect distinct institutional contexts in different parts of the globe, including different tax regimes, variations in state investment in social welfare, and divergent norms and expectations around charitable giving.

Authors such as Friedman (1970) initially criticized charitable giving for effectively stealing from shareholders. More recently, attention has turned to **strategic philanthropy** (C. Smith 1994) and **cause-related marketing** (Varadarajan and Menon 1988) as ways of aligning charitable giving with firm self-interest. Under such initiatives, firms select suitable recipients of funding not so much according to need, but according to their potential for improving the firm's competitive context, enhancing its reputation, and other instrumental ends (Porter and Kramer 2006). Although this is a logical response to doubts about the business value of community involvement, it does suggest certain limitations to philanthropy as a means of satisfying broader civic roles and responsibilities. As we said in Chapter 2, this form of community involvement is very much within a limited view of corporate citizenship. Although it benefits communities and civil society, it does not usually allow them much voice in shaping corporate action, potentially leading to exploitation rather than empowerment (Muthuri 2008). Essentially, according to our depiction of different modes of stakeholder engagement in Chapter 5, this is a form of *one-way support* from business to civil society.

Business–CSO collaboration

In addition to these one-way philanthropic gestures, closer and more interactive relations between civil society and corporations have also risen to prominence in recent years. This move towards business–CSO collaboration has included dialogue between business and civil society actors, such as when major regeneration or construction projects are planned, and strategic alliances between business and civil partners on matters such as supply-chain management and certification. These developments have included various civil society actors, including environmental NGOs such as WWF, aid charities such as Oxfam, labour organizations such as the ILO (International Labour Organization), and various local and community groups. Some examples involving multinational companies and CSOs are described in **Figure 10.6**.

Whilst reliable figures on the number of collaborations between CSOs and corporations are not readily available, there is general agreement that their incidence and scope has increased quite dramatically over the last ten years or so (Selsky and Parker 2005; *Ethical Performance* 2006). There is also considerable evidence to suggest that the *degree of interaction* between commercial and civil organizations has intensified—from basic 'transactional' approaches to more 'integrative' relationships (Austin 2000). It is often suggested that CSOs are moving from being passive recipients of corporate philanthropy, or 'brand-for-hire' endorsers of existing company products, to more strategic roles in developing corporate policies and sharing resources and capabilities in order to contribute to joint value creation (Kolk et al. 2008). Brugmann and Prahalad (2007) demonstrate that business and CSOs may even go so far as to co-create new businesses together—an issue that we will explore in more depth in the following section on 'social enterprise'.

Given the history of boycotts, strikes, occupations, protests, and other conflicts, businesses and CSOs might seem at first to be rather strange, and somewhat uneasy, bedfellows. However, there are a number of reasons why they have sought to work more closely together (see Elkington and Fennell 2000). For businesses, these reasons include consumer expectations, an interest in leveraging CSO credibility, a desire to head off potentially negative publicity, and the potential for introducing new thinking into the organization. For CSOs, the reasons include a need for better resources, improved access to markets, disenchantment with governments, and access to corporate supply chains.

Name of initiative	Country	Main CSO(s) involved	Main corporation(s) involved	Launch	Aims and objectives
Change for Good	International	UNICEF	Major airline carriers incl. Alitalia, British Airways, Cathay Pacific, JAL, Quantas	1987	To collect unused currency from passengers and convert it into life-saving materials and services for needy children
Marine Stewardship Council (MSC)	International	Originally developed by WWF-UK, now MSC is an independent CSO in itself	Unilever (at outset), now thousands of retailers, suppliers and restaurants globally	1997	Establishment of standards and independent certification for sustainable fishing
Ethical Trading Initiative	UK/ International	15 NGOs & 3 trade unions incl. International Confederation of Free Trade Unions, Anti-Slavery International & Christian Aid	50+ companies, incl. Gap, Jaeger, Monsoon, Tesco, Body Shop	1998	To define best practice in ethical trade and enable firms to implement labour standards in international supply chains
Juice	UK	Greenpeace	Npower	2001	Development of a 'clean' electricity product which is based on renewable energy sources.
Sustainable Coffee	US/ International	The Rainforest Alliance	Kraft Foods	2003	To bring coffee beans certified for social and environmental sustainability into Kraft's mainstream brands, including Kenco Yuban, and Carte Noir.
International Business and Poverty Reduction	Indonesia	Oxfam	Unilever	2004-5	Development of a research programme to explore the nature of Unilever's Indonesia business and its impacts on people living in poverty.
HSBC Climate Partnership	International	The Climate Group, Earthwatch Institute, Smithsonian Tropical Research Institute, WWF	HSBC	2007	To combat climate change by 'inspiring action by individuals, businesses and governments worldwide', including programmes in education, research, conservation, and engagement with business, government and communities.
Green Works	US	Sierra Club	Clorox	2008	Endorsement of 'green' line of cleaning products

Figure 10.6. Some examples of business–CSO collaboration

In many respects, such collaborations appear to be very welcome, and in general have been afforded a very positive response in the academic and business press (Selsky and Parker 2005). We can see in such developments the potential for greater discussion, debate, and reflection on business ethics by the different partners. This raises the prospect of those from different sectors gaining greater understanding of the different facets of problems and learning to engage with competing, even conflicting, perspectives in order to build mutually acceptable solutions. Clearly, this has strong resonance with a **discourse ethics** approach to resolving ethical problems. However, as we shall now see, the value of this approach will depend on a number of other factors.

VISIT THE WEBSITE for a short response to this feature

? THINK THEORY

Think about business–CSO collaboration from the perspective of discourse ethics. What should the conditions of such collaborations be from this theoretical perspective?

Limitations of business–CSO collaboration

Several authors have suggested potential limitations to business–CSO collaboration. Possible drawbacks include problems of potential 'culture clash' between such culturally diverse organizations (Crane 1998) and the difficulties of ensuring consistency and commitment (Elkington and Fennell 2000). Similarly, Ackers and Payne (1998) identify risks such as continuing hostility and power imbalances between the 'partners'.

The question of *power imbalance* is a crucial one here in addressing the potential for a discourse ethics approach to bring benefits to the two parties. Typically, one would expect business partners to be considerably more powerful than CSOs in terms of size, capital, political influence, and other key power resources. However, such a perspective tends to overlook the important power that CSOs wield in terms of specific knowledge, communications expertise, and public credibility (Arts 2002). Certainly, though, where large companies and relatively more dependent CSOs work together, there is a danger that the relative influence of the two parties will be skewed towards corporate interests, and rewards may be unevenly shared. Thus, despite the good intentions of both parties, the rhetoric of 'partnerships' might often mask somewhat more traditional and asymmetric relations between the two sectors (Seitanidi and Ryan 2007). In addition, it has been argued that business–CSO alliances might favour the interests of companies and CSOs in developing countries over those in less developed countries (Bendell and Murphy 2000).

We might also look to the *distribution of the benefits* of partnerships. Darcy Ashman (2001), for example, suggests that the benefits of many CSO–business partnerships are garnered more by the partners than they are by the constituencies they are supposed to be aiding. Examining ten cases of collaboration in Brazil, India, and South Africa, Ashman (2001) reveals that although both businesses and CSOs tended to reap benefits in terms of improved public images, better external relations, gains in resources, and organizational capacity-building, the development impacts on community beneficiaries were less predictable and considerably less emphatic. In a similar vein, Pearson and Seyfang (2001) argue that the benefits of international labour codes agreed by businesses and CSOs have tended to do more for the public image of Western MNCs than they have for the pay and conditions of workforces in developing countries.

Finally, another key risk in business–CSO collaboration is the prospect it raises of *corporations co-opting CSO partners*. This is a particular concern, since it threatens the independence that makes the civil sector such an important balance to corporate (and government) power. Through working with business, CSOs lay themselves open to the accusation of 'sleeping with the enemy' and thereby forfeiting some of their legitimacy and public credibility (Zadek 2001: 47–50). This, in fact, is part of a broader ethical problem of **CSO independence** that requires further elaboration.

CSO independence

For the relations between CSOs and businesses to function effectively, whether those relations are adversarial or collaborative, requires that the parties remain independent of one another. On the one hand, CSOs are unlikely to be able to occupy the moral high ground and pose a credible challenge to corporate abuses unless they are, and are seen to be, sufficiently distant from their corporate adversaries. On the other hand, if CSOs become too closely involved in working with corporations, they might lose the public credibility that made them attractive partners for business in the first place. For example, the decision by the US environmental group, the Sierra Club, to endorse a range of 'green' Clorox cleaning products in 2008 prompted accusations that the CSO had 'sold out'—especially since the rank-and-file membership, and even the organization's corporate accountability committee, were not consulted prior to the deal being announced (Entine 2008b).

In many ways, though, the issue of CSO independence goes yet deeper. If we return to our earlier categorization of civil society as the 'third sector', the idea that CSOs provide social and political pluralism in order to create and sustain a civilized society is clearly compromised if the third sector loses its independence from the other sectors (market and government). The very purpose of CSOs as representatives of the diversity of interests in society is potentially weakened once they begin to lose their unique position outside of the market sector. This is particularly problematic in a society where the power of corporations and of the market is so substantial that working with them can often be the most effective way of achieving real change. As many CSOs have found, if you want to improve the working conditions of workers in developing countries, or prevent the destruction of tropical rainforests, the best way to do so is to leverage the purchasing power of corporations in the West. But what happens when the former 'poacher' becomes the 'gamekeeper' (Zadek 2001: 80)?

There is clearly a certain degree of ambivalence here. Whilst CSOs might want to harness the power of the market (usually through corporations) to achieve social ends, the market can be seen to 'contaminate' the primarily moral orientation of the civil sector (Eikenberry and Kluver, 2004). As Kaler (2000) suggests, the power of many campaigning groups to tap into public opinion and influence business is in itself derived from the avowedly moral stance that they take—and in particular, their ability to relate to people as moral agents rather than just as consumers. The ethical challenge for CSOs, then, is to retain their distinctly moral orientation, whilst making a positive and constructive contribution to business practice—a delicate balance by any standards.

Thus far, most CSOs appear to have been relatively successful at doing this. Sometimes they will do so by setting up a separate 'business' unit within the organization, such as Amnesty International's Business Group, or by forming specific task forces charged with developing business relations, whilst the rest of the organization gets on with its usual campaigning role. Clearly, though, such a development involves CSOs (and, for that matter, corporations) in a certain degree of schizophrenia, i.e. they often need to be both friends and foes to corporations, sometimes even at the same time (Elkington and Fennell 2000). Perhaps the most fundamental problem here, though, is one of *CSO accountability*, a problem that we discussed in some depth earlier in the chapter. After all, the proposition that CSOs should remain to some extent independent of corporations is based on an assumption that they have a specific task to fulfil on behalf of a certain constituency—and that this task is compromised by a loss of independence. This issue is even more pronounced when CSOs do not merely partner with business, but actually transform into a business, as we shall now see.

Social enterprise

The escalating number of CSO alliances with businesses suggests an increased attention in the sector to using market-based solutions to address social problems. Indeed, the growing influence of business strategies and tools within civil society is undeniable (Eikenberry and Kluver 2004). One facet of this has been the more business-like approach to philanthropy that is evident in the emergence of **venture philanthropy** (or 'philanthrocapitalim' as it is sometimes referred to)—namely the application of venture capital techniques to grant making (Moody 2008). Bodies such as the Bill and Melinda Gates Foundation or Google.org, the social venture arm of the Google company, are good examples of this, given their focus on social return on investment, active engagement with grantees, commitment to innovation and technology, and belief in the power of business ideas to address major problems such as poverty, global health problems, climate change, and education.

Beyond the changing landscape of philanthropy, civil society has also incorporated business methods into the very fabric of new organizational forms. The emergence of **social enterprise** as a distinct model of CSO has been a significant development to have occurred within civil society since the 1990s (Defourny and Nyssens 2006). Due to a variety of factors, including challenges in accessing secure funding, dissatisfaction with existing delivery mechanisms for social programmes, pressure from funders, and competition from business in the social sector, there has been increasing attention to the development of civil society *businesses* (Brugmann and Prahalad 2007; Dees, 1998; Seelos and Mair 2005).

As a relatively new phenomenon, the definition of social enterprise (also known as 'social enterpreneurship' or 'social business') remains rather fuzzy, but several key characteristics distinguish social enterprises from either traditional CSOs or from business enterprises. These are summarized in **Figure 10.7**. As the table shows, social

	Social Enterprise	Civil society organization	Corporation
Aims	Social and economic value creation	Social value creation	Economic value creation
Role of profit	Profit earning; limits on profit distribution	Non-profit making	Profit maximizing
Activities	Production and trade of social goods and services	Production of social goods and services, campaigning, advocacy, research, grant-giving, etc.	Production and trade of goods and services
Funding	Self-funding (at least partially)	Grants, donations, or membership dues	Self-funding
Governance	Based on participation and democracy amongst stakeholders	Based on participation and democracy amongst stakeholders	Based on accountability to providers of capital

Figure 10.7. Key differences between social enterprise, CSOs, and corporations
Sources: Dees (1998); Defourny and Nyssens (2006); Nicholls (2006)

enterprises occupy something of a middle ground between a conventional business and a civil society organization (whether promotional or sectional). Some elements they share with the former—such as the production and trade of goods and services for a profit—whilst others they share with the latter—such as having a distinct social purpose. In many respects, then, social enterprise is not so dissimilar from the co-operative movement that we discussed in Chapter 6—and indeed, some social enterprises have actually gone on to adopt a co-operative structure. However, despite there being some overlap, there are also differences—the central one being that whilst co-operatives are primarily concerned with looking after the interests of their members, social enterprises typically have a broader set of social goals and stakeholder obligations (Defourny and Nyssens 2006).

Social enterprise has emerged in recent years as a novel way of embedding dual social and economic goals in the very nature of organizations. Rather than looking to traditional corporations to voluntarily address social problems, social enterprises are designed to do so from the outset. As such, the phenomenon has been met with considerable attention and enthusiasm (Nicholls 2006). Several of the fair trade companies that we discussed in the previous chapter, such as Café Direct and Traidcraft, can be regarded as successful social enterprises. Other well-known examples include the Grameen Bank in Bangladesh, the Aravind Eye Hospital in India, and the US-based company, One Laptop Per Child. In many cases, social enterprise has been associated with bottom-of-the-pyramid strategies for addressing poverty that we first introduced in Chapter 8.[15]

In the main, social enterprises have to date tended to emerge from 'social entrepreneurs' operating within civil society. For instance, the founders of the children's education and development charity, Free the Children, set up the social enterprise, Me to We, to market ethical clothing and educational products as a way of creating a sustainable funding stream for the charity.[16] However, large corporations are also now beginning to take an interest in developing social enterprise initiatives with CSO partners, moving towards what Brugmann and Prahalad (2007) term 'a new social compact'. **Ethics in Action 10.2** illustrates some of these developments, suggesting a picture of rather mixed success so far.

Social enterprises can bring a number of benefits to civil society, including the development of more sustainable and diverse funding streams, the introduction of innovative solutions to social problems, greater efficiency and better targeting of services to client needs. However, their novel form also throws up some particular ethical challenges. Some of the most important of these are the following (see Dees 1998; Eikenberry and Kluver 2004; Foster and Bradach 2005):

- **Compromise of social mission**. The demands of the commercial marketplace can place stress on the social goals and purpose of the organization, leading to 'mission drift' away from its founding mission.
- **Moral legitimacy**. As we showed earlier in the chapter, civil society tends to be afforded greater trust than business. Therefore, the more business-like social enterprises become, the less moral legitimacy they may hold for key stakeholders.
- **Escalation of risk.** Given their role in critical social arenas such as health, education, housing, and poverty, CSOs typically operate in a context of quite highly managed risk. Social enterprise, however, tends to emphasize greater risk taking and innovation, which can pose threats to both essential services and clients.
- **Prioritization of profitable markets.** The need to secure sustainable sources of revenue encourages social enterprises to focus on potentially profitable social goods and services, where clients are willing to pay, rather than unprofitable areas where clients might be more needy.

Such risks pose important challenges for managers in social enterprises. Given that in many countries, social enterprises do not even have explicit legal recognition as a distinct social form, institutional pressures may well encourage them towards being increasingly understood and practised in more narrow commercial and revenue-generation terms (Dart 2004). However, in being aware of the potential pitfalls, social entrepreneurs can at least steer clear of the major dangers and press for broader institutional change. Indeed, civil society has increasingly taken a stronger role in the regulation of commercial enterprise, as we shall now see.

Civil regulation

In the last chapter, we saw how some regulation of business could be achieved outside government. At that juncture, we looked mainly at self-regulation by business, corporations 'policing' their suppliers, and even competitors regulating each other through industry partnerships and programmes. As we have already seen in the current chapter, civil society can also be a source of regulation of corporations. Whether through protests and boycotts or various forms of collaboration, CSOs increasingly appear to have the power to shape, influence, or curb business practice. Some authors refer to this as 'civil regulation' (e.g. Bendell 2000b; Zadek 2001; Vogel 2008). As Bendell (2000b) argues, civil society effects regulation by creating norms for business and then enforcing them in some way.

Civil regulation, then, goes somewhat further than just the *relations* that CSOs have with business. Rather, we also have to look at the *outcomes* of these processes. Sometimes these outcomes are company or project specific, sometimes they have more lasting impact. For example, it is evident that many of these conflicts and collaborations have led to the establishment of codes of conduct intended to govern corporate action. Such codes clearly encompass aspects of norm creation and enforcement that are more institutionalized and lasting than say a single change in corporate policy made as a result of boycott action. As Schneidewind and Petersen (1998) suggest, business collaboration with civil society can help to build social and political structures that might even change the rules for other business actors. More recently, we have also witnessed similar developments at the global level (Dahan et al. 2006; Vogel 2008).

The *Ethical Trading Initiative* (ETI), for example, commits its members to adopting its code of practice on workplace standards, and requires that members report on their performance against its provisions. **Figure 10.8** presents the core activities of the initiative, and shows how it includes a mixture of rule definition, awareness raising, provision of resources and tools to enable effective operation, and a method for ensuring compliance with its rules. These activities essentially act as regulatory forces on member organizations, since failure to abide by them would, at least in principle, lead to companies being thrown out of the initiative. Whilst this is rare, Levi Strauss was suspended for a year from the ETI in 2007 for refusing to sign up to a principle guaranteeing workers a 'living wage'. The firm claimed that the definition of a living wage was ill-defined and not completely actionable, whereas the ETI argued that 'what is important for us is that they demonstrate a commitment and don't walk away from those problems' (Butler 2007).

Probably the main drawback of this and other examples of civil regulation is their **voluntary** nature. Whereas state regulation is obligatory and usually includes some form of punishment for non-compliance (such as a fine), civil regulation relies on the voluntary commitments of companies. Many companies will not choose to join, and even among those that do, there is always the option to leave if their priorities change. For example, in 2009, the UK retailer Boots pulled out of the ETI due to a change in strategy regarding its approach to ethical sourcing—but vehemently denied that the move was in any way related to its transfer of ownership into private equity (Mathiason 2009). Although some form of censure is available for civil actors in these kinds of circumstances—they can publicize the incidents, create bad publicity, and even initiate protests, boycotts, and other forms of direct action—this constitutes a relatively 'soft' form of regulation compared to traditional government modes.

Despite such limitations, civil society has certainly taken an increasingly important role in forming codes of practice and even some more formal elements of rule setting and regulation (Zadek 2001). As we intimated in the previous section on globalization, given the

VISIT THE WEBSITE for links to useful sources of further information

ETHICS IN ACTION 10.2 http//:www.ethicalcorp.com

Ethical CORPORATION

Social innovation: good for you, good for me

John Russell, 9 April 2008

Muhammad Yunus has for more than 30 years challenged business leaders to find radical ways of creating new markets in poor countries. The Nobel Peace Prize winner's latest book, *Creating a World Without Poverty: Social Business and the Future of Capitalism*, is no less ambitious. It explores how big companies can invest in external partners to develop products and services that will benefit the poor.

Yunus outlines the concept of a 'social business', which he defines as a 'no loss, no dividend' company with social objectives. Social business ventures are set up by a 'social entrepreneur', such as Yunus, who combines the risk-taking of enterprise with an explicit mission to address urgent problems, such as access to healthcare, sanitation, education and so on. The new products and services that these inventive individuals devise are examples of 'social innovation'.

Unlike charities, social businesses do not need to keep applying to governments or foundations for grants. They support themselves by selling goods and services at cost, or at a small profit—all of which is reinvested to fund their expansion. But to do this, social entrepreneurs must find investors willing to help take a new idea to scale. Now multinational companies are emerging as an important source of funding for social innovation. Big companies are looking for exciting and potentially lucrative new ways to meet their sustainability goals.

The archetypal social business—in the Yunus sense of a no-loss, no-dividend company—is Danone Grameen Foods, a joint venture set up two years ago between Yunus's own Grameen group and the French food and drink multinational Danone. The partners have developed an affordable, fortified yoghurt for poor children in Bangladesh. The yoghurt is high in calcium and other nutrients that children lack. It is cheap because it is produced locally, cutting down on expensive refrigeration.

As a social business, Danone Grameen Foods measures its success in terms of 'social dividend' or 'social return on investment'—its positive impact on the rate of market failure that it was set up to redress. In this case, the dividend and return are the improvement in child health in Bangladesh and the number of jobs its activities supports (see below). The first yoghurt processing plant in Bogra will in three to four years support 1,600 jobs, while the company plans to build 50 plants over the next ten years. Danone invested $1 million in the Bogra plant—a tiny amount for a company with revenue of €14.5 billion in its latest full year.

For that investment it has seen significant returns that are hard to measure financially. Danone says it has learnt how to cut energy and save money in its supply chain and how to sell the idea of nutrition to the poor in emerging markets. And then there is the reputation rub-off of being associated with Yunus, founder of the Grameen Bank and now something of a celebrity for his pioneering work on microfinance.

Partner problems

Acquisition in some cases might be the preferred option for companies wanting to avoid the potential pitfalls of partnering with mission-driven social entrepreneurs. Intel's decision in January to withdraw from One Laptop Per Child (OLPC) is a case of a partnership that was not meant to be. The initiative, announced by social entrepreneur Nicholas Negroponte at Davos in 2005, aimed to put a $100 laptop in the hands of 150 million children in poor countries within four years. Three years later the project is struggling to take off, with just a few thousand children using the cheap laptops in pilot projects around the world. Chip maker Intel ploughed millions of dollars into OLPC and joined the board in July 2007. But the partnership was never a good fit, as the laptops run on chips made by Intel's rival AMD. Having quit the association with OLPC, Intel continues to develop its own low-cost laptop, the Classmate, which is priced at $200–$300.

One reason why partnerships between companies and social entrepreneurs are yet to take off could be mutual ignorance of each other. 'This is quite new territory for business,' says International Business Leaders' Forum director Ros Tennyson, who advises companies on partnerships. 'Most do not know what the term "social entrepreneurship" means.' She says business must listen to social entrepreneurs 'if it is to get beyond simply philanthropic funding of a good idea'. But, she adds, social entrepreneurs, too, must be flexible and understanding of companies. 'They need to develop a genuine interest in business drivers and priorities in order to conduct purposeful and equitable conversations.'

Microfinance is typically the most fertile common ground on which companies and social entrepreneurs can meet. Thanks to Grameen Bank, the model has been shown to work at a small, local level, in the commercial sense that most borrowers are able to repay their loans. More and more banks are interested in helping to expand microfinance networks, using them as a bridge into emerging markets where most people do not have access to bank accounts. Companies outside of financial services are using microfinance networks to extend their distribution and sales reach into remote areas of emerging markets, as Unilever is doing in India.

Microfinance remains the 'paradigmatic example' of social entrepreneurship, says Stephan Chambers, chairman of the Skoll Centre for Social Entrepreneurship at the University of Oxford. He adds: 'And in some senses, it's the problem that the field has. It is still in its infancy and it's still trying to figure out what are the next half a dozen really good examples.' Chambers compares the state of social entrepreneurship to Silicon Valley before the internet boom. 'There's lots of energy, lots of activity, lots of investment, lots of creativity—and so far one billion-dollar company.' He adds: 'Someone is going to be the next Muhammad Yunus. And as soon as that starts to happen there will be loads of them.'

Sources

Ethical Corporation, John Russell, 9 April 2008, http://www.ethicalcorp.com.

VISIT THE WEBSITE for a short response to this feature

? THINK THEORY

Think about social enterprise in relation to the sectional and promotional groups that we summarized earlier in the chapter. Go back to Figure 10.3 and figure out how social enterprise would compare with the other two types of CSO across each of the dimensions listed in the table.

We define best practice in ethical trade

All corporate members of ETI agree to adopt the ETI Base Code of labour practice, which is based on the standards of the International Labour Organisation (ILO). We work out the most effective steps companies can take to implement the Base Code in their supply chains. We learn by doing, and by sharing our experience. Our projects and working groups develop and try out new ideas, often piloting these approaches on the ground in sourcing countries. By taking part in these groups as well as in roundtable discussions, our members collectively establish good practice in ethical trade. We then develop training and resources to capture this learning, providing practical tools to help companies to put their ethical trade policies into effect.

We help workers to help themselves

Codes of labour practice can, and should, help create space for workers to bargain with management through trade unions. In several countries around the world we are supporting initiatives that raise workers' awareness of their rights and helping create work cultures where workers can confidently negotiate with management about the issues that concern them. We also broker resolutions where there are major breaches of trade union rights by companies that supply our members.

We build strategic alliances that make a difference

Finding effective and sustainable solutions to workers' issues requires joint action between companies, suppliers, trade unions, NGOs and governments. We build alliances in key sourcing countries and internationally, to address problems that occur not only in individual workplaces, but also affect entire countries and industries.

We persuade and influence key players

Retailers and brands are responsible for using their buying power to influence their suppliers' employment practices. Governments, employers, trade unions, consumers and the media also have a distinct and vital role. We raise awareness of how everyone can play a part in protecting workers' rights and work closely with governments and international labour agencies to influence policy and legislation.

We drive improvements in member companies' performance

In today's global economy, all companies have issues in their supply chains. By joining ETI, a company is acknowledging these issues and making a commitment to tackling them. Our member companies report annually on their efforts and the results they are achieving at farm or factory level.

We expect them to improve their ethical trade performance over time, and have a robust disciplinary procedure for companies that fail to make sufficient progress or to honour their membership obligations.

Figure 10.8. Core activities of the Ethical Trading Initiative

Source: Ethical Trading Initiative, 'What We Do': www.ethicaltrade.org
Reproduced with permission

apparent absence of effective global government, this is especially the case with transnational regulations, such as those dealing with environmental management or labour conditions. Although the business literature has been fairly slow to acknowledge this development, even here the growing influence of civil society in the institutional arrangements facing international business has been recognized (e.g. Doh and Teegen 2002; Dahan et al. 2006). Certainly, CSOs can now at the least be considered to be part of the group of actors shaping the rules, norms, and practices of international business—assigning them a place in what writers in the politics literature tend to call systems or regimes of 'global governance' (e.g. Nickel 2002; Bernstein and Cashore 2007; Vogel 2008). We shall examine the implications of this further in the next chapter when we move on to discuss more generally the role of government and regulation in shaping the context of business ethics.

The key point to take away from this section is that civil society can act as a conduit through which individual citizens can exert some kind of leverage on, or gain a form of participation in, corporate decision-making and action. When we speak of corporate citizenship in its extended sense, the idea that corporations are increasingly involved in governing various citizens' rights suggests that those citizens might need a way of registering their desires and wishes in some way. Voting and consumer choices are two avenues; participation in civil society is another. As we shall see in the final section, this issue of participation also has important ramifications for notions of sustainability.

■ Civil society, business, and sustainability

Civil society has been at the forefront of the development of sustainability theory and practice. This is hardly surprising when we consider that each of the three elements of sustainability—social, environmental, and economic—have been typical foci for CSOs of various kinds, from humanitarian NGOs (social issues), to development agencies (economic and social issues), and environmental activists (environmental issues). Moreover, many environmental and other CSOs are now actually dedicating themselves to advancing the cause of sustainability itself, rather than focusing on specific issues. For example, the mission of Friends of the Earth International is to 'challenge the current model of economic and corporate globalization, and promote solutions that will help to create environmentally sustainable and socially just societies'.[17]

It is, then, the representative nature of the stake held by CSOs that makes them so integral to sustainability in business. At best, corporations can only really claim to represent economic interests. However, progress towards sustainability requires that a wider set of interests are also represented and incorporated in business decisions. Certainly, government is one actor that can do this, but given the retraction of the state and the growth in civil society influence, CSOs also increasingly fulfil this role for social, environmental—and to a lesser extent, economic—interests. As we saw with some of our examples of business–CSO collaboration in the previous section, diverse social, environmental, and economic interests can be brought together to develop solutions that are more balanced on the sustainability scorecard. Of course, it is contestable whether business has to necessarily work *with* civil society to achieve sustainable solutions, but at the very least civil actors have a role to play in encouraging business to take notice of and address particular dimensions of sustainability.

The problem here, though, is that because CSOs are advancing particular interests, they cannot necessarily be expected to agree on what actions are likely to be the most appropriate for corporations to take. Sustainability remains contested in most, if not all, areas where corporations might be expected to act. Hence, if corporations are serious about addressing sustainability, one principal challenge is inevitably going to be how best to balance the **competing interests** of different civil actors. At another level, even once the competing interests of civil society have been taken into account, corporations are still left with the problem of deciding the extent of community and NGO **participation** in decision-making. Finally, some argue that the importance of civil society to sustainable business is so great that companies should not simply resign themselves to the existence of CSOs, but should actively seek to **sustain civil society** through their actions.

Balancing competing interests

Civil society is made up of a wide variety of disparate actors, each of which may be promoting single issues that comprise different aspects of sustainability. While some, such as Amnesty International or Burma Campaign, will primarily advocate social issues, others, such as the WWF, will promote environmental issues, and others, such as business associations, will promote economic interests. This means that sustainable business needs to take account of such competing interests simultaneously—representing a major challenge for any organization. For example, in recent years, civil interests have clashed in a number of key industries—the energy industry, aviation, agriculture, and tourism—being just some of the examples. If we look to one particularly interesting example, the alternative energy industry, we can see how some of these competing interests might play out.

The energy industry has been the scene of contestation between civil groups for many years, involving a range of issues around oil extraction, power station location, nuclear power, and more recently, alternative energy generation, such as wind, wave, and solar power. If we just take the example of wind power, a number of competing civil interests are evident. Many governments and national and international environmental NGOs, for example, actively promote investment in wind-power technologies because they offer clean renewable energy. Similarly, local governments, development agencies, farming groups, and landowners have generally been supportive of wind-farm development because of the financial rewards, jobs, and investment that they bring. However, some local environmental organizations, community groups, conservation groups, and tourism promoters have opposed the erection of wind turbines, arguing that they despoil the countryside and disrupt bird and wildlife. As one recent media article put it, wind farms have become a battle of 'green v green' (Lynas 2008).

In some parts of the world, this has led to wind farm developments arousing much controversy, and many of them have been blocked. In the UK, for example, campaigns have led to a substantial proportion of proposed projects being refused permission, and relatively few have yet to be built (see **Figure 10.9**). As a result, in 2007, just 2% of the UK's energy came from wind power, compared with 29% in Denmark, 20% in Spain, and 15% in Germany.[18] Significantly, Denmark appears to have avoided planning protests by developing wind power through a modest step-by-step approach which initially saw four

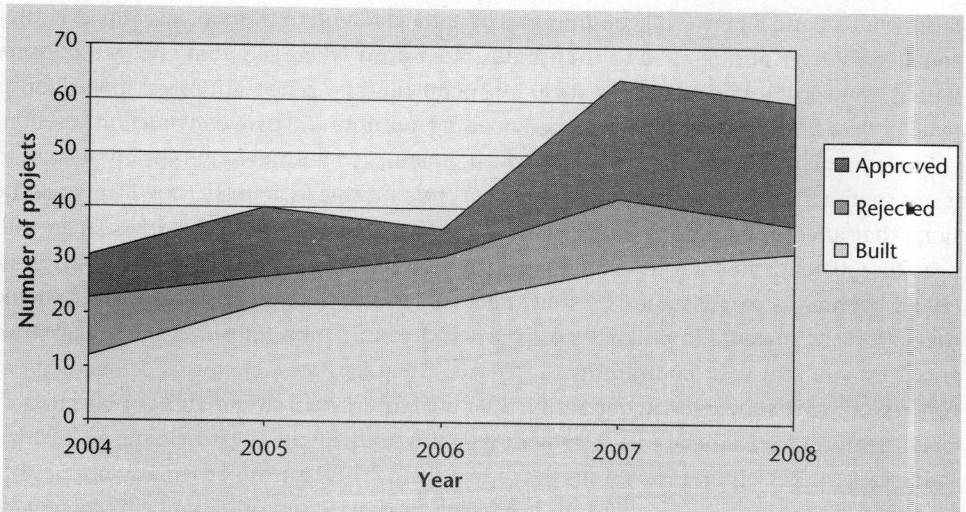

Figure 10.9. Number of wind-farm projects in the UK
Source: Original data sourced from British Wind Energy Association: www.bwea.com

out of five Danish turbines being erected by individuals on their own land rather than in large concentrated wind farms (Houlder 1999).

The debate about wind farms looks set to continue, especially with governments across the developed world struggling to meet their commitments to reducing climate change emissions, and increasingly concerned about 'energy security' because of their reliance on sources from the Middle East, Central Asia, Africa, and other relatively unstable parts of the globe. As a result, some civil society groups have cautiously begun promoting the merits of nuclear energy again, which has predictably given rise to further clashes with other CSOs over the safety, feasibility, financing, and geographical location of the various options.[19]

> **? THINK THEORY**
>
> Think about the triple bottom line of sustainability and set out the various stakeholders that represent the different interests involved in wind power. Is it possible to determine which of the elements of sustainability are deemed more legitimate, or are the most strongly represented, by the stakeholders involved?

VISIT THE WEBSITE for a short response to this feature

Fostering participation and democracy

As the wind-generation industry shows, the range of interests represented by different civil actors often puts them at odds with each other, especially when different facets of the triple bottom line of sustainability are at issue. We have focused here on an 'upstream' activity—i.e. resource extraction and utilization—since it is often here where different interests are most evident, and where local communities in particular tend to be involved. However, we could easily have also referred to the various other areas where different civil actors have fought over specific business issues, including plant closures, gene technology applications, retail park or housing developments, road building, mining, and dam construction.

In some ways, though, the key issue for sustainability in business–civil society relations is not so much that civil groups agree, but that they are able to actively *participate* in decisions that affect them. Many authors writing about sustainability in business stress the need for greater democracy in corporations through community participation. As Bendell (2000b) contends: 'organizations ... that affect you and your community, especially when they affect the material foundations of your self-determination, must be able to be influenced by you and your community ... What are required are new forms of democratic governance so that people can determine their own futures in a sustainable environment.' CSOs clearly have a crucial role to play in enabling individuals to participate, at least in some way, in the corporate decisions that affect them. This issue is particularly important for those groups or interests that might typically not have any other voice in corporate decision-making. The natural environment, non-human species, and future generations are all sustainability stakeholders that need CSOs to represent their interests.

Although evidence suggests that corporations tend to limit the degree of participation that civil groups and other stakeholders can exercise—often concentrating more on simply consulting or placating them (Banerjee 2000; Cumming 2001)—this does at least provide a *possible* mechanism for participation, although certainly not a guaranteed one. However, whilst arguments about the accountability and representativeness of CSOs themselves are likely to persist, their role in bringing a plurality of interests to bear on corporations undoubtedly makes them important actors in democratizing the evolving sustainability agenda.

Sustaining civil society

As we can see then, in one way or another, whether as irritant or inspiration, CSOs play a vital role in encouraging business towards more sustainable practice. Sometimes this is played out in direct business–CSO relationships, sometimes via their work influencing government regulation of business, and sometimes simply through demonstrating how sustainability can be achieved through social enterprise. Therefore, for companies serious about sustainability, the health and vitality of civil society are crucial.

A flourishing civil society is something that corporate managers in most developed countries take for granted. Therefore their role in ensuring that CSOs prosper is likely to require the typical forms of charity, volunteering, and collaboration that we discussed above. However, in developing and transitional economies, the situation can be very different. As we discussed before, countries such as China have a very underdeveloped civil society, and this situation is replicated across numerous other contexts, including Russia, Eastern Europe, the Middle East, and Central Asia. In these contexts, corporations may find that they need to develop capacity amongst local NGOs to deal with sustainability issues. For example, Sekem, an Egyptian agricultural company that promotes sustainable development, helped create the Egyptian Biodynamic Association, a CSO that promotes the organic-agriculture movement among the country's farmers and provides them with research and training (Valente and Crane 2009). Similarly, the large Russian aluminium producer, SUAL (Siberian-Ural Aluminum Company), was involved in a major sustainability initiative, setting up and supporting local community organizations and independent NGOs in the areas in which it operates (Zhexembayeva et al. 2007).

This kind of high engagement with the sustaining of civil society itself may seem like a step too far for most companies. However, the importance of a strong civil society, as well as other 'countervailing forces' to business—such as government and the media—should not be underestimated in attempts to tackle sustainability challenges. By their very nature, sustainability problems are complex and multidimensional, often requiring change across a number of arenas. Without an active and effective civil society, corporate sustainability initiatives may lack the legitimacy and impact necessary to develop meaningful solutions.

■ Summary

In this chapter, we have discussed the role that civil society plays in business ethics. We have taken a fairly broad definition of what constitutes civil society in order to include the whole gamut of organizations outside business and government that have confronted corporations over various aspects of business ethics. These CSOs have been shown to have a somewhat different stake in the corporation compared with the other stakeholders we have looked at so far. Specifically, the representational nature of CSO stakes makes their claim rather more indirect than for other constituencies.

In examining the ethical issues arising in business–CSO relations and the attempts by business to deal more responsibly with civil society, we have charted a gradual shift in the nature of these relations. Business and civil society appear to have moved from a primarily confrontational engagement to a more complex, multifaceted relationship that still involves confrontation but also includes charitable giving, collaboration, social enterprise, and aspects of civil regulation. Regardless of the nature of this interaction, though, we argued that for citizens, local communities, and other groups typically excluded from the decision processes of business, CSOs can act as important conduits through which their interests can be expressed and advanced within business. Although civil groups themselves may not even always agree with each other, the contribution they make to engendering a pluralistic context for business decision-making and action appears to be vital to our understanding of business ethics.

Study questions

1 What are civil society organizations, and what relevance do they have for business ethics?

2 Select one civil society organizations that you have some knowledge of. Who or what does this organization purport to represent—does this make it a promotional or a sectional group? In what ways is the organization accountable to its various stakeholders?

3 'It is simply not really the company's choice who is and is not a stakeholder' (Zadek 2001: 163). Evaluate this statement in the context of civil society organizations as stakeholders of business.

4 What is a social enterprise? What are the main opportunities and challenges faced by social enterprises in achieving social outcomes?

5 Explain the concept of civil regulation. How appropriate is this term for describing the nature of civil society activities?

6 What role do civil society organizations play in enhancing business sustainability?

Research exercise

Select a CSO with which you are familiar and conduct some research on its main activities with and/or against business.

1 What are the main tactics and approaches used by the CSO in its relations with business?
2 Would you say its approach has shifted at all over time? Explain your answer.
3 How effective and ethical do you think the CSO's approach has been?

Key readings

VISIT THE WEBSITE for links to further key readings

1 **Brugmann, J. and Prahalad, C.K. 2007. Cocreating business's new social compact. Harvard Business Review, 85 (2): 80–90.**

This article provides a host of examples from across the world of business partnership with civil society, particularly in the area of social enterprise and poverty alleviation. Mainly intended for a practitioner audience, it lacks an objective appraisal or critical perspective, but offers an inspirational account of future trends.

2 **Eikenberry, A.M. and Kluver, J.D. 2004. The marketization of the nonprofit sector: civil society at risk? Public Administration Review 64(2): 132–40.**

Adopting a distinctly critical perspective, this article provides a comprehensive overview of the threats posed by the increasing commercial orientation of civil society. An excellent companion piece to the Brugmann and Prahalad article.

Case 10

VISIT THE WEBSITE for links to useful sources of further information

From conflict to collaboration? Greenpeace's Greenfreeze campaign

This case examines Greenpeace's attempts to develop a solutions-oriented approach to introducing more sustainable technologies in the refrigerants industry. The case details the NGO's initial collaboration with the former East German manufacturer Foron to develop the 'climate-friendly' Greenfreeze refrigerant, and their subsequent negotiations with companies to diffuse the technology across the globe. The case provides the opportunity to examine the approaches open to civil society organizations in attempting to influence corporate policy, and in particular their roles and responsibilities in shaping the rules and norms of global business practice.

When General Electric, the company renowned for its 'Ecomagination' environmental innovation programme, announced in 2008 that it would launch North America's first climate-friendly refrigerator by 2010, it marked a major turning point not only for the giant American manufacturer but for the campaigning pressure group, Greenpeace. In an industry dominated by big corporations, it was Greenpeace that had worked for the best part of two decades to get its clean refrigerant, 'Greenfreeze', commercialized and then diffused throughout the global refrigeration industry. The civil society organization, best known for its occupations and protests, had shown that it could also help to develop markets and promote new technologies.

The emergence of Greenfreeze

Greenfreeze is a refrigerant, i.e. a type of coolant used in fridges, freezers, air conditioners, and other types of cooling appliances. It was first developed by scientists at the Dortmund Institute of Hygiene in Germany in 1989. At this time, most of the refrigeration industry was starting to move from refrigerants using CFCs (which contributed to ozone depletion) to HCFCs (which still contributed to ozone depletion, but less so) and ultimately to HFCs (which did not contribute to ozone depletion). However, all of these alternatives, regardless of their impact on the ozone, contributed significantly to climate change. In fact, some HFC gases are up to 11,000 times more harmful to the climate than carbon dioxide, the most widely known greenhouse gas. However, although Greenfreeze succeeded in avoiding both of the main environmental problems of existing refrigerants (and their supposed replacements), the refrigeration industry took almost no notice at all of the new technology, and the Dortmund project was abandoned.

It was at this point that Greenpeace became involved in the story. The organization is probably best known for its dramatic campaigning activities on the high seas—saving whales, attempting to block nuclear tests, and storming oil platforms, among other things. But in 1992, when Greenpeace entered the Greenfreeze story, it decided to take a different approach to its usual confrontational, protest-based methods. Seeing the significant potential of the new technology, it decided to take it upon itself to champion hydrocarbons to refrigerator manufacturers. So, it was Greenpeace that gave Greenfreeze its distinctive name, and it was Greenpeace that attempted to resurrect the stalled development programme of the new technology.

The task of converting the refrigeration industry was, however, a daunting one. Most of the industry infrastructure, including the manufacturers and their suppliers, was set up for the existing refrigerants and so the major players refused to 'leapfrog' to an entirely new technology. Moreover, the powerful chemical industry, which supplied refrigerants to the fridge and air-conditioner manufacturers, was actively pushing HFCs as the replacement of choice for CFCs. Chemical manufacturers had little interest in developing Greenfreeze commercially, since the mixture could not be patented (because it consisted of two common gases) and the technology was free.

In the end, only the former East German manufacturer, Foron Household Appliances, was willing to experiment with the new technology. Like many former East German firms after reunification, Foron was close to bankruptcy, but agreed to work with the Greenfreeze technology as a last resort. In May 1992, Greenpeace secured an arrangement between Foron and the Dortmund Institute, and commissioned ten prototype greenfreeze refrigerators. Before work could be completed though, the German authorities announced that Foron would be liquidated. Greenpeace and Foron rapidly organized a press conference, and almost overnight produced the first Greenfreeze fridge to present at the conference. Greenpeace also launched a grassroots campaign to persuade consumers and the media, and at the last moment, Foron was saved and secured additional funding to keep going.

Overcoming barriers

Having overcome its first initial barrier, Greenpeace was to face many more in the years to come. At first, even its own staff posed a threat and the organization faced an internal revolt over the collaboration with Foron. Endorsing any kind of company was a significant departure from Greenpeace's usual confrontational style, and was viewed by many inside the organization as a 'sell-out'. One member referred to the response as a 'bloody internal battle', not least because Greenfreeze represented the first main attempt by Greenpeace to leverage the market to try and create positive change in an industry.

The main resistance, however, came from the chemical and refrigerator industries. At first they launched press and communications campaigns, warning manufacturers and retailers that the technology was unproven, unfeasible, inefficient, and potentially dangerous—'a potential bomb' no less! However, Greenpeace's publicity machine generated over 70,000 advance orders from consumers, and eventually the claims against Greenfreeze were dropped, as Greenpeace successively managed to persuade the government and scientists to test (successfully) for product safety. By the end of 1992, Greenfreeze was certified by the German safety standards authority, and the following February, Foron's 'Green Cooler' fridge, using Greenfreeze technology, was awarded the prestigious 'Blue Angel' eco-label.

By 1994, all German manufacturers declared that they would abandon HCFCs and HFCs for Greenfreeze. Greenpeace, of course, heralded this as a major success, but for Foron, the wider adoption meant that the company rapidly lost its competitive advantage. The Greenfreeze technology was available free to anyone (and even Greenpeace received no financial remuneration or royalty for developing the product) so as the more sophisticated rivals adopted the new technology, Foron's precarious financial position and lack of marketing clout left it in a weak market position. The company eventually declared bankruptcy in 1996, and its refrigerator division was purchased by the Dutch firm ATAG.

Greenpeace, meanwhile, took its Greenfreeze campaign into the rest of Europe, and ultimately worldwide. As it did so, most manufacturers would initially resist the technology, but with some smart manoeuvring from the civil society organization, most would eventually switch. Greenpeace had quickly discovered that its leverage was greatest when it targeted the big brands using refrigeration technology rather than the manufacturers, whose business tended not to deal very often with the end consumer. A milestone in the campaign involved the 2000 Sydney Olympic Games, where Greenpeace targeted the Games' sponsors, including Coca-Cola and McDonald's, branding them 'dirty Olympic sponsors'. The organization even set up a website, CokeSpotlight, modelled on the anti-McDonald's McSpotlight site (see Case 1) and released postcards and badges aping the style of the famous 'Enjoy Coca-Cola' slogan, with the acerbic 'Enjoy Climate Change'. Before long Coca-Cola announced a new refrigeration policy that would see all of its fridges and dispensing machines converted to Greenfreeze.

Similarly, McDonald's responded to the campaign and in 2003, opened its first HFC-free restaurant in Denmark. The next major milestone came in 2004 when Unilever, a leading producer of frozen food and ice-cream, joined Coca-Cola and McDonald's in launching its Refrigerants Naturally! initiative, the main objective of which was to phase out HFCs in their point-of-sale cooling equipment. By 2009, Unilever had installed 400,000 new refrigeration units throughout its global operations, whilst Coca-Cola had introduced 42,000 climate friendly-vending machines. Not content with this, Greenpeace moved on to targeting major retail brands such as Tesco, Sainsbury's, and Iceland in the UK, all of which eventually made commitments to phase out HFCs.

Greenfreeze goes global ... almost

In the rest of the world, too, Greenpeace was active in promoting Greenfreeze. Developing countries had posed a particular problem, since Western multinationals were using their older CFC and HCFC-based technologies in countries such as China and India. However, in China, Greenpeace played a pivotal role in 'matchmaking' governmental agencies and international donors (such as the World Bank, the German Ministry for Development Aid, and the US Environmental Protection Agency) with key international and local manufacturers. By 2003, the market share of Greenfreeze technology in China had leapt to 35%, and this has continued to grow steadily ever since. Although progress in other developing countries was also initially hampered by various factors, including technical challenges, industry resistance, and government inertia, the technology has now been adopted in most major developing countries, including Argentina, Brazil, Indonesia, and India. Indeed, by 2008, some 300 million of the world' s refrigerators employed Greenfreeze technology, amounting to nearly 40% of all domestic refrigerators. Through a smart mix of government lobbying, media pressure, consumer activism, and behind the scenes dialogue, Greenpeace had succeeded in getting the technology adopted by virtually of all the leading manufacturers in Europe, Japan, China, Australia, India, and South America—almost everywhere in fact except North America.

The continued resistance of North American producers to make the switch to climate-friendly refrigerants remained the last major hurdle for Greenpeace. As the world's largest emitter of greenhouse gases, the US represents a key battleground for climate change campaigners, yet even with major food and beverage manufacturers beginning to switch to alternative refrigerators, US manufacturers continued to stall. Ironically, one of the main problems was the obstacle posed by the Environmental Protection Agency's (EPA) approval process for green alternatives. US manufacturers were clearly reluctant to navigate through the necessary bureaucracy to try and secure EPA approval for the new technology.

However, in 2008, things started to change at last when Ben & Jerry's, the ice cream company owned by Unilever, partnered with Greenpeace to test out the US's first Greenfreeze-cooled freezers in two of its scoop shops as part of a trial 'market test' allowance from the EPA. Then, later the same year, when GE announced its intention to bring Greenfreeze-style refrigerators to the US for the first time, it looked like the long wait might finally be over. However, with EPA approval still to be granted, and the company aiming only to use the technology in one of its high end models, Greenpeace may still need to exercise its well-rehearsed carrot and stick approach to facilitate greater diffusion in the key US market.

Questions

1. Set out the tactics used by Greenpeace in the Greenfreeze campaign. Can you discern an overall strategy used by the organization?
2. To what extent would you say that Greenpeace had changed from a conflict-based approach to a more collaborative mode of engagement?
3. Who are Greenpeace's stakeholders in this case? What responsibilities, if any, would you say that they had to these stakeholders?
4. How would you assess Greenpeace's relative advantages in pursuing the Greenfreeze campaign compared to a company attempting to diffuse an innovation?
5. In what ways, and in which industries (if any), is the notion of a 'civil regulator' a useful way of describing Greenpeace's role in this case? Elaborate on your answer by looking at the way the campaign was carried out in different parts of the world.

Sources

Cowe, R. 2004. Enemies find a better way to cool off: global warming: Greenpeace's partnership with Unilever has boosted sales of refrigerators that do not contribute to climate change. *Financial Times*, 18 Nov.: 13.

Greenpeace global website: http://www.greenpeace.org.

Murray, S. 2005. Campaigners use peace as a weapon—partnerships: pressure groups need activists who can do deals with the enemy. *Financial Times*, 5 May: 4.

Refrigerants Naturally! website: http://www.refrigerantsnaturally.com.

Stafford, E.R., Hartman, C.L. and Liang, Y. 2003. Forces driving environmental innovation diffusion in China: the case of Greenfreeze. *Business Horizons*, 46 (2), March–April: 47–56.

Stafford, E.R. and Hartman, C.L. 2001. Greenpeace's 'greenfreeze campaign': hurdling competitive forces in the diffusion of environmental technology innovation. In K. Green, P. Groenewegen, and P.S. Hofman (eds.), *Ahead of the curve*, 107–31. Dordrecht: Kluwer.

Stafford, E.R., Polonsky, M.J., and Hartman, C.L. 2000. Environmental NGO–business collaboration and strategic bridging: a case analysis of the Greenpeace–Foron alliance. *Business Strategy and the Environment*, 9: 122–35.

Notes

1 For a further look at some of this definitional debate, see Candler, G.G. 2000. The professions and public policy: expanding the third sector. *International Political Science Review*, 21 (1): 43–58.

2 These figures are for 2008. For US data, see Table 25, 'Tax-Exempt Organizations and Nonexempt Charitable Trusts, Fiscal Years 200–2008', at http://www.irs.gov. For UK data, see the Charity Commission's 'Register of Charities' at http://www.charity-commission.gov.uk.

3 See Ethics Resource Center (2008), *2007 national nonprofit ethics survey: an inside view of nonprofit sector ethics*, Arlington, VA: Ethics Resource Center.

4 See Schor, E. 2008. US Christian group boycotts McDonald's for association with gay organisation. *Guardian*, 15 July: http://www.guardian.co.uk.

5 See BBC 2009. Shell settles Nigeria deaths case. *BBC News*, 9 June: http://www.bbc.co.uk/news.

6 For details of the Survival International campaign, go to: http://www.survival-international.org/about/barefoot. For details of the anti-NGO campaign, see http://rtnetworking.org/ngo/index.htm.

7 For example, the Co-operative Bank, The Ethical Consumerism Report 2005 (http://www.co-operativebank.co.uk) reported that 28% of UK consumers had claimed to have boycotted at least one product in the past year, whilst a 2005 international online opinion poll on 15,500 consumers in 17 countries conducted by GMI Poll (http://www.gmi-mr.com) reported that 36% of consumers worldwide were boycotting products.

8 For the Boycott Israel list, go to http://www.inminds.co.uk/boycott-israel.php. For Ethical Consumer's list of current boycotts, see http://www.ethicalconsumer.org/Boycotts.aspx.

9 See BBC 2002. US warns companies over Israel boycott. *BBC News*, 5 Nov.: http://www.bbc.co.uk/news.

10 See http://www.icftu.org for more details.

11 For more information see http://www.thecoca-colacompany.com/citizenship/conservation_partnership.html.

12 For more information, see http://www.foei.org.

13 See http://www.attac.org.

14 See http://www.vodafonefoundation.org.

15 For examples and case study descriptions of poverty-related social enterprise, see Brugmann and Prahalad (2007) and Seelos and Mair (2005).

16 For details on Me to We, see http://www.metowe.com. More information on Free the Children can be found at http://www.freethechildren.com.

17 See Friends of the Earth International website at http://www.foei.org.

18 BBC. 2009. RSPB calls for more UK wind farms. *BBC News*, 24 Mar.: http://www.bbc.co.uk/news.

19 BBC. 2006. Nuclear power plants get go-ahead. *BBC News*, 11 July: http://www.bbc.co.uk/news.

11

Government, Regulation, and Business Ethics

In this chapter we will:

- Discuss the specific stake that governments have in corporate activity by outlining the double agency that governments assume.
- Explain the ethical issues and problems faced in business–government relations, paying particular attention to practices commonly criticized in the media and public discourse.
- Identify the shifts in these issues and problems in the context of globalization.
- Further develop the notion of corporate citizenship by analysing the changing role of business and CSOs in the regulatory process and discuss various alternative routes for regulating corporate behaviour.
- Examine the challenges posed by sustainability to business–government relations and show the importance of strong governmental regulation for achieving potentially sustainable solutions.

■ Introduction

With the growth in corporate attempts to influence government policy through lobbying, political donations, and even bribery, the issue of business relations with government has increasingly become a key facet of business ethics. Is it acceptable for corporations to use their considerable power to shape government policy? Is the government jeopardizing its role in protecting the public interest when politicians sit on the board of corporations? Should powerful business interest groups such as the oil industry or the food industry actively contribute to the development of regulation that is supposed to ensure they operate in society's best interest? These are all crucial questions for business ethics when looking at relations with the government. And as we shall see, they represent some of the most pressing problems confronting us in an era of globalization, where the lack of a 'global government' makes the 'policing' of multinational corporations increasingly problematic.

In this chapter, we will analyse in more depth some of these ideas that have been bubbling up throughout this book—the increasingly political role taken up by corporations, the involvement of private actors in the regulation of business ethics, the weakening of the state in protecting our social, political, and civil rights, etc.—as well as examining some new (but related) issues that arise when looking at the business–government relation, such as corporate lobbying and party financing. Government has a crucial role to play in establishing the 'rules of the game' by which we judge business ethics. However, as we shall see in this chapter, in the era of globalization, the traditional boundaries between business and government have blurred to such an extent that defining these rules has become a matter of ethical concern in itself.

■ Government as a stakeholder

Government is frequently presented as a major stakeholder in business, but before we proceed to specify the nature of this stake, it is important that we define a few terms a little more precisely.

Defining government, laws, and regulation

We have actually come across government several times already in this book. For a start, government is involved in issuing laws regulating business practice. Back in Chapter 1, for example, when we made our initial definition of business ethics, we pointed out that business ethics tended to begin where the law ended. This would suggest that government takes on the role of setting at least the baseline of acceptable practice in business. As we shall see shortly, the government also effectively provides business with a 'licence to operate' in its jurisdiction.

When talking about 'the government' in this context, though, we have to be aware that we are actually talking about a whole group of different actors, institutions, and processes.

In democratic societies, the government would include all legislative and executive bodies that act on the basis of parliamentary consent. Furthermore, the incorporation of those functions pertains to various *levels*: it would start with the legislative bodies at the transnational level, such as the United Nations or the European Commission; it would then include the *national government*, but also in many cases *regional governments*, such as the Welsh Assembly, or the government of a Canadian Province; finally, it would also relate to *local or municipal authorities*.

In short, we can define 'government' as follows:

The government consists of a variety of institutions and actors at different levels that share a common power to issue laws.

By laws, you should remember that in the context of business ethics, we are basically concerned with the codification of what society deems are appropriate and inappropriate actions. This suggests the following definition:

Laws serve as a codification into explicit rules of the social consensus about what a society regards as right and wrong.[1]

Looking specifically at laws codifying right and wrong *business* practices, it is important to recognize that the law is only one aspect of the broader area of regulation of business. Although laws are of some relevance to business ethics, it is the role of regulation that it is most vital to understand. This is because it is regulation more generally, rather than the law specifically, which tends to operate in the *grey areas* of business ethics. After all, once we have a clear legal ruling on certain business practices, they are no longer really matters of business ethics. But those still open to other forms of non-legally binding regulation certainly are. So what exactly do we mean by regulation here?

Regulation is all about the *rules* governing business behaviour. It includes laws and acts, but also pertains to other forms of formal or informal *rule-making and enforcement*. This includes broader governmental policies, concepts, goals, and strategies, all of which ultimately enable or restrict the activities of business actors. For example, in the UK, there are specific laws dealing with issues of discrimination in the workplace, including the Sex Discrimination Act 1975 and the Race Relations Act 1976. In addition to these legally binding rules, though, there are also other *regulatory instruments* that are intended to encourage compliance with non-discrimination through non-legally-binding (hence 'weaker') modes of influence. For instance, until the introduction of the Employment Equality (Age) Regulations in 2006, anti-ageism in the UK was tackled by a voluntary code rather than by a specific law. Not all regulation is therefore enforced through the law; sometimes it operates by creating norms that define 'acceptable' behaviour, but which essentially only operate through social enforcement or encouragement.

Originally, most regulation would be issued and enforced by governmental bodies in the narrow sense such as parliament, ministries, and public authorities. However, if we look at the way many financial markets are regulated, we find that the majority of rules that govern the actors in these markets are not in fact issued by the government at all, but by a *private* body, such as the Financial Services Authority in London or the Securities and Exchange Commission in New York. In a similar vein, in the last two chapters we have raised the prospect of corporations and civil society organizations becoming involved in regulatory activity. Later in this chapter, we will discuss in more detail the role of *private actors* in regulatory processes. To begin with, though, it is important to clearly state that regulation is no longer the solitary prerogative of the government: it can be *delegated* to other parties.

These two clarifications—that regulation is about certain types of rules, and that it operates through governmental and non-governmental actors—lead us to the following definition:

> **Regulation can be defined as rules that are issued by governmental actors and other delegated authorities to constrain, enable, or encourage particular business behaviours. Regulation includes rule definitions, laws, mechanisms, processes, sanctions, and incentives.**

This leads us to one final clarification about the relationship between business and government. When talking about government, the terms 'political' and 'politics' typically arise. Originally, these terms described the governance of the Greek people, the 'polis', and consequently included issuing laws, running the economy, (international) diplomacy, etc. In the course of time, however, 'politics' has become a somewhat ambiguous concept, with all sorts of connotations, such as in 'office politics' or 'political correctness', etc. In this chapter, however, we will use the word 'politics' in its original sense. Therefore, when we discuss how companies are getting more and more involved in 'politics', we mean that they increasingly act in areas that have traditionally been the prerogative of governments.

Let us start then by clarifying the nature of the relationship between business and government, and in particular, the specific stake held by the government in corporations.

Basic roles of government as a stakeholder

When talking with managers about the government, or even simply skimming through the business press, it does not take long to realize that people in business tend to have a very ambiguous role towards the government. On the one hand, business likes to complain about an over-active government, perhaps because it demands 'excessive' taxes, or because it restricts their activities, for example by blocking mergers or raising new standards for product safety. On the other hand, business also expects the government to be constantly active in protecting their interests, such as improving the infrastructure, or keeping foreign competitors out of the market.

If we look to this relation from the government's perspective, the situation is by no means any more straightforward. While politicians like to surround themselves with powerful business leaders and are quite aware of the fact that a booming economy helps their chances at the ballot box, they also have to consider the interests of their electorate, who expect governments to 'police' business and to make sure that it acts for the benefit of society.

We could go on and find numerous examples of the rather complex, interwoven, and often quite contradictory ties between business and government. However, when

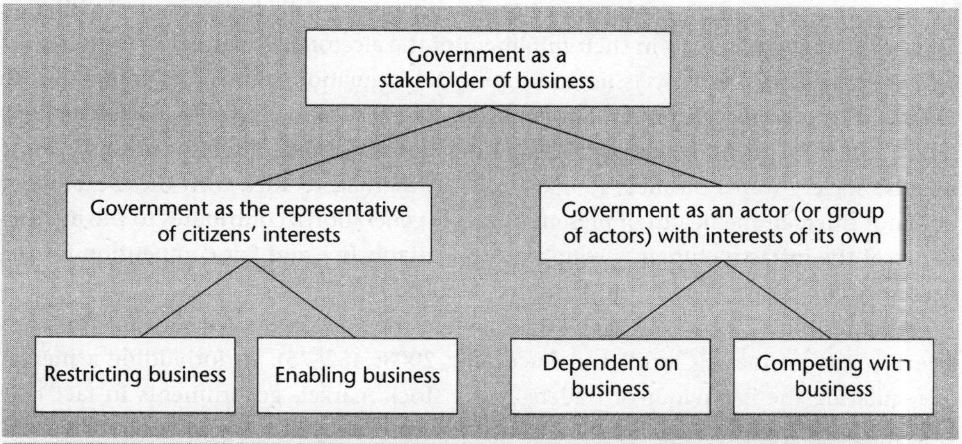

Figure 11.1. Government as a stakeholder of business

discussing stakeholder theory in Chapter 2, we determined that a stakeholder of a corporation could be defined by the fact that it benefits or is harmed by the corporation, and/or that its rights were affected by the corporation. Applying this to government, we have to ask the question: how is government affected by business and how are certain governmental rights influenced by corporate action?

In order to sort out this slightly complicated relationship, we have to differentiate the two basic roles of government, which are shown in **Figure 11.1**. These are government as a representative of citizens' interests and government as an actor (or group of actors) with interests of its own.

Government as a representative of citizens' interests

Unlike many other stakeholders, such as shareholders, employees, or suppliers, government in principle represents an *entire community*, since it is elected by the citizens of a certain town, region, country, or even continent (such as the European Parliament). In this respect, governments are similar to CSOs, which we discussed in the previous chapter, in that they administer and represent the interest of a wider community. In this role as the *representative of citizens' interests*, government mainly defines the conditions for the *licence to operate* of business. That said, we have to recognize that this aspect of the governmental role is of different strength in different political systems. In democratic systems, governments have a fairly strong incentive to act in their citizens' interests as they face elections on a regular basis. In more authoritarian or dictatorial systems, governments might be less concerned about this part of their role. However, even in such systems, governments cannot survive long term if they constantly violate the interests of their citizens, as the examples of the fall of communism 20 years ago, the end of apartheid in South Africa in the 1990s, or the recent regime change in Zimbabwe have shown.

In practice, this definition of the licence to operate normally becomes most visible in areas where governments—in their fulfilment of the electorate's mandate—try to *restrict business*. For example: they issue environmental regulation that forces companies to install filters or to recycle rather than dump waste; they impose taxes on corporate profits; and they investigate whether a merger bid is in the public interest. All this is done because society wants business to operate in a way that, to stick with these examples: does not threaten the health of present or future generations; contributes to the maintenance of the infrastructure in a country; or maintains free and fair competition for the benefit of consumers (Thorne McAlister et al. 2008: 110–23).

The latter aspect, however, is closely linked to the positive side of the government's role towards business (Carroll and Buchholtz 2008: 452–75). In forbidding a merger or regulating the behaviour of traders at the stock market, governments in fact take over a key role in *enabling business* activities in the first place. For instance, if the EU commissioner for competition forbids a merger and thus avoids the gradual emergence of monopolies, he or she makes sure that there is still competition and—ultimately—still a free market as such. In fact, if we look to most of the regulatory functions of governments with regard to business, they in fact have an enabling role more than anything else: markets can only function if basic rules are established and an appropriate regulatory framework exists.

Enabling role of the government, however, is by no means confined to markets and other directly economic issues. It also pertains to a number of broader rules in society, such as a reliable and fair legal system, and efficient sanctioning mechanisms for illegal behaviour. Economic transactions rely heavily on safe expectations about the behaviour of the transaction partners. One of the problems of so-called less developed countries is that a weak government does not tend to provide the stability that encourages foreign investors to enter these markets. An extreme case currently is Iraq, where the lack of stable governmental rule has made it increasingly unattractive for companies to invest in, despite significant business opportunities in reconstruction and exploitation of its resources. Striking examples are also some economies in Eastern Europe and Central Asia, most notably some parts of the former Soviet Union. Here, the implosion of the communist regime has resulted in a political and legal vacuum that (among many other problems) has resulted in poorly enforced regulation and escalating corruption, which together make it increasingly difficult to attract foreign investment to foster economic growth.

There is, of course, some debate about the *degree* of governmental responsibility for a functioning economy (Carroll and Buchholtz 2008: 449–55). The options range from a passive, *laissez-faire* hands-off approach where government just sets the rules and controls the compliance of economic actors, to the other extreme where government assumes a forceful role in 'industrial policy' by actively interfering with the economy. The former approach was dominant in Anglo-American style economies for a considerable time, while many European governments have long operated a much more hands-on approach (Matten and Moon 2008). The financial crisis of the late 2000s, however, seems to have changed this: especially in the US and the UK, governments have effectively taken control over a number of banks and other companies. Whether this actually represents a general sea change in governmental approaches, though, remains to be seen. Looking beyond the Western context to regions such as South and East Asia, state influence, if not ownership, of business remains high—a phenomenon that we will return to later in this chapter.

Government as an actor (or group of actors) with interests of its own

The motivations for government to take an active role in the economy might be quite strong at times, but it is important to understand that this is not only because they are acting directly in the interests of their electorate. Government can also be seen as an actor (or group of actors), with interests of its own. One reason for this is that governments normally have a self-interest to be re-elected. One could also argue that, in most democracies, the control of the government by the electorate is somewhat indirect. This certainly applies to transnational governments such as the European Commission, but is increasingly an issue in many countries globally. As a result of this situation, we have to assume that government's stake in business in not only as an (indirect) representative of its electorate, but also as a (direct) stakeholder with its own rights and interests.

As such, governments are first and foremost interested in a booming economy. Bill Clinton's famous election slogan 'It's the economy, stupid!'—meaning that government success will mostly be judged in terms of competence in running the economy—could be said to be largely true now for many countries. This actually makes governments very *dependent on business*. On the one hand, their electoral success depends on maintaining high employment, increasing incomes, and expanding business activities. On the other hand, none of these things is *directly* influenced, let alone achieved, by government alone. This situation makes government a rather weak and dependent stakeholder, which businesses are often only too aware of. This was clearly illustrated in the 2008 election campaign in the US and the subsequent struggles and pressures on the Obama administration. Even though Obama was highly critical of the dealings of many banks, his administration ultimately had no choice but to provide a multi-trillion dollar 'bail-out' package, since the collapse of the banking system would have had unacceptable consequences for the economy and wider society. Another example is the strong interest of the German government in finding a new owner for the German subsidiary of General Motors, Opel, in 2009. The company employs 25,000 people in the former industrial heartlands of Germany and no government in an election year can afford to passively let employment nosedive so dramatically.

Government in this role, however, is not only *dependent* on business, but also *competes with business*. If we think about the privatization of telecommunications, the ownership of television companies, or the increasing usage of private companies in national healthcare provision, we can see that business increasingly has also either taken over from, co-operated with, or competed with public organizations in certain industries. This has probably been displayed nowhere more visibly than in the war in Iraq, where from 2003, many traditional tasks of the US Army have been outsourced to private contractors and where many army units have keenly experienced pressure to compete for their own jobs (Elms and Phillips 2009).

One could argue that in this context, governments are similar to those stakeholders described in Chapter 9, especially competitors. However, the delicate nature of the relations between business and governments when they compete in the same industry derives from their different and/or unequal positions of power. Government enjoys considerable authority and institutional power, since it can define industry rules and exercise legislative power. Corporations, on the other hand, might sometimes enjoy economic advantages, since they potentially have recourse to additional sources of finance for investment that government may be unable or unwilling to generate through taxation.

Having now set out in some detail the two main aspects of the stake held by government, we shall proceed to look at the ethical issues and problems this complex relation inevitably raises.

■ Ethical issues in the relation between business and government

From the discussion above, it should already be fairly obvious that the stake (or stakes) held by government puts it in an ambiguous position regarding its relation with business. However, most of the ethical issues that arise in this relation pertain to the *closeness* of business–government relations. In particular, critics have questioned whether cosy relations between business and government can jeopardize the government's ability to fulfil its role of protecting the public's interest. **Ethical Dilemma 11** gives you an opportunity to think about some of these problems in a specific example of 'close' business–government relations.

We will start with the basic issues here—essentially problems of legitimacy and accountability—and as we proceed through this section, we will examine the ethical case for different types and levels of business–government interaction. Towards the end of the section, we will then turn our attention to some further ethical issues that arise from government attempts at privatization and deregulation of industry.

Identifying the basic problems and issues: legitimacy, accountability, and modes of influence

Probably the main source of ethical problems in business–government relations lies in the fact that government has a fiduciary relation to society in general. What this means is that government is entrusted with the responsibility to act in society's best interests. As **Figure 11.2** shows, governments here is in a somewhat bi-polar situation (Mitchell 1990; Stigler 1971). First, government is in a mutually dependent relation with *society*: government receives consent from society and acts upon this to enact a regulatory environment that protects society's interests. But government also has a relation with *business* where both partners are mutually dependent on each other for

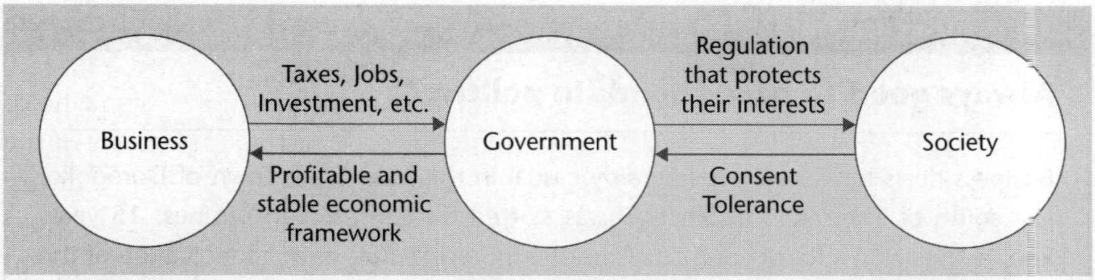

Figure 11.2. Government between business and society's interests

certain things: government is expected to provide a profitable and stable economic environment for business to act in; business is expected to provide taxes, jobs, and economic investment in return.

For government, the main ethical issue here lies in the necessity of carrying out the mandate society has given it (in a democracy, this would be established through the electoral process) and to live up to what it has promised to its constituents. One aspect of this, of course, is its constraint and enabling of business. However, sometimes the relation that government has with business can threaten its ability to live up to its duty to society. As Robert Reich (2007) argues, many of the decisions taken by the US government are not the reflection of citizen's voices but the result of special business interests who have lobbied government officials or paid for their campaigns. The activist and journalist Naomi Klein (2007), in her recent book *The Shock Doctrine*, shows how in many countries, business has gained key influence over governments and provides many examples from developed, as well as developing, countries.

What it boils down to, though, is that business obviously can have a significant influence on the implementation and direction of governmental policies. It is therefore no surprise that the issue of 'public sector ethics' has gained enormous momentum (Dobel 2007). The main ethical consideration arising from this situation is twofold: first, there is the problem of *legitimacy* of business influence; and second, the issue of *accountability*.

The *legitimacy* of business influence on government has two sides. On the one hand, business is perfectly entitled to expect a stable legal and economic framework for its activities. On the other hand, if these demands interfere with the mandate of government to act in the interests of their citizens, the line is clearly crossed. This then leads directly to the aspect of *accountability*: since the government acts as a representative of society's interests, the public has a right to be informed about governmental decisions with other constituencies (such as business), and to be able to determine whether it is acting in its interests or not.

Although not the same, accountability and legitimacy are fairly closely related to each other. Accountability will always be a problem when the influence of business on government is perceived as potentially illegitimate. We have discussed the issue of accountability of corporations earlier in Chapter 2, and to a certain degree, this is an issue in all business relations with stakeholders. However, the difference

AN ETHICAL DILEMMA 11

Always good to have friends in politics?

Business deals have always been fairly casual in the little Greek town of Dorodoko, just south of Thessalonica. Since Costas started his construction business 15 years ago, he has won a lot of contracts from the municipal authority: redecoration of the town hall, a new kindergarten, even a nice chunk of the new circular road around town—all of which kept his 20 employees busy, and helped Costas and his family to enjoy a fairly decent lifestyle. Sitting on the patio of his eighteenth-century farmhouse and slowly watching the fumes of his Cohiba Cigar vanishing into the Mediterranean sunset, he feels quite at ease—if only there had not been this meeting with Dionisis this afternoon.

Dionisis is an old friend of Costas from his childhood days. But while Costas had to start working at 15 years old, building houses with his father, Dionisis had become a teacher. However, he had soon got bored and before long, he went into politics. For ten years now, Dionisis has been the mayor of Dorodoko—but despite his lofty position, the two friends have continued to get on very well.

They normally meet once a month in the backroom of a local café, share some ouzo, and exchange gossip. Of course, they also talk about business, and knowing what is coming up in mayoral office has always helped Costas to tailor his bids to the municipal authority's priorities. Not that Dionisis had directly pushed things for him—but among friends, they talked about projects and Costas was clever enough to integrate this information into his bids. Of course, he has known how to show his old mate some gratitude: when Dionisis needed something to be fixed at his house, it never took one of Costas's employees more than half an hour to turn up and sort it out. And when Dionisis gave a party for his fiftieth birthday last year, Costas took over the entire catering for 200 people, including drinks—but this was just a 'birthday present' for his friend.

But today, things were different. Dionisis knew that Costas urgently needed new contracts to keep his company running; and so he mentioned the new municipal swimming pool that is about to be built. Dionisis also mentioned that the project manager from another construction company, whom he had met last Sunday after church, had offered to build Dionisis a swimming pool in his own house, if his company won the contract. Now Costas knows all too well that this has been Dionisis' dream for years. Not that Dionisis had asked for anything, but there was a funny tone about him telling Costas of his little chat about the pool.

Costas could easily fiddle the bills for labour and materials in such a way that a small swimming pool in a private house could be 'hidden' in the accounting of a project of the dimensions of the tendered municipal one. But after all, wasn't that taking things a little bit too far? On the one hand, there are his employees and their families: there is not much other work in the pipeline. And doing a favour for an old mate here and there can't be a crime. Plus, Dionisis is ultimately in charge of a lot more future projects. On the other hand, renewing Dionisis' roof after last year's storms was already quite something he did for him. But building a swimming pool clearly is a bigger investment than any of the favours he's provided before. What will his employees say? And if they don't say anything, what will they think? And what about the rest of the people of Dorodoko?

The more he thinks about it, the more angry he gets—at his competitor for offering the swimming pool; at Dionisis for being so cheeky; and at himself for having been gradually dragged into this somewhat puzzling relationship. He decided to discuss the matter with his lovely wife Cassandra as soon as she returns from her shopping trip to Thessalonica later that night. Maybe she would have some good ideas about how to sort out the dilemma...

Questions

1 What are the main ethical issues in this case?

2 What are the main ethical arguments for and against building the swimming pool for Dionisis?

3 Would the situation be different if Dionisis were a regular business customer rather than the mayor?

4 If you were Cassandra, how would you advise Costas to proceed?

in accountability in business–government relations is that the problem is not just business accountability to its stakeholders, but also the accountability of both parties to society about their relationship. As **Ethics Online 11** shows, the internet has become a crucial platform in providing more transparency and accountability around business–government relations.

In the following, we will analyse some of the more common practices where these concerns of legitimacy and accountability arise from the relationship between business and government. Although both partners are able to influence the other, the main concerns for business ethics are where business has influence on government. This can happen in a variety of ways.

Modes of business influence on government

There are numerous ways that business can influence government. William Oberman (cited in Getz 1997: 59) distinguishes among different ways according to the following criteria:

- **Avenue of approach to decision-maker.** Business influence can range from very *direct* approaches to political decision-makers in person to more *indirect* forms of influence, such as advocacy advertising or media editorial that supports or challenges political decisions.

VISIT THE WEBSITE for links to useful sources of further information

ETHICS ONLINE 11

Holding business and governments accountable

In the struggle to hold business and government accountable in their dealings with each other, or to tackling the complicity of business in human rights abuses by governments, the internet has become a critical instrument. There has been a veritable avalanche of sites emerging on the web that monitor all sorts of corporate ethical infractions, in particular issues of corruption and collusion with oppressive regimes.

The different actors in this virtual arena are quite a mixed bag. There are groups such as the London-based Business and Human Rights Resource Centre, which seeks to provide a neutral platform for information. They offer a balanced perspective by, for instance, inviting corporations to comment on allegations published on the site. It is certainly the most global source of information on business and human rights, with recently added content in the French and Spanish languages. In a similar category, we can place Transparency International (TI), a global civil society organization dedicated to fighting corruption. TI is best known for its annual Corruption Perception Index (p. 413) and Bribe Payers Index (p. 510), which are freely available to consult on their website, and have become invaluable yardsticks for assessing corruption issues internationally. The organization also reports on stories of corruption around the world, and offers resources for those seeking to address problems of corruption, including business–government bribery.

Another site seeking to offer balanced evidence of business–government relations is the US-based Center for Public Integrity, whose mission is to 'produce original investigative journalism about significant public issues to make institutional power more transparent and accountable'. Among the organization's campaigns is The Climate Change Lobby, which provides data on the firms, business associations, and other special interests seeking to influence the climate change debate in the US through governmental lobbying. Featuring a searchable database of companies and lobbyists, anyone can find out who has paid how much, and when, to make their case to government about climate change issues. The data provided on the site show that in 2008 nearly 800 companies and organizations spent some $90 million on lobbying on climate change in the US, hiring more than 2,000 lobbyists to work on their behalf in the process. Top of the list was the American Coalition for Clean Coal Electricity (a coalition of nearly 50 companies), which spent almost $10 million solely on climate change lobbying in 2008.

In addition to those sites providing a national focus, some websites specialize in particular sectors, such as Bankwatch, which attempts to provide greater transparency on the role of the financial industry in supporting projects in developing countries with questionable effects on the environment or human rights. Other players focus on specific issues, an example being Intellectual Property Rights Watch, which reports on a host of ethical issues around the involvement of business and other special interests in the design and implementation of intellectual property rights policy. Based in Switzerland and reporting mainly in English, the organization also provides reports in French, Spanish, Arabic, and Mandarin.

Organizations such as these have clearly started to play an important role in generating and disseminating news, data, and insights into specific elements of business–government relationships. In so doing, they help facilitate, at least in some small way, accountability between governments, corporations, and citizens.

Sources

Bankwatch website: http://www.bankwatch.org/.
Business and Human Rights Resource Centre: http://www.business-humanrights.org/Home.
Centre for Public Integrity: http://www.publicintegrity.org.
Climate Change Lobby website: http://www.publicintegrity.org/projects/entry/1182/.
Intellectual Property Watch website: http://www.ip-watch.org/.
Transparency International website: http://www.transparency.org/.

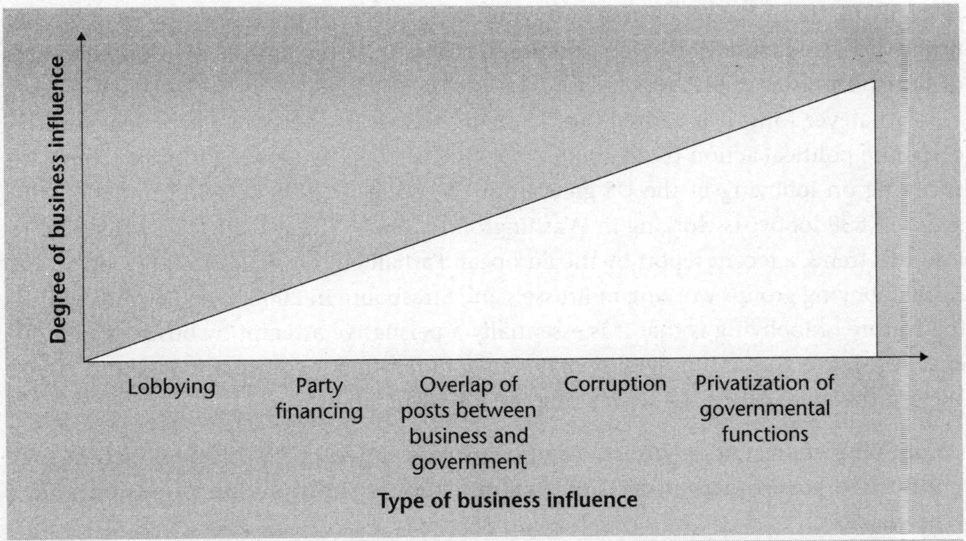

Figure 11.3. Business influence on government

- **Breadth of transmission.** Influence can also be *public* (and therefore visible to all), or *private*, where politicians are approached behind closed doors.
- **Content of communication.** Finally, influence can either be *information-oriented*, that is, focusing more on communication of information to persuade decision-makers, or *pressure-oriented*, which would involve more coercive types of approaches.

Ethical problems of accountability and legitimacy tend to arise primarily in *direct* forms of *private* influence. Beginning with the weakest form of such influence—lobbying—we will explore progressively stronger influences that involve more pressure-oriented content, such as party donations, until we arrive at corruption, where government policy is virtually dictated (or 'captured') by business through illicit payments and other forms of bribery. Beyond corruption, we go on to discuss the problems of privatization and deregulation, which see business not so much merely *influencing* government as actually *replacing* it entirely. These different levels of influence that we will be examining are represented in **Figure 11.3.** As we shall see, these various modes bring with them a range of ethical problems and issues.

Lobbying

The weakest form of direct, private business influence on government is normally called 'lobbying' (McGrath 2005; Vining et al. 2005). For corporations, this area has become increasingly important, and today many major corporations employ professional lobbyists, or have what is called a 'PA expert', a person or even a unit that is responsible for 'public affairs' (van Schendelen 2002), and which manages the corporation's attempts to communicate with and persuade government officials about issues relevant to the business.[2] Other lobbying takes place through specialized lobbying firms, such as Burson-Marsteller, or umbrella organizations, such as the Confederation of British Industry (CBI).

In whatever form it is carried out, lobbying has clearly become a prevalent form of corporate political action (Lord 2000). Lobbying is a rapidly growing industry: the total spending on lobbying in the US grew from US$1.4bn in 1998 to 3.3bn in 2008, with some 14,838 lobbyists working in Washington in 2008.[3] Though the US is often said to lead this trend, a recent report by the European Parliament estimates 15,000 lobbyists in 2,500 lobbying groups working in Brussels and Strasbourg in 2007.[4] The key distinguishing feature of lobbying is that it is essentially a persuasive attempt by business to influence legislators through providing *information* rather than explicit *pressure* (Lord 2000). We can therefore define the term along the following lines:

Lobbying represents a direct, usually private, attempt by business actors to influence governmental decision-making through information provision and persuasion.

This 'information' can be in the form of specific data, analyses, or opinions on business-related public policy issues. However, the persuasive nature of this provision of information often also introduces considerable pressure on government decision-makers. For this reason, although lobbying might be considered an important part of the policy-making process, it has often been regarded as a somewhat questionable activity (AccountAbility 2005). However, the practice occurs in various guises, some more questionable than others, and includes a broad range of instruments and processes. To get a more concrete picture, then (and a more comprehensive idea of the ethical implications of lobbying), we might consider the different types of lobbying (see McGrath 2002).

- **Atmosphere setting.** This is essentially an awareness-raising process intended to enhance government appreciation of industry issues and products, and to create a climate or 'atmosphere' amenable to further influence. This may include events, dinners, or information rallies that create visibility for the interests of industry in the government sphere.

- **Monitoring.** With an ever-increasing amount of regulation, especially at the EU level, an important part of lobbying consists of building up relations with politicians in order to receive reasonably detailed and up-to-date or 'advance' information about ongoing legislative trends and processes.

- **Provision of information to policy-makers.** Government actors involved in policy-making cannot hope to know everything about the industries they are dealing with. As a result, they often seek out detailed, first-hand information from the very companies that are the subjects of proposed regulation. Strong relations between lobbyists and policy-makers frequently mean that lobbyists are involved in the provision of this information.

- **Advocacy and influencing.** The ultimate goal of lobbying, of course, is not only to inform, but ultimately, to have an influence on decision-makers. Business might attempt to do this by offering policy-oriented expertise and 'consultancy', often through industry associations, since they tend to have expert knowledge on certain issues.

- **Application of pressure**. Finally, business lobbying may use the opportunity to communicate with government actors to provide 'information' that is intended to put pressure on them to act in a certain way. This may include implicit or explicit 'warnings' about the potential consequences of particular policies, such as the likelihood of job losses or other politically sensitive outcomes.

In the case of these last three aspects of lobbying, it is not always entirely clear where relatively harmless information provision turns into advocacy, or even more questionable forms of pressurization. In order to do so, we often have to examine specific examples in a particular context. Let us take a look, then, at a couple of illustrations of successful lobbying in action.

- When President Obama started to draft the first plans to reform healthcare in the US, the industries related to this project sent 3,300 lobbyists to Washington to influence the reform package. This adds up to no fewer than six lobbyists for each member of congress, and a total of US$263m in lobbying expenditure just in the first six months of 2009 (Salant and O'Leary 2009). It is hard to imagine that this influence will not have substantial effects on how the reform will finally shape up. Naturally, the pharmaceutical industry, private healthcare providers, and other companies have interests which are not necessarily compatible with Obama's initial promise to provide affordable healthcare to all US citizens. It will be exciting to observe the outcome of this ongoing legislative process.
- In 2003, the revised EU directive on cosmetics regarding animal testing was adopted (Directive 2003/15/EC) after 13 years of controversy and intense debate between animal rights groups, industry, and trade unions. One of the major successes of the lobbying of European cosmetic companies, most prominently the French firm L'Oréal, was that the ban would only really be effective from 2009.[5] Commentators argued that the lobbying strategy of the industry, based on both scientific research (proving that animal testing was not yet dispensable for safe cosmetics), as well as economic advice (claiming massive competitive disadvantages against US and Japanese competitors), represented an exemplar of effective corporate political action (Dahan 2005).

These forms of lobbying are quite frequent and industry appears to be especially keen on using 'information', such as estimates or opinions on possible job losses or threats to competitiveness, to encourage governments to withdraw or substantially revise regulation.

But how should we assess lobbying from an ethical perspective (see Ostas 2007)? It is obvious that weaker forms of lobbying, such as monitoring of legislative processes or communication with decision-makers in government, are fairly unproblematic. In a certain sense, they could even be argued to improve regulatory outcomes, and may indeed be desirable. However, there is a case to be made about the relative ease of the ability of business interest groups to gain access to political decision-makers, compared with other interest groups, such as civil society organizations, who may lack the resources or presumed *legitimacy* to exercise influence.

The main ethical problem, however, probably consists of the fact that the involvement of corporations is not 'for free' and may suggest, especially over the long term, a reciprocal arrangement along the lines of 'I'll scratch your back and you scratch mine'. One could suggest, then, that lobbying threatens the relations of *trust* between governments as supposed 'agents' and representatives of their electorate. The example of lobbyists shaping the healthcare reforms in the US or L'Oréal influencing EU regulations certainly raises the question of whether their 'private' interests are the same as those of the wider 'public' electorate.

There is, however, still a further aspect. Many regulatory processes are fairly invisible to outsiders, and lobbying is often based on close personal ties between politicians and business. Corporations often use their 'recreational skills' (Dahan 2005) to gain access to politicians in a more relaxed, casual, and informal setting. Typical examples would be invitations to holiday resorts or big sporting events. For instance, in the build-up to the FIFA Word Cup in 2006, the German public prosecution authorities investigated the CEO of the utilities conglomerate EnBW for giving away free tickets to politicians.[6] This case stirred up considerable unrest among politicians in Germany, especially given a context where many of the newly privatized utility companies still depended quite heavily on governmental regulation and support.

It should also be noted that the relations established by corporate lobbyists are not only used in the context of legislative processes. These relations can also impact upon other government activities, such as governmental purchasing decisions, most notoriously in the area of defence technology (Andrews 1996). If BAE Systems, a major defence contractor, 'advises' the UK government on which technological option might be the most viable for a certain defence issue, this is hardly neutral advice (see also **Case 11** at the end of this chapter). As we saw in Chapter 9, such *conflicts of interest* are a common problem affecting supplier relations of one sort or another, and lobbying clearly raises the potential for business–government relations to be exposed to similar dilemmas.

VISIT THE WEBSITE for a short response to this feature

? THINK THEORY

Which ethical theory would you find to be best suited to judge whether the lobbying activity of a corporation or industry association is morally right or wrong? What would constitute 'responsible lobbying' according to this perspective?

Party financing

A similar situation occurs when industry makes donations to political parties. Like lobbying, donations to parties by business can raise conflict of interest problems. For instance, in 2002, the UK government's decision to award a £32m smallpox vaccination contract to the UK pharmaceutical company Powderject without seeking competitive tenders raised eyebrows in the media, given that the firm's CEO Paul Drayson had just donated £100,000 to the UK Labour Party. Whilst Powderject and the Labour Party were both cleared of any impropriety by independent enquiries, the case got a further twist when Drayson was given a peerage (a seat in the House of Lords) in 2004 and only six weeks later, again gave another £500,000 cheque to the Labour Party (White 2004). Lord Drayson later became the minister for defence procurement, and then minister for science and innovation in the Labour government, thereby further muddying the lines between business and government.

Practices such as these have led to widespread cynicism about business donations to political parties. Again, the key issue is the legitimacy of these donations: even if parties are perfectly accountable for these donations—and in a number countries, politicians are forced to disclose party donations—the temptation to link political decisions to financial support is substantial. Ultimately, some of these party 'donations' could easily be seen as a 'fee' to obtain a certain political decision or other personal favours—which of course raises the prospect of *preferential treatment*, and might even go so far as to threaten the very notion of democratic process.

Again, as we saw in Chapter 9, there are a number of ways we can look at such 'gifts' to try and determine whether they are acceptable, including the intention of the gift-giver, the impact on the receiver, and the perception of other parties. For business too, though, this situation is clearly a dilemma: while having good relations with political parties seems to be a necessity in many industries, the instrument of party financing can be a double-edged sword. It gains influence—but it could also severely harm the company's image and perhaps encourage questionable behaviour on the part of employees.

The ethical dilemma for corporations becomes even more complicated given that they are not the only ones who work hard at gaining influence with political parties: in an attempt to professionalize their strategies, CSOs have also increasingly sponsored political parties and events (Harris and Lock 2002). This partly brightens the moral terrain of party financing, since corporations then are more or less part of a general trend in society—although again the problem of the differential resources available to business actors compared with civil actors needs to be raised.

Of course, one possible way of dealing with these problems is for corporations to simply introduce rules that forbid political donations. This indeed has been the response of BP, one of the world's largest oil companies, which has completely banned any funding of political parties in Europe and—more delicately—in the US.[7] Although such a move is certainly to be commended for making a stand on an issue of increasing contestability, there might be said to be more to BP's decision that first meets the eye. With its tax contributions, spending power, and over 100,000 employees worldwide, BP is a typical representative of a group of MNCs that do not necessarily need to do extra party financing in order to be worthy of governmental attention. In addition, BP has been able to take advantage of close relations with the UK government through personnel shifts between the two organizations (Maguire and Wintour 2001), a widespread phenomenon, often referred to as 'revolving doors'. This has created close informal ties between the company and the government, and of course, these ties conceivably allow the same kind of lobbying efforts that we mentioned earlier, without actually needing to particularly invest in formal 'lobbying'. But this, as we shall now see, raises a different kind of conflict of interest problem at the individual level.

Overlap of posts between business and government: individual conflicts of interest

'Revolving doors' between business and government are not just common in Europe or North America, but also in other parts of the world. In Japan, it is a common phenomenon for politicians to change into careers in the private sector and vice versa (Hayes 2009). However, if a company's managers go to work in government, we might reasonably ask whether they are acting for the government (as an agent of the general public) or for the company (as an agent for its shareholders). Clearly, this overlapping of posts raises quite substantial individual-level conflicts of interest when the two agency relations involved clash.

It is not only business people working for the government that is the problem though. The overlap works both ways. Many senior politicians also tend to find themselves on the (supervisory) boards of large companies. Quite a number of ministers voted out of office in the 2005 elections in Germany are now in executive positions in major German companies. In France, which still has a considerably high government ownership of corporations, the overlap of interests between business and government is so substantial that some elements of the media identify a 'crippling cronyism' in the French government.[8]

One of the more acute cases is that of Silvio Berlusconi in Italy. During his times in power between 2001 and 2006 and since his re-election in 2008, Berlusconi, as the owner of Italy's three major television stations and largest publishing house, had been able to virtually dominate the media and thereby marginalize criticism of his government.[9] Various contestable bills have been debated in parliament without major media coverage inside the country. Moreover, revelations in 2009 about Berlusconi's alleged improprieties with prostitutes led to a swathe of writs from the Prime Minister in an effort to block coverage in the (non Berlusconi-owned) newspaper *La Republicca*, as well as several foreign magazines and newspapers. A controversial documentary, *Videocracy*, released the same year and which was highly critical of Berlusconi's influence on democracy and the media in Italy, was also refused airing by national TV networks RAI and Mediaset because it was 'offensive' to the reputation of their boss.[10]

The ethics of occupying a dual role in business and politics is therefore somewhat questionable. On the one hand, one could argue that it has certain advantages if politicians have had experience of the business world and vice versa. It certainly makes politicians more aware of the economic realities underlying many of the issues about which they have to decide. It might be suggested even that industry experience can provide politicians with a more professional style of work and decision-making compared to what normally dominates the rather bureaucratic structures of the public domain. All these factors could enable a more efficient approach to political work and therefore might be argued to be in the best interests of society. Close links between business and politics might also be an advantage in industries and projects whose success is strongly reliant on political factors. Examples could be entry into foreign markets, where the principle 'the flag goes and the trade follows' seems to have been a successful approach for some countries and industries. This more *utilitarian argument* would, in fact, see some benefit in a close overlap between business and politics.

On the other hand, there are also quite significant ethical problems linked to such a close amalgamation of business and politics. Famous for these inter-linkages was the George W. Bush administration in the US, where many senior officials had close ties to oil, defence, and finance companies. For example, Hank Paulsen, the US Secretary of State responsible for solving the financial crisis of 2008, was the former CEO of Goldman Sachs, and many at the time questioned his independence in deciding about the fate of his former company and its Wall Street rivals (Gapper 2008). Whatever the rights and wrongs of incidents such as these, it makes obvious the problems that can arise when we have politicians who are entitled to set the rules of the economic game also acting as players in the game. If a company or an industry is able to influence and manipulate the rules towards its own interests, this potentially violates the principle of justice, most notably the notion of *procedural justice*. This particular type of justice underlies the set-up of modern democracies, since it focuses particularly on fairness and equality in the treatment of all parties involved in the political process. Democratic institutions are tailored towards the representation and the pursuit of the interests of all members of society and not just towards those with the most economic power.

Corruption of governmental actors by business

So far, we have been discussing forms of business influence on government that, although they may be in the grey areas of business ethics, are pretty much legal in most countries. However, a more extreme form of business influence that occurs quite widely, but tends to be more often classified as illegal, is the direct payment of bribes to government officials by businesses. Where this is intended to 'buy' an influence on regulation, we refer to this as 'corruption'. According to Transparency International:[11]

Corruption is the abuse of entrusted power for private gain.

Corruption can occur in many contexts and sectors, but when talking about government corruption in relation to business, we are mainly concerned with activities where private firms shape the formulation, implementation, or enforcement of public policies or rules by payments to public officials and politicians. In a certain sense, corruption is the most direct, private, and straightforward way of influencing governments. The offer of bribes and other forms of corruption to gain influence over politicians is a major problem in many parts of the world. The international anti-corruption pressure group, Transparency International, produces an annual *Corruption Perceptions Index* (CPI),

Country rank	Country	CPI score	Country rank	Country	CPI score
1	Denmark	9.3	40	South Korea	5.6
1	New Zealand	9.3	45	Czech Republic	5.2
1	Sweden	9.3	54	South Africa	4.9
4	Singapore	9.2	55	Italy	4.8
5	Finland	9.0	57	Greece	4.7
5	Switzerland	9.0	58	Lithuania	4.6
7	Iceland	8.9	58	Poland	4.6
7	Netherlands	8.9	58	Turkey	4.6
9	Australia	8.7	147	Russia	2.1
9	Canada	8.7	166	Zimbabwe	1.8
11	Luxembourg	8.3	171	Congo, Democratic Republic	1.7
12	Austria	8.1	171	Equatorial Guinea	1.7
12	Hong Kong	8.1	173	Chad	1.6
14	Germany	7.9	173	Guinea	1.6
14	Norway	7.9	173	Sudan	1.6
16	Ireland	7.7	176	Afghanistan	1.5
16	United Kingdom	7.7	177	Haiti	1.4
18	Belgium	7.3	178	Iraq	1.3
18	Japan	7.3	178	Myanmar	1.3
18	USA	7.3	180	Somalia	1.0
23	France	6.9			
23	Uruguay	6.9			
26	Slovenia	6.7			
27	Estonia	6.6			
28	Spain	6.5			
32	Portugal	6.1			
33	Israel	6.0			
35	United Arab Emirates	5.9			
39	Taiwan	5.7			

Score relates to perceptions of the degree of corruption among government officials as seen by business people, country experts, and risk analysts, and ranges between 10 (highly clean) and 0 (highly corrupt).

Figure 11.4. 2008 Corruption Perception Index (CPI) for selected countries

Source: adapted from 2008 Corruption Perception Index. Copyright 2008 Transparency International: the global coalition against corruption. Used with permission. For more information, visit http://www.transparency

a listing of different states and the degree to which their public officials and politicians are perceived to be susceptible to corruption. Some highlights of the 2008 CPI are shown in **Figure 11.4**.

As the CPI shows, government officials in countries such as Denmark, New Zealand, Sweden, and Singapore are among those perceived to be least susceptible to corruption, whilst countries with ongoing conflict, high levels of poverty, and failed institutions, such as Somalia, Iraq, Haiti, and Sudan, score very low. However, it is not just poverty (as some argue) which influences a country's place on the scale. In the 2008 ranking, both Germany and the UK fell in the rankings, due in part to the impact of major cases of corruption discussed in this book— Siemens in Germany (Case 4) and BAE in the UK (Case 11).

In the light of the above, the ethics of such practices probably should be beyond much doubt. However, the dilemma for corporations in highly corrupt countries seems to be largely unavoidable. One might argue that when so many economic actors effectively 'buy' public officials, it becomes a necessity for all businesses to do so. This argument, however, leads us directly into the controversy about ethical absolutism and relativism we introduced back in Chapter 3, and which has arisen a number of times throughout this book. Ultimately, from the perspective of Western democracies, this situation is beyond what we would regard as an ethically acceptable situation given the corrosive effects of corruption on societies. Moreover, if instead of the rule of law, there is the rule of the most powerful corporations, then individual business is subject to governmental arbitrariness and despotism. When property rights are not granted, and contracts are not reliable, business ultimately becomes very difficult and uncertain (Hellman and Schankerman 2000). From an ethical theory perspective, this is a good example of Kant's theory, most notably the first maxim of the categorical imperative: if state capture becomes a 'universal law', a normally functioning economy becomes nearly impossible.

? THINK THEORY

Corruption has also been addressed from the perspective of consequentialist theories. How would these apply to state capture as discussed here?

VISIT THE WEBSITE for a short response to this feature

Ethical issues in the context of privatization and deregulation

If corruption sometimes represents situations where business can dictate certain aspects of government policy, then privatization takes us into a situation where government effectively cedes responsibility for the provision of certain goods and services to business completely. Although we certainly wouldn't want to suggest that privatization raises the same kind of fundamental ethical problems as corruption, there are a number of issues and dilemmas that we need to address.

Starting in the US and the UK during the 1980s, the world has experienced a strong move towards privatization of public industries such as public transport, postal services, telecommunications, and utility supply. This development coincided with, and was partly due to, quite substantial deregulation of certain industries and markets. This deregulation led to a situation where private businesses were allowed to enter industries that formerly were dominated, if not totally controlled, by public organizations. Similar developments took place later in the rest of Europe, Australasia, and Latin America and are still ongoing in many developing countries (Klein 2007). In a similar vein, the fall of the iron curtain propelled the major state-owned companies of Eastern Europe and the former Soviet Union into the privately owned capitalist system, entailing more or less similar consequences.

The common perception of state ownership is that large public service monopolies tend to be inflexible, bureaucratic, and typically deliver average quality at high costs (Wong 2009). So, for instance, the owner of Capita, one of the major players in the privatized public services industry in the UK, boasted after privatization that it takes his company seven hours to reach a decision that would have taken seven weeks in the civil service.[12] However, the results of the process of privatization have been mixed: while some of the newly privatized companies and industries, especially in the area of telecommunications and utilities, have been quite successful, other privatized corporations struggle and have not been able to provide reasonable quality and profitability. The picture is even more mixed from an ethical point of view (Jones 2001). Let's consider some of the common issues:

- **Privatization profits**: An issue of extensive debate has been the price at which formerly public companies should be 'sold' to private owners. If too high a price is charged, the new owners may feel exploited if their investment subsequently attracts a far lower valuation than their initial investment. For example, when Deutsche Telekom (owner of the T-Mobile brand) was privatized, the share price immediately sank dramatically below the price of the initial public offering (IPO), thereby infuriating shareholders. If too low a price is charged, a small group of investors taking over a former public utility might end up making huge profits on what were essentially public assets that ultimately belonged to the taxpayer. For instance, privatizations in Russia during transition resulted in super-rich oligarchs and an impoverished state and citizenry. Apart from the fact that stock-market prices ultimately are not predictable, a key ethical challenge in privatizing state-owned companies is to find a *fair price*.

- **Citizens turned consumers**. Postal services or public transport—just to name two examples—were originally under the care of governments because these services were considered a component of the social entitlements of citizens. One reason the state became involved in such services was to ensure that provision of basic services was supplied to all, regardless of where they lived, or the cost of providing the service. However, a privatized postal service might argue that it cannot run a post office in rural Lapland or a Himalayan mountain village because there are only a few families in the village. They have to take these decisions on an economic rather than a political basis—which may mean that these families will no longer have a post office or bus service. In the absence of regulation, these issues typically cause public outrage and confront corporations with difficult ethical dilemmas.

- **Natural monopolies.** Telecommunications, railways, and other utilities that deliver their services via networks—be they cables, rails, or tubes—cannot easily be privatized and opened up to competition because of the degree of integration that is necessary for them to function effectively. To give a simple example, it is technically and economically infeasible for a new rail company to build a new rail network next to a competitor's. For this reason, such industries are sometimes called *natural monopolies*. Generally, under the privatization of natural monopolies, access to and prices for using such networks are largely determined by governmental policy. However, experience shows that corporations may exploit this situation by either overcharging customers or delivering poor quality.

Next to full-on privatization, there has recently been considerable debate on so-called **public–private partnerships** (PPP). This is partly a reaction to unsuccessful privatization, which sometimes resulted in the opposite of the desired goals of better quality services and lower prices. The central idea of PPPs is that the government is still responsible for a considerable part of the project, while private companies bring in the investment. In the UK, PPPs have been quite extensively introduced, while many other countries seem rather reluctant to take up these initiatives. Well-known UK examples are in the area of public transport, most notably the reform of the London Underground (Shaoul 2002), in civil services, and in healthcare (Grimshaw et al. 2002).

The analysis of both planned and realized PPP projects, though, is not overly impressive. The overwhelming evidence in the UK on PPPs—carried out under the label of the 'Private Finance Initiative' (PFI)—seems to suggest a sharp rise in costs of public service, with the result that in one major poll, only 17% of respondents continued to view this approach to public service with any favour (Serwotka and Sinnott 2006). The general result seems to be that the profit-maximization rationale of the private sector seems to dominate PPPs at the expense of quality and effectiveness for consumers and citizens.

Regardless of the possibility of raising ethical problems, it would appear that privatization, deregulation, and public–private partnerships are likely to continue to be a major feature of the economic landscape for firms, whether at home or further afield in developing countries. Just how far the privatization process has gone can be seen in the discussion of private military contractors in **Ethics in Action 11.1**. As this shows, governments are increasingly recognizing that new regulation is sometimes necessary to manage the involvement of private actors in providing public services. Moreover, as we shall now see, such developments are also part of a broader shift in relations between the state and business that has arisen from the process of globalization.

? THINK THEORY

What difference does it make to the notion of ethical duty if a company sells consumer goods or if it provides a public service, as described in this section? Apply Kant's ethics of duty in assessing the differences, in particular the aspect of human dignity.

VISIT THE WEBSITE for a short response to this feature

VISIT THE WEBSITE for links to useful sources of further information

ETHICS IN ACTION 11.1 http://www.ethicalcorp.com

Private military—new rules of engagement

Peter Davies, 6 October 2008

Ethical CORPORATION

The UK government is under pressure from a House of Commons committee to introduce legislation in 2008 to govern the private military sector. The foreign affairs select committee, in its annual report published in July 2008, called on the government 'to announce its intention to introduce the relevant legislation in the forthcoming Queen's speech'. In the US, too, the legislative framework for private military companies is tightening. In 2007, the House of Representatives amended the Military Extraterritorial Jurisdiction Act (MEJA), which had been passed in 2000 and permitted the justice department to go into US district courts to prosecute employees of the defence department, contractors and subcontractors who commit crimes overseas. In 2008, a companion bill, the Security Contractor Accountability Act, had been introduced to the Senate by (then still Senator) Barack Obama. Although there are a number legislative hurdles yet to be cleared before these bills pass into law, they give a strong indication of the way the wind is blowing.

Blackwater fallout

The current flurry of activity has been prompted by a series of incidents involving private contractors operating in Iraq and Afghanistan. Probably the most high-profile occurred in September 2007. A group of guards from a firm called Blackwater were accompanying a US official back to the Green Zone. Exactly what happened is a matter of debate, but 17 people died when the guards opened fire as their convoy entered a busy square in central Baghdad. Unsurprisingly, this incident sparked outrage. Iraq's minister for human rights, Wijdan Salim, called for the men to be tried for murder in Iraq; a US human rights group, the Centre for Constitutional Rights, said it would sue Blackwater for war crimes; and the state department ordered a review of its security arrangements. Following a ten-month inquiry, the US justice department indicated in August that it may well indict some of the Blackwater staff involved in the incident.

The episode highlighted the sheer scale of the private security sector. The July report from the UK committee observes: 'The war in Iraq has led to a proliferation of the use of private security firms by the government and its allies.' In 2006, a War on Want report estimated that there were three British private security guards for every British soldier deployed in Iraq.

It is estimated that there are 190,000 private contractors in Iraq—compared to 168,000 US troops in the country at the height of the 'surge' earlier this year. And it is not just in Iraq that this sector is burgeoning. According to Doug Brooks, president of the International Peace Operations Association (IPOA), the industry's trade body, the business of providing services in the field in peacekeeping and stability operations globally is worth about $20 billion a year. The industry encompasses a wide range of activity. The IPOA estimates that, globally, 90% of contractors provide support and logistics services to international operations in war-zones. A further 5% are engaged in security sector reform programmes, and only 5% are actually providing private security services. This said, there is considerable divergence in estimates of the numbers of

PMC operatives there are in Iraq. According to Peter Singer, a defence analyst with the Brookings Institution, there are nearly 50,000 armed private security guards working in Iraq; but the IPOA's Brooks puts the figure at 20,000. The US defence department estimates that there are no more than 10,000 in Iraq and Afghanistan combined.

Foreign contractors seem to have courted controversy. KBR, which provides logistical support to US forces, is facing allegations of abuse. One of its employees, Jamie Leigh Jones, alleges that she was gang-raped by colleagues in Iraq. In August this year, a Washington law firm filed a lawsuit against KBR alleging that the company and its Jordanian subcontractor engaged in human trafficking of 13 Nepali workers.

It is not surprising therefore that pressure is building on both sides of the Atlantic to regulate security companies—it is estimated that as many as 85% of firms in this sector are based either in the UK or the US. Peter Frankental of Amnesty International says: 'At present these companies enjoy impunity because they cannot be prosecuted in British courts for crimes committed overseas.' Unsurprisingly, his organisation welcomes the recommendations of the foreign affairs select committee report, which 'support our view that legislation should be in place to bring to justice private military and security contractors for serious crimes committed abroad'.

Perhaps more surprisingly, the security sector itself also welcomes the prospect of tighter regulation. The IPOA's Brooks say: 'There has to be a legitimate system of accountability. We have our own process of self-regulation, but that will always be supplemental to the legal framework. When people hire our companies, they need to know they are properly regulated.' This final point cuts to the heart of the question of why there are so many private-sector contractors in Iraq and Afghanistan. The answer is simple: post-conflict reconstruction is hard and slow work, and having troops committed overseas for long periods is politically unacceptable. Reconstruction of Iraq will take many more years, if not decades. If it is not politically acceptable to have troops in-theatre, then the work will have to be done by private contractors. And it is not just Iraq. In countries such as Sudan, the former Yugoslavia and Haiti, ongoing development is and will continue to be supported by private contractors. The private security sector looks certain to continue to grow, and ensuring that these companies behave properly, and do not make delicate situations worse, is vital.

On 17 September 2008, representatives of 17 nations meeting in Montreux, Switzerland, endorsed a set of rules and good-practices to ensure private military companies comply with international human rights law. The 'Montreux Document', which is not legally binding, outlines existing international laws relating to private military and security companies. It also lists 70 good practices that states could follow to meet their obligations under these laws. States that signed the document were: Afghanistan, Angola, Australia, Austria, Canada, China, France, Germany, Iraq, Poland, Sierra Leone, South Africa, Sweden, Switzerland, the UK, Ukraine, and the US.

Sources

Ethical Corporation, Peter Davies, 6 October 2008, http://www.ethicalcorp.com.

VISIT THE WEBSITE for a short response to this feature

? THINK THEORY

Think about private military contractors (PMCs) from the perspective of the extended view on corporate citizenship (Chapter 2). What are the specific areas in which PMCs become involved in the governance of citizen's rights? What consequences should that entail for the way they do business? How do you evaluate what has been done so far?

Globalization and business–government relations

Back in Chapter 1, we defined globalization as 'the progressive eroding of the relevance of territorial bases for social, economic, and political activities, processes, and relations'. The erosion of the territorial base has some specific consequences for the role of governments in the age of globalization. The British political scientist, Anthony McGrew, has described this in terms of a transition from a traditional, i.e. national context to a global one, which he calls 'the post-Westphalian' setting (Held and McGrew 2000; McGrew 1997a, 1997b). In the following, we will use McGrew's analysis of this transition in order to set out the implications of globalization for business relations with government.

From the national to the global context

McGrew argues that since the Westphalian peace treaties in the seventeenth century, the identity of nation, society, and state has been the leading pattern of political organization in the 'civilized' world. Hence, for the last 400 years or so, we have tended to think of ourselves as being part of nation states, and if we are talking about 'society' in a certain part of the world, we could equally talk about 'the French', 'the Swedes', or 'the Chinese', etc. As Ulrich Beck (1997: 49–55) contends, society and social life mainly took place within the 'container of the nation state'.

However, as we have seen throughout this book, when globalization deterritorializes social, economic, and political action, the significance of these nation states is weakened. This fundamentally challenges the traditional context of the 'Westphalian setting' and in some areas, and for some issues, moves us into a global context, or 'post-Westphalian' setting. This transition, which is summarized in **Figure 11.5(a)**, can be described in terms of the following features:

- **Society**. McGrew's argument is basically that the national and the globalized world order co-exist. In many respects, we still think of ourselves as 'the French', 'the British', or 'the Japanese', but in others our society is viewed in a transnational context. For example, a French person may also think of herself as 'a Sony employee', a British person as 'a Peugeot owner', or a Japanese person as 'a Greenpeace member'. These latter identities are distinctly transnational, rather than being tied to a nation state. Hence, when we consider issues in a globalized context, the notion of 'society' is no longer an entity confined simply to national borders. It is rather a more or less worldwide community conceptualized by authors like Luhmann (1998) as a '*world society*'.

a) Changing context

	National context (Westphalian setting) ↔	**Globalized context (Post-Westphalian setting)**
Society	Nation	World Society
Holder of political power	Monopoly by national governments	Multitude of governmental, civil society, and private actors
Manifestation of political activity	National regulation (laws)	Systems of transnational negotiations (e.g. EU directives, codes of conduct)
Addressee of regulation	Social actors (e.g. domestic companies, citizens)	Nation states (e.g. EU member states) Private transnational actors (e.g. MNCs)
Intensity of regulation	Decreasing (e.g. deregulation, privatisation)	Increasing
Democratic control of political power	Higher	Lower

b) Changing roles

	National context (Westphalian setting) ↔	**Global context (Post-Westphalian setting)**
Role of the state	Dominant (as Regulator)	Dependent (as addressee of regulation)
Role of the company	Dependent (as addressee of regulation)	Dominant (e.g. corporate power of withdrawal)
Types of regulation	Imperative regulation	Nation states: imperative regulation Private transnational actors: private, self-controlled regulation

Figure 11.5. Globalization, government and business: changing context and roles

- **Holder of political power**. This change entails certain consequences for the political control of society. In the traditional national context, governments of states possessed the monopoly of political power, since they were the only authority that could set rules by issuing regulation. This is radically altered through globalization, since society and social interaction can transcend the territorial boundaries of the state and might thus escape the scope of national governments. Political power beyond the nation state is rather broadly distributed and loosely shared (Scherer et al. 2006). As we saw in the last chapter, it is often MNCs and CSOs that are the main organizations that wield influence on a global level. Therefore, there are a *multitude of governmental, civil society, and private actors* holding political power.

- **Manifestation of political activity**. What this means is that we still have national regulation, but we also find national governments setting up *systems of transnational negotiations*—the European Union, or the North American Free Trade Agreement (NAFTA) for example—and we also see CSOs and MNCs involved in setting up regulatory efforts, such as international codes of conduct.

- **Addressee of regulation**. Given such transnational negotiations, it is not only social actors such as citizens and domestic companies who are subject to regulation (as we see in the case of national regulation), but also *nation states* and *private transnational actors* such as MNCs. Indeed, one of the reasons that European countries such as the UK or Denmark are rather suspicious of the European Union is that it involves them in being subject to regulation from another level of government. Significantly, this often applies to regulation targeted at environmental protection, human rights, and various other issues of consequence to business ethics.

- **Intensity of regulation**. If we look at individual countries, there have been strong moves towards deregulation and by this, efforts to decrease the level of regulation at the national level. We have discussed above the reasons and ethical implications at the national level. At the same time, however, we also see that the level of regulation at the transnational and global level is *increasing*, not only for nation states (e.g. by EU regulation), but also for private actors (e.g. by codes of conducts of the OECD).

- **Democratic control of political power**. The decreasing power and relevance of national governments in the globalized context leads to a central, yet frequently overlooked, problem: the principles of democratic control of political power are eroded. As soon as political actors like CSOs, MNCs, or supranational bodies act beyond the scope of the nation state, where in most industrialized countries political power is controlled by the electorate, these actors are no longer directly accountable to those over whom they exert their power.

These then are essentially the main aspects of the shift identified by McGrew. As we have already mentioned, one of the key things to remember here is that both contexts continue to co-exist; it is simply that in the global context, the role and nature of regulation are substantially different from at the national level. Let us now go on to see how these differences reshape the roles and relations between business and government.

Shifting roles for business and government in a global context

The main consequence of globalization is that it begins to reverse the roles of government and corporations (**see Figure 11.5(b)**). In the national context, states are in the politically dominant position, since they are regulators of economic actors (the 'addressees' of regulation). In the global context, though, nation states also become addressees of all kinds of transnational regulation.

Companies, on the other hand, seem to gain a specific increase in political power through globalization (Fuchs 2005). The main reason for this is not predominantly that they find themselves in a position where they could wilfully discard or violate national regulation. Rather, it is based on a phenomenon that Beck (1998) has described as the 'corporate power of transnational withdrawal', namely that in a global economy, corporations can quite easily threaten governments that they will relocate to another country if certain 'undesirable' regulations—such as health and safety standards—are enforced. As national governments depend on corporations in terms of employment and tax payments, this situation puts companies in a position of relative power.

Another source of political power of companies, however, is based on the fact that many MNCs have considerable *economic* power of their own. Corporations can have a substantial influence on global developments simply because of their size, scope, and resources. **Ethics on Screen 11** illustrates some of the tensions and ethical infractions in business–government relations in a globalized economy.

The consequences of these changing contexts and changing roles is that business finds itself in a situation where it still operates within the traditional national context, as well as being a key actor at the global level. Let us now look at the types of regulation this exposes business to.

Business as an actor within the national context (Westphalian setting)

Businesses are still located within nation states and they are therefore still subject to national law, which we have called *imperative regulation* in **Figure 11.5(b).** By imperative regulation, we mean that the regulation is mandatory and imposed from above. The ability of governments to use this traditional element of politics remains powerful in areas where companies do not dispose of strong internationalization options (Rugman and Verbeke 2000). Furthermore, the increase in transnational regulation still results in a considerable increase in imperative regulation at the national level. Governments are responsible for the national implementation of, for instance, the Kyoto Protocol or certain EU directives. Since these treaties apply to many countries simultaneously, the power of transnational withdrawal for companies is certainly limited.

As with all categorizations, however, we should add that these developments are always subject to certain dynamics. We write this in 2009 in the midst of the financial crisis and a remarkable surge in the importance of direct intervention by governments in the business world. In many Western countries, most notably the US and the UK, governments now own substantial parts of the banking system and are directly involved in restructuring other industries. This, however, raises some rather distinct ethical issues, in particular for governments. While the investment of taxpayers' money was legitimized by the failure of these companies and its impacts on the economy as a whole, the temptation for governments as the owner of businesses has always been to intervene and use these assets for the short-term political gain of politicians in power. As Simon Wong (2009) has pointed out, the UK government has probably the most cutting-edge approach to these issues: transparency in the goals of ownership and an arm's-length approach appear to be the most important elements of a successful governmental role. Crucial for this was the set-up of UK Financial Investments (UKFI) as a separate company which manages the engagements in a similar way to an investment fund.

VISIT THE WEBSITE for links to useful sources of further information

ETHICS ON SCREEN 11

The Constant Gardener

A firecracker. The sort of movie the Oscars were designed for.

Peter Bradshaw, *Guardian*

Focus Features/The Kobal Collection

The Constant Gardener has all the ingredients of a Hollywood blockbuster: a best-selling novel as the basis for the script (by John Le Carré); a plot full of intrigue and excitement; a dramatic African location; and great performances from Ralph Fiennes (who plays British Diplomat Justin Quayle) and Rachel Weisz (his wife Tessa), who won an Oscar as Best Supporting Actress for her role. Brazilian director, Fernando Meirelles, who took much of his unique cinematography from his earlier *City of God (Cidade de Deus)* to *The Constant Gardener*, manages to grippingly intertwine this story about the realities of global capitalism with a romantic and intelligently scripted love story.

The film centres around the testing of a drug by a British pharmaceutical multinational in the Kenyan slums. 'Dypraxa' is designed for HIV tests and the trials are to find out whether it could also serve as a hugely profitable anti-tuberculosis drug. While Justin, on his first assignment as a junior diplomat to the British Embassy in Kenya, is very much part of the networks between 'big pharma', the British government, and Kenyan government officials, his wife Tessa sides with the disenfranchized and poor victims in Nairobi's shantytowns. Her mysterious death at the beginning of the film sets the scene for Justin's own journey into the murky waters of personal and professional betrayal.

The film exposes the roles and responsibilities of large multinational companies, most notably in relation to the world's poor, and health issues in particular. It also showcases the complexity of business–government relations, both in the global North where governments depend on companies in securing employment, and in the South where a whole new set of ethical problems are faced, including poverty, corruption, and development. It also highlights the task of NGOs in today's global economy, in particular their role as moral conscience and advocate for the disenfranchized masses in the developing world. Interestingly, the film also exposes the different protagonists to situations where, individually, they have to take an ethical decision running against the expectations of 'the system', i.e. a functional, amoral bureaucracy.

On closer examination, the film is not, of course, without flaws. Meirelles certainly has not avoided painting the characters in a somewhat overwrought and stereotypical fashion and does not exactly avoid the usual clichés. Without going so far as Jean-Pierre Garnier, CEO of 'big pharma' company GlaxoSmithKline, who found the movie 'entertaining, but it has nothing to do with the real world, not even 10 per cent of it', one might wonder if the attack on pharmaceutical companies is not a bit too simplistic. Despite its critics, the industry has made a significant contribution to global health issues, and recently has arguably made considerable inroads into many of the issues evoked by the film. However, the film enthusiastically plays out the anti-big pharma debate to a global audience, and neatly dovetails it into broader concerns about the relations between multinationals and governments in the global economy.

If anything, then, the film can probably best be considered as a comment on the wider context of politics and power in the post-cold war system of global capitalism. Intertwined with a romantic thriller, beautifully shot scenes of life and landscapes on the poverty-stricken continent, the movie certainly makes for highly entertaining and at times deeply moving viewing.

Sources

Wachman, R. 2006. Big pharma's constant Garnier. *Observer*, 30 Apr.

Jeffries, S. 2005. 'I do give a damn' (Interview with David Cornwell aka John Le Carré). *Guardian*, 6 Oct

Bradshaw, P. 2005. The Constant Gardener. *Guardian*, 20 Oct.

http://www.theconstantgardener.com.

Business as an actor within the national context of authoritarian/oppressive regimes

Considering business–government relations in the context of globalization, though, it is necessary to also highlight situations where business becomes an actor in authoritarian and oppressive regimes. Recent discussions of this issue have focused on countries such as Zimbabwe, Nigeria, China, Burma, and Sudan. The crucial ethical dilemma here is that MNCs that want to operate in these countries have to collaborate to a certain degree with the regime. This is shown quite visibly in the case of internet providers such as Yahoo! or Google in China (see **Case 5**).

Next to collaborating, MNC presence in these countries also can be said to contribute to the economic stability and wealth of the existing regime. Therefore, even without directly collaborating with the regime, the presence of Western companies can be deemed to be contributing to their support. With the rise of MNCs from India, China, and Brazil, finding an ethical approach is by no means uncontroversial, as the case of Sudan and its government's alleged human rights abuses in Darfur has shown. While many Western pension funds have started to divest in companies involved in Sudan and many companies have pulled out of the country, this vacuum is filled by other players with different perspectives on human rights, such as Chinese companies (Ethical Corporation 2006).

As Nien-hê Hsieh (2009) argues, MNCs in those contexts have a duty to contribute to the establishment of background institutions which normally protect human rights in democratic systems. He points to a number of areas where MNCs have a moral duty to become involved:

- Upholding human rights through normal business operations. This argument was used specifically in the case of MNCs in apartheid South Africa in the 1970s and 1980s, where in particular MNCs from the US refused to adopt the apartheid rules in their operations.

- Contributing to economic development. As we have seen in **Figure 11.4**, there is some form of link between poor governance and poverty. By operating in a developing country, a MNC can bring wealth and economic development to a country. This would also include MNCs becoming involved in providing education, infrastructure, or healthcare to the communities in which they operate.

- Direct involvement in creating background institutions for good governance. Companies such as Statoil in Venezuela or BP in Azerbaijan have run or sponsored programmes to train local judges or policemen in human rights and good governance. This might also include the encouragement of workers to join or found trade unions and other CSOs.

VISIT THE WEBSITE for a short response to this feature

? THINK THEORY

Reflect on the role of Western MNCs operating in oppressive regimes and countries with poor governance. What argument, based on the ethical theories in Chapter 3, can you make in favour of an obligation for MNCs to build fair background institutions in those countries?

Business as an actor in the global context (post-Westphalian setting)

At a global level, we argued earlier that corporations assume a more dominant role, while governments—bound by their confinement to territorial boundaries—have only limited influence beyond national boundaries. The central ethical problem here is that business can find it easier in less developed countries than in Western democracies to negotiate about tax levels, environmental and health and safety standards, or human rights. The result of this process is the so-called 'race to the bottom' (Rudra 2008) between developing countries, trying to attract foreign investment by offering lower and lower levels of standards (Scherer and Smid 2000).

While the general public seems to have quite generally accepted that these ethical issues exist and that the deterioration in standards is a real issue (e.g. Hertz 2001b; Korten 1995; Klein 2007), there are a several authors who contest this evidence (e.g. Rugman 2000). While some argue along the lines of decreased levels of pollution in the developing countries during the last decades (e.g. Wheeler 2001), others point to the fact that MNCs in developing countries have a positive influence on environmental standards. So, for instance, Christman and Taylor (2001) argue that MNCs in China actually improve environmental performance, since they introduce their environmental management systems (such as ISO 14000) in their Chinese subsidiaries.

While this argument in itself is only partly convincing (environmental management systems tend to be process standards rather than a performance measures) it nevertheless leads us in an interesting direction. Although governments in developing countries may be unlikely to provide 'imperative' regulation that *forces* companies into more ethical behaviour—either because they do not dare or do not care—we increasingly witness that business *itself* assumes an active role in setting up certain types of regulation. We will have a closer look at these regulatory innovations in the next section as they are very closely linked to the corporate role as a citizen in civil society.

Business–government relations in international trade regimes

Despite the general point we made that governmental power at the transnational level is rather limited, there are however a number of transnational governmental institutions that have quite a significant influence on business. These can be regional bodies, such as the European Union (EU), the North American Free Trade Agreement (NAFTA), and the Association of South East Asian Nations (ASEAN), or global players, such as the World Trade Organization (WTO) and the World Bank. The general role of these bodies is to enable trade and exchange of goods and services. For business, this can be a double-edged sword: on the one hand, these regional or global bodies may enable firms to access cheap labour, reach larger markets, and other new opportunities. At the same time, these institutions increase competition and in some ways limit business, especially those outside the respective regional space. It is therefore no surprise that the regular meetings, for instance, of the WTO, in which new regulation is discussed, are heavily lobbied by business, which often even has a direct mandate to take part in these negotiations (Woll and Artigas 2007)

Arguably, one of the most influential regional bodies is in fact the EU, as quite considerable legislative powers have been delegated from the member states to EU level. This not only concerns a lot of regulation on health, safety, and the environment, but the EU Commission is particular active in making sure that fair competition is upheld in European markets for goods and services. This becomes particularly visible in the case of mergers and acquisitions, where the EU has a legacy of forbidding many planned mergers for fear of creating monopolies in certain markets.

■ Corporate citizenship and regulation: business as key player in the regulatory game

As we have seen in this chapter, the situation for companies is that imperative regulation at the national level remains important, but has decreased in intensity, whilst transnational regulation is still limited but has intensified. These transitions, coupled with concerns about 'over-regulation' stifling business innovation, have led to a fertile debate about how to improve the rule-making process governing social and environmental issues in business.

As a result, various innovations and new styles of regulation have emerged. These innovations pose a significant challenge to corporations in terms of how they might think about the notion of corporate citizenship. Specifically, the new regulatory approach usually includes business (next to other actors) in the regulatory process itself. And because regulation is essentially about creating rules to benefit society, this inevitably involves corporations more heavily in the *governing of citizenship rights*. In Chapter 2, we likened this to a *political role* for corporations in the era of globalization.

There are a number of different labels by which this new trend in regulation is described. The most common one would be *self-regulation* (Doyle 1997), sometimes known as 'reflexive regulation' (Orts 1995). Here, the central idea is that the actors are involved in setting up the very regulation that they themselves will be subsequently affected by. A typical example here is the regulation of financial markets in the UK, which is handled by the Financial Services Authority—a self-regulating industry body rather than a government organization.

This, then, is closely related to the idea of *privatization*, since regulation is no longer a task only for public (government) actors, but also for private actors such as industry associations and CSOs (Knill and Lehmkuhl 2002; Ronit 2001). Moreover, much of this regulation is *voluntary* in that business gets involved in these regulatory processes not because they are forced to do so by government, but because they see it as being in their own self-interest (Van Calster and Deketelaere 2001). Regulation might therefore be regarded as 'softer' and more flexible, since it can adjust reasonably easily to new circumstances, issues, and actors (Martínez Lucio and Weston 2000). Accordingly, some authors have suggested that these regulatory processes allow the actors to embark on *learning legislation*, which incorporates past experiences and feeds these into the ongoing rule-making process (Wagner and Haffner 1999).

As Orts and Deketelaere (2001) point out, this innovative approach to regulation is foremost a European approach, and one that has only fairly recently been adopted in other parts of the world and, most notably, on the global level. This collaborative approach has a long tradition in Europe and is often referred to by the term *corporatism* (Molina and Rhodes 2002). In particular, then, it has been countries such as France, Germany, and the Netherlands that have been among the early adopters of this approach since the 1970s.

There are a number of reasons why these new forms of regulation have emerged. According to van Calster and Deketelaere (2001), the main goals for those trying to introduce new types of rule-making in this area are:

- **Encouragement of a pro-active approach from industry**. Industry as an addressee of regulation (and hence the one that has to adapt to it) has typically been integrated rather late into the rule-making process—if at all. This means that governmental regulation has not always offered much encouragement for business and has not usually been very enthusiastically welcomed by corporations. Self-regulation therefore has tried to encourage earlier and more pro-active engagement from industry in the rule-making process, and has tried to make more use of the market to encourage ethical behaviour.
- **Cost-effectiveness.** Another goal of self-regulation is to cut down on bureaucracy and costs by co-operating more closely with business. To give a recent example: rather than telling companies which technology to use, or to measure the emissions at every single smoke stack, the introduction of a limited amount of tradable emission certificates for a certain industry has the same result without the costly administration and compliance control (Smalley Bowen 2003).
- **Faster achievement of objectives.** The average time for a proposal to be adopted by the EU is two years, followed by another two years for transposition by the member states. One of the urges to change the regulatory process is to shorten this time lag. When engaging industry in regulation, the assumption is that the aims are attained faster since it offers a shortcut through the different institutions.

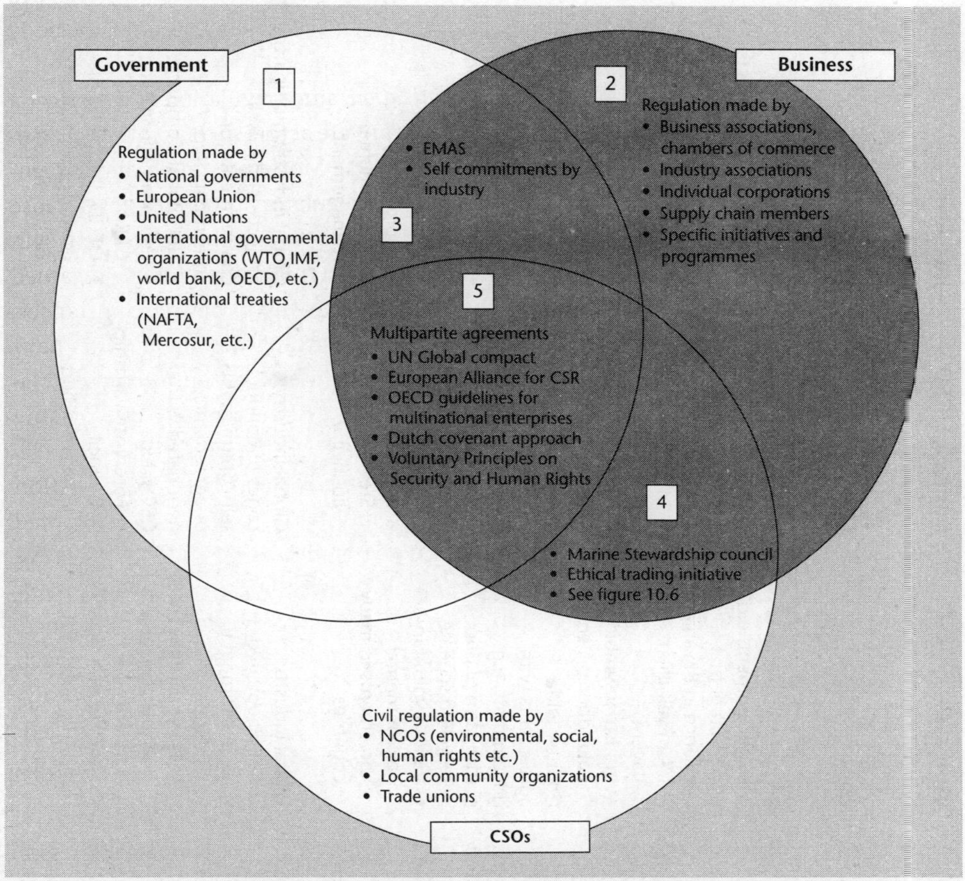

Figure 11.6. Players in the regulatory game and selected examples of private regulatory efforts

Figure 11.6 provides an overview of the changing field of regulation affecting business. It is based on Figure 10.1 in the previous chapter, which depicts the three main institutional sectors in society—government, business, and civil society. Figure 11.6 shows the relevant actors in each sector and gives some typical examples of the regulatory processes they are involved in. We have shaded the business sphere because this is the area that relates specifically to business *self-regulation*.

While this figure shows the different actors, **Figure 11.7** provides a closer view on the *combinations* of actors, and at different *levels* of regulatory behaviour. Specifically, we look at regulation that involves the following combinations:

- Government.
- Business.
- Business and government.

Regulatory actor group involved (Segment in Fig. 11.4)	**Government** (1)	**Business** (2)	**Business + Government** (3)	**Business + CSO** (4)	**Business + Government + CSO** (5)
Local/regional level	Regional 'imperative' regulation, e.g. • Anti pollution • Waste management	Codes of conduct for SMEs or local subsidiaries of corporations, etc.	Regional agreements with government, e.g. • Environmental alliance in Bavaria ("Umweltallianz Bayern) • Industrial symbiosis Kalundborg, Denmark	Regional agreements with CSOs, e.g. • Local Agenda 21 projects • Mediation projects, e.g. noise reduction at many airports	Regional multipartite agreements and projects, e.g. • Business in the Community (BITC) initiatives • Local development projects
National level	National 'imperative' regulation, e.g. • 35hr week in France • Dual waste management in Germany (Green Dot) • Closure of nuclear power stations in Sweden	Country wide self regulation, e.g. • BDI (Confederation of German Industry) commitment to reduce greenhouse gases • Financial market regulation by the FSA in UK	Country wide agreements with government, e.g. • Irish farm plastic recycling scheme • Various voluntary environmental agreements in many countries	Country wide agreements with CSOs, e.g. • Trade union agreements with business • Marine Stewardship council	Country wide multipartite agreements and projects, e.g. • Covenant for Work in Germany • Dutch covenant approach in environmental management
International/ global level	International 'imperative' regulation, e.g. • GATT • EU regulation on European works councils	Global industry codes of conduct, e.g. • Chemical industry: Responsible Care Programme, • ISO 14000 • ISO 26000	Global industry codes, negotiated with governmental organisations, e.g. • EMAS (environmental management system standard) • Sporting goods industry codes of conduct	Global industry codes of conduct, self-commitments or agreements, negotiated with CSOs, e.g. • Forest Stewardship Council • Ethical Trading Initiative	Global industry multipartite projects, codes, self-commitments, or agreements, e.g. • UN Global Compact • European Alliance for CSR • OECD, ILO codes of conduct for multinational corporations

Figure 11.7. Examples for regulatory outcomes on different levels in a multi-actor setting

- Business and civil society.
- Business, government, and civil society.

At the following levels:

- Local/regional level.
- National level.
- International/global level.

Further details on the various approaches and examples are provided in the sections following.

Governments as regulators (segment 1)

First of all, we find governmental bodies as key actors in regulation. As we indicated earlier in this chapter, imperative regulation by government is still quite widely practised. This certainly applies to *national* governments and also to *regional* legislation.

Beyond this, there is growing importance for bodies above the national level (sometimes called the 'supranational' level) such as the EU or treaty systems such as NAFTA. There is still quite some debate about the power and future of nation states but there is certainly evidence that the regulatory power of nation states, although diminished by globalization, will continue to be a significant influence on business (Taplin 2002). Figure 11.7 shows some of the recent examples where national governments in Europe have issued legislation that has had significant influence on business activities.

However, if we analyse the role of governmental organizations with global scope such as the UN or the OECD, we see that their approach to regulation gets increasingly innovative in the sense described above. There are certainly strong 'reflexive' elements, since they tend to integrate business and CSOs in their regulation. Furthermore, as these organizations lack efficient mechanisms for sanctioning non-compliance with their regulation, much of it is voluntary. Exceptions are the World Bank and the IMF (International Monetary Fund), since they have the power to either grant or withdraw considerable amounts of money to developing nations (Woods 2001), and through this, also have considerable leverage on companies doing business in these countries.

Self-regulation by business (segment 2)

In discussing the roles of various actors in the field of regulation, it is apparent that the roles of business and government have increasingly become intertwined. The amount of regulation exclusively set by government is shrinking, as is the share of regulation that is exclusively set by business.

However, at the *local* level, there are still a considerable amount of rules and norms that corporations set for themselves (and for other corporations), such as the codes of conduct introduced by small businesses, or the social and environmental rules imposed on local subsidiaries and suppliers by large corporations.

Typical examples for *national*-level efforts of self-regulation can be found in the area of environmental issues: so, for instance, in order to avoid costly and restrictive regulation in the realization of the national goals for carbon dioxide reduction, the Confederation of German Industry (BDI) committed itself to the reduction of greenhouse gasses far beyond the level originally requested by the government (Eberlein and Matten 2009). Apart from those commitments with regard to environmental goals (see further examples in ten Brink 2002), self-regulation of business practices is also very common in the financial industry (Doyle 1997) and in the area of corporate governance (see Chapter 6).

On the *global* level, there have been numerous initiatives where industry has been involved as a key actor among others. As Figure 11.7 shows, most of these global initiatives are stimulated either by CSOs and/or governments. There are, however, a few initiatives that have been driven primarily by industry and where the enforcement and implementation of regulation is primarily the responsibility of business.

The most long-standing example is probably the *Responsible Care Programme*.[13] This was initiated by the International Council of Chemical Association (ICCA), which is the global industry confederation of all major national Chemical Industry Associations. Responsible Care was begun as a response to the devastating chemical-related disasters in Bhopal, Basle, and Seveso in the 1980s, and was adopted by the ICCA in 1991. The programme prescribes in quite some detail a large array of measures, practices, and policies intended to ensure responsible management in the industry. Member firms of the industry's national associations have to adopt these measures in order to be allowed to use the Responsible Care logo. As of 2009, the chemical industry associations of 53 countries worldwide had adopted the programme, thereby making its implementation for member firms mandatory.

An equally important standard that has been developed by industry is the *ISO 14000* standard series of the International Standard Organization in Switzerland.[14] These standards basically accredit environmental management systems for business as a way of setting rules for good practice in environmental management (Gibson 1999; Stenzel 1999). This is the most widely implemented environmental standard on a global level, mainly due to the fact that many corporations, especially MNCs, specify ISO 14000 certification for their suppliers (Corbett and Kirsch 2001). There is quite a debate in the literature about the actual value of this programme, since it basically defines the nature of an environmental management system rather than ensuring actual improvements in environmental performance (Rondinelli and Vastag 2000; Stenzel 1999). The most recent initiative by ISO is the development of a new standard on corporate social responsibility, *ISO 26000*,[15] which is currently being discussed in a complex and multi-layered process of consultation with a wide array of global representatives from business, industry associations, trade unions, governments, and CSOs (Castka and Balzarova 2008). The standard is expected to be released in 2010 (see **Ethics in Action 3.2**).

In fact, where business engages in pure self-regulation such as this, the literature remains somewhat ambivalent about the likely benefits (e.g. King and Lenox 2000; Tapper 1997). These approaches seem to have worked primarily in situations where corporate self-interest would suggest these measures anyway. So, for instance, the self-commitment of the German industry to reduce carbon dioxide emissions was easy to fulfil, because large producers of these gases in East Germany were about to close down anyway in the early 1990s (Eberlein and Matten 2009).

Regulation involving business, governmental actors, and CSOs (segments 3, 4, and 5)

Voluntary environmental agreements and other regulatory approaches between business and government have become quite common tools in many countries at a regional, national, and transnational level. Increasingly, business also co-operates with CSOs in these areas, as we saw in the last chapter.

More specifically, at the *regional* level, examples include the UK business membership organization, Business in the Community, which often combines business and local civil society or government partners in local community programmes.[16] We have also already discussed regional cooperations such as the Kalundborg industrial eco-system in Denmark (pp. 430–1), which involves business collaboration with the municipal authority to develop effective resource exchange. Other typical examples of these kinds of local collaborations are 'mediation projects' (Renn et al. 1995). These are programmes that seek to develop rules to manage the social and environmental impacts of large projects such as airport extensions in densely populated areas (Sack 2001).

On the *national* level, some of the more powerful CSOs are trade unions, which often take a key role in negotiating national pay conditions and—if necessary—initiate industrial action. Several other examples have been discussed in Chapter 10 (see Figure 10.6). A specific, and in many respects unique, approach to national environmental regulation has been developed in the Netherlands. Often called the *covenant approach*, it aims to involve business, government, and other stakeholders in the specification, implementation, and monitoring of environmental regulation (Orts and Deketelaere 2001). Sometimes also referred to as the 'polder model' (after the land reclamation areas where the approach has often been used) (Glasbergen 2002), covenants focus on bringing relevant stakeholders together to find a consensus on acceptable processes and outcomes. There is some debate about the long-term success and the transferability of this approach, especially as some of the outcomes have not been overly satisfactory. There seems to be something of a trade-off between a rather smooth and quick way of regulating on the one hand, and the risk that the consensus comes with the price of watered-down standards on the other.

Finally, at the *global* level, we have seen the emergence of what David Detomasi (2007: 321) calls 'global public policy networks', whereby 'the strengths of state, market, and civil society actors combine to create an effective international governance system that overcomes the weaknesses afflicting each individually'. Typically, the main instrument used in such networks to regulate the social, ethical, and environmental impacts of business are *codes of conduct*. We have already discussed these at some length in Chapter 5, including questions of effectiveness and the plausibility of developing worthwhile global codes of ethics. Nearly all large global governmental and multi-partite organizations, such as the UN, the OECD, the ILO (International

Labour Organization), the FAO (Food and Agriculture Organization), and the WHO (World Health Organization), have issued codes intended to provide some degree of rule-setting for corporations in areas beyond the control of the nation state (Christmann and Taylor 2002; Kolk et al. 1999).

Indeed, there is such a rapidly expanding number of codes that it is hardly possible to provide a complete overview of this mushrooming field of regulation. In one study of codes relevant to MNCs, Fransen and Kolk (2007) identified almost 50 corporate responsibility standards issued over the past decade, including six from intergovernmental organizations, seven from CSOs, 14 from business associations, and a further 22 multiple-stakeholder standards. This, of course, is in addition to the hundreds of individual company codes operated by companies across the globe.

International codes of conduct are quite varied in nature and content (Simma and Heinemann 1999; Fransen and Kolk 2007). A growing number of codes focus on the institution of the *MNC*, issued either by specific corporations themselves or by other bodies, one of the most well-known being the 'OECD Guidelines for Multinational Enterprises' of 2000. Others focus on *industries or products*, such as the 'Electronics Industry Code of Conduct' issued by an industry coalition in 2004, the 'Equator Principles' in the Finance industry (see p. 272), or the 'Voluntary Principles on Security and Human Rights',[17] launched in 2000 as the result of a consultation process which involved the governments of the USA and UK, extractive and energy companies from those countries, and NGOs. Finally, some codes target certain undesired practices, such the 'UN Declaration Against Corruption and Bribery in International Commercial Transactions', developed in 1996.

As we have argued earlier in the book, the usefulness and effectiveness of codes of all varieties remain contested. Their main weakness as regulatory instruments lies in their non-mandatory, non-legally binding character. Codes do, however, provide a signal for corporations, as well as for CSOs, about what could be regarded as a consensus on ethical behaviour at a global level. Certainly, the guidelines issued by the OECD and the UN serve these purposes—and companies violating these codes can be subjected to considerable public pressure. They therefore provide a clear yardstick that corporations can refer to in order to prevent or deflect allegations of unethical conduct. However, given the proliferation of codes in the last ten years, there are recent approaches to move away from these codified attempts at global regulation towards more local, interaction-based approaches. **Ethics in Action 11.2** discusses the UN Global Compact as a more recent attempt to explore a different trajectory to fill the lack of regulatory bodies at the global level.

In the final analysis, then, it would appear that the whole area of business involvement in self-regulation is multifaceted, multi-level, and highly dynamic. That business *is* involved in regulation is clear—thereby providing support for the argument that corporations have increasingly become involved in the protection (or otherwise) of citizens' rights and interests. What remains unclear, though, is whether voluntary initiatives by corporations can ever succeed in providing suitable and sufficient protection for citizens. In the final section, we shall address this question to the specific context of sustainability.

■ Governments, business, and sustainability

Back in Chapter 1, we defined sustainability as 'the long-term maintenance of systems according to environmental, economic, and social considerations'. This definition certainly captures the broad understanding of the concept in business, politics, and wider parts of society. Reaching towards the end of the book, however, we should add that this definition by no means satisfies everybody, nor is it how it was originally thought of. Sustainability was certainly first considered a pre-eminently *ecological concept* prescribing rules and principles for the usage of natural resources in such a way which allows future generation to survive on this planet (see Pearce and Turner 1990).

The central idea of sustainability is to prescribe and implement new usage of natural resources (Turner 1993). With regard to *renewable resources*, such as wood, agricultural products, water, or air, the key principle would be not to use those resources beyond their capacity of regeneration. With *non-renewable resources*, however, such as coal, oil, minerals, metals, and other key resources of modern industry, the original rules of 'strict' sustainability would suggest that none of these resources should be used if they would put future generations at a lower level of ability to meet their needs than the present generation. In the case of metals and other recyclables, this would result in fairly strict rules for circulating these resources in the economy; with regard to oil or coal, the consequences are more severe. Since resources such as these will ultimately be depleted, we have to be extremely cautious about their use. While some have argued that sustainability does not allow their usage at all, others have proposed that we might use them only if we provide future generations with new technologies that would allow them to have the same level of welfare that we presently enjoy.

Without going into too much detail, sustainability in this sense is quite a tough and—from a business perspective—somewhat threatening concept. This applies particularly to industries that rely on non-renewable resources, such as the mining, oil, or chemical industries. There has been some research that shows that the mutation of the sustainability concept from the original ecological view towards a 'softer' concept has been particularly driven by industry. For example, Mayhew (1997) showed how the World Business Council of Sustainable Development—a key player at the Rio Summit—introduced a systematically watered-down definition of sustainable development and by this gave a new, more industry-friendly meaning to the concept. By linking sustainability not only to ecological, but also to social and economic criteria, the strict rules for using resources are loosened and the concept becomes far more open to deliberation and discretion.

Some authors, therefore, argue that the original agenda of sustainability has been 'hijacked' by industry and made less threatening and more ready to serve as a buzzword for corporate public relations (Welford 1997). Dirk Matten (1998: 8–10), for instance, showed how the German chemical industry association (VCI) introduced the industry-friendly rendition of sustainable development into its discourse through a series of conferences throughout the mid-1990s. The VCI skilfully broadened the agenda for sustainability, defining it as a 'persistent, enduring, severe, intensive, incisive and effective development'—which ultimately allows for all kinds of interpretations!

VISIT THE WEBSITE for links to useful sources of further information

ETHICS IN ACTION 11.2

The UN Global Compact: talking about global regulation

The UN has been a player in the global regulation of companies for quite some time. Though backed by national governments as an institution, the codes and regulations of the UN itself have never been able to tackle effectively the various ethical, social, and environmental problems caused by corporations, particularly in the developing world. The UN simply lacks the power, the institutional infrastructure, and the global acceptance by all national governments to be an effective 'ethics police' on a global level. Most of the regulatory efforts of the main UN agency for these issues, the UN Centre on Transnational Corporations, were not able to gain consent from all UN members. As a result, the agency was eventually closed down in 1993.

In a new attempt to address the ethical problems linked to corporate activities on a global scale, in 2000 the UN launched an initiative called 'The UN Global Compact'. Rather than pursuing the top-down approach of earlier regulatory efforts, the Global Compact starts from the bottom up by working directly with corporations. As it states on the organization's webpage, the initiative is a 'strategic platform for participants to advance their commitments to sustainability and corporate citizenship', but it is 'not designed, nor does it have the mandate or resources, to monitor or measure participants' performance'. At its inception, the Global Compact was based on nine principles; a tenth on anti-corruption was added in 2004:

- **Human Rights**

  Business is asked to:

  1 Support and respect the protection of international human rights within their sphere of influence; and

  2 Make sure their own corporations are not complicit in human rights abuses.

- **Labour**

  Business is asked to uphold:

  3 Freedom of association and the effective recognition of the right to collective bargaining;

  4 The elimination of all forms of forced and compulsory labour;

  5 The effective abolition of child labour; and

  6 The elimination of discrimination in respect of employment and occupation.

- **Environment**

  Business is asked to:

  7 Support a precautionary approach to environmental challenges;

  8 Undertake initiatives to promote greater environmental responsibility;

  9 Encourage the development and diffusion of environmentally friendly technologies.

- **Anti-Corruption**

  Business is asked to:

  10 Work against all forms of corruption, including extortion and bribery.

Companies that are willing to join have to (a) provide a letter from their CEO indicating a commitment to these ten principles; and (b) provide evidence annually of the firm's 'Communication on Progress' (COP) in implementing the principles to all stakeholders. In return, the companies are allowed to use the UN's 'We Support the Global Compact' logo for their corporate publicity.

The UN considers the Global Compact to be a facilitator of dialogue and learning between business, government, and CSOs. It achieves this by establishing *learning forums* at a global, national, and local level, as well as *policy dialogues*, for instance on the role of business in conflict zones or on business and sustainable development. Here, multi-partite participants engage in building working groups to further discuss and break down the issues on a concrete business level. Another initiative consists of *partnership projects*, where business, public sector actors, and CSOs get involved in specific projects to tackle ethical problems in business. More recently, activities have included annual reports on company progress and increased peer review of members' progress in regional learning networks.

As of 2009, the initiative has grown to more than 6,700 participants, including over 5,200 businesses in 130 countries around the world. Georg Kell, its executive director, argues that as a voluntary, facilitating initiative rather than a mandatory, imperative form of regulation, the compact has proven to be far more successful at gaining corporate 'buy-in' than any preceding initiative. The Compact, though, sees itself not as a substitute but as a network supplementing regulation at a global level.

It was this approach that initially raised considerable criticism. Several CSO groups have argued that signing up to the ten principles does not commit corporations to very much, since compliance is not monitored and defection is substantially not sanctioned. Ultimately, the critics see the Global Compact as a cheap 'bluewash' for corporations (meaning they cover up or 'wash' their problems with the blue of the UN flag), and a rather naïve approach to globalization that ignores the compelling economic rationalities of liberalized world markets.

Meanwhile, after becoming the largest such initiative in the world in terms of membership, the Global Compact has implemented a more formal structure of self-governance, including a board with representatives from business, civil society, labour, and the United Nations. The initiative also sought to bolster its integrity by firming up the rules of membership and ensuring that failure to provide a COP would result in a non-communicating or inactive status for participants, and possibly a de-listing. In order to address the rather problematic funding situation, in 2006 the Compact set up a foundation with the goal of raising $1m annually from members to fund tool development for companies and to strengthen local networks, in particularly in developing countries (50% of the members are from non-OECD countries).

The relative success of the Global Compact in engaging with business has led to the emergence of more focused sector initiatives from the UN that apply a similar strategy. Realizing the importance of financial markets in pushing responsible corporate behaviour, the 'UN Principles for Responsible Investment' were launched in April 2006 (see p. 272). The latest offshoot is the 'UN Principles of Responsible Management Education' (PRME), which was launched in 2007. This is a set of six principles that business schools should follow in their education of future business leaders. In its first two years of operation, around 250 business schools in more than 50 countries had signed up to PRME.

Sources

McIntosh, M., Waddock, H., and Kell, G. (eds.) 2004. *Learning to talk: corporate citizenship and the development of the UN Global Compact*. Sheffield: Greenleaf.

Monbiot, G. 2000. Getting into bed with business: the UN is no longer just a joke. *Guardian*, 31 Aug.: 18.

Rasche, A. and G. Kell (eds.) 2010. *The United Nations Global Compact: achievements, trends and challenges*. Cambridge: Cambridge University Press.

Willamson, H. 2003. Signing up to corporate citizenship. *Financial Times*, 12 Feb.: 12.

UN Global Compact website: http://www.unglobalcompact.org.

Principles for Responsible Management Education website: http://www.unprme.org.

VISIT THE WEBSITE for a short response to this feature

? THINK THEORY

Relate the UN global compact to the concepts of business–society relations, as outlined in Chapter 2. Where does the global compact fit into these concepts? Which areas does it not cover? By using these concepts, try to give a critical assessment of the future potential and chances of the global compact.

Given this more or less subtle resistance of industry to sustainability, it is no wonder that the strongest impulse towards regulating for sustainability has come from governments. Mainly as a result of the Rio Summit in 1992 (the forerunner to the 2002 Johannesburg Summit), the industrialized world witnessed an avalanche of legislation in the 1990s aimed at tightening environmental standards for industry. The central ethical debate here focuses on the question of whether governments need to address sustainability primarily by imperative regulation or if voluntary, market-based approaches provide the more efficient and fair outcomes in pursuit of a more sustainable economy. We will illustrate these aspects by analysing the role of business and governments in the area of climate change and in the area of commodity management with regard to food security.

Global climate change legislation and business responses: support versus obstruction

One of the key political arenas of sustainability has been the debate on the regulation of global climate change (Begg, van der Woerd, and Levy 2005; Levy and Newell 2005). As early as 1992, global warming and changes in the global climate were centre stage at the Rio Summit. Levy and Egan (2000) suggest that by this time, the World Business Council of Sustainable Development (a coalition of 160 international companies) had already subtly lobbied against any concrete measures to be implemented on a global level. However, as the political debate moved on, the Kyoto Protocol was ultimately signed in 1997 by nearly 200 countries. The protocol foresaw significant reductions by 2012 in the emission of greenhouse gases, most notably carbon dioxide. In 2009, the Kyoto process was followed up by the Copenhagen Climate Change Summit, which aimed to reach an agreement on policies for the period after 2012.

Reductions in carbon dioxide, however, represent a severe threat for some industries. Kolk and Levy (2001) illustrate that among the fiercest opponents of imperative regulation was the oil industry, which is fundamentally implicated in greenhouse gas emissions through the burning of fossil fuels. As a result, the industry founded the Global Climate Coalition (GCC) in 1989 in order to lobby against governmental regulation to cut back on greenhouse gas emissions. Depending on the home country context, however, companies have subsequently followed rather different trajectories (Eberlein and Matten 2009; Kolk and Pinske 2007).

Counted as among the main members of the GCC were the American companies ExxonMobil and Texaco, as well as the European companies BP and Shell, which left the GCC in 1996 and 1998, respectively. Despite their industry's profound scepticism towards regulating against greenhouse emissions, both European companies had to face the fact that their governments, and most notably the EU, were bound to implement Kyoto at some stage. Moreover, they faced considerable stakeholder pressure from CSOs and others to step back from the obstructive position of the GCC. This constructive engagement of industry towards climate change in Europe has hitherto gained further momentum. In 2005, the EU introduced the EU Green House Gas Emission Trading Scheme (EU ETS) in order to reach the goals of the Kyoto treatment and European companies were heavily involved in lobbying efforts to shape the regulation. The EU ETS, on the one hand, represents one of the strictest approaches to managing climate emissions globally. On the other hand, it uses a market mechanism to reach these targets and leaves considerable freedom to business as to how exactly they want to address the issue.

The strategy of the companies in Canada, the US, and Australia has been quite different, since they saw considerable mileage in lobbying their governments to refrain from implementing climate protection legislation. ExxonMobil placed advocacy advertisements in the US press that questioned the 'uncertain' science of global warming, warned that regulation would 'restrict life itself', and argued that technological innovation and the market could meet any 'potential risks' of climate change (Livesey 2002). One of the first acts of the Bush administration was to pull the US out of the Kyoto agreement and the policies of the State Department on climate change in the early 2000s were directly based on the position of the GCC (Kolk and Pinske 2007).

With the publication by the UK Treasury of the Stern Report (2006), which documented the severe economic impacts of climate change, as well as the general shift in attitude on climate change by new governments in the US and Australia in 2008, the resistance seemed to have softened. A growing number of companies have understood that measures to tackle climate change will be inevitable and that they might as well be part of the process as opposed to resisting the inevitable. This is accompanied by the fact that implementation of climate change policies has given rise to new business opportunities, for example in solar and wind technologies, or alternative ways of powering cars, as the success of hybrid vehicles has shown.

Achieving sustainability: securing the global supply of food and water

Another area of concern for governments in many countries, developed and developing nation alike, is the conservation of a sustainable livelihood for its citizens. Among the key challenges here are the conservation of freshwater resources and the issue of food security. In both areas, business plays a key role which has given rise to a number of ethical concerns.

An initial issue arising in the 1970s and 1980s in the industrialized world was the increasing water pollution caused by business, most notably the chemical industry. While these issues have been more or less successfully addressed through increased regulation and oversight, water pollution remains a major concern in rapidly industrialized countries such as China or India.

A more recent ethical debate has concerned the privatization of water management and supply in many countries across the world (see also case 2). The most spectacular example of the ethical challenges of water privatization can be found in Bolivia (Spronk 2007). As many state-owned water suppliers in developing countries are challenged with corruption issues, efficiency problems, and poor quality service, the World Bank has typically pushed countries towards privatization of the water supply. When Bolivian water was privatized in the early 2000s, American and French MNCs took over, and began charging high fees or else refused to connect to the grid neighbourhoods that could not afford to pay. When, as part of their supply-chain management, the companies successfully lobbied the government to outlaw the use of rainwater, this led to violent protests and, ultimately, a change of government in the country. Similar cases have also been reported from the developed world (Whitford and Clark 2007) and it highlights that corporations, in taking over these crucial services, end up embroiled in the administration of a fundamental human right, which in the absence of effective governmental oversight, imposes new and different responsibilities on them. Potential solutions to the problem seem to lie in novel, tripartite community enterprises, where Western MNCs bring capital and know-how and local governments and CSO provide the infrastructure and human capital (Nwankwo et al. 2007).

In addition to water, with well over 6 billion people on the planet, the issue of food security is also becoming a growing sustainability concern for governments world wide.

Together with the depletion of key resources such as fish stocks, and the increasing proliferation of toxic chemicals such as DDT in the food chain, the issue is thought to be one of the major political challenges for the future. Again, the corporate sector plays a key role here, as most elements of the global supply chains for food are run by private corporations.

A major issue which has put substantial strain on poorer countries is the volatility of global commodity markets for wheat and rice (Dorosh 2008). This has been exacerbated by another sustainability issue, namely the rise of biofuels to substitute for fossil fuels. While the experts are divided on whether biofuels present a genuine threat to food security (McNeely et al. 2009), it is obvious that a good many of the decisions on these issues will have to be taken by private corporations, even if governments continue to play a role in setting the parameters and constraints on addressing these ethical issues.

■ Summary

In this chapter, we have looked in some depth at the stake held by government in business, and set out how the role of government, and its central task of issuing regulation for business, affects this stakeholder relationship. We have seen that 'government' today is quite a complex set of actors and institutions that act on various levels, from local or regional level to a transnational or even global stage.

During the course of the chapter, we have discussed the complex role of governments and the interdependencies and mutual interests that they have with business. As an actor that is primarily obliged to pursue the interest of the electorate, or society, the dominant ethical challenges in business–government relations are the issues of legitimacy and accountability. This particularly focuses on the question of how much influence business should be allowed on governmental actors, and by what means this influence is enacted. We discussed various forms of business intervention in governmental decision-making, from lobbying, to party financing, up to far stronger forms of state capture and corruption.

We then had a closer look at the way globalization shifts the roles of business and government in regulating issues of relevance to business ethics. We discussed the notion of the 'post-Westphalian' context, which conceptualizes the impact of globalization on the power of nation-state governments to shape business behaviour. We linked these shifts particularly to the new role of corporations as active players in the regulatory game, and discussed the various options and innovations in regulation open to business and other players. We concluded that in terms of corporate citizenship, business was actually placed in a *political* role that in certain respects, was akin to that of governments. We qualified this new role, though, when analysing the role of government in initiating sustainable practices in business. While business is a key player in governments' attempts to implement sustainable development business, short-term interests may often hamper these initiatives, as we have seen particularly in the area of climate change regulation.

Study questions

1. What is regulation? What does it mean to say that actors other than government engage in regulation?
2. Explain the two basic roles of government that determine its stakeholder relationship with corporations.
3. What are the potential ethical problems associated with corporate lobbying of government?
4. 'Corporations should never do business with authoritarian or oppressive regimes. It is simply beyond the boundaries of ethical acceptability.' Critically examine this argument, outlining practical ways in which business can make decisions about which countries to do business in.
5. Why have corporations been increasingly involved in setting regulation for social and environmental issues and what are the main ethical challenges associated with their involvement?
6. Are strong governments necessary to achieve an effective response to climate change? Explain using examples from contemporary business practice.

Research exercise

Conduct some research on the responsible care programme of the chemical industry (http://www.icca-chem.org).

1. Explain the main details of the programme.
2. To what extent is the programme illustrative of self-regulation?
3. What are the advantages and disadvantages of self-regulation compared to government regulation for ensuring ethical conduct in the chemical industry?
4. Would you say the programme is likely to be sufficient to ensure ethical conduct in the chemical industry? If not, what else is necessary?

Key readings

VISIT THE WEBSITE for links to further key readings

1. **Detomasi, D. A. 2007. The multinational corporation and global governance: modeling global public policy networks. *Journal of Business Ethics*, 71: 321–34.**

   This article provides a concise overview and conceptualization of the role of private business in many regulatory processes. It maps out the important players in global regulatory arenas and provides an evaluation of the strengths and weaknesses of each of them and how collaboration between players can improve the outcome of global business regulation.

2. **Fransen, L.W. and Kolk, A. 2007. Global Rule-Setting For Business: A Critical Analysis Of Multi-Stakeholder Standards. *Organization*, 14 (5): 667–84.**

   A useful companion piece to the first selection, this article sets out some of the different types of standards used in setting rules for global business and examines, in particular, the supposed benefits of multiple stakeholder initiatives in terms of membership, governance, and implementation. It offers a helpful and quite critical comparison of multiple stakeholder codes against other types of standards, using evidence from a comprehensive inventory of codes developed over the past decade.

Case 11

Dispensing 'the less orthodox inducements'—BAE Systems and the global defence industry

VISIT THE WEBSITE for links to useful sources of further information

This case is concerned with a series of major scandals that have rocked the defence industry, most notably concerning the UK company, BAE Systems. The case discusses the company's dealings with governments across the world, and examines the specific ethical challenges of the global defence industry. The case provides the opportunity to examine the ethics of close business–government relations, and offers the chance to explore the difficulty of changing long-standing patterns of interaction between business and government.

Luxury cars, posh hotels, lavish parties, prostitutes, secret agents, and corrupt officials—if the media reports around UK defence technology company, BAE Systems, and its long-standing business relations with Saudi Arabia are anything to go by, the recent history of the firm has all the ingredients of a Hollywood blockbuster. But this is no movie. Critics contend that between 2002 and 2004 gifts and payments worth more than £60m were paid to members of the Saudi royal family, £17m alone to the key Saudi arms purchaser, Prince Turky bin Nasser, funding a global jet-setter's lifestyle for him, his family, and his 35-strong entourage of servants, drivers, and bodyguards.

The money was allegedly paid to secure the latest instalment in the 'Al Yamamah' (The Dove) project, which, according to former BAE chair Sir Richard Evans, has provided BAE with no less than £43bn of revenue since 1986. The project started shortly after the US Congress had banned arms exports to Saudi Arabia by US firms, leaving a large chunk of the global arms market to competitors. It is said to have kept BAE afloat in the 1990s, at a time when, after the fall of the iron curtain, the defence expenditure of most governments slumped considerably. Investigators, however, have calculated that more than £6bn may have been distributed over a 20-year span in corrupt commissions to secure the Al Yamamah deals. The interest in this case shown by prosecutors, the media, and NGOs is not just fuelled by the magnitude of the alleged payments, but also by the conspicuous role of the British government in the scandal.

Furthermore, the Al Yamamah scandal is only one of many allegations BAE has faced over the years. Allegedly, the company has tried to sell electric-shock batons fit for torturing to Saudi Arabia; delivered fighter planes to Indonesia that were subsequently used to oppress freedom fighters in East Timor; and secured deals with widely criticized regimes in Zimbabwe and Tanzania. Even in 2008, the company was still being subjected to new revelations about supposed illicit payments. According to a police document leaked to the UK's *Guardian* newspaper, the company secretly paid more than £100m on 'financially incentivising' South African politicians to purchase a controversial fleet of warplanes, at a time when the country was in the grip of crippling unemployment and an AIDS epidemic.

The defence industry and business–government relations

To understand the nature of alleged corruption in cases such as the BAE Al Yamamah deals, it is helpful to look at the peculiarities of the defence industry, most notably the close relationships that defence companies need to nurture with governments. Looking at the *demand side* of the market, not only does the industry nearly exclusively sell to governments, in most countries the parliament also has to agree the level of spending and often even the type of equipment that should be bought. Furthermore, governments often demand offset deals from defence companies, asking them to produce some part of the equipment domestically in order to secure employment and some benefits for the respective local economy. For instance, it was reported that BAE was able to secure a £1.5bn deal in South Africa in 1999 because it offered the best local offset deal to the government.

On the *supply side*, again governments of the arms-exporting countries are deeply involved. The UK, which is the world's second largest arms exporter, has a special unit in the government department for UK Trade and Investment to promote its defence companies, the Defence Export Services Organization (DESO). Most deals also involve the government's Export Credits Guarantee Department (ECGD) to secure loans and provide payment guarantees to exporters. Furthermore, with tens of thousands of UK jobs being provided by the defence sector, securing employment is often a strong driver in governmental support for its domestic arms industry. The development of new defence systems increasingly involves international co-operation—BAE has customers and partners in over a hundred countries—which again involves governmental consent and support in an area of potential concern to national security. As a result, relations between defence companies and their home governments are close and unsurprisingly, BAE chair Evans was known to be one of the few businessmen who could see the prime minister on request.

Given this context, it is perhaps not surprising that the defence industry has maintained its claim to notoriety for being a hotbed for all sorts of ethical dilemmas and controversies. A limited number of very powerful buyers (mostly governments) and a limited numbers of competitors (often co-operating with each other in at least some area of their business) have led to a situation where we cannot really talk of a 'free' market. Many deals rely on long-term business relationships and strong personal relations, such that the arms industry is 'a bit like a cottage industry' where 'everybody knows everyone else and everything is connected', as BAE chair Evans was once quoted.

There are other reasons too why the defence industry has had a chequered ethical history. Given the sensitivities around security issues, most deals are concluded in secret. Moreover, the number of contracts is relatively few, but almost always of a very high value, making every transaction a major business-critical event. Such dynamics also make it relatively easy to hide commissions and other payments. As a result, it comes as little surprise that the industry, though only accounting for 1% of global trade, accounts for about half of all bribes paid globally, according to an estimate by the US Department of Commerce.

The mechanics of corruption in the defence industry typically follow a common pattern. Companies looking to bribe public officials will often use local agents and front companies to dispense 'the less orthodox inducements', as one industry executive termed them. These are often recorded as 'commissions', 'marketing services', and other terms, and are usually financed by slush funds or simple overcharging on the contracts. In the Al Yamamah deal, for instance, payments were reportedly made through a complex web of front companies, including BAE's man in Saudi-Arabia (a former Royal Air Force wing commander), the agency 'Travellers World Ltd.', and another BAE company, Robert Lee International. Rather than handing out cash directly, these agencies are supposed to have picked up the royal Saudi family's fairy-tale bills for shopping sprees, presidential suites in the world's finest hotels, Rolls-Royces, Aston-Martins, and private jets—to name just some of the key items. According to investigative journalists, the cash for all these payoffs came from overcharging—a supposition supported by accidentally released UK documents which reveal that the basic price of the planes was inflated by 32%, to allow for an initial £600m in commissions.

The UK government's anti-corruption efforts target BAE

Despite the obviously close relationships between the government and defence companies, corruption is also a major issue for governments to deal with. In the 2000s, the UK government sought to strengthen its anti-corruption efforts. This led to the introduction of new anti-bribery regulations in 2001, which made it illegal for UK companies to pay bribes. However, despite the tougher regulatory stance, the Serious Fraud Office (SFO), which investigates bribery claims, received no additional budget from the government, and to date has failed to bring a single prosecution to court for bribery. Finally, in 2006, the UK government gave the issue greater attention by setting up an 'anti-corruption squad', with a mooted £1m annual budget.

One of the key investigations of the SFO over the past decade has been the allegations of corruption at BAE, in particular the deals with Saudi Arabia. A full-scale investigation was launched in 2003 and according to media reports, by 2006 the organization had spent around £2m investigating BAE and was making 'excellent progress'. However, in December 2006, with the SFO on the brink of accessing key Swiss bank accounts involved in the alleged payments, the UK government forced a sudden reversal and pressured the SFO into dropping the investigation completely. Claiming that the 'wider public interest ... outweighed the need to maintain the rule of law', the government's dramatic intervention was defended on the grounds of 'national security'. Among the reasons given were that the Saudi government had threatened to stop sharing intelligence with British authorities about Al-Qaida terrorist activities if the investigations continued. According to the UK prime minister, this meant that British lives could be at risk unless the case was dropped. The Saudis were also alleged to have threatened to pull out of the next stage of Al Yamamah, worth another £6bn to BAE, and offer it to a French defence rival—a prospect which had prompted frantic lobbying from BAE in efforts to halt the SFO inquiry.

The decision by the government to close down the investigations brought fierce criticism from anti-corruption campaigners and prompted a strong rebuke from the OECD. However, following a judicial review, the tide appeared to be turning against BAE again when the decision to shut down the investigation was judged 'unlawful' by the high court in April 2008—only for the ruling to be overturned by the House of Lords three months later.

BAE seeks to rebuild its tarnished image

Despite their successes in having the SFO inquiry stopped, BAE emerged from the affair with a severely tarnished reputation, and a number of critical ethical challenges ahead. Having been rather hostile towards its critics in the past, the company began to adopt a somewhat more conciliatory approach in the late 2000s. Most notably, the company hired the former chief justice Lord Woolf to head a committee to review the company's ethical conduct. His report, published in May 2008, confirmed that BAE's leaders 'acknowledged that the company did not in the past pay sufficient attention to ethical standards and avoid activities that had the potential to give rise to reputational damage'. He also reported that the firm had 'a greater culture of secrecy ... than is necessary or desirable'. Although criticized in some quarters for bypassing judgement on BAE's past corruption scandals, Woolf proposed 23 recommendations for enhancing business ethics at the company, which it is committed to implementing by 2011.

By summer 2009, four of the 23 points had been addressed, including the appointment of a managing director for corporate responsibility, the implementation of a global code of conduct, a more robust system of vetting external agents, and an externally assured corporate responsibility report. To make this happen, 60 executive staff had been seconded to work at least part time on implementing Woolf's recommendations.

According to the newly appointed corporate responsibility officer, though, the next step appears to be the toughest: to address the root of corruption by changing the firm's business model. Rather than working with local agents—who often are the linchpin of corruption—BAE wants to cut out the middleman altogether. This would imply that a significant part of its operations in engineering, manufacturing, and sales would need to be moved to countries with whose governments BAE would then be able to deal directly.

Whether such radical changes will be realistic to implement remains to be seen. There are certainly encouraging examples: BAE's main US rivals, Boeing and Lockheed Martin, which had similar scandals decades ago, today count among the models of ethics and compliance practice. For BAE though, the legacy of the past may be even harder to escape. With corruption investigations under way in several countries, including the US and Austria, the truth or otherwise about the firm's 'less orthodox inducements' may still come to light.

Questions

1 What types of business–government relations are alluded to in this case? Identify the key factors in business–government relations that make the defence industry particularly vulnerable to ethical misconduct.

2 Identify the main stakeholders in this case and describe the key ethical dilemmas faced by each of the different actors involved.

3 To what extent can BAE be blamed for its part in the alleged bribery, or are the UK and Saudi governments ultimately more responsible for any wrongdoing?

4 Describe and evaluate the efforts by BAE and the UK government to address the problem of corruption

5 If you were hired by BAE to advise on its ethical challenges, what would your recommendations be?

Sources

Leigh, D. 2006. Specialist police to tackle graft overseas. *Guardian*, 23 June.
Lilley, S. 2003. BAE System's Dirty Dealings. *Corporate Watch*, 11 Nov.: http://www.corpwatch.org.
Russell, J. 2009. A call to arms. *Ethical Corporation*, July/August: 35–6.
The Economist. 2002. Odd industry out. *The Economist*, 20 July.
The *Guardian's* 'BAE files': http://www.guardian.co.uk/world/bae.

Notes

1 Unless we explicitly state otherwise, it should be noted that we chiefly talk about democratic political systems with some form of parliamentary representation.
2 Public affairs is not to be confused with PR (public relations), which is primarily a promotional activity for the corporation. In contrast, public affairs usually focuses on the management of government and community relations more broadly. This may well include PR, but public affairs is distinguished by its focus on government relations. See Carroll and Buchholtz (2008: 153–86).
3 Source: Center for Responsive Politics, http://www.opensecrets.org/lobbyists/ (accessed 26 Aug. 2008).
4 European Parliament Draft Report 2007/2115(INI).
5 Osborn, A. and Gentleman, A. 2003. Secret French move to block animal-testing ban. *Guardian*, 19 Aug.: http://www.guardian.co.uk.
6 Ott, K. 2006. Staatsanwaltschaft ermittelt wegen verschenkter WM-Tickets. *Süddeutsche Zeitung*, 8 May.
7 See their Code of Conduct at http://www.bp.com.
8 Tieman, R. 2006. Crisis exposes crippling cronyism at heart of the French state. *Observer*, 25 June.
9 Jones, G. 2002. Conflicts continue: pressure mounts on prime minister to sell his TV stations. *Financial Times*, 22 July: 4.
10 See Hooper, J. 2009. Berlusconi declares war on European media over sex scandal reports. *Guardian*, 28 Aug.: http://www.guardian.co.uk; Walters, B. 2009. TV network's attempt to stifle Silvio Berlusconi documentary backfires. *Guardian*, 3 Sept.: http://www.guardian.co.uk.
11 See http://www.transparency.org.
12 *Guardian*. 2003. Fiascos that haunt 'can do' company. *Guardian*, 15 Feb.: 13.
13 For more details, go to the website of the initiative: http://www.responsiblecare.org.
14 For more details, go to the website of the initiative: http://www.iso.org.
15 ibid.
16 For more details, see the Buiness in the Community website: http://www.bitc.org.uk.
17 See http://www.voluntaryprinciples.org.

12

Conclusions and Future Perspectives

In this chapter we will:

- Reiterate the role, meaning, and importance of business ethics.
- Summarize the influence of globalization on business ethics.
- Assess the value of the notion of sustainability.
- Discuss the role and significance of stakeholders as a whole for ethical management.
- Review the implications of corporate citizenship thinking for business ethics.
- Summarize the contribution of normative ethical theories to business ethics.
- Consider the benefits of thinking about ethical decision-making.
- Assess the role of specific tools for managing business ethics.

■ Introduction

We hope by now that you have a pretty good idea of what business ethics is all about, and what some of the main issues, controversies, concepts, and theories are that make business ethics such a fascinating subject to study. There is always a danger, though, that in reading a book such as this, you are left at the end thinking something like: 'fine, each individual chapter makes sense, but how does it all fit together?' In this last chapter, we will therefore attempt to remedy this by setting out a brief overview of the key topics of the book, and providing a round-up of our discussions during the preceding 11 chapters. We will in particular return to the subjects introduced in Part A of the book—such as globalization, sustainability, stakeholder theory, corporate citizenship, ethical theory, and management tools, etc.—and summarize how we have applied, developed, examined, and critiqued them in the context of individual stakeholders in Part B of the book. This final chapter should therefore help you to apply an overall perspective to your revision of the book.

■ The nature and scope of business ethics

By now you should be quite aware that the simple question of 'what is business ethics?' does not exactly lend itself to a simple answer. In Chapter 1, we defined the subject of business ethics as 'the study of business situations, activities, and decisions where issues of right and wrong are addressed'. Clearly, the range of such situations, activities, and decisions here is immense. We have certainly discussed most of the main ones, but existing problems sometimes go away, or become more a matter of legislation, and new problems continue to arise, either because of new technologies, changes in business practices or markets, exposure to different cultures, changing expectations, or simply the arising of new opportunities for ethical abuse. Consequently, it is never possible to determine the exact extent of the business ethics subject—and nor indeed should it be.

The question of business ethics and the law that we first introduced in Chapter 1 has been substantially expanded upon throughout the book. In particular, we would like to reiterate the importance of seeing business ethics as largely, but by no means exclusively, starting where the law ends. We have actually showed this relation to be an increasingly complex one, with corporations sometimes supplementing or replacing the law-making process with self-regulation, and sometimes challenging, resisting, and subverting legalistic approaches to enforcing ethical behaviour. Whichever way we look at it then, the relationship between business ethics and the law would appear to be an area of continued change and evolution in the years to come. This, if anything, is likely to make the whole issue of business ethics even more important, particularly given the increasing scope for international businesses to act in a range of contexts where state influence over ethical behaviour is limited or on the wane.

■ Globalization as a context for business ethics

One of the main subjects covered in Chapter 1 was the context for business ethics provided by globalization. We quite carefully worked towards a definition of the 'G-word' at the beginning of the book—and the subsequent chapters vividly illustrated that 'deterritorialized' economic, social, and political activities dramatically reshape the role and context of business ethics. As we particularly emphasized in each of the stakeholder chapters in Part B, globalization results in a very specific demand for innovation in all firm–stakeholder relations.

The first aspect of globalization is that much corporate activity takes place in multiple national contexts. We have explained how shareholders, employees, consumers, suppliers, competitors, CSOs, and governments might all conceivably be located in other continents. This, as we said in Chapter 1, typically exposes companies to different *cultural* and *legal* environments that leave considerable discretion to managers in determining and upholding ethical standards. A particular focus for us in discussing the consequences of globalization has therefore been on emerging economies, such as China and India, which have attracted such a major proportion of global trade, and developing countries, where some of the effects of unethical practice can be most extreme. Throughout the book, we have quite extensively discussed ethical issues in the context of emerging and developing economies, and it is fairly reasonable to expect them to remain towards the top of the business ethics agenda for the foreseeable future.

On a second level, we suggested at the outset that globalization creates a social space beyond the governing influence of single nation states. We particularly reiterated this in the context of global financial markets in Chapter 6 and the global regulation of corporations in Chapters 10 and 11. For many business ethics problems, no single nation state is able to regulate and control corporate actors, especially in contexts such as global financial markets. We have argued that a firmer governmental grip on such spaces is somewhat unlikely to happen in the near future. We also revealed and explored some of the mechanisms that lead to a situation where many other corporate activities escape the direct control of nation states. This 'transnational space' creates an interesting arena where corporate actors appear to currently dominate the scene. This does not mean that ethical norms are not present here, but these spaces lack governmental authorities to organize and control corporate action. We have, especially in Chapters 10 and 11, discussed ways of filling this gap, by self-regulation, or by selected initiatives of global CSOs, or even by initiatives driven by the UN. The latter arena, however, still leaves ample space for corporations, and further challenges them from an ethical point of view. The initiatives discussed in the book, and even more so their limits, show that there still remains much to be desired in terms of the global regulation and enforcement of business ethics. This, again, will no doubt be an area of increasing activity and interest in the future.

■ Sustainability as a goal for business ethics

The next major issue we raised in Chapter 1 was that of sustainability as a goal for business ethics. Throughout the chapters of the second half of the book, we discussed the nature of this goal, its challenges, and suggested some of the steps that corporations might take in order to enhance sustainability in the context of different stakeholder relations. We have found that in different contexts, contributions can be made in the different 'corners', as it were, of the sustainability triangle (see Figure 1.9, p. 33), as well as in providing a more even balancing of the triple bottom line of sustainability. Initial, but significant, progress in sustainability reporting, sustainability share indexes, industrial ecosystems, product recapture, and civil and intergovernmental regulation has been made, and bodes reasonably well for the future.

However one looks at it, though, the challenge posed by sustainability for business ethics is a huge one. Appropriate balancing of the triple bottom line is extremely difficult to engineer, even when (as is quite rare) corporations have the will to attempt it. Some of our discussions around sustainability in the area of employees, consumers, suppliers, etc. have been quite speculative and potentially threatening to existing corporate ways of thinking, organizing, and behaving. Ultimately, sustainability implies goals that lie beyond the time horizons of business, and which might be thought to jeopardize traditional bottom line goals. Progress towards sustainable solutions therefore appears to be possible, but slow, tentative, and at present, often merely exploratory.

What remains to be said, then, of the goal of sustainability? Our reflections in Chapter 11 have already been rather critical on the role of corporations in the sustainability area. This leaves us to reiterate two main conclusions. First, the triple bottom line definition of sustainability obfuscates the fact that corporations tend to focus primarily on *economic* aspects, and even the majority of those actors pressing for greater sustainability tend to mainly emphasize *environmental* dimensions, at the expense of *social* interests. There is often a trade-off between the different elements, and in the context of developing countries especially, many of those likely to be affected lack sufficient power and influence to have their interests effectively heard and represented.

Secondly, without strong governments issuing legislation and/or developing new institutional arrangements (such as carbon markets), business progress is unlikely to be sufficient to meet sustainability goals. As much as we have identified the eroding effects of globalization and increasing corporate power on governmental authority, sustainability is likely to demand that governmental actors—perhaps in concert with CSOs and corporations—retain a significant degree of influence over the globalizing economy.

■ Corporate citizenship and business ethics

Back in Chapter 2, we also introduced the concept of corporate citizenship (CC) as the latest step in a number of developments in conceptual frameworks for ethical behaviour in business. Indeed, the subtitle of this book suggests that much of the content is about how to manage CC in an era of globalization. When first talking about the concept, two major points were evident. On the one side, CC in the 'extended' view identifies the corporate involvement in the governance of *citizenship rights*, most notably social, civil, and political rights. On the other hand, we have reiterated throughout the book that alongside this role, the question of accountability automatically surfaces. We have discussed these issues throughout the book, especially in Part B, raising a number of serious issues for consideration.

With regard to the first claim—that corporations take up the governing of citizenship—Chapters 6 to 11 have provided a convincing, though nonetheless varied, impression. When discussing the relationship to shareholders, we identified quite a substantial influence of corporations over civil rights, most notably the right to property of this constituency. We then made an extensive survey of the various rights corporations have to govern for their employees, many of which touched on their social and civil rights.

In the area of consumers and CSOs, corporations often provide a channel through which the public expresses its political choices rather than going to the ballot box. Corporate involvement in lobbying, as well as self-regulation and voluntary codes of conduct, further underlines their role in areas of politics traditionally occupied predominantly by governments.

In the context of competitors and suppliers, corporations might like to use practices that ultimately focus on infringing or circumventing the mechanisms of the market. In so doing, they can determine prices and the range of choices that we as citizens ultimately have. Corporations, in this area, assume some responsibility over the way markets operate and remain functioning. Large corporations, in particular, have significant influence over their suppliers, and through this, can dictate the way in which products are manufactured. If a large corporation requires certain ethical standards from its suppliers, such as environmental quality or human rights protections, they have considerable power to shape the manner in which the entitlements of third parties are actually enacted.

On the side of accountability, the picture developed over the previous 11 chapters of this book is not so very bright. We have identified considerable power on the part of shareholders through their right to vote and initiate shareholder activism. In some forms of governance, such as is found in continental Europe, or in worker co-operatives, employees too can exert a reasonable amount of influence on corporations. Such 'industrial democracy' (Engelen 2002), however, tends to remain limited to the rather narrow scope of societal interest that is closely linked to the interest of the corporation as a whole.

Consumers too have some, albeit quite limited, influence on corporations, since their approval or disapproval of the company's stance on certain ethical issues can be expressed through the market. But certainly, the most direct control of corporations in this respect requires the involvement of CSOs and formal campaigns of action. Indeed, it is exactly this sector that will probably play a central role in holding corporations accountable for the way in which they participate in society in the future. Nonetheless, the lack of accountability and legitimacy of CSOs themselves arguably remains one of the weaker foundations of CSOs' power to act as proxies for citizens.

Consequently, the relation between companies and governments seems to be the most problematic one. It is apparent that under-resourced governments have ceded some influence and power to corporations—even in terms of their own party funding—but recent events have suggested something of a revitalization of the governmental role. If anything, our discussions highlight the major gap between the influence of corporations on citizenship rights and the subsequent control and accountability issues involved for citizens. Throughout the book, we clearly identify this institutional void; however, we also show some potential ways in which each stakeholder group can use existing links in order to fill this gap.

The contribution of normative ethical theories to business ethics

In Chapter 3, we introduced normative ethical theories, suggesting that in a pluralistic perspective, they can provide a number of important considerations for ethical decision-making in business. In so doing, we had already watered down a little the inherent claim of traditional ethical theories—that they provide codified rational solutions to every problem. Indeed, as you have progressed through the book, it should have become extremely clear that these theories rarely provide us with a clear-cut, unambiguous, and non-controversial solution. As such, this book could be argued to be closer to a postmodern perspective than anything else: ethical theories are at best tools to inform the 'moral sentiment' of the decision-maker and as such cannot predetermine solutions from an abstract, theoretical, or wholly 'objective' point of view. Ultimately, ethical decisions are taken by actors in everyday business situations. Ethical theories might help to structure and rationalize some of the key aspects of those decisions, but their status never can be one that allows a moral judgement or decision to be made without effectively immersing in the real situation. This is one of the key reasons that we introduced the Ethics on Screen and Ethics Online features into recent editions of the text since the medium of film and the interactive potential of the web allow us to immerse ourselves into 'real life' situations and, as it were, live the reality of ethical decision-making in business.

By positioning the role of ethical theory on this level, we by no means intend to play down the role of normative ethical theory though (as a postmodernist would). These theories first of all help the individual actor to rationalize moral sentiments, and to verbalize moral considerations in concrete business situations. Thus, we have emphasized the important role of ethical theory throughout the book, yet at the same time we have tried to encourage you to develop a critical perspective on theory. When discussing cases, ethics in action vignettes, and ethical dilemmas, our hope is that you will have discovered the value of ethical theories for communicating your views, and also for understanding the views and perspective of others. Here, perhaps the main value of ethical theories lies in the fact that they help to rationalize and enable a discourse about ethical considerations in business decisions.

Influences on ethical decision-making

In Chapter 4, we examined descriptive ethical theories. This helped us to understand the way in which people in organizations actually made decisions about business ethics. In the subsequent chapters, we have made evident the enormous range and complexity of ethical problems that continue to occur in business, suggesting that the factors influencing unethical decision-making continue to have a substantial role to play.

Given the increasing internationalization of business discussed throughout the book, we might first suggest that the national and cultural influences on decision-making, at both the individual and situational level, will become more important, but less clear-cut. Personal religious and cultural factors are increasingly challenged and re-shaped by global business practices, and the influence of a specific, local, national context also shifts in the context of 'foreign' MNCs with global codes of practice.

Indeed, many of the more important influences identified in Chapter 4 were context-based, and were often informal and cultural aspects, such as the moral framing of ethical issues in the workplace, organizational norms, and work roles. This suggests that more formal efforts to target improved ethical decision-making, such as codes of conduct and voluntary regulation, might ultimately have fairly limited impact unless they presage a more profound culture shift in business organizations. Some prospects for hope might be evident here when we consider that the mere fact of actively taking part in designing codes and rules could conceivably lead businesses to a deeper consideration of values in the longer term. Perhaps this is a little optimistic, but the opportunities for doing so would be enhanced if corporations continue to open themselves up to discourse with stakeholders—especially those that might challenge the dominant corporate mindset.

■ The role of management tools in business ethics

In Chapter 5, the last chapter in the first part of the book, we discussed the management of business ethics. Therefore, unlike, for instance, a book on finance or marketing, Crane and Matten has just one chapter dedicated to what we would traditionally call management instruments and tools. This might strike you as odd, especially if you are a business or management student, but it shows that business ethics is about more than just managing with tools and techniques. To our mind, it is much more about expanding horizons, deepening understandings, and developing critical thinking about business practices. The chapter on tools also suggests that business ethics is not really a separate branch of management at all. After all, it should be pretty clear by now that business ethics pertains to every traditional branch or aspect of management, such as marketing, finance, strategy, etc. and more constitutes an additional set of criteria for typical decisions, and a different way of looking at 'normal' business situations.

This is not to say that the explicit management of business ethics is not important, and we have traced some of the potential for tools and techniques in the second part of the book. A crucial role, for example, is likely to be played by new forms of social auditing and reporting, particularly in helping customers, CSOs, and shareholders evaluate the corporation's performance against ethical criteria. This is closely linked to new forms of stakeholder dialogue that we discussed in Chapter 5. Employee participation, shareholder democracy, or business–CSO partnership, among other things that we discussed in Part B, clearly require active engagement by corporations with their stakeholders.

Another of the tools that we have made frequent reference to throughout Chapters 6 to 11 is codes of ethics. These are certainly one of the most commonly used tools of business ethics, and as we have discussed, the general lack of governmental regulation in a growing number of business areas means that codes are necessary to fill the rule-making gap. Certainly, in industry at the moment, codes of various sorts have been the subject of enormous effort and interest. As we have discussed throughout the book, though, it remains to be seen where this development might lead, and what real impact it might actually have on the ground. Indeed, the multiplication and proliferation of more and more codes might actually be counterproductive to the original purpose of making decision-making more clear, and companies more transparent and accountable.

■ The role of different stakeholder constituencies in business ethics

In Chapter 2, we introduced a number of important concepts that help us to frame business ethics. Perhaps the most important of these was stakeholder theory, especially given that the major stakeholder constituencies of the corporation provided the structure for Part B of the book. Notwithstanding the fact that many managers will in practice probably deal with stakeholders on a much more instrumental basis, in the main, we have primarily developed a *normative* approach to stakeholder theory, namely the idea that certain groups have intrinsic rights and interests that need to be considered by managers. This has been an important element of the discussion in the second part of the book, not least because stakeholder rights often form the basis of many ethical issues and problems faced by business.

In Chapters 6 to 11, we discussed each individual stakeholder group separately, and it might appear as if they were all equally important to the corporation. Although in a certain sense they are, their significance certainly varies in different contexts, issues, and topics. *Shareholders* certainly remain a key stakeholder group for the corporation, especially at a time when globalized financial markets confront companies with the necessity to source their capital on a global level. With countries outside the US increasingly adopting a shareholder value ideology, the prospects of assigning a dominant role for shareholders appear to be advancing, nothwithstanding a growing interest in alternative systems—partly, it has to be said, caused by the financial crisis of the late 2000s. Another challenging area here is the topic of shareholder activism. Certainly, the field of SRI is an area of growing importance for corporations, and major institutional investors are increasingly responding to demands to add ethical criteria to their investment decisions.

Employees count among the most long-standing stakeholder groups of every business operation. In Europe and some other national contexts, there is still considerable ground for expecting employees to be a dominant stakeholder group, especially given the strong legal position this group generally has. However, new working practices, increased flexibilization, and challenges to legally codified protections, all appear to have weakened the stake of employees somewhat in recent years. In the developing world, employee rights might be yet more open to contestation and abuse, requiring considerable attention to new practices and protections.

The role of *consumers* is particularly interesting, since although they have always been of utmost *instrumental* importance to business, their *normative* claims would seem to be somewhat weaker than those of certain other constituencies. Whilst consumers might easily simply transfer their attention to another product or supplier, groups such as employees, suppliers, and local communities are more 'locked in' to the corporation and cannot so easily switch to an alternative. Nonetheless, it is easy to miss the fact that although the satisfaction of consumers appears to be in the self-interest of corporations, there is still much scope for exploitation and abuse of consumer rights. That said, the power of (some) consumers to exercise ethical purchasing is likely to sustain corporations' attention to consumers' ethical concerns.

The stake of *suppliers* appears to be one that although quite strong in certain contexts and industries, often has little legal protection, and will in practice often depend on the relative power balance with the corporation. *Competitors*, meanwhile, have one of the more contestable stakes in a firm, and although they have certain in-built rights that need to be considered, will often be one of the lowest priorities for corporations. Interestingly, in environmentally exposed industries, competitors might be more strongly considered, because of their role in setting up take-back and recycling schemes, just as suppliers might play a major role where integrated networks of recovery are intended. With an increasing trend towards just-in-time production and specialization, as well as strategic alliances and joint ventures, certain industries are more closely tied to their competitors and suppliers than others—a tendency that may also vary across different cultures and countries.

The stake of *CSOs* and *governments* is certainly the most complex and dynamic at the current time. CSOs, on the one hand, have heralded and pushed crucial ethical issues in the past, even initiating long-term processes of change on the part of corporations to respond, adopt, and incorporate the issues at stake. Over the course of time, CSOs have contributed to mainstreaming business ethics, but the legitimacy of their stake remains open to contestation in specific cases. The relation of business with government meanwhile seems to be developing in an even more controversial direction. While governments may have lost some of their traditional power in issuing and enforcing regulation, they have by no means decreased in importance as a stakeholder. The crucial innovation, though, is that the relationship develops more into a partnership rather than the previously dependent role of business. This applies to the national level, but increasingly also to the global level as well, as the UN Global Compact, for example, illustrates quite well.

■ Trade-offs and conflicts between different stakeholder groups

One final point that should be made clear at this stage is that one of the most challenging tasks for ethical management is to achieve an effective and appropriate balance between *competing* stakeholder expectations and claims. Different stakeholders are likely to diverge in the demands they place on corporations, making even a supposedly 'ethical' response a matter of some disagreement. Moreover, as we saw in Chapter 5, companies may well make their assessments based on largely instrumental grounds, meaning that those unable or unwilling to influence the corporation may be neglected, regardless of any intrinsic rights they might have.

On the surface, expectations of shareholders could be seen as clashing with all other stakeholders' interests nearly by default, as many of the latter are most likely to have a negative impact on profits, at least in the short term. Looking at the negative side, one could argue, based on the numerous scandals we have discussed in this book (particularly in Chapter 6), that whenever shareholders are negatively affected, we also see that other stakeholders, most notably employees and local communities, suffer as well from corruption and mismanagement. Looking at the ongoing popularity of ethical—or as we also termed it—socially responsible investment (SRI), we could argue that some of the most widely discussed and applied topics in business ethics in the business press are exactly those that attempt to reconcile shareholders interests with those of other stakeholders. This 'business case' for business ethics is important, but it is critical that ethical issues are not always simply relegated to instrumental reasoning. Real rights and real responsibilities are at stake here.

More broadly, claims for more sustainability, accountability, and good citizenship from companies can be interpreted as demands for a better accommodation of competing and conflicting interests of their various stakeholders. In a sense, managing business ethics is almost always a matter of navigating a path through situations of multiple expectations and values that are in conflict. An essential starting point in this process is the acknowledgement and understanding of these divergent positions—and therefore finding a way of enabling stakeholders to give voice to their values. Here we can expect quite a bit of development over the coming years, in an arena sometimes couched in terms of 'stakeholder dialogue' or more optimistically 'stakeholder democracy' (Matten and Crane 2005). In the latter debate, the political metaphor of democracy is applied to the corporate engagement with stakeholders, suggesting that businesses are increasingly expected to allow all their stakeholders opportunities to voice their interests and provide legitimate engagement in the governing of the corporation. In the context of our argument in this section, one of the key effects of these patterns of interaction would be to involve companies in a transparent process of simultaneous responses to divergent claims from various stakeholder constituencies.

■ Summary

In this chapter, we have reviewed the main themes that were introduced in Part A of the book, and have synthesized and summarized the main contributions subsequently made to these themes in Part B. We have concluded that the nature and scope of business ethics is likely to remain complex and ever evolving, with the prospect that the subject will be increasingly important in the years to come. We explained how globalization has dramatically reshaped the role and context of business ethics, whilst sustainability has presented an important, yet extremely challenging, goal for business ethics to contend with. We then provided a summary of the different stakeholder contributions to our understanding of corporate citizenship thinking. In the remainder of the chapter, we assessed the contribution of ethical theory, ethical decision-making, and business ethics management to our discussions in Part B. Here, we highlighted the need for a pragmatic, pluralistic approach that was both sensitive to the variety of contexts that corporations and managers are involved in, and that went beyond mere adherence to codified laws and procedures. Finally, we analysed the relative importance and relevance of each of the different stakeholder groups discussed in Part B, then went on to emphasize the profound problems of balancing competing stakeholder interests.

We hope that in reading this book, and thinking and talking about the issues and ideas that were raised, you will be better equipped to respond to the complex, yet fascinating, problems of business ethics. At the very least, we would like to think that we've opened your eyes to new problems and perspectives and hopefully excited you about the real-world challenges of business ethics. If the theories, concepts, and tools that you've learned along the way enable you to make better ethical decisions—by using empathy, imagination, and good judgement—then so much the better. The world of business ethics awaits you.

Study questions

1. What do you think will be the major new ethical issues and problems that businesses will have to face over the next decade?
2. Compare the challenges posed by globalization and sustainability to business ethics thinking and practice. Which do you think will prove to be the greatest challenge?
3. What are the particular ethical problems and issues that are likely to be faced by companies from emerging economies? What approaches to business ethics thinking and practice are likely to be appealing and suitable for such companies?
4. What are the major implications of corporate citizenship ideas for each major stakeholder group? How well placed is each group to influence the decisions and actions of corporations?
5. What are the benefits and drawbacks of adopting a pluralistic approach to normative ethical theory in business ethics?
6. Account for the prevalence of ethical codes in global business. To what extent do you consider such a development to be beneficial to the improvement of business ethics?

Research exercise

Select a controversial mining project currently under way in your country, or involving a multinational company domiciled in your country and undertake research on the main stakeholders and ethical issues involved in the project. You might want to consult websites of major extraction companies, such as Alcoa, Anglo American, Barrick Gold, BHP Billiton, Freeport, or Rio Tinto, and/or review websites dedicated to responsibility issues in mining such as the following:

Miningwatch Canada: http://www.miningwatch.ca

Latin American Mining Conflict Watch: http://www.conflictosmineros.net

Mines and Communities: http://www.minesandcommunities.org

1. Who are the main stakeholders involved in the project, and what are their main concerns and interests?
2. Provide a ranking of these stakeholders according to either instrumental or normative principles, listing the criteria used in your ranking.

3 What methods has the company adopted so far in incorporating the interests of these stakeholders in its decision-making?

4 How would you recommend it proceed to enhance its stakeholder democracy?

Key readings

VISIT THE WEBSITE for links to further key readings

1 **Ip, P.K. 2009. The challenge of developing a business ethics in China. *Jou nal of Business hics*, 88 (Supplement 1): 211–24.**

Whilst the US has arguably had the biggest influence on twentieth-century business ethics, the future of the subject looks set to be bound up with developments in emerging economies, especially in China. This article discusses the challenge of developing business ethics in China by examining recent ethical scandals in the country and exploring some of their root causes. It concludes by offering some thoughts on what a uniquely Chinese version of business ethics might look like in the future.

2 **Matten, D. and Crane, A. 2005. What is stakeholder democracy? Perspectives and issues. *Business hics: A u opean Re iew*, 14 (1): 6–13.**

This article provides a broad overview of the current debate on corporate accountability, openness, and transparency to stakeholders. As an introductory essay to a special journal issue, it aims to present the fundamental challenges and issues of the field, and guides the interested reader to more in-depth analysis of selected areas of interest.

REFERENCES

AccountAbility. 2005. *Towards responsible lobbying: leadership and public policy*. London: AccountAbility.

Ackers, P. and Payne, J. 1998. British trade unions and social partnership: rhetoric, reality and strategy. *International Journal of Human Resource Management*, 9 (3): 529–50.

Adams, J. 2008. Chinese union. *Newsweek*, 14 February 2008: http://www.newsweek.com.

Agle, B.R. and Caldwell, C.B. 1999. Understanding research on values in business. *Business and Society*, 38 (3): 326–89.

Aguilera, R.V., Williams, C.A., Conley, J.M., and Rupp, D.E. 2006. Corporate governance and social responsibility: a comparative analysis of the UK and the US. *Corporate Governance*, 14 (3): 147–58.

Albert, M. 1991. *Capitalisme contre capitalisme*. Paris: Le Seuil.

Ali, S.H. 2000. Shades of green: NGO coalitions, mining companies and the pursuit of negotiating power. In J. Bendell (ed.), *Terms for endearment: business, NGOs and sustainable development*. Sheffield: Greenleaf.

Allenby, B.R. 1993. *Industrial ecology*. New York: Prentice Hall.

Altman, B.W. and Vidaver-Cohen, D. 2000. A framework for understanding corporate citizenship. Introduction to the special edition of Business and Society Review 'corporate citizenship and the new millennium'. *Business and Society Review*, 105 (1): 1–7.

Anand, V., Ashforth, B.E., and Joshi, M. 2004. Business as usual: the acceptance and perpetuation of corruption in organizations. *Academy of Management Executive*, 18 (2): 39–53.

Anderson, E. and Jap, S.D. 2005. The dark side of close relationships. *MIT Sloan Management Review*, 46 (3): 75.

Anderson, R., Guerrera, F., Hall, B., and Parker, G. 2009. Europe moves to curb executive salaries. *Financial Times*, 7 February 2009: http://www.ft.com.

Andrews, L. 1996. The relationship of political marketing to political lobbying. *European Journal of Marketing*, 30 (10/11): 68–91.

Arrow, K.J. and Hurwicz, L. 1977. *Studies in resource allocation processes*. Cambridge and New York: Cambridge University Press.

Arthur, C. 2008. Phorm fires privacy row for ISPs. *Guardian*, 6 March: http://www.guardian.co.uk.

Arts, B. 2002. 'Green alliances' of business and NGOs: new styles of self-regulation or 'dead-end roads'? *Corporate Social Responsibility and Environmental Management*, 9: 26–36.

Artz, K.W. 1999. Buyer-supplier performance: the role of asset specificity, reciprocal investments and relational exchange. *British Journal of Management*, 10 (2): 113–26.

Ashman, D. 2001. Civil society collaboration with business: bringing empowerment back in. *World Development*, 29 (7): 1097–113.

Assael, H. 1995. *Consumer behaviour and marketing action* (5th edn.). Cincinnati: South-Western College.

Auger, P. and Devinney, T.M. 2007. Do what consumers say matter? The misalignment of preferences with unconstrained ethical intentions. *Journal of Business Ethics*, 76 (4): 361–83.

—— —— and Louviere, J.J. 2006. Global segments of socially conscious consumers: do they exist? Paper presented at the Corporate Responsibility and Global Business: Implications for Corporate and Marketing Strategy, London Business School, 13–14 July.

Austin, J. 2000. *The collaboration challenge: how nonprofits and businesses succeed through strategic alliances*. San Francisco: Jossey-Bass.

Badaracco, J.L., Jr. and Webb, A.P. 1995. Business ethics: a view from the trenches. *California Management Review*, 37 (2): 8–29.

Badenhorst, J.A. 1994. Unethical behaviour in procurement: a perspective on causes and solutions. *Journal of Business Ethics*, 13 (9): 739–45.

Bahena, A. 2009. *What role did credit rating agencies (CRAs) play in the financial crisis*? Des Moines, Ia.: University of Iowa Center for International Finance and Development.

Bakan, J. 2004. *The corporation: the pathological pursuit of profit and power*. London: Constable and Robinson.

Baker, G. and Chandler, D. (eds.). 2005. *Global civil society*. London and New York: Routledge.
Balch, O. 2009. Access all areas. *Ethical Corporation*, April: http://www.ethicalcorp.com.
Ballwieser, W. and Clemm, H. 1999. 'Wirtschaftsprüfung'. In W. Korff (ed.), *Handbuch der Wirtschaftsethik*: 399–416. Gütersloh: Gütersloher Verlagshaus.
Banerjee, S.B. 2000. Whose land is it anyway? National interest, indigenous stakeholders, and colonial discourses. *Organization & Environment*, 13 (1): 3–38.
—— 2009. Necrocapitalism. *Organization Studies*, 29 (12): 1541–63.
Barkawi, A. 2002. Benchmarking sustainability investments am Beispiel der Dow Jones Sustainability Indexes. In R. von Rosen (ed.), *Ethisch orientierte Aktienanlage—Nische oder Wachstumsmarkt?*: 88–98. Frankfurt: Deutsches Aktieninstitut.
Barrett, E. 1999. Justice in the workplace? Normative ethics and the critique of human resource management. *Personnel Review*, 28 (4): 307–18.
Bart, C.K. 1997. Sex, lies and mission statements. *Business Horizons*, November–December: 9–18.
Basil, D.Z., Runte, M.S., Easwaramoorthy, M. and Barr, C. (2009). Company support for employee volunteering: a national survey of companies in Canada. *Journal of Business Ethics*, 85: 387–398.
Baskerville-Morley, R.F. 2005. A research note: the unfinished business of culture. *Accounting, Organizations, and Society*, 30: 389–91.
Baudrillard, J. 1997. *The consumer society*. London: Sage.
Baughn, C.C. and Buchanan, M.A. 2001. Cultural protectionism. *Business Horizons*, 44 (6): 5–15.
Bauman, Z. 1989. *Modernity and the holocaust*. Cambridge: Polity Press.
—— 1991. The social manipulation of morality. *Theory, Culture and Society*, 8 (1): 137–52.
—— 1993. *Postmodern ethics*. London: Blackwell.
Baumhart, R.C. 1961. How ethical are businesses? *Harvard Business Review*, July–August: 6.
BBC. 2009. Rating agency warning on UK debt, 21 May: http://www.bbc.co.uk/news.
Beauchamp, T.L. 1997. Goals and quotas in hiring and promotion. In T.L. Beauchamp and N.E. Bowie (eds.), *Ethical theory and business* (5th edn.): 379–87. Upper Saddle River, NJ: Prentice Hall.
—— and Bowie, N.E. 1997. *Ethical theory and business* (5th edn.). Upper Saddle River, NJ: Prentice Hall.
Becht, M. and Röell, A. 1999. Blockholdings in Europe: an international comparison. *European Economic Review*, 43: 1049–56.
Beck, U. 1992. *Risk Society: towards a new modernity*. London: Sage.
—— 1997. *Was ist globalisierung*? Frankfurt/Main: Suhrkamp.
—— (ed.). 1998. *Politik der globalisierung*. Frankfurt/Main: Suhrkamp.
Becker, B. and Westbrook, D.A. 1998. Confronting asymmetry: global financial markets and national regulation. *International Finance*, 1 (2): 339–55.
Becker, H. and Fritzche, D.J. 1987. Business ethics: a cross-cultural comparison of managers' attitudes. *Journal of Business Ethics*, 6: 289–95.
Beekun, R.I. and Badawi, J.A. 2005. Balancing ethical responsibility among multiple organizational stakeholders: the Islamic perspective. *Journal of Business Ethics*, 60 (2): 131–45.
Begg, K., van der Woerd, F., and Levy, D.L. (eds.). 2005. *The business of climate change: corporate responses to Kyoto*. Sheffield: Greenleaf.
Belal, A.R. 2002. Stakeholder accountability or stakeholder management: a review of UK firms' social and ethical accounting, auditing and reporting (SEAAR) practices. *Corporate Social Responsibility and Environmental Management*, 9: 8–25.
Bendell, J. (ed.). 2000. *Terms for endearment: business, NGOs and sustainable development*. Sheffield: Greenleaf.
—— 2000. Civil regulation: a new form of democratic governance for the global economy? In J. Bendell (ed.), *Terms for endearment: business, NGOs and sustainable development*: 239–54. Sheffield: Greenleaf.
—— 2000. Introduction: working with stakeholder pressure for sustainable development. In J. Bendell (ed.), *Terms for Endearment: Business, NGOs and Sustainable Development*. Sheffield: Greenleaf.
—— 2005. In whose name? The accountability of corporate social responsibility. *Development in Practice*, 15 (3/4): 362–74.
—— and Murphy, D.F. 2000. Planting the seeds of change: business-NGO relations on tropical deforestation. In J. Bendell (ed.), *Terms for endearment: business, NGOs and sustainable development*. Sheffield: Greenleaf.
Berle, A.A. and Means, G.C. 1932. *The modern corporation and private property*. New York: Transaction.
Bernstein, A. 2000. Too much corporate power? *Business Week*, 11 September: 52–60.

Bernstein, S. and Cashore, B. 2007. Can non-state global governance be legitimate? An analytical framework. *Regulation & Governance*, 1 (4): 347–71.

Binford, L. 2009. From fields of power to fields of sweat: the dual process of constructing temporary migrant labour in Mexico and Canada. *Third World Quarterly*, 30 (3): 503–17.

Birchfield, V. and Freyberg-Inan, A. 2005. Organic intellectuals and counter-hegemonic politics in the age of globalisation: the case of ATTAC. In C. Eschle and B. Maiguashca (eds.), *Critical theories, international relations and 'the anti-globalization movement'*: 154–73. London: Routledge.

Bird, F.B. and Waters, J.A. 1989. The moral muteness of managers. *California Management Review*, Fall: 73–88.

Blakely, R., Richards, J., Rossiter, J., and Beeston, R. 2007. MI5 alert on China's cyberspace spy threat. *The Times*, 1 December: http://www.timesonline.co.uk.

Bloom, P.N. and Perry, V.G. 2001. Retailer power and supplier welfare: the case of Wal-Mart. *Journal of Retailing*, 77 (3): 379–97.

Blowfield, M. 1999. Ethical trade: a review of developments and issues. *Third World Quarterly*, 20 (4): 753–70.

Boatright, J.R. 2009. *Ethics and the conduct of business* (6th edn.). Upper Saddle River, NJ: Pearson Education.

Boele, R., Fabig, H., and Wheeler, D. 2000. The story of Shell, Nigeria and the Ogoni people—a study in unsustainable development. I—Economy, environment and social relationships. Paper presented at the Academy of Management Conference. Toronto.

Boli, J. and Lechner, F.J. (eds.). 2000. *The globalization reader*. Malden, Mass. and Oxford: Blackwell.

Borgerson, J.L. 2007. On the harmony of feminist ethics and business ethics. *Business and Society Review*, 112 (4): 477–509.

Borgmann, A. 2000. The moral complexion of consumption. *Journal of Consumer Research*, 26, March: 418–22.

Bowie, N.E. 1991. New directions in corporate social responsibility. *Business Horizons*, 34, July–August: 56–65.

Boyd, C. 1996. Ethics and corporate governance: the issues raised by the Cadbury Report in the United Kingdom. *Journal of Business Ethics*, 15: 167–82.

Braithwaite, T. and Urry, M. 2008. A taste of change for M&S food suppliers. *Financial Times*, 6 June: http://www.ft.com.

Brammer, S. and Pavelin, S. 2005. Corporate community contributions in the United Kingdom and the United States. *Journal of Business Ethics*, 56 (1): 15–26.

—— Williams, G., and Zinkin, J. 2007. Religion and attitudes to corporate social responsibility in a large cross-country sample. *Journal of Business Ethics*, 71 (3): 229–43.

Braverman, H. 1974. *Labor and monopoly capital: the degredation of work in the twentieth century*. New York: Monthly Review Press.

Brown, M.B. 1993. *Fair trade*. London: Zed Books.

Brown, M.T. 2005. *Corporate integrity: rethinking organizational ethics and leadership*. Cambridge: Cambridge University Press.

Brugmann, J. and Prahalad, C.K. 2007. Cocreating business's new social compact. *Harvard Business Review*, 85 (2): 80–90.

Buchanan, D. and Huczynski, A. 1997. *Organizational behaviour* (3rd edn.). London: Prentice-Hall.

Buchholz, R.A. 1998. The ethics of consumption activities: a future paradigm? *Journal of Business Ethics*, 17 (8): 871–82.

Buck, T. and Morrison, S. 2005. Microsoft poised to ship unbundled Windows. *Financial Times*, 8 June: http://www.ft.com.

Burke, R.J. and Black, S. 1997. Save the males: backlash in organizations. *Journal of Business Ethics*, 16: 933–42.

Butler, S. 2007. Levi's suspended by ethical group in living wage row. *The Times*: http://www.timesonline.co.uk.

Cannon, T. 1994. *Corporate responsibility*. London: Pearson.

Cappelli, P. 2009. The future of the U.S. business model and the rise of competitors. *Academy of Management Perspectives*, 23 (2): 5–10.

Carney, M. 2008. The many futures of Asian business groups. *Asia Pacific Journal of Management*, 25 (4): 595–613.

Carr, A. 1968. Is business bluffing ethical? *Harvard Business Review*, 46 (January–February): 143–53.

Carroll, A.B. 1979. A three dimensional model of corporate social performance. *Academy of Management Review*, 4: 497–505.

—— 1991. The pyramid of corporate social responsibility: toward the moral management of organizational stakeholders. *Business Horizons*, July–August: 39–48.

—— 1998. The four faces of corporate citizenship. *Business and Society Review*, 100 (1): 1–7.

—— 2008. A history of corporate social responsibility: concepts and practices. In A. Crane, A. McWilliams, D. Matten, J. Moon and D. Siegel (eds.), *The Oxford handbook of corporate social responsibility*: 19–46. Oxford: Oxford University Press.

—— and Buchholtz, A.K. 2009. *Business and society: ethics and stakeholder management* (7th edn.). Cincinnati: South-Western.

Cashore, B. 2002. Legitimacy and the privatization of environmental governance: how non-state market-driven (NSMD) governance systems gain rule-making authority. *Governance*, 15 (4): 503–29.

Cassell, C., Johnson, P., and Smith, K. 1997. Opening the black box: corporate codes of ethics in their organizational context. *Journal of Business Ethics*, 16: 1077–93.

Cassimon, D. 2001. Financing sustainable development using a feasible Tobin Tax. *Journal of International Relations and Development*, 4 (2): 157–73.

Castka, P. and Balzarova, M.A. 2008. ISO 26000 and supply chains—on the diffusion of the social responsibility standard. *International Journal of Production Economics*, 111: 274–86.

Cerin, P. and Dobers, P. 2001a. Who is rating the raters? *Corporate Environmental Strategy*, 8 (2): 1–3.

—— —— 2001b. What does the performance of the Dow Jones Sustainability Group Index tell us? *Eco-Management and Auditing*, 8: 123–33.

Chen, A.Y.S., Sawyers, R.B., and Williams, P.F. 1997. Reinforcing ethical decision making through corporate culture. *Journal of Business Ethics*, 16: 855–65.

Cheney, G. 1995. Democracy in the workplace: theory and practice from the perspective of communication. *Journal of Applied Communication*, 23: 167–200.

Chenting, S. 2003. Is Guanxi orientation bad, ethically speaking? A study of Chinese enterprises. *Journal of Business Ethics*, 44 (4): 303–15.

Chertow, M.R. 2007. 'Uncovering' Industrial Symbiosis. *Journal of Industrial Ecology*, 11 (1): 11–30.

Chhabara, R. 2008. Workplace equality—putting harassment on notice. *Ethical corporation*, 22 October: http://www.ethicalcorp.com.

Christie, P.M.J., Kwon, I.-W.G., Stoeberl, P.A., and Baumhart, R. 2003. A cross-cultural comparison of ethical attitudes of business managers: India, Korea and the United States. *Journal of Business Ethics*, 46 (3): 263–87.

Christmann, P. and Taylor, G. 2002. Globalization and the environment: strategies for international voluntary environmental initiatives. *Academy of Management Executive*, 16 (3): 121–37.

Chryssides, G. and Kaler, J. 1996. *Essentials of business ethics*. London: McGraw-Hill.

Claessens, S. and Fan, J.P.H. 2002. Corporate governance in Asia: a survey. *International Review of Finance*, 3 (2): 71–103.

Clark, C.E. 2000. Differences between public relations and corporate social responsibility: an analysis. *Public Relations Review*, 26 (3): 363–80.

Clarke, T. 2007. *International corporate governance: a comparative approach*. London: New York: Routledge.

Clarkson, M.B.E. 1995. A stakeholder framework for analyzing and evaluating corporate social performance. *Academy of Management Review*, 20 (1): 92–117.

Claydon, T. 2000. Employee participation and involvement. In D. Winstanley and J. Woodall (eds.), *Ethical issues in contemporary human resource management*: 208–23. Basingstoke: Macmillan.

Cludts, S. 1999. Organization theory and the ethics of participation. *Journal of Business Ethics*, 21: 157–71.

Coffee, J.C., Jr. 2001. The rise of dispersed ownership: the roles of law and the state in the separation of ownership and control. *Yale Law Journal*, 111 (1): 1–82.

Collier, J. 1995. The virtuous organization. *Business Ethics: A European Review*, 4 (3): 143–9.

—— and Esteban, R. 1999. Governance in the participative organization: freedom, creativity and ethics. *Journal of Business Ethics*, 21: 173–88.

Collier, R. 2001. A hard time to be a father? Reassessing the relationship between law, policy, and family (practices). *Journal of Law and Society*, 28 (4): 520–45.

Collins, J.W. 1994. Is business ethics an oxymoron? *Business Horizons*, September–October: 1–8.

Cooper, B. 2009. Analysis: pensions—the ultimate employee benefit. *Ethical Corporation*, June.

Cooper, C. 1996. Hot under the collar. *Times Higher Education Supplement*, 21 June: 12–16.
Cooper, R.W., Frank, G.L., and Kemp, R.A. 2000. A multinational comparison of key ethical issues, helps and challenges in the purchasing and supply management profession: The key implications for business and the professions. *Journal of Business Ethics*, 23 (1/1): 83–100.
Corbett, C.J. and Kirsch, D.A. 2001. International diffusion of ISO 14000 certification. *Production and Operations Management*, 10 (3): 327–42.
Cowe, R. 2002. Wanted: shareholders with a global conscience. *Observer – Business*, 24 November: 6.
Cowton, C.J. 1994. The development of ethical investment products. In A.R. Prindl and B. Prodhan (eds.), *Ethical conflicts in finance*: 213–32. Oxford: Blackwell.
—— 1999a. Accounting and financial ethics: from margin to mainstream. *Business Ethics: A European Review*, 8 (2): 99–107.
—— 1999b. Playing by the rules: ethical criteria at an ethical investment fund. *Business Ethics: A European Review*, 8 (1): 60–9.
Cox, A., Sanderson, J., and Watson, G. 2000. *Power regimes: mapping the DNA of business and supply chain relationships*. Stratford-upon-Avon: Earlsgate Press.
Cragg, W. and Greenbaum, A. 2002. Reasoning about responsibilities: mining company managers on what stakeholders are owed. *Journal of Business Ethics*, 39: 319–35.
Crain, K.A. and Heischmidt, K.A. 1995. Implementing business ethics: sexual harassment. *Journal of Business Ethics*, 14: 299–308.
Crane, A. 1998. Culture clash and mediation: exploring the cultural dynamics of business–NGO collaboration. *Greener Management International* (24): 61–76.
—— 2000. *Marketing, morality and the natural environment*. London: Routledge.
—— 2001a. Corporate greening as amoralization. *Organization Studies*, 21 (4): 673–96.
—— 2001b. Unpacking the ethical product. *Journal of Business Ethics*, 30: 361–73.
—— 2005a. In the company of spies: when competitive intelligence gathering becomes industrial espionage. *Business Horizons*, 48 (3): 233–40.
—— 2005b. Meeting the ethical gaze: challenges for orienting to the ethical market. In R. Harrison, T. Newholm, and D. Shaw (eds.), *The ethical consumer*. London: Sage.
—— Knights, D., and Starkey, K. 2008. The conditions of our freedom: Foucault, organization, and ethics. *Business Ethics Quarterly*, 18 (3): 299–320.
—— and Livesey, S. 2003. Are you talking to me? Stakeholder communication and the risks and rewards of dialogue. In B. Husted (ed.), *Unfolding stakeholder thinking*, Vol. II. Sheffield: Greenleaf.
—— Matten, D., and Moon, J. 2008. *Corporations and Citizenship*. Cambridge: Cambridge University Press
—— and Spence, L. (2008). *Competitive intelligence: ethical challenges and good practice*, London: Institute of Business Ethics.
Cranford, M. 1998. Drug testing and the right to privacy: arguing the ethics of workplace drug testing. *Journal of Business Ethics*, 17: 1805–15.
Cumming, J.F. 2001. Engaging stakeholders in corporate accountability programmes: a cross-sectoral analysis of UK and transnational experience. *Business Ethics: A European Review*, 10 (1): 45–52.
Cywinski, M. 2008. Influence of large corporations on government too strong, survey says. *CanadaOne*, 19 January: http://www.canadaone.com.
Dahan, N. 2005. A contribution to the conceptualization of political resources utilized in corporate political action. *Journal of Public Affairs*, 5: 43–54.
—— Doh, J.P., and Guay, T. 2006. The role of multinational corporations in transitional institutional building: a policy network perspective. *Human Relations*, 59: 1571–600.
Dahler-Larsen, P. 1994. Corporate culture and morality: Durkheim-inspired reflections on the limits of corporate culture. *Journal of Management Studies*, 31 (1): 1–18.
Daly, H.E. 1991. *Steady state economics* (2nd edn.). Washington: Island Press.
—— and Cobb, J.B.J. 1989. *For the common good: redirecting the economy towards community, the environment, and a sustainable future* (1st edn.). Boston: Beacon Press.
Dart, R. 2004. The legitimacy of social enterprise. *Nonprofit Management and Leadership*, 14 (4): 411–24.
David, F.R. 1989. How companies define their mission. *Long Range Planning*, 22 (1): 90–7.
Davies I. 2007. The eras and participants of fair trade: an industry structure/stakeholder perspective of growth of the fair trade industry. *Corporate Governance*. 7(4): 455–470.
Davies, I.A. and Crane, A. 2003. Ethical decision-making in fair trade companies. *Journal of Business Ethics*, 45 (1/2): 79–92.
—— —— 2010. CSR in SMEs: investigating employee engagement in fair trade companies. *Business Ethics: A European Review*, forthcoming.

Davis, K. 1973. The case for and against business assumption of social responsibilities. *Academy of Management Journal*, June: 312–22.

Dawar, N. and Frost, T. 1999. Competing with giants. *Harvard Business Review*, 77, March–April: 119–29.

Dawson, D. 2005. Applying stories of the environment to business: what business people can learn from the virtues in environmental narratives. *Journal of Business Ethics*, 58 (1/3): 37–49.

De George, R.T. 1999. *Business ethics* (5th edn.). Upper Saddle River, NJ: Prentice Hall.

Dearlove, D. 2006. Money scandals focus minds on need for ethics. *The Times*, 19 January.

Dees, J.G. 1998. Enterprising nonprofits. *Harvard Business Review*, 76 (1): 54–67.

Defourny, J. and Nyssens, M. 2006. Defining social enterprise. In M. Nyssens (ed.), *Social enterprise: at the crossroads of market, public policies and civil society*.. London and New York: Routledge.

Delmas, M.A. and Montiel, I. 2009. Greening the supply chain: when is customer pressure effective? *Journal of Economics and Management Strategy*, 18 (1): 171–201.

Derry, R. 1987. Moral reasoning in work-related contexts. In W.C. Frederick (ed.), *Research in corporate social performance*. Greenwich, CT: JAI Press.

Des Jardins, J.R. and Duska, R. 1997. Drug testing in employment. In T.L. Beauchamp and N.E. Bowie (eds.), *Ethical theory and business* (5th edn.): 309–19. Upper Saddle River, NJ: Prentice-Hall.

Desmond, J. 1998. Marketing and moral indifference. In M. Parker (ed.), *Ethics and organizations*. London: Sage.

—— and Crane, A. 2004. Morality and the consequences of marketing action. *Journal of Business Research*, 57: 1222–30.

—— McDonagh, P., and O'Donohoe, S. 2000. Counter-culture and consumer society. *Consumption, Markets and Culture*, 4 (3): 241–79.

Detomasi, D. 2007. The multinational corporation and global governance: modelling global public policy networks. *Journal of Business Ethics*, 71 (3): 321–34.

Devlin, J.F. 2005. A detailed study of financial exclusion in the UK. *Journal of Consumer Policy*, 28: 75–108.

Dhir, A.A. 2009. Towards a race and gender-conscious conception of the firm: Canadian corporate governance, law and diversity, *CLPE Research Paper*, Vol. 01/2009. Toronto: Osgoode Hall Law School.

Diamond, J. 2008. What's Your Consumption Factor? *New York Times*, 2 January: http://www.nytimes.com.

Dickinson, R.A. and Carsky, M.L. 2005. The consumer as economic voter. In R. Harrison, T. Newholm, and D. Shaw (eds.), *The ethical consumer*: 25–36. London: Sage.

Dobel, J.P. 2007. Public management as ethics. In E. Ferlie, L.E. Lynn and C. Pollitt (eds.), *The Oxford handbook of public management:* 156–81. Oxford: Oxford University Press.

Dobson, A. 1996. Environmental sustainabilities: an analysis and typology. *Environmental Politics*, 5 (3): 401–28.

Doh, J.P. and Guay, T.R. 2006. Corporate social responsibility, public policy, and NGO activism in Europe and the United States: an institutional-stakeholder perspective. *Journal of Management Studies*, 43 (1): 47–73.

—— and Teegen, H. (eds.). 2003. *Globalization and NGOs: transforming business, government, and society*. Westport, CT: Praeger Publishers.

Dommeyer, C.J. and Gross, B.L. 2003. What consumers know and what they do: an investigation of consumer knowledge, awareness, and use of privacy protection strategies. *Journal of Interactive Marketing*, 17 (2): 34.

Donaldson, T. 1989. *The ethics of international business*. New York and Oxford: Oxford University Press.

—— 1996. Values in tension: ethics away from home. *Harvard Business Review*, September–October: 48–62.

—— 2008. Hedge fund ethics. *Business Ethics Quarterly*, 18 (3): 405–16.

—— and Preston, L.E. 1995. The stakeholder theory of the corporation: concepts, evidence, and implications. *Academy of Management Review*, 20 (1): 65–91.

Donleavy, G.D., Lam, K.C.J., and Ho, S.S.M. 2008. Does East meet West in business ethics: an introduction to the special issue. *Journal of Business Ethics*, 79 (1/2): 1–8.

Dorosh, P.A. 2008. Food price stabilisation and food security: international experience. *Bulletin of Indonesian Economic Studies*, 44 (1): 93–114.

Doyle, C. 1997. Self-regulation and statutory regulation. *Business Strategy Review*, 8 (3): 35–42.

Drumwright, M. 1994. Socially responsible organizational buying. *Journal of Marketing*, 58, July: 1–19.
du Gay, P. 2000. *In praise of bureaucracy*. London: Sage.
Durán, J.L. and Sánchez, F. 1999. The relationships between the companies and their suppliers. *Journal of Business Ethics*, 22 (3): 273–80.
Durkheim, E. 1993. *The division of labour in society*. Glencoe, Ill.: Free Press.
Eaglesham, J. 2000. Staff privacy in the spotlight: workplace surveillance. *Financial Times*, 9 October: 22.
Easton, G. 1992. Industrial networks: a review. In G. Easton (ed.), *Industrial networks: a new view of reality*: 3–27. London: Routledge.
Eberlein, B. and Matten, D. 2009. Business responses to climate change regulation in Canada and Germany—lessons for MNCs from emerging economies. *Journal of Business Ethics*, 86 (2): 241–55.
Edelman. 2009. *2009 Edelman Trust Barometer*. http://www.edelman.com.
Edwards, M. and Fowler, A. (eds.). 2002. *The Earthscan reader on NGO management*. London: Earthscan.
Edwards, V. and Lawrence, P. 2000. *Management in Eastern Europe*. Basingstoke: Palgrave.
Eikenberry, A.M. and Kluver, J.D. 2004. The marketization of the nonprofit sector: civil society at risk? *Public Administration Review*, 64 (2): 132–40.
EIRIS. 2009. *Emerging markets investor survey report: An analysis of responsible investment in emerging markets*. London: EIRIS.
Elankumaran, S., Seal, R., and Hashmi, A. 2005. Transcending transformation: enlightening endeavours at Tata Steel. *Journal of Business Ethics*, 59 (1): 109–19.
Elkington, J. 1999. *Cannibals with forks: the triple bottom line of 21st century business*. Oxford: Capstone.
—— and Fennell, S. 2000. Partners for sustainability. In J. Bendell (ed.), *Terms for endearment: business, NGOs and sustainable development*: 150–62. Sheffield: Greenleaf.
Ellerman, D. 1999. The democratic firm: an argument based on ordinary jurisprudence. *Journal of Business Ethics*, 21: 111–24.
Elms, H. and Phillips, R.A. 2009. Private security companies and institutional legitimacy: corporate and stakeholder responsiblity. *Business Ethics Quarterly*, 19 (3): 403–32.
Emmelhainz, M.A. and Adams, R.J. 1999. The apparel industry response to 'sweatshop' concerns: a review and analysis of codes of conduct. *Journal of Supply Chain Management*, Summer: 51–7.
Enderle, G. 1996. A comparison of business ethics in North America and continental Europe. *Business Ethics: A European Review*, 5 (1): 33–46.
Engelen, E. 2002. Corporate governance, property and democracy: a conceptual critique of shareholder ideology. *Economy and Society*, 31 (3): 391–413.
Entine, J. 2003. The myth of social investing: a critique of its practice and consequence for corporate social performance research. *Organization and Environment*, 16 (3): 352–68.
—— 2008a. Crunch time for ethical investing. *Ethical Corporation*, November: 24–7.
—— 2008b. Sell-out at the Sierra Club. *Ethical Corporation*, 1 September: http://www.ethicalcorp.com.
Eschle, C. and Maiguashca, B. (eds.). 2005. *Critical theories, international relations and 'the anti-globalization movement'*. London: Routledge.
Ethical Corporation. 2006. Can investor activism have any effect on Sudan? *Ethical Corporation*, June: 6–7.
—— 2009. Ethical Corporation Institute reveals innovations in training: Novartis employees play video games to learn about code of ethics. *Ethical corporation*, 12 March: http://www.ethicalcorp.com/content.asp?ContentID=6396.
Ethical Performance. 2006. Ethical performance best practice. *Ethical performance*, 8: 4–18.
Ethics Resource Center. 2007. *National business ethics survey 2007: an inside view of private sector ethics*. Arlington, VA: Ethics Resource Center.
—— 2008. *National government ethics survey 2007: an inside view of public sector ethics*. Arlington, VA: Ethics Resource Center.
ETI. 2009. Our members. *Ethical Trading Initiative*. http://www.ethicaltrade.org.
Evan, W.M. and Freeman, R.E. 1993. A stakeholder theory of the modern corporation: Kantian capitalism. In W.M. Hoffman and R.E. Frederick (eds.), *Business ethics: readings and cases in corporate morality*: 145–54. New York: McGraw-Hill.
Evans, D. and Salas, C. 2009. Flawed credit ratings reap profits as regulators fail investors. *Bloomberg News*, 29 April.
Faulks, K. 2000. *Citizenship*. London: Routledge.
Featherstone, M. 1991. *Consumer culture and postmodernism*. London: Sage.

Ferner, A. and Hyman, R. 1998. *Changing industrial relations in Europe*. Oxford: Blackwell.
Ferrell, O.C., Fraedrich, J., and Ferrell, L. 2008. *Business ethics: ethical decision making and cases* (7th edn.). Boston: Houghton Mifflin.
—— and Gresham, L.G. 1985. A contingency framework for understanding ethical decision-making in marketing. *Journal of Marketing*, 49: 87–96.
—— —— and Fraedrich, J. 1989. A synthesis of ethical decision models for marketing. *Journal of Macromarketing*, 9 (2): 55–64.
Fineman, S. and Clarke, K. 1996. Green stakeholders: industry interpretations and response. *Journal of Management Studies*, 33 (6): 715–30.
Fisher, J. 2007. Business marketing and the ethics of gift giving. *Industrial Marketing Management*, 36 (1): 99–108.
Fiss, P.C. and Zajac, E.J. 2004. The diffusion of ideas over contested terrain: the (non)adoption of a shareholder value orientation among German firms. *Administrative Science Quarterly*, 49: 501–34.
Fitzgerald, R. 1999. Employment relations and industrial welfare in Britain: business ethics versus labour markets. *Business and Economic History*, 28 (2): 167–79.
Focus. 2009. Wiedeking, der Top-Verdiener Europas. *Focus online*, 16 July.
Ford, R.C. and Richardson, W.D. 1994. Ethical decision making: a review of the empirical literature. *Journal of Business Ethics*, 13 (3): 205–21.
Forstater, M. 2006. Green jobs. *Challenge*, 49 (4): 58–72.
Foster, W. and Bradach, J. 2005. Should nonprofits seek profits? *Harvard Business Review*, 83 (2): 92–100.
Fraedrich, J., Thorne, D.M., and Ferrell, O.C. 1994. Assessing the application of cognitive moral development to business ethics. *Journal of Business Ethics*, 13 (10): 829–38.
Frankental, P. 2002. The UN Universal Declaration of Human Rights as a corporate code of conduct. *Business Ethics: A European Review*, 11 (2): 129–33.
—— 2006. Why socially responsible investment requires more risk for companies rather than more engagement. In R. Sullivan and C. Mackenzie (eds.), *Responsible investment*: 241–6. Sheffield: Greenleaf.
Fransen, L.W. and Kolk, A. 2007. Global rule-setting for business: a critical analysis of multi-stakeholder standards. *Organization*, 14 (5): 667–84.
Frederick, W.C. 1994. From CSR_1 to CSR_2: The maturing of business-and-society thought. *Business & Society*, 33 (2): 150–64.
Freeman, R.E. 1984. *Strategic management: a stakeholder approach*. Boston: Pitman.
French, P. 1979. The corporation as a moral person. *American Philosophical Quarterly*, 16: 207–15.
—— 2008. Philanthropy—China starts to give. *Ethical Corporation*, 12 November.
Frenkel, S.J. and Scott, D. 2002. Compliance, collaboration and codes of practice. *California Management Review*, 45 (1): 29–49.
Friedman, M. 1970. The social responsibility of business is to increase its profits. *New York Times Magazine*, 13 September.
—— 1999. *Consumer boycotts*. New York: Routledge.
Fuchs, D. 2005. Commanding heights? The strength and fragility of business power in global politics. *Millennium: Journal of International Studies*, 33 (3): 771–801.
Fuller, D.A. 1999. *Sustainable marketing: managerial-ecological issues*. Thousand Oaks, Ca: Sage.
Furman, F.K. 1990. Teaching business ethics: questioning the assumptions, seeking new directions. *Journal of Business Ethics*, 9: 31–8.
Gabriel, Y. and Lang, T. (eds.). 2006. *The unmanageable consumer* (2nd edn.). London: Sage.
Gadsden, A. 2008. Earthquake rocks China's civil society. *Far Eastern Economic Review*, June: http://www.feer.com.
Galbraith, J.K. 1974. *The new industrial state* (2nd edn.). Harmondsworth: Penguin.
Gapper, J. 2008. Whatever is good for Goldman ... *Financial Times*, 24 September: http://www.ft.com.
Gellerman, S.W. 1986. Why 'good' managers make bad ethical choices. *Harvard Business Review*, July–August: 85–90.
Getz, K.A. 1997. Research in corporate political action: integration and assessment. *Business & Society*, 36 (1): 32–72.
Geyer, R. and Jackson, T. 2004. Supply loops and their constraints: the industrial ecology of recycling and reuse. *California Management Review*, 46 (2): 55–73.
Ghoshal, S. 2005. Bad management theories are destroying good management practices. *Academy of Management Learning and Education*, 4 (1): 75–92.
Gibson, R.B. (ed.). 1999. *Voluntary initiatives and the new politics of corporate greening*. Peterborough, Ontario: Broadview Press.

Gichure, C.W. 2006. Teaching business ethics in Africa: what ethical orientation? The case of East and Central Africa. *Journal of Business Ethics*, 63 (1): 39–52.

Gilligan, C. 1982. *In a different voice*. Cambridge, Mass.: Harvard University Press.

Gini, A. 1997. Moral leadership: an overview. *Journal of Business Ethics*, 16 (3): 323–30.

Gladwin, T.N., Kennelly, J.J., and Krause, T.S. 1995. Shifting paradigms for sustainable development: implications for management theory and research. *Academy of Management Review*, 20 (4): 874–907.

Glasbergen, P. 2002. The green polder model: institutionalizing multi-stakeholder processes in strategic environmental decision-making. *European Environment*, 12: 303–15.

Gnuschke, J.E. 2008. Is the Green Revolution for real this time? Will green jobs be created in sufficient numbers to offset declines in other parts of the economy? Will green jobs replace real estate as the engine for the next round of economic expansion? *Business Perspectives*, 19 (3): 6–9.

Goff, C. 2006. New standards in project finance. *Ethical Corporation*, May: 32–3.

Goolsby, J.R. and Hunt, S.D. 1992. Cognitive moral development and marketing. *Journal of Marketing*, 56 (1): 55–68.

Gopal, P. 2009. Now hiring: green-collar workers. *BusinessWeek Online*: 23 July 2009: http://www.businessweek.com.

Gordon, J.N. 2002. What Enron means for the management and control of the modern business corporation: some initial reflections. *University of Chicago Law Review*, 69: 1233–50.

Gordon, K. and Miyake, M. 2001. Business approaches to combating bribery: a study of codes of conduct. *Journal of Business Ethics*, 34: 161–73.

Gorz, A. 1975. *Ecologie et politique*. Paris: Editions Galilée.

Gould, S.J. 1995. The Buddhist perspective on business ethics: experiential exercises for exploration and practice. *Journal of Business Ethics*, 14 (1): 63–72.

Graham, G. 1990. *Living the good life: an introduction to moral philosophy*. New York: Paragon.

Gray, R.H. 1992. Accounting and environmentalism: an exploration of the challenge of gently accounting for accountability, transparency and sustainability. *Accounting, Organizations and Society*, 17 (5): 399–426.

—— Bebbington, J., and Collinson, D. 2006. NGOs, civil society and accountability: making the people accountable to capital. *Accounting, Auditing and Accountability Journal*, 19 (3): 319–48.

Gray, R., Dey, C., Owen, D., Evans, R., and Zadek, S. 1997. Struggling with the praxis of social accounting: stakeholders, accountability, audits and procedures. *Accounting, Auditing and Accountability Journal*, 10 (3): 325–64.

Greening, D.W. and Turban, D.B. 2000. Corporate social performance as a competitive advantage in attracting a quality workforce. *Business & Society*, 39 (3): 254–80.

Greenwood, M.R. 2002. Ethics and HRM: a review and conceptual analysis. *Journal of Business Ethics*, 36: 261–78.

Greyser, S.A. 1972. Advertising: attacks and counters. *Harvard Business Review*, 50, March–April: 22–36.

Griffin, J.J. and Mahon, J.F. 1997. The corporate social performance and corporate financial performance debate: twenty-five years of incomparable research. *Business & Society*, 36 (1): 5–31.

Grimshaw, D., Vincent, S., and Willmott, H. 2002. Going privately: partnership and outsourcing in UK public services. *Public Administration*, 80 (3): 475–502.

Gross-Schaefer, A., Trigilio, J., Negus, J., and Ro, C.-S. 2000. Ethics education in the workplace: an effective tool to combat employee theft. *Journal of Business Ethics*, 26: 89–100.

Grunig, J.E. and Hunt, C. 1984. *Managing public relations*. New York: Holt, Rinehart, and Winston.

Guardian. 2008. The Guardian executive pay survey. *Guardian*, 12 September.

Guerrera, F. 2009. Welch denounces corporate obsessions. *Financial Times*, 13 March.

Guide, V.D.R., Jr. and Wassenhove, L.N.V. 2006. Closed-loop supply chains: an introduction to the feature issue (part 1). *Production and Operations Management*, 15 (3): 345–50.

Gunter, B., Oates, C., and Blades, M. 2005. *Advertising to children on TV: content, impact, and regulation*. London: Routledge.

Gustafson, A. 2000. Making sense of postmodern business ethics. *Business Ethics Quarterly*, 10 (3): 645–58.

Habermas, J. 1983. Diskursethik – Notizen zu einem Begründungsprogramm. In J. Habermas, *Moralbewusstsein und kommunikatives Handeln*: 53–125. Frankfurt/Main: Suhrkamp.

Håkansson, H. and Snehota, I. 2006. No business is an island: the network concept of business strategy. *Scandinavian Journal of Management*, 22 (3): 256–70.

Hall, M.H., Barr, C.W., Easwaramoorthy, M., Sokolowski, S.W., and Salamon, L.M. 2005. *The Canadian nonprofit and voluntary sector in comparative perspective*. Toronto: Imagine Canada.

Hallaq, J.H. and Steinhorst, K. 1994. Business intelligence methods—how ethical. *Journal of Business Ethics*, 13: 787–94.

Handfield, R.B. and Baumer, D.L. 2006. Managing conflict of interest issues in purchasing. *Journal of Supply Chain Management*, 42 (3): 41–50.

Harding, J. 2001a. Feeding the hands that bite. *FT.com*, 15 October.

—— 2001b. Globalization's children strike back. *FT.com*, 10 September.

—— 2001c. The by-product of globalization. *FT.com*, 12 October.

Harris P. and Lock, A. 2002. Sleaze or clear blue water? The evolution of corporate and pressure group representation at the major UK party conferences. *Journal of Public Affairs*, 2 (2): 136–51.

Hart, S.L. and Sharma, S. 2004. Engaging fringe stakeholders for competitive imagination. *Academy of Management Executive*, 18 (1): 7–18.

Hart, T.J. 1993. Human resource management—time to exorcise the militant tendency. *Employee Relations*, 15 (3): 29–36.

Hartman, C.L. and Stafford, E.R. 1997. Green alliances: building new business with environmental groups. *Long Range Planning*, 30 (2): 184–96.

Hartman, L.P. 1998. The rights and wrongs of workplace snooping. *Journal of Business Strategy*, 19 (3): 16–20.

Haslam, P.A. 2007. The corporate social responsibility system in Latin America and the Caribbean. In A. Crane and D. Matten (eds.), *Corporate Social Responsibility—A Three Volumes Edited Collection*, Vol. 3: 236–53. London: Sage.

Hauskrecht, A. 1999. Die asiatische Währungs- und Finanzkrise. In Landeszentrale für Politische Bildung (ed.), *Globalisierung als Chance*: 35–40. Stuttgart: Landeszentrale für Politische Bildung.

Hawkes, C. 2007. Regulating and litigating in the public interest: regulating food marketing to young people worldwide: trends and policy drivers. *American Journal of Public Health*, 97 (11): 1962–73.

Hayes L.D. 2009. *Introduction to Japanese politics* (5th edn.). Armonk, NY: M.E. Sharpe.

Hayman, J.R. 2009. Flexible work arrangements: exploring the linkages between perceived usability of flexible work schedules and work/life balance. *Community, Work & Family*, 12 (3): 327–38.

Heartfield, J. 2005. Contextualizing the 'anti-capitalism' movement in global civil society. In G. Baker and D. Chandler (eds.), *Global civil society*: 85–99. London and New York: Routledge.

Hediger, W. 1999. Reconciling 'weak' and 'strong' sustainability. *International Journal of Social Economics*, 26 (7/8/9): 1120–43.

Heery E. 2000. The new pay: risk and representation at work. In D. Winstanley and J. Woodall (eds.), *Ethical issues in contemporary human resource management*: 172–88. Basingstoke: Macmillan.

Heilman, M.E. 1997. Sex discrimination and the affirmative action remedy: the role of sex stereotypes. *Journal of Business Ethics*, 16 (9): 877–89.

Heiskanen, E. and Pantzar, M. 1997. Toward sustainable consumption: two new perspectives. *Journal of Consumer Policy*, 20: 409–42.

Held, D. and McGrew, A.G. 2000. *The global transformation reader: an introduction to the globalization debate*. Cambridge: Polity Press.

Hellman, J.S. and Schankerman, M. 2000. Intervention, corruption and capture. *Economics of transition*, 8 (3): 545–76.

Herrera, D. 2004. Mondragon: a for-profit organization that embodies Catholic social thought. *Review of Business*, 25 (1): 56–68.

Hertz, N. 2001a. Better to shop than to vote? *Business Ethics: A European Review*, 10 (3): 190–3.

—— 2001b. *The silent takeover*. London: Heinemann.

Higgins, M. and Tadajewski, M. 2002. Anti-corporate protest as consumer spectacle. *Marketing Intelligence and Planning*, 40 (4): 363–71.

Higgs-Kleyn, N. and Kapelianis, D. 1999. The role of prefessional codes in regulating ethical conduct. *Journal of Business Ethics*, 19: 363–74.

Hilhorst, D. 2002. Being good at doing good? Quality and accountability of humanitarian NGOs. *Disasters*, 26 (3): 193–212.

Hill, C.W.L. and Jones, G.R. 2007. *Strategic management: an integrated approach* (7th edn.). Boston: Houghton Mifflin.

Hill, R.P., Ainscough, T., Shank, T., and Manullang, D. 2007. Corporate social responsibility and socially responsible investing: a global perspective. *Journal of Business Ethics*, 70 (2): 165–74.

Hingley, M.K. 2005. Power to all our friends? Living with imbalance in supplier–retailer relationships. *Industrial Marketing Management*, 34 (8): 848–58.

Hof, R.D. and Green, H. 2002. How Amazon cleared the profitability hurdle. *BusinessWeek Online*, 4 Feb.

Hoffman, W.M., Driscoll, D.-M., and Painter-Morland, M. 2001. Integrating ethics. In C. Bonny (ed.), *Business ethics: facing up to the issues*: 38–54. London: *The Economist* Books.

Hofstede, G. 1980. *Culture's consequences: international differences in work related values*. Beverly Hills, Calif.: Sage.

—— 1994. *Cultures and organizations: software of the mind*. London: Harper Collins.

Holbrook, M.B. 1987. Mirror, mirror on the wall, what's unfair in the reflections on advertising? *Journal of Marketing*, 51, July: 95–103.

Holland, M. 1993. *European integration: from community to union*. London: Pinter.

Hopkins, W.E. and Hopkins, S.A. 1999. The ethics of downsizing: perceptions of rights and responsibilities. *Journal of Business Ethics*, 18: 145–56.

Hosmer, L.T. 1987. *The ethics of management*. Boston:Irwin Press.

Houlder, V. 1999. Wind power's zephyr builds to gale force. *Financial Times*, 25 June: 13.

Hsieh, N.-h. 2009. Does global business have a responsibility to promote just institutions? *Business Ethics Quarterly*, 19 (2): 251–73.

Hughes, A. 2001. Global commodity networks, ethical trade and governmentality: organizing business responsibility in the Kenyan cut flower industry. *Transactions of the Institute of British Geographers*, 26 (4): 390–406.

Hughes, A. 2005. Corporate strategy and the management of ethical trade: the case of the UK food and clothing retailers. *Environment and Planning A*, 37: 1145–63.

Hummels, H. 1998. Organizing ethics: a stakeholder debate. *Journal of Business Ethics*, 17: 1403–19.

Hunt, S.D. and Vitell, S.J. 1986. A general theory of marketing ethics. *Journal of Macromarketing*, 6, Spring: 5–16.

Hyatt, J.C. 2005. Birth of the ethics industry. *Business Ethics*, Summer: 20–6.

International Labour Organization. 1998. *World employment outlook*. Geneva: ILO.

Ip, P.K. 2009. The challenge of developing a business ethics in China. *Journal of Business Ethics*, 88 (Supplement 1): 211–24.

Iwata, E. 2006. How Barbie is making business a little better. *USA Today*, 26 March: http://www.usatoday.com.

Jackall, R. 1988. *Moral mazes*. Oxford: Oxford University Press.

Jackson, T. 2000. Management ethics and corporate policy: a cross-cultural comparison. *Journal of Management Studies*, 37 (3): 349–69.

—— 2001. Cultural values and management ethics: a 10 nation study. *Human Relations*, 54 (10): 1267–302.

Jensen, M. and Meckling, W. 1976. Theory of the firm: managerial behaviour, agency costs and ownership structure. *Journal of Financial Economics*, 3: 305–60.

Jeschke, M. 2007. Mining sector. In W. Visser, D. Matten, M. Pohl, and N. Tolhurst (eds.), *The A–Z of corporate social responsibility—the complete reference of concepts, codes and organisations*: 326–8. London: John Wiley.

Johnson, G. and Scholes, K. 2002. *Exploring corporate strategy* (6th edn.). Harlow: Pearson Education Ltd.

Johnson, P. and Smith, K. 1999. Contextualising business ethics: anomie and social life. *Human Relations*, 52 (11): 1351–75.

Jones, A. 2001. Social responsibility and the utilities. *Journal of Business Ethics*, 34: 219–29.

Jones, C., Parker, M. and ten Bos, R. 2005. *For business ethics*. London: Routledge.

Jones, I.W. and Pollitt, M.G. 1998. Ethical and unethical competition: establishing the rules of engagement. *Long Range Planning*, 31 (5): 703–10.

Jones, T.M. 1991. Ethical decision making by individuals in organizations: an issue-contingent model. *Academy of Management Review*, 16: 366–95.

Kaldor, M., Anheier, H., and Glasius, M. (eds.). 2002. *Global civil society 2002*. Oxford: Oxford University Press.

Kaler, J. 1999a. Understanding participation. *Journal of Business Ethics*, 21: 125–35.

—— 1999b. What's the good of ethical theory? *Business Ethics: A European Review*, 8 (4): 206–13.

—— 2000. Reasons to be ethical: self-interest and ethical business. *Journal of Business Ethics*, 27: 161–73.

Kalinowski, T. 2008. TTC Union slams drug testing idea. *The Star*, 13 September.

Kaptein, M. and Schwartz, M.S. 2008. The effectiveness of business codes: a critical examination of existing studies and the development of an integrated research model. *Journal of Business Ethics*, 77 (2): 111–27.

Karnani, A. 2007. The mirage of marketing to the bottom of the pyramid: how the private sector can help alleviate poverty. *California Management Review*, 49 (4): 90–111.

Keane, J. 2003. *Global civil society?* Cambridge: Cambridge University Press.

Kelemen, M. and Peltonen, T. 2001. Ethics, morality and the subject: the contribution of Zygmunt Bauman and Michel Foucault to 'postmodern' business ethics. *Scandinavian Journal of Management*, 17 (2): 151–66.

Kelleher, K. 2006. Wind power generating a higher profile. *TheStreet.com*, 7 May: http://www.thestreet.com.

Kempson, E. and Whyley, C. 1999. *Kept out or opted out? Understanding and combating financial exclusion.* Bristol: Policy Press.

Kieselbach, T. and Mader, S. 2002. Occupational transitions and corporate responsibility in layoffs: a European research project (SOCOSE). *Journal of Business Ethics*, 39: 13–20.

Kilbourne, W., McDonagh, P., and Prothero, A. 1997. Sustainable consumption and the quality of life: a macromarketing challenge to the dominant social paradigm. *Journal of Macromarketing*, 17 (1): 4–24.

Kimber, D. and Lipton, P. 2005. Corporate governance and business ethics in the Asia-Pacific region. *Business & Society*, 44 (2): 178–210.

King, A.A. and Lenox, M.J. 2000. Industry self-regulation without sanctions: the chemical industry's Responsible Care Program. *Academy of Management Journal*, 43 (4): 698–716.

—— —— and Terlaak, A. 2005. The strategic use of decentralized institutions: exploring certification with the ISO 14001 management standard. *Academy of Management Journal*, 48 (6): 1091–106.

Kirrane, D.E. 1990. Managing values: a systematic approach to business ethics. *Training and Development Journal*, November: 53–60.

Klein, N. 2000. *No logo: taking aim at the brand bullies.* London: Flamingo.

—— 2007. *The shock doctrine: the rise of disaster capitalism.* Toronto: Alfred A. Knopf Canada.

Kline, J.M. 2005. *Ethics for international business.* London: Routledge.

Knill, C. and Lehmkuhl, D. 2002. Private actors and the state: internationalization and changing patterns of governance. *Governance: An International Journal of Policy, Administration, and Institutions*, 15 (1): 41–63.

Knoepfel, I. 2001. Dow Jones Sustainability Group Index: a global benchmark for corporate sustainability. *Corporate Environmental Strategy*, 8 (1): 6–15.

Koch, E. 2000. *Globalisierung der wirtschaft.* Munich: Vahlen.

Koehn, D. 1999. What can Eastern philosophy teach us about business ethics? *Journal of Business Ethics*, 19: 71–9.

Kohlberg, L. 1969. Stage and sequence: the cognitive development approach to socialization. In D. Goslin (ed.), *Handbook of socialization theory and research*: 347–80. Chicago: Rand McNally.

Kolk, A. and Levy, D. 2001. Winds of change: corporate strategy, climate change and oil multinationals, *European Management Journal*, 19 (5): 501–9.

Kolk, A. and Pinske, J. 2007. Multinational's political activities on climate change. *Business & Society*, 46 (2): 201–28.

—— van Tulder, R. and Kostwinder, E. 2008. Business and partnerships for development. *European Management Journal*, 26: 262–73.

—— —— and Welters, C. 1999. International codes of conduct and corporate social responsibility: can transnational corporations regulate themselves? *Transnational Corporations*, 8 (1): 143–80.

Korten, D.C. 1995. *When corporations rule the world.* London: Earthscan.

Koslowski, P. 2000. The limits of shareholder value. *Journal of Business Ethics*, 27: 137–48.

Kotler, P. and Lee, N. 2005. *Corporate social responsibility: doing the most good for your company and your cause.* Hoboken, NJ: Wiley.

Kotter, J.P. 1990. What leaders really do. *Harvard Business Review*, 68, May–June: 103–11.

KPMG International. 2008. *KPMG International Survey of Corporate Responsibility Reporting 2008.* http://www.kpmg.com.

Kumar, S. and Malegeant, P. 2006. Strategic alliance in a closed-loop supply chain, a case of manufacturer and eco-non-profit organization. *Technovation*, 26: 1127–35.

Kurucz, E., Colbert, B., and Wheeler, D. 2008. The business case for corporate social responsibility. In A. Crane, A. McWilliams, D. Matten, J. Moon, and D. Siegel (eds.), *The Oxford handbook of corporate social responsibility*: 83–112. Oxford: Oxford University Press.

Laczniak, G.R. and Murphy, P.E. 1993. *Ethical marketing decisions: the higher road.* Boston: Allyn and Bacon.

Lambert, D.M. 2008. *Supply chain management: processes, partnerships, performance* (3rd edn.). Sarasota, FL: Supply Chain Management Institute.

Lang, R. (ed.). 2001. *Wirtschaftsethik in Mittel- und Osteuropa*. Munich: Rainer Hampp.

Larsson, L. 2007. Public trust in the PR industry and its actors. *Journal of Communication Management*, 11 (3): 222–34.

Lasprogata, G., King, N.J., and Pillay, S. 2004. Regulation of electronic employee monitoring: identifying fundamental principles of employee privacy through a comparative study of data privacy legislation in the European Union, United States and Canada. *Stanford Technology Law Review*, 4: http://stlr.stanford.edu/STLR/Articles/04_STLR_04.

Lee, M. and Koh, J. 2001. Is empowerment really a new concept? *International Journal of Human Resource Management*, 12 (4): 684–95.

Legge, K. 1998. Is HRM ethical? Can HRM be ethical? In M. Parker (ed.), *Ethics and organization*: 150–72. London: Sage.

—— 2000. The ethical context of HRM: the ethical organization in the boundaryless world. In D. Winstanley and J. Woodall (eds.), *Ethical issues in comtemporary human resource management*: 23–40. Basingstoke: Macmillan.

Lemke, F., Goffin, K., and Szwejczewski, M. 2003. Investigating the meaning of supplier-manufacturer partnerships: an exploratory study. *International Journal of Physical Distribution and Logistics Management*, 33 (1/2): 12.

Lertzman, D. and Vredenburg, H. 2005. Indigenous peoples, resource extraction and sustainable development: an ethical approach. *Journal of Business Ethics*, 56 (3): 239–54.

Levitt, T. 1970. The morality (?) of advertising. *Harvard Business Review*, 48, July–August: 84–92.

Levy, D. and Egan, D. 2000. Corporate politics and climate change. In R.A. Higgott, G.R.D. Underhill, and A. Bieler (eds.), *Non-state actors and authority in the global system*: 138–53. London: Routledge.

Levy, D.L. and Newell, P. 2005. *The business of global environmental governance*. Cambridge, Mass.: MIT Press.

Lewicka-Strzalecka, A. 2006. Opportunities and limitations of CSR in the postcommunist countries: Polish case. *Corporate Governance: The International Journal of Effective Board Performance*, 6 (4): 440–8.

Livesey, S.M. 2002. Global warming wars: rhetorical and discourse analytic approaches to ExxonMobil's corporate public discourse. *Journal of Business Communication*, 39 (1): 118–49.

Locke, R. and Romis, M. 2007. Improving work conditions in a global supply chain. *MIT Sloan Management Review*, Winter: 54–62.

Loe, T.W., Ferrell, L., and Mansfield, P. 2000. A review of empirical studies assessing ethical decision making in business. *Journal of Business Ethics*, 25 (3): 185–204.

Lord, M.D. 2000. Corporate political strategy and legislative decision-making. *Business & Society*, 39 (1): 76–93.

Louche, C. and Lydenberg, S. 2006. Socially responsible investment: differences between Europe and the United States. Vlerick Leuven Gent Working Paper Series 2006/22.

Lovins, A.B., Lovins, L.H., and Hawken, P. 1999. A road map for natural capitalism. *Harvard Business Review*, May–June: 145–58.

Luce, E. and Merchant, K. 2003. India orders ban on advert saying fairer equals better for women. *Financial Times*, 20 March: http://www.ft.com.

Luhmann, N. 1998. Der Staat des politischen Systems. In U. Beck (ed.), *Perspektiven der Weltgesellschaft*: 345–80. Frankfurt/Main: Suhrkamp.

Lynas, M. 2008. Green v green. *Guardian*, 24 April: http://www.guardian.co.uk.

Lyotard, J.-F. 1984. *The postmodern condition: a report on knowledge*. Manchester: Manchester University Press.

Lysonski, S. and Gaidis, W. 1991. A cross-cultural comparison of the ethics of business students. *Journal of Business Ethics*, 10: 141–50.

MacIntyre, A. 1984. *After virtue: a study in moral theory*. Notre Dame, Ill.: University of Notre Dame Press.

Mackenzie, C. 1998. The choice of criteria in ethical investment. *Business Ethics: A European Review*, 7 (2): 81–6.

Maguire, K. and Wintour, P. 2001. The other woman in Blair's life walks out on him for job with BP. *Guardian*, 9 November.

Maier, M. 1997. Gender equity, organizational transformation and challenger. *Journal of Business Ethics*, 16: 943–62.

Maignan, I. 2001. Consumers' perceptions of corporate social responsibilities: a cross-cultural comparison. *Journal of Business Ethics*, 30 (1/1): 57–72.

—— and Ferrell, O.C. 2000. Measuring corporate citizenship in two countries: the case of the United States and France. *Journal of Business Ethics*, 23: 283–97.

—— —— 2001. Antecedents and benefits of corporate citizenship: an investigation of French businesses. *Journal of Business Research*, 51: 37–51.

—— —— and Hult, G.T.M. 1999. Corporate citizenship: cultural antecedents and business benefits. *Journal of the Academy of Marketing Science*, 27 (4): 455–69.

Majumder, S. 2006. Furore reflects India's caste complexities. *BBC News*, 20 May: http://www.bbc.co.uk/news.

Marshall, T.H. 1965. *Class, citizenship and social development*. New York: Anchor Books.

Martínez Lucio, M. and Weston, S. 2000. European works councils and 'flexible regulation': the politics of intervention. *European Journal of Industrial Relations*, 6 (2): 203–16.

Mathiason, N. 2009. Private equity owned Boots ends ethical pledge. *Guardian*, 13 June: http://www.guardian.co.uk.

Matten, D. 1998. Sustainable Development als betriebswirtschaftliches Leitbild: Hintergründe—Abgrenzungen—Perspektiven. In H. Albach and M. Steven (eds.), *Betriebliches Umweltmanagement*: 1–23. Wiesbaden: Gabler.

Matten, D. and Crane, A. 2005a. Corporate citizenship: towards an extended theoretical conceptualization. *Academy of Management Review*, 30 (1): 166–79.

—— —— 2005b. What is stakeholder democracy? Perspectives and issues. *Business Ethics: A European Review*, 14 (1): 6–13.

—— and Moon, J. 2008. 'Implicit' and 'explicit' CSR: a conceptual framework for a comparative understanding of corporate social responsibility. *Academy of Management Review*, 33 (2): 404–24.

Mayhew, N. 1997. Fading to grey: the use and abuse of corporate executives' 'representational power'. In R.J. Welford (ed.), *Hijacking environmentalism—corporate responses to sustainable development*: 63–95. London: Routledge.

McCabe, D.L., Dukerich, J.M., and Dutton, J.E. 1991. Context, values and moral dilemmas: comparing the choices of business and law school students. *Journal of Business Ethics*, 10 (2): 951–60.

—— and Treviño, L.K. 1993. Academic dishonesty: honor codes and other situational influences. *Journal of Higher Education*, 64: 522–38.

McEwan, T. 2001. *Managing values and beliefs in organisations*. Harlow: Pearson Education.

McGrath, C. 2002. Comparative lobbying practices: Washington, London, Brussels. Paper presented at the Political Studies Association annual conference, University of Aberdeen.

—— 2005. Towards a lobbying profession: developing the industry's reputation, education and representation. *Journal of Public Affairs*, 5: 124–35.

McGrew, A.G. 1997a. Democracy beyond borders? Globalization and the reconstruction of democratic theory and practice. In A.G. McGrew (ed.), *The transformation of democracy? Globalization and territorial democracy*: 231–66. Cambridge: Polity Press.

—— 1997b. Globalization and territorial democracy: an introduction. In A.G. McGrew (ed.), *The transformation of democracy? Globalization and territorial democracy*: 1–24. Cambridge: Polity Press.

McIntosh, M. and Thomas, R. 2002. *Corporate citizenship and the evolving relationship between non-governmental organisations and corporations*. London: British-North American Committee.

McKinsey Quarterly 2006. The McKinsey Global Survey of Business Executives: Business and Society. *McKinsey Quarterly*, (2): 33–9.

—— 2008. From risk to opportunity – how global executives view sociopolitical issues, *McKinsey Quarterly*, September: http://www.mckinseyquarterly.com.

McMurtry, J.J. 2009. Ethical value-added: fair trade and the case of Café Femenino. *Journal of Business Ethics*, 86: 27–49.

McNeely, J.A., Solh, M., Hiremath, R.B., Kumar, B., Suarez, P.A.Z., Uprety, K., Abdulrahim, M.A., Ruf, F., and Legoupil, J.-C. 2009. Viewpoints: 'Can the growing demand for biofuels be met without threatening food security?'. *Natural Resources Forum*, 33 (2): 171–3.

McPhail, K. 2001. The *other* objective of ethics education: re-humanising the accounting profession—a study of ethics education in law, engineering, medicine and accountancy. *Journal of Business Ethics*, 34: 279–98.

McWilliams, A. and Siegel, D. 2000. Corporate social responsibility and financial performance: correlation or misspecification? *Strategic Management Journal*, 21 (5): 603–9.
Meadows, D.H., Meadows, D.L., Randers, J., and Behrens, W.W. 1974. *The limits to growth*. London: Pan.
Meglino, B.M. and Ravlin, E.C. 1998. Individual values in organizations: concepts, controversies, and research. *Journal of Management*, 24 (3): 351–89.
Mellahi, K. and Wood, G. 2002. *The ethical business*. Basingstoke: Palgrave.
Michalos, A.C. 1988. Editorial. *Journal of Business Ethics*, 7: 1.
Millington, A., Eberhardt, M., and Wilkinson, B. 2005. Gift giving, Guanxi and illicit payments in buyer–supplier relations in China: analysing the experience of UK companies. *Journal of Business Ethics*, 57: 255–68.
Milne, G.R. and Culnan, M.J. 2004. Strategies for reducing online privacy risks: why consumers read (or don't read) online privacy notices. *Journal of Interactive Marketing*, 18 (3): 15–29.
Milner, S. 2002. An ambiguous reform: the Jospin government and the 35-hour-week laws. *Modern and Contemporary France*, 10 (3): 339–51.
Mintzberg, H. 1983. The case for corporate social responsibility. *Journal of Business Strategy*, 4 (2): 3–15.
Mitchell, R.K., Agle, B.R., and Wood, D.J. 1997. Toward a theory of stakeholder identification and salience: defining the principle of who and what really counts. *Academy of Management Review*, 22 (4): 853–86.
Mitchell, W.C. 1990. Interest groups: economic perspectives and contribution. *Journal of Theoretical Politics*, 2: 85–108.
Moilanen, T. and Salminen, A. 2007. *Comparative study of the public-service ethics of the EU member states*. Helsinki: Finnish Ministry of Finance.
Molina, O. and Rhodes, M. 2002. Corporatism: the past, present and future of a concept. *Annual Review of Political Science*, 5: 305–31.
Monks, R.A.G. and Minow, N. 2004. *Corporate governance* (3rd edn.). Malden, Mass.: Blackwell.
Mont, O. 2004. *Product-service systems: panacea or myth?* Lund: International Institute for Industrial Environmental Economics.
Moody, M. 2008. 'Building a culture': the construction and evolution of venture philanthropy as a new organizational field. *Nonprofit and Voluntary Sector Quarterly* 37 (2): 324–52.
Moon, J. 1995. The firm as citizen: corporate responsibility in Australia. *Australian Journal of Political Science*, 30 (1): 1–17.
—— and Vogel, D. 2008. Corporate social responsibility, government, and civil society. In A. Crane, A. McWilliams, D. Matten, J. Moon, and D. Siegel (eds.), *The Oxford handbook of corporate social responsibility*: 303–23. Oxford: Oxford University Press.
Moore, E.S. 2004. Children and the changing world of advertising. *Journal of Business Ethics*, 52 (2): 161–7.
Moore, G. 1999a. Corporate moral agency: review and implications. *Journal of Business Ethics*, 21: 329–43.
—— 1999b. Tinged shareholder theory: or what's so special about stakeholders? *Business Ethics: A European Review*, 8 (2): 117–27.
Moore, J. 1990. What is really unethical about insider trading? *Journal of Business Ethics*, 9: 171–82.
Moore, K. and Lewis, D. 1999. *Birth of the multinational enterprise: 2000 years of business history—from Assur to Augustus*. Copenhagen: Copenhagen Business School Press.
Moore, M. 2008. China's pioneering eco-city of Dongtan stalls. *Telegraph*, 18 October: http://www.telegraph.co.uk.
Morris, D. 2004. Defining a moral problem in business ethics. *Journal of Business Ethics*, 49: 347–57.
Muller, A. and Whiteman, G. 2009. Exploring the geography of corporate philanthropic disaster response: a study of Fortune global 500 firms. *Journal of Business Ethics*, 84: 589–603.
Murphy, D. 2007. More Saudi women join the workforce, but limits remain strict. *Christian Science Monitor*, 24 April: http://www.csmonitor.com.
Murphy, D.F. and Bendell, J. 1997. *In the company of partners: business, environmental groups and sustainable development post-Rio*. Bristol: Policy Press.
Muskin, J.B. 2000. Interorganizational ethics: standards of behavior. *Journal of Business Ethics*, 24: 283–97.

Muthuri, J.N. 2008. Participation and accountability in corporate community involvement programmes: a research agenda. *Community Development Journal*, 43 (2): 177–93.

—— Matten, D., and Moon, J. 2009. Employee volunteering and social capital: contributions to corporate social responsibility. *British Journal of Management*, 20 (1): 75–89.

Nader, R. 1984. Reforming corporate governance. *California Management Review*, 26 (4): 126–32.

Nanto, D. 2008. *The U.S. financial crisis: the global dimension with implications for U.S. policy (November 10, 2008)*. Washington: Congressional Research Service.

Nelson, J. and Prescott, D. 2003. *Business and the millennium development goals: a framework for action*. London: The International Business Leaders Forum.

New, S. 1998. The implications and reality of partnership. In Dale (ed.), *Working in partnership: best practice in customer-supplier relations*: 9–20. Aldershot: Gower Publishing.

Newell, P. and Frynas, J.G. 2007. Beyond CSR? Business, poverty and social justice: an introduction. *Third World Quarterly*, 28 (4): 669–81.

Newton, L.H. 1992. The many faces of the corporate code. Paper presented at the Conference on Corporate Visions and Values.

Nicholls, A. 2006. Introduction. In A. Nicholls (ed.), *Social entrepreneurship: new models of sustainable social change*. Oxford, Oxford University Press.

—— and Opal, C. 2005. *Fair trade: market-driven ethical consumption*. London: Sage.

Nickel, J.W. 2002. Is today's international human rights system a global governance regime? *Journal of Ethics*, 6 (4): 353–72.

Nielsen, R.P. 2006. Introduction to the special issue. In search of organizational virtue: moral agency in organizations. *Organization Studies*, 27 (3): 317–21.

—— 2008. The private equity-leveraged buyout form of finance capitalism: ethical and social issues and potential reforms. *Business Ethics Quarterly*, 18 (3): 379–404.

Nomani, F. 2008. Islamic finance: law, economics. *International Journal of Middle East Studies*, 40 (2): 349–51.

Nozick, R. 1974. *Anarchy, state, and utopia*. New York: Basic Books.

Nwankwo, E., Phillips, N., and Tracey, P. 2007. Social investment through community enterprise: the case of multinational corporations involvement in the development of Nigerian water resources. *Journal of Business Ethics*, 73 (1): 91–101.

Nyaw, M.-K. and Ng, I. 1994. A comparative analysis of ethical beliefs: a four country study. *Journal of Business Ethics*, 13 (7): 543–55.

O'Dwyer, B. and Owen, D.L. 2005. Assurance statement practice in environmental, social and sustainability reporting: a critical evaluation. *British Accounting Review*, 37 (2): 205–29.

O'Fallon, M.J. and Butterfield, K.D. 2005. A review of the empirical ethical decision-making literature: 1996–2003. *Journal of Business Ethics*, 59 (4): 375–413.

O'Neill, O. 2002. *A question of trust: the BBC Reith lectures 2002*. Cambridge: Cambridge University Press.

OECD. 2001. Codes of corporate conduct—an expanded review of their contents. Paris: Organisation for Economic Co-operation and Development.

Ogbonna, E. and Harris, L.C. 1998. Managing organizational culture: compliance or genuine change? *British Journal of Management*, 9: 273–88.

—— and Wilkinson, B. 1996. Inter-organizational power relations in the UK grocery industry: contradictions and developments. *International Review of Retail, Distribution and Consumer Research*, 6 (4): 395–414.

Orlitzky, M. 2008. Corporate social performance and financial performance: a research synthesis. In A. Crane, A. McWilliams, D. Matten, J. Moon, and D. Siegel (eds.), *The Oxford handbook of corporate social responsibility*: 113–36. Oxford: Oxford University Press.

—— Schmidt, F.L., and Rynes, S.L. 2003. Corporate social and financial performance: a meta-analysis. *Organization Studies*, 24 (3): 403–11.

O'Rourke, A. 2003. A new politics of engagement: shareholder activism for corporate social responsibility. *Business Strategy and the Environment*, 12 (4): 227–39.

Orts, E.W. 1995. A reflexive model of environmental regulation. *Business Ethics Quarterly*, 5 (4): 779–94.

—— and Deketelaere, K. 2001. Environmental contracts and regulatory innovation. In E.W. Orts and K. Deketelaere (eds.), *Environmental Contracts*: 1–35. Dordrecht et al.: Kluwer.

Ostas, D.T. 2007. The law and ethics of K street—lobbying, the first amendment, and the duty to create just laws. *Business Ethics Quarterly*, 17 (1): 33–63.

Ottensmeyer, E.J. and Heroux, M.A. 1991. Ethics, public policy, and managing advanced technologies: the case of electronic surveillance. *Journal of Business Ethics*, 10: 519–26.
Oulton, W. 2006. The role of activism in responsible investment—the FTSE4Good indices. In R. Sullivan and C. Mackenzie (eds.), *Responsible investment*: 196–205. Sheffield: Greenleaf.
Owen, D.L. 2005. Corporate social reporting and stakeholder accountability: the missing link. *ICCSR Research Paper Series* (32–2005).
Owen, D.L. and O'Dwyer, B. 2008. Corporate social responsibility: the reporting and assurance dimension. In A. Crane, D. Matten, A. McWilliams, J. Moon, and D. Siegel (eds.), *The Oxford handbook of corporate social responsibility*: 384–409. Oxford: Oxford University Press.
Packard, V. 1957. *The hidden persuaders*. New York: Pocket Books.
Pagell, M. and Wu, Z. 2009. Building a more complete theory of sustainable supply chain management using case studies of 10 exemplars. *Journal of Supply Chain Management*, 45 (2): 37–56.
Paine, L.S. 1994. Managing for organizational integrity. *Harvard Business Review*, March–April: 106–17.
Palazzo, B. 2002. US–American and German business ethics: an intercultural comparison. *Journal of Business Ethics*, 41: 195–216.
Parker, B. 1998a. *Globalization and business practice: managing across boundaries*. London: Sage.
Parker, M. 1998b. Business ethics and social theory: postmodernizing the ethical. *British Journal of Management*, 9 (special issue): S27–S36.
Parkin, F. 1982. *Max Weber*. London: Routledge.
Parkinson, J.E. 1993. *Corporate power and responsibility*. Oxford: Oxford University Press.
Parkinson, J.E. 2003. Models of the company and the employment relationship. *British Journal of Industrial Relations*, 41 (3): 481–509.
Paulson, H. 2001. The gospel of globalisation. *Financial Times*, 13 November: 25.
Pava, M.L. 1998. The substance of Jewish business ethics. *Journal of Business Ethics*, 17 (6): 603–17.
Pearce, D. 1999. *Economics and environment: essays on ecological economics and sustainable development*. Cheltenham: Edward Elgar.
—— and Turner, K. 1990. *Economics of natural resources and the environment*. New York: Harvester Wheatsheaf.
Pearce, J.A., II. 2009. The profit-making allure of product reconstruction. *MIT Sloan Management Review*, 50 (3): 59–65.
Pearson, R. and Seyfang, G. 2001. New hope or false dawn? Voluntary codes of conduct, labour regulation and social policy in a globalizing world. *Global social policy*, 1 (1): 49–78.
Peattie, K. and Crane, A. 2005. Green marketing: legend, myth, farce or prophesy? *Qualitative Market Research: An International Journal*, 8 (4): 357–70.
Peloza, J. and Hassay, D.N. 2006. Intra-organizational volunteerism: good soldiers, good deeds and good politics. *Journal of Business Ethics*, 64 (4): 357–79.
Pfeffer, J. and Salancik, G.R. 1978. *The external control of organizations: a resource dependence perspective*. New York: Harper and Row.
Phillips, B.J. 1997. In defense of advertising: a social perspective. *Journal of Business Ethics*, 16: 109–18.
Picard, R.G. 2004. A note on economic losses due to theft, infringement, and piracy of protected works. *Journal of Media Economics*, 17 (3): 208–17.
Pijper, P. 1994. *Creative accounting: the effectiveness of financial reporting in the UK*. London: Macmillan.
Pojman, L.P. 1997. The moral status of affirmative action. In T.L. Beauchamp and N.E. Bowie (eds.) *Ethical theory and business* (5th edn.): 374–79. Upper Saddle River, NJ: Prentice Hall.
Pollay, R.W. 1986. The distorted mirror: reflections on the unintended consequences of advertising. *Journal of Marketing*, 50, April: 18–36.
Porter, M.E. 1980. *Competitive strategy: techniques for analysing industries and competitors*. New York: Free Press.
—— and Kramer, M.R. 2006. Strategy and society: the link between competitive advantage and corporate social responsibility. *Harvard Business Review*, December: 78–92.
Prahalad, C.K. and Hammond, A. 2002. Serving the world's poor, profitably. *Harvard Business Review*, 80 (9): 48–57.
Premeaux, S.R. and Mondy, R.W. 1993. Linking management behavior to ethical philosophy. *Journal of Business Ethics*, 12: 349–57.
Preuss, L. 1999. Ethical theory in German business ethics research. *Journal of Business Ethics*, 18: 407–19.
—— 2005. *The green multiplier: a study of environmental protection and the supply chain*. Basingstoke: Palgrave Macmillan.

Puppim de Oliveira, J.A. and Vargas, G. 2006. Corporate citizenship in Latin America: new challenges for business (special issue). *Journal of Corporate Citizenship* (21).

Rabelo, F.M. and Vasconcelos, F.C. 2002. Corporate governance in Brazil. *Journal of Business Ethics*, 37 (3): 321–35.

Rabcuin, M. 1997. Lyin' T(*)gers, and 'Cares', oh my: the case of feminist integration of business ethics. *Journal of Business Ethics*, 16: 247–61.

Ram, M. 2000. Investors in people in small firms: case study evidence from the business services sector. *Personnel Review*, 29 (1): 69–91.

Rawls, J. 1971. *A theory of justice*. Cambridge, Mass.: Harvard University Press.

Reece, J.W. 2001. Business and the civil society: the missing dialectic. *Thunderbird International Business Review*, 43 (5): 651–67.

Reed, D. 2002. Corporate governance reforms in developing countries. *Journal of Business Ethics*, 37 (3): 223–47.

Reeves, R. 2005. Do the right thing. *Management Today*, 1 July: http://www.clickmt.com.

Reich, R.B. 2007. *Supercapitalism: the transformation of business, democracy and everyday life*. New York: Alfred A. Knopf.

Reitz, H.J., Wall, J.A., Jr., and Love, M.S. 1998. Ethics in negotiation: oil and water or good lubrication? *Business Horizons*, May–June: 5–14.

Renn, O., Webler, T., and Wiedemann, P.M. (eds.). 1995. *Fairness and competence in citizen participation*. Dordrecht: Kluwer.

Rest, J.R. 1986. *Moral development: advances in research and theory*. New York: Praeger.

Rice, G. 1999. Islamic ethics and the implications for business. *Journal of Business Ethics*, 18 (4): 345–58.

Rifkin, J. 1995. *The end of work*. New York: Tarcher Putnam.

Rivoli, P. 1995. Ethical aspects of investor behaviour. *Journal of Business Ethics*, 14: 265–77.

Roberts, S. 2003. Supply chain specific? Understanding the patchy success of ethical sourcing initiatives. *Journal of Business Ethics*, 44 (2/3): 159–70.

Robin, D.P. and Reidenbach, R.E. 1987. Social responsibility, ethics and marketing strategy: closing the gap between concept and application. *Journal of Marketing*, 51, January: 44–58.

Robins, N. and Humphrey, L. 2000. Sustaining the rag trade. London: International Institute for Environment and Development.

Robinson, W. 2005. Ethical considerations in flexible work arrangements. *Business and Society Review*, 110 (2): 213–24.

Rokeach, M. 1973. *The nature of human values*. New York: Free Press.

Romar, E.J. 2004. Globalization, ethics, and opportunism: a Confucian view of business relationships. *Business Ethics Quarterly*, 14 (4): 663–78.

Rondinelli, D. and Vastag, G. 2000. Panacea, common sense, or just a label? The value of ISO 14001 environmental management systems. *European Management Journal*, 18 (5): 499–510.

Roner, L. 2009. Responsible downsizing. *Ethical Corporation*, February: http://www.ethicalcorp.com.

Ronit, K. 2001. Institutions of private authority in global governance. *Administration & Society*, 33 (5): 555–78.

Rosenthal, S.B. and Buchholz, R.A. 2000. *Rethinking business ethics: a pragmatic approach*. New York: Oxford University Press.

Rossouw, G. 2005. Business ethics and corporate governance in Africa. *Business & Society*, 44 (1): 94–106.

Rothenberg, S. 2007. Sustainability through servicizing. *MIT Sloan Management Review*, 48 (2): 83–91.

Rothschild, J. and Miethe, T.D. 1999. Whistle blower disclosures and management retaliation: the battle to control information about organization corruption. *Work and Occupations*, 26 (1): 107–28.

Rowan, J.R. 2000. The moral foundation of employee rights. *Journal of Business Ethics*, 24: 355–61.

Rowley, T.J. 1997. Moving beyond dyadic ties: a network theory of stakeholder influences. *Academy of Management Review*, 22 (4): 887–910.

Roy, R. and Whelan, R.C. 1992. Successful recycling through value-chain collaboration. *Long Range Planning*, 25 (4): 62–71.

Royle, T. 2005. Realism or idealism? Corporate social responsibility and the employee stakeholder in the global fast-food industry. *Business Ethics: A European Review*, 14 (1): 42–55.

Rudelius, W. and Buchholz, R.A. 1979. Ethical problems of purchasing managers. *Harvard Business Review*, March–April: 8–14.

Rudolph, B. 1999. Finanzmärkte. In W. Korff (ed.), *Handbuch der Wirtschaftsethik*: 274–92. Gütersloh: Gütersloher Verlagshaus.

Rudra, N. 2008. *Globalization and the race to the bottom in developing countries: who really gets hurt?* Cambridge, UK and New York: Cambridge University Press.

Ruggie, J. 2008. Protect, respect and remedy: a framework for business and human rights. *Innovations*, Spring: 189–212.

Rugman, A.M. 2000. *The end of globalisation*. London: Random House.

—— and Verbeke, A. 2000. Six cases of corporate strategic responses to environmental regulation. *European Management Journal*, 18 (4): 377–85.

Russell, J. 2006. A charter for success. *Ethical Corporation*, June: 11.

Sack, D. 2001. Jobs, Lärm, Mediation: Zur demokratischen Partizipation bei glokalen Großprojekten. In M. Berndt and D. Sack (eds.), *Glocal Governance?* 219–37. Opladen: Westdeutscher Verlag.

Salamon, L.M., Haddock, M.A., Sokolowski, S.W., and Tice, H.S. 2007. Measuring civil society and volunteering: initial findings from implementation of the UN handbook on nonprofit institutions, *Working Paper No. 23*. Baltimore: Johns Hopkins Center for Civil Society Studies.

Salant, J.D. and O'Leary, L. 2009. Six lobbyists per lawmaker work on health overhaul. *Bloomberg News*, 14 August.

Sandberg, A. (ed.). 1995. *Enriching production: perspectives on Volvo's Uddevalla plant as an alternative to lean production*. Aldershot: Avebury.

Sarkar, J. and Sarkar, S. 2000. Large shareholder activism in corporate governance in developing countries: evidence from India. *International Review of Finance*, 1 (3): 161–94.

Schaefer, A. and Crane, A. 2005. Addressing sustainability and consumption. *Journal of Macromarketing*, 25: 76–92.

Scherer, A.G. and Palazzo, G. 2008a. Globalization and CSR. In A. Crane, A. McWilliams, D. Matten, J. Moon, and D. Siegel (eds.), *The Oxford handbook of corporate social responsibility*: 413–31. Oxford: Oxford University Press.

—— —— (eds.). 2008b. *Handbook of research on global corporate citizenship*. Cheltenham: Edward Elgar.

—— —— and Baumann, D. 2006. Global rules and private actors—towards a new role of the TNC in global governance. *Business Ethics Quarterly*, 16 (3): 505–32.

—— and Smid, M. 2000. The downward spiral and the U.S. model business principles: why MNEs should take responsibility for improvement of worldwide social and environmental conditions. *Management International Review*, 40 (4): 351–71.

Schlosser, E. 2001. *Fast food nation*. Boston: Houghton Mifflin.

Schmidt, G. and Williams, K. 2002. German management facing globalization: the 'German model' on trial. In M. Geppert, D. Matten, and K. Williams (eds.), *Challenges for European managment in a global context: experiences from Britain and Germany*: 281–93. Basingstoke: Palgrave.

Schneider, M.C. and Buchenau, M.W. 2009. Wiedeking kämpft um Machterhalt. *Süddeutsche Zeitung*, 25 May.

Schneidewind, U. and Petersen, H. 1998. Changing the rules: business–NGO partnerships and structuration theory. *Greener Management International*, 24: 105–14.

Scholte, J.A. 2005. *Globalization: a critical introduction* (2nd edn.). Basingstoke: Palgrave.

Schrader, U. 1999. Consumer acceptance of eco-efficient services. *Greener Management International*, 25: 105–21.

Schumacher, E.F. 1974. *Small is beautiful: a study of economics as if people mattered*. London: Abacus.

Schwartz, M. 2000. Why ethical codes constitute an unconscionable regression. *Journal of Business Ethics*, 23: 173–84.

Schwarzer, C.E., May, D.R., and Rosen, B. 1995. Organizational characteristics and HRM policies on rights: exploring the patterns of connections. *Journal of Business Ethics*, 14: 531–49.

Scott, K., Park, J., and Cocklin, C. 2000. From 'sustainable rural communities' to 'social sustainability': giving voice to diversity in Mangakahia Valley, New Zealand. *Journal of Rural Studies*, 16: 443–6.

Seelos, C. and Mair, J. 2005. Social entrepreneurship: creating new business models to serve the poor. *Business Horizons*, 48: 241–6.

Seitanidi, M. M. and Ryan, A. 2007. A critical review of forms of corporate community involvement: from philanthropy to partnerships. *International Journal of Nonprofit and Voluntary Sector Marketing*, 12: 247–66.

Selsky, J.W. and Parker, B. 2005. Cross-sector partnerships to address social issues: challenges to theory and practice. *Journal of Management*, 31 (6): 1–25.

Sen, S., Gurhan-Canli, Z., and Morwitz, V. 2001. Withholding consumption: a social dilemma perspective on consumer boycotts. *Journal of Consumer Research*, 28 (3): 399–417.

Serwotka, M. and Sinnott, S. 2006. The perils of privatisation. *Guardian*, 26 June: http://www.guardian.co.uk.

Sethi, S.P. 2002. Standards for corporate conduct in the international arena: challenges and opportunities for multinational corporations. *Business and Society Review*, 107 (1): 20–40.

Shankman, N.A. 1999. Reframing the debate between agency and stakeholder theories of the firm. *Journal of Business Ethics*, 19: 319–34.

Shaoul, J. 2002. A financial appraisal of the London underground public–private partnership. *Public Money and Management*, April–June: 53–60.

Shapiro, B.R. 1998. Economic espionage. *Marketing Management*, 7 (1): 56–8.

Sharp Paine, L. 1993. Children as consumers: the ethics of children's television advertising. In J.A. Quelch (ed.), *Ethics in marketing*. Homewood, Ill.: Irwin.

Shaw, B. 1995. Virtues for a postmodern world. *Business Ethics Quarterly*, 5 (4): 843–63.

Shaw, D. and Newholm, T. 2001. Voluntary simplicity and the ethics of consumption. *Psychology and marketing*, 19 (2): 167–85.

Shrivastava, P. 1995. Ecocentric management for a risk society. *Academy of Management Review*, 20 (1): 118–37.

Sillanpää, M. 1998. The Body Shop values report: towards integrated stakeholder auditing. *Journal of Business Ethics*, 17: 1443–56.

—— and Wheeler, D. 1997. Integrated ethical auditing: The Body Shop International. In S. Zadek, P. Pruzan, and R. Evans (eds.), *Building corporate accountability: emerging practices in social and ethical accounting, auditing and reporting*: 102–28. London: Earthscan.

Simma, B. and Heinemann, A. 1999. Codes of conduct. In W. Korff et al. (eds.), *Handbuch der Wirtschaftsethik*, Vol. 1: 403–18. Gütersloh: Gütersloher Verlagshaus.

Simms, M. 1994. Defining privacy in employee health screening cases: ethical ramifications concerning the employee/employer relationship. *Journal of Business Ethics*, 13: 315–25.

Simpson, R. 1998. Presenteeism, power and organizational change: long hours as a career barrier and the impact on the working lives of women managers. *British Journal of Management*, 9 (special issue): 37–50.

—— 2000. Presenteeism and the impact of long hours on managers. In D. Winstanley and J. Woodall (eds.), *Ethical issues in contemporary human resource management*: 156–71. Basingstoke: Macmillan.

Sims, R.R. and Brinkmann, J. 2002. Leaders as moral role models: the case of John Gutfreund at Salomon Brothers. *Journal of Business Ethics*, 35 (4): 327–39.

—— —— 2003. Enron ethics (or: Culture matters more than codes). *Journal of Business Ethics*, 45 (3): 243–56.

Sinclair, A. 1993. Approaches to organizational culture and ethics. *Journal of Business Ethics*, 12: 63–73.

Singhapakdi, A. and Vitell, S.J. 1990. Marketing ethics: factors influencing perceptions of ethical problems and alternatives. *Journal of Macromarketing*, 10 (1): 4–18.

Sison, A.J.G. 2000. Integrated risk management and global business ethics. *Business Ethics: A European Review*, 9 (4): 288–95.

Sklair, L. 1991. *Sociology of the global system*. Baltimore: John Hopkins University Press.

Smalley Bowen, T. 2003. Reducing pollution—it's a bargain. *Financial Times*, 2 February: 16.

Smith, A. 1793. *An inquiry into the nature and causes of the wealth of nations*. London: A Sraten and T. Cadell.

Smith, C. 1994. The new corporate philanthropy. *Harvard Business Review*, May–June: 105–16.

—— and Pun, N. 2006. The dormitory labour regime in China as a site for control and resistance. *International Journal of Human Resource Management*, 17 (8): 1456–70.

Smith, L. 2005. Too few black and Asian faces at the top. *Guardian*, 17 November: 29.

Smith, N.C. 1990. *Morality and the market: consumer pressure for corporate accountability*. London: Routledge.

—— 1995. Marketing strategies for the ethics era. *Sloan Management Review*, 36 (4): 85–97.

—— 2003. Corporate social responsibility: whether or how? *California Management Review*, 45 (4): 52–76.

—— and Cooper-Martin, E. 1997. Ethics and target marketing: the role of product harm and consumer vulnerability. *Journal of Marketing*, 61, July: 1–20.

—— and Quelch, J.A. 1993. *Ethics in marketing*. Homewood, Ill.: Irwin.

Smith, S. and Barrientos, S. 2005. Fair trade and ethical trade: are there moves towards convergence? *Sustainable Development*, 13: 190–8.

Solomon, A. and Lewis, L. 2002. Incentives and disincentives for corporate environmental disclosure. *Business Strategy and the Environment*: 154–69.

Solomon, R.C. 1999. *A better way to think about business: how personal integrity leads to corporate success*. New York: Oxford University Press.

Solymossy, E. and Masters, J.K. 2002. Ethics through an entrepreneurial lens: theory and observation. *Journal of Business Ethics*, 38 (3): 227–41.

Somers, M.J. 2001. Ethical codes of conduct and organizational context: a study of the relationship between codes of conduct, employee behaviour and organizational values. *Journal of Business Ethics*, 30: 185–95.

Sorge, A. 2005. *The global and the local: understanding the dialectics of business systems*. Oxford: Oxford University Press.

Sorrell, T. 1998. Beyond the fringe? The strange state of business ethics. In M. Parker (ed.), *Ethics and Organizations*: 15–29. London: Sage.

Spar, D. and Yoffie, D. 1999. Multinational enterprises and the prospects for justice. *Journal of International Affairs*, 52 (2): 557–81.

Sparkes, R. 2001. Ethical investment: whose ethics, which investment? *Business Ethics: A European Review*, 10 (3): 194–205.

Spence, L. J. 2000. What ethics in the employment interview? In D. Winstanley and J. Woodall (eds.), *Ethical issues in contemporary human resource management*: 43–58. Basingstoke: Macmillan.

—— 2002. Is Europe distinctive from America? An overview of business ethics in Europe. In H. von Weltzien Hoivik (ed.), *Moral leadership in action*: 9–25. Cheltenham: Edward Elgar.

—— 1999. Does size matter? The state of the art in small business ethics. *Business Ethics: A European Review*, 8 (3): 163–74.

—— Coles, A.-M., and Harris, L. 2001. The forgotten stakeholder? Ethics and social responsibility in relation to competitors. *Business and Society Review*, 106 (4): 331–52.

—— and Lozano, J.F. 2000. Communicating about ethics with small firms: experiences from the U.K. and Spain. *Journal of Business Ethics*, 27 (1/2): 43–53.

Spencer, J.W. 2008. The impact of multinational enterprise strategy on indigenous enterprises: horizontal spillovers and crowding out in developing countries. *Academy of Management Review*, 33 (2): 341–61.

Spicer, A., Dunfee, T.W., and Bailey, W.J. 2004. Does national context matter in ethical decision-making? An empirical test of integrative social contracts theory. *Academy of Management Journal* 47 (4): 610–20.

Spronk, S. 2007. Roots of resistance to urban water privatization in Bolivia: the 'new working class,' the crisis of neoliberalism, and public services. *International Labor and Working-Class History*, 71: 8–28.

Stansbury, J. and Barry, B. 2007. Ethics programs and the paradox of control. *Business Ethics Quarterly*, 17 (2): 239–61.

Stanworth, C. 2000. Flexible working patterns. In D. Winstanley and J. Woodall (eds.), *Ethical issues in contemporary human resource management*: 137–55. Basingstoke: Macmillan.

Stark, A. 1994. What's the matter with business ethics? *Harvard Business Review* (May–June): 38–48

Starkey, K. 1998. Durkheim and the limits of corporate culture: whose culture? Which Durkheim? *Journal of Management Studies*, 35 (2): 125–36.

Steinmann, H. and Löhr, A. 1994. *Grundlagen der Unternehmensethik*. Stuttgart: Schäffer-Poeschel.

Stenzel, P.L. 1999. Can the ISO 14000 series environmental management standards provide a viable alternative to government regulation? *American Business Law Journal*, 37: 238–98.

Stern, N.H. 2006. *The economics of climate change*. http://www.hm-treasury.gov.uk/stern_review_report.htm.

Stigler, G.J. 1971. The theory of economic regulation. *Bell Journal of Economics and Management Science*, 2: 3–21.

Stoney, C. and Winstanley, D. 2001. Stakeholding: confusion or Utopia? Mapping the conceptual terrain. *Journal of Management Studies*, 38 (5): 603–26.

Sullivan, C. and Lewis, S. 2001. Home-based telework, gender, and the synchronization of work and family: perspectives of teleworkers and their co-residents. *Gender, Work and Organizations*, 8 (2): 123–45.

Sullivan, R. (ed.). 2003. *Business and human rights*. Sheffield: Greenleaf.
—— Mackenzie, C., and Waygood, S. 2006. Does a focus on social, ethical and environmental issues enhance investment performance? In R. Sullivan and C. Mackenzie (eds.), *Responsible investment*: 55–61. Sheffield: Greenleaf.
Swash, R. 2009. Filesharing mum ordered to pay nearly $2m. *Guardian*, 19 June: http://www.guardian.co.uk.
Sweney, M. 2008. Apple has another iPhone ad banned after 'really fast' claims. *Guardian*, 27 November: http://www.guardian.co.uk.
Tandon, R. and Srivastava, S.S. 2003. *Invisible yet widespread: the non-profit sector in India* (revised edn.). New Delhi: PRIA.
Taplin, I. 2002. The effects of globalization on the state-business relationships: a conceptual framework. In M. Geppert, D. Matten, and K. Williams (eds.), *Challenges for European management in a global context*: 239–59. Basingstoke: Palgrave.
Tapper, R. 1997. Voluntary agreements for environmental performance improvement: perspectives on the chemical industry's responsible care programme. *Business Strategy and the Environment*, 8: 287–92.
Taylor, R. 2000. How new is socially responsible investment? *Business Ethics: A European Review*, 9 (3): 174–9.
—— 2001. Putting ethics into investment. *Business Ethics: A European Review*, 10 (1): 53–60.
Teather, D. 2005. Ahold agrees to pay $1.1bn to settle US accounting scandal. *Guardian*, 29 November.
ten Bos, R. 1997. Business ethics and Bauman ethics. *Organization Studies*, 18 (6): 997–1014.
—— and Willmott, H. 2001. Towards a post-dualistic business ethics: interweaving reason and emotion in working life. *Journal of Management Studies*, 38 (6): 769–93.
ten Brink, P. (ed.). 2002. *Voluntary environmental agreements*. Sheffield: Greenleaf.
Terrachoice. 2009. *The seven sins of greenwashing: environmental claims in consumer markets*. Toronto: Terrachoice Group Inc.
The Co-operative Bank. 2008. *Ethical Consumerism Report 2008*, 29 November: http://www.goodwithmoney.co.uk.
The Economist. 2000. NGOs: sins of the secular missionaries. *The Economist*, 354 (8155), 29 January: 25–7.
—— 2008a. A special report on corporate social responsibility. *The Economist*, 386 (8563), 19 January: 1–24.
—— 2008b. Asset-backed insecurity. *The Economist*, 19 January: 78–80.
Thomas, A. 2004. The rise of social cooperatives in Italy. *Voluntas: International Journal of Voluntary and Nonprofit Organizations*, 15 (3): 243–63.
Thompson, C.J. 1995. A contextualist proposal for the conceptualization and study of marketing ethics. *Public Policy and Marketing*, 14 (2): 177–91.
Thompson, P. and McHugh, D. 2002. *Work organizations* (3rd edn.). Basingstoke: Palgrave.
Thorne LeClair, D. and Ferrell, L. 2000. Innovation in experiential business ethics training. *Journal of Business Ethics*, 23 (3/1): 313–22.
Thorne McAlister, D., Ferrell, O.C., and Ferrell, L. 2008. *Business and society. A strategic approach to corporate social responsibility* (3rd edn.). Boston: Houghton Mifflin.
Topping, A. 2009. Disabled worker wins case for wrongful dismissal against Abercrombie & Fitch. *Guardian*, 13 August.
Torrington, D. 1993. How dangerous is human resource management? A reply to Tim Hart. *Employee Relations*, 15 (5): 40–53.
Tremlett, G. 2009. Spain's Costa Brava uses Bahamas photograph in ad campaign. *Guardian*, 11 February: http://www.guardian.co.uk.
Treviño, L.K. 1986. Ethical decision making in organizations: a person-situation interactionist model. *Academy of Management Review*, 11 (3): 601–17.
—— and Brown, M.E. 2004. Managing to be ethical: debunking five business ethics myths. *Academy of Management Executive*, 18 (2): 69–81.
—— Hartman, L.P., and Brown, M. 2000. Moral person and moral manager: how executives develop a reputation for ethical leadership. *California Management Review*, 42 (4): 128–42.
—— and Nelson, K.A. 2007. *Managing business ethics: straight talk about how to do it right* (4th edn.). Hoboken, NJ: Wiley.

—— Weaver, G.R., Gibson, D.G., and Toffler, B.L. 1999. Managing ethics and legal compliance: what works and what hurts. *California Management Review*, 41 (2): 131–51.

—— and Youngblood, S.A. 1990. Bad apples in bad barrels: a causal analysis of ethical decision making behavior. *Journal of Applied Psychology*, 75 (4): 378–85.

Tsalikis, J. and Fritzsche, D.J. 1989. Business ethics: a literature review with a focus on marketing ethics. *Journal of Business Ethics*, 8: 695–743.

Turner, K. (ed.). 1993. *Sustainable environmental economics and management: principles and practice*. London: Belhaven Press.

Unerman, J. and O'Dwyer, B. 2006. On James Bond and the importance of NGO accountability. *Accounting, Auditing and Accountability Journal*, 19 (3): 305–18.

UN. 2005. *2005 Report on the world situation*. New York: United Nations Publications.

—— 2008. *Embedding Human Rights in Business Practice II*. New York: UN Global Compact.

Valente, M. and Crane, A. (2009) 'Private, but public', *The Journal Report: Business Insight*, Spring, March 23: http://www.sloanreview.mit.edu/business-insight.

Van Calster, G. and Deketelaere, K. 2001. The use of voluntary agreements in the European Community's environmental policy. In E.W. Orts and K. Deketelaere (eds.), *Environmental contracts*: 199–246. Dordrecht et al.: Kluwer.

van Gerwen, J. 1994. Employers' and employees' rights and duties. In B. Harvey (ed.), *Business ethics: a European approach*: 56–87. London: Prentice Hall.

van Luijk, H.J.L. 1990. Recent developments in European business ethics. *Journal of Business Ethics*, 9: 537–44.

—— 2001. Business ethics in Europe: a tale of two efforts. In R. Lang (ed.), *Wirtschaftsethik in Mittel- und Osteuropa*: 9–18. Munich: Rainer Hampp.

van Schendelen, R. 2002. The ideal profile of the PA expert at the EU level. *Journal of Public Affairs*, 2 (2): 85–9.

van Tulder, R. and Kolk, A. 2001. Multinationality and corporate ethics: codes of conduct in the sporting goods industry. *Journal of International Business Studies*, 32 (2): 267–83.

Varadarajan, P.R. and Menon, A. 1988. Cause-related marketing: a coalignment of marketing strategy and corporate philanthropy. *Journal of Marketing*, 52, July: 58–74.

Verstegen Ryan, L. 2005. Corporate governance and business ethics in North America: the state of the art. *Business & Society*, 44 (1): 40–73.

Vining, A.R., Shapiro, D.M., and Borges, B. 2005. Building the firm's political (lobbying) strategy. *Journal of Public Affairs*, 5: 150–75.

Visser, J. 2006. Union membership statistics in 24 countries. *Monthly Labor Review*, January: 38–49.

Visser, W. 2006. Revisiting Carroll's CSR pyramid: an African perspective. In E.R. Pedersen and M. Huniche (eds.), *Corporate citizenship in developing countries: new partnership perspectives*. Copenhagen: Copenhagen Business School Press.

—— 2008. CSR in developing countries. In A. Crane, A. McWilliams, D. Matten, J. Moon, and D. Siegel (eds.), *The Oxford handbook of corporate social responsibility*: 473–99. Oxford: Oxford University Press.

—— McIntosh, M., and Middleton, C. (eds.). 2006. *Corporate citizenship in Africa—lessons from the past; paths into the future*. Sheffield: Greenleaf.

Vitell, S., Nwachukwa, S., and Barnes, J. 1993. The effects of culture on ethical decision making: an application of Hofstede's typology. *Journal of Business Ethics*, 12: 753–60.

Vives, A. 2007. Social and environmental responsibility in small and medium enterprises in Latin America. In A. Crane and D. Matten (eds.), *Corporate social responsibility—a three volumes edited collection*, Vol. 3: 245–66. London: Sage.

Vogel, D. 1992. The globalization of business ethics: why America remains different. *California Management Review*, 35 (1): 30–49.

—— 1998. Is US business obsessed with ethics? *Across the board*, November–December: 31–3.

—— 2005. *The market for virtue: the potential and limits of corporate social responsibility*. Washington: Brookings Institution Press.

—— 2008. Private global business regulation. *Annual Review of Political Science*, 11 (1): 261–82.

Waddock, S.A. and Graves, S.B. 1997. The corporate social performance–financial performance link. *Strategic Management Journal*, 18 (4): 303–19.

Wagner, G.R. and Haffner, F. 1999. Ökonomische würdigung des umweltrechtlichen instrumentariums. In R. Hendler, P. Marburger, M. Reinhardt, and M. Schröder (eds.), *Rückzug des Ordnungsrechtes im Umweltschutz*: 83–127. Berlin: Erich Schmidt.

Wagner, S. and Lee, D. 2006. The unexpected benefits of Sarbanes–Oxley. *Harvard Business Review*, 84, April: 133–40.

Wallace, M. 1989. Brave new workplace: technology and work in the new economy. *Work and Occupations*, 16 (4): 363–92.

Walsh, J.P. 2008. CEO compensation and the responsibilities of the business scholar to society. *Academy of Management Perspectives*, 22 (2): 26–33.

Wang, H., Appelbaum, R. P., Degiuli, F., and Lichtenstein, N. 2009. China's New Labour Contract Law: is China moving towards increased power for workers? *Third World Quarterly*, 30 (3): 485–501.

Wansink, B. and Chandon, P. 2006. Can 'Low-Fat' Nutrition Labels Lead to Obesity? *Journal of Marketing Research*, 43 (4): 605–17.

Warner, M. and Sullivan, R. (eds.). 2004. *Putting partnerships to work. Strategic alliances for development between government, the private sector and civil society*. Sheffield: Greenleaf.

Wartick, S.L. and Cochran, P.L. 1985. The evolution of the corporate social performance model. *Academy of Management Review*, 10: 758–69.

Watson, T.J. 1994. *In search of management: culture, chaos and control in managerial work*. London: Routledge.

—— 1998. Ethical codes and moral communities: the gunlaw temptation, the Simon solution and the David dilemma. In M. Parker (ed.), *Ethics and Organizations*: 253–68. London: Sage.

—— 2003. Ethical choice in managerial work: the scope for moral choices in an ethically irrational world. *Human Relations*, 56 (2): 167–85.

Watts, J. 2009. China plastic bag ban 'has saved 1.6m tonnes of oil'. *Guardian*, 22 May: http://www.guardian.co.uk.

Weaver, G., Treviño, L.K., and Cochran, P.L. 1999a. Corporate ethics practices in the mid-1990s: an empirical study of the Fortune 1000. *Journal of Business Ethics*, 18: 283–94.

—— —— —— 1999b. Corporate ethics programs as control systems: influences of executive commitment and environmental factors. *Academy of Management Journal*, 42 (1): 41–57.

Webb, T. 2006. Is Asian corporate governance improving? *Ethical Corporation*, May: 25–6.

Weber, J. 1990. Managers' moral reasoning: assessing their responses to three moral dilemmas. *Human Relations*, 43 (7): 687–702.

Weber, M. 1905. *Die protestantische Ethik und der 'Geist' des Kapitalismus*, Vols. 21 and 22. Tübingen: Archiv für Sozialwissenschaft und Sozialpolitik.

—— 1947. *The theory of social and economic organization* (T. Parsons, trans.). Oxford: Oxford University Press.

Webley, S. 2001. Values-based codes. In C. Moon and C. Bonny (eds.), *Business ethics: facing up to the issues*: 159–69. London: *The Economist* Books.

—— (ed.). 2008. *Use of codes of ethics in business: 2007 survey and analysis of trends*. London: Institute of Business Ethics.

—— and Le Jeune, M. 2005. *Corporate use of codes of ethics: 2004 survey*. London: Institute of Business Ethics.

Welford, R.J. 1997. *Hijacking environmentalism: corporate responses to sustainable development*. London: Routledge.

Werhane, P.H. 1998. Moral imagination and the search for ethical decision-making in management. *Business Ethics Quarterly*, Ruffin Series (1): 75–98.

Whawell, P. 1998. The ethics of pressure groups. *Business Ethics: A European Review*, 7 (3): 178–81.

Wheeler, D. 2001. Racing to the bottom? Foreign investment and air pollution in developing countries. *Journal of Environment and Development*, 10 (3): 225–45.

—— Fabig, H., and Boele, R. 2002. Paradoxes and dilemmas for stakeholder responsive firms in the extractive sector: lessons from the case of Shell and the Ogoni. *Journal of Business Ethics*, 39: 297–318.

White, M. 2004. On May 1 Paul Drayson was given a peerage. On June 17 he gave Labour a £500,000 cheque. *Guardian*, 25 August.

Whitford, A.B. and Clark, B.Y. 2007. Designing property rights for water: mediating market, government, and corporation failures. *Policy Sciences*, 40 (4): 335–51.

Whitley, R. (ed.). 1992. *European business systems*. London: Sage.

—— 1999. *Divergent capitalisms: the social structuring and change of business systems*. Oxford: Oxford University Press.

—— 2009. U.S. capitalism: a tarnished model? *Academy of Management Perspectives*, 23 (2): 11–22.

Whittington, R. and Mayer, M. 2002. The evolving European corporation: strategy, structure and social science. In K. Williams (ed.), *Challenges for European management in a global context*: 19–41. Basingstoke: Palgrave.

Wickramasekara, P. 2008. Globalisation, international labour migration and the rights of migrant workers. *Third World Quarterly*, 29 (7): 1247–64.

Wienen, I. 1999. *Impact of religion on business ethics in Europe and the Muslim world: Islamic versus Christian tradition*. Oxford: Peter Lang.

Winstanley, D., Clark, J., and Leeson, H. 2002. Approaches to child labour in the supply chain. *Business Ethics: A European Review*, 11 (3): 210–23.

Witkowski, T.H. 2005. Antiglobal challenges to marketing in developing countries: exploring the ideological divide. *Journal of Public Policy and Marketing*, 24 (1): 7–23.

Woll, C. and Artigas, A. 2007. When trade liberalization turns into regulatory reform: the impact on business–government relations in international trade politics. *Regulation & Governance*, 1: 121–38.

Wong, S.C.Y. 2004. Improving corporate governance at SOEs: an integrated approach. *Corporate Governance International*, 7 (2): 6.

—— 2009. Government ownership: why this time it should work. *McKinsey Quarterly* (June): http://www.mckinsey.com.

Wood, D.J. 1991. Corporate social performance revisited. *Academy of Management Review*, 16: 691–718.

—— and Logsdon, J.M. 2001. Theorising business citizenship. In M. McIntosh (ed.), *Perspectives on corporate citizenship*: 83–103. Sheffield: Greenleaf.

Woodruffe, H. 1997. Compensatory consumption: why women go shopping when they're fed up and other stories. *Marketing Intelligence and Planning*, 15 (7): 325–34.

Woods, N. 2001. Making the IMF and the World Bank more accountable. *International Affairs*, 77 (1): 83–100.

Wootliff, J. and Deri, C. 2001. NGOs: the new super brands. *Corporate Reputation Review*, 4 (2): 157–65.

World Commission on Environment and Development. 1987. *Our common future*. Oxford: Oxford University Press.

World Economic Forum. 2002. *Global corporate citizenship: the leadership challenge for CEOs and Boards*. Geneva: World Economic Forum and The Prince of Wales Business Leaders Forum.

World Trade Organization. 2008. *International Trade Statistics 2008*. Geneva: WTO.

Woywode, M. 2002. Global management concepts and local adaptations: working groups in the French and German car manufacturing industry. *Organization Studies*, 23 (4): 497–524.

Wray-Bliss, E. and Parker, M. 1998. Marxism, capitalism and ethics. In M. Parker (ed.), *Ethics and organizations*. London: Sage: 30–52.

Wylie, I. and Ball, C. 2006. Out with the old? *Guardian*, 25 February: 3.

Yang, G. 2005. Environmental NGOs and institutional dynamics in China. *China Quarterly*, 181: 46–66.

Yaziji, M. and Doh, J. 2009. *NGOs and corporations: conflict and collaboration*. Cambridge: Cambridge University Press.

Yip, G. 1995. *Total global strategies*. London: Prentice Hall.

Young, N. 2002. Three 'C's: civil society, corporate social responsibility, and China. *China Business Review*, January–February: 34–8.

Zadek, S. 1998. Balancing performance, ethics and accountability. *Journal of Business Ethics*, 17: 1421–41.

—— 2001. *The civil corporation: the new economy of corporate citizenship*. London: Earthscan.

—— 2004. The path to corporate responsibility. *Harvard Business Review*, 82, December: 125–32.

—— Pruzan, P., and Evans, R. (eds.). 1997. *Building corporate accountability: emerging practices in social and ethical accounting, auditing and reporting*. London: Earthscan.

Zhao, X. and Belk, R.W. 2008. Politicizing consumer culture: advertising's appropriation of political ideology in China's social transition. *Journal of Consumer Research*, 35 (2): 231–44.

Zhexembayeva, N., Fedoseeva, O., and Martyschenko, S. 2007. Towards a revolution in cross-boundary partnership: complex socio-economic development in the Regions of SUAL Group Presence. *Centre for Business as an Agent of World Benefit Newsletter*, 3 (2): worldbenefit.case.edu/forum2006/documents/Forumfinaloutput.doc.

Wilson, R. 1999. [illegible] Islamic [illegible]

—— 2005. Government ownership [illegible] World Bank [illegible]

[illegible] and Chen, C. 2007. [illegible] Corporate Reputation Review, [illegible]

SUBJECT INDEX

C

D

AUTHORS INDEX

COUNTRIES AND REGIONS INDEX

COMPANIES, ORGANIZATIONS, AND BRANDS INDEX